The *Athletic-Minded*™ Traveler

Where to Work Out and Stay When Fitness is a Priority

Over 500 Recommended Hotels and Fitness Venues

2ND EDITION

Jim Kaese
and
Paul Huddle

Athletic-Minded Traveler, LLC
SAN DIEGO, CALIFORNIA

THE ATHLETIC-MINDED TRAVELER

Where to Work Out and Stay When Fitness is a Priority

By Jim Kaese and Paul Huddle

Published by:
Athletic-Minded Traveler LLC
Post Office Box 33188
San Diego, CA 92163-3188
www.athleticmindedtraveler.com

Quantity discounts are available on bulk purchases of this book for corporate, club, organization sales promotions, premiums and gifts. Special editions, including personalized covers, can be created. For information, contact your local bookseller or Athletic-Minded Traveler LLC, online or at (877) 27-BOOKS.

The Authors and Publisher have made every effort to ensure the accuracy of the information provided throughout this book. The same Authors and Publisher disclaim any and all liability for any reason including but not limited to miscalculations, misinformation, false facts, errors, omissions and/or changes at the properties, routes and/or facilities discussed or mentioned inside this book, whether due to mistake, negligence or any other cause. The Authors and Publisher also disclaim any liability for any injury, physical or emotional, suffered during or as a result of exercise or activity inside, near or around such properties, routes and facilities. Exercise at any level is a strenuous activity. You should consult your health professional before beginning any exercise routine or program.

Printed in Canada

ISBN 0-9753060-7-3
ISBN 13: 978-0-9753060-8-6
LCCN 2004108665

Edited by Erin Kaese and Connie Kearney
Book Design and Production by Beth Hagman
Cover by Kristin Mayer
Cover Photos: Gym, Peninsula Hotel, Chicago, Illinois
Pool, YMCA Aquatic Center, Orlando, Florida

ACKNOWLEDGEMENTS

As an important and closely held endeavor, we entrusted very few to help formulate and complete this book. Their wondrous talents and painstaking diligence have resulted in a work more substantial and helpful to others than we ever imagined. We are honored by their significant contributions.

Erin Kaese, *Editor and Content Contributor* — without your words, hard work and inspiration, this immense undertaking would have remained an unachievable dream and a book without soul.

Beth Hagman, *Book Designer* — your innovative vision and dedication to "getting it right" have created overwhelming pride and excitement.

Connie Kearney, *Editor* — envious of your many abilities, we are most appreciative of your invaluable wisdom, keen eye for detail and willingness to selflessly share your talents.

Kristin Mayer, *Cover Designer* — though the saying goes, "Don't judge a book by its cover," we will happily tell others to do so with ours. Thank you, sincerely.

We additionally appreciate all of our friends and family across the country who shared their homes, opinions and support.

CONTENTS

CONTENTS CONTINUED

PREFACE

As extensive business and leisure travelers, we have repeatedly confronted the perils of working out while on the road. Unlike home, where we rely on a dependable health club, a familiar lap pool and a favorite running route, out-of-town exercise introduces the unknown and is plagued by misinformation and rhetoric. All too often, we have encountered scantily equipped rooms advertised as "state-of-the-art" fitness centers, suffered through excessive flip-turning in 15-yard pools billed as "Olympic-size," and endured "suggested jogging routes" burdened by frequent traffic stops.

Frustrated, we embarked on a mission: To uncover the BEST places for healthy-minded individuals to work out and stay when traveling to the most popular U.S. destinations. Downtowns, major business districts, vacation hotspots — we visited them all to ensure that your workout plans will not be derailed. More than just listing fitness options, we wanted athletic-minded travelers to discover accommodations matching their personal preferences, budgets AND athletic needs. As fitness enthusiasts, we want to have it all — the right hotel, the right workout and the right location.

Sound too good to be true? Nonsense. It took a lot of hard work, but wait till you read what we found.

After scouring information on over 2,200 hotel and fitness locations and personally touring nearly 1,100 that made our first cut, we uncovered a variety of fantastic "stay and play" options. Our "Gold," "Silver" and "Bronze" hotel recommendations are the best of the best, divided into three price categories (Expensive, Moderately Expensive and Least Expensive). To cover the fitness spectrum beyond hotels, we recommend appealing and convenient health clubs, community centers, YMCAs, lap pools and running routes.

Unlike many reference guides that provide general information without suggestions, The Athletic-Minded Traveler only *recommends*. We eliminated the "crop" and provide frank opinions on the "cream," so your travel decisions are simplified. Choose your city, your price range, your sport, and let this book be your guide.

You can wave good-bye to closet-size workout rooms, worn machines and short pools and say hello to 500+ hotels, health clubs and community centers that will accommodate your healthy lifestyle. Exercise is certainly more enjoyable when you know where to go and what to expect. We're leading you to the Gatorade, it's up to you to drink.

USING THIS BOOK

OVERVIEW

A total of 78 popular travel destinations located in 50 U.S. cities are covered. Larger metropolitan areas typically have more than one desirable destination, and we provide recommendations for each. For example, the New York City chapter includes recommendations for Central Park, Midtown, Union Square and Downtown — all frequent stops for business and leisure travelers.

After each city's introduction, we categorize the hotels by area (e.g., Downtown, Central Park), and then by price (Expensive, Moderately Expensive and Least Expensive). Within each price category, hotels are identified by Gold, Silver and Bronze rankings. The bigger the city, the more "medals" awarded. Smaller cities may have only one recommended hotel in each price category, or all of the recommended hotels may fit into one price category. In addition, we note occasional times when two hotels garner the same medal.

To arrive at our hotel recommendations, we evaluated accommodation quality, amenities provided, location convenience, cost AND fitness options. For health clubs and pools, we assessed the quality and quantity of equipment, venue size/dimensions, facility aesthetics and cost. Because all accommodations in each price category are recommended, athletic-minded travelers are assured of a reliable lodging AND workout option. It is a combination of the two that made it our winner and hopefully yours, too!

RATINGS

Hotels

Below each hotel's vitals (address, phone, website) we summarize its unique features and describe our reasons for the recommendation — the more interesting the property, the more ink it receives. Each hotel with a notable on-site fitness option has an accompanying chart detailing quantity and brands of machines, amount and type of weights, pool characteristics, hours and cost, etc. Keep in mind, hotels add equipment and machines break down, so the numbers may change. However, fitness-focused hotels will remain fitness-focused hotels, so our nominees should always be superior choices.

Hotels without a chart have either no on-site gym or no exercise option worthy of a detailed breakout. These "chart-free" hotels are recommended from a fitness perspective due to their relationships with and proximity to nearby fitness centers. For some, the related health clubs are physically connected to the hotel, while others are a short walk away. Regardless, these hotel/health club combinations are often more appealing than a stand-alone hotel with an in-house workout room.

Off-Site Fitness Venues

Health club descriptions and other recommended off-site workout options (e.g., lap pools, community centers, YMCAs) are organized under the BEYOND HOTELS section following the hotel listings. Detailed descriptions are provided, along with corresponding charts identifying amenities, types and brands of equipment, lap pool characteristics and facility information (e.g., hours, cost, classes, etc.). With very few exceptions, we personally viewed, counted and noted this information — so have confidence in its accuracy. Unlike the hotel charts, which provide a specific number of machines, our health club winners typically supplied too many machines to count. Therefore, we focused on brands and quality, unless the center was small enough to make counting practical.

Running Routes

Each city chapter concludes with a short description of local running routes (and quarter-mile tracks) that are convenient to the area covered. Although a few routes require a short drive, most are reachable on foot from your hotel.

Appendix: Ironman

For those of you who are the elite of the amateur endurance world (some would say crazy), there is a special appendix that covers most race towns on the Ironman North America circuit. Though much of this information is race specific, you will find some general data on health clubs and restaurants as well. However, these cities, hotels and fitness venues did not receive the same scrutiny as the rest of the book's destinations — the information is simply a compilation of experiences from years of travel to these locales.

HELPFUL HINTS

- Always bring your room key and a photo I.D. to off-site fitness venues.
- Call ahead to verify hours, class schedules, prices etc. at all off-site fitness venues, especially lap pools.
- Bring a swim cap to health club and community center pools (YMCAs often require one).
- Many off-site venues do not provide towels and locks, so bring your own or call first
- IHRSA is a not-for-profit organization that your home club may belong to. Find out, because you may be entitled to access and/or a discount at many clubs. Check with your local club and/or this website: www.healthclubs.com for membership status.
- When typing in the listed websites, put www before all domain names to ensure proper site routing.

ABBREVIATIONS & DEFINITIONS

ACCOMMODATIONS

Expensive - Used to describe a hotel's rates — typically $200/night or more, but can vary tremendously depending on city, season and demand (e.g., convention, event etc.).

Moderately Expensive - Typically $130-$200/night, but varies.

Least Expensive - Typically under $130/night, but varies.

EQUIPMENT

Fan - An upright bike with a front wheel that creates wind.

Free Weights - Includes strength equipment for bench press and other exercises using a barbell and circular plate weights (dumbbells are categorized separately).

Hammer - A category of equipment that denotes plate-loaded machines, typically manufactured under the Hammer Strength brand, but also made by Cybex and other companies. Circular "plate" weights with a hole cut out of the middle are placed on these machines for strength exercises.

LF - Life Fitness, a major exercise brand and equipment manufacturer.

Machines - Stack-loaded strength stations where users vary the weight by placing a pin into the weight's hole. Weights are usually in 10 lb increment "bricks." Air pressurized (Keiser) and computerized resistance machines (Life Circuit) are also listed in this category.

Multi - A single stack-loaded unit (think 10 pound bricks and pin placement) with the capability of multiple weight exercises (usually 3 or more).

Old - Indicates a worn machine and/or old model.

XC ski - Cross country skiing aerobic machine

POOL

Clock - A swim pace clock is provided.

Fins - A form of swim fins are provided.

Grade - The overall quality of a pool considering length, aesthetics and amenities. A is the best, F is the worst.

Kick - Swim kickboards are provided.

"m" and **"yd"** - meters and yards.

Masters - A Masters Swim group is offered.

Pull - Swim pull-buoys are provided.

Vary - Usually pertains to hours of a venue. Many schools and community centers modify hours per season, events, etc. You should call ahead to verify.

The magic word is... CONFIDENCE!

Albuquerque

33 Locations Reviewed

ALBUQUERQUE, NEW MEXICO

Red or green? Visitors to the Land of Enchantment will undoubtedly encounter this dilemma. As one of the most frequently asked questions in New Mexico, only three answers suffice: red, green or Christmas. This simple inquiry has even been certified as New Mexico's official question by the state legislature.

What the heck are we talking about? Little edibles that pack a powerful punch... chile peppers.

As the State's #1 cash crop, 60% of all chile peppers consumed in the U.S. are grown in New Mexico. The booming popularity of salsa in the American diet has helped to double production since the early 1980s. In fact, salsa surpassed ketchup as the #1 condiment in the U.S. in the mid '90s. New Mexico annually ships as much as 100,000 tons of these green and red fire sticks.

Despite differences in taste (red tends to be sweeter), both shades grow on the same plant. The rosy chile is simply a green pepper that's left on the plant longer. While both hues can vary in spiciness, some greens can be hotter than reds — and vice versa. Both draw their heat from the same source: capsaicin. In true Darwinian fashion, this fiery chemical evolved in the pepper's center and membrane to protect it from hungry predators. Over time, the seeds absorb capsaicin, making the little pods blaze with spice as well.

Low in fat and high in vitamins A and C, chile peppers are more than spicy additions to a Southwestern meal. From the ancient Mayans to present day Hawaiians, capsaicin is recognized for its healing properties and is widely used to treat illnesses such as arthritis, asthma, swollen feet, blood clots and heart attacks.

So, red or green with your entree? You make the call. Those indecisive travelers who answer, "Christmas," will receive a mix of both.

Because hotels are spread across this sprawling city, we have listed recommendations for three popular business districts: Downtown, North (5 miles north of Downtown along I-25), and Near Northeast (3 miles east along I-40). With no high-end, luxury hotels, our recommendations fall into the Moderate and Least Expensive categories.

DOWNTOWN

MODERATELY EXPENSIVE

GOLD: Hyatt Regency

330 Tijeras, Albuquerque, NM 87102
(505) 842-1234 • albuquerque.hyatt.com

CARDIO

TREADMILLS: **3 LF • 2 True**
RECUMBENT BIKE: **4 LF**
ELLIPTICAL: **2 Precor**
STEPPER: **2 Tectrix • 2 StairMaster** - old

STRENGTH

MACHINES: **8 Cybex**
DUMBBELLS: **5-50 lbs**

SWIM

GRADE: **D+**
SPECS: **2x18yd • Outdoor • 82°**

OTHER

HOURS: POOL **6a-10p** • GYM **24**
COST: **Free**
TV: **Yes**

Located across from the convention center and the Sports and Wellness Club at the Galleria, Hyatt Regency is downtown Albuquerque's premier hotel. All 395 rooms are attractively decorated in pastel tones of salmon and blue, with contemporary furnishings and expansive city or mountain views. We liked the hint of Southwest flavor and think you will, too.

Hyatt's 3rd floor is the hub of all things aerobic. Despite the business ambiance of white workplace ceilings and walls, the workout room's equipment is above average in quantity and quality. The ellipticals, recumbent bikes and True treadmills are in good condition. However, the other cardio machines show wear. Fortunately, Hyatt's strength equipment is anything but weak, with a full assortment of new, stack-loaded weight stations and dumbbells. With no upright bikes, cyclists must recline or head to Sports and Wellness for additional options.

Outside the workout room in the fresh Albuquerque air, swimmers can lap in the "tweener." This 18-yard box is satisfactory for a brief visit but too short for a lengthy stay. The absence of floating lane lines does not help, but two bottom stripes guide the route. Its consistent 82° temperature affords year-round use. Make peace with this wet offering — it's the longest lap pool in downtown Albuquerque. (Sports and Wellness' pool is shorter at 14 meters.)

If Downtown is your destination, this Hyatt is the place to work your body and rest your head. Keep in mind, though, that straying a few miles from the city center will improve your workout choices (see North and East below).

Note: Starbucks is in the lobby, and a Subway is across the street.

SILVER: Doubletree

201 Marquette Avenue NW, Albuquerque, NM 87102
(505) 247-3344 • doubletreealbuquerque.com

This hotel, with its 295 rooms, offers nothing special, save its delicious signature chocolate chip cookies. The accommodations and amenities are standard but, for those in town on business, the underground walkway to the Albuquerque Convention Center is convenient.

Athletic-minded guests will appreciate the proximity (3-minute walk) to Sports and Wellness, since Doubletree's paltry option consists of 6 older cardio machines and 1 multi-gym. The room's inferno-like temperature, created by the glaring afternoon sun, doesn't help matters.

Swimmers, you're out of luck as well. This hotel does not have a lap pool, and Sports and Wellness' 14-meter box is no attraction. Your best bet is to stay at the Hyatt or check out another business district.

Note: Admission to Sports and Wellness is $8.

CARDIO

TREADMILLS: **2 True**
UPRIGHT BIKE: **1 StarTrac**
RECUMBENT BIKE: **1 Tectrix**
ELLIPTICAL: **1 True**
STEPPER: **1 Cybex**

STRENGTH

MACHINES: **1 Cybex Multi**

SWIM

SPECS: **Outdoor • Not lap**

OTHER

HOURS: **6a-9p**
COST: **Free**
TV: **Yes**

LEAST EXPENSIVE

GOLD: La Posada de Albuquerque (re-opening April 2007)

125 Second Street NW, Albuquerque, NM 87102
(505) 242-9090 • laposada-abq.com

The Hyatt, Doubletree and La Posada are located within several blocks of one another and less than a block from the convention center. Hilton's property in Albuquerque's hub is the most bare-bones of the trio, offering 1930s style rooms with an Old Southwest flavor. Many of the rooms afford queen size beds only, so be sure to confirm the sleeping configuration when booking.

La Posada offers no on-site gym. Instead, it sells guests $8 passes to Sports and Wellness across the street in the Galleria Mall. Normally, hotels provide health club passes for free or at a discount to compensate guests for sub-par facilities. Not here. La Posada's $8/day fee is identical to the rate Sports and Wellness charges every Tom, Dick and Jane staying at the Hyatt or Doubletree. Go figure.

BEYOND HOTELS DOWNTOWN

Sports and Wellness Club at the Galleria

40 First Plaza NW, Albuquerque, NM 87102
(505) 242-1500 • nmsw.com/downtown

Sports and Wellness Club at the Galleria is a small fitness center in the heart of downtown Albuquerque catering primarily to weekday office workers. Plenty of cardio and strength equipment adorns two separate sweat areas. Inside the club, exercisers will find most of the endurance apparatus set up to the right of the reception desk, weights on the left. An overhead balcony is an additional locale for bikes and NordicTracks.

CARDIO

TREADMILLS: **StarTrac**
UPRIGHT BIKE: **LF**
RECUMBENT BIKE: **LF**
ELLIPTICAL: **Precor • StarTrac • Reebok**
STEPPER: **StairMaster**
ROWING: **Concept II**
OTHER: **NordicTrack**

STRENGTH

FREE WEIGHTS: **Yes**
MACHINES: **Cybex • Free Motion**
DUMBBELLS: **3-100 lbs**

SWIM

GRADE: **F**
SPECS: **3x14m • Indoor • 76-80°**
TOYS: **Kick**

OTHER

CLASSES: **Yes**
HOURS: M-F **5a-9p** • SAT **8a-2p** • SUN **Closed**
COST: **$8**
TV: **Yes**
EXTRAS: **Basketball**

Although some machines are squeezed into the facility's nooks and crannies, most stations sit in open and well-lit spaces. We counted 7 new recumbent bikes, 7 4600PT series steppers, 6 youthful treadmills and a bunch of useful ellipticals. Plate-loaded weight machines such as Hammer Strength were noticeably absent, but there are plenty of stack-loaded stations, free weights and dumbbells to satisfy strength trainers.

Swimmers should look elsewhere for a lap option. Sports and Wellness' 14-meter Napoleon has no floating lines (it does have bottom stripes) and not much heat — a crisp 76°. If the cold doesn't undermine your stroke, the back and forth required to accrue meaningful yardage may make you regret getting wet.

NORTH

LEAST EXPENSIVE

GOLD: **Drury Inn**

4310 The 25 Way Northeast, Albuquerque, NM 87109
(505) 341-3600 • druryhotels.com

Just off Interstate 25 and approximately 5 miles north of downtown Albuquerque, New Mexico's first Drury property opened in May 2003. The hotel's tidy accommodations, free hot breakfasts, complimentary internet access and gratis evening snacks give visitors a bang for their buck.

This Drury's tiny exercise room stocks only 3 treads and a recumbent bike, so driving 5 minutes to Defined Fitness is a road worth taking for serious exercise hounds. Just 7 bucks admission gets you everything your heart desires and your muscles need.

Note: Mimi's Café (good breakfasts) is adjacent to the hotel, and PF Chang's (lunch & dinner) is a half block away.

SILVER: Nativo Lodge

6000 Pan American Freeway NE, Albuquerque, NM 87109
(505) 798-4300 • nativolodge.com

About a mile north along Interstate 25 from Drury Inn, Nativo's 151-room accommodation comes with unique furnishings and colors that impart a Native American style. And the place is inexpensive! Often $75 to $100 will secure a bed for a night.

On the workout front, guests should head to Defined Fitness. Your commute is 5 minutes in the car — giving you a worthwhile fitness upgrade to Nativo's uncomfortably petite workout room, which contains 3 cardio machines and a few dumbbells.

BEYOND HOTELS NORTH

Defined Fitness

4930 McLeod NE, Albuquerque, NM 87109
(505) 888-7097 • defined.com

Sporting a stadium-like, four-tiered cardio and weight area, this club gets high marks for its ingenuity and creative décor. Out-of-town exercisers will benefit from the deluge of cutting-edge strength equipment, complete with stack and plate-loaded weight machines, dumbbells and bench/squat racks. Designed to maximize floor space, cardio machines are arranged on multi-tier levels overlooking the weight space. About 30 pieces are organized on each level, all facing overhead TVs. Similar to the strength stations, the endurance apparatus is new, new, new, and in plentiful supply.

Swimmers get to join the fitness frenzy in this club's attractive 25-yard lap pool. Five lanes are separated by floating lines and bottom stripes, with kickboards adding variety to your freestyle training. A pace clock was nowhere to be found, so those planning to knock out base intervals should bring the wristwatch.

Note: Bring your own towel, too.

CARDIO

TREADMILLS: **Precor**
UPRIGHT BIKE: **LF**
RECUMBENT BIKE: **LF**
ELLIPTICAL: **Precor**
STEPPER: **StairMaster • Stepmill**
ROWING: **Concept II**
OTHER: **Crossrobic**

STRENGTH

FREE WEIGHTS: **Yes**
HAMMER: **Yes**
MACHINES: **Cybex • Free Motion**
DUMBBELLS: **3-140 lbs**

SWIM

GRADE: **B**
SPECS: **5x25yd • Indoor • 82-86°**
TOYS: **Kick**

OTHER

CLASSES: **Yes**
HOURS: M-TH **4:30a-12a** • F **4:30a-10p** • SAT **7a-8p** • SUN **8a-7p**
COST: **$8**
TV: **Yes**

NEAR NORTHEAST

LEAST EXPENSIVE

GOLD: **Hampton Inn University/Midtown**
2300 Carlisle NE, Albuquerque, NM 87110
(505) 837-9300 • hamptoninn.com

GOLD: **Radisson Hotel & Conference Center**
2500 Carlisle NE, Albuquerque, NM 87110
(505) 888-3311 • radisson.com

Located along I-40 approximately 4 miles east of downtown Albuquerque, Radisson and Hampton are your best stay/workout options outside the city center with their affordable rates and exercise convenience. Both offer rooms with standard floor plans, basic amenities and typical hotel décor.

Sports and Wellness' first-class health facility is in their "backyard." It's a good thing, too, because neither budget accommodation has a worthwhile gym of its own — Hampton does not have one at all. Radisson guests get in free, while Hampton guests pay $3 (average Joe pays $12/day).

So take your pick. You cannot go wrong. Though Hampton offers complimentary continental breakfasts each morning, Radisson usually prices out about $20/night cheaper.

CARDIO

TREADMILLS: **LF • StarTrac**
UPRIGHT BIKE: **LF**
RECUMBENT BIKE: **LF**
ELLIPTICAL: **Precor • StarTrac • Reebok**
STEPPER: **StairMaster**
ROWING: **Concept II**
OTHER: **XC Ski**

STRENGTH

FREE WEIGHTS: **Yes**
MACHINES: **Cybex • Free Motion**
DUMBBELLS: **5-110 lbs**

SWIM

GRADE: **B**
SPECS: **6x25yd • Indoor/Outdoor • 81-83°**
TOYS: **Kick • Pull • Clock**

OTHER

CLASSES: **Yes**
HOURS: M-TH **5a-10p** • F **5a-9p** • SAT-SUN **7a-7p**
COST: **Free Radisson • $3 Hampton • $12 Others • $30/week**
TV: **Yes**

BEYOND HOTELS
NEAR NORTHEAST

Sports and Wellness
Midtown
4100 Prospect NE
Albuquerque, NM 87110
(505) 888-4811 • nmsw.com

A difficult place to find unless you are staying at the Radisson or Hampton, Sports and Wellness (Midtown) is a full-service health club offering impressive equipment, a hospitable environment and friendly staff. Although not luxurious, this facility is twice the size of its downtown sister club and houses an ample quantity of recently-purchased exercise equipment. We counted at least 12 treadmills, 10 recumbent bikes, ten 4400PT series steppers and 9 ellipticals. Weight buffs should not despair. Sports and Wellness serves up enough strength apparatus to make hardcore muscle-heads whimper. New Cybex and Free Motion stack-loaded weight stations are on the floor, as well as a wide range of dumbbells and plenty of free weights. Although we did not see any plate-loaded Hammer Strength equipment, the other weight hardware compensates well.

Our fish-like friends are not left out, either. They receive access to a year-round, outdoor, 6 lane, 25-yard lap pool. You may be wondering, "Year-round? What about Albuquerque's crisp winters?" Sports and Wellness keeps swimmers in business by inflating a dome to form a bubble over the water box during the cold months. A pace clock and toys are here as well.

RUNNING ROUTES

Albuquerque's Rio Grande River location and its surrounding foothills provide ample running trails and paths. However, accessing these beautifully scenic routes from local hotels is not overly convenient and involves a solid warm-up to arrive.

Downtown

Those bunking Downtown should look to the Bosque (which means forest) path that follows the Rio Grande north for 6 paved miles. The route's reward is the Rio Grande Nature Center State Park's 270 acres of forest, meadows and marsh — and more running trails! Runners can access the path in Old Town. Unfortunately, this beautiful park is a solid 6+ miles (mostly west) from the other business districts.

Montgomery Park

Montgomery Park, which is within 2 miles of NE hotels, is a potential start/end for striders looking for some green, little traffic and potential camaraderie. One of the City's running groups meets here for 5k and 10k workouts.

Sandia Foothills

The Sandia Foothills Open Space is another popular destination and connects to the Tramway Path. Again, the distance is a good 4+ miles to the east of the North and Near Northeast districts. For Radisson dwellers, it is a straight shot north on Carlisle and East on Montgomery. The views are excellent.

Tramway Bike Path

Yes this is named a "bike path," but joggers are commonly found on this popular paved route. Located on the east side of Albuquerque, the Tramway Path runs along the Sandia Mountains, providing wonderful views and a welcome distraction. A couple of wooden bridges can be found along the way, as well as a few traffic intersections which will break your stride. Nevertheless, this is an enjoyable Albuquerque option.

Atlanta

ATLANTA, GEORGIA

Far from its roots as a plantation and farming town, Atlanta's economy is now driven by corporate heavyweights like Coca-Cola, Delta, Home Depot and UPS, all of which headquarter in the "Home of the Brave(s)." Blending deep Southern tradition with all that is modern, Atlanta is known as the capital of the "New South." Transplants flock to what some describe as the "next great international city" to enjoy its temperate climate, cosmopolitan flair and job opportunities. As host of the 1996 Olympics, Atlanta solidified itself as a world-renowned city and simultaneously added the word "ya'll" into many vocabularies.

Contributing to Atlanta's character and universality is its rich African American history, exemplified by the life and work of Dr. Martin Luther King, Jr. whose birthplace in the revitalized Sweet Auburn neighborhood received the National Historic Landmark designation in 1976 and is now home to the Martin Luther King Center for Nonviolent Social Change.

DOWNTOWN

New York, San Francisco, Boston and Chicago all boast vibrant urban centers that buzz around the clock. Densely populated and flush with dining, entertainment, business, recreational, shopping and cultural attractions, no suburb can conceivably rival such amenities. These cities have "It," and every other large U.S. city wants "It" too. Atlanta is no different, and has attempted to cultivate a similar allure for its Downtown. Efforts are yielding returns, as evidenced by the surge in new housing developments amid office skyscrapers. However, despite being spotlighted by the 1996 Olympics, downtown Atlanta remains more a business hub than anything else. Its Peachtree Center is a convenient dining and shopping venue and a number of other trendy eateries are sprinkled throughout. But neighboring Buckhead still draws hip locals and tourists looking for "It."

73 Locations Reviewed

EXPENSIVE

GOLD: **Westin Peachtree Plaza**

210 Peachtree Street, Atlanta, GA 30303
(404) 659-1400 • westin.com

CARDIO
TREADMILLS: **5 Cybex**
UPRIGHT BIKE: **1 Cybex**
RECUMBENT BIKE: **2 Cybex**
ELLIPTICAL: **3 Precor**
STEPPER: **2 Cybex**

STRENGTH
MACHINES: **18 Cybex**
DUMBBELLS: **5-50 lbs**

SWIM
SPECS: **In/Out • Not lap**

OTHER
HOURS: **6a-10p**
COST: **Free**
TV: **Yes**
EXTRA: **$16 pass to Peachtree**

Wow! These rooms are breathtaking. Towering 73 stories, this landmark Westin's floor-to-ceiling windows bring you close to the sun and moon. Within walking distance of everything downtown Atlanta offers and connected to the Peachtree Center, the 1,068-room Westin is an attraction in itself. The 73rd floor Sun Dial revolving restaurant, 10th floor retractable-roof swimming pool, in-lobby Starbucks, superb fitness center and phenomenal views throughout will tempt you to relax inside — all day long.

Westin's 10th floor "L"-shaped complimentary gym supplies a commendable mix of newer exercise equipment. Although most cardio machines are located on the shorter and narrower end of the "L," athletes have plenty of elbow room. Don't fret the lack of free weights. By providing dumbbells, 18 separate Cybex stations and one pulley system, Westin has your muscle-pumping routine covered. Despite the glamour of the pool, it is not lap designed. So swimmers and those still in search of more should purchase a $16 pass from the front desk and walk 7 minutes to the massive and impressive Peachtree Athletic Club.

Note: Due to its size, this hotel gets very busy (e.g., elevators, check-in, room service, etc.) — but this potential downside is more than offset by the Westin's guaranteed upside.

SILVER: **Omni Hotel Downtown at CNN Center**

100 CNN Center, Atlanta, GA 30303
(404) 659-0000 • omnihotels.com

This already substantial Centennial Park hotel became a 1,000+ room behemoth when it opened a twin tower in 2004. While the second spire is more luxurious, the addition may have created a lodging giant too big for its britches. We waited nearly 5 minutes for an elevator and, at times, endured close to 10 rings before our phone calls to the front desk were answered. We wonder how long room service takes... Nevertheless, the luxurious Omni spoils guests with floor-to-ceiling windows, premium bedding with high thread count sheets, spacious work desks and marble bathrooms. Moreover, the splendid workout options cannot be overlooked and easily substantiate its runner-up position in this price category.

The in-house fitness center is a welcome sight to athletic eyes. The cutting-edge cardio and strength equipment is gassed up, oiled and ready to be worked. Some machines have attached plasma television screens and, thankfully, the programming includes more than CNN.

If Omni's gym does not float your boat, ship out to the Turner Athletic Club in the attached CNN Center Atrium. Hotel guests can access Turner's facility for a $10 fee. Swimmers should head straight over, since the Omni has no lap pool.

CARDIO

TREADMILLS: **6 Precor**
UPRIGHT BIKE: **1 Precor**
RECUMBENT BIKE: **2 Precor**
ELLIPTICAL: **4 Precor**

STRENGTH

MACHINES: **8 Cybex**
DUMBBELLS: **5-50 lbs**

SWIM

SPECS: **Outdoor • Not lap**

OTHER

HOURS: **6a–12a**
COST: **Free**
TV: **Yes**
EXTRA: **$10 Pass to Turner**

BRONZE: Ritz Carlton

181 Peachtree Street, Atlanta, GA 30303
(404) 659-0400 • ritzcarlton.com/hotels/atlanta_downtown

This Ritz Carlton barely made our cut. The diminutive 4th floor workout room's machine count is anemic and, unlike fine wine, the equipment fails to improve with age. The absence of ellipticals, recumbent bikes and free weights is glaring. But it is difficult to berate the Ritz clan too severely given their impeccable service, high thread count bedding, 24-hour room service and warm hospitality. This location even provides a 24-hour "technology butler" whose duties include helping frustrated guests with any computer problems day or night.

CARDIO

TREADMILLS: **4 Trotter**
UPRIGHT BIKE: **2 Cybex**
STEPPER: **2 Cybex • 2 Tectrix • 1 StairMaster**

STRENGTH

MACHINES: **4 Cybex**
DUMBBELLS: **2.5-50 lbs**

OTHER

HOURS: M-F **5a-10p** • SAT-SUN **7a-10p**
COST: **Free**
TV: **Yes**

Stay here if you long for Ritz service and comforts, but plan to walk 7 minutes to Peachtree Athletic Club to sweat. It'll cost you $20/day.

MODERATELY EXPENSIVE

GOLD: Hilton

255 Courtland Street NE, Atlanta, GA 30303
404-659-2000 • atlanta.hilton.com

Not to be outdone in size by the Omni and Westin, Hilton's big momma tops out at 1,224 rooms. We often avoid such grand scale hotels but, in downtown Atlanta, the theme seems to be bigger is better.

With the Hilton brand you can count on the basics: a comfortable but plain room, standard furnishings, average amenities and

CARDIO

TREADMILLS: **3 LF - old**
UPRIGHT BIKE: **4 LF**
RECUMBENT BIKE: **1 LF**
ELLIPTICAL: **1 LF**
STEPPER: **3 StairMaster**

STRENGTH

FREE WEIGHTS: **Yes**
MACHINES: **7 Hoist**
DUMBBELLS: **5-45 lbs**

SWIM

SPECS: **Outdoor • Not lap**

OTHER

HOURS: **5:30a-10p**
COST: **$7**
TV: **Yes**
EXTRAS: **$15 pass to Peachtree; • Tennis • Basketball**

average service. To our surprise, Hilton Atlanta overcame this penchant for mediocrity with its wonderfully equipped fitness and recreation center. Although the bland décor garners no rave reviews, we praise the amount and variety of equipment inside. Most gear is youthful and in good working order. Free weights are a rarity for hotel gyms, and Hilton goes for the Gold with its approximately 300 lbs. of iron for bench press exercises and the like.

While the stated guest fee payable at the fitness center desk is $7/day, there's frequently no attendant on duty, so a freebie may be in order.

The Hilton's across-the-street location from the Peachtree Athletic Club is another bonus — it is the closest hotel to downtown's best health facility. Purchase a pass from the Hilton for $15.

SILVER: Hyatt Regency

265 Peachtree Street NE, Atlanta, GA 30303
(404) 577 1234 • atlantaregency.hyatt.com

CARDIO

TREADMILLS: **5 Cybex**
UPRIGHT BIKE: **2 LF**
RECUMBENT BIKE: **1 LF - old**
ELLIPTICAL: **3 Precor**
STEPPER: **2 StairMaster**

STRENGTH

MACHINES: **4 Hoist**
DUMBBELLS: **5-50 lbs**

SWIM

SPECS: **Outdoor • Not lap**

OTHER

HOURS: **5a-11p**
COST: **Free**
TV: **Yes**
EXTRAS: **$15 pass to Peachtree**

With all of this heavyweight competition, did you really think Hyatt would put a boutique accommodation on its corner? No way! Scaling in at 1,260 guest rooms, Hyatt is the bulkiest on downtown's block. And, typically for large convention-type hotels, Hyatt goes "basic" with its room décor and furnishings. Nothing too bad, but nothing too wonderful either.

Unlike the accommodations, the fitness center is a champ. On the lobby level, the free facility boasts 20-foot ceilings and a fair amount of high-quality equipment. While this is a larger than typical hotel gym, the online description of 5,000 square feet is a stretch. Our guess is approximately 1,500 square feet? No matter, size is not always paramount — it is the equipment inside that matters most. Hyatt's new Precors, StairMasters and other machines make this facility a force to be reckoned with.

If you don't like what you see, you can always walk 5 minutes to Peachtree. Hyatt will sell you a $15/day pass or 3 days/$40.

BRONZE: **Sheraton**

165 Courtland Street, Atlanta GA 30303

(404) 659-6500 • sheratonatlantahotel.com

If you are shopping for a deal, keep your eye on Sheraton. Depending on the date, we saw king/non-smoking rooms going for as little as $109/night during the week — $50/night less than Sheraton's moderately priced rivals. Its 2002 renovation yields a fresh appearance and creative quarters. The 765 playfully decorated rooms afford guests large work desks, ergonomic chairs and colorful bedding. Surprisingly, the unusual salmon and purple tones combine well and create a unique, warm vibe.

CARDIO

TREADMILLS: **4 Cybex**
UPRIGHT BIKE: **3 Tectrix**
RECUMBENT BIKE: **3 Tectrix**
ELLIPTICAL: **4 Trotter**
STEPPER: **2 Tectrix**

STRENGTH

MACHINES: **6 Cybex - old**

SWIM

SPECS: **Indoor • Not lap**

OTHER

HOURS: **24**
COST: **Free**
TV: **Yes**
EXTRAS: **$15 pass to Peachtree**

Sheraton certainly did not make our list for its debilitated workout room. Walking in, we hunched to avoid a ceiling collision. Okay... slight exaggeration. The roof was not THAT low, but the lack of adequate height was noticeable and confining. The exercise equipment was nothing to stand tall about, either. All of the machines were worn, some were really old and none was inviting. Sheraton's saving grace is its proximity to Peachtree Athletic Club, a 3-minute walk from the hotel entrance. The front desk will sell you a pass for $15.

LEAST EXPENSIVE

GOLD: **Best Western Inn at the Peachtree**

330 West Peachtree Street, Atlanta, GA 30308

(404) 577-6970 • bestwestern.com

In search of a downtown Atlanta hotel under $100/night that offers clean and reasonably furnished rooms with a decent workout option? Look no further than Best Western. Don't expect upscale accommodations at these prices, but you will receive a free continental breakfast each morning and the opportunity to purchase a $15/day pass to the Peachtree Athletic Club. So hand over your cash at the front desk and walk 7 minutes to this foolproof facility. If you were wondering about an on-site gym... don't bother.

BEYOND HOTELS DOWNTOWN

Peachtree Center Athletic Club

227 Courtland Street, Atlanta, GA 30303

(404) 523-3833 • peachtreeac.com

The saying, "Don't judge a book by its cover," applies to this downtown Atlanta health club. Located on top of a multi-story parking garage, we would never have guessed that this structure harbors

CARDIO

TREADMILLS: **StarTrac**
UPRIGHT BIKE: **LF • Tectrix**
RECUMBENT BIKE: **LF**
ELLIPTICAL: **LF • StarTrac**
STEPPER: **StairMaster**
ROWING: **Concept II**
OTHER: **Gravitron • XC Ski**

STRENGTH

FREE WEIGHTS: **Yes**
HAMMER: **Yes**
MACHINES: **Cybex • Free Motion • Nautilus**
DUMBBELLS: **3-120 lbs**

SWIM

GRADE: **B+**
SPECS: **4x25m • Indoor • 82°**
TOYS: **Kick • Clock**

OTHER

CLASSES: **Yes**
HOURS: M-F **5:30a-10p** • SAT **8:30a-7p** • SUN **9:30a-6p**
COST: **$20 • Discounts w/hotel pass**
TV: **Yes**
EXTRAS: **1/13 mile indoor track • Basketball • Racquetball**

a workout gold mine. In fact, until the garage elevators delivered us into the 72,000 square foot, spick-and-span fitness nirvana, we feared we were lost.

You will feel like a big shot athlete gearing up for your professional training session when entering this two-story, wide-open facility, filled with the latest and greatest equipment. Whatever your heart desires, Peachtree has it. From its top-of-the-line computerized cardio machinery to its cutting-edge body sculpting free weights to the competition-level lapper that hosts a Masters group, athletic-minded travelers can indulge in any fitness frenzy. If you are in the mood to shoot some hoops or engage in group fun, Peachtree houses a full basketball court and offers more than 60 aerobic classes each week.

This is the best club we toured in metro Atlanta and one of the top fitness centers in the Southeast. Before heading over, be sure to purchase a discounted admission pass from the front desk of your respective hotel. Most offer a discount of $3 to $5 off Peachtree's $20/day rate.

Note: This club offers a full line of reasonably-priced spa and salon services. Peachtree participates in the Wellbridge Reciprocal Program so, if your home club is a Wellbridge member, admission is on the house. Check with your gym.

Turner Athletic Club

100 CNN Center NW, Atlanta, GA 30303
(404) 827-0571

Only Omni hotel guests receive guest privileges at this average facility. Because Omni's complimentary in-house gym will satisfy most travelers' athletic demands, Turner Club is recommended primarily for those seeking a lap swim venue or a more significant strength session (additional free weights and stack-loaded machines).

Omni's website claims Turner's lap pool is 25-meters — but several conversations with Turner staff and our inspection confirm that the indoor water rectangle is only 20 meters. Nevertheless, this pool presents a decent swim option with floating lane lines, bottom stripes, kickboards and pull-buoys. If you are planning to do intervals, bring a watch; we did not notice a pace clock on deck.

Turner's cardio and weight offering is more impressive than its lapper. Weight buffs especially will salivate over the gym's 14 Hammer Strength machines, ton of free weights, wide assortment of dumbbells and over 20 Cybex stack-loaded weight stations. The cardio does not disappoint, either, with over 15 new treadmills, 11 youthful bikes, 11 fresh ellipticals and seven 4400 series StairMaster steppers. And, who knows, maybe you'll get to "spot" for your favorite CNN news anchor.

CARDIO

TREADMILLS: **LF**
UPRIGHT BIKE: **LF**
RECUMBENT BIKE: **LF**
ELLIPTICAL: **Precor • LF**
STEPPER: **StairMaster**
ROWING: **Concept II**

STRENGTH

FREE WEIGHTS: **Yes**
HAMMER: **Yes**
MACHINES: **Cybex**
DUMBBELLS: **5-100 lbs**

SWIM

GRADE: **C+**
SPECS: **4x20m • Indoor • 80-84°**
TOYS: **Kick • Pull**

OTHER

CLASSES: **Yes**
HOURS: M/W **6a-11p** • T/TH **6a-12a** • F **6a–9p** • SAT-SUN **8a-6p**
COST: **$10 • $35/week Omni only**
TV: **Yes**
EXTRAS: **1/10 mile indoor track**

BUCKHEAD

This posh area 6 miles north of downtown Atlanta attracts affluent locals and out-of-towners with over 1,400 retail stores and chic dining spots. If your Atlanta trip allows time for personal indulgence, staying in fashionable Buckhead affords innumerable opportunities for entertainment and fun — especially on weekends.

Despite being home to the world's largest 10K run (Peachtree Road Race-55,000 participants), Buckhead's workout options do not rival downtown's Peachtree Athletic Club. However, our research did uncover several peachy fitness prospects for you to enjoy.

By the way, if you find yourself in town over the Fourth of July and are considering joining in the 10K fun — forget about it! The competition to participate is as fierce as the race itself, with sellouts occurring three months prior to the race's start.

EXPENSIVE

GOLD: **Hotel Intercontinental**
3315 Peachtree Road NE, Atlanta, GA 30326
ichotelsgroup.com/buckhead

Opened in November 2004, this is a stellar member of the upscale Intercontinental chain. All rooms are colored in soft/relaxing tones, and the decor is both tasteful and practical. Bathrooms display high-grade fixtures, but we'd like to see a little more sink counter space.

CARDIO

TREADMILLS: **5 LF**
RECUMBENT BIKE: **2 LF**
ELLIPTICAL: **4 LF**

STRENGTH

MACHINES: **5 LF**
DUMBBELLS: **Yes**

SWIM

Outdoor • Not lap

OTHER

COST: **Free**
TV: **Yes**

When it comes to sweating, our expectation for any upscale hotel includes an appealing workout room with an assortment of quality equipment. Intercontinental's gym and spa combination makes the grade with high-end, modern cardio and strength apparatus. Personal viewing screens are a nice touch.

We always like having the option of getting a massage as a reward for our healthy lifestyle — Intercontinental can make that happen here, too.

SILVER: Ritz Carlton

3434 Peachtree Road, Atlanta, GA 30326
(404) 237-2700 • ritzcarlton.com/hotels/atlanta_buckhead

CARDIO

TREADMILLS: **6 Cybex**
UPRIGHT BIKE: **3 Cybex - 2 old • 2 Tectrix**
ELLIPTICAL: **2 Cybex**
STEPPER: **2 Cybex**

STRENGTH

FREE WEIGHTS: **Yes**
MACHINES: **10 Cybex**
DUMBBELLS: **5-50 lbs**

SWIM

GRADE: **D+**
SPECS: **3x20yd • Indoor • 84°**

OTHER

HOURS: M-F **6a–10p** • SAT-SUN **7a–10p**
COST: **Free**
TV: **Yes**

The Ritz's incredible room comforts, plush surroundings and phenomenal service invite the "L" word (laziness) to creep into your body and mind. Although we cannot rely on its fitness center to inspire, the abundance of shopping, entertainment and unique dining spots surrounding this hotel should elevate your heart rate.

The tiny workout room stocks a mix of old and new Cybex equipment exclusively, so any Life Fitness or Precor fetish will go unsatisfied. Free weights are always a welcome sight, and we credit Ritz for supplying a sufficient amount.

The 20-yard indoor lap pool has bottom stripes but no floating lines or equipment, so serious swimmers looking for more length should consider Crunch Fitness. While this Bally-owned private club will cost $17/day for entry, lap swimmers have no other conveniently located regulation size alternatives.

BRONZE: Grand Hyatt

3300 Peachtree Road, Atlanta, GA 30305
(404) 365-8100 • grandatlanta.hyatt.com

Although a notch below Ritz's luxury, Grand Hyatt's attractive rooms, reliable service and prime location do not disappoint. Lenox Square and Phipps Plaza malls are both within a mile and the hotel's complimentary shuttle can zip you there.

Grand's best workout feature is the 400 lbs. of free weights and accompanying bench/rack in a pint-sized fitness room. The weight machines and dumbbells are sufficient, but the cardio machines need upgrading. Most are older models and not befitting a luxury hotel. Joggers, cyclists and steppers will get by on the frail equipment, but elliptical romantics will be without their beloveds.

Swimmers and those looking for a more elaborate fitness fix should travel to Crunch Fitness and LA Fitness, respectively. Crunch will cost $17 (7 minute walk), and LA Fitness charges $20 (take the shuttle).

CARDIO

TREADMILLS: **4 LF**
UPRIGHT BIKE: **3 LF - 2 old**
RECUMBENT BIKE: **3 LF**
STEPPER: **2 LifeStep • 1 LF**

STRENGTH

FREE WEIGHTS: **Yes**
MACHINES: **8 Maxicam**
DUMBBELLS: **5-50 lbs**

SWIM

SPECS: **Outdoor • Not lap**

OTHER

HOURS: **24**
COST: **Free**
TV: **Yes**

MODERATELY EXPENSIVE

GOLD: Doubletree

3342 Peachtree Road NE, Atlanta, GA 30326
(404) 231-1234 • doubletree.com

GOLD: Courtyard

3332 Peachtree Road NE, Atlanta, GA 30326
(404) 869-0818 • courtyard.com

Located across the street from one another and within 3 blocks of Tower Place Mall, Courtyard's fitness room misses the mark and Doubletree has none. However, each offers guests complimentary passes to a health club that is within a 5-minute walk. Doubletree sends you to Crunch and the Courtyard works with Buckhead Athletic Club. The accommodations are typical for their respective chains, so pick the one with the cheaper rate and include the walk in your plan.

Swimmers, Crunch is your best option, as it offers the only regulation lap pool in the Buckhead area.

LEAST EXPENSIVE

GOLD: Amerisuites

3242 Peachtree Road NE , Atlanta, GA 30305
(404) 869-6161 • amerisuites.com

SILVER: Hampton Inn Buckhead

3398 Piedmont Road NE, Atlanta, GA 30305
(404) 233-5656 • hamptoninn.com

Despite a "Least Expensive" classification, these hotels garner our overall pick for the best places to stay and work out in Buckhead. Each offers clean rooms, free continental breakfasts and access to Buckhead's best health club — LA Fitness (Amerisuites $10, Hampton Inn $15). So your workout will be located located across a parking lot from both hotels (2-minute walk from Amerisuites and 5 from Hampton). Hampton also offers a $5 pass to Crunch. Amerisuites appears to be a newer hotel and is closer to LA Fitness, so we give it the edge. Regardless, book either with confidence.

Note: Jason's Deli, located just north of LA Fitness is a yummy and healthy eatery offering more than just sandwiches. We think you'll like it.

BEYOND HOTELS BUCKHEAD

Crunch Fitness

3365 Piedmont Road, Atlanta, GA 30305
(404) 262-2120 • crunch.com

CARDIO

TREADMILLS: **LF**
UPRIGHT BIKE: **LF**
RECUMBENT BIKE: **StarTrac**
ELLIPTICAL: **LF • Precor**
STEPPER: **StairMaster • Precor**

STRENGTH

FREE WEIGHTS: **Yes**
HAMMER: **Yes**
MACHINES: **Cybex**
DUMBBELLS: **5-100 lbs**

SWIM

GRADE: **C+**
SPECS: **5x25m • Indoor • 78-81°**
TOYS: **Kick • Pull**

OTHER

CLASSES: **Yes**
HOURS: M-F **5:30a-10:30p** • SAT-SUN **8a-8p**
COST: **$17** • **Free Doubletree & Courtyard**
TV: **Yes**
EXTRAS: **1/17 mile indoor track • Basketball • Racquetball • Boxing ring**

This Bally-owned facility, located on the south end of Tower Place Mall (near the movie theater) has some weaknesses, but the positives definitely prevail. First, the good news: Crunch is a full-service gym housing a ton of cardio and weight equipment, a 25-meter indoor pool, basketball and racquetball courts and a variety of classes. Thirty-three treadmills, 24 ellipticals, 18 Cybex weight machines and 8 Life Fitness 9500 series upright bikes exemplify the massive selection of modern apparatus.

Now, the bad news: The machines are crammed together, forcing you to get cozy with your workout neighbor; the weight areas are disorganized with dumbbells spread throughout the floor; and the pool is dark and dreary. Then there are the locker rooms... plan to clean up back at your hotel. During rush hours, this gym can get busy. And if you are not staying at the Courtyard or Doubletree, you must fork over $17 to gain access.

LA Fitness

3232 Peachtree Road NE, Suite A, Atlanta, GA 30305
(404) 233-8311 • lafitness.com

This is the best club in Buckhead without a lap pool, and we encourage all but swimmers to consider the Amerisuites for your bed and LA Fitness for your gym.We have yet to come across a disappointing LA Fitness, and this representative of the expanding franchise is no exception. The décor is warm and inviting, the staff is friendly and the equipment is modern and in large supply.

Highlights include 50 stack-loaded weight machines, 21 Hammer Strength machines, 20 treadmills and 14 ellipticals.

Classes are offered daily and are included in your complimentary guest pass from Amerisuites or Hampton Inn. All others wishing to work out here must have $15 ready.

CARDIO

TREADMILLS: **StarTrac**
UPRIGHT BIKE: **LF**
RECUMBENT BIKE: **LF**
ELLIPTICAL: **LF • Precor**
STEPPER: **StairMaster • Stepmill**
ROWING: **Concept II**

STRENGTH

FREE WEIGHTS: **Yes**
HAMMER: **Yes**
MACHINES: **Cybex • LF • Nautilus • BodyMaster**
DUMBBELLS: **5-125 lbs**

OTHER

CLASSES: **Yes**
HOURS: M-F **5a-10p** • SAT-SUN **8a-8p**
COST: **$15 • Free Hampton & Amerisuites**
TV: **Yes**

RUNNING ROUTES

DOWNTOWN

Piedmont Park

Atlanta's summertime weather can be downright stifling, but the upside is that winter's bite is fairly benign. Our suggestion is to consult with the hotel front desk for an out-and-back route.

However, just north of Downtown (2-3 miles) is Piedmont Park, a highly rated jogging spot. Take Piedmont north to 14th to this large, 185-acre recreation space complete with tennis courts, baseball diamonds, pool and, of course, a nice 2.2+ mile exterior loop with a shorter 1.2 mile interior loop.

Piedmont Park is also the finishing point for the Peachtree Classic 10K, so those runners looking for some additional mileage can follow Peachtree Road to Buckhead (you can take the MARTA back Downtown).

Freedom Park

Another venue is Freedom Park, about 2 miles NE of Downtown and less crowded than Piedmont. This 45-acre park sports well maintained paved paths for runners and bikers. The park runs along North Avenue and Freedom Parkway. In addition, runners can access "PATH," Atlanta's expanding paved trail network.

BUCKHEAD

Piedmont Park

Buckhead runners can also take advantage of Piedmont Park's offering (see above). If you fancy tracing the Peachtree Classic's 10k course, it is easy to follow. Begin at Lenox Square and follow Peachtree Road south to 14th Street, Piedmont Park's entrance. Peach logos on the sidewalks mark the route, and there are mile-markers along the way.

Chastain Park

After Piedmont, the 158-acre Chastain Park is the second most popular running spot, offering a 2.5+ mile loop. However, runners must clock about 3 miles to get there from Buckhead. The Park is located at Wieuca Road and Powers Ferry Road and is set in one of Buckhead's most affluent neighborhoods, next to a golf course.

Austin

32 Locations Reviewed

AUSTIN, TEXAS

As a culturally rich urban community with a small town neighborhood feel, Austin frequently appears on "best cities to live" lists. Natives who hunger for the outdoors are satiated by "Texas' Playgrounds" — 14,000 acres of parks and 150 miles of lakes. Early morning runs around Town Lake, midday trail rides in the Barton Creek greenbelt and a late afternoon dip in one of the City's natural spring swimming holes are all possibilities. However, Austin thrives on much more than a recreational diet. Art gallery perusing along Sixth Street, retail therapy on Congress Avenue and live singing performances in the Warehouse District spice up this city's mix.

The latest ingredient added to Austin's melting pot came courtesy of the technology boom. High heels and wingtips substitute for Birkenstocks in the burgeoning "Silicon Hills." Anchored by corporate heavyweights such as Dell, Cirrus Logic and Inquisite, a parade of high-tech companies continues to march into town. In true Austin style, business deals and negotiations are as likely to occur on tennis courts and running trails as in boardrooms.

Cycling shoes are another fashionable slip-on, thanks to Austin's most esteemed athlete, Lance Armstrong. Bicycle routes, lanes and trails abound throughout the Lone Star State's capital, making it one of America's most alluring cycling cities. On the off chance you see Lance training one morning, holding his wheel (for those non-cycling geeks, this means riding behind him) for a few seconds will impart water cooler bragging rights about "working out" with the "Big Texan."

Finding athletic endeavors in this fitness friendly town is an easy "feet" — just don't forget your shoes.

EXPENSIVE

GOLD: Intercontinental Stephen F. Austin

701 Congress Avenue, Austin, TX 78701
(512) 457-8800 • austin.intercontinental.com

GOLD: Driskill

604 Brazos Street, Austin, TX 78701
(512) 474-5911 • driskillhotel.com

Intercontinental

CARDIO

TREADMILLS: **3 Cybex**
UPRIGHT BIKE: **2 Cybex**
RECUMBENT BIKE: **2 Cybex**
ELLIPTICAL: **1 Cybex**
STEPPER: **2 Cybex**

STRENGTH

MACHINES: **6 Cybex**
DUMBBELLS: **5-50 lbs**

SWIM

GRADE: **D-**
SPECS: **1x13yd • Indoor • 78-82°**

OTHER

HOURS: **6a-11p**
COST: **Free**
TV: **Yes**

Driskill

CARDIO

TREADMILLS: **2 StarTrac**
RECUMBENT BIKE: **2 StarTrac**
ELLIPTICAL: **2 Precor**
STEPPER: **2 StairMaster**

STRENGTH

MACHINES: **5 Hoist**
DUMBBELLS: **5-50 lbs**

OTHER

HOURS: **24**
COST: **Free**
TV: **Yes**

These two hotels in the heart of Austin offer a very similar lodging and workout experience. Guests at both will enjoy luxurious and historic accommodations.

Intercontinental goes for a 1920s look and feel, while Driskill marches further back in time, offering rooms with late 19th Century Victorian features.

On the workout front, the "Stephen F.," as locals call it, boasts a larger exercise room and more equipment than the Driskill. However, before you start dialing reservations, picky workout fiends may favor Driskill's wider assortment of brands, as Stephen F. stocks Cybex exclusively. Both fitness centers house newer apparatus, but noticeably absent from Driskill's red-and-black-walled gym is an upright bike.

Guests of either hotel desiring a more elaborate workout can walk 3 minutes to Gold's Gym — a new and improved version.

Swimmers can get a little water action at the Intercontinental's 13-yard, bottom-striped square. Bring the abacus to track the shortened laps. For better swim options, see the community alternatives in the "Beyond Hotels" section that follows.

Bottom line, our recommendation is to book according to price. If no real discrepancy exists, go with the Intercontinental. Or dismiss both and stay at the Hilton.

MODERATELY EXPENSIVE

GOLD: **Hilton** Austin Convention Center
500 East 4th Street, Austin, TX 78701
(512) 482-8000 • hilton.com

Built with the business traveler and conventioneer in mind, this modern and contemporary Hilton in the heart of Downtown opened December 2003.

Like a sportscar's aroma fresh off the lot, this youthful Hilton smells of luxury. Marble flooring in the lobby, common area wood paneling and fashionably appointed guest rooms contribute to the hotel's splendid scent. The room rates don't stink, either — $100/night cheaper than the "Expensive" hotels and about $30/night less than Embassy Suites.

Hilton's 8th floor fitness center is nicely designed, with cheery colors, wide open spaces and spanking new equipment. Traveling athletes must pay a vexing $10 access fee ($15 per stay), but take the medicine, because Hilton provides the best hotel workout prescription in town. While we are not crazy about the True brand machines, if ever a workout facility tempted us to use them, this is it. Hilton supplies sweat-aholics with 16 gleaming models of this less popular brand along with an estimated 350 pounds of free weights (bench and racks included).

The outdoor pool deck and hot tub are attractive features but not practical for lap swimmers. Those with a water workout in mind will need to sniff out one of the community alternatives.

CARDIO

TREADMILLS: **6 True**
UPRIGHT BIKE: **2 True**
RECUMBENT BIKE: **3 True**
ELLIPTICAL: **5 True**
STEPPER: **1 StarTrac**

STRENGTH

FREE WEIGHTS: **Yes ~ 350 lbs**
MACHINES: **9 Paramount**
DUMBBELLS: **5-75 lbs**

SWIM

SPECS: **Outdoor • Not lap**

OTHER

HOURS: **24**
COST: **$10 • $15/stay**
TV: **Yes**

SILVER: **Embassy Suites Hotel** Downtown
300 South Congress Avenue, Austin, TX 78704
(512) 469-9000 • embassysuites.com

On the south side of Town Lake, Embassy's atrium-style hotel features guest rooms typical for this mid-range brand. Since downtown's heart is just north of Town Lake, this city's real flavor is a good 10-15 minute walk away.

You will not have to wander far, however, to nibble Embassy's complimentary made-to-order breakfast served each morning in the lobby. Free booze and snacks are also offered during the hotel's evening happy hour.

Keep walking past Embassy's in-hotel workout option. The tiny room's dated machines are better suited to a fitness museum. Fortunately, management recognizes this weakness and offers guests free passes to Gold's Gym on 6th Street, a 15-20 minute walk. We like this new and improved Gold's, but we wish it was closer.

LEAST EXPENSIVE

GOLD: **Homestead Studios & Suites Downtown**
507 South First Street, Austin, TX 78704
(512) 476-1818 • homesteadhotels.com

This hotel is an extended stay facility, which means quarters include a complete kitchen, cookware, free local calls and on-site laundry. On top of that, Homestead offers its rooms for under $100/night, which is low for downtown Austin. Without a gym, Homestead provides guests with free passes to Gold's on 6th Street. Similar to the Embassy Suites, with a location on Town Lake's south shore, plan on a 15-20 minute walk to Gold's and downtown's hub.

BEYOND HOTELS

Gold's Gym
101 West 6th Street, Austin, TX 78701
(512) 479-0044 • goldsgym.com

CARDIO

TREADMILLS: **Precor • StarTrac**
UPRIGHT BIKE: **Precor • StarTrac**
RECUMBENT BIKE: **LF • Tectrix**
ELLIPTICAL: **Precor**
STEPPER: **StairMaster • Tectrix**
ROWING: **Concept II**

STRENGTH

FREE WEIGHTS: **Yes**
HAMMER: **Yes**
MACHINES: **Cybex • Free Motion • Icarian**
DUMBBELLS: **5-110 lbs**

OTHER

CLASSES: **Yes**
HOURS: M-F **24** • SAT **8a-8p** • SUN **10a-8p**
COST: **Free Embassy & Homestead • $16.24 Others**
TV: **Yes**

If the name Gold's Gym calls to mind images of intimidating body builders and massive muscle heads, you have this small Austin club all wrong. Located on the main drag of 6th Street, this reinvented Gold's appeals to all exercise enthusiasts with its high energy flair, stock of good-quality cardio equipment and top-of-the-line weights. In the Precor brand alone, Gold's supplies 15 treads, 14 ellipticals and 2 upright bikes. Weight trainers will be impressed by the 9 Hammer Strength machines and plenty of free weights. Group exercisers enjoy an assortment of classes (including spin), but swimmers are left out of the fun. The club does not include a lapper.

With a $16.24/day fee, Gold's is not cheap. So staying at a hotel that offers a free pass is smart (e.g., Embassy and Homewood).

Barton Springs Pool
2101 Barton Springs Road, Austin, TX 78704 (in Zilker Park)
(512) 476-9044
www.ci.austin.tx.us/parks/bartonsprings.htm

The sports-minded town of Austin is filled with enviable community swim options. About 2 miles from Downtown, the 3-acre

SWIM

GRADE: **B (open water)**
HOURS: **5a-10p** • TH **5-9a & 7-10p**
COST: **$3**

Barton is a fresh water spring which averages 68° year round. Termed a "pool," it is really a dammed off 100-foot wide x 1/8-mile long lake, making it an ideal spot to practice your open water technique — if you can tolerate the chill. During Austin's hot summer days, you'd better show up early, because the midday sun brings out the floating rafts, noodles and children.

Note: Barton is free from November to March and $3 other months.

Deep Eddy Pool

401 Deep Eddy Drive, Austin, TX
(512) 472-8546 • www.deepeddy.org

SWIM

GRADE: **B+**
HOURS: M-F **6a-8p** • SAT-SUN **10a-8p**
COST: **$3**

Deep Eddy is Texas' oldest pool, and its tip-top shape offers swimmers endless lap potential during its February through October season. Fed by an artesian well, Deep Eddy has 8 lanes and 33-1/3-yards of length with floating lines and bottom stripes. The water temperature typically ranges from 68-72 degrees, so getting in is an awakening experience. However, completing a few base intervals should chase the numbness from your body.

Note: After your swim, have a meal at Magnolia Café on 6th Street across from the park entrance. We heard the breakfasts were great and, judging from the line outside, many others have heard the same.

Big Stacy Pool Stacy Neighborhood Pool

800 E. Live Oak Street, Austin, TX
(512) 445-0304
www.ci.austin.tx.us/parks/pools_schedule.htm#Stacy

SWIM

GRADE: **B**
HOURS: M-F **6a-8p** • SAT-SUN **12-7p**
COST: **Free**
TOYS: **Pull**

Longing for a toasty outdoor swim in the winter? As the only free and heated public pool in Austin, this is your place.

Three miles from Downtown, the pool offers 6 lanes of 33-yard lap swimming marked by floating lines and bottom stripes in water that is typically maintained at 80 degrees. The place is nothing fancy — just a pool with a fence around it. Pull-buoys are the only toys provided and, if you plan to swim intervals, bring a watch as a pace-clock is not on deck.

To get here, exit at the Oltorf-IH35 intersection. It's a little tricky, so be sure to consult the hotel staff before heading over.

24 Hour Fitness Hancock Center (Sport)

1000 East 41st Street, Austin, TX 78751
(512) 458-2424 • 24hourfitness.com

CARDIO

TREADMILLS: **LF**
UPRIGHT BIKE: **LF**
RECUMBENT BIKE: **LF**
ELLIPTICAL: **LF • Precor**
STEPPER: **StairMaster • Stepmill**
ROWING: **Concept II**

STRENGTH

FREE WEIGHTS: **Yes**
HAMMER: **Yes**
MACHINES: **Cybex • Free Motion**
DUMBBELLS: **5-125 lbs**

SWIM

GRADE: **B**
SPECS: **3x25yd • Indoor • 82°**
TOYS: **Kick • Clock**

OTHER

CLASSES: **Yes**
HOURS: **24**
COST: **$15**
TV: **Yes**
EXTRAS: **Basketball**

This great workout option is for those willing to drive to — and pay for — a cutting-edge fitness center without large crowds. Opened in 2003, 24 Hour Fitness stocks a plethora of fresh, ultramodern machines and equipment. All of the best brands are under one roof, including 31 Nautilus Nitro weight machines, 22 Life Fitness treadmills, 12 Precor ellipticals and 12 Hammer Strength free weight machines.

Swimmers get a 3 lane, 25-yard pool that is not as scenic as Austin's outdoor community swimming holes but usually less crowded.

The club is located on the back side of the Hancock Center Mall, off 41st Street, about a 5-minute drive north of Downtown. Admission is $15.

RUNNING ROUTES

Town Lake

Town Lake's "hike and bike" path is a runner's dream that can be accessed easily from all downtown hotels. The 10-mile loop is scenic and outfitted with mile markers, drinking fountains and restrooms. For those looking for a little less mileage, the bridges along the way provide shorter loop options. The Town Lake path also connects to the Barton Creek Greenway, a great off-road running option. Runners will be very happy here.

For more information, or to view trail maps online, check out runtex.com.

Baltimore

BALTIMORE, MARYLAND

In an area of the country where catching crabs is a good thing, Baltimore's Chesapeake Bay blue hard shell crabs provide a tasty and fun meal for locals and tourists alike. Never mind the soft shell version, which is the same crab plucked from the sea before it can grow (molt) a new and larger hard cover. The real fun occurs while the ornery crustacean remains in its rigid form. Diners are encouraged to don a bib, utilize a mallet, eat with their hands and make a mess — high-chairs are optional.

For those interested in a more unique preparation, local restaurants in this crabby harbor go overboard with options such as steamed crab, crab cakes, crab soup, deviled crab, grilled crab, crab omelets... we could go on. If you can't find a crab dish to enjoy in Baltimore, then forget it — you're never going to fancy eating the cranky saltwater critter.

Come to think of it, exercising and cracking crab have something in common... they both take an awful lot of work for a little bit of result.

29 Locations Reviewed

EXPENSIVE

GOLD: Renaissance Harborplace

202 East Pratt Street, Baltimore, MD 21202
(410) 547-1200 • renaissancehotels.com

CARDIO

TREADMILLS: **4 Precor**
RECUMBENT BIKE: **1 Precor**
ELLIPTICAL: **2 Precor**

STRENGTH

FREE WEIGHTS: **Yes**
MACHINES: **6 Cybex**
DUMBBELLS: **5-50 lbs**

SWIM

SPECS: **Indoor • Not lap**

OTHER

HOURS: **24**
COST: **Free**
TV: **Yes**

This luxury high-rise hotel commands the best location in downtown Baltimore. On the Inner Harbor, across the street from the Gallery Shops at Harborplace and connected to Harborplace Pavilion, Renaissance guests enjoy convenient access to all of the city center's retail shops, restaurants and attractions. The price of admission may be high, but the Renaissance delivers with a smile. Comfortable bedding, adequate workspace and sparkling bathrooms are this 622-room hotel's staples. Many of the units have spectacular views of the Bay.

Renaissance's December 2003 decision to relocate its in-house fitness center from the pool deck to a 4th floor expanse was music to our ears. This new and improved room receives plenty of sunshine via large windows with exceptional views. In conjunction with the move, ownership spent a good chunk of cash on brand-new, first-rate equipment for guests to enjoy. We are especially fond of the stack-loaded weight machines, wide array of dumbbells and large supply of free weights. With the general manager's office a mere 5 paces away, you know this workout facility is monitored and immaculately maintained by the engineering and housekeeping crews.

Swimmers must walk 10 minutes to Brick Bodies for a 20-meter dip or drive 10 minutes to Meadowbrook for a 50-meter option, as Renaissance has no lap option on-site.

Note: Need an additional perk to tip the scales in favor of this top-rated hotel? Starbucks is just off the lobby.

SILVER: Hyatt Regency

300 Light Street, Baltimore, MD 21202
(410) 528-1234 • baltimore.hyatt.com

A respectable showing by Hyatt, this modern hotel is connected via skybridge to the Baltimore Convention Center and Inner Harbor. Similar to many of its brethren, this Hyatt's rooms surround a 14-story atrium. Its 486-guest quarters offer contemporary elegance in stylish blue and gold tones, black marble bathroom vanities and floor-to-ceiling windows. The motif is more business than leisure, but the ambiance is far from boring.

More proof that bigger is not always better: Hyatt's independently run Nautilus Health Club stocks more equipment in a larger space than the Renaissance, but falls well short of its rival's state-of-the-art quality. On Hyatt's 4th floor, guests are hit with a $10/day exercise tariff before setting foot on a treadmill.

Weaving our way through the tightly-packed club, we noticed a lack of newly purchased equipment. The York stack-loaded weight stations and most of the cardio machines exhibit signs of wear and tear. With an enormous dumbbell set and plenty of free weights lining the floor, strength is clearly this club's emphasis.

Swimmers must look to Brick Bodies or Meadowbrook for a lap session.

CARDIO

TREADMILLS: **2 Cybex • 1 StarTrac**
UPRIGHT BIKE: **2 LF**
ELLIPTICAL: **3 Reebok**
STEPPER: **2 LifeStep**

STRENGTH

FREE WEIGHTS: **Yes**
HAMMER: **Yes**
MACHINES: **14 York**
DUMBBELLS: **5-125 lbs**

SWIM

SPECS: **Outdoor • Not lap**

OTHER

CLASSES: **Yes**
HOURS: M-F **6a-9p** • SAT-SUN **8a-5p**
COST: **$10**
TV: **Yes**
EXTRAS: **1/8 mile outdoor track • Basketball • Tennis**

MODERATELY EXPENSIVE

GOLD: **Radisson Plaza Lord Baltimore**

20 West Baltimore Street, Baltimore, MD 21201
(410) 539-8400 • radisson.com

Located 5 blocks from the Inner Harbor, Radisson welcomes visitors in search of a pleasing accommodation at more affordable prices. The historic building's classic turn-of-the-century style prevails throughout its 439 rooms. Cream tones and antique furnishings decorate guest quarters in a manner that satisfies but does not wow the senses. This 19th Century era hotel keeps pace with modern times by providing complimentary, high-speed internet access in its lobby bar and in-house Starbucks.

CARDIO

TREADMILLS: **4 LF**
UPRIGHT BIKE: **2 LF**
RECUMBENT BIKE: **1 LF**
ELLIPTICAL: **1 LF**
STEPPER: **1 Universal** - old

STRENGTH

MACHINES: **1 Multi**
DUMBBELLS: **5-50 lbs**

OTHER

HOURS: **6a-11p**
COST: **Free**
TV: **Yes**

Radisson's otherwise dreary lower-level exercise room is brightened by several good-quality Life Fitness cardio machines. Although there are no free weights, an ample set of dumbbells and a mediocre multi-gym are on-site. Brick Bodies is directly across the street, but we recommend first inspecting Radisson's fitness center, since it may have all you need. A sweat at Brick runs $10.

Though Brick owns a 20-meter lap pool, swimmers who want an "A" rated facility and don't mind a short drive should consider a Meadowbrook commute.

SILVER: **Wyndham Inner Harbor**

101 West Fayette Street, Baltimore, MD 21201

(410) 752-1100 • wyndham.com

CARDIO

TREADMILLS: **3 LF - old**

UPRIGHT BIKE: **2 LF**

STEPPER: **2 LifeStep • 1 LF**

STRENGTH

MACHINES: **5 Nautilus • 3 Hoist**

SWIM

SPECS: **Outdoor • Not lap**

OTHER

HOURS: **24**

COST: **Free**

TV: **Yes**

This enormous, modern hotel sits across the street from Brick Bodies, cementing its runner-up spot in the category. Both Wyndham and Radisson have a central Baltimore location, convenient to the Baltimore Arena and 10 minutes by foot to the Inner Harbor.

Wyndham's 707 rooms are uninspiring. Guests will find basic accoutrements plus a Herman Miller Aeron office chair and higher than average ceilings. At 200 square feet, the units are somewhat small, so open the window shades to expand the quarters with natural light.

Don't expect any inspiration from the in-house gym, either. While the rather depressing room contains a scant number of newer weight machines, most of the cardio equipment is on social security. Non-finicky athletes may be able to punch in a meager weight workout using the gym's stack-loaded weight stations. However, with no free weights or dumbbells, getting a full body strength session is a challenge. We strongly recommend forking over the $10 fee, showing your room key and exercising at Brick Bodies. Actually, if you don't mind a little farther walk to Brick, Tremont Plaza's less expensive accommodations may present an overall better package.

Swimmers willing to drive should consider a trip to Meadowbrook's stellar aquatic center (5-10 minutes).

LEAST EXPENSIVE

GOLD: **Tremont Plaza**

222 Saint Paul Street, Baltimore, MD 21202

(410) 727-2222 • tremontsuitehotels.com

It was difficult to find a desirable downtown Baltimore hotel under $100/night. Those with rates under a C-note are more "roach" than "motel." Tremont Plaza is the best budget option we discovered. Not to be confused with Tremont Park, the Plaza is a 37-story, all-suite hotel about a 10-minute walk from the Inner Harbor. There are studio, one-bedroom and two-bedroom suites, each with a kitchenette and stylish interior. The least expensive studios at 500 square feet have plenty of space for 2 people. A café/deli on Tremont's ground floor offers delicious and healthy hot/cold food items.

Forget about working out in the 4th floor exercise room. Stocked with 4 disappointing machines in a diminutive square space, traveling athletes will welcome the 5-minute walk to Brick Bodies. You'll pay $10 — just show your room key.

Swimmers, think about freestyling at Meadowbrook instead. It's worth the 5-10 minute drive.

SILVER: Days Inn Inner Harbor

100 Hopkins Place, Baltimore, MD 21201
(410) 576-1000 • daysinnerharbor.com

With guest room doors that open into interior hallways (not outside), this Days Inn is a good representative of the budget hotel chain. The guest quarters are comparable to Wyndham's, save the Herman Miller office chair. And, with a renovation completed in 2003, the rooms provide an almost cozy feel.

Four pieces of distressed equipment sit in the hardly occupied workout room. To repeat what's becoming a familiar battle cry in this town, "Head to Brick Bodies!" From Days, it requires close to a 12-minute walk.

Note: Remember to bring your room key.

BEYOND HOTELS

Brick Bodies Fitness Center

218 North Charles Street, Baltimore, MD 21201
Center Plaza, corner of Charles and Fayette Streets
(410) 547-0053 • brickbodies.com

Located in the Charles Center office tower's plaza level, Brick's mediocre health club is short on space and even shorter on high-quality equipment. Before you get too down on Baltimore's only "walkable" full-service fitness facility, let us give you the positives. The club sports an abundance of strength equipment, including stack-loaded weight stations, free weights and a wide range of dumbbells. And, while the weight machines are older models, they still perform. Endurance exercisers must search for the few buried treasures in the rough cardio sea, but, rest assured, several gems will pique your interest. Best bets may be Brick's 6 newer Life Fitness bikes or 6 Life Fitness treads.

CARDIO

TREADMILLS: **LF**
UPRIGHT BIKE: **LF**
RECUMBENT BIKE: **LF**
ELLIPTICAL: **LF**
STEPPER: **StairMaster - old • Stepmill**
ROWING: **Concept II**

STRENGTH

FREE WEIGHTS: **Yes**
HAMMER: **Yes**
MACHINES: **Eagle**
DUMBBELLS: **5-100 lbs**

SWIM

GRADE: **C+**
SPECS: **4x20m • Indoor • 84°**
TOYS: **Kick • Pull • Clock**

OTHER

CLASSES: **Yes**
HOURS: M-F **6a-10p** • SAT-SUN **9a-3p**
COST: **$10 Hotels • $15 Others**
TV: **Yes**
EXTRAS: **Basketball • Squash**

Swimmers coming to Brick must settle for a 20-meter lapper. Floating lines and bottom stripes divide the lanes and toys are available for freestyle variety. Overall, keep your expectations in check for this average club, and you will come away satisfied.

Note: Brick's website includes a variety of helpful photos.

Meadowbrook Aquatic Center

5700 Cottonworth Avenue, Baltimore, Maryland 21209
(410) 433-8300 • mbrook.com

SWIM

GRADE: #1 **A** • #2 **A**
SPECS: #1 **8x50m • Indoor • 80°**
#2 **8x50m • Outdoor • 80°**
TOYS: **Kick • Pull • Clock**
MASTERS: **Yes**

OTHER

HOURS: M-F **5:30a-9:30p** • SAT **6a-8p** • SUN **10a-7p**
COST: **$12**

Downtown Baltimore has a dearth of appealing lap pools, with Brick Bodies' 20-meter shorty as best in show. A non-recommended health club holds the only other downtown lapper (Merritt Club/ Downtown Athletic Club), but the $20/day access charge for its even shorter 20-yard pool, as well as its inferior fitness equipment, drops it from contention. Not satisfied with these options, we put in some overtime and found an additional venue that shines. If you have a car and do not mind a 10-minute drive, head to Meadowbrook Aquatic Center for a $12 water rendezvous.

This enormous gym and aquatic center (a lot more swim than gym) boasts an indoor AND outdoor 50-meter lap pool. Though Meadowbrook's indoor pool is open year round, Mother Nature forces the outdoor pool's closure from October through mid May. Meadowbrook normally arranges the pools with a short and long-course combination, setting up a bulkhead that jets out into the middle. With this design, simultaneous 25-yard, 25-meter and 50-meter swimming can occur in one competition-quality pool. Check out Meadowbrook's website for great photos and a more detailed description. Bottom line is that this is a fantastic lap option.

True to its title, swimming is clearly emphasized over exercise equipment. The fitness center is nothing more than a narrow corridor suspended over the pools decorated with a few old machines. So come here for the water, or else you'll go home with a whine.

RUNNING ROUTES

Inner Harbor

Baltimore's Inner Harbor is the place to run, but striders will have to mind the traffic on this street and sidewalk course. The approximate 6-miler out-and-back route begins at the Inner Harbor. Pratt Street is a main east/west thoroughfare that will get you to the Harbor. Run south on Light Street to Key Hwy and Fort Avenue to Fort McHenry and back. The scenic route will take you past some of Baltimore's sights, including Federal Hill Park.

BIRMINGHAM, ALABAMA

Here's a question for you trivia buffs: Who is Birmingham's most famous professional athlete? Need a clue? Recognized throughout the world, he played pro baseball and owns six world championship rings. Have the answer? Keep reading.

Known stateside as "Pittsburgh of the South," Birmingham is named after the British city famous for its considerable iron and coal industries. When the mill horns sound, locals spend their "R&R" fishing from bass boats, golfing on tightly cut fairways and cheering for their favorite NASCAR drivers. This is the heart of Dixie after all — so, although Birmingham played host to the 2004 U.S. Olympic marathon qualifications, we were not surprised to discover that Downtown's five hotels did not include anything close to full-service gyms. In local speak, "the pickins ar' gonna be slim for y'all who do that goofy runnin' in place stuff." While providing worthwhile exercise opportunities do not appear to be the hotels' priority, their employees and the rest of Birmingham compensate with big hearts and Southern hospitality.

Don't despair, we did find a great workout place for y'all — the Downtown YMCA.

ANSWER: *Michael Jordan played for the AA Birmingham Barons after his first retirement from basketball.*

DOWNTOWN

Central Business District/UAB

A total of five hotels offer rooms in downtown Birmingham: Tutwiler, Crowne Plaza, Sheraton, Radisson and Pickwick. The first three are located in Birmingham's central business district, while Radisson and Pickwick are a couple miles away in the University of Alabama area. With no hotel providing a useful on-site gym, athletic-minded travelers will want to stay conveniently close to Birmingham's best workout option — the Downtown YMCA. Tutwiler, Crowne Plaza and Sheraton are within walking distance. The UAB hotels are not. Therefore, we recommend eliminating Radisson and Pickwick from consideration even if business on UAB's campus brought you to town.

Birmingham

7
Locations Reviewed

MODERATELY EXPENSIVE

GOLD: Tutwiler A Wyndham Historic Hotel

2021 Park Place North, Birmingham, AL 35203
(205) 322-2100 • wyndham.com

In the heart of Birmingham's business district and within a 3-minute walk to the Downtown YMCA, Tutwiler is an historic hotel offering turn-of-the-century elegance in a prime locale. As this city's most upscale property, Tutwiler provides guests with pillow-top mattresses, high speed internet access (surcharge) and Herman Miller Aeron desk chairs. The somewhat dreary rooms could use some brightening, so open the curtains as far as they will go and let in the sunshine.

Tutwiler does not have any workout facility in-house, but it will cover your admission fee at the Downtown YMCA 2 blocks away. Stop by the front desk for your free pass and bring a picture I.D.

SILVER: Crowne Plaza

2101 Fifth Avenue North, Birmingham, AL 35203
(205) 324-2101 • crowneplaza.com

CARDIO

TREADMILL: **2 StarTrac**
UPRIGHT BIKE: **1 StarTrac**
RECUMBENT BIKE: **1 StarTrac**
STEPPER: **1 StarTrac**

STRENGTH

MACHINES: **3 York**

OTHER

HOURS: **24**
COST: **Free**
TV: **Yes**

Only a block away from the Tutwiler, and with comparable room rates, Crowne's best feature is its central location. When a hotel's website highlights in-room standards like televisions, clock radios, telephones and private bathrooms, you know amenities are in scarce supply. However, this property's guest quarters are clean, cozy and the best alternative if Tutwiler is full.

Without a "fee arrangement" with the Downtown YMCA, we hoped Crowne would have a respectable on-site workout option. Unfortunately, its basement fitness facility did not meet our standards. The cellar's gloomy room provides little equipment and even less ambiance. While the StarTrac machines are fairly new, it would be difficult for us to exercise here knowing that an impressive Y is around the corner. Since Crowne does not cover the Y's $15 fee and its room quality is a notch below, choosing Tutwiler is the smart choice.

BRONZE: Sheraton

2101 Richard Arrington Jr. Blvd. N., Birmingham, AL 35203
(205) 324-5000 • sheraton.com/birmingham

Connected to the Birmingham Jefferson Convention Complex on the outskirts of Downtown, the Sheraton is barely within walking distance to the Downtown YMCA (10-15 minutes). A large hotel with a business motif, Sheraton's 770 guest rooms are simply designed with standard furnishings and dull patterns.

On the 3rd floor, the glass-enclosed exercise room is more greenhouse than fitness center. Two walls of floor-to-ceiling windows allow passers-by and those at the pool to watch you sweat. Inside the workout bubble, Sheraton provides 6 low-quality True brand machines and one always-popular upright fan bike. So, athletic-minded guests should head out the door for a 10 to 15-minute YMCA trek. And, since you are not staying at the Tutwiler, have your $15 ready.

CARDIO

TREADMILL: **4 True**
UPRIGHT BIKE: **1 Fan**
RECUMBENT BIKE: **1 True**
ELLIPTICAL: **1 True**

STRENGTH

MACHINES: **1 Multi**
DUMBBELLS: **5-40 lbs**

SWIM

SPECS: **Indoor • Not lap**

OTHER

HOURS: **6a-10p**
COST: **Free**
TV: **Yes**

BEYOND HOTELS

Downtown YMCA

2101 Fourth Avenue North, Birmingham, AL 35203
(205) 324-4563 • ymcabham.org

Downtown Birmingham actually has two YMCAs: Downtown and Five Points. The Downtown location is larger, provides better equipment, has longer hours and is within walking distance of the three hotels listed above.

The Downtown YMCA is a four-floor facility loaded with cutting-edge equipment, an indoor track, a full-length basketball court and a quality lap pool. Recently remodeled, the bright and stylish third floor fitness room is stocked with 26 stack-loaded weight stations, 8 Life Fitness 9500 treadmills, and 4 each of uprights, recumbents and ellipticals. Free weights are here in force, too, along with pulley systems and a full set of dumbbells.

For those with a penchant for group training, this Y offers a broad range of classes including aerobics and spin.

Swimmers will be satisfied by the 25-yard lap pool with 6 lanes separated by floating lane lines and bottom stripes. A high ceiling and plenty of windows give the indoor rectangle an outdoor vibe. To be safe, bring a swim cap; many Ys will not let you swim without one.

Note: Hours are limited on Sunday, so plan your day accordingly.

CARDIO

TREADMILLS: **LF • StarTrac**
UPRIGHT BIKE: **StairMaster • LF**
RECUMBENT BIKE: **LF**
ELLIPTICAL: **LF • Precor - old**
STEPPER: **StairMaster**
ROWING: **Concept II**
OTHER: **Crossrobic**

STRENGTH

FREE WEIGHTS: **Yes**
HAMMER: **Yes**
MACHINES: **LF • Cybex • Nautilus • BodyMaster**
DUMBBELLS: **5-100 lbs**

SWIM

GRADE: **B**
SPECS: **6x25yd • Indoor • 84°**
TOYS: **Kick • Pull • Clock**

OTHER

CLASSES: **Yes**
HOURS: M-F **5a-9p** • SAT **8a-5p** • SUN **1-5p**
COST: **$15 • Free Tutwiler**
TV: **Yes**
EXTRAS: **1/10 mile indoor track • Basketball • Racquetball**

RUNNING ROUTES

Highland Avenue Loop

While running in any Downtown area presents the usual urban challenges of stoplights, cars, pollution, etc., we understand there is a decent 5+ mile route that locals call the Highland Avenue Loop. Unfortunately, you will likely want to note and confirm the path!

It starts at Downtown's Linn Park. If you head south, you will pass through Downtown's heart, up a hill to the 5 Points South area, then left on Highland, which will turn into 32nd. Follow 32nd to 2nd Avenue South. If you are not lost at this point, you will pick up 20th again. Take a right and you will be back to Linn Park. The allure is the neighborhood's historic homes.

Lane Park

An out-and-back run is also a possibility in Birmingham. The 7-miler starts at the Radisson (20th and 6th). Head south on Highland, which becomes Arlington Avenue, to Cahaba Road. When you hit Mountain Brook Parkway, turn around...

Boston

BOSTON, MASSACHUSETTS

In this sports-crazy town, most locals (male and female alike) can happily relay last night's game rundown, including scores, highlights and favorite players' stats. The Red Sox get most of the ink, but Bostonians love their multiple Super Bowl Champion Patriots, '80s dynasty Celtics and the "Big Bad Bruins." While these teams capture headlines throughout the year, Boston's "little" marathon on Patriot's Day puts Beantown on the running world's map, too. Boston without athletics would be like peanut butter without jelly, a workout without sweat, yin with no yang.

Do not mistake Boston natives for simple-minded sports fans, however. Despite their funny accents, these season ticket holders are likely to showcase diplomas from the esteemed hometown institutions of Harvard, MIT, Wellesley, Boston University, Tufts and Boston College. Quantum physics, Black-Scholes option pricing and Newton's laws of motion are easily understood by this high IQ crew. Now, if only they could devise a systematic scheme to defeat those darn Yankees!

42 Locations Reviewed

EXPENSIVE

GOLD: **Ritz Carlton** Boston Common

10 Avery Street, Boston, MA 02111
(617) 574-7100 • ritzcarlton.com/hotels/boston_common

Make sure you book the right one! Beantown sports two Ritz properties located on opposite sides of Boston Common. The athletic-minded traveler's choice by far is the Avery Street Ritz. Situated in the Theater District and connected to the Sports Club/LA, it hits a home-run with the best stay/play option in Boston.

The guest accommodations are far from traditional, and we are big fans. Mauve and cream tones dominate the crisp, cool and chic surroundings. All 192 soundproofed rooms come equipped with feather beds, down pillows, large marble tiled baths, complimentary bottled water and CD/cassette players. And it just gets better...

The fabulous on-site 100,000 square foot Sports Club/LA will satiate any exercise craving. While your room key grants workout privileges, there are potential access fees. Business travelers booking via a corporate account (confirm with guest reception) are in luck — the $10 fee is waived. Leisure travelers are hit with a $10/day per room charge. Two people staying in one room pay $10 total or $5 each per day. We are perturbed by expensive "full-service" hotels that impose fees for their workout option, but this expense is well worth it. Sports Club/LA delivers an unparalleled fitness experience, and it's the best Boston has to offer.

SILVER: **Four Seasons**

200 Boylston Street, Boston, MA 02116
(617) 338-4400 • fourseasons.com/boston

CARDIO

TREADMILLS: **6 Precor**
UPRIGHT BIKE: **2 Precor**
RECUMBENT BIKE: **1 Precor**
ELLIPTICAL: **2 Precor**
STEPPER: **2 Precor**

STRENGTH

MACHINES: **9 Cybex**
DUMBBELLS: **1-50 lbs**

SWIM

GRADE: **D**
SPECS: **2x15yd • Indoor • 84°**
TOYS: **Kick**

OTHER

HOURS: **24** • POOL **6a-10p**
COST: **Free**
TV: **Yes**

The upscale Four Seasons brand speaks for itself. Count on exceptional service, wonderful rooms, a quality workout option — and, unfortunately, really expensive rates. Overlooking the Boston Public Garden, this particular property has all of the above, including a top-notch gym.

The 8th floor fitness center houses a moderate number of high-end cardio and weight stations in a happy environment. Cardio fans will be satisfied with the sweat options and can tune into their favorite programs via each machine's individual plasma screen. Strength buffs may feel short-changed by the absence of free weights, but the other muscle apparatus is first rate. While its machines are the best on the market and added touches such as complimentary fruit and flavored water substantiate its runner-up ranking, they are not enough to propel Four Seasons ahead of the phenomenal Ritz-Sports Club/LA combination.

Swimmers are out of luck, unless they can withstand the flip turns required to accrue any real yardage in the 15-yard indoor Napoleon. For guests seeking more, check out the off-site options. Wang's Y is the closest.

MODERATELY EXPENSIVE

GOLD: Doubletree Hotel

821 Washington Street, Boston, MA 02111
(617) 956-7900 • doubletreebostonhotels.com

Located in the heart of downtown Boston, and within convenient walking distance to the Theater District, China Town and the Public Garden, this Doubletree is a fitness fan winner due to its Wang YMCA "connection." Doubletree describes its guest quarters as having an "Asian flair," but our spin is simply rooms painted in shades of white and red. While bed headboards do suggest the Orient, the rest of the furnishings are standard, business-hotel fare. We are certainly not complaining — all 267 rooms are quite pleasing, and we were satisfied with our tour. We just like nitpicking the creative marketing.

With no exercise room of its own, Doubletree presents guests with complimentary passes to the adjacent Wang YMCA, conveniently accessed via the hotel's elevators. While this club "ain't no Sports Club/LA," its variety of high-end equipment and functional lap pool make Doubletree the best Boston option in this price category.

SILVER: Colonnade

120 Huntington Avenue, Boston, MA 02116
(617) 424-7000 • colonnadehotel.com

In what we deem a "photo finish," the Colonnade is a very close 2nd to Doubletree. The latter slips into the Gold slot with its free access to the Wang Y's regulation lap pool. But those not prioritizing a swim and/or preferring a home base closer to Boston's shopping and dining venues will likely favor the Colonnade. In fact, gourmets will appreciate this hotel's restaurant offering — the well-known Brasserie Jo, created by famed Chef Jean Joho. This 285-room upscale property is convenient to Copley Square, Copley Place Mall and first rate dining and entertainment attractions — not to mention its 3 block distance from the Boston Marathon finish line. Soft tones of blue and red, antique-style furnishings and large windows create pleasing rooms.

The recently renovated 5th floor fitness center offers a solid number of newer Precor cardio machines in a cheery atmosphere filled with natural light. Although no free weights are on Colonnade's

CARDIO

TREADMILLS: **5 Precor**
UPRIGHT BIKE: **1 Precor**
RECUMBENT BIKE: **1 Precor**
ELLIPTICAL: **3 Precor**
STEPPER: **2 Precor**

STRENGTH

MACHINES: **5 Icarian**
DUMBBELLS: **5-50 lbs**

SWIM

SPECS: **Outdoor • Not lap**

OTHER

HOURS: **6a-10p**
• Will open after hours
COST: **Free**
TV: **Yes**

strength stage, its decent range of dumbbells and several acceptable stack-loaded weight stations are useful stand-ins for muscle play.

If the hotel's gym does not satisfy your workout desires, the high-quality Fitcorp club across the street serves up a worthy alternative for $20/day (or print a 1-time free pass from the club's website).

Swimmers, while the closest lap option is the Central YMCA (10-15 minute walk), you may prefer a longer commute to the Wang Y. The Central Y's pool is regulation length, but it breaks all sorts of aesthetic laws. So consider cabbing it to Doubletree's neighborhood and swimming at the Wang YMCA ($6-$10 cab fare). Trust us, you will be much happier.

LEAST EXPENSIVE

GOLD: Midtown Hotel

220 Huntington Avenue, Boston, MA 02115
(617) 262-1000 • midtownhotel.com

You can judge this hotel by its cover. Midtown's urban, motor-lodge exterior carries over to its motel-ish interior. With guest room doors opening into interior hallways, expect clean and basic but nothing else from this 159-room property. So why recommend it? Priced under $100/night, Midtown's budget friendly rates and central location are winning attributes.

The hotel is within 2 long blocks of Copley Place Mall, Symphony Hall and, most importantly, Fitcorp — a worthy off-site fitness venue. And 5-10 minutes on foot will put you at Northeastern University's doorstep. Commuters will appreciate Midtown's complimentary guest parking and the nearby "T" station (Boston's public subway system), which affords cheap and convenient transportation to the City's major attractions.

Midtown has no on-site fitness room, but no matter your workout question, a 5-minute walk in either direction along Huntington Avenue resolves it. Cardio and strength buffs should head in a northeasterly direction to Fitcorp, located across the street from the Colonnade hotel ($20/day, or print a 1-time freebie from the club's website).

Fish-like friends should proceed southeast to Boston Central YMCA. Finicky breeds may prefer the longer commute and added cab cost to lap it up in Wang YMCA's superior water box.

SILVER: John Hancock Conference Center

40 Trinity Place, Boston, MA 02116
(617) 933-7700 • jhcenter.com

A great Copley Square location, inexpensive rates, free continental breakfasts and $5 admission to a nearby corporate fitness center earn John Hancock runner-up honors in this category. The Conference Center's primary focus is hosting large business meetings and events, so its 64 rooms are secondary in importance, and guests get what they pay for. No high thread count sheets, feather beds or plush amenities decorate these rooms. Your skeleton accommodations include a bed, desk and bathroom. What more do you want for less than a "C-note" in downtown Boston?

Hotel guests looking to unwind with a good sweat have no onsite option, but the ground floor of the building just opposite the Conference Center presents a notable alternative, the John Hancock Fitness Center. After paying the bargain $5/day admission tariff, athletic-minded travelers can satisfy non-chlorinated exercise yearnings. Those in search of this chemical must taxi over to the Wang YMCA.

Note: John Hancock Fitness Center is closed on weekends.

BEYOND HOTELS

Sports Club/LA

4 Avery Street at Tremont
Boston, MA 02111
(617) 375-8200
thesportsclubla.com

Are you kidding me? This place is unbelievable! At Sports Club/LA you will find hundreds of high-end machines (many with plasma televisions attached) throughout a beautifully decorated and well-managed state-of-the-art facility. With its art filled walls, contemporary vibe and limited membership, we almost forgot we were in a health club! You may notice a smattering of the "BP" crowd roaming the floors, but most exercisers were sweating hard rather than hardly sweating.

Since this "everything including the kitchen sink," club boasts fitness amenities too plentiful to describe here, check out its website to preview the fitness goodies. With the strength area alone topping 10,000

CARDIO

TREADMILLS: **LF**
UPRIGHT BIKE: **LF**
RECUMBENT BIKE: **LF**
ELLIPTICAL: **LF • Precor**
STEPPER: **StairMaster • Stepmill**
ROWING: **Concept II**
OTHER: **VersaClimber**

STRENGTH

FREE WEIGHTS: **Yes**
HAMMER: **Yes**
MACHINES: **LF • Free Motion • Cybex • Icarian**
DUMBBELLS: **3-105 lbs**

SWIM

GRADE: **B+**
SPECS: **8x25yd • Indoor • 80-82°**
TOYS: **Kick • Pull**
MASTERS: **Yes**

OTHER

CLASSES: **Yes**
HOURS: M-F **5:30a-10:30p** • SAT-SUN **7a-7:30p**
COST: **$10 Ritz • $35 Other hotels**
TV: **Yes**
EXTRAS: **Basketball • Squash • Cafe**

square feet and Sports Club's endurance space hosting more than 150 cardio pieces, we can confidently write, "if you want it, they have it."

Swimmers will love to call this pool home. Eight lanes of 25-yard swimming divided by floating lines and bottom stripes mark the territory. Our only whine is that the pool's narrow lanes make sharing difficult. But, in this exclusive club, swimmers are rarely forced to double up. If you can afford the Ritz, stay there and work out here. You'll be happier than a pig in mud.

Note: Depending on your Ritz reservation, access may be free (at most, Ritz guests pay $10/day/room). Those staying at other accommodations must bring a referral letter from their hotel and $35 (arrange with the Sports Club before heading over).

Wang YMCA

8 Oak Street West, Boston, MA 02116
(617) 426-2237 • ymcaboston.org

CARDIO

TREADMILLS: **LF • Precor**
UPRIGHT BIKE: **LF**
RECUMBENT BIKE: **LF**
ELLIPTICAL: **LF • Precor**
STEPPER: **LF • StairMaster**
ROWING: **Concept II**

STRENGTH

FREE WEIGHTS: **Yes**
HAMMER: **Yes - 1**
MACHINES: **LF • Free Motion • Nautilus**
DUMBBELLS: **5-100 lbs**

SWIM

GRADE: **B**
SPECS: **5x25yd • Indoor • 84°**
TOYS: **Kick • Pull • Clock**

OTHER

CLASSES: **Yes**
HOURS: M-F **5a-10p** • SAT **6a-7p** • SUN **9a-5p**
COST: **Free Doubletree • $10 Others**
TV: **No**
EXTRAS: **Basketball**

This relatively young YMCA (opened 2000) is located in Boston's Theater District and Chinatown. It's connected to the Doubletree, so hotel guests can access the Y through an in-house elevator. Talk about convenient! Most Y facilities are built to serve the surrounding community, and this one is no exception. During the day, high school gym classes and after school programs utilize the basketball courts and some of the aerobic equipment. Thankfully, the youngsters are well-supervised and separated from adult exercisers.

Although the fitness layout is rather muddled, with equipment strewn across two balconies overlooking the basketball courts, the cutting-edge Precor and Life Fitness machines are familiar and appreciated. We counted 17 treadmills, 8 ellipticals, 4 upright bikes and 2 StairMaster 4600PT steppers. The weight area could use a little "TLC," but strength connoisseurs will get by on over 17 stack-loaded weight stations, an ample number of free weights and a wide range of dumbbells.

Wang's 5-lane, 25-yard pool complete with bottom stripes and floating lines will spark swimmers' spirits. Kickboards and pull-buoys break up long distance monotony, and a pace clock is on deck to help you through base intervals. While the aquatic center's ceilings are uncomfortably low and air ducts visible, you will forget about these aesthetic moles once your head is under water.

Busting out $10-$15 to work out here may be tough, but Doubletree's free pass makes the decision a no-brainer for its guests. Have fun!

Fitcorp Prudential Center

800 Boylston Street, Boston, MA 02199
(617) 262-2050 • fitcorp.com

A pool is the only missing feature at this grade "A" health club. Fitcorp's 31,000 square foot Prudential Center venue opened in 2003 as the "flagship" facility for Boston's largest locally-owned fitness provider. Management has done a tremendous job filling two stories of colorfully designed workout space with the best workout brands on the market.

CARDIO

TREADMILLS: **LF • StarTrac**
UPRIGHT BIKE: **LF**
RECUMBENT BIKE: **LF**
ELLIPTICAL: **LF • Precor**
STEPPER: **StairMaster**
ROWING: **Yes**

STRENGTH

FREE WEIGHTS: **Yes**
HAMMER: **Yes**
MACHINES: **LF • Free Motion**
DUMBBELLS: **5-120 lbs**

OTHER

CLASSES: **Yes**
HOURS: M-TH **5:30a-10p**
• F **5:30a-9p**
• SAT **8a-7p** • SUN **9a-6p**
COST: **$20 • 1st time web freebie**
TV: **Yes**

Of course, a newer club means "just out of the box" equipment. Our favorites here include over 25 stack-loaded weight stations, a cycling room with Keiser spin bikes and a large assortment of Hammer Strength machines. Expect a high caliber experience from this Fitcorp branch. The club caters to a business clientele, so you are unlikely to see the "BP" crowd here. Fitcorp leaves the hoopla to its competitors.

To get inside, you must meander through the Prudential Center Mall. If you are bashful in your fitness attire, grab your sweats. Otherwise, prance that hard body and make those Cinnabon eaters jealous. On the upside, you can get some shopping done on your return commute.

Your sweat will run $20/day, but you can print a one-time freebie off the web.

YMCA Central

316 Huntington Avenue, Boston, MA 02115
(617) 536-6950 • ymcaboston.org

This multi-level Y is located on the northeastern edge of Northeastern University. The ground level's freshly painted walls, new flooring and host of modern cardio and weight machines will attract fitness fans like bees to honey. Fourteen new Precor treadmills, 11 youthful ellipticals, 6 StairMaster 4600PT series steppers and 6 good-quality upright bikes are samples of the machines adorning this renovated space.

CARDIO

TREADMILLS: **Precor**
UPRIGHT BIKE: **LF**
RECUMBENT BIKE: **Stratus**
ELLIPTICAL: **LF • Precor • Reebok**
STEPPER: **LF • StairMaster • Stepmill**
ROWING: **Concept II**

STRENGTH

FREE WEIGHTS: **Yes**
HAMMER: **Yes**
MACHINES: **LF • Free Motion • Nautilus**
DUMBBELLS: **5-100 lbs**

SWIM

GRADE: **D+**
SPECS: **3x25yd • Indoor • 81-84°**
TOYS: **Kick • Clock**
MASTERS: **Yes**

OTHER

CLASSES: **Yes**
HOURS: M-W **5a-11p** • TH-F **5a-9p** • SAT-SUN **7a-7p**
COST: **$10**
TV: **No**
EXTRAS: **Basketball • Racquetball**

However, the basement is in a 1960s time warp. Rusty weights, paint-chipped walls and a black rubber floor dominate the visual landscape. A good number of machines are provided, but the unpleasant atmosphere may force you back upstairs in a hurry. We don't know about the women's locker room, but the men's "lounge" featured a 1970s TV (complete with rabbit-ears) sitting across from an old poker table.

Unfortunately, the 25-yard lap pool is part of the mess. While 3 wide lanes marked with bottom stripes and floating lines offer plenty of room for swimmers, this water venue is ancient, grungy and unpleasant. Only really hardcore freestylers will be able to overlook the flaws. $10/day is the going guest rate.

John Hancock Fitness Center

197 Clarendon Street, Boston, MA 02117
(617) 275-0265 • fitcorp.com

CARDIO

TREADMILLS: **StarTrac - old • Trotter - old**
UPRIGHT BIKE: **LF • StarTrac**
RECUMBENT BIKE: **LF**
ELLIPTICAL: **Precor - old**
STEPPER: **StairMaster - old**
ROWING: **Yes**

STRENGTH

FREE WEIGHTS: **Yes**
MACHINES: **Cybex • Nautilus**
DUMBBELLS: **3-100 lbs**

OTHER

CLASSES: **Yes**
HOURS: M-F **6a-8p • Closed weekends**
COST: **$5 JH Conf Center only**
TV: **Yes**

This health club (managed by Fitcorp) is a small executive fitness center offered primarily for those working in the surrounding buildings (it is located opposite the John Hancock Tower on the ground floor). Though neither its size nor equipment will amaze you, it is a cheap ($5/day) option for those staying at the John Hancock Conference Center. Other non-members are not permitted.

The club makes good use of its rather meager space and mixes mostly older cardio equipment with a few newer pieces (bikes). Its 10 treadmills, 7 ellipticals and 5 step machines appear 5+ years old. The strength apparatus, including the 18 stack-loaded weight stations, is newer and higher quality.

Aerobics classes, including cycling, are available for those in need of a little group therapy. Lunch hour appears to be the busiest time, so stay away if you can.

RUNNING OPTIONS

City Run

Boston Common serves up a hilly, 1-mile loop around its perimeter. And adjacent to our nation's oldest park is its first Public Garden, a scenic escape filled with cherry trees, statues, a lagoon and charming suspension bridge. After you have satisfied yourself with Boston's more natural offerings, consider additional mileage and head to touristy Copley Square with its majestic hotels, museum, statuary and, in late spring through early autumn, a Farmers Market. While Boston Common and the Public Garden offer mixed surfaces, the jog to Copley and around its hoopla will be on city streets — watch out for traffic.

Charles River

Now that you have toured Boston's more historic attractions, it is time to get serious with your mileage. From Watertown Square to the Science Museum, athletes can log a 17.2 mile round trip course on the Charles River's paved path. Running along this scenic river is a great way to greet Boston, and for those of you who get short of breath quickly, several bridges along the way present shorter loop opportunities. The Esplanade (parallel to Storrow Drive) is along the way and affords a great view of MIT.

Back Bay Fens

This 50-acre green oasis located between the Charles River and Northeastern University is another venue for nature seeking striders. Runners can look forward to an abundance of plants, trees, roses, gardens and a short jogging circuit — but 50 acres is not that large. You will likely have to pick a few streets to stride on if your goal is to rack up some serious mileage.

Boston Marathon

We could not close our Boston chapter without some mention of this famous and highly coveted race. While you could run all or part of the course almost any time under your own steam, to run the Boston Marathon on Patriot's Day is a major thrill — and a major undertaking.

Did you know that Boston's marathon is the oldest American marathon? It's also one of the largest — so large, in fact, that, for the opportunity to log those 26.2 miles, you must run a qualifying time in a certified marathon.

Qualifying times are figured according to age, and they change from year to year. For example, a 47-year-old male needs to clock under 3 hours and 30 minutes in a qualifying race before he will be allowed to register for the Boston Marathon. Ladies are allotted 30 more minutes in each age category to get the green light for April's race day — Patriot's Day — Marathon Monday.

While most are familiar with President's Day, Memorial Day, Independence Day and Veteran's Day, the anniversary of the American Revolutionary War escapes mention by those living ouitside New England. The skirmishes between British troops and the Minute Men at Concord occurred in April, 1775 — now commemorated as the Patriot's Day holiday.

So, as you gaze at the athletic-minded striding along Boston's course, look for signs of patriotism — many runners sport creative costumes!

BOULDER, COLORADO

Besides its big-time image in the fitness and endurance sporting worlds, Boulder is a quaint and artsy college town located 30 miles northwest and 75 feet above Denver.

A passion for the outdoors is a common thread for residents of this diversely populated burg. How could it not be? Its myriad trails, streams, fields, bike lanes and mountains present an unparalleled setting for vitality, and this city's 95,000 citizens thrive on an athlete's diet. Although cycling and running appear the most popular entrées, Boulderites cover the workout menu from Apricots to Zucchini. We would not be surprised if cross-training was invented here!

So why, in this town where fitness is front and center, are the hotel and health club exercise pickings more slim than supreme? Our hunch is that it's difficult for these businesses to compete against Mother Nature's well-run — and complimentary — outdoor gym. Travelers will best be served by heeding the well-known adage, "when in Rome..." and heading outside, where the CU Buffaloes roam.

Do not despair, gym rats. We have not abandoned you. Although tracking down worthy prospects in Boulder was nearly as challenging as running a sub-4 minute mile, we identified several spry venues. And, though we do not claim membership in this esteemed group of fleet feet, we trust that your hooves will be kept busy in Boulder.

EXPENSIVE

BRONZE: Marriott

2660 Canyon Boulevard, Boulder, CO 80302
(303) 440-8877 • marriott.com

The Bronze rating is no mistake. Marriott's strongest attribute is its location. About a mile from Boulder's Pearl Street shopping and entertainment district, the Marriott is a tidy hotel in an agreeable, touristy spot. But athletic-minded travelers may find Millennium or Homewood Suites more convenient for working out, as well as a better bang for the buck. Marriott describes its 157 rooms as having "Southwestern décor" but, last we checked, cheap-looking office-style furniture and busy patterns do not match this region's style. No matter, the lack of charm will provide further motivation for you to explore the wonderful Boulder town.

A real exercise session will compel you off-site, since Marriott's workout room is nearly nonexistent. A couple of junky cardio machines and a small dumbbell set waste away in the dinky closet of a room. So make like a fugitive and escape to one of the nearby trailheads or Flatiron Athletic Club. Driving to the gym takes about 5 minutes and admission is $10 ($5 discount) — a smart investment for this sharp club.

MODERATELY EXPENSIVE

GOLD: Millennium Harvest House

1345 28th Street, Boulder, CO 80302
(303) 443-3850 • millenniumhotels.com

CARDIO

TREADMILLS: **1 StarTrac**
UPRIGHT BIKE: **1 LF**
RECUMBENT BIKE: **1 LF**
ELLIPTICAL: **1 Precor**
STEPPER: **2 StairMaster - old**

STRENGTH

MACHINES: **1 Cybex Multi**

SWIM

GRADE: **C+**
SPECS: **4x25yd • Indoor • 82–84°**
TOYS: **Kick • Clock**

OTHER

HOURS: **6a-11p**
COST: **Free**
TV: **Yes**

Situated near the Marriott and about a mile away from engaging Pearl Street, Millennium is a resort-style hotel covering 16 acres just east of the University of Colorado campus. With rustic Western furnishings, rough-cut beams, leather lamps and colorful quilted bedspreads, Millennium's 269 guest rooms are the most attractive in Boulder. The fresh mountain breeze flowing into your room is an additional on-the-house perk.

The hotel provides mountain bike rentals and a small workout room, but Millennium's best fitness feature is its 25-yard indoor lap pool. With 4 lanes divided by floating lines and bottom stripes, this rectangle is the only lap pool you will find at a Boulder hotel. Though it will not knock your Speedos off, as a hotel pool it receives good marks.

Unfortunately, the quality of the exercise room does not impress. Lacking free weights and dumbbells, the only cardio machines worth your sweat equity are an upright bicycle, an elliptical trainer and a treadmill. Fortunately, the hotel is less than 3 miles from Flatiron Athletic Club, so those looking for a full-body workout should hustle over or take to the nearby paths for a challenging run.

Note: Flatiron will cost $15/day. Guests do not receive a discount.

SILVER: Homewood Suites by Hilton

4950 Baseline Road, Boulder, CO 80303
(303) 499-9922 • homewoodsuites.com

For those Boulder visitors who prioritize a convenient workout location ahead of a short walk to dining and entertainment attractions (Pearl Street) and unique accommodations, Homewood is your place. The hotel's mixed use (residential/office) setting does not provide much in the way of festive diversions, so a quick car ride is necessary in order to sample Boulder's artsy side. However, a pair of shoes and 20 paces is all it takes to arrive at Boulder's best fitness complex — the Flatiron Athletic Club.

While Homewood's décor will not win any style awards, its 112 suites are clean and comfortable. Guests enjoy separate living and sleeping rooms, full-size refrigerators, microwave ovens and kitchenettes. The hotel also treats patrons to a complimentary hot breakfast buffet each morning plus a free social hour Monday through Thursday that offers warm nibbles, beer, wine and soft drinks.

Because of its proximity to Flatiron, pay no attention to Homewood's in-house exercise room. Its second-hand treadmill and poor quality bike should be put out of their misery. At Flatiron, a discounted rate of $10 will put you shoulder-to-shoulder with some of the world's premier endurance athletes. Resist the temptation to gawk. It's a health club, not a race expo.

LEAST EXPENSIVE

GOLD: Boulder Broker Inn

555 30th Street, Boulder, CO 80303
(303) 444-3330 • boulderbrokerinn.com

Across the street from the University's dorms and 2 miles from Pearl Street's shopping and entertainment venues, the Broker Inn is a sensible accommodation for those on a budget. The standard rooms are not easy on the eyes, with cabin-like wood paneled walls and ruffled curtains framing the beds' headboards. The more expensive suites are in better shape, but the point of staying here is to conserve cash, right? You will do just that with the hotel's free hot breakfasts during the week, but weekend chow will cost you.

Without an in-house gym, Broker Inn resolves workout dilemmas by selling $5 passes to the 24 Hour Fitness club located around the corner. There's no pool, but all other cardio and weight machines are in stock. Although walking to 24 is a no brainer, do not plan on hoofing it to Pearl Street. You're too far away.

SILVER: **Holiday Inn Express**

4777 North Broadway, Boulder, CO 80304
(303) 442-6600 • hiexpress.com

While this hotel is way out on the northwest edge of town, it is the closest lodging option to some of the best running trails in the country. Running addicts may want to consider staying here. Everyone else, don't bother — better options exist. Holiday Inn Express provides guests with basic rooms and standard amenities in addition to its complimentary "Express Start" breakfasts. Its tiny workout room houses 3 worthless machines. If you want weights and more, drive 10 minutes to Flatiron.

Note: The Foothill Trail begins about 2 blocks west of the hotel toward the mountains. Pick a direction and have at it.

BEYOND HOTELS

Flatiron Athletic Club

505 Thunderbird Drive, Boulder, CO 80303
(303) 499-6590 • flatironathleticclub.com

CARDIO

TREADMILLS: **LF**
UPRIGHT BIKE: **LF**
RECUMBENT BIKE: **LF**
ELLIPTICAL: **LF • Precor • Cybex**
STEPPER: **StairMaster**
ROWING: **Concept II**

STRENGTH

FREE WEIGHTS: **Yes**
MACHINES: **Cybex • Magnum • Nautilus**
DUMBBELLS: **3-120 lbs**

SWIM

GRADE: #1 **A** • #2 **C+**
SPECS: #1 **6x25m • Outdoor • 80°**
#2 **4x23yd • Indoor • 83°**
TOYS: **Kick • Pull • Clock**
MASTERS: **Yes**

OTHER

CLASSES: **Yes**
HOURS: M-TH **5:30a-11p**
• F **5:30a-10p** • SAT-SUN **7:30a-8p**
COST: **$10 Homewood/Marriott**
• **$15 Others**
TV: **Yes**
EXTRAS: **1/8 mile indoor track**
• **Tennis** • **Racquetball**
• **Cafe**

With over 50,000 square feet of workout space, plenty of the latest and greatest cardio and weight equipment, competition-quality indoor and outdoor lap pools, an exclusive Masters swim program coached by Jane Scott (wife of triathlon legend Dave Scott), a modern Pilates studio, a useful 1/8-mile indoor track, courts for all racquet sports and a tasty grill/snack bar, this club is fitness heaven. Whew!

Formerly an ice skating rink, the real estate is now devoted to making athletic-minded individuals stronger, faster and happier. Flatiron is all business in its approach to fitness, so do not expect lavish surroundings and luxurious amenities designed to appease a perfectly-coiffed BP crowd. Exercisers come here to work out and to work out hard. Because Flatiron is Boulder's best health club, don't be surprised if you find yourself asked to spot for some of endurance sports' better-known athletes. Seeing these studs and studettes here is an indication of the club's superior quality. Count on cutting-edge everything.

24 Hour Fitness

2950 Baseline Road, Boulder, CO 80303
(303) 443-2639 • 24hourfitness.com

We recommend this club only if you are staying at the Boulder Broker Inn ($5 entry fee) or are a member of the 24 Hour Fitness chain. Otherwise, Flatiron is a far superior alternative.

We are not implying that this gym is weak. It is stuffed with a great assortment of today's modern cardio and weight apparatus. Flatiron is just top-of-the-food-chain good.

On 24's two fitness floors, workout fanatics will find a litany of good cardio machines, better strength equipment and a variety of daily exercise classes. Most of the endurance selection is on the ground level, while free weights and weight stations are on top. It is a smaller facility for this expanding franchise, but solid nonetheless.

Swimmers, there's no pool here. Head to Flatiron.

CARDIO

TREADMILLS: **LF**
UPRIGHT BIKE: **LF**
RECUMBENT BIKE: **LF**
ELLIPTICAL: **LF • Precor**
STEPPER: **StairMaster**
ROWING: **Concept II**

STRENGTH

FREE WEIGHTS: **Yes**
HAMMER: **Yes**
MACHINES: **Cybex • Free Motion • Icarian • Bodymaster**
DUMBBELLS: **5-120 lbs**

OTHER

CLASSES: **Yes**
HOURS: M-TH **24** • F **Close 11p** • SAT **6a-10p** • SUN **7a-10p**
COST: **$5 Boulder Broker • $10 others**
TV: **Yes**

OTHER WORKOUT OPTIONS

Although Flatiron and 24 Hour Fitness are the "best bets" for out-of-town exercisers, Boulder's health club scene has additional players. For your convenience, the other major clubs/community centers in the area are listed in no particular order.

Rally's Health Club (rallysportboulder.com)

On the small side, Rally's maze-like interior feels like working out in someone's house. There is a decent outdoor 4x25-yard outdoor lap pool, however. $10, IHRSA members only.

YMCA (ymcabv.org)

You get no frills at the Y, and the interior is nothing fancy. Still, there are good bikes, weak steppers and ellipticals in the workout room and a nice 4x25-yard pool. The Y will set you back $12.

Pulse (boulderpulse.com)

Very small inside, Pulse has a weights focus, no pool and weak cardio machines. But its location is good, just off Pearl Street ($12).

Eastside Community Center (303-441-4400)

Great 8x25-yard pool, plenty of free weights, Body Master weight machines, Eastside is only $6/day. However, the cardio equipment is weak — especially steppers and bikes.

Northside Community Center (303-413-7260)

With an 8x25 yard B+ pool, Northside is okay for weights, but lacking cardio — especially bikes. There are a few good LF ellipticals and treadmills ($6).

RUNNING ROUTES

Local Trail Map

Boulder is loaded with multi-use paths. Striders should pick up a city and area map that details the numerous routes in and out of town. Most hotels have this handy guide. One favorite central Boulder route begins at Scott Carpenter Park (30th and Colorado) and heads north for miles. South-siders can pick up one of the paths that head toward Baseline Reservoir. Foothill Trail is recommended on the north side; it begins 2 blocks west of the Holiday Inn Express.

Charlotte

CHARLOTTE, NORTH CAROLINA

It did not take long for us to understand why people make Charlotte their home and companies establish their headquarters in the "Queen City" (e.g., Bank of America, Lowe's, Wachovia). Named after England's Queen Charlotte, the town's dynamic "Uptown" city center (yes, Uptown means Downtown here), beautiful tree-lined residential neighborhoods and numerous sporting and nightlife amusements contribute to its allure. However, Charlotte's best attribute comes not from fancy buildings or expensive attractions, but rather from the people themselves who truly make this city feel like a home away from home.

We generally hear Charlotte locals described as warm and friendly, but that is an understatement. As we strolled along Uptown's sidewalks, we were initially taken aback by the number of locals who wished us a "good morning." But in no time this simple gesture made us feel welcome. Ask for directions and your guide will not walk away until they are satisfied you know the way. Pull out a Charlotte attractions map in a restaurant and don't be surprised when your server asks if you need recommendations. This city is an example of Southern hospitality at its finest, and the workout options are pretty darn good, too.

29 Locations Reviewed

EXPENSIVE

GOLD: Hilton & Towers

222 East Third Street, Charlotte, NC 28202
(704) 377-1500 • hilton.com

This heart of Uptown hotel posed an interesting dilemma for us. While it unquestionably provides the best hotel workout option in Charlotte, the rooms could use a makeover, and guests receive basic amenities and good service. With its fairly pricey nightly rates, we believe visitors may expect more from their accommodations. But if you're like most of our members, you prioritize workouts over hotel features, and the internally connected Uptown YMCA provides a fantastic sweat option for a reasonable $10. So Hilton gets the nod, but it was definitely a photo finish. Those who prefer more upscale accommodations may be happier at one of our other recommended hotels.

SILVER: Omni Hotel

132 E. Trade Street, Charlotte, NC 28202
(704) 377-0400 • omnihotels.com

CARDIO

TREADMILLS: **8 StarTrac**
UPRIGHT BIKE: **1 LF • 2 StarTrac**
RECUMBENT BIKE: **4 StarTrac**
ELLIPTICAL: **6 Precor**
STEPPER: **4 StairMaster • 2 Stepmill**
ROWING: **3 Concept II**

STRENGTH

FREE WEIGHTS: **Yes**
MACHINES: **11 LF**
DUMBBELLS: **5-100 lbs**

SWIM

HOTEL: **Outdoor • Not lap**
TOWER CLUB: **None**

OTHER

CLASSES: **Yes**
HOURS: M-TH **5:30a-9p** • F **5:30a-7p** • SAT **8:30a-4p** • SUN **11a-3p**
COST: **$6 • $20/week**
TV: **Yes**
EXTRAS: **Basketball • Racquetball**

Though the Uptown YMCA provides Charlotte's best overall workout alternative, Omni's independently owned Tower Club will completely satisfy even the most finicky exercise fiends. Admission costs $6/day or $20/week, and the facility is worth the nominal fee. Other than private members, only Omni guests have access privileges, so crowds are not a problem.

Tower Club provides every modality to make your heart tick a few beats faster — except a pool. In its two-story open and airy space, this club supplies a large assortment of free weights, modern machines and numerous classes (e.g., cycling).

With pricing and location similar to Hilton's, Omni guests enjoy fancier room décor, softer bedding and superior amenities for a more luxurious hotel experience. So if Omni's equipment breakdown appeals to you, and you are a stickler for high thread-count sheets, drop Hilton into the #3 slot and move Omni and Westin up.

Swimmers staying at the Omni can still use the Y's pool. Just bring your I.D., $10 and a Speedo — it's only a 5-minute walk.

Note: Omni's own workout room is worth missing.

BRONZE: **Westin**
601 South College Street, Charlotte, NC 28202
(704) 375-2600 • westin.com

On the edge of Uptown and across the street from Charlotte's Convention Center, this Westin caters primarily to business travelers. But this is not your grandfather's convention hotel! Westin gets kudos for designing and decorating a massive 700-room accommodation with a modern vision and contemporary style. Rooms take on a 21st Century minimalist motif and come equipped with Westin's signature Heavenly Beds and Baths. And, happily, the attractive décor spills over into the fitness center's environment as well.

CARDIO
TREADMILLS: **6 LF**
UPRIGHT BIKE: **1 LF**
RECUMBENT BIKE: **2 LF**
ELLIPTICAL: **3 LF**

STRENGTH
MACHINES: **12 LF**
DUMBBELLS: **5-50 lbs**

SWIM
SPECS: **Indoor • Not lap**

OTHER
HOURS: **24**
COST: **$5**
TV: **Yes**

Westin's 24-hour gym costs $5/day and supplies youthful Life Fitness equipment exclusively. Large windows provide plenty of light and third-floor city views. Though the center offers a decent quantity of machines, those desiring a stepper, free weights, classes or a lap pool need to look elsewhere. We suggest the Aquatic Center for swimmers and the Uptown YMCA for all others — both require a 10-minute walk.

Note: Those not conducting business at the convention center may find the Westin a bit out of the way. A 5-10 minute walk is in order for any exploration of Charlotte's hub.

MODERATELY EXPENSIVE

GOLD: **Courtyard City Center**
237 S. Tryon Street, Charlotte, NC 28202
(704) 926-5800 • courtyard.com

In the heart of Uptown and all of its attractions, Courtyard receives the Gold due to its proximity to and relationship with the Uptown YMCA.

This Courtyard is typical for the Marriott-owned brand, offering free coffee in the lobby, clean rooms, high-speed internet access and a forgettable in-house workout facility. The 5 sub-par cardio machines and one crummy multi-gym will not satisfy serious exercisers. Fortunately, hotel management has negotiated an $8/day workout deal with the Uptown YMCA (2-minute walk). While you save only $2 off the regular price, management's effort to arrange a discount shows Courtyard is thinking about the ath-

CARDIO
TREADMILLS: **2 StarTrac**
UPRIGHT BIKE: **1 StarTrac**
RECUMBENT BIKE: **1 StarTrac**
STEPPER: **1 StarTrac**

STRENGTH
MACHINES: **1 Multi**

SWIM
SPECS: **Outdoor • Not lap**

OTHER
HOURS: **6a-11p**
COST: **Free**
TV: **Yes**
EXTRAS: **$8 pass to Y**

letic-minded traveler, and we appreciate it. Before heading over, purchase the voucher from the front desk.

SILVER: **Doubletree Hotel** Charlotte Gateway Village

895 W. Trade Street, Charlotte NC 28202
(704) 347-0070 • doubletree.com

CARDIO

TREADMILLS: **2 LF**
RECUMBENT BIKE: **1 LF**
ELLIPTICAL: **1 LF**

STRENGTH

MACHINES: **LF**

OTHER

COST: **Free**
TV: **Yes**
EXTRAS: **$8/day pass YMCA**

Doubletree is a worthy lodging option for those conducting business in the nearby office buildings of Uptown's growing Gateway Village district. About a mile from the heart of Downtown, this up-and-coming multi-use development includes residences, retail stores and office buildings. While we do not recommend staying in this somewhat out-of-the-way location if your business is in the heart of the City or at the Convention Center, those with meetings in this area will not find a more conveniently located hotel.

Recently renovated, the Doubletree gleams with attractive style and furnishings. The deep maroon and beige tones throughout the rooms are comforting — and so is the staff.

The workout room received the welcome addition of new Life Fitness equipment, so Doubletree's management gets a gold star in our book for not leaving out athletic-minded travelers. The treadmills even have personal televisions attached.

Still, some sweat fiends may want more equipment; if you're one of them, you will find the Gateway Village YMCA just across the street. It's a fantastic supplement to Doubletree's own fitness offering. Bring $8, your room key, and a lock if you need a locker.

BRONZE: **Residence Inn** Uptown

404 S. Mint Street, Charlotte, NC 28202
(704) 340-4000 • residenceinn.com

Although the Carolina Panthers' Ericsson Stadium is about the only attraction close to this isolated property, the Residence Inn provides free shuttle service and passes to the very impressive Mecklenburg Aquatic Center. This outstanding swimming venue may provide enough incentive for our fish-like friends to overlook the hotel's weak location and stay here anyway. But, for our water-resistant amigos, we doubt the hotel's free breakfasts and in-room kitchenettes will make up for the lousy location and terrible in-house gym.

LEAST EXPENSIVE

GOLD: **Hampton Inn Uptown**
530 East Second Street, Charlotte, NC 28202
(704) 373-0917 • hamptoninn.com

SILVER: **Hilton Garden Inn Uptown**
508 East Second Street, Charlotte, NC 28202
(704) 347-5972 • hiltongardeninn.com

These neighboring hotels offer guests very similar accommodations, but Hampton edges out the competition by providing complimentary breakfast each morning. This is the budget category, so rooms are not outfitted with many extras, but you should get clean quarters and service with a smile at both.

Neither hotel has an attractive fitness option, so plan to buy the $8 discounted pass to the Uptown YMCA at your hotel's front desk.

If swimming is your thing, take advantage of the closer and better pool at Mecklenburg Aquatic Center. The fee is identical and the walk over is 5 minutes (10 minutes to the Y).

BEYOND HOTELS

Uptown YMCA

301 South College Street, Charlotte, NC 28202
(704) 716-6400 • ymcacharlotte.org

Uptown YMCA's front entrance is accessible from inside the adjacent Hilton or through One First Union Center. In return for a $10 admission fee ($8 Courtyard, Hampton, Hilton Garden Inn) guests receive complete access to this cutting-edge club, one of the larger and more modern Ys we have seen.

In addition, staff commented that exercisers rarely wait for machines even during the busy 11:30 a.m. to 1 p.m. lunch hour. For a good visual of the club's innards, check out its website.

The person in charge of ordering the Y's equipment must be allergic to Life Fitness machines, as all other brands are here except this heavyweight. While loyalists might be ini-

CARDIO

TREADMILLS: **Precor • Cybex**
UPRIGHT BIKE: **Cybex**
RECUMBENT BIKE: **Cybex • StairMaster • Stratus**
ELLIPTICAL: **Precor • StarTrac**
STEPPER: **StairMaster • Stepmill**
ROWING: **Concept II**
OTHER: **Versa Climber**

STRENGTH

FREE WEIGHTS: **Yes**
HAMMER: **Yes**
MACHINES: **Cybex • Nautilus • Free Motion**
DUMBBELLS: **3-100 lbs**

SWIM

GRADE: **B**
SPECS: **5x25yd • Indoor • 81°**
TOYS: **Kick • Pull • Clock • Fins**
MASTERS: **Yes**

OTHER

CLASSES: **Yes**
HOURS: M-TH **5a-9p** • F **5a-8:30p** • SAT **8a-6p** • SUN **1-5p**
COST: **Varies per hotel**
TV: **Yes**
EXTRAS: **1/9 mile indoor track • Basketball • Deli**

tially disappointed, the Y stocks an assortment of other high-quality equipment, including 17 Cybex bikes, 14 Precor ellipticals, 10 Precor treadmills and 8 StairMaster steppers. Life Fitness fanatics, this may be a good opportunity to expand your exercise repertoire.

Weight equipment is just as abundant as cardio, so those wishing to pump up the pecs will have plenty of choices too.

Swimmers will enjoy the highly rated 25-yard pool, complete with essential equipment and timing devices. The lapper was completely empty during our tour and we got the impression that the water remains still for most of the day.

YMCA Gateway Village

900 West Trade Street, Charlotte, NC 28202
(704) 716-4700 • ymcacharlotte.org

CARDIO

TREADMILLS: **Cybex**
UPRIGHT BIKE: **Cybex**
RECUMBENT BIKE: **Cybex**
ELLIPTICAL: **Precor**
STEPPER: **StairMaster**
ROWING: **Concept II**

STRENGTH

FREE WEIGHTS: **Yes**
HAMMER: **Yes**
MACHINES: **Cybex**
DUMBBELLS: **3-100 lbs**

OTHER

CLASSES: **Yes**
HOURS: M-TH **5:30a-9p** • F **5:30a-7p** • SAT **8a-4p** • SUN **Closed**
COST: **$8 w/Doubletree key**
TV: **Yes**

Conveniently located across the street from the Doubletree, guests are provided access to the 27,000 square foot Y after paying $8 and showing their hotel keys. Along with out-of-towners, the clean and bright facility attracts many office workers from the neighboring businesses.

The ground floor of the two-level club is predominantly open space with cardio, free weights and weight machines dispersed nicely. Unlike Doubletree's exercise room, the Y provides a slew of new machines, including 12 stack-loaded weight machines, 10 ellipticals, 8 treadmills and 8 bikes. Downstairs, sweat fiends will find the club's group exercise studios, where numerous classes such as spinning and aerobics are offered.

Despite its many advantages, Gateway has two drawbacks: It does not have a pool and it is closed on Sundays. If these two shortcomings do not concern you and your business is in the Gateway Village, Doubletree is your place to stay and the Gateway Y is your place to play.

Note: Bytes Café across the lobby serves yummy breakfast, lunch and dinner buffets.

Mecklenburg County Aquatic Center (MCAC)

800 East 2nd Street, Charlotte, NC 28202
(704) 336-3483 • parkandrec.com

This place is a swimmers' utopia. While a free parking lot makes driving convenient, the center is within walking distance of many uptown hotels. The closest on our list are the Hampton Inn and Hilton Garden Inn, respectively. Guests are charged $8, but the fee is waived if you're staying at the Residence Inn.

The competition pools are contained in a fieldhouse-type building with high ceilings and bleachers on one side. On Tuesdays and Thursdays from 5:30 a.m. to 1:30 p.m., 8 lanes of long course (50m) are set up in the main pool. At all other times, swimmers follow a short course layout with 18 lanes x 25 yards. This fantastic swimming facility receives our highest rating and is a rare find in the middle of a downtown urban area.

CARDIO

TREADMILLS: **Precor**
UPRIGHT BIKE: **Precor**
RECUMBENT BIKE: **Precor**
ELLIPTICAL: **Precor**
STEPPER: **Precor**

STRENGTH

MACHINES: **Nautilus**
DUMBBELLS: **5-70 lbs**

SWIM

GRADE: **A**
SPECS: **8x50m • Indoor • 80°**
TOYS: **Kick • Pull • Clock**
MASTERS: **Yes**

OTHER

HOURS: **Call**
COST: **Free Residence Inn • $8 Others**
TV: **Yes**
EXTRAS: **88° Therapy pool**

Ask Tom Malchow if he likes this pool. He set the Butterfly World Record here in June 2000.

Other features include basic locker and shower facilities, an 88° therapeutic pool and a 104° hot tub. A small workout room filled with expensive cardio and weight equipment offers a viable exercise option for any anti-swimming traveling companions. The Precor brand of machines is always a welcome sight, and this gym supplies just enough of them to make you smile.

Towels are not provided, so bring one along. Locks are not supplied either, but most people leave their duffel bags on the pool deck, bleachers or workout room floor.

Finally, because the pool is used by local swim teams, we highly recommend calling in advance to confirm the facility's availability. Practices and meets can sometimes occupy the entire pool.

RUNNING ROUTES

McDowell/Dilworth

Running in this urban center will be on sidewalks and streets. For a nice out-and-back run, head south on McDowell Road and then east on Dilworth, which will take you through a historic, residential community. The homes are beautiful and plenty of intersecting roads provide ample alternatives to create loops.

McAlpine Creek Park

Located at 8711 Monroe Road, McAlpine Creek Park is about a 15-20 minute drive from Downtown. It offers runners a 462-acre playland, with a 3-acre lake, 8 soccer fields, a 2-mile bike trail and a fishing pier. Best of all, McAlpine also sports a 5k championship cross-country course. The route is marked fairly well, so you should not have problems finding the way. Call (704) 568-4044 for information.

Catawba River Front Trail

About 20 minutes west of Charlotte, Catawba River Front Trail is mostly enjoyed as a mountain bike haven. However, it also serves up over 8 miles of single track paths. It is by no means flat, and your quads will get a workout in this densely landscaped area. Consider bringing some breadcrumbs along to help you find your way back to the car if you don't complete the loop. Or, better yet, bring someone along who has a good sense of direction. Ask your hotel for driving directions.

CHICAGO, ILLINOIS

Architectural books encourage visiting Sears Tower, cultural magazines suggest touring the Chicago Art Institute and shopping guides rave about Michigan Avenue's highbrow stores. But taking in a Cubs game at legendary Wrigley Field is our #1 "must do" for Windy City travelers.

Originally built in 1914 with seating for 14,000, Wrigley is one of baseball's grandfathers — the second oldest park behind Boston's Fenway (1912). Throughout its history, the Friendly Confines has staged some of baseball's most notable events: Babe Ruth hit his famous "called home run" in 1932; Ernie Banks slugged his 500th homer in 1970; Pete Rose smacked his record tying 4,191st career hit in 1985; and Steve Bartman interfered with a foul ball to foil the beloved Cubbies' advancement to the World Series in 2003.

Still located on its Clark and Addison Street corner and now accommodating 40,000 fans, Wrigley is the centerpiece of a young and vibrant urban neighborhood. Locals love nothing more than settling in for an afternoon of beer drinking and hotdog eating — cherished pursuits in celebration of America's greatest pastime.

This ballpark's one-of-a-kind features and long-standing traditions, combined with its famously die-hard fans, create an unrivaled sporting venue. The 1937 center field scoreboard is still changed by hand. Players chasing fly balls battle the ivy that flourishes along the red brick home run wall. "Take Me Out to the Ballgame" is led by celebrity cantors in tribute to the Cubs' (and White Sox) legendary broadcaster, Harry Caray. Wrigley's "bleacher bums" were the first to throw an opposing team's home run ball back onto the field. And "Wait 'til next year," has been the October battle cry ever since the underdog Cubbies' last World Series Championship in 1908.

When you walk up to Wrigley, it's like going on a first date; when you're inside, it's like being at home; and when you leave it's like saying good-bye to an old friend. See you soon, ol' buddy... see you soon.

87 Locations Reviewed

DOWNTOWN

EXPENSIVE

GOLD: The Peninsula

108 E. Superior Street, Chicago, IL 60611
(312) 337-2888 • chicago.peninsula.com

CARDIO

TREADMILLS: **6 StarTrac**
UPRIGHT BIKE: **2 Cybex**
RECUMBENT BIKE: **1 Cybex**
ELLIPTICAL: **5 LF**
STEPPER: **2 Cybex**

STRENGTH

FREE WEIGHTS: **Yes**
MACHINES: **10 Cybex • 2 Free Motion**
DUMBBELLS: **1-65 lbs**

SWIM

GRADE: **B+**
SPECS: **3x25m • Indoor • 82°**
TOYS: **Kick • Pull • Fins**

OTHER

CLASSES: **Yes**
HOURS: M-F **6a-10p** • SAT-SUN **7a-8p**
COST: **Free**
TV: **Yes**

This unbelievably posh accommodation will spoil you. Steps away from Michigan Avenue's upscale shopping on the aptly named Magnificent Mile and within 10 minutes' walk of Oak Street Beach, Peninsula's location has it all.

Built in 2001, the palatial hotel's 339 guest quarters enchant with luxurious décor, contemporary style and modern electronic gizmos. Like a swank gadget store, the technologically advanced rooms captivated us. We especially enjoyed soaking in the full-size tub while controlling the bathroom's television, speakerphone and music system from a reachable wall pad. Twenty-four-hour room service, afternoon tea, 4 distinct restaurants and a tony (and rather smoky) bar comprise the hotel's cuisine options. Although worker bees at such luxury venues sometimes front a hoity-toity attitude, the staff here is friendly and helpful.

Peninsula's spa and fitness center covers the 19th and 20th floors. Commanding Magnificent Mile views, its light hardwood floors, bright walls and sparkling new exercise equipment will inspire you. Though Precor elliptical addicts may be disappointed by the best sellers' absence (Life Fitness is supplied instead), plenty of other high-end machines and weights are available for the taking — including ~350 pounds of plate free weights for bench press. Daily classes are offered for those seeking like-minded travelers' company.

Swimmers will be awed. Peninsula's indoor, 3 lane, 25-meter lap option complete with floating lines and bottom stripes is a beauty. Don't fret the online picture, which omits the lane divisions. Photographers purposely removed the "ugly" lines and stripes for "artistic" reasons. The rest of the photo is accurate, including the high ceilings and bright atmosphere — making this water box one of the best *hotel* lappers in the country.

SILVER: Park Hyatt

800 N. Michigan Avenue, Chicago, IL 60611
(312) 335-1234 • parkchicago.hyatt.com

Located near The Peninsula, Park Hyatt is a close second to its Chitown competitor. With identical location perks and equally impressive skyline views, travelers will not miss out on any luxury at this wonderful hotel property on Old Water Tower Square. Flat screen televisions, lap top computer re-chargers, CD/DVD players, dual-spouted walk-in showers, double bathroom sinks and high thread count sheets outfit Park's 202 rooms.

CARDIO

TREADMILLS: **5 Precor**
UPRIGHT BIKE: **2 LF**
RECUMBENT BIKE: **2 Cybex**
ELLIPTICAL: **3 Precor**
STEPPER: **1 StairMaster**

STRENGTH

FREE WEIGHTS: **Yes**
MACHINES: **11 Cybex**
DUMBBELLS: **3-75 lbs**

SWIM

GRADE: **B**
SPECS: **2x25yd • Indoor • 84°**
TOYS: **Kick • Pull • Fins • Clock**

OTHER

HOURS: **24** • POOL **5:30a-11p**
COST: **Free**
TV: **Yes**

While leaving the stylishly modern quarters may prove difficult, the 7th floor fitness center should kickstart athletic-minded travelers. Inside the complimentary 24-hour facility, guests longing for a sweat will need no introduction to the familiar top-of-the-line machines. While Park Hyatt makes available the popular Precor elliptical and StairMaster Free Climber (as well as a good number of Cybex weight stations and free weights), we give the nod to Peninsula due to its larger and more aesthetically pleasing gym.

Our fish-like friends will happily lap it up in the 25-yard pool. While 3 lanes are provided with floating lines and bottom stripes, only 2 are full length — the third is roughly 5 yards or so shorter. Every toy is on deck, as well as a pace clock for intervals.

MODERATELY EXPENSIVE

GOLD: Embassy Suites Lakefront

511 N. Columbus Drive, Chicago, IL 60611
(312) 836-5900 • chicagoembassy.com

Do not confuse this stellar accommodation with its sister property on Ontario Street. This Embassy Suites hits a "Moderately Expensive" home run for athletic-minded travelers. And its location, within 3 blocks of Michigan Avenue, the lakefront and Navy Pier, is convenient to all Chicago attractions. Opened in 2001, this 17-story atrium hotel is one of the nicest Embassys we have seen — and we've toured quite a few. Guests can count on Embassy's separate sleeping area floor plans in all 455 rooms, along with kitchenettes, microwaves, refrigerators and impressive city views. Each morning starts with Embassy's trademark full breakfast buffet of waffles, omelets, cereals and juices — a perfect reward after a hard sweat.

CARDIO

TREADMILLS: **4 LF**
UPRIGHT BIKE: **1 LF**
RECUMBENT BIKE: **1 LF**
ELLIPTICAL: **1 LF - old**
STEPPER: **1 LF - old**

SWIM

GRADE: **D**
SPECS: **0x21yd • Indoor • 81-84°**

OTHER

HOURS: **6a-10p**
COST: **Free**
TV: **Yes**
EXTRAS: **$10 pass Holmes Place**

While the lobby-level workout facility may serve up a quick aerobic session, it has no strength equipment. Athletic-minded travelers will appreciate Embassy's connection to the adjacent Holmes Place Health Club. For a reasonable $10/day admission, Embassy guests receive full privileges to this Grade "A" fitness center opened in 2002 (Embassy Diamond members get in free).

Embassy's 21-yard indoor pool is a desperate swimmer's lap option but, with no lane lines or bottom stripes, straight swimming is difficult. A better swim bet is heading to Holmes and enjoying a proper lap session in its phenomenal 25-meter water box.

Note: Embassy guests can also seek shelter from cold Chicago winter days at the 21-screen movie theater next door.

SILVER: Hilton Chicago

720 S. Michigan Avenue, Chicago, IL 60605
(312) 922-4400 • hilton.com

CARDIO

TREADMILLS: **4 Quinton • 2 StairMaster • 2 LF - old**
UPRIGHT BIKE: **2 LF**
RECUMBENT BIKE: **2 Tectrix • 3 LF - old**
ELLIPTICAL: **7 Precor**
STEPPER: **5 StairMaster**
OTHER: **Gauntlet**

STRENGTH

FREE WEIGHTS: **Yes**
HAMMER: **Yes**
MACHINES: **8 Nautilus**
DUMBBELLS: **3-80 lbs**

SWIM

GRADE: **C-**
SPECS: **3x20yd • Indoor • 83°**
TOYS: **Kick • Pull**

OTHER

HOURS: **5:30a-9p**
COST: **$13**
TV: **Yes**
EXTRAS: **1/18 mile indoor track**

As the Chicago Marathon's host hotel for the past several years, Hilton understands athletic-minded travelers' needs and preferences. While its South Loop locale does not afford the same convenient access to Michigan Avenue's upscale shopping and dining, this somewhat quieter area of the Windy City puts guests in the midst of Grant Park, the Art Institute and the Loop's skyscrapers, theaters and shopping. Chicago's downtown continues to grow as more attractions make their way south of the Chicago River.

This 1,544-room Hilton always bustles. Conventioneers, leisure travelers, holiday party go-ers — on any given night you see revelers en route to some function or party. Fortunately, the rooms provide a cozy and quiet retreat with brightly colored walls and carpets, premium bedding and antique style furnishings. We always leave well rested.

Hilton's gym is good but not quite as impressive as the Embassy/Holmes Place combo — especially in light of Hilton's vexing $13/day access fee. However, with high ceilings, a wide-open room and an indoor 1/18 mile track encircling the machines, the venue is aesthetically pleasing. Given the rather steep tariff, we expected to find a plethora of top-of-the-line machinery and a vast array of weights. Hilton comes close, but its mix of old and new cardio stations is disappointing. The strength alternatives, however, have a younger average age, so those with a lifting routine in mind should find ample opportunities to make their bodies bulge.

Swimmers catch a break by not having to pay a fee to get wet. Three lanes are divided by floating lines, but no stripes are marked on the pool's bottom. The length is a little short at 20 yards, so prepare for more flip turns and laps. And bring a watch if you plan on swimming intervals, since no pace clock is available.

BRONZE: Intercontinental

505 N. Michigan Avenue, Chicago, IL 60611
(312) 944-4100 • chicago.intercontinental.com

On the south end of Michigan Avenue's Magnificent Mile, Intercontinental offers a more historic lodging experience compared to its modern skyscraping neighbors. Staying at this fine hotel will keep you within a half-mile walk of this area's luxury shopping and exquisite dining venues. Intercontinental's 807 rooms are divided between two towers, the historic and the newer main building. Providing a little more pizzazz with its amber walls, polkadot comforters and contemporary furnishings, we favor the main building's guest quarters. If you land in the historic tower, don't despair. These rooms are attractive as well, with marble baths, antique décor and separate tubs and showers.

CARDIO

TREADMILLS: **6 LF**
UPRIGHT BIKE: **2 LF • 2 LF - old**
RECUMBENT BIKE: **2 LF**
ELLIPTICAL: **1 LF**
STEPPER: **2 LF • 2 LifeStep • 1 StairMaster - old**
ROWING: **1 - old**

STRENGTH

FREE WEIGHTS: **Yes**
MACHINES: **10 Cybex**
DUMBBELLS: **3-50 lbs**

SWIM

GRADE: **B-**
SPECS: **5x25yd • Indoor • 80°**
TOYS: **Kick • Pull**

OTHER

HOURS: **24 • POOL Shortened hours**
COST: **$12 • $16/stay • POOL Free**
TV: **Yes**

The value of Intercontinental's on-site fitness center depends upon your workout plan. The separate weight and cardio equipment rooms are rather small and almost "cave-ish," and many of the cardio machines are older models. However, if you can bear the tight quarters, you will find quite a few fitness diamonds in the rough. Your best bets will be the bikes, elliptical trainer and strength equipment. Certainly the highlight of Intercontinental's exercise center, the 25-yard ornately designed lap pool is reminiscent of an ancient Roman bathhouse. Vintage tiles and handcrafted designs will have swimmers daydreaming about stroking in the center of a 19th Century fountain (without the spouting water, of course). During our tour, 5 lanes were marked with bottom stripes, but only 3 were separated by floating lines. Though the pool is unique, many of our other listed swim venues are superior. Those intending to swim intervals should bring a watch, as no pace clock is supplied.

Note: While Intercontinental charges an irritating $12/day or $16/stay fee for use of its gym, swimming pool access is free.

LEAST EXPENSIVE

GOLD: **Holiday Inn** Chicago Mart Plaza

350 N. Orleans Street, Chicago, IL 60654
(312) 836-5000 • chicago.martplaza.holiday-inn.com

CARDIO

TREADMILLS: **3 LF**
UPRIGHT BIKE: **2 LF**
RECUMBENT BIKE: **3 LF**
ELLIPTICAL: **4 LF**

STRENGTH

MACHINES: **1 Multi**

SWIM

GRADE: **D**
SPECS: **3x17yd • Indoor • 81-84°**

OTHER

HOURS: **5a-11p**
COST: **Free**
TV: **Yes**
EXTRAS: **$25 access East Bank**

Attached to the Merchandise Mart via skybridge, this Holiday Inn is just across the river from Chicago's business "Loop" and about 8 blocks from Michigan Avenue's shops and attractions. Taxis are abundant, so shoppers shouldn't fret the 1 mile distance from Magnificent Mile. A $5 cab ride will get you there in a jiffy. Although no Holiday Inn showers guests with lavish amenities or loads of perks, this one garners our Gold due to its reasonable rates, clean and inviting accommodations and its across-the-street location from one of the country's largest and best health clubs — East Bank Club.

If you are in a hurry and need a quick cardio hit, Holiday's 16th floor exercise room may suffice. Its 12 Life Fitness 9500 series cardio machines are new and in good shape. However, those with a strength routine or lap swim in mind will not be satisfied. The on-site pool is a 17-yard shorty (bottom stripes, but no floating lines), and the multi-exercise weight unit should be replaced. To satiate any — and we mean any — exercise craving, walk 3 minutes to the unbelievable East Bank Club. Admission is steep at $25/day ($20 IHRSA), but consider it your personal fitness amusement park — you have to see the place to believe it!

Note: Have the concierge call East Bank or provide you with something in writing before heading over.

BEYOND HOTELS DOWNTOWN

East Bank Club

500 N. Kingsbury Street, Chicago, IL 60610
(312) 527-5800 • eastbankclub.com

After belonging to this esteemed club for several years, we recall its scene nearly as well as its stellar equipment. The East Bank bunch ranges from hard core sweat fiends clad in typical gym shirt/short combos to the BP set with freshly coiffed hair, a strong layer of cologne and, in some cases, we kid you not, high-heeled gym shoes. In case you're wondering, we did not belong to this latter group.

The enormous facility stretches across 2 full city blocks and houses an unbelievable assortment of fitness equipment, exercise classes and dining options, along with a full-service spa. And you know a facility is massive when it boasts an indoor 1/4-mile track! Add to this 8 indoor tennis courts, 2 competition-quality 25-yard lap pools (1 indoor/1 outdoor), 4 racquetball courts, an indoor driving range, a formal restaurant and a large café — get the picture? Notice, we have not even discussed the strength and cardio options!

East Bank's cardio floor — just the cardio floor — is larger than 20,000 square feet. The latest and greatest endurance machines line the room with Precor and Life Fitness leading the charge. If you see Oprah sweating off some stress, tell her you have a great book to recommend. Strength enthusiasts will find an incredible supply and variety of stack-loaded weight stations, computerized resistance machines, free weights and Hammer Strength plate-loaded equipment. It's all here... just leave a trail of breadcrumbs to help you find your way around.

Swimmers, you're in luck. You not only have 2 wonderful lap pools, but you can also count on a full assortment of toys and a pace clock on deck.

Only guests at a few Chicago hotels may join in the fun, and

CARDIO

TREADMILLS: **Precor • LF • NordicTrack**
UPRIGHT BIKE: **LF**
RECUMBENT BIKE: **LF**
ELLIPTICAL: **LF • Precor**
STEPPER: **StairMaster • Stepmill**
ROWING: **Concept II**

STRENGTH

FREE WEIGHTS: **Yes**
HAMMER: **Yes**
MACHINES: **Cybex • Free Motion • BodyMaster • Technogym**
DUMBBELLS: **5-120 lbs**

SWIM

GRADE: #1 **B** • #2 **A**
SPECS: #1 **4x25yd • Indoor • 80°**
#2 **5x25yd • Outdoor • 78-80°**
TOYS: **Kick • Pull • Fins • Clock**
MASTERS: **Yes**

OTHER

CLASSES: **Yes**
HOURS: M-F **5:15a-11p** • SAT **6:45a-9p** • SUN **7:30a-8:30p**
COST: **$25 Select hotels • $20 IHRSA**
TV: **Yes**
EXTRAS: **1/4-mile indoor track • Basketball • Racquetball • Tennis • Golf • Cafe**

Holiday Inn–Mart Plaza is one of them. Although $25 might seem steep, your body is worth it!

Note: Members of IHRSA clubs are additionally welcome for $20/day (check www.healthclubs.com or ask staff at your home club).

Holmes Place Health Club

355 E. Grand Avenue, Chicago, IL 60611
(312) 467-1111 • holmesplace.com

CARDIO

TREADMILLS: **LF • StarTrac**
UPRIGHT BIKE: **LF**
RECUMBENT BIKE: **LF**
ELLIPTICAL: **LF • Precor**
STEPPER: **StairMaster**
ROWING: **Concept II**

STRENGTH

FREE WEIGHTS: **Yes**
HAMMER: **Yes**
MACHINES: **LF • Free Motion • Magnum • Technogym**
DUMBBELLS: **3-100 lbs**

SWIM

GRADE: **B+**
SPECS: **3x25m • Indoor • 80-82°**
TOYS: **Kick**

OTHER

CLASSES: **Yes**
HOURS: M-TH **5:30a-10p** • F **5:30a-9p** • SAT-SUN **8a-6p**
COST: **$10 Embassy only**
TV: **Yes**

Adjacent to the Lakefront Embassy Suites, this European fitness franchise impresses. While its size fails to rival East Bank's behemoth, Holmes' recently-opened full-service fitness center is more modern and swank. Plasma screens adorn the walls, light hardwood floors provide a stylish terra firma and plush locker rooms contribute upscale primping facilities.

Holmes' cardio and strength equipment defines "cutting edge." Whether you prefer a sweat standing up, sitting down or some position in between, this place has you covered. Plenty of classes are offered as well, for those needing group therapy.

Swimmers are treated with equal respect by Holmes' 25-meter lap pool. Three lanes are divided by floating lines and bottom stripes, so swimming straight is no sweat. Kickboards add variety, but bring a watch for intervals — one of the few items missing is a pace clock.

Note: Embassy guests must purchase a $10 pass from the hotel. If you are not staying at Embassy Suites, you cannot get in.

SCHAUMBURG

Located about 20 miles west of Downtown, Schaumburg is dense with business offices, corporate campuses and economic hotels. One of the largest indoor malls in the country (Woodfield) calls this suburban neck of the woods home, providing shopping and dining variety to visitors. And nearby Busse Woods is a runners' paradise, with close to 20 miles of paved and dirt paths.

Stay here only if you need to, but know that we've got your workout covered.

LEAST EXPENSIVE

GOLD: Hawthorn Suites

1251 E. American Lane, Schaumburg, IL 60173
(847) 706-9007 • hawthornschaumburg.com

A stay at Hawthorn Suites puts travelers within walking distance of Woodfield Mall's shopping and dining, Busse Woods' running paths (~1mile) and the enormous Lifetime Fitness exercise mecca, where guests receive complimentary access — a $25/day value! The perks don't stop there. All 135 suites offer kitchenettes, microwaves and modern furnishings. Add to the portfolio free breakfasts, free local calls and free parking.

Skip Hawthorn's tiny exercise room and head straight to Lifetime Fitness (5-minute walk) or Busse Woods for your daily detox. Both are phenomenal options, especially considering they're free.

SILVER: Comfort Suites

1100 E. Higgins Road, Schaumburg, IL 60173
(847) 330-0133 • choicehotels.com

We recommend Comfort primarily because it is the closest hotel to Lifetime Fitness — practically next door. Although guests do not receive free admission passes (Hawthorn is the only freebie purveyor), Comfort's inexpensive nightly rates make a $25/day workout tack-on affordable.

This is not your typical "frill-less" Comfort Inn. Opened in July 2003, this Comfort Suites impresses with charming furnishings, in-room refrigerators and microwaves, free local calls and a yummy, complimentary breakfast spread of scrambled eggs, hash browns, cereals and juices.

Don't bother with the barely serviceable workout room on-site. Instead, walk over to Lifetime Fitness and spend the $25 — you know you'll be happy afterward. (Runners, don't forget about Busse Woods.)

BEYOND HOTELS SCHAUMBURG

Lifetime Fitness

900 E. Higgins Road, Schaumburg, IL 60173
(847) 517-7171 • lifetimefitness.com

This burgeoning chain knows how to design health clubs. Massive in size and with state-of-the-art style, Lifetime Fitness will wow you. Hundreds of cardio pieces line the warehouse-sized fitness floor and weights are supplied in tons. Featuring 4 different brands of ellipticals and stack-loaded weight machines, the club is like an exercise equipment showroom. Suffice it to say, Lifetime covers all fitness bases.

Swimmers will be captivated by Lifetime's 5 lane, 25-meter lapper which sports floating lines and bottom stripes in comfort-

CARDIO

TREADMILLS: **LF • Woodway**
UPRIGHT BIKE: **LF**
RECUMBENT BIKE: **LF**
ELLIPTICAL: **LF • Precor • StarTrac**
STEPPER: **StairMaster • Stepmill**
ROW: **Concept II**

STRENGTH

FREE WEIGHTS: **Yes**
HAMMER: **Yes**
MACHINES: **Cybex • Icarian • BodyMaster**
DUMBBELLS: **5-130 lbs**

SWIM

GRADE: **B**
SPECS: **5x25m • Indoor • 80°**
TOYS: **Kick • Pull • Clock**

OTHER

CLASSES: **Yes**
HOURS: M-F **6a-9p** • SAT-SUN **9a-9p**
COST: **Free Hawthorn Suites • $25 Others**
TV: **Yes**
EXTRAS: **Basketball • Racquetball • Climbing Wall • Cafe**

able 80° water. A pace clock is on deck and, if you don't see any kickboards, ask the aquatics office for a loaner.

Hawthorn guests receive free admission passes from their hotel, while all other exercisers must pay $25.

Note: Though the club is open 24 hours for members, guests have shorter hours — see the chart.

RUNNING ROUTES

CHICAGO

Lake Michigan

Jogging in the Windy City is a piece of cake... or, should we say, slice of deep dish pizza? A flat paved path runs along Lake Michigan's shore for 18.5 scenic miles. Start jogging east from your hotel to reach an access point. From the Magnificent Mile, enter through Lake Shore Drive pedestrian underpasses at Oak Street Beach or Ohio Street. Heading north on the path will take you to Sheridan Road and the Roger's Park neighborhood, while a southerly out-and-back brings Hyde Park into play. The scenery is better to the left (north), but you will find it somewhat more crowded.

SCHAUMBURG

Busse Woods

Runners staying in Schaumburg will enjoy Busse Woods' 11 miles of paved paths and nearby 9 miles of added trails. From your hotel, head east along Higgins Road, jog under the I-290/Rt. 53 highway and you'll see the path. Take it in either direction through the nearby forests and meadows.

CINCINNATI, OHIO

While we may be fitness fiends, we also admit that "pigging out" is an infrequent, yet sometimes merited reward. In the City affectionately known as "Porkopolis," the eating ritual is embraced, and natives ham it up with annual festivals, community events and local competitions — all in honor of its hog heritage.

During the early 19th Century, a multitude of slaughterhouses sprouted up all over the Ohio River basin, which is not surprising, considering the hog was the state's chief livestock and corn its principal crop. Cincinnati soon became the pork-packing capital of the world, giving rise to its swine notoriety. "Let your corn walk to market," became a popular expression, underscoring the industry's growth and importance.

Because Cincinnati owed its economic livelihood to the mud-loving glutton, the hog took on an exalted status among townsfolk. Laws were passed to support this burgeoning trade — the most conspicuous being the requirement to dispose of all trash onto the streets in order to feed roving hogs! Locals could hardly snort at the filth and stench with this visible industry literally bringing home the bacon.

Today, locals piggyback their ancestry onto entertaining events like the Flying Pig Marathon, the Porkopolis BBQ Festival and the Big Pig Gig Art Show. And, since we have found a few good places in Porkopolis for you to stay and work out, no squealing will be allowed.

EXPENSIVE

GOLD: **Hilton** Netherland Plaza

35 West Fifth Street, Cincinnati, OH 45202
(513) 421-9100 • hilton.com

This opulent Hilton property, listed on the National Register of Historic places, evokes Old World charm and culture. In the heart of downtown Cincinnati, the 550-room classical giant recently completed a full-scale room renovation, refreshing the traditional dark red tones with more modern whites and greens. While the furnishings may reflect a historic Victorian motif, modern conveniences such as free high-speed internet access are available. In addition, the connected Tower Place Mall offers upscale shopping and a food court.

The privately owned and operated Gym at Carew Tower is Hilton's workout option, but it is also available to others for a fee. Recently refurbished, this weight-intense club provides exercisers with a full variety of workout pleasures. It's the primary reason for the hotel's top ranking. To get inside, take the elevators to the lower level arcade, follow the overhead signs to The Gym's entrance, and enjoy.

Note: Lap swimmers must walk 10 minutes to the YWCA because the gym's pool is not a lapper.

SILVER: **Westin**

21 East Fifth Street, Cincinnati, OH 45202
(513) 621-7700 • westin.com/cincinnati

CARDIO

TREADMILLS: **4 LF**
UPRIGHT BIKE: **1 LF**
RECUMBENT BIKE: **1 LF**
ELLIPTICAL: **1 LF**
STEPPER: **1 LF**

STRENGTH

MACHINES: **3 LF**
DUMBBELLS: **5-50 lbs**

SWIM

SPECS: **Indoor • Not lap**

OTHER

HOURS: **24**
COST: **Free**
TV: **Yes**

While the Hilton goes for a classic feel, the Westin exudes a contemporary vibe with leather upholstered headboards, modern furniture and a fashionable lobby. Though both are in the "Expensive" category, if you prefer the Westin's present-day style, prepare to lay down more 21st Century cash. Our research indicates a \$60-\$70 premium to be "in vogue."

The modern theme carries over to Westin's wonderfully equipped 17th floor fitness facility. Recently purchased machines await your arrival with well-oiled parts and individually attached plasma TVs, all in an aesthetically pleasing room. Life Fitness is the brand of choice, so Precor and Cybex aficionados will have to look elsewhere or expand their horizons. (You could have worse problems.)

Swimmers, your dipping dreams will only come true at downtown's YWCA, a 5-minute walk.

MODERATELY EXPENSIVE

GOLD: **Marriott** Cincinnati River Center

10 West RiverCenter Boulevard, Covington, KY 41011
(859) 261-2900 • marriott.com

Options like these prove we have really done our homework! Located on the south bank of the Ohio River in Kentucky and directly across from the heart of Downtown, it only takes a short 1/4-mile drive across the Roebling Suspension Bridge to put you in Cincinnati. The commute is made even easier by Marriott's complimentary shuttle service during weekday business hours.

CARDIO

TREADMILLS: **4 Cybex**
UPRIGHT BIKE: **2 Tectrix • 1 Cybex**
RECUMBENT BIKE: **3 Tectrix**
ELLIPTICAL: **2 Trotter**
STEPPER: **2 Tectrix**

STRENGTH

FREE WEIGHTS: **Yes**
MACHINES: **17 Cybex**
DUMBBELLS: **3-75 lbs**

SWIM

GRADE: **C**
SPECS: **2x25yd • Indoor • 78-82°**

OTHER

HOURS: **6a-11p • Will unlock after hours**
COST: **Free**
TV: **Yes**

Marriott's guest rooms will not win any style awards with ordinary furnishings and unattractive décor, but the worthy gym is in contention for the blue ribbon. Equipment is organized in a long and narrow room with newer cardio machines and stack-loaded weight stations stealing the show. Staggered by the quantity of Cybex units, we had to count them twice to ensure 17 was the correct number. Equally impressive is Marriott's willingness to provide free weights for bench press and squat reps. The cardio machines are in good condition, but some are the cheaper Trotter and Tectrix brands. The air temperature seemed a little chilly, so bring along a layer to shed once you break a sweat.

Swimmers will be intrigued, but not delighted, by the 25-yard pool. Without floating lines, swimmers must navigate the two lanes using the wide stripes on the pool's bottom. We did not see any toys or a pace clock, so those planning on base interval training should bring a wristwatch.

LEAST EXPENSIVE

GOLD: **Millennium** - Downtown

150 West Fifth Street, Cincinnati, OH 45202
(513) 357-5800 • millenniumhotels.com

Millennium Hotels took over the old Four Points property and provided a much needed facelift. Connected via skywalk to the Cincinnati Convention Center, the hotel is centrally located in the midst of downtown's hustle and bustle.

The 872-guest quarters offer a pleasant in-room experience with warm pastel colors, stylish furniture, and a choice between "standard" and "club" rooms. For the extra dough, club rooms provide

CARDIO
TREADMILLS: **3 LF**
RECUMBENT BIKE: **2 LF**
STEPPER: **3 LifeStep**

STRENGTH
MACHINES: **Multigym**

OTHER
COST: **Free**
TV: **Yes**

a little more luxury and panache (eg, high speed internet access, upgraded bath amenities, and a few perks), but the "standard" version is no slouch.

The hotel's on-site fitness room affords exercise fiends an opportunity to sweat — especially on the newer treadmills and recumbent bikes. But the LifeStep steppers and Universal weight machine may leave some guests, especially those desiring a serious strength workout, wanting more. No worry, Millenium's convenient location puts you within a 2-minute walk of The Gym at Carew Tower —the best fitness center Downtown.

If you belong to an IHRSA member health club back home (e.g., 24 Hour Fitness), admission will cost only $8. However, if IHRSA does not come to your rescue, a workout here will run $20/day. While a little steep, the room rate savings should keep the check book in balance.

Swimmers, head to the Y.

Note: To determine whether your health club is an IHRSA member, go to www.healthclubs.com.

BEYOND HOTELS

The Gym at Carew Tower (Hilton)

441 Vine Street Suite 100-LL, Cincinnati, OH 45202
(513) 651-1442 • thegymatcarewtower.com

CARDIO
TREADMILLS: **LF • Precor**
UPRIGHT BIKE: **Precor**
RECUMBENT BIKE: **Precor**
ELLIPTICAL: **Precor**
STEPPER: **StairMaster • Tectrix • LifeStep**
ROWING: **Yes**

STRENGTH
FREE WEIGHTS: **Yes**
HAMMER: **Yes**
MACHINES: **Cybex**
DUMBBELLS: **3-150 lbs**

SWIM
SPECS: **Indoor • Not lap**

OTHER
CLASSES: **Yes**
HOURS: M-F **5:30a-9:30p** • SAT **8a-6p** • SUN **10a-4p**
COST: **Free Hilton • $8 IHRSA • $10 Others**
TV: **Yes**

The executive-size Gym has undergone a recent renovation and ownership change that should spark the interest of travelers and locals alike. Though it is not a large facility, The Gym's new owners know what counts — equipment, equipment, equipment.

Most cardio machines are new and in good condition, though a few old friends like the StairMaster 4000PTs are in the mix. Weights are not taken lightly here, so muscle pump buffs will find strength in the club's offering of 22 Cybex stack-loaded weight stations, 8 Hammer Strength machines and 2 dumbbell sets progressing up to 150 pounds.

Swimmers are left out of the fun, however. While the cozy center does provide a pool, it is not nearly long enough for any meaningful lapping. The YWCA is a better swim alternative.

While Hilton guests get in for free, all other exercisers must pay $10 for entry, or $8 with IHRSA membership (healthclubs.com).

Downtown YWCA

898 Walnut Street, Cincinnati, OH 45202
(513) 241-7090 • ywcacincinnati.org/health.html

Recommended only for its swimming pool, this YWCA's fitness room stocks equipment that likely predates the 8-track tape player.

Triathletes and swimmers looking for a little water action will find the lap pool adequate, but well short of spectacular.

While the facility is housed in a historic building, the pool area is brightened by a fresh coat of paint and some general "sprucing up." Four lanes are separated by floating lines and bottom stripes, and all swim toys are provided. We did not notice a pace clock, however, so wear a watch for intervals. The locker rooms are clean and carpeted, so a quick chlorine rinse after your swim should not offend the senses. Bring your I.D., swim cap (just to be safe) and $7.

SWIM

GRADE: **B-**
SPECS: **4x25yd • Indoor • 84°**
TOYS: **Kick • Pull • Fins**
MASTERS: **Yes**

OTHER

HOURS: M-F **6a-8p** • SAT **9a-5p** • SUN **Closed**
COST: **$7**

RUNNING ROUTES

Eden Park

The 186-acre Eden Park sports approximately 4-6 miles of running trails. A 15-minute run from most Downtown hotels will get you there. For a more scenic route, follow Vine Street to Central Parkway/Reading Road. Gilbert Avenue is more direct, but it tends to be congested. Once you arrive, you will be greeted by lakes, gardens and a 172-foot high water tower. The historic park is also home to the Cincinnati Art Museum, Art Academy, Playhouse in the Park, a Pavillion and Conservatory. There are also several memorials located throughout the park, the most interesting being the Presidential Grove, which is marked by 5 memorial tree plantings.

Roebling Bridge

In addition, due to Porkopolis' location on the Ohio River, jaunting across the Roebling Suspension Bridge is another run option. Depending upon your starting point (OH, KY), there is a paved path you can pick up at the entrance of Downtown's Sawyer Point Park. The path crosses to Kentucky via the bridge and takes runners through quiet and charming residential streets along Riverside Drive. Non-runners may appreciate the Sawyer Point facilities, which include an outdoor skating rink, performance pavillion, 8 outdoor tennis courts, 3 sand volleyball courts, a spectacular playground and a "water feature."

Eastern Avenue

Eastern Avenue is a potential out-and-back route, as it parallels the river. You'll get about 4 miles until Eastern forks in another direction.

Note: As always, check your route with the hotel. Most will have maps available.

Cleveland

CLEVELAND, OHIO

In the late 1930s, high school classmates and native Clevelanders Joe Shuster and Jerry Siegel invented Clark Kent and his famous superhuman split personality. Siegel was a science fiction junkie, and Shuster a fledgling artist. Both envisioned comic strips as a means to further their respective passions — Siegel developed the content, while Shuster fashioned the illustrations. In their early collaborations, this unique character was portrayed as a world-conquering villain. Yes, that's right — Superman started out as a bad guy.

Only after the two tried to take Superman into newspapers and magazines did they make him over into the fearless "champion of the suppressed." After several years of rejection, the duo caught a break from an upstart comic book called Action, which agreed to introduce our now famous hero and his superhuman feats in its June 1938 issue. As the saying goes, the rest is history.

Several days without exercise can have the same debilitating effect on an athlete that Kryptonite has on Superman. Fortunately, Cleveland has several good stay and play options where you can work on getting faster than a speeding bullet and more powerful than a locomotive. Don't forget your cape!

26 Locations Reviewed

EXPENSIVE

GOLD: **Ritz Carlton**

1515 West Third Street, Cleveland, OH 44113
(216) 623-1300 • ritzcarlton.com/hotels/cleveland

CARDIO

TREADMILLS: **2 Quinton - old**
RECUMBENT BIKE: **2 Tectrix**
ELLIPTICAL: **1 LF**
STEPPER: **1 LF • 1 Tectrix**

STRENGTH

FREE WEIGHTS: **Yes ~250 lbs**
MACHINES: **4 Paramount**
DUMBBELLS: **5-50 lbs**

SWIM

GRADE: **D-**
SPECS: **2x15yd • Indoor • 81-84°**
TOYS: **Kick**

OTHER

HOURS: **24**
COST: **Free**
TV: **Yes**

For snooty-toots who accept nothing less than 300 thread count Egyptian cotton bedding, this Ritz option is especially for you. Although the Residence Inn, Radisson and Hyatt offer better workout alternatives, those preferring more luxury will appreciate the Ritz's impeccable service and upscale accommodations. You'll be pampered with marble baths, feather beds, complimentary shoeshines and 24-hour room service.

Unfortunately, persnickety guests will not be pleased by the 7th floor workout room. Disappointing for any 4-star hotel, Ritz drops the fitness ball by stocking low-end brands of cardio equipment. Premium machines such as Precor, Cybex and/or Life Fitness should be here rather than Quinton and Tectrix. Ritz also carries no upright bikes but, just prior to printing, an elliptical finally arrived. Though a decent quantity of free weights decorates the room, only 4 stack-loaded weight stations are supplied. While we may be pushing the finicky envelope with this last criticism, the other deficiencies are significant. Luckily, Ritz guests can walk 5 minutes through an indoor shopping mall and be treated to a worthy workout at Tower City Fitness. It will cost $10.

Swimmers have a lap option at Ritz, but it is also less than premium. Though the pool's bottom has lane stripes, its length amounts to only 46 feet (about 15 yards) — barely accommodating a dozen strokes. Look to the YMCA for the only true lap pool available to downtown Cleveland travelers.

Note: Just prior to publishing, we were informed by Ritz staff that an upright bike and 2 new treads were "on the way." Call and check with the gym attendant to make sure the delivery actually occurred.

MODERATELY EXPENSIVE

GOLD: **Residence Inn**

527 Prospect Avenue, Cleveland, OH 44115
(216) 443-9043 • residenceinn.com

Conveniently connected to the Colonial Market Place, this quaint Residence Inn occupies an historic building in the heart of Downtown. Guests receive a number of perks during their stay, including fully equipped kitchenettes and cooking/eating utensils, refrigerators, microwaves and free high-speed internet access. In the lobby, patrons are treated to complimentary hot breakfasts and evening social hours with free nibbles and beverages. One unique feature of this Residence Inn is the billiards room (two tables).

Since the 2nd floor exercise room barely offers more machines than the billiards room has tables, we were pleased to find that visitors are granted complimentary access to the Fitworks Fitness Center located in the adjacent Colonial Market Place. This is downtown Cleveland, so "Market Place" does not mean sprawling suburban buildings — think small arcade. Door to door, it will take you no longer than 2 minutes.

Swimmers receive no water relief at Fitworks. Your lap destiny awaits at the YMCA and requires a commute — 15 minutes on foot, 5 minutes on a bus or 3 minutes in a car.

SILVER: Hyatt Regency

420 Superior Avenue, Cleveland, OH 44114
(216) 575-1234 • cleveland.hyatt.com

Across the street from downtown's Colonial Market Place and 6 blocks from the convention center, this hotel is housed in another historic arcade-style building. Although Hyatt's contemporary decor and vaulted ceilings create an upscale look in its 293 rooms, we rank Residence a notch higher for its litany of free perks — including free Fitworks access.

Nevertheless, Hyatt's arcade-level exercise room is no slouch. Similar to its guest quarters, contemporary furnishings, bright colors and new flooring create a pleasant environment. Although free weights are not supplied, Hyatt gets kudos for stocking new, cutting-edge cardio equipment and weight machines. It is a noteworthy option, just not as elaborate or thorough as Fitworks.

Swimmers, your YMCA commute is 15 minutes on foot, 5 minutes on a bus, or 3 minutes in a car.

CARDIO

TREADMILLS: **3 LF**
UPRIGHT BIKE: **2 LF**
RECUMBENT BIKE: **2 Nautilus**
ELLIPTICAL: **2 Precor**
STEPPER: **1 LF**

STRENGTH

MACHINES: **6 Cybex**
DUMBBELLS: **5-50 lbs**

OTHER

HOURS: **5a-10p**
COST: **Free**
TV: **Yes**

BRONZE: Marriott at Key Center

127 Public Square, Cleveland, OH 44114
(216) 696-9200 • marriott.com

If you want to see what a $10 million hotel renovation looks like, stay a few nights at the Marriott Downtown Cleveland. You won't be disappointed. This 25-story accommodation limped onto our original Cleveland recommended list (pre-renovation), but we're happy to report significant upgrades.

Marriott spoils its guests with rooms featuring new plasma tele-

CARDIO

TREADMILLS: **3 LF**
UPRIGHT BIKE: **2 Spin**
RECUMBENT BIKE: **1 LF**
ELIPTICAL: **1 LF**

STRENGTH

MACHINES: **7 LF**
DUMBBELLS: **3-50 lbs**

SWIM

SPECS: **Indoor • Not lap**

OTHER

HOURS: **24/7**
COST: **Free**
TV: **Yes**
EXTRAS: **AMT run map • $10/day access to Key Club**

visions, upscale bath and shower facilities, classy interior decorating, premium bedding, and functional features for the business traveler (e.g., plenty of AC outlets, wireless internet, and ample work space). You'll look forward to retiring to these impressive quarters after a hard day's work. And, you'll enjoy waking up for an early sweat at the renovated onsite gym.

On the fourth floor, athletic-minded guests will find a 24-hour exercise facility with the latest and greatest in cardio and strength equipment. We've toured larger fitness centers and many with fancier accoutrements, but rarely do we find a hotel gym with better machines. The elliptical, recumbent bike and treadmills look to be 2005 models and all have plasma televisions built-in (bring your own headphones). Those in search of a muscle pump session should be satisfied by a well-rounded assortment of selectorized weight machines and dumbbells up to 50 pounds. The one flaw here is that the adjacent indoor pool and hot tub add quite a bit of heat and humidity to the area (as well as a hint of chlorine aroma in the air), but hotel management is trying to fix the problem.

Lap swimmers will not find Marriott's pool conducive to back and forth stroking, so ask the front desk or concierge to help with admission to the neighboring Key Club. It has a 25-yard option.

Last, if the weather is good, head outdoors for a downtown Cleveland jog. After learning about AthleticMindedTraveler.com, hotel management asked us to suggest running routes for their guests. There's a fun route that meanders around Cleveland Browns' stadium, past the Rock 'n' Roll Hall of Fame, and along Lake Erie (look for our color card maps at the gym and front desk).

LEAST EXPENSIVE

GOLD: Radisson Hotel Gateway

651 Huron Road, Cleveland, OH 44115
(216) 377-9000 • radisson.com

This Radisson is a clean hotel with no frills and Mission-style accommodations. In this case "Mission-style" is just a fancy description for old. Hotel guests receive an antique bed and desk in a small room. That's it. But you are saving money, right?

Red flags go up and alarms ring whenever an exercise center's location is designated with a room number. Radisson's room #221 offering substantiates this concern. Inside, you will find a mere

3 worn cardio machines and one multi-gym. Fortunately, Radisson management recognizes this shortcoming and supplies guests with free passes to Fitworks across the street in the Colonial Market Place.

Swimmers should make a beeline to the YMCA (15 minutes on foot, 5 minutes on a bus or 3 minutes in a car).

BEYOND HOTELS

Tower City Fitness Center

1500 W. 3rd Street, Suite 550, Cleveland, OH 44113
(216) 771-6900 • towercitycenter.com

For Ritz guests, this appealing workout facility is tough to find via the indoor mall and walkway that connects the hotel, so we suggest a more direct route. Exit the Ritz and cross the street to MK Ferguson Plaza (5th floor). For all others, look for the Plaza building.

Catering to the 9 to 5 bunch, Tower City has an intimate club feel and resembles an attractive office space. After accepting your $10 donation, a friendly staff greets and encourages you to hit the machines. Tower offers an ample quantity of cardio and strength equipment, featuring 25 new Cybex stack-loaded weight machines, 12 Cybex treadmills and 9 Precor ellipticals. For those in search of group exercise, Tower offers some classes (no spin) and will allow you to join in without an additional fee.

Swimmers, as usual, you are left out of the fun. YMCA is your only alternative.

CARDIO

TREADMILLS: **Cybex**
UPRIGHT BIKE: **Cybex**
RECUMBENT BIKE: **Cybex**
ELLIPTICAL: **Precor**
STEPPER: **Cybex**
ROWING: **Yes**

STRENGTH

FREE WEIGHTS: **Yes**
HAMMER: **Yes**
MACHINES: **Cybex**
DUMBBELLS: **5-100 lbs**

OTHER

CLASSES: **Yes**
HOURS: M-TH **5:30a-9p** • F **5:30a-8p** • SAT **9a-5p** • SUN **1-5p**
COST: **$10**
TV: **Yes**

Fitworks Fitness Center - Colonial Marketplace

530 Euclid Avenue, Cleveland, OH 44115
(216) 344-9267 • fitworks.com/colonialmarketplace

In the middle of the Colonial Market Place, Fitworks is conveniently located for guests of the Residence Inn and the Radisson hotel — and you get in for free! Unsatisfied Hyatt guests are welcome, too, for $10/day.

With its 2 floors of dedicated sweat space, Fitworks is downtown Cleveland's best gym without a lap pool. Although not a huge space, the first floor cardio zone houses a fair number of high quality machines. The 8 Life Fitness and 6 Precor ellipticals are club favorites, as are the 12 Life Fitness bikes.

CARDIO

TREADMILLS: **LF**
UPRIGHT BIKE: **LF**
RECUMBENT BIKE: **LF**
ELLIPTICAL: **LF • Precor**
ROWING: **Concept II**

STRENGTH

FREE WEIGHTS: **Yes**
HAMMER: **Yes**
MACHINES: **Cybex • Free Motion • Strive**
DUMBBELLS: **3-115 lbs**

OTHER

CLASSES: **Yes**
HOURS: M-F **5a-8p** • SAT **8a-5p** • SUN **Closed**
COST: **Free Res. Inn & Radisson • $10 Others**
TV: **Yes**

The second floor gives a favorable first impression, but downstairs is where the real action is. Over 30 stack-loaded weight stations beg for attention along with a ton of free weights and 7 Hammer Strength plate-loaded free weight machines. Again, because space is rather limited, the equipment can get tight in spots. But, overall, expect a positive workout experience at this reliable fitness destination.

Swimmers, no pool. Go to the Y.

The Club at Key Center

127 Public Square, Cleveland, OH 44114
(216) 241-1272 • theclubatkeycenter.com

CARDIO

TREADMILLS: **Woodway • StarTrac**
UPRIGHT BIKE: **LF**
RECUMBENT BIKE: **LF • Cybex**
ELLIPTICAL: **StarTrac**
STEPPER: **StairMaster • Tectrix**
ROWING: **Concept II - old**

STRENGTH

FREE WEIGHTS: **Yes**
HAMMER: **Yes**
MACHINES: **Cybex**
DUMBBELLS: **5-120 lbs**

SWIM

GRADE: **B-**
SPECS: **2x25m • Indoor • 80-82°**
TOYS: **Kick • Clock**

OTHER

CLASSES: **Yes**
HOURS: M-TH **5:30a-9p** • F **5:30a-8p** • SAT **8a-5p** • SUN **9:30a-3p**
COST: **$10 maybe**
TV: **Yes**

An executive fitness center devoted primarily to those employed in the nearby office high-rises, this little "Club" packs a big punch. While Marriott guests must "work it" to work out, the Club's restrictive guest policy (no guests except possibly Marriott patrons, $10/day) ensures an uncrowded facility. Marriott guests must call ahead and receive permission — and it's not a sure thing.

The narrow "U"-shaped club presents an attractive strength area with 15 Cybex weight stations and plenty of free weights. Unfortunately, the quality of the cardio equipment does not match the weight apparatus. Eight treadmills and 5 ellipticals make up the bulk of the supply.

Besides the Y, this club is the only other facility downtown to offer a legitimate lap pool. Its 2 lane, 25-meter version barely fits the space but, once you are in the water, it is smooth sailing. Although a pace clock was on deck during our tour, it appeared broken, so bring a watch just in case. A floating line separates the two bottom striped lanes.

YMCA Downtown

2200 Prospect Avenue, Cleveland, OH 44115
(216) 344-7700 • ymcacleveland.org

The Y's 1-1.5 mile distance from downtown hotels is a drawback, but if swimming brings you here, consider adding cardio or weights to make the trek more worthwhile. In addition to a 2 lane, 25-yard lapper, the Y provides a great selection of endurance and strength machinery in a hospitable environment. We especially appreciated seeing newer bikes, ellipticals and stack-loaded weight stations.

Getting wet in the Y's average pool is no bargain at $15/day. Floating lines and bottom stripes divide the water traffic, which is typically light outside the lunch hour. The pool's aesthetics are old-school, with a brown tile deck and plain surroundings. Just dull your senses and grind out the yards — because, other than the red-tape filled Club at Key Center, the Y sports the only regulation lap pool in downtown Cleveland.

CARDIO

TREADMILLS: **LF • Precor - old**
UPRIGHT BIKE: **LF**
RECUMBENT BIKE: **LF**
ELLIPTICAL: **LF • Precor**
STEPPER: **Tectrix • Stepmill**
ROWING: **Concept II**

STRENGTH

FREE WEIGHTS: **Yes**
MACHINES: **Magnum**
DUMBBELLS: **5-55 lbs**

SWIM

GRADE: **C**
SPECS: **2x25yd • Indoor • 82-84º**
TOYS: **Kick • Pull • Clock**

OTHER

CLASSES: **Yes**
HOURS: M-F **5:30a-9p** • SAT **8a-5p** • SUN **10a-5p**
COST: **$15**
TV: **Yes**
EXTRAS: **1/26 mile indoor track**

RUNNING ROUTES

When the weather permits, runners can take to the outdoors and run along the Cuyahoga River or Lake Erie. Street running is also fare game and we suggest a perimeter loop around Tower City.

Lakefront Bike Trail

To access the 9-mile Lakefront Bike Trail, head toward the Lake and Marginal Road. East 9th Street is a good thoroughfare. Run northeast and, in about 4+ miles, you will come to Edgewater Park on Lake Shore Blvd., whose upper and lower areas are connected by a paved path and fitness course. In addition, the park is home to a large pavilion, a statue of Conrad Miza (the oldest monument in Cleveland) and a swimming beach.

Cuyahoga River

If you want to run down by the river, ask your hotel for the best route to the "Flats," Cleveland's up-and-coming riverfront and warehouse district. Your route will likely include some hilly terrain marked by 19th Century warehouses and other historic sights. Keep in mind that years and years ago this river was toxic — polluted by the industry that lines its banks. Don't worry, it has been cleaned up.

Big Creek Reservation

If you have a car and fancy more scenic mileage, seek out Big Creek Reservation and its 7+ miles of trails. It is about 5 miles southwest of Downtown. The reservation runs parallel to Pearl Road and is located in Brooklyn, Parma, Parma Heights, Middleburg Heights and Strongsville. Runners will likely find Lake Isaac, a natural basin formed by glacial movements, a spectacular sight. Because the trails are "all-purpose," mountain bikers and hikers are frequent users.

COLORADO SPRINGS, COLORADO

In the eastern Rocky Mountain foothills at 6,100 feet elevation, Colorado Springs is home to some of our country's most beautiful landscape, fastest athletes and bravest military personnel. Snow-capped mountain crests, rolling hills and meandering streams set this city's stage, and Pike's 14,000-foot Peak is its most dramatic actor. Overwhelming to many, Pike's purple mountain majesty inspired Katherine Lee Bates to pen "America the Beautiful" after her ascent to its summit.

Colorado Springs is also center stage for the United States Olympic Training Center, whose ample props sharpen America's quickest swimmers, strongest weightlifters, most accurate marksmen and fastest runners. Olympic hopefuls live and train year round in multi-million-dollar facilities housing over 500 amateur athletes and coaches. Most of the property is open to the public for daily tours. Call (888) 659-8687 for times.

However, all is not fun and games in Colorado Springs. With the military as this city's largest employer, about 1/3 of all working residents set their alarm clocks for 0600 hours instead of 6 a.m. Five military bases occupy the resolute side of town, including the 18,500-acre U.S. Air Force Academy and the North American Aerospace Defense Command (NORBA), perhaps the most secretive military organization known to exist. NORBA is the primary tracking and defense alert station for missiles, space satellites and aircraft attacks. Unbelievably, it is situated inside and below Cheyenne Mountain (just like in the movies!). NORBA's 15 steel buildings are constructed to withstand massive shelling and/or nuclear attack and are capable of supporting 800 personnel for 30 days with an independent supply of air, water and power.

Though not quite as secretive, Colorado Springs' workout options will support athletic-minded travelers for well over 30 days.

24 Locations Reviewed

EXPENSIVE

GOLD: The Broadmoor

1 Lake Avenue, Colorado Springs, CO 80906
(719) 634-7711 • broadmoor.com

CARDIO

TREADMILLS: **3 Precor • 1 Trotter**
UPRIGHT BIKE: **2 Precor**
RECUMBENT BIKE: **2 Precor • 2 Cybex**
ELLIPTICAL: **6 Precor**
STEPPER: **1 Tectrix**
ROWING: **2 Concept II**

STRENGTH

FREE WEIGHTS: **Yes**
MACHINES: **15 Cybex**
DUMBBELLS: **3-50 lbs**

SWIM

GRADE: **B**
SPECS: **2x25yd • Outdoor • 84°**
TOYS: **Kick**

OTHER

CLASSES: **Yes ($)**
HOURS: **5:30a-9p**
COST: **Free**
TV: **Yes**
EXTRAS: **Tennis • Golf**

This place is awe inspiring. Originally built as a casino in 1891, this five-star resort is a regal presence at the foot of Cheyenne Mountain.

About a 10-minute drive from Downtown, Broadmoor is located on the southern edge of Colorado Springs. While room rates vary tremendously by season ($200/night winter to $350/night in the summer for a basic room), the resort's impeccable quality and its flawless staff are consistent year round.

Behind Broadmoor's lobby and front building, a vast body of undisturbed water creates a centerpiece for the property. The serene lake is surrounded by low-rise hotel buildings that house different levels of classically appointed accommodations. We don't know about you, but as soon as we see a lake our first thought is not, "Oh, how beautiful." Rather, it is, "Open water swimming?" To our disappointment, a "no-touch, look only" policy governs this potential freestyle venue.

Our temptation to test this rule quickly fizzled after getting a load of Broadmoor's impressive fitness center and lap pool. The separately housed and attended facility provides athletic-minded visitors a wide assortment of youthful cardio machines, a large quantity of weight stations and free weight equipment and a full menu of daily classes, including spin ($10/class).

The club's outdoor 2 lane, 25-yard lap pool is a swimmer's treat. Floating lane lines and bottom stripes divide the water in this year round rectangle. During the winter months, leave some extra clothing on deck to fend off that Rocky Mountain chill.

After working out, we like nothing better than a professional rubdown. On-site massage therapists pamper guests with their magic hands and soothing aura — completing the wonderful Broadmoor experience.

Note: 36 holes of golf are on-site, with another 18 scheduled to re-open in 2006.

MODERATELY EXPENSIVE

GOLD: Cheyenne Mountain Resort

3225 Broadmoor Valley Road, Colorado Springs, CO 80906
(719) 538-4000 • cheyennemountain.com

Within a few miles of Broadmoor, Cheyenne Mountain Resort is a fantastic lodging alternative to its higher-priced, luxury neighbor. Although Cheyenne's accommodations are not as glamorous, the active pursuits offered on property are comparable. The resort's 316 rooms are clustered into 8 lodges scattered about the grounds. Each guest unit provides typical hotel accommodations. The dark blue-green carpeting and unattractive bedspreads are far from chic, but the mountain views should lift your spirits.

CARDIO

TREADMILLS: **5 StarTrac**
UPRIGHT BIKE: **4 Tectrix**
RECUMBENT BIKE: **3 Tectrix**
ELLIPTICAL: **4 Precor**
STEPPER: **2 Climbmax**

STRENGTH

FREE WEIGHTS: **Yes**
MACHINES: **9 Total - • Cybex • Paramount • Free Motion**
DUMBBELLS: **3-75 lbs**

SWIM

GRADE: #1 **A** • #2 **B**
SPECS: #1 **8x50m • Outdoor • 83°**
#2 **6x25yd • Indoor • 83°**
TOYS: **Kick • Pull • Fins • Clock**

OTHER

CLASSES: **Yes ($)**
HOURS: M-TH **5:30a-10p** • F **5:30a-8p** • SAT-SUN **7a-8p**
COST: **Free**
TV: **Yes**
EXTRAS: **Tennis • Racquetball • Golf**

Cheyenne's complimentary fitness center mixes new weight equipment with slightly worn cardio machines and offers a variety of classes (e.g., spin, yoga) for an additional fee. Management has obviously spent more money on the strength equipment than endurance machines, and we understand why. In this captivating country, we believe most people prefer to run/bike/walk outdoors soaking up the beautiful scenery.

Swimmers, hold on to your Speedos! Yes, there is a 35-acre lake but it only has a small, reserved swimming area. You will be better served by the lap pools. If you are in residence between the end of May and the middle of September, Cheyenne provides an 8 lane, 50-meter outdoor competition quality lap pool complete with backstroke flags, pace clock and all of your favorite toys. Year round, the resort offers an indoor 25-yard option, too, but getting a true Olympic-size water box is a rare treat.

Note: Golf and spa services are additional offerings, and the Resort's Sunday Brunch is noted as one of the best in Colorado Springs.

SILVER: Antlers Hilton

4 South Cascade Avenue, Colorado Springs, CO 80903
(719) 473-5600 • antlers.com/colsprings

As the best lodging option for those staying in downtown Colo-

CARDIO

TREADMILLS: **4 Trotter**
UPRIGHT BIKE: **1 Tectrix**
RECUMBENT BIKE: **1 LF - old**
ELLIPTICAL: **1 Precor**
STEPPER: **2 LifeStep**

STRENGTH

MACHINES: **6 Maxicam - old**
DUMBBELLS: **3-50 lbs**

SWIM

GRADE: **D**
SPECS: **3x14yd • Indoor • 83°**

OTHER

HOURS: **5a-11p**
COST: **Free**
TV: **Yes**

rado Springs, Hilton offers proximity to the City's offices and quaint retail establishments. Enchanting shops and cafes provide visitors endless opportunities to spread their wealth. We especially enjoyed our lunch at The Cottage on Kiowa Street.

While Hilton's 292 rooms are conservatively furnished with little flair or style, guest quarters are roomy and offer expansive city or mountain views that pleased our senses. Unfortunately, we cannot say the same for the in-house workout room.

The 2nd floor fitness center's best feature is its spectacular view of Pike's Peak. Good news for camera carrying tourists, but bad news for hard-core workout enthusiasts. The cardio machines are eviction worthy save the one Precor elliptical. Worn but barely adequate weight machines are also on deck.

Swimmers do not get better news. The "lap" pool's length is barely 14 yards. Three stripes are on the pool's bottom, but no floating lines or toys are provided.

What to do? Walk across the street to World Gym for a $5 sweat session. No lapper is on-site, but the club carries everything else.

LEAST EXPENSIVE

GOLD: La Quinta Inn South

2750 Geyser Drive, Colorado Springs, CO 80906
(719) 527-4788 • laquinta.com

SILVER: Fairfield Inn South

2725 Geyser Drive, Colorado Springs CO 80906
(719) 576-1717 • fairfieldinn.com

Close to the Broadmoor area on the south side of Colorado Springs, these two wallet-friendly hotels provide similar accommodations and pile on the freebies (e.g., local calls, hot breakfasts, parking). La Quinta's guest rooms open to interior hallways, Fairfield's to the outside. Additionally, a strip mall with restaurants, movie theaters and a Target is within walking distance of both.

Neither hotel has an exercise room worth mentioning; however, both are within 3 miles of an impressive, full-service 24 Hour Fitness (5-minute drive). At $15/day, the admission fee is a little steep, but the comps and $60-$70/night room rates should make up the difference.

BRONZE: **Clarion Hotel**

314 West Bijou Street, Colorado Springs, CO 80905
(719) 471-8680 • choicehotels.com

Recommended primarily for its downtown location and free passes to the YMCA, Clarion is a budget accommodation providing 202 basic rooms, standard amenities and typical hotel décor. Located just off highway I-25, this property is beyond walking distance to downtown's quaint cafés and shops but remains a convenient lodging option for those fit travelers wanting to be close to the City's heart.

Bypass Clarion's in-house workout center. Its few pieces of rundown cardio equipment in a miniature room are far from useful. Fortunately, the hotel provides guests with complimentary passes to sweat at the 1 mile away YMCA.

BEYOND HOTELS

World Gym Downtown

25 N. Cascade, Suite 90, Colorado Springs, CO 80903
(719) 329-1111 • worldgymcs.com

CARDIO

TREADMILLS: **StarTrac • NordicTrack**
UPRIGHT BIKE: **LF**
RECUMBENT BIKE: **LF**
ELLIPTICAL: **Precor**
STEPPER: **Stepmill**
ROWING: **Concept II**

STRENGTH

FREE WEIGHTS: **Yes**
HAMMER: **Yes - leg only**
MACHINES: **Free Motion**
DUMBBELLS: **3-100 lbs**

OTHER

CLASSES: **Yes**
HOURS: M-F **5a-8p** • SAT **9a-2p** • SUN **Closed**
COST: **$5**
TV: **Yes**

Our eyebrows were skeptically furrowed as we descended wooden steps into this basement-level club. However, upon reaching reception, we were pleasantly surprised by the cheery art deco motif and sufficient supply of contemporary equipment. For those of you who may have encountered World Gym in other locales, this gym is not part of that chain.

The club makes the best of its diminutive size by providing ample space around an assortment of machines, including a 10x15-foot spinning studio. Fitness fanatics will find 10 good treads, 7 excellent ellipticals, 5 decent recumbent bikes and a full line of Free Motion weight stations, among other cutting-edge equipment.

Since the tariff is cheap at $5, guests of the Hilton should come here in a heartbeat.

Note: Limited hours on Saturdays, and Sundays the club is closed.

YMCA Downtown

207 North Nevada, Colorado Springs, CO 80903
(719) 473-9622 • ppymca.org/downtown.htm

CARDIO

TREADMILLS: **Precor**
UPRIGHT BIKE: **StairMaster**
RECUMBENT BIKE: **StairMaster**
ELLIPTICAL: **Precor**
STEPPER: **StairMaster • Stepmill**
ROWING: **Concept II**

STRENGTH

FREE WEIGHTS: **Yes**
HAMMER: **Yes**
MACHINES: **Magnum • Paramount • Strive**
DUMBBELLS: **5-120 lbs**

SWIM

GRADE: **B-**
SPECS: **6x25yd • Indoor • 83°**
TOYS: **Kick • Pull • Clock**
MASTERS: **Yes**

OTHER

CLASSES: **Yes**
HOURS: M-F **5a-9:30p • SAT 7a-8p • SUN 1-5p**
COST: **Free Y members & Clarion only**
TV: **Yes**

Although YMCA reception staff initially informed us that outside guests were not permitted to work out, the manager on duty subsequently explained that guests of Clarion hotel (~1 mile away) are granted free admission with a pass provided by the hotel.

If you are not staying at Clarion, you cannot work out here. For those left out of the Y's loop, know that we recommend the Y primarily for its 6 lane, 25-yard lap pool with wide lanes, floating lines and bottom stripes. Otherwise, exercising at the less crowded and less expensive World Gym is just as good as the Y (and more convenient to Hilton guests).

Inside the Y, endurance and strength buffs will be impressed by Y's selection of new cardio and weight equipment. Eight treadmills, 6 ellipticals, five 4400 series steppers, 4 upright bikes and 4 recumbent bikes line the room. A ton of stack-loaded weight machines, free weights and dumbbells are offered as well.

Note: Y members from other cities can work out here for free.

24 Hour Fitness Sport

1892 Southgate Road, Colorado Springs, CO 80906
(719) 633-2442 • 24hourfitness.com

This is a fantastic health club. Newer 24 Hour Fitness facilities like this one offer the best equipment on the market in a large, lofty, industrial-type environment. Additionally, its strip mall location affords ample parking.

Inside, a ton of floor-space is dedicated to every sweat option imaginable. We counted over 20 treadmills, more than 19 bikes and at least 15 ellipticals — plus a whole lot more. Of course, daily classes are offered, and the huge spinning studio made us want to saddle up immediately.

Swimmers will delight in the 25-meter pool which, according to staff, is under appreciated, so no crowd worries here. Floating lines and bottom stripes mark the lanes.

Our only criticism of this fabulous club is the fairly high rent at $15/day. If your home club belongs to IHRSA, admission drops to $7 (check healthclubs.com). Fortunately, 24 has the equipment muscle backing it up.

CARDIO

TREADMILLS: **LF • StarTrac**
UPRIGHT BIKE: **LF • Cybex**
RECUMBENT BIKE: **LF • Cybex**
ELLIPTICAL: **LF**
STEPPER: **Cybex • StairMaster • Stepmill**
ROWING: **Yes**

STRENGTH

FREE WEIGHTS: **Yes**
HAMMER: **Yes**
MACHINES: **Free Motion • Paramount**
DUMBBELLS: **5-125 lbs**

SWIM

GRADE: **B**
SPECS: **3x25m • Indoor • 80-84°**
TOYS: **Kick • Pull**

OTHER

CLASSES: **Yes**
HOURS: **24**
COST: **$15 • $7 IHRSA**
TV: **Yes**

RUNNING ROUTES

BROADMOOR

North Cheyenne Cañon Park

For those luxuriating at the Broadmoor, its acreage and lake are convenient for some quick mileage, but we suggest lacing up and exploring the 1-mile-away North Cheyenne Cañon Park, which sports 8+ miles of natural surface trails. This natural beauty is located just west of the hotel and is not for the elevation faint of heart.

Quail Lake

Unfortunately North Cheyenne's scenic trail is a solid 3+ miles from the other listed hotels. An alternative destination is Quail Lake, located a short mile east of these hotels. Access is off Cheyenne Mountain Blvd. The mileage is rather meager here — a 1 mile loop — but can be added to with the adjacent park.

DOWNTOWN

Monument Valley Park

Colorado Springs is a runners' paradise. Winter's bite and thin air are added challenges. For those nesting Downtown, Monument Valley Park is nearly within shouting distance and provides 4+ miles of running fun.

There are several loops within the park, as well as a fitness course. Combining the north and south loops accrues the 4+ miles.

For serious striders, you are in luck. The Park boasts an access point to the Santa Fe Trail (Pike's Peak Greenway), which runs more than 10+ miles north, most of it paved and fairly flat.

DALLAS, TEXAS

Home to arguably the world's most recognizable sports franchise, "Big D" loves its modern day Cowboys. It's a Sunday religion for some, and game-day parishioners claim that the 2.5-acre hole in Texas Stadium's roof was cut out so God could watch his favorite team.

Though the love for "America's Team" may not extend much beyond the Lone Star State's borders, one thing is for sure — everyone has an opinion about this NFL football franchise. Love 'em or hate 'em, it is difficult to find a sports enthusiast who sits on the fence when asked about the players or its eccentric personnel.

As one of the early expansion teams, the Dallas Cowboys have been successful pioneers in the sport both on and off the field. With the most Super Bowl appearances (8) and victories (5, tied with S.F. 49ers), the Cowboys' performance on the gridiron is unmatched. However, the club owes much of its notoriety and financial status to decisions made in corporate boardrooms, not in gametime huddles.

One of the first teams to use marketing and promotion to increase brand awareness and broaden its revenue base, the Cowboys kicked off a blitz of image enhancing strategies in the 1970s. Tex Schramm (GM 1960-1989) was the brain behind many clever entrepreneurial concepts, perhaps his most successful being the creation of the world famous Dallas Cowboy Cheerleaders. He also developed the largest radio broadcast network for any sports team and conceptualized the Cowboys' "Ring of Honor," which recognizes outstanding contributions from former personnel by showcasing their names above the Cowboy bench at Texas Stadium. So far, 12 names appear in the Ring — the most recent being Tex Schramm himself, who was inducted several months prior to his death in June 2003.

As Chicago Bears fans, writing a complimentary piece on the oh-so-humble Cowboys is tough — but we must give credit where credit is due.

UPTOWN & MARKET CENTER

If you can afford it, we highly recommend the two Uptown hotels over the other Dallas options. An Uptown base promises easy access to the trendy restaurants, shops and bars on McKinney Avenue as well as the jogging routes through Turtle Creek Park. Even if your business is in the heart of Downtown, the Crescent Court and Hotel ZaZa are just a mile away, making for an easy commute into the City.

A couple of miles north of Downtown is the Market Center area, home to the World Trade Center and the Dallas Trade Mart. More of a business destination, the streets are primarily lined by hotels and convention-type venues. If your dealings are in the Market Center zone, stay here. If not, both Uptown and Downtown offer more opportunities for fun.

EXPENSIVE

GOLD: Crescent Court Hotel

400 Crescent Court, Dallas, TX 75201
(214) 871-3200 • crescentcourt.com

CARDIO

TREADMILLS: **8 NordicTrack**
UPRIGHT BIKE: **4 Tectrix • 1 Fan**
RECUMBENT BIKE: **2 Tectrix**
ELLIPTICAL: **6 Precor**
STEPPER: **6 StairMaster**
OTHER: **1 Gravitron • 1 VersaClimber**

STRENGTH

FREE WEIGHTS: **Yes**
HAMMER: **Yes**
MACHINES: **13 Cybex**
DUMBBELLS: **5-100 lbs**

SWIM

SPECS: **Indoor • Not lap**

OTHER

CLASSES: **Yes**
HOURS: M-TH **6a-9p** • F **6a-8p** • SAT **8a-7p** • SUN **8a-6p**
COST: **$10**
TV: **Yes**
EXTRAS: **Gym clothes provided**

Pulling into Crescent Court's cobblestone circular drive bespeaks the endless European luxury that awaits travelers checking into this glamorous hotel. Located a short walk from the trendy restaurants and shops of McKinney Avenue, Crescent Court occupies some of the best hotel real estate in Dallas.

Inside, guests are treated to charming common areas and rooms that exude a simple elegance. Creature comforts include French doors that open to airy balconies, high thread count Egyptian cotton sheets and refrigerators upon request.

The 22,000-square foot spa and fitness center is an exerciser's dream. Although the hotel strikes the healthy minded with a punitive $10/day access charge, we can accept the Court's "sentence" knowing that the equipment is first rate. High-end machinery sparkles like new, and some cardio stations provide for individual television viewing. Though running through nearby Turtle Creek Park is encouraged, those remaining indoors will be delighted by Crescent Court's top-of-the-line Nordic-

Track incline treadmills. An assortment of free weights should also get your heart and muscles pumping, especially Hammer Strength machines, which are seldom seen in hotels.

Forget your workout gear? No sweat. In addition to serving up machines and weights, Crescent supplies complimentary attire.

Swimmers, no lap option here. So plan on driving 3 minutes to Bally Total Fitness and springing $10 to get inside.

SILVER: Hotel ZaZa

2332 Leonard Street, Dallas, TX 75201
(214) 468-8399 • hotelzaza.com

CARDIO
TREADMILLS: **3 LF**
RECUMBENT BIKE: **1 LF**
ELLIPTICAL: **1 Sohn**

STRENGTH
MACHINES: **6 LF**
DUMBBELLS: **3-40 lbs**

SWIM
SPECS: **Outdoor • Not lap**

OTHER
HOURS: **24**
COST: **Free**
TV: **Yes**
EXTRAS: **$10 pass to Bally**

An upscale hotel with flair, Hotel ZaZa exhibits refreshing creativity. Across the street from its luxury rival, ZaZa matches the Crescent Court's fabulous location in Uptown Dallas. The 146 smoke-free guest quarters are individually designed and decorated in rich purples, blues and reds. High ceilings, Frette linens and unique furnishings top off these bold rooms for an overall impressive effect.

The recent makeover of ZaZa's on-site gym was long overdue, but at least it was done with a panache typical of the hotel's decor. ZaZa does nothing boring, and the gym has a unique flavor — check out the pix on our website. We're happy to learn that the renovation and update included the purchase of new high end cardio and strength equipment. If you want more from your sweat or a group class, drive 3 minutes to Bally's. You can get your groove on there for $10/day.

Swimmers, since ZaZa's pool is not a lapper, head to Bally Fitness.

MODERATELY EXPENSIVE

GOLD: Wyndham Anatole Market Center

2201 Stemmons Freeway, Dallas, TX 75207
(214) 748-1200 • wyndham.com

While this massive convention hotel may not be on par with the two luxury accommodations above, the Anatole's workout option rivals some of the best clubs in Dallas. Hardly Asian-influenced as its website suggests, the Anatole's guest quarters' conservative colors and basic furnishings create an atmosphere no more unique than another reality TV show. Housing 1,614 rooms located just off the Stemmons Freeway (I-35), it's not exactly ideal for travelers who want a cozy boutique hotel experience. In fact, the much smaller Wyndham Market Center down the street offers just that with its charming room décor, less expensive nightly rates and same access fee to Anatole's well-equipped fitness center.

If you do select the Anatole, liven it up by working out and swimming at the separately owned and operated Verandah Club in the hotel's "backyard." It's a massive facility with a good mix of sweat options. Bring $15 + tax to get in.

LEAST EXPENSIVE

GOLD: Wyndham Dallas Market Center

2015 Market Center Boulevard, Dallas, TX 75207
(214) 741-7481 • wyndham.com

Only a quarter mile from the Anatole, this Wyndham represents an overall better hotel choice versus its sister property. The 227 recently renovated guest rooms outfitted with pillow top mattresses, Herman Miller Aeron chairs and mini-refrigerators (upon request) afford a warm and comfortable stay.

Skip this hotel's next-to-nothing on-site exercise room. The pathetic equipment is not even tune-up worthy. Instead, plan to pay $15 at the Verandah Club to indulge your workout craving. We suggest making the short trek on foot, since parking is limited — or have the Wyndham's shuttle drive you.

SILVER: Fairfield Inn Dallas Market Center

2110 Market Center Boulevard, Dallas, TX 75207
(214) 760-8800 • fairfieldinn.com

Let the freebies begin! Across the street from the Wyndham DMC and near the Anatole's Verandah Club, Fairfield is small on cost and big on comps. Guests enjoy free continental breakfasts, free high-speed internet access, free local phone calls, free 24-hour coffee and tea service, free 3-mile shuttle transport (M-F) and free parking. Yahooo! We gave the nod to Wyndham for their superior bedding and room amenities, but we would have no problem staying here instead.

Your fee to work out at Verandah is the same $15 + tax that everyone else pays, including guests of the Anatole. Take the shuttle or walk 7 minutes.

BEYOND HOTELS UPTOWN & MARKET CENTER

Bally Total Fitness Turtle Creek II

3232 McKinney Avenue, #400, Dallas, TX 75204
(214) 871-7700 • ballytotalfitness.com

Recommended primarily as a swim option for those staying in the Turtle Creek neighborhood (ZaZa and Crescent Court), Bally offers an aesthetically pleasing 25-meter outdoor lap pool. Floating lane lines and bottom stripes mark the four lanes, but do not expect to find any swim goodies or a pace clock. Ten bucks gets you through the door — and remember your stopwatch if base intervals are in your plans.

The full-service gym contains an array of cardio machines, weight equipment and classes. But we saw buckets on the floor for a leaking ceiling, dirty locker rooms and worn machines. Do not let these indoor glitches frighten you away from a swim, however. We endorse the outdoor pool with confidence.

SWIM

GRADE: **B**
SPECS: **4x25m • Outdoor • 78-82°**

OTHER

HOURS: M-F **5:30a-10p** • SAT-SUN **8a-7p**
COST: **$10**

24 Hour Fitness

2425 McKinney Avenue, Dallas, TX 75201
(214) 871-0708 • 24hourfitness.com

A free pass from Hotel ZaZa or $10 will get you in the door of this modern health club. The newer exercise center has a cutting-edge, industrial feel with its loft-like ceilings and abundant equipment. Housing everything but a pool, workout fiends will be flying high with close to 20 newer treadmills, 13 barely-worn Precor ellipticals, 12 youthful Hammer Strength machines, 10 fresh upright bikes and an assortment of other unspoiled equipment.

Early Sunday morning appears to be a great time to sweat; during our tour we counted a modest seven people in the entire gym.

CARDIO

TREADMILLS: **StarTrac**
UPRIGHT BIKE: **LF**
ELLIPTICAL: **LF • Precor**
STEPPER: **StairMaster • Stepmill**
ROWING: **Concept II**

STRENGTH

FREE WEIGHTS: **Yes**
HAMMER: **Yes**
MACHINES: **Cybex • Free Motion • Icarian • Strive**
DUMBBELLS: **5-120 lbs**

OTHER

CLASSES: **Yes**
HOURS: M-TH **24** • F **5a-9p** • SAT-SUN **8a-8p**
COST: **Free ZaZa • $10 Others**
TV: **Yes**

Verandah Club

2201 North Stemmons Freeway, Dallas, TX 75207
(214) 761-7878

Located behind the Anatole hotel on the back edge of its tree-lined estate, Verandah is an 82,000 square foot athletic enthusiasts' playground. Follow the 1/8 mile jogging loop to the club's doors. Once inside, land and water lovers alike will revel in an assortment of workout options that make hearts pitter-patter.

Although many of the cardio machines are older models, most appear to be functioning well. New Precor ellipticals, StarTrac bikes and StairMaster Free Climbers are in the mix too, exemplifying the Club's ongoing replacement process. Strength equipment is a highlight with free weights, new Cybex machines and an extensive dumbbell set, all useful for a well-rounded routine.

CARDIO

TREADMILLS: **StarTrac - old**
UPRIGHT BIKE: **StarTrac • Fan**
RECUMBENT BIKE: **StarTrac**
ELLIPTICAL: **Precor • StarTrac**
STEPPER: **StairMaster • Stepmill • Tectrix**
ROWING: **Concept II**
OTHER: **Gravitron**

STRENGTH

FREE WEIGHTS: **Yes**
MACHINES: **Cybex • Free Motion**
DUMBBELLS: **5-100 lbs**

SWIM

GRADE: **B+**
SPECS: **7x25m • Indoor • 82-84°**
TOYS: **Kick • Pull • Clock**

OTHER

CLASSES: **Yes**
HOURS: M-F **5:30a-9:30p** • SAT-SUN **7a-8p**
COST: **$15 +tax • $35/3-day**
TV: **Yes**
EXTRAS: **1/8 mile outdoor path • Basketball • Tennis**

Swimmers can look forward to frolicking in a fantastic 25-meter pool complete with floating lane lines, bottom stripes and all the toys that your heart desires.

Bring your water bottle to help swallow the $15 + tax access fee — because even staying at the Anatole does not afford a discount! Reduced fee multi-day passes are available, however ($35/3-day).

DOWNTOWN

Glamorized by both real and fictional billionaires (H. Ross Perot, Mark Cuban and JR Ewing), and host to arguably the most renowned and ritzy retailer, we expected Downtown to be more razzle-dazzle and less run-of-the-mill. The City's business hub is just that — all business, without nearly as many of the leisure, dining and social opportunities that characterize Uptown.

On weekends especially, the heart of this city resembles a deserted concrete jungle, except perhaps for the Saturday beeping of credit card machines emanating from Neiman Marcus' flagship store. Shopping is very much a sport in Dallas, and this luxury-goods outpost consistently ropes in dolled-up locals with its unabashed ostentation. So stay in Uptown for more Big D flavor, but if you want to save a few bucks and be within walking distance of Downtown's businesses, several noteworthy hotel/workout options make our list — and a few restaurants may make yours.

EXPENSIVE

GOLD: **Westin City Center**
650 North Pearl Street, Dallas, TX 75201
(214) 979-9000 • westin.com/citycenterdallas

Catering to the corporate crowd, Westin's attractive hotel offers a lodging experience typical for this upscale chain. Heavenly

Beds, conservative décor and 24-hour room service are sample amenities. This property also features an indoor skating rink in the connected atrium plaza, as well as a recently renovated exercise facility. While we appreciate all these extras, the hotel's best asset is its proximity to downtown businesses.

CARDIO
TREADMILLS: **4 LF**
UPRIGHT BIKE: **2 LF**
ELLIPTICAL: **1 LF**

STRENGTH
MACHINES: **1 LF Multi**
DUMBBELLS: **5-50 lbs**

OTHER
HOURS: **24**
COST: **Free**
TV: **Yes**
EXTRAS: **Indoor ice rink**

The Westin reopened its fitness room in March 2004 after blowing out a couple of walls and ordering brand new Life Fitness equipment. Unfortunately, we visited just prior to its completion, so we did not view the final product. We did confirm two facts, however: The new center's size is slightly larger than a guest room, and our equipment numbers are accurate.

Despite a new and improved room, most will gladly leave it behind if the local Gold's Gym (3-minute walk) reopens. This fabulous facility recently closed, and we understand it may be taken over by another company, so the name might change — but it was one of the coolest health clubs we have toured. Check the status with the concierge.

Swimmers and those looking for a larger gym while Gold's is closed should plan to make the 15-minute trek to the YMCA.

Note: With one side of the hotel overlooking a 15-story indoor atrium housing an ice skating rink, light sleepers and others desiring quiet quarters should request a room on the opposite side of the hotel.

SILVER: Fairmont Hotel

1717 North Akard Street, Dallas, TX 75201
(214) 720-2020 • fairmont.com/dallas

Do not let the Fairmont's location confuse you. Despite an address on the 1700 block of Akard, it actually is across the street from the 601 N. Akard YMCA. You can imagine our surprise when, after touring the Y and gearing up for the "11 block" walk to the Fairmont, the hotel magically appeared! With room rates just under $200/night, the Fairmont slides into the moderately priced category but, make no mistake, the accommodations are still well-to-do. Italian-style interiors and mahogany wood furnishings are this Fairmont's décor preference, with accents in deep shades of red.

CARDIO
TREADMILLS: **3 Precor**
UPRIGHT BIKE: **1 Tectrix**
RECUMBENT BIKE: **2 Tectrix**
ELLIPTICAL: **3 Precor**
STEPPER: **1 Tectrix**

STRENGTH
MACHINES: **9 Cybex**
DUMBBELLS: **10-50 lbs**

SWIM
SPECS: **Outdoor • Not lap**

OTHER
HOURS: **5a-11p**
COST: **Free**
TV: **Yes**

The lower level fitness center is a disappointing mix of old and new equipment. While the timeworn cardio machines appear to "run," we recommend issuing pink slips. Those looking for a weight workout will find the 9 newer Cybex machines and a respectable dumbbell set more appealing.

With a moderate price, near first-class accommodations and convenient proximity to the Downtown Y, Fairmont is a clear award winner in this category. Because hotel guests no longer receive discounted Y admission, plan to fork over $15 for a more extensive sweat session or swim.

LEAST EXPENSIVE

GOLD: Adam's Mark

400 North Olive Street, Dallas, TX 75201
(214) 922-8000 • adamsmark.com/dallas

CARDIO

TREADMILLS: **7 LF**
UPRIGHT BIKE: **1 LF - old**
RECUMBENT BIKE: **2 LF**
STEPPER: **3 LF • 2 LifeStep**

STRENGTH

MACHINES: **11 LF**

SWIM

SPECS: **Indoor & Outdoor • Not lap**

OTHER

HOURS: **5a-11p**
COST: **Free**
TV: **Yes**

The twin tower Adam's Mark is a gigantic complex housing 1,840 rooms. As a less expensive hotel, Adam's does not offer much beyond basic amenities. However, its location is tough to beat, near downtown businesses and a stone's throw away from 24 Hour Fitness.

We were hopeful about the hotel's in-house exercise center after catching sight of the large number of Life Fitness weight stations. Sadly, the spell was quickly broken when we saw aged treadmills and other cardio machines in dire need of replacement. Head to 24 Hour Fitness for a proper sweat, or head to the YMCA.

Swimmers should walk 10-15 minutes down San Jacinto Street to the YMCA for the only regulation lap pool in downtown Dallas ($15/day).

BEYOND HOTELS DOWNTOWN

24 Hour Fitness Super Sport

700 North Harwood, Dallas, TX 75201
(214) 220-2423 • 24hourfitness.com

You have to see this 24 Hour Fitness! Located above a parking garage on the 10th floor of the Bryantower, this 24 is a bit difficult to find, so call ahead to confirm directions from your origination point. Once you do discover this hidden treasure, you will not believe your eyes. The Westin and Adam's Mark are closest, but no hotel receives discounted access for its guests — all non-members pay $20/day or $10/day for multiple day passes.

As you enter the ultra-modern 40,000 square-foot arena, your view is all equipment. The reception area is perched a good 30 feet above the enormous fitness court and provides a birds-eye view of the wide open, natural light filled space stuffed with top-of-the-line machines. Athletes can feast on a spread of equipment that includes nearly 20 each of treadmills, ellipticals, weight apparatus and bikes. Classes are included in your access fee, but bring your own sweat/shower towel for a clean up.

Swimmers will have to hike to the YMCA as this 24 Hour Fitness is pool-less.

YMCA – Downtown Dallas

601 North Akard, Dallas, TX 75201

(214) 954-0500 • downtowndallasymca.org

Across from the Fairmont, the YMCA provides the best lap pool in downtown Dallas and a more elaborate workout option for nearby hotel guests. Admission is a little steep at $15/day, but the Y delivers a powerful punch of superior equipment in its 21st Century facility.

Except for older 4000PT StairMaster steppers, the floor's cardio units are recent models. Most impressive is the collection of 12 Hammer Strength free weight machines and 33 stack-loaded weight stations.

The Y's downside is the rather indiscreet location of the men's locker room, which forces male Speedo sporters to parade through the cardio area en route to the pool. But the potential awkwardness is well worth it, because our aquatic friends will be rewarded with a more than adequate water box. Women, don't worry, no procession is required!

Although 8 lanes are divided by floating lines and bottom stripes, a portable staircase intrudes on lane 1. All the bells and whistles we expect from a competition pool are here, including a pace clock, toys and backstroke flags.

Weekend warriors should note the limited hours on Sundays. We would hate for you to be all dressed up in your Speedo with no place to go.

CARDIO

TREADMILLS: **LF • StarTrac**
UPRIGHT BIKE: **LF • Fan**
RECUMBENT BIKE: **LF**
ELLIPTICAL: **LF • Precor**
STEPPER: **StairMaster**
ROWING: **Concept II**
OTHER: **Gravitron**

STRENGTH

FREE WEIGHTS: **Yes**
HAMMER: **Yes**
MACHINES: **Cybex • Free Motion • HighTech**
DUMBBELLS: **3-110 lbs**

SWIM

GRADE: **B**
SPECS: **8x25m • Indoor • 82°**
TOYS: **Kick • Pull • Fins • Clock**
MASTERS: **Yes**

OTHER

CLASSES: **Yes**
HOURS: M-F **5:30a-9p** • SAT **7:30a-5:30p** • SUN **1-5:30p**
COST: **$15**
TV: **Yes**
EXTRAS: **Basketball • Racquetball**

RUNNING ROUTES

UPTOWN

Turtle Creek Trail

For those luxuriating in the Uptown area, this greenbelt provides up to 5 miles of running paths in an out-and-back format. Hotels should have a map on hand that outlines the best route.

DOWNTOWN

Katy Trail

Take to the streets or seek out the Katy Trail, which is part of this city's revitalization process. The trail runs through the heart of downtown Dallas and will eventually cover more than 17 miles. Runners can pick up the trail from Maple Ave. (near Reverchon Park), which is approximately 1 mile from downtown's heart. Most hotels have maps. See www.dallascityhall.com/dallas/eng/html/hike_and_bike_trail_map.html.

OTHER

White Rock Lake

If you have a car and crave more mileage, White Rock Lake, located 5 miles northeast of Downtown, offers a 9-mile loop and is a local favorite.

Denver

DENVER, COLORADO

Oxygen is one of the first elements we learn about in grade school. Humans breathe it, plants produce it, fire consumes it and the higher you go the less you'll find of it. At Denver's 5,280 feet of elevation, oxygen and air density levels run about 15% lower than at sea level. Doesn't sound like much? Consider this: An 8 minute/mile jogger's pace will slow to a 9:15 minute/mile with the same level of effort. A golfer who normally drives the ball 250 yards will carry close to 300 yards. And a major league pitcher, accustomed to the air density's "grab" on a curve ball, will watch it break 25% less.

Golfers will be psyched and pitchers disappointed, but what about endurance enthusiasts? Many have researched the physical consequences of altitude, and most arrive at the same conclusion. During the first 24 hours in a higher elevation, the body withstands any adverse symptoms. After 7 days the body has acclimated. It is during the interval in between when athletes suffer the most, with day 1 producing minimal impact and days 2 and 3 causing the most. On day 4, recovery begins.

So, if you plan to run in a thin-air marathon or compete in a high altitude soccer match, book your travel plans strategically. The Raiders are known to arrive in Denver as late as NFL rules allow. Soccer teams playing in Mexico City (7,500 ft. elevation) typically fly in 12-16 hours before game time. You may not have this luxury, but just remember that the Mile High City's altitude is a breeze compared to places like La Paz, Bolivia, where international athletic events are hosted at 12,000 feet!

33 Locations Reviewed

DOWNTOWN

Downtown Denver's hustle and bustle runs a mile along the 16th Street promenade. It's a top tourist spot, where visitors meander inside modern retail stores and funky coffee shops. Hip restaurants line both sides of the street. Unlike the unusual boutiques found along L.A.'s Melrose Avenue or in NYC's SoHo district, most stores here represent trendy national chains. Thankfully, the numerous restaurants are unique.

Making an easy walking tour even more convenient is a free shuttle bus service that transports shoppers from one end to the other — the only motorized vehicles allowed on this street. All hotels recommended below are within a few short blocks of this desirable locale.

EXPENSIVE

GOLD: The Brown Palace

321 17th Street, Denver, CO 80202
(303) 297-3111 • brownpalace.com

"Simple, yet elegant" is the term that came to mind during our tour through this hotel. Brown Palace is one of Downtown Denver's landmark hotels, and guests are treated to a stay marked by appealing accommodations and impeccable service.

Guest rooms aren't in danger of being too haughty or fancy, and that's okay in our book.

Brown's fitness center requires a walk across a skybridge to the neighboring Comfort Inn. The equipment inside is above average, but the main draw for athletic-minded guests of this property is the hotel's relationship with the exclusive Denver Athletic Club. Brown guests get in for $15/day and the Club is only a 5-minute walk away.

See the Comfort Inn's chart for equipment specifics.

SILVER: Magnolia

818 17th Street, Denver, CO 80202
(303) 607-9000 • themagnoliahotel.com

If you appreciate creativity and long for a unique hotel experience, consider Magnolia for your mile-high stay. Replete with Art Deco common areas and contemporary rooms, this hotel exudes class and keeps its guests comfortably close to the 16th Street promenade (1 block) and convention center (4 blocks).

All 224 rooms spotlight cozy bedding, colorful surroundings and fun patterns. The standard units are somewhat small, but not atypical for an urban hotel. The morning menu is less elaborate than Embassy's, but Magnolia guests do not miss the freebie train. Complimentary continental breakfasts, free cocktails and hors d'oeuvres in the evening and gratis nighttime cookies and milk are all on the menu. And for those needing an a.m. espresso jolt, Starbucks is next door.

Originality extends into Magnolia's cylindrical, blue-lit fitness room. Though the unusual lighting may challenge readers, we give a "thumbs-up" to the concept and space. Magnolia's equipment supply is rather sparse, and the in-stock steppers are dated; however, enough good quality machines are here to accommodate a quick "tune-up."

CARDIO

TREADMILLS: **2 LF**
UPRIGHT BIKE: **2 LF**
RECUMBENT BIKE: **2 LF**
STEPPER: **2 LF - old**

STRENGTH

MACHINES: **1 Hoist multi**
DUMBBELLS: **3-60 lbs**

OTHER

HOURS: **5:30a-10p**
COST: **Free**
TV: **Yes**

If the gym is not up to your standards or you're in the mood for a swim, don't worry. For a full-service sweat and dip, walk 5 minutes to the phenomenal Athletic Club at Denver Place. Unlike Embassy's indoor walk, Magnolia guests will have to endure Mother Nature's wrath during Denver's winter, so wear a hat.

Without a discount, the fare is $15. Unless your home club belongs to IHRSA — then it is $10 (check www.healthclubs.com).

MODERATELY EXPENSIVE

GOLD: Adam's Mark Downtown

1550 Court Place, Denver, CO 80202
(303) 893-3333 • adamsmark.com

Adjacent to Denver's 16th Street promenade and 4 blocks from the convention center, the Mark's best feature is its location. Despite its enormous size, (1,225 rooms), conventioneers often fill vacancies which drive up prices. So be sure to compare rates prior to booking.

The hotel's business traveler focus is obvious, with accommodations that are anything but fancy. Expect dark wood furniture, floral pattern bedding and generally dull decor.

CARDIO

TREADMILLS: **4 LF - 1 old**
UPRIGHT BIKE: **3 LF - 2 old**
ELLIPTICAL: **1 LF - old**
STEPPER: **2 Tectrix**

STRENGTH

MACHINES: **5 LF • 5 mix**
DUMBBELLS: **5-50 lbs**

SWIM

SPECS: **Outdoor • Not lap**

OTHER

HOURS: **24**
COST: **Free**
TV: **Yes**

The guest suite sized 5th floor gym will impress strength enthusiasts with its 10 modern stack-loaded weight stations and ample set of dumbbells. However, cardio fiends are not so lucky — the 8 endurance machines are in poor condition. So, in what is becoming a familiar yodel in this mountain town, "Head to Athletic Club at Denver Place for a more elaborate workout or swim."

The outdoor walk will take 10-15 minutes and you'll need $15 to get inside ($10 IHRSA). Once you arrive, ACDP will make you forget all of your worries by providing a topnotch workout facility.

Note: While the Denver Athletic Club (DAC) is much closer than the Ath-

letic Club at Denver Place (ACDP), access is only granted to those staying at The Brown Palace, Teatro and Comfort Inn hotels (see Comfort Inn for details). No others are permitted.

SILVER: **Holiday Inn** Downtown

1450 Glenarm Place, Denver, CO 80202
(303) 573-1450 • holiday-inn.com/den-downtown

Holiday Inn's accommodations and proximity to downtown's 16th Street promenade satisfy. Guest rooms are typical for this moderately priced chain, with basic bedding, conservative décor and standard amenities. In a 21-story high-rise, some units afford spectacular city views.

Fitness fans will not be inspired by the small 6th floor workout room. Although 2 acceptable treadmills and one worthy Life Fitness 9500 series elliptical are inside, the other equipment serves no purpose. Most athletic-minded travelers (swimmers included) will prefer walking 10 minutes to Athletic Club at Denver Place. Fifteen bucks will get you in the door — it's worth the trip. Observant visitors may notice another health club just down the street, but Denver Athletic Club only allows access to guests of the Brown Palace, Teatro and Comfort Inn hotels — darn!

Note: The Holiday Inn is contemplating a gym upgrade, so call if an on-site option is important.

LEAST EXPENSIVE

GOLD: **Comfort Inn** Downtown

401 17th Street, Denver, CO 80202
(303) 296-0400 • comfortinndenver.com

CARDIO

TREADMILLS: **5 LF**
UPRIGHT BIKE: **1 LF - old**
RECUMBENT BIKE: **2 LF - old**
ELLIPTICAL: **1 - new**
STEPPER: **2 LF - old**

STRENGTH

MACHINES: **9 Cybex**
DUMBBELLS: **7.5-50 lbs**

OTHER

HOURS: **5a-10p**
COST: **Free**
TV: **Yes**
EXTRAS: **$15 pass to DAC**

Comfort Inn presents a budget friendly accommodation convenient to the 16th Street promenade. The 231 guest rooms are what we expected for the price, but the hotel's generous offering of creature comforts deserves some ink — free high-speed internet access, free local calls, 24-hour room service and complimentary continental breakfasts.

Best of all, Comfort is managed by the same company as the attached Brown Palace hotel — a luxury property that did not make our list. What's the significance? Comfort guests can purchase $15 passes to the exclusive Denver Athletic Club (different than the Athletic Club at Denver Place) from Brown's front desk. Only one other Denver hotel receives this exclusive privilege.

Muscle-pumpers may not need the pass. Comfort's in-house gym contains 9 newer Cybex stack-loaded weight machines and an ample set of dumbbells. However, cardio junkies will grumble at the mediocre treadmills and frown at the other worn machines. Fortunately, Denver Atheltic Club is only 5-10 minutes walk away. Plan to use DAC and make yourself un-"Comfort"-able with a real workout — swimmers, too, since Comfort Inn has no pool.

BEYOND HOTELS

Athletic Club at Denver Place (ACDP)

1849 Curtis Street, Denver, CO 80202
(303) 294-9494 • acdp.com

Denver Athletic Club (DAC)

1325 Glenarm Place, Denver, CO 80204
(303) 534-1211 • denverathleticclub.org

Athletic-minded travelers have it made in this mile-high city. Unlike other large towns where we struggle to find one conveniently located, solid workout venue, downtown Denver boasts two! Choose either club for fitness bliss. Each provides a ton of new, cutting-edge equipment in an aesthetically pleasing environment. Two charts (at right and on the following page) illustrate what's in store for you.

Most of DAC's cardio equipment is manufactured by Life Fitness and Technogym — 2 firms that produce good quality products. Expect to find Life Fitness' 9500 series and Technogym's most recent models. You may even glimpse NBA players roaming the halls, as the Denver Nuggets occasionally utilize DAC's basketball court for practices.

Luckily, ACDP will let anyone in for a fee and provides a greater variety of machines. Be sure to try the Cybex Arc Trainer ellipticals — quickly becoming endurance favorites.

ACDP

CARDIO

TREADMILLS: **StarTrac**
UPRIGHT BIKE: **LF • Cybex • Spin**
RECUMBENT BIKE: **LF**
ELLIPTICAL: **Precor • Cybex**
STEPPER: **StairMaster • Stepmill**
ROWING: **Concept II**
OTHER: **XC Ski • Crossrobic**

STRENGTH

FREE WEIGHTS: **Yes**
HAMMER: **Yes**
MACHINES: **Cybex • Free Motion**
DUMBBELLS: **1-120 lbs**

SWIM

GRADE: **B**
SPECS: **3x25m • Indoor • 81°**
TOYS: **Kick • Pull • Clock**
MASTERS: **Yes**

OTHER

CLASSES: **Yes**
HOURS: M-F **5a-10p** • SAT-SUN **7a-7p**
COST: **$10 Embassy & IHRSA • $15 Others**
TV: **Yes**
EXTRAS: **Basketball • Racquetball**

DAC is significantly smaller in terms of square footage, but its pool is larger and slightly more appealing — though both clubs' water boxes have floating lane lines, bottom stripes and a ton of toys. Most of the more desirable hotels only offer access to ACDP, so if you want to work out at the more exclusive DAC you must stay at the

DAC

CARDIO

TREADMILLS: **LF • Technogym**
UPRIGHT BIKE: **LF • Technogym • Tectrix**
RECUMBENT BIKE: **LF • Technogym • Tectrix**
ELLIPTICAL: **LF • Precor**
STEPPER: **StairMaster • Stepmill**
ROWING: **Concept II**
OTHER: **XC Ski • Gauntlet**

STRENGTH

FREE WEIGHTS: **Yes**
HAMMER: **Yes**
MACHINES: **Cybex • Technogym**
DUMBBELLS: **5-110 lbs**

SWIM

GRADE: **A**
SPECS: **8x25m • Indoor • 82°**
TOYS: **Kick • Pull • Clock**
MASTERS: **Yes**

OTHER

CLASSES: **Yes**
HOURS: M-F **6a-9:30p** • SAT-SUN **7:30a-8p**
• 24 hours members only
COST: **$15 pass 3 hotels only -**
• Comfort Inn • Brown Palace • Hotel Teatro
TV: **Yes**
EXTRAS: **1/16 mile indoor track**
• Basketball • Racquetball
• Grill

elegant Brown Palace, the modest Comfort Inn or one other non-recommended property. Locals split 50/50 over which club is superior. Bottom line, you can't go wrong, so it comes down to your hotel preference.

Although members of DAC are provided 24 hour access, hotel guests wanting to sweat must come over during the hours listed in the chart.

RUNNING ROUTES

In addition to two fantastic health clubs, downtown Denver offers some brilliant running routes. The most popular and easiest to access is the Cherry Creek Trail. This paved route begins in Confluence Park (NW) and runs parallel to Cherry Creek. Many of the auto intersections are avoided by underpasses. At the 13-mile mark, joggers will arrive at Cherry Creek State Park (water/bathrooms), where an additional 10 miles of tree-lined trails can be tackled by our ultra-distance friends. Remember the altitude!

DES MOINES, IOWA

Yes, we are aware that Des Moines is the third insurance capital of the world (behind London and Hartford). And we are familiar with the history and political significance of the Iowa Caucus.

Pause for yawning here.

What we find most fascinating about the Hawkeye state capital is its ongoing battle against Salt Lake City for the title of Jell-O gelatin capital of the world!

In 1999, Des Moines was awarded this jiggly honor by Jell-O's manufacturer Kraft Foods. Though New York consistently slurps the most sweet in terms of total quantity, Des Moines took the U.S. lead in per capita Jell-O gelatin consumption that year. A prevalence of church functions, frequent family-related events and the 3rd largest senior-citizen population in the country are factors thought to have contributed to Des Moines' jellied reign. While we could not find any actual numbers, suffice it to say that having a serving of Jell-O each week in these parts is not uncommon.

Dismayed former champion Salt Lake City viewed Des Moines' usurpation of the title as a Jell-O shot to the face. Determined to win back the wiggly claim to fame, Salt Lake launched an all-out gelatin-slinging barrage before the Iowans knew what hit them. Utah newspapers ran stories about the upset. Salt Lake restaurants held Jell-O recipe contests. BYU students gathered signatures petitioning for Jell-O as the official state snack. Their sticky effort succeeded and, along with its other sub-first titles, Des Moines is now considered the second Jell-O capital of the world.

EXPENSIVE

GOLD: Suites at 800 Locust

800 Locust Street, Des Moines, IA 50309
(515) 288-5800 • 800locust.com

CARDIO

TREADMILLS: **3 LF**
UPRIGHT BIKE: **1 LF**
RECUMBENT BIKE: **2 LF**
ELLIPTICAL: **1 LF**
STEPPER: **2 LF**

STRENGTH

MACHINES: **11 LF**
DUMBBELLS: **3-50 lbs**

OTHER

HOURS: **24**
COST: **Free**
TV: **Yes**

In the heart of downtown Des Moines, the Suites at 800 Locust offer a conveniently located boutique accommodation worth the few extra dollars.

Each room is uniquely designed and furnished with pillow top mattresses and deluxe linens, but we think the designers may have been colorblind. Many of the guest quarters are outfitted in garish tones and combine busy patterns with dark green or bright red carpeting. Though we refrained from laughing aloud, the hues definitely had us chuckling. Fortunately, the Suites' exercise room had us smiling for all the right reasons.

Inside the lower-level fitness center, guests will enjoy a fine sweating experience. The 40x40 foot well-organized space contains a solid selection of new Life Fitness weight and cardio equipment. All of the endurance machines are this brand's top-of-the-line 9500 series and the vast assortment of stack-loaded weight stations makes full body conditioning possible.

Although no pool is on-site, swimmers are about 7 blocks away from YMCA's regulation 25-yard lapper.

After your workout, take advantage of the Suites' relaxing sauna, whirlpool, and massage services plus the fruit basket for a quick sugar fix.

SILVER: Embassy Suites

101 E. Locust Street, Des Moines, IA 50309
(515) 244-1700 • embassysuitesdesmoines.com

As the closest hotel property to downtown's YMCA, Embassy's location on the Des Moines River provides quick access to the Capitol, City Hall and the river running path.

In typical Embassy fashion, its atrium-designed hotel offers 234 guest suites with separate living and sleeping areas, mini-refrigerators and microwave ovens. Though you can zap an afternoon snack or even dinner, Embassy takes care of your breakfast each morning with a complimentary cooked-to-order meal.

When it comes time to work off that free omelet and hash browns, skip Embassy's puny and ill-equipped workout room, with its 2 Sohn treadmills and 4 other haggard cardio machines. Since the YMCA is less than a 5-minute walk away, the $5 admission fee is a no-brainer.

MODERATELY EXPENSIVE

GOLD: Fort Des Moines

1000 Walnut Street, Des Moines, IA 50309
(515) 243-1161 • hotelfortdesmoines.com

For those wanting to spend a little less money, Fort Des Moines affords a comfortable lodging experience in a central locale. The 244 guest units will not win any style awards, but they are comparable to the other rooms in downtown Des Moines. For some reason, hotels in this Hawkeye town have a "thing" for green carpeting. Fort Des Moines follows suit, offering many rooms in this loud Leprechaun tint.

While we were not wowed by the tiny fitness room's one good Precor elliptical and several other second-rate machines, travel writer happiness did ensue when we confirmed staff's claim that a lap pool is on-site. Fort Des Moines' swim option is an above-ground tank, approximately 20 yards in length. Though a floating lane line or two would be nice, wide stripes on the pool's bottom will keep you swimming straight. You will not write home about this pool, but hotels with legitimate lappers (20 yards or longer) deserve special recognition, as they are an endangered species. Swimmers wanting an extra 5 yards should walk 5 minutes to the YWCA. (The YW's fitness center and pool may be closing. If so, the YM is the alternative.)

CARDIO

TREADMILLS: **1 Precor - old**
UPRIGHT BIKE: **2 Fan**
ELLIPTICAL: **1 Precor**
STEPPER: **1 Tectrix**
OTHER: **1 Dip Machine**

SWIM

GRADE: **C-**
SPECS: **2x20yd • Indoor • 82°**

OTHER

HOURS: **7a-12a**
COST: **Free**
TV: **Yes**

Note: Cardio and weight enthusiasts should hop on the free hotel shuttle or walk 15 minutes to the Riverfront YMCA.

LEAST EXPENSIVE

SILVER: Quality Inn & Suites

929 3rd Street, Des Moines, IA 50309
(515) 282-5251 • qualityinn.com

While we firmly believe that you will be happier doling out a little extra dough at any of our other listed hotels, we recommend Quality because it is the closest budget hotel to the Riverfront YMCA — and consequently the best in this category. Overall the property has been improved with a recent renovation and sprucing, but it's still a basic accommodation that gets the job done, and not much more.

Getting to the YMCA will still take 10 to 15 minutes on foot, so "closest" does not mean convenient.

BEYOND HOTELS

Riverfront YMCA

101 Locust St., Des Moines, IA 50309
(515) 282-9622 • desmoinesymca.org/Riverfront

CARDIO

TREADMILLS: **Precor**
UPRIGHT BIKE: **Tectrix • Fan**
RECUMBENT BIKE: **LF**
ELLIPTICAL: **Precor • LF**
STEPPER: **LifeStep • StairMaster - old**
ROWING: **Concept II**

STRENGTH

FREE WEIGHTS: **Yes**
MACHINES: **Cybex**
DUMBBELLS: **5-120 lbs**

SWIM

GRADE: **C**
SPECS: **4x25yd • Indoor • 82-84°**
TOYS: **Kick • Pull • Clock**

OTHER

CLASSES: **Yes**
HOURS: M-F **5a-10p** • SAT **7a-6p** • SUN **9a-6p**
COST: **$5 w/ID & Hotel Key • $10 w/ID only**
TV: **Yes**
EXTRAS: **1/19 mile indoor track • Basketball • Racquetball • Cafe**

While this facility is where most downtown workers get their lunchtime sweat on, it did not appear too crowded during our feeding-time visit on a Thursday afternoon.

Unlike the YWCA across town, this YM provides members and guests with newer cardio and weight equipment in an open/airy atmosphere complete with light hardwood flooring and exposed brick walls. At least 40 cardio machines decorate the space, along with plenty of free weights and reliable weight stations.

With low ceilings and a dated coat of paint, the indoor pool is somewhat dreary. Nevertheless, the 4-lane rectangle is a functional venue for our agua-adoring amigos. Floating lines and bottom stripes mark the path and a decent supply of toys will keep you busy. A pace clock is also available for those wanting to work through some base intervals.

Do not forget your picture I.D. and hotel room key to ensure the $5 admission fee. Without a key, your rate doubles to $10. Without an I.D., you will not get in.

Note: The Y's café serves sandwiches, wraps and hot items.

RUNNING ROUTES

Except for the bitter cold winters, it is all desirable running in this Midwestern town. In the unlikely event that you get lost, Iowans are some of our country's friendliest folk, so don't be bashful about asking for directions. Locals love to help.

River Trail

The Des Moines River snakes through downtown and offers miles of running fun along the Des Moines River Trail. You can find additional routes in the many large parks inside the city limits. Macrae Park is south of most hotels (SW 9th and Davis) and offers tennis courts, ice skating and other outdoor pursuits.

Water Works Park

Fleur Drive (or Grand) is a convenient thoroughfare to get you going in the right direction, either to the River or toward Water Works Park and Gray's Lake. We suggest heading west and then south on Fleur to Water Works Park.

From the downtown hotels, it is 1 to 1.5 miles to Water Works. Inside this 1,500 acre wooded area, runners can pick up the 2-mile loop around Gray's Lake or follow the Raccoon River for additional mileage.

Saylorville Trail

If you elect to run with the river, the Saylorville Trail is on the east side. Head north and this path will take you through several parks. Each trail segment has a different name, so ask your hotel where you can best access the path. Also, the Des Moines Marathon and Half Marathon courses run through Water Works and finish on the Des Moines River — meaning that there is plenty of convenient mileage to be had right from Downtown's doorstep.

Detroit

DETROIT, MICHIGAN

Don't miss one of Motor City's most enduring enterprises. No, we are not referring to GM's headquarters, or to a Ford factory, nor are we plugging the Michigan-based Dominos or Little Caesar's. But food IS on our minds. When you're in this city, count on "Big Boy" to put a smile on your face and tasty eats in your stomach.

These family eateries are longstanding Michigan favorites, and the darling pick for local "best of" lists. Though we certainly agree with "best wait staff" and "best thick milk shake," we scratch our heads over "best spot for a last date." While the original Big Boy franchise opened in California, the Wolverine State boasts the greatest number of these yummy diner-like joints... which is not surprising, since Detroit houses its corporate headquarters.

Where did this unlikely name and cute child-like icon with its appetizing grin and slicked-back hair come from? Founder Bob Wian named his restaurant franchise after a chubby kid who frequented his original diner. Amused by the boy's happy-go-lucky character, roly-poly cheeks and tummy hanging over his pants, Bob — who had difficulty remembering the lad's name — simply called him "Big Boy." Big Boy's appearances on the big screen in "Austin Powers" and on the silk-screen with trendy T-shirts have generated a cult-like following. Locals befriend the endearing Big Boy at an early age, but it's not too late for you.

Note: Due to its size, we covered six popular business destinations around Detroit: Downtown, Auburn Hills, Birmingham, Dearborn, Southfield and Troy.

88 Locations Reviewed

DOWNTOWN

While public and private efforts have been made to add something — anything — to the Motor City's hub, it is still a vibe-less concrete morass. Detroit's metropolitan area is so large that most visitors stay in the surrounding suburbs. Wherever you choose to snooze, familiarize yourself with the infamous "Michigan Left" — a forced U-turn of sorts designed to avoid left turns at busy intersections — and be prepared for Detroit's notorious traffic snarls.

MODERATELY EXPENSIVE

GOLD: **Marriott** Renaissance Center

Renaissance Center, Detroit, MI 48243
(313) 568-8000 • marriott.com

CARDIO

TREADMILLS: **7 StarTrac**
UPRIGHT BIKE: **2 StarTrac**
RECUMBENT BIKE: **2 StarTrac**
ELLIPTICAL: **3 LF**
STEPPER: **2 StarTrac**

STRENGTH

MACHINES: **8 Hoist**
DUMBBELLS: **Uni**

OTHER

HOURS: **24**
COST: **Free**
TV: **Yes**

This Marriott tries to manage solid service notwithstanding its huge size. It's getting there. The enormous, 72-story convention hotel is located in the heart of downtown Detroit in the Renaissance Center, known locally as the "Ren Cen." Its 1,298 colorful rooms, contemporary furnishings and floor-to-ceiling windows with either city or river views are comfortable.

The on-site workout room contains good condition machines. The dumbbells are the multi-weight variation (the square-ish, one piece dumbbell that can be added to or subtracted from to vary the weight), which are inconvenient, especially when your routine calls for changing weights. We suggest you look to the Hoist stack-loaded machines for any strength work.

Swimmers, and those wanting a more elaborate alternative, are advised to drive or taxi 5 minutes to FitnessWorks in the New Center area of town. There, you will happily find everything your heart and lungs desire ($12).

LEAST EXPENSIVE

GOLD: **Hotel St. Regis**

3071 West Grand Boulevard, Detroit, MI 48202
(313) 873-3000 • hotelstregisdetroit.com

We are reluctant to put Gold next to this hotel's name. But with the dearth of appealing properties in downtown Detroit, this bare-bones New Center hotel got our nod for its across-the-street location from the phenomenal FitnessWorks athletic center. Do not confuse this Hotel St. Regis with the high-end Starwood St. Regis properties

— there is a world of difference. This is a BUDGET accommodation, and we mean BUDGET. All 221 rooms are scantily clad, with ancient-looking furnishings and drab colors. Room rates rarely exceed $100/night and are often in the $70/night ballpark. St. Regis' location is especially convenient for those with business at Wayne State University or those taking in a show at Fisher Theatre.

When it is time for your sweat, bypass the in-house workout room and make a beeline to FitnessWorks. Twelve bucks grants entry to this wonderful health club. Tons of machines, daily classes and a fantastic lap pool — it's all here.

Bottom line: If you are looking to save some money, need to stay in/near downtown Detroit and are not picky about your accommodations, stay at the Hotel St. Regis.

BEYOND HOTELS DOWNTOWN

FitnessWorks

6525 2nd Avenue, Detroit, MI 48202
(313) 972-4040 • fitnessworksclub.com

About a 5-minute drive from most of Downtown's hotels (St. Regis is across the street), FitnessWorks is a stellar 42,000 square-foot health club in Detroit's New Center area. Easily Downtown's best exercise facility, out-of-towners can satiate their workout desires for a mere $12/day.

More than 18 Precor ellipticals, 15 treadmills and 10 bikes are available to build your endurance. And under the same high-ceilings, nearly 40 stack-loaded weight stations, a wide range of dumbbells and plenty of free weights call for action. If exercising in groups is your preferred workout method, FitnessWorks hosts a broad selection of classes.

Swimmers should flock to this club's marvelous pool. Bright and attractive, the highly rated water venue provides 5 lanes of 25-yard swimming. During our tour, only 3 of the 5 lanes were divided by floating lines, but swimming here does not appear overly popular, so do not worry about lane sharing (all 5 lanes have bottom stripes). We found kickboards and pull-buoys on deck; however, those swimming intervals will want to bring a watch.

CARDIO

TREADMILLS: **Precor**
UPRIGHT BIKE: **LF • Fan**
RECUMBENT BIKE: **Precor • Reebok**
ELLIPTICAL: **Precor • Reebok**
STEPPER: **Tectrix**
ROWING: **Concept II**
OTHER: **NordicTrack**

STRENGTH

FREE WEIGHTS: **Yes**
MACHINES: **Cybex • Free Motion • Life Circuit**
DUMBBELLS: **5-100 lbs**

SWIM

GRADE: **B+**
SPECS: **5x25yd • Indoor • 83°**
TOYS: **Kick • Pull**

OTHER

CLASSES: **Yes**
HOURS: M-TH **5:30a-9p** • F **5:30a-8p** • SAT **8a-2p** • SUN **Closed**
COST: **$12**
TV: **Yes**
EXTRAS: **1/12 mile indoor track • Basketball • Racquetball**

AUBURN HILLS

LEAST EXPENSIVE

GOLD: **Hampton Inn**

1461 North Opdyke Road, Auburn Hills, MI 48326
(248) 370-0044 • hamptoninn.com

Hampton Inn is a reliable brand — not a lot of fancy frills but plenty of good ol' fashioned hospitality. Expect standard rooms with basic features and a full menu of freebies. Complimentary high-speed internet access, gratis local calls and free continental breakfasts each morning are always appreciated.

This Hampton separates itself from surrounding hotels by offering one additional, and important comp, free passes to the stellar North Oakland YMCA (a $20/day value). Plan on the 5-minute drive, because Hampton's in-house workout room is not so reliable.

Note: You must get the pass from the hotel's front desk.

BEYOND HOTELS AUBURN HILLS

North Oakland YMCA

3378 East Walton Boulevard, Auburn Hills, MI 48326
(248) 370-9622 • ymcametrodetroit.org

CARDIO

TREADMILLS: **LF • StairMaster**
UPRIGHT BIKE: **LF**
RECUMBENT BIKE: **LF**
ELLIPTICAL: **LF • Precor • Cybex**
STEPPER: **StairMaster • Stepmill**

STRENGTH

FREE WEIGHTS: **Yes**
MACHINES: **Cybex**
DUMBBELLS: **5-100 lbs**

SWIM

GRADE: **B+**
SPECS: **5x25yd • Indoor • 84-86°**
TOYS: **Kick • Pull • Clock**

OTHER

CLASSES: **Yes**
HOURS: M-F **5:30a-10p** • SAT **7a-6p** • SUN **9a-6p**
COST: **Free Hampton • $20 Others**
TV: **Yes**
EXTRAS: **1/12 mile indoor track • Basketball**

Opened in September 2003, Auburn Hills' modern and young Y has everything you need from A to Z. The fresh atmosphere is complemented by an unblemished line of top-notch cardio and strength equipment, 2 basketball courts and a 25-yard lap pool. Hampton guests receive privileges on the house, and all others must pay $20/day.

We always enjoy touring new facilities, and this family-friendly Y is no exception. Everything is just out of the box, including nearly 20 treadmills, 15 Precor ellipticals, 4 Cybex ArcTrainers, 4 Life Fitness 9500 series upright bikes and 3 StairMaster 4600PT model steppers. If strength training is your plan, the Y offers a great assortment of stack-loaded weight machines — we counted 28. While free weights are housed in a separate, smaller room, enough plates and benches are inside to get you by.

Swimmers may not always appreciate the Y's multi-generational friendliness. The lap pool shares water with the kid's fun pool and waterslide. Often only 2 of the 5 lanes are separated by floating lines, but this varies throughout the day and week (all 5 lanes have bottom stripes). On weekends especially, coveted smooth and calm waters are rattled by waves and splashing from the kid's section. Nevertheless, it is still an above average swim option.

Note: You must bring your I.D. to get in — even Hampton Inn guests.

BIRMINGHAM

EXPENSIVE

GOLD: The Townsend

100 Townsend Street, Birmingham, MI 48009
(248) 642-7900 • townsendhotel.com

CARDIO

TREADMILLS: **2 Precor - old**
RECUMBENT BIKE: **2 Cybex**
ELLIPTICAL: **2 Precor**

STRENGTH

MACHINES: **9 Cybex**
DUMBBELLS: **3-25 lbs**

OTHER

HOURS: **24**
COST: **Free**
TV: **Yes**
EXTRAS: **Free Access to Oakland • $15 Beverly Hills**

The Townsend is one of the most lavish accommodations in metropolitan Detroit. This quaint suburb's upscale shops and cafes are the Townsend's neighbors, and Oakland County's corporate community is a short drive away.

The hotel exterior appears modern with its brown brick façade and large windows, but setting foot inside brings you to the 19th Century. All 150 rooms feature Old World charm, Victorian style and luxurious furnishings. Egyptian cotton sheets, 24-hour room service, marble tubs and Aveda toiletries are Townsend comforts.

Unfortunately, the hotel's workout facility does not measure up to the premium surroundings. Strength enthusiasts have more machines to play with, but the cardio selection is disappointing. Upright bikes and step machines are noticeably absent, and the 2 treadmills are worn, despite online "cutting edge" references. Townsend's saving grace is its satisfying ellipticals and recumbent bikes — not huge in quantity, but adequate for a hotel of this size.

For athletic-minded travelers wanting to invest in a longer and more full-service workout, several options are available. The Oakland Athletic Club is a 5-minute walk with access complimentary to Townsend guests. However, those willing to spend $15/day and drive 5 minutes can treat themselves to the larger and more exclusive Beverly Hills Health Club ($7.50/day if IHRSA).

Lap swimmers must look to Beverly Hills, since the Oakland Athletic Club has no pool, and the nearby Birmingham YMCA does not permit guests. You can beg and plead with the membership office and you might get in. If so, a "B-rated" 5x25-yard lapper awaits.

LEAST EXPENSIVE

GOLD: Hamilton Hotel

35270 Woodward Avenue, Birmingham, MI 48009
(248) 642-6200 • hamiltonhotel.com

A 5-minute walk from Birmingham's main drag, Hamilton is a small, 64-unit mid-rise hotel. It competes with Holiday Inn Express just down the street, and our guess is that it is ahead. Hamilton's rooms are not going to win any style awards, but guests will enjoy a litany of freebies from this clean and reliable accommodation. Complimentary high-speed internet access and bottled water are provided in every room, along with refrigerators and triple-sheeted beds. While you can stash a few snacks in the fridge, don't worry about breakfast fare, because Hamilton covers the morning meal. Far from continental, the free gourmet buffet includes French toast, waffles, cereals and juices.

With its 6 machines and small dumbbell set, Hamilton's workout room is not very useful. Athletic-minded guests should walk 7 minutes to the Oakland Athletic Club for a proper sweat ($10).

Lap swimmers belonging to an IHRSA club at home can freestyle at the Beverly Hills Club for $7.50 (5-minute drive). If your club is not a part of IHRSA, getting wet on this trip can be a challenge — requiring that you commute to one of our other covered areas, convince the Birmingham Y to make an exception to their "members only" policy (248-644-9036) or stay at the Townsend, which allows you to swim at Beverly for $15.

BEYOND HOTELS BIRMINGHAM

CARDIO

TREADMILLS: **Precor**
UPRIGHT BIKE: **LF • Fan**
RECUMBENT BIKE: **LF - old**
ELLIPTICAL: **Precor • Reebok**
STEPPER: **StairMaster • LF • Stepmill**
ROWING: **Concept II**
OTHER: **Crossrobic • Gravitron**

STRENGTH

FREE WEIGHTS: **Yes**
HAMMER: **Yes**
MACHINES: **Trotter**
DUMBBELLS: **10-120 lbs**

OTHER

CLASSES: **Yes**
HOURS: M-TH **5:30a-9:30p** • F **5:30a-8:30p** • SAT-SUN **7a-6:30p**
COST: **Free Townsend • $10 Other hotels • $15 Others**
TV: **Yes**

Oakland Athletic Club

355 N. Old Woodward Ave. #290
Birmingham, MI 48009
(248) 540-9596
oaklandathleticclub.net

As Birmingham's closest health club, Oakland has everything athletes need to strengthen their hearts and muscles. By no means a huge facility, this understated center has an office vibe and prides itself in offering good-quality equipment to its members. Townsend guests are granted free access, and others are charged $15/day.

Although several older pieces remain part of the fitness floor inventory (e.g., recumbent bikes), most machines are youthful and in excellent condition. We counted 13 treadmills, 8 StairMaster 4400 series steppers, 7 ellipticals and 6 upright bikes. Plenty of free weights are available for hard-core strength routines and a serviceable selection of stack-loaded weight stations complement the plates.

The only athletic feature missing is a pool, so swimmers must seek chlorinated water elsewhere.

Beverly Hills Club

31555 Southfield Road, Beverly Hills, MI 48025
(248) 642-8500 • beverlyhillsclub.net

Beverly is the largest and most upscale private health club in this section of Motor Town. Unfortunately, the only out-of-towners lucky enough to share its fitness wealth are guests of the Townsend ($15) and members of a hometown IHRSA club ($7.50, check www.healthclubs.com).

If you can get in, your heart will pitter patter with workout excitement, then thump from exercise fatigue. Inside the 90,000 square foot facility, fitness fans can choose among a vast selection of cutting-edge cardio machines (e.g., 15 treadmills and 14 ellipticals), new stack-loaded weight stations (25) and a ton of free weights. Although Beverly serves up a great spinning studio with modern bikes available for anytime use, we saw no computerized uprights on the main fitness floor.

CARDIO

TREADMILLS: **LF • StarTrac • NordicTrack**
UPRIGHT BIKE: **Spin**
RECUMBENT BIKE: **StarTrac**
ELLIPTICAL: **Precor**
STEPPER: **StairMaster • Stepmill**

STRENGTH

FREE WEIGHTS: **Yes**
HAMMER: **Yes - Leg**
MACHINES: **Cybex**
DUMBBELLS: **5-115 lbs**

SWIM

GRADE: **B**
SPECS: **3x25yd • Indoor • 80°**
TOYS: **Kick • Pull • Clock**

OTHER

CLASSES: **Yes**
HOURS: M-TH **5:30a-11p** • F **5:30a-10p** • SAT-SUN **7a-7p**
COST: **$15 Townsend • $7.50 IHRSA • No others**
TV: **Yes**
EXTRAS: **1/16 mile indoor track • Basketball • Tennis**

Beverly does not leave swimmers high and dry. Its 3 lane, 25-yard lapper is well marked with floating lines and bottom stripes. All necessary toys are here, as well as a pace clock for interval work.

DEARBORN

EXPENSIVE

GOLD: Ritz Carlton

300 Town Center Drive, Dearborn, MI 48126
(313) 441-2000 • ritzcarlton.com

CARDIO

TREADMILLS: **3 Cybex**
UPRIGHT BIKE: **2 Cybex**
ELLIPTICAL: **1 Cybex**
STEPPER: **1 Cybex**

STRENGTH

MACHINES: **8 Cybex**
DUMBBELLS: **5-70 lbs**

SWIM

SPECS: **Indoor • Not lap**

OTHER

HOURS: **24**
COST: **Free**
TV: **Yes**
EXTRAS: **$15 access Fairlane**

The Ritz is near the top of metropolitan Detroit's hotel food chain. Other than Birmingham's Townsend hotel, finding a true luxury property in the Motor City is as difficult as locating a mint-condition '53 Corvette. After visiting a host of wonderfully unique Ritz properties across the country, we can tell you that the Dearborn representative weighs in light on the luxury scale — nice but nothing too special.

The 308 rooms are suited up in shades of cream and brown, sport marble baths, afford premium feather bedding and provide high-speed internet access (fee). However, the plain and conservative décor may disappoint those accustomed to more upscale Ritz trappings.

The hotel has upgraded its fitness room to include several new machines, but the room remains dark and space constrained. Cybex is the name of the workout game here, so Precor and Life Fitness fans will have to make do. We highly recommend Cybex's ArcTrainer elliptical machine — and know a few converts. Three of Ritz's stack-loaded weight stations are leg apparatus, and an ab-bench can help with the six-pack.

Those wanting more cardio or strength can walk a half-mile to the Fairlane Club ($15) or drive 1.5 miles to the Ford Community Center ($10). Both are great alternatives, so let your budget and commute dictate your exercise fate.

Ritz's on-site 40-foot indoor Napoleon is nowhere near lap length. Swimmers planning to accrue real yardage must consider off-site options — there are two. During the summer (Memorial Day to Labor Day), the nearby Fairlane Club's appealing 3 lane, 25-yard outdoor option ($15) is open for your business, and the Ford Community Center's wonderful 6 lane, 25-yard water box is available year round ($10). While Fairlane has an indoor pool also, it's a 50-foot shorty.

We always prefer to swim outside, so during the summer we would front the extra $5 for a dip in Fairlane's water box under the Midwest sun. Throughout the rest of the year, head over to Ford with confidence.

MODERATELY EXPENSIVE

GOLD: Hyatt Regency

600 Town Center Drive, Dearborn, MI 48126
(313) 593-1234 • hyatt.com

Located near the Ritz and Fairlane Town Center Shopping Mall, Hyatt's Gold standing is due to its proximity to (and relationship with) the quarter-mile away Fairlane Club, where Hyatt guests are permitted access for $15/day. Spending a night in one of Hyatt's 772 rooms is satisfying. The large, high-rise hotel caters to the business traveler with its standard floorplans and furnishings. No free breakfasts, no complimentary high-speed internet access and no premium bedding. It's tidy, relatively quiet and convenient.

CARDIO

TREADMILLS: **2 LF - old • 2 True - old**
UPRIGHT BIKE: **2 LF**
RECUMBENT BIKE: **1 LF**
ELLIPTICAL: **2 LF**
STEPPER: **1 LF**

STRENGTH

MACHINES: **3 LF**

SWIM

SPECS: **Indoor • Not lap**

OTHER

HOURS: **6a-11p**
COST: **Free**
TV: **Yes**
EXTRAS: **$10/day Bally's & Dearborn**

Hyatt's workout room is marginal. Separated by a brick wall, the equipment shares space with Hyatt's small indoor pool. Half of the machines are old and worn models, while the 3 newer bikes were missing pedal straps — a pet peeve. Taking advantage of Hyatt's arrangement with Bally's ($10), or driving 5 minutes to Dearborn's Ford Community Center ($10), is an easy decision.

Lap swimmers can head to Dearborn's Ford Community Center — a great pool and only $10 admission.

LEAST EXPENSIVE

GOLD: Hampton Inn

20061 Michigan Avenue, Dearborn, MI 48124
(313) 436-9600 • hamptoninn.com

SILVER: Courtyard by Marriott

5200 Mercury Drive, Dearborn, MI 48126
(313) 271-1400 • marriott.com

Both hotels are within 1.5 miles of the fantastic Ford Community Center — a $10/day state-of-the-art workout facility. Upholding their respective brands, each accommodation offers clean rooms, reliable service and complimentary high-speed internet access. These budget friendly abodes earn no raves for their in-house workout rooms. We give Hampton the nod because it normally runs slightly cheaper than Courtyard, and its free continental breakfasts are a nice perk.

Book either with confidence and remember that staying here

instead of the Ritz or Hyatt lines your pockets with an extra $75-$150/night.

BEYOND HOTELS DEARBORN

Fairlane Club

5000 Fairlane Woods Drive, Dearborn, MI 48126
(313) 336-4400 • fairlaneclub.com

CARDIO

TREADMILLS: **StarTrac • Woodway**
UPRIGHT BIKE: **StarTrac • Tectrix**
RECUMBENT BIKE: **LF**
ELLIPTICAL: **Precor • Reebok**
STEPPER: **Tectrix • StairMaster** - old **• Stepmill**
ROWING: **Concept II**
OTHER: **Gravitron • Crossrobic • NordicTrack**

STRENGTH

FREE WEIGHTS: **Yes**
HAMMER: **Yes**
MACHINES: **Cybex**
DUMBBELLS: **2-130 lbs**

SWIM

GRADE: #1 **B** • #2 **D**
SPECS: #1 **3x25yd • Outdoor • 82°**
#2 **2x17yd • Indoor • 82°**
TOYS: **Kick • Pull**

OTHER

CLASSES: **Yes**
HOURS: M-F **5:30a-10p** • SAT-SUN **7a-9p**
COST: **$15 Ritz/IHRSA • No others**
TV: **Yes**
EXTRAS: **1/14 mile indoor track • Basketball • Racquetball • Tennis • Cafe**

This private, upscale country club employs a "members only" policy. Luckily, an exception is made for guests of the Ritz Carlton and one other non-recommended hotel. For $15/day, Ritz patrons can revel in Fairlane's equipment largesse.

On its fitness floor, exercisers are treated to an exceptional selection of cutting-edge machines in an open and lofty environment. Over 50 cardio pieces line the space, including 15 treadmills, 10 ellipticals and 5 bikes. Strength apparatus is here in force as well, with 10 Hammer Strength plate-loaded machines, bench and squat racks and approximately 20 Cybex stack-loaded stations.

Topping off the sweat prospects is an array of cardio and strength classes.

A lap swim option is only viable from Memorial Day to Labor Day. The warm weather marks the opening of Fairlane's 25-yard outdoor pool, with lanes divided by floating lines and bottom stripes. Although the rectangle can support 6 lanes, only 3 are typically set up each day. Bring a watch if base intervals are in your plans, because no pace clock is on deck. Fairlane does house a year-round indoor pool, but its short length (50 feet or ~17 yards) will not satisfy serious lap swimmers.

Ford Community Center

15801 Michigan Avenue, Dearborn, MI 48126
(313) 943-2350 • dearbornfordcenter.com

Look for the neon sign on the south side of Michigan Avenue (the center shares a parking lot with the Dearborn Police) for this modern glass, office-looking building. Ford certainly knows how to build things, and it did a great job with this new community facility, which houses a performing arts center as well as a community health club and pool.

The fitness floor's atrium-like space is well organized, with cutting-edge Precor cardio equipment. We counted 13 treadmills, 10 ellipticals, 8 recumbent bikes and 2 uprights. Beyond the endurance machines, but in the same atrium, Ford's strength equipment sparkles. Only one free weight bench and squat rack are on the premises; however, 8 Hammer Strength machines and more than 15 stack-loaded weight stations service a full-body pump. The indoor 1/11-mile track is a nice addition and is popular during Detroit's bitter winters. This is a family club, so mind the strollers, which are allowed on the track from 9-11 a.m.

CARDIO

TREADMILLS: **Precor**
UPRIGHT BIKE: **Precor • Fan**
RECUMBENT BIKE: **Precor**
ELLIPTICAL: **Precor**
STEPPER: **Stepmill**
ROWING: **Concept II**

STRENGTH

FREE WEIGHTS: **Yes**
HAMMER: **Yes**
MACHINES: **Magnum • Free Motion**
DUMBBELLS: **5-80 lbs**

SWIM

GRADE: **B+**
SPECS: **6x25yd • Indoor • 79-82°**
TOYS: **Kick • Pull • Clock**

OTHER

CLASSES: **Yes**
HOURS: M-F **6a-10p** • SAT **8a-8p** • SUN **9a-6p**
COST: **$10 w/hotel key • $42/week**
TV: **Yes**
EXTRAS: **1/11 mile indoor track • Basketball • Outdoor jog path • Climbing wall • Food Bar**

You'll do flip-turns of joy in this fantastic water box — one of the best lap pools in metro Detroit. Six lanes of 25-yard swimming are offered, with floating lines and bottom stripes. Be sure to bring your hotel room key and I.D. along with your $10.

SOUTHFIELD

MODERATELY EXPENSIVE

Embassy Suites

28100 Franklin Road, Southfield, MI 48034
(248) 350-2000 • embassysuites.com

You can rely on Embassy for a positive lodging experience. All 239 suites have separate living and sleeping areas affording extra space to spread out your belongings or the family. Microwaves and refrigerators are convenient, and free high-speed internet access is provided in all rooms. Don't forget the yummy, complimentary breakfasts and happy hours that are served each day in the hotel lobby.

Athletic-minded guests, pay no mind to the ineffective on-site workout room. Instead, take advantage of Embassy's exclusive privileges ($8) at the nearby Franklin Athletic Club. You can walk, but beware the busy streets and consider driving 2 minutes. Just show your room key and pay at the fitness center.

BEYOND HOTELS SOUTHFIELD

Franklin Athletic Club

29350 Northwestern Highway, Southfield, MI 48034
(248) 352-8000 • franklinclub.com

CARDIO

TREADMILLS: **LF • Precor • StarTrac**
UPRIGHT BIKE: **LF**
RECUMBENT BIKE: **LF • Cybex**
ELLIPTICAL: **Precor • LF**
STEPPER: **LF • StairMaster • StarTrac**
ROWING: **Yes**

STRENGTH

FREE WEIGHTS: **Yes**
HAMMER: **Yes**
MACHINES: **Cybex • Life Circuit**
DUMBBELLS: **3-110 lbs**

SWIM

GRADE: #1 **B** • #2 **D+**
SPECS: #1 **3x25m • Outdoor • 82º**
#2 **4x18m • Indoor • 85º**
TOYS: **Kick • Pull • Fins • Clock**

OTHER

CLASSES: **Yes**
HOURS: M-F **5:30a-10p** • SAT-SUN **5:30a-9p**
COST: **$8 Embassy • $15 IHRSA • No others**
TV: **Yes**
EXTRAS: **1/12 mile indoor track • Racquetball**

This place must be the largest health club in Michigan. Emphasizing racquet sports, the facility's 225,000 square feet of workout bliss boasts 13 tennis courts, a number of racquetball courts and a full service restaurant and bar. But those seeking a cardio sweat, strength routine or lap swim are not the least slighted.

Over 20 treadmills, 12 ellipticals and 12 bikes pack the arena-like fitness floor. Life Fitness is the brand of choice, which most fitness fans value — us included. The club hosts a variety of aerobic and strength classes and houses separate yoga and spin studios.

Swimmers will not be overly excited by Franklin's lap option. At 18 meters, it's a little short of our preferred distance of 25 yards, but floating lines and bottom stripes lead the way. And we did find a full assortment of toys and a pace clock on deck. During summer, the liquid options improve with Franklin's outdoor 25-meter lapper. Usually, 3 lanes are set up with floating lines and bottom stripes, but call to ensure a water aerobics class isn't occupying the entire pool.

Note: This is a members' only club with an exception made for Embassy guests ($8) and IHRSA club members ($15).

TROY

MODERATELY EXPENSIVE

GOLD: Embassy Suites

850 Tower Drive, Troy, MI 48098
(248) 879-7500 • embassysuites.com

Just west of Highway 75, Embassy's proximity to the awesome Lifetime Fitness club is its winning attribute. Guests enjoy typical Embassy hospitality in its 251 separate living and sleeping suites, equipped with refrigerators and microwave ovens. While you may be tempted to zap a late night snack, don't fuss with breakfast. Embassy cures your morning cravings with a complimentary full buffet featuring waffles, eggs, cereals and juices. Evening happy hours present free hors d'oeuvres and drinks.

Embassy's gym will not, however, cure your exercise cravings. The hotel's complimentary shuttle will whisk you to one of Detroit's best health clubs — Lifetime Fitness. Admission is steep at $25/day, but this club is a fitness amusement park with all sorts of rides.

SILVER: Residence Inn

2600 Livernois Road, Troy, MI 48083
(248) 689-6856 • marriott.com

A few miles south of Embassy Suites, Residence Inn offers similar quality accommodations and a free off-site workout option. In keeping with the brand's theme, this 152-room property offers two-room suites, fully equipped kitchens, refrigerators and microwaves. Though never astonishing with jaw-dropping luxury or over-the-top décor, Residence Inn is a trusty hotel option. Count on leaving well rested and with a full stomach — a free hot full breakfast buffet is offered each morning (weekly BBQs, too).

Most satisfying are the complimentary passes to Bally Total Fitness — 7-minute walk/3-minute drive. A good representative for an inconsistent health club franchise, this fitness perk is the main reason Residence earned our vote.

Swimmers must drive 10 minutes to Lifetime Fitness, since Bally has no pool. Shoppers may want to visit nearby Somerset Collection Mall — Neiman's, Saks, Nordstrom, etc.

Note: Be sure to bring your I.D. and the passes provided by the hotel.

LEAST EXPENSIVE

GOLD: Drury Inn

575 W. Big Beaver Road, Troy, MI 48084
(248) 528-3330 • druryhotels.com

Another bare bones accommodation with a bunch of freebies, Drury Inn is located two parking lots away from Bally Fitness. Guest perks include free local calls, free high-speed internet access and free hot breakfasts each morning — somewhat less extensive than Residence's buffet, but good nonetheless.

Although the hotel does not offer free admission passes to Bally, several conversations with club personnel confirmed that Drury guests wanting to work out at Bally need only make a small retail purchase (e.g., bottle of water or an energy bar) to gain admission. This arrangement is very reasonable, since this facility's usual daily rate for non-members is $20.

Swimmers, plan on driving 10 minutes to Lifetime, because Bally Fitness has no pool.

Bottom line, this may be the best and most convenient stay/play option in Troy.

Note: Shoppers will appreciate the 2-minute drive proximity to Somerset Collection Mall's upscale chain retailers.

BEYOND HOTELS TROY

Lifetime Fitness

4700 Investment Drive, Troy, MI 48098
(248) 267-1000 • lifetimefitness.com

CARDIO

TREADMILLS: **LF • Cybex**
UPRIGHT BIKE: **LF • Cybex**
RECUMBENT BIKE: **LF • Cybex**
ELLIPTICAL: **Cybex • Precor • Reebok**
STEPPER: **StairMaster • Stepmill**
ROWING: **Concept II**

STRENGTH

FREE WEIGHTS: **Yes**
HAMMER: **Yes**
MACHINES: **LF • Cybex • BodyMaster • Icarian**
DUMBBELLS: **3-130 lbs**

SWIM

GRADE: **B+**
SPECS: **5x25m • Indoor • 80-82°**
TOYS: **Kick • Pull • Clock**

OTHER

CLASSES: **Yes**
HOURS: **6a-9p**
COST: **$25**
TV: **Yes**
EXTRAS: **Basketball • Climbing wall**

Wow! If you have never been inside a Lifetime Fitness mega-health club, you are in for a treat. All are monstrous facilities with too many machines to count and every athletic modality you can imagine.

Lifetime's 88,000 square foot Troy property is no exception, sporting over 50 treadmills, a ton of free weights and a highly rated lap pool. The fitness floor's strength section resembles a Las Vegas sports book with its 6 wide screen televisions hanging high on the walls.

There's even a 45-foot rock-climbing wall for those looking to scale heights.

The club's lap pool received a high rating, featuring 5 lanes separated by floating lines and bottom stripes over its 25-meter course. Kickboards and pull-buoys are provided.

The $25/day admission is expensive. But you should experience this club at least once, and you can expense it, right?

Bally Total Fitness Columbia Center

203 W. Big Beaver Road, Troy, MI 48084
(248) 524-6474 • ballytotalfitness.com

Bally is the runt of the litter compared to Lifetime Fitness, so expect less equipment and more of a crowd. Although this franchise often puts out an "iffy" product, the Troy club is a good representative for an inconsistent chain.

Plenty of cardio and strength equipment fills 2 floors. For example, we counted approximately 50 stack-loaded weight machines — all ready to make you strong. A plethora of classes are offered as well, for those seeking strength in numbers.

CARDIO

TREADMILLS: **LF**
UPRIGHT BIKE: **LF**
RECUMBENT BIKE: **LF**
ELLIPTICAL: **LF • Precor**
STEPPER: **StairMaster - old**

STRENGTH

FREE WEIGHTS: **Yes**
HAMMER: **Yes**
MACHINES: **LF • Maxicam • Icarian**
DUMBBELLS: **3-100 lbs**

OTHER

CLASSES: **Yes**
HOURS: M-TH **5:30a-11p** • F **5:30a-10p** • SAT-SUN **7a-7p**
COST: **Free Residence Inn • Free w/Retail purchase • $20 Others**
TV: **Yes**

Residence Inn guests get in free with passes provided by the hotel. Drury patrons and other travelers will typically be provided access after making a small retail purchase. (If all else fails, have $20 ready.)

Unlike many Bally Fitness gyms, the staff here appears to understand the plight of an athletic-minded traveler and is willing to help.

Note: Bring your photo ID.

RUNNING ROUTES

Downtown

They don't call it the Motor City for its jogging routes, that's for sure. Running in metro Detroit requires creativity and a willingness to stride on residential streets and along busy highways.

Plan to head out from your hotel and direct yourself along what appear to be the least traveled roads (check with the concierge first).

While efforts are underway to complete the 3.5-mile RiverWalk, which will run from Joe Louis Arena to the Belle Isle Bridge, runners must cab over to Belle Isle (~$6) for any fun. Approximately 3 miles of paths await — meager, we know. Consult with the hotel concierge and keep in mind that any mileage should be logged during daylight hours only. Completion of the project is scheduled for late 2005.

Paint Creek Trail

Those staying in the Troy/Auburn Hills area may be interested in driving to the Paint Creek Trail — a crushed limestone path that runs from Rochester Park in downtown Rochester to Lake Orion (approx. 9 miles).

HOUSTON, TEXAS

Thousands of our nation's brightest engineers, mathematicians and scientists dream of moving to Houston. Why? Does this Texas town have beautiful year-round weather? No. Is the City free of traffic jams and pollution? Hardly. Is this oil and gas hub also a recreational or cultural mecca? Nope.

So what could possibly explain Houston's gravitational force — that has the best of the best eager to uproot? Four letters: NASA.

NASA's Johnson Space Center in Houston is home to the Astronaut Training Center and Mission Control. Knowing it will invest $600,000 to $1,000,000 in each candidate's first year of training, NASA painstakingly scrutinizes 10,000 applicants every two years to select 20 prospective astronauts. Most have "astronomical" I.Q.'s and resumés an inch thick.

Of the 144 cosmos currently on the payroll, only about 60% have endured the physical demands of life beyond Earth's atmosphere. Exposure to dangerous levels of radiation, changes in atmospheric pressure and living in zero gravity all take a toll. It is not unusual for astronauts to grow 2 inches taller, lose 30% of their fitness and suffer a 20% bone loss while in space. To delay this environmental onslaught, astronauts are encouraged to exercise during their mission.

En route, space shuttle voyagers stick to their fitness regimen by pedaling on a stationary bike. Those who stay at the International Space Station (ISS) exercise at the most exclusive and private health club in the universe. That's right, along with its astronomical and scientific functions, the ISS provides a workout room containing one treadmill, one cycle ergometer and a weight training device. Unfortunately, no amount of exercise in space will prepare the human body for its homecoming.

Once returning to Earth, cosmonauts suffer debilitating symptoms of poor balance, lightheadedness and nausea. Approximately 40% cannot stand for more than 10 minutes without fainting! It takes nearly a month for the human body to begin readjusting to our environment.

Sounds a little like how we feel after an Ironman triathlon. Maybe we should apply to NASA… though that I.Q. thing might pose a problem.

DOWNTOWN

"Houston, we do NOT have a problem." When it comes to working out in America's 4th largest city, travelers with a bent for exercise will be pleased with the choices. We found several downtown hotels housing attractive fitness centers with healthy helpings of equipment. For swimmers and those staying in an accommodation without a good gym, the Downtown YMCA will launch you into workout bliss.

EXPENSIVE

GOLD: **Hilton Americas**

1600 Lamar, Houston, TX 77010
(713) 739-8000 • hilton.com

CARDIO

TREADMILLS: **6 LF**
RECUMBENT BIKE: **4 LF**
ELLIPTICAL: **3 LF**
STEPPER: **2 LF**

STRENGTH

FREE WEIGHTS: **Yes**
MACHINES: **14 Nautilus**
DUMBBELLS: **5-65 lbs**

SWIM

SPECS: **Indoor • Not lap**

OTHER

HOURS: **6a-10p**
COST: **$6**
TV: **Yes**
EXTRAS: **Basketball • Tennis**

Squeezing out Four Seasons for the Gold, Hilton earns the "Honor" with its newer and slightly nicer fitness center as well as a nightly pricetag that's roughly $100/night lower. Hilton's 24-story high-rise offers 1,200 soundproofed guest quarters in conservative beige and cream tones. It opened its doors in December 2003, and the rooms and accoutrements still retain that fresh scent and appearance. However, as is often the case with newer properties, some kinks are still being "worked out" with respect to service and amenities.

Connected to the Brown Convention Center and 6 blocks from Minute Maid Field, Hilton's location is opportune for business and sporting events, but a taxi ride will be in order to sample downtown's Main Street restaurants and shopping. Those preferring to waddle home after a filling steak dinner should allot 15 to 20 minutes. Tack on a couple minutes more if you indulged in a chocolate soufflé.

Whether you are repenting last evening's feeding frenzy or just looking to start your day with vigor, you will flip over Hilton's 23rd floor fitness center's fabulous views and equipment. Six bucks introduces you to a great assortment of sparkling new cardio and weight machines and approximately 400 lbs. of free weights. Cycling geeks must go recumbent, as upright bikes are noticeably absent.

With no lap pool, swimmers should taxi or drive to the YMCA. The 20-minute walk is long and boring.

Note: Hilton Americas was the host hotel for the 2004 Super Bowl.

SILVER: **Four Seasons**
1300 Lamar Street, Houston, TX 77010
(713) 650-1300 • fourseasons.com/houston

Although it is never a lock to make our list, Houston's version of this spectacular hotel chain definitely belongs near the top. In the heart of Houston's business district and a 5-minute walk from downtown's Main Street shopping and entertainment district, Four Seasons pampers guests with its trademark luxury and service. The least expensive room tops $300/night, so you may need a second job to cover the bill, however. Make sure you reserve the sleeping arrangement you desire, because many entry-level units come with only one queen-size bed. All guests enjoy high thread count sheets, marble baths, 24-hour room service and complimentary Towncar service within the downtown area.

CARDIO
TREADMILLS: **6 StarTrac**
UPRIGHT BIKE: **2 LF**
RECUMBENT BIKE: **2 LF**
ELLIPTICAL: **5 Precor**
STEPPER: **2 StairMaster - old**

STRENGTH
MACHINES: **9 Cybex**
DUMBBELLS: **5-50 lbs**

SWIM
GRADE: **D**
SPECS: **2x18yd • Outdoor • 82-84°**

OTHER
HOURS: **24**
COST: **Free**
TV: **Yes**

When we visited the 4th floor workout center, Peyton Manning was pushing reps on the plentiful Cybex machines. We pulled out our pen to rate this facility, and a grim expression came over Peyton's face — due either to a particularly challenging set or because he feared we were about to swoop in for an autograph!

If the club is good enough for a Pro Bowl quarterback, it has to be good enough for us, right? Maybe. Although Four Seasons does offer a good variety of equipment in a hospitable environment, free weights are nowhere to be found, and the step machines are old. However, all other cardio and weight stations are in great condition, and many of the aerobic machines have attached TV screens.

Outside the fitness center on the 4th floor deck, a 2-lane, 18-yard pool begs for action. The website lists the pool length at 65 feet, but we paced off only 18 yards (54 feet). The lanes are marked by two narrow bottom stripes without floating lines. You decide whether the pool is Speedo worthy. We don't think so, unless you're in dire need of some quick yardage. Our recommendation is to take a $5 taxi ride to the YMCA and frolic in its regulation size rectangle.

MODERATELY EXPENSIVE

GOLD: **Crowne Plaza**
1700 Smith Street, Houston, TX 77002
(713) 739-8800 • crowneplaza.com

Crowne Plaza sits on the southwest edge of Houston's financial district and is a bit isolated from the rest of Downtown. While walking to Main Street's restaurants, shops and entertainment venues is out of the question, the impressive Downtown YMCA is conveniently located across the street.

Decorated with stodgy furnishings in fuddy-duddy patterns, Crowne's guest units are more befitting a "davenport" than a "sofa." Still, we can't turn our noses up too high. The rooms are tidy and the workout option is first rate.

You didn't think we meant Crowne's in-house gym, did you? If so, clear your mind.

The on-site weakling containing 5 SportsArt cardio pieces (a feeble brand) and a no-name multi-gym will galvanize those with a penchant for athletics to high-tail it to the nearby Y. Along with your $8 ($2 discount), bring a picture I.D. — and a swim cap if you plan to get wet.

SILVER: Residence Inn

904 Dallas Street, Houston, TX 77002
(832) 366-1000 • residenceinn.com

Opened in June 2003, Residence Inn occupies some of the most centrally located real estate in downtown Houston. Adjacent to Main Street, Residence guests can take advantage of more than 60 eclectic restaurants and lively bars in the City's social center. A 10-minute saunter is in order to reach either the YMCA or convention center.

A stay at one Residence Inn guarantees familiarity with all of this Marriott brand's properties. Fully-equipped kitchens, suites with separate living and sleeping areas and complimentary full-breakfast buffets are standard goodies. Though you will seldom find unique and creative décor, downtown Houston's Residence Inn, like most others, offers clean rooms and reliable service.

Another common feature of this chain is its paltry workout rooms. Again, Houston's Residence fits the mold, but fortunately the Downtown YMCA is 6 blocks away. Ten bucks gets you in the door.

LEAST EXPENSIVE

GOLD: Holiday Inn Express Downtown

1810 Bell Avenue, Houston, TX 77003
(713) 652-9400 • hiexpress.com

Staying on the cheap never comes with many frills, so don't expect any from this convention center area Holiday Inn Express. The rooms are basic, with unappealing bedspreads and simple furnishings, but are clean, nonetheless. While asking Jeeves to fetch room service is not possible, complimentary continental breakfast is provided each morning in the lobby. The cinnamon rolls are the highlight.

This hotel is on the southeast fringe of Downtown, so travelers should plan to take a taxi to any destination other than the convention center, including the 11 blocks to the Y ($10). The fitness room here is definitely "Express"; one blink of an eye and you miss it.

BEYOND HOTELS DOWNTOWN

YMCA Downtown

1600 Louisiana Street, Houston, TX 77002
(713) 659-8501 • ymcahouston.org

Closest to the Crowne Plaza (just across the street) and within 1.5 miles of all other hotels, this fantastic Y is the best health club in downtown Houston. The ceilings are a little lower than we prefer, but we cannot quibble with the stellar equipment. Twenty-five treadmills, 15 ellipticals and 10 each of upright bikes, recumbent bikes and step machines twinkle throughout the gym's cardio areas. Those looking to pump iron will be impressed by the assortment of free weights, dumbbells and 37 Cybex weight stations. Classes are offered, too, with cycling and aerobics topping the charts.

The Y includes swimmers in the fun by offering an above-average lap pool with floating lines and bottom stripes. Most of the toys are provided on deck. Bring your swimsuit and goggles, along with picture I.D. and $10 (a few hotels offer a $2 discount).

CARDIO

TREADMILLS: **Precor**
UPRIGHT BIKE: **Precor**
RECUMBENT BIKE: **Precor**
ELLIPTICAL: **Precor**
STEPPER: **Precor**
ROWING: **Concept II**

STRENGTH

FREE WEIGHTS: **Yes**
HAMMER: **Yes**
MACHINES: **Cybex**
DUMBBELLS: **5-130 lbs**

SWIM

GRADE: **B-**
SPECS: **4x25yd • Indoor • 82°**
TOYS: **Kick • Pull • Fins • Clock**
MASTERS: **Yes**

OTHER

CLASSES: **Yes**
HOURS: M-F **5a-10p** • SAT **8a-6p** • SUN **10a-6p**
COST: **$8 w/hotel discount • $10 Other**
TV: **Yes**
EXTRAS: **Basketball • Racquetball**

GALLERIA AREA/UPTOWN

Eight miles from Downtown Houston, the Galleria Mall is the 5th largest shopping complex in the country and Houston's #1 tourist attraction. Those with some free time may want to stay in this part of the City's universe to explore the stunning architecture and endless number of shops.

Other than Main Street and Minute Maid Park, Downtown is primarily a business destination filled with office skyscrapers, highrise hotels and the convention center.

Conversely, Galleria entertains with numerous restaurants, plenty of tourist attractions and enough retail square footage to satisfy a marathoner. Workout options are just as good, if not better than Downtown, so be sure to bring the sweat gear no matter which side of town you end up in.

EXPENSIVE

GOLD: Houstonian

111 North Post Oak Lane, Houston, TX 77024
(713) 680-2626 • houstonian.com

CARDIO

TREADMILLS: **8 Precor • 8 StarTrac**
UPRIGHT BIKE: **13 LF • 1 Precor**
RECUMBENT BIKE: **12 LF • 1 StarTrac**
ELLIPTICAL: **15 Precor • 5 LF • 2 StarTrac**
STEPPER: **5 StairMaster • 3 Cybex**
ROWING: **2 Concept II**
OTHER: **Gravitron**

STRENGTH

FREE WEIGHTS: **Yes**
HAMMER: **Yes**
MACHINES: **35 Cybex • Free Motion • Technogym • Nautilus**
DUMBBELLS: **5-120 lbs**

SWIM

GRADE: **B+**
SPECS: **6x25yd • Outdoor • 82°**
TOYS: **Kick • Pull • Clock**
MASTERS: **Yes**

OTHER

CLASSES: **Yes**
HOURS: M-F **5a-10p** • SAT-SUN **6a-9p**
COST: **Free**
TV: **Yes**
EXTRAS: **1/9 mile indoor track • Tennis • Racquetball • Spa**

Take refuge from the hustle and bustle of America's 4th largest city at this hotel, club and spa. Referring to the Houstonian as another luxury hotel is like referring to a rare Ferrari as just a nice car. Frequently the affluent host of outdoor weddings, this private and exclusive resort's park-like setting radiates beauty and tranquility.

In its 280 guest rooms, the Houstonian successfully creates a classically elegant look and feel without the stiffness and frump we have observed in many high-end Southern properties. Narrow floor-to-ceiling windows provide views of the acreage and invite in plenty of natural light. Our favorite feature is the compound's 125,000 square foot health club. Complimentary to guests, this massive fitness facility is a hop, skip and jump away from the hotel lobby. Inside, exercise nuts will crack with pleasure when eyeing the stellar equipment, modern facilities and awesome lap pool.

The cardio and weight nerve center is within the perimeter of the Houstonian's 1/9 mile indoor track. Twenty-two ellipticals, 16 treadmills, 14 upright bikes and 8 step machines stand at attention. Those in search of a strength session will benefit from the mix of 35 stack-loaded weight stations and 12 Hammer Strength free weight machines. Though you are apt to encounter "social exercisers," those enhanced with a little silicone or an extra shot of cologne, the club's ample space and generous number of machines offer shelter.

Swimmers will do flip-turns over the Houstonian's outdoor lap pool. Marked with floating lines and bottom stripes, the 25-yard rectangle is a competition level pool with all the bells and whistles, except for backstroke flags. And if your technique is in need of refining, Olympic Bronze Medalist Laura Walker will be happy to chime in with her thoughts for a slight fee — she teaches a weekly class.

Additional highlights of this urban paradise include: the Trellis Spa and Salon, playing privileges at the private Redstone Golf Club (home of the Shell Houston Open) and access to a multitude of tennis, paddle, racquetball and basketball courts. Who knew Houston could be so much fun?

SILVER: **Westin** Galleria

5060 West Alabama Street, Houston, TX 77056
(713) 960-8100 • westin.com/galleria
University Club • (713) 621-4010

Driving up to this overbearing, concrete hotel with its unsightly, above-ground attached parking structure hardly inspires the awe of pulling into the Houstonian's landscaped sanctuary. However, the saying "never judge a book by its cover" should be included somewhere in this hotel's marketing material, because the Westin's inside looks nothing like its façade suggests, especially the rooms.

Completing a renovation in June 2003, Westin refashioned its 487 guest quarters with a contemporary minimalist flair. In a pleasing contrast to the rooms' brown tones and clean lines, fluffy white comforters flow over the trademark Heavenly Beds. We like the end product — a look that combines comfort with a touch of panache.

CARDIO

TREADMILLS: **11 Mixed brands**
UPRIGHT BIKE: **3 Precor • 1 Technogym**
RECUMBENT BIKE: **3 LF • 2 Reebok • 2 Technogym**
ELLIPTICAL: **6 Precor**
STEPPER: **3 StairMaster • 2 Reebok • 1 LF**
ROWING: **2 Concept II**
OTHER: **3 Gauntlet • 1 XC Ski**

STRENGTH

FREE WEIGHTS: **Yes**
HAMMER: **Yes**
MACHINES: **18 Cybex & LF**
DUMBBELLS: **5-100 lbs**

SWIM

GRADE: **D-**
SPECS: **4x17yd • Outdoor • 72°**

OTHER

CLASSES: **Yes**
HOURS: M-F **4:30a-9:30p • SAT 7a-7p • SUN 8a-7p**
COST: **$11** • POOL **Free**
TV: **Yes**
EXTRAS: **1/5 mile outdoor track**

Along with an outdoor pool and 1/5 mile outdoor track (faux putting green surface), Westin offers guests workout privileges at the independently-owned University Club for an $11 fee. Inside this smallish facility (separate building), exercisers will be satisfied by a mix of equipment brands and styles. If ever there were a 31-flavor style health club, this place would be it. Though not sporting nearly as many machines as the Houstonian, it offers more variety, almost to the point of confusion with the different brands of treadmills. Most machines are new and in good working order, so once you decide on the ride, it should purr.

The 17-yard cold bath/lap pool, measured by our unofficial pacing, serves as a get-wet option for our desperate, thick-skinned, fishy friends. Those requiring a longer and warmer swim box should drive to 24 Hour Fitness or stay at the Houstonian to begin with. The prices appear fairly comparable.

BRONZE: Intercontinental Hotel

2222 West Loop South, Houston, TX 77027
(713) 627-7600 • houston.intercontinental.com

CARDIO

TREADMILLS: **4 LF**
UPRIGHT BIKE: **1 LF**
RECUMBENT BIKE: **2 LF**
ELLIPTICAL: **2 Precor • 1 LF**
STEPPER: **1 StairMaster**

STRENGTH

MACHINES: **5 Cybex**
DUMBBELLS: **5-50 lbs**

SWIM

SPECS: **Outdoor • Not lap**

OTHER

HOURS: **24**
COST: **Free**
TV: **Yes**

Where the New England Patriots caught their zzz's before their 2004 Super Bowl triumph, the Intercontinental offers upscale accommodations and a full-service fitness center decked out with newly purchased machines in an appealing atmosphere. Within a few blocks of the Galleria, guests can fully gratify their retail cravings as well.

The 5th floor, 24-hour facility scores a touchdown with its healthy supply of equipment but misses the extra point by not providing free weights or Hammer Strength machines. Both Houstonian and Westin confirm their leading stats with a superior number of weight stations.

Lap swimmers should bypass Intercontinental's 5th floor outdoor pool, a family-style, leisure rectangle without lane lines or bottom stripes. 24 Hour Fitness is your best option (~ a mile away).

MODERATELY EXPENSIVE

GOLD: Residence Inn by the Galleria

2500 McCue Street, Houston, TX 77056
(713) 840-9757 • residenceinn.com

This Residence Inn was formerly an apartment complex, which explains its residential location behind several office towers. Within a couple blocks of the Galleria, the Inn recently added 99 rooms via an additional wing. In its core, Residence's suite doors open to interior hallways, while the doors in the new wing open to the outside, giving the property a "motel-ish" appearance.

The floor plans are typical for this Marriott-owned chain, with separate living and sleeping areas, spacious bathrooms and fully equipped kitchenettes. While you may want to cook lunch or dinner, don't worry about breakfast; Residence covers that pro bono with its hearty breakfast buffet.

As a special treat for its athletic-minded guests and in compensation for its pathetic exercise room, Residence provides complimentary passes to the 1-mile away 24 Hour Fitness. On the way over, you will drive past Bally's. Keep the foot on your accelerator, because 24 Hour is a better and nicer club.

Note: Free high-speed internet access is also offered in the rooms.

SILVER: **Hilton Hotel – Post Oak**

2001 Post Oak Boulevard, Houston, TX 77056
(713) 961-9300 • Hilton.com

Make sure you book the right Hilton — only the Post Oak location provides complimentary passes to Bally Total Fitness.

Nothing is fancy about this hotel. The 449 rooms are decorated in a contemporary style with private balconies and standard furnishings. But its workout option separates it from the crowd. When you have free access to an across-the-street Bally Total Fitness, why even pay attention to a less-than-mediocre in-house workout room containing a few pieces of equipment? We wouldn't — and we advise you to do the same.

Don't even think of having the free shuttle take you over — it's less than a 3-minute walk. Be careful crossing the busy street!

LEAST EXPENSIVE

GOLD: **Hampton Inn Galleria**

4500 Post Oak Parkway, Houston, TX 77027
(713) 871-9911 • hamptoninn.com

About a mile away from Galleria's hub, Hampton Inn offers affordable rooms, free local calls and continental breakfasts in a location convenient to the area's businesses and attractions.

The best freebie is the complimentary workout for the way-above-average 24 Hour Fitness located just shy of a mile away. The walk will take 10-15 minutes, so feel free to stroll right by the in-house gym. With 3 cardio pieces and a multi-gym, this little guy does not offer big athletes much. Pick up your "sweat slip" at the front desk and enjoy the gratuitous conditioning at 24 Hour Fitness.

SILVER: **Homestead Suites Galleria**

2300 West Loop South, Houston, TX 77027
(713) 960-9660 • homesteadhotels.com

This property is closer to the Galleria Mall than the Hampton, but its category rival's accommodations are a step above Homestead's. Homestead's guest quarters accommodate extended stays by offering fully equipped kitchens.

However, the 136-room hotel makes our list primarily due to its relationship with 24 Hour Fitness. Approximately one mile away from this Grade "A" full-service health club, Homestead guests can obtain free passes from the front desk.

BEYOND HOTELS GALLERIA AREA/UPTOWN

24 Hour Fitness Super-Sport

1550 Post Oak Boulevard, Houston, TX 77056
(713) 840-1436 • 24hourfitness.com

CARDIO

TREADMILLS: **StarTrac**
UPRIGHT BIKE: **LF**
RECUMBENT BIKE: **LF**
ELLIPTICAL: **Precor**
STEPPER: **StairMaster • LF • Stepmill**
ROWING: **Concept II**

STRENGTH

FREE WEIGHTS: **Yes**
HAMMER: **Yes**
MACHINES: **LF • Free Motion • Nautilus • Life Circuit**
DUMBBELLS: **5-120 lbs**

SWIM

GRADE: **B**
SPECS: **4x25yd • Indoor • 80°**
TOYS: **Kick • Pull • Clock**

OTHER

CLASSES: **Yes**
HOURS: M-TH **24** • F **Closes 11pm** • SAT-SUN **7a-8p**
COST: **Free Residence, Hampton, Homestead • $10 IHRSA • $20 Others**
TV: **Yes**

Rivaling Houstonian's exclusive health club, this elaborate 24 Hour Fitness pushes the exercise industry envelope. New, top-of-the-line equipment is offered in astounding quantities. Close to 30 treadmills, 15 bikes, 11 ellipticals and 10 steppers contribute to 24's cardio collection. Nearly 60 stack-loaded weight stations and 20 Hammer Strength free weight machines decorate the muscle building areas. The entire club conveys a high-energy, urban vibe with bright colors and wide-open spaces.

Swimmers will not be disappointed by 24 Hour's lap pool. Four lanes of 25-yard swimming are divided by floating lane lines and bottom stripes. While we saw no toys on deck, staff assured us that kickboards and pull-buoys are available... somewhere.

We have listed hotels that provide free passes to this stellar workout venue but, if you choose another accommodation, admission is $20 (IHRSA $10).

Bally Total Fitness

1980A South Post Oak Boulevard, Houston, TX 77056
(713) 960-1037 • ballytotalfitness.com

Guests at the Doubletree across the street from this Bally Fitness are entitled to free access with a pass from the hotel. Even though Bally may be closer to your hotel than 24 Hour Fitness, we suggest all but Doubletree guests go to 24 Hour.

More relaxed than most of its clubs, this Bally provides a ton of equipment in a small but hospitable environment. Forty-five stack-loaded weight stations, 20 treadmills and 11 recumbent bikes are a few examples of the breadth of its machines.

It's an executive-size club, so swimmers at Bally Fitness will not find a pool. We suggest that thirsty friends stay at a hotel that has arranged complimentary access to 24 Hour Fitness — unless you do not mind the $20 fee for getting wet in 24's pool.

CARDIO

TREADMILLS: **StarTrac • LF**
UPRIGHT BIKE: **LF**
RECUMBENT BIKE: **LF**
ELLIPTICAL: **LF • Precor**
STEPPER: **Precor**
ROWING: **Schwinn**

STRENGTH

FREE WEIGHTS: **Yes**
HAMMER: **Yes**
MACHINES: **LF • Cybex • Magum • Strive**
DUMBBELLS: **5-100 lbs**

OTHER

CLASSES: **Yes**
HOURS: M-F **5a-9p** • SAT-SUN **8a-8p**
COST: **Free Hilton w/pass • $10 Others**
TV: **Yes**

RUNNING ROUTES

DOWNTOWN

Buffalo Bayou

Buffalo Bayou is more of a "tweener" in terms of locale — between Downtown and Galleria — and offers up to 5+ miles of running fun. The Bayou borders the south end of Memorial Park and the western edge of Downtown. We understand that it is approximately 12 blocks from the Four Seasons and that most hotel staff can point you in the right direction.

Garage Run

A more unusual option for downtown dwellers is what is known as the Garage Run. We heard that the Houston Track Club performs repeat loops up and down the car ramps of an 8-story downtown parking garage, hence the name. Call (713) 977-6626 for information.

Allen Parkway

Bordering Memorial Park and the Buffalo Bayou is Allen Parkway, a local favorite running route. Runners can log 5+ miles on its residential route. From Downtown, pick up the parkway (within a half-mile of hotels, ask your concierge) and head west. Turning around at Shepherd will give you ~6 miles.

GALLERIA

Memorial Park

Memorial Park (I-10W and I-610 at Memorial Drive) sports a 3-mile loop named the Seymour Lieberman Jogging Trail, as well as a 400 meter track within the park. Rice University, which is nearby, boasts a higher quality track. And if you would like a little company, we understand that the Houston running club starts an 8-miler Saturday and Sunday mornings at 8 a.m. (meet at park's pool). As you can tell with the running club's usual distance, Memorial Park's 1,500 acres afford plenty of add-on mileage.

Rice University Area

About 3.5 miles south of Downtown, runners can stride along the 3-mile tree-lined path around Rice University and/or tour around Hermann Park, a Houston cultural and recreational hub. The park not only sports a friendly 2-mile perimeter loop, but it is also home to a golf course, outdoor theatre, zoo, museum and elaborate gardens. Runners in search of more distance can head to the southeast corner of the park (near the golf center) and pick up the 13-mile Bray's Bayou Trail.

INDIANAPOLIS, INDIANA

In the Hoosier state, where entire towns drive for miles to support their local basketball teams, high school and college hoops are king. NBA legend Larry Bird, who grew up in rural French Lick, is this state's crowned prince. And Bobby Knight, love him or hate him, is the Hoosier's most infamous demagogue — though the General's pontificating emanates from Texas since his banishment from Indiana University.

This sports mecca is not all about farm town roundball. A variety of other high profile amateur competitors and Olympic hopefuls make their pilgrimage to the state capital for title shots. Indiana University's Natatorium holds the USA Olympic Swimming Trials and National Championships, the IU Michael Carroll Stadium hosts the National Track and Field Championships, and Downtown's Velodrome sponsors the Indoor Cycling National Championships. Athletic-minded travelers should hold onto their headbands and Speedos: The facilities used for such elite competitions remain open to the public throughout the year! That's right, staying in downtown Indy affords exercise fiends the opportunity to trace the footsteps and swim strokes of previous Gold, Silver and Bronze medal winners. Some accommodations are within a 10-15 minute walk, and all are no more than a short drive away.

With all these star athletes in temporary residence, there must be a strength and endurance facility of equal caliber, right? Absolutely. Indianapolis delivers the goods with its superb National Institute for Fitness and Sport (NIFS).

These access privileges are especially welcome because, with a few exceptions, downtown hotels' fitness prospects are as weak as a marathoner's legs after crossing the finish line. For those who have never experienced noodle limbs after 26.2 miles, trust us — that's weak!

EXPENSIVE

GOLD: Marriott Downtown

350 West Maryland Street, Indianapolis, IN 46225
(317) 822-3500 • marriott.com

CARDIO
TREADMILLS: **6 Cybex**
UPRIGHT BIKE: **2 Cybex**
RECUMBENT BIKE: **2 Cybex**
ELLIPTICAL: **1 Precor**
STEPPER: **1 Cybex**

STRENGTH
MACHINES: **7 Cybex**
DUMBBELLS: **5-40 lbs**

SWIM
SPECS: **Indoor • Not lap**

OTHER
HOURS: **24**
COST: **Free**
TV: **Yes**

This large conventioneer accommodation caters to the business traveler. Located in the heart of downtown Indy, Marriott's 19-story hotel is connected to the Indianapolis Convention Center and the RCA Dome. Boasting 615 guest units, Marriott is far from intimate and cozy. But the hotel does succeed in combining contemporary colored furnishings with down-home charm and service. We certainly noticed and appreciated the "Hoosier hospitality" during our tour. And our caffeine/sugar addiction welcomed a grande, triple-shot, vanilla latte at the in-lobby Starbucks.

Marriott's on-site fitness facility is the best hotel gym in town. Following the accommodation's overriding theme, the 3rd floor center is all business. Although free weights and StairMaster brand steppers are missing, the gym's high-end equipment is recently purchased and in good condition. Three of the 7 new Cybex machines are leg apparatus. And for you night owls, the facility remains open 24 hours.

For those wanting to lap swim or sample an elite gym, walk 10-15 minutes to NIFS and/or the Natatorium. Ask the front desk for specific directions and a map.

SILVER: Westin

50 South Capitol Avenue, Indianapolis, IN 46204
(317) 262-8100 • westin.com

CARDIO
TREADMILLS: **4 LF**
UPRIGHT BIKE: **1 LF**
RECUMBENT BIKE: **1 LF**
ELLIPTICAL: **1 LF**
STEPPER: **1 LifeStep**

STRENGTH
MACHINES: **1 LF Multi**
DUMBBELLS: **5-50 lbs**

SWIM
SPECS: **Indoor • Not lap**

OTHER
HOURS: **24**
COST: **Free**
TV: **Yes**

Also connected to the Indiana Convention Center via skybridge, Westin neighbors the Marriott in the hub of downtown Indianapolis. It's another high-rise business-themed accommodation, with 573 modern and tastefully decorated rooms equipped with the hotel's signature Heavenly Beds and Heavenly Baths. Sleep-deprived guests should expect a night full of zzz's on Westin's high thread count, pillow top, down stuffed dream creators. Shower soakers will enjoy some relaxing wet time with the double-head sprayers.

Room service is 24-hours/day, and so is access to the fitness center. Westin allocated two small rooms for traveling athletes to sweat and muscle pump. Precor and Cybex lovers will be disappointed by the exclusive Life Fitness collection. However, Westin's low mileage cardio machines are a solid and reliable option for endurance junkies. Weight lifters, unfortunately, must settle for dumbbells and a multi-gym or head to NIFS.

Lap swimmers must head to the Natatorium.

Westin is on the cusp of walking distance to these off-site workout options — plan on 15 minutes. NIFS and the Natatorium have ample parking, so driving might be the preferred option, especially in the winter months. While Westin's accommodations are more luxurious than Marriott's, its inferior gym and extra 5-minute walking distance to Indy's spectacular off-site workout options garner it the Silver.

MODERATELY EXPENSIVE

GOLD: Courtyard Downtown

501 West Washington Street, Indianapolis, IN 46204
(317) 635-4443 • courtyard.com

Two Courtyards sit within a half-mile of one another in downtown Indy. Both make the cut so, if you book the wrong one, don't sweat it. As the closest hotel to NIFS and the Natatorium, Courtyard Downtown receives the Gold. When comparing Courtyard's pricing to the previous two listings, consider its free parking — a likely $15-$20/night additional savings. Except for a TGI Friday's restaurant and Hertz rental desk adjacent to the hotel lobby, everything about this property is typical: rooms, amenities and services, including complimentary high-speed internet access. In other words, do not expect to be swept off your feet with a unique experience.

Unfortunately, this Courtyard's on-site gym is also typically paltry. Three forgettable machines placed in a closet-sized room will not provide a proper workout experience. Thank goodness your ETA to NIFS and the Natatorium is a mere 5-7 minutes on foot.

SILVER: Courtyard at the Capitol

320 North Senate Avenue, Indianapolis, IN 46204
(317) 684-7733 • courtyard.com

SILVER: Residence Inn on the Canal

350 West New York Street, Indianapolis, IN 46202
(317) 822-0840 • residenceinn.com

These neighboring properties are 4 blocks away from downtown's main drag but still within walking distance of Indy's restaurants and shopping. The Courtyard at the Capitol runs about $20/night less than the Residence Inn (and $20-$50/night less than Courtyard Downtown) but, if you have a family to feed, the latter's free breakfast each morning will quickly make up the Andrew Jackson. Both offer complimentary parking and typical accommodations for their respective brands.

Courtyard's workout option is slightly more elaborate than Residence Inn's. Both provide equipment in tiny rooms, but Courtyard's bikes and treads (Precor) appear newer and more friendly (foot straps provided).

Since the hotels are both Marriott-owned, staying at one and exercising at the other is an option; however, athletic-minded travelers will surely prefer the 7-10 minute walk to the off-site fitness venues.

LEAST EXPENSIVE

We found no worthy downtown accommodations under $110/night. The hotels priced in this range often charged for parking, which brings the nightly rates into the same "Moderately Expensive" ballpark. More importantly, these same hotels had terrible in-house workout options and are beyond walking distance to NIFS and the Natatorium.

BEYOND HOTELS

National Institute for Fitness & Sport (NIFS)

250 University Boulevard, Indianapolis, IN 46202
(317) 274-3432 • nifs.org

CARDIO

TREADMILLS: **NordicTrack • Cybex**
UPRIGHT BIKE: **LF • Cybex • Fan**
RECUMBENT BIKE: **LF • Cybex**
ELLIPTICAL: **Precor • Cybex • Reebok**
STEPPER: **StairMaster**
ROWING: **Concept II**
OTHER: **XC Ski**

STRENGTH

FREE WEIGHTS: **Yes**
HAMMER: **Yes**
MACHINES: **Cybex • Free Motion**
DUMBBELLS: **3-110 lbs**

OTHER

CLASSES: **Yes**
HOURS: M-TH **5:30a-10p** • F **5:30a-9p** • SAT-SUN **7a-6p**
COST: **$12 • $30/week**
TV: **Yes**
EXTRAS: **1/8 mile indoor track • Basketball**

This spectacular 65,000 square foot facility is nearly as unique as an Olympic gold medal. Most cardio and weight equipment are located in the center of the facility's 6-lane, 1/8 mile, Mondo-surface indoor track. The volume of machines is incredible. There are more than 100 cardio pieces alone!

Equipment highlights include 37 Cybex weight stations, 25 Free Motion weight machines, 12 Precor ellipticals and 10 StairMaster Free Climbers.

The rest of the club is equally impressive. Basketball fans will revere the NBA-size court also located in the center of the indoor track. Free weights, along with several benches and racks, are relegated to a rather cramped, yet sufficient, room. And over 40 fitness classes are offered each week, including cycling, yoga and Pilates.

What does this fitness frenzy cost? Twelve bucks a day or $30/ week. Put it in the trip's budget — you'll be happy you did.

Note: For a sneak peek of this club's innards, check out its website. Also, parking is located in a garage just north of NIFS, adjacent to the Natatorium.

Indiana University Natatorium

901 West New York Street, Indianapolis, IN 46202
(317) 274-3518 • iunat.iupui.edu

SWIM

GRADE: #1 **A** • #2 **B+**
SPECS: #1 **8x50m • Indoor • 78°**
#2 **6x33m • Indoor • 85-88°**
TOYS: **Kick • Pull • Clock**
MASTERS: **Yes • 3x/day**

OTHER

HOURS: **Vary/Call**
COST: **$6**

We were so awed by this facility, we forgot to take notes. No worries, a place like this leaves a lasting imprint. The Natatorium boasts 2, 50-meter pools (1 competition and 1 instructional) and a diving well complete with various height platforms and boards. With 90 American and 11 world records set in these waters, it is no surprise that this pool is considered one of the world's fastest. Your base intervals should be a breeze in this water box and, if you need additional inspiration, imagine the stadium packed with 5,000 screaming fans!

During summers, the competition pool remains at a long course, 50-meter configuration. Throughout the rest of the year, count on 2, 25-yard set-ups. The instructional pool usually remains at 33 meters year round but, at 88°, it is rather warm. If you have a camera crew in tow, they can observe and film via six underwater main pool viewing windows — just like an aquarium!

This place is all about the first-rate pools, so do not expect anything plush from the locker rooms. But at $6/day, we are not complaining (10 visit pass is $24). The "Nat" does offer a small fitness center, but the older machines and rusty weights are not worth your sweat equity, especially given that NIFS is a close neighbor.

Although the pools are closed on Saturdays, lap swim times are available during the other 6 days of the week. Given this facility's caliber, we strongly suggest calling ahead to verify lane availability.

IU Michael A. Carroll Track & Soccer Stadium

1001 West New York Street, Indianapolis, IN 46202
(317) 274-9749 • sportcomplex.iupui.edu

Want to get in a track workout while in Indy? From April to November, you can challenge yourself on one of the fastest outdoor tracks in the world. This truly state-of-the-art facility can accommodate over 12,000 fans and includes a regulation size soccer field inside the 400-meter Mondo-surface oval. To enter, you must pay

$3.50 at the Natatorium reception desk. You can reach the track via a tunnel connecting it to the Natatorium. Four world and 8 American Track and Field records have been broken on these grounds. Imagine your favorite running star racing next to you, and you will best that PR!

RUNNING ROUTES

Canal Walk

While the first rate track at Carroll Stadium will undoubtedly attract sprinters, distance runners will likely prefer Indy's scenic circuits. The Canal Walk runs 11 blocks between 11th and Washington Streets and connects to White River State Park on the west side of White River. Accrue mileage along the Walk and then head to the park, where you will be treated to city views, trails and large grassy areas. The Park is home to many cultural and educational sites including the City's zoo, several museums and a theater. Runners should not miss the half-mile River Promenade located just behind the zoo. This corridor is paved by huge limestone blocks that have famous landmarks carved into them.

White River Greenway

Indianapolis plans to link Downtown and its Canal Walk to the White River Greenway's miles of trails. As it stands, to reach the wonderfully peaceful 5+ mile Central Canal Towpath, runners must clock about 3-4 miles. 30th Street is the nearest access point to the path's southern end — near Riverside Park, which is also a great venue. If you fancy a beautiful, wooded course, consult with your hotel for the best route — it is northwest of Downtown.

Jacksonville

JACKSONVILLE, FLORIDA

If this up-and-coming town failed to serve up a good workout option, we could then cleverly write, "This town doesn't have Jack!" Get it? Alas, the few hotels in downtown "Jax," as natives call it, provide decent exercise alternatives of their own or have arrangements in place with nearby health clubs.

Frequently found on "best cities to live in" lists, Jacksonville can rightfully brag about its miles of beautiful beaches, gorgeous weather, incredible golf courses and vibrant city center. Jacksonville Landing and Southbank Riverwalk are two shopping, dining and entertainment venues that anchor Downtown's ongoing revitalization.

However, with only 5 hotels dotting the landscape, Jax had better pick up its pace. Where are all the 2005 Superbowl fans going to stay? Those hunting for a room that particular February weekend may end up exclaiming, "This town doesn't have Jack!"

24 Locations Reviewed

DOWNTOWN

MODERATELY EXPENSIVE

GOLD: **Omni**

245 Water Street, Jacksonville, FL 32202
(904) 355-6664 • omnihotels.com

CARDIO

TREADMILLS: **2 Precor**
RECUMBENT BIKE: **1 Precor**
ELLIPTICAL: **2 Precor**

STRENGTH

MACHINES: **3 Cybex**
DUMBBELLS: **10-50 lbs**

OTHER

EXTRAS: **$10/day YMCAs**

This is a very nice Omni, but we have seen nicer (Chicago, Atlanta, San Diego). The 16-story hotel sits in downtown's business district and is the closest accommodation to two YMCAs. The rooms are classically appointed with puffy comforters and cherry wood furniture. Traveling with a friend of the four-legged kind? Sharing your bed is encouraged, but ordering room service is not. And Omni retracts the welcome mat for furry ones tipping the scales over 25 lbs.

As for your workout, in Summer 2004 as part of a hotel-wide renovation, Omni embarked upon a complete overhaul of its exercise facility, expanding the size and purchasing new equipment. The changes further enhance Omni's top ranking. Most equipment is Precor and a few of the cardio machines have TVs attached.

Meanwhile you have two additional options—each costing $10/day. Either walk across the street to the Bank of America Building YMCA (closed weekends), or jog/drive an approximate mile to the full-service Yates YMCA. Our recommendation depends on what is most important to you. Budget concerns? Sweat for free at the hotel. Looking for size and variety? Go to Yates. Finally, if Omni's gym does not satisfy and Yates is too far, head across the street (remember, weekdays only).

SILVER: **Hyatt Regency**

225 Coast Line Drive East, Jacksonville, FL 32202
(904) 633-9095 • hyatt.com

CARDIO

TREADMILLS: **6 LF**
UPRIGHT BIKE: **2 LF**
RECUMBENT BIKE: **2 LF**
STEPPER: **2 LF**

STRENGTH

MACHINES: **9 LF**

SWIM

SPECS: **Outdoor • Not lap**

OTHER

HOURS: **6a-11p**
COST: **Free**
TV: **Yes**

Close to Alltel Stadium, this 966-room Hyatt was a sensible choice as host hotel for the 2005 Super Bowl. The property offers views of the St. John's River and is within walking distance of Jacksonville Landing's amusements. If you are really organized, check out jacksonvillelanding.com, where you can request a coupon book prior to your visit.

Guest rooms are decorated in a Floridian

style that we have never been fond of. Light wood, pastel colors and flowery prints appear cheap during the day and ugly at night. On the upside, we do like the look of the fitness center's equipment.

While the room is not very attractive, the quality and selection of equipment are. The 19th floor views aren't too shabby, either. Newer treadmills and recent-model uprights, recumbents and steppers round out a solid cardio offering. We also appreciate the large number of Life Fitness weight stations, but Hyatt dropped the medicine ball by failing to purchase ellipticals, dumbbells or free weights.

Swimmers must drive less than 5 minutes to the Yates YMCA, as Hyatt's outdoor pool is not a lapper.

BRONZE: Hilton Riverfront

1201 Riverplace Boulevard, Jacksonville, FL 32207
(904) 398-8800 • hilton.com

Along with Hampton Inn and Radisson, Hilton's property is located on the south shore of the St. John's River — across the water from downtown Jacksonville. Because these properties are more isolated from the City's hubbub, they are often priced lower than their 'cross River competition.

Guest room balconies and the on-site Ruth's Chris' Steakhouse are unique features of an otherwise ordinary Hilton. Request a north facing room and you will be treated to a tremendous skyline with river views.

CARDIO
TREADMILLS: **2 Landice**
UPRIGHT BIKE: **3 LF**
STEPPER: **3 LF**

STRENGTH
MACHINES: **1 Multi**

SWIM
SPECS: **Outdoor • Not lap**

OTHER
HOURS: **24**
COST: **Free**
TV: **Yes**
EXTRAS: **$5 pass to Univ. Club**

The in-house gym is open 24 hours but not recommended. Other than Life Fitness 9100 upright bikes, we were disappointed with the equipment offering. Instead, walk down the driveway to the adjacent Riverplace Tower, pay $5 and exercise in the petite University Athletic Club. It's worth the Abe Lincoln.

Swimmers will have to drive 5 minutes to the Yates YMCA.

LEAST EXPENSIVE

GOLD: Hampton Inn I-95 Central

1331 Prudential Drive, Jacksonville, FL 32207
(904) 396-7770 • hamptoninn.com

On the south river bank (see Hilton, above), the Hampton has nothing special and no workout room on-site. But freebies, as usual, are on its menu. Guests receive complimentary continental breakfasts and passes to the University Athletic Club in the Riverplace Tower across the street.

Those looking for a more elaborate workout or a lap swim session should drive 5 minutes to the Yates YMCA.

SILVER: **Radisson Riverwalk Hotel**
1515 Prudential Drive, Jacksonville, FL 32207
(904) 396-5100 • radisson.com

CARDIO
TREADMILLS: **2 Precor - old**
UPRIGHT BIKE: **1 Tectrix - old**
RECUMBENT BIKE: **3 Tectrix - old**
STEPPER: **1 Tectrix - old**

STRENGTH
DUMBBELLS: **5-15 lbs**

SWIM
SPECS: **Outdoor • Not lap**

OTHER
HOURS: **24**
COST: **Free**
TV: **Yes**
EXTRAS: **$5 pass to Univ. Club**

"Budget accommodations at a budget price" is what came to mind while touring this South Bank property. Despite Radisson's comparable rooms and two outdoor tennis courts, we still favor Hampton because of its freebies.

The Radisson does have a workout room, but make like an amnesiac and forget about it — the 7 decrepit cardio machines will hopefully soon find a home in the fitness hall of yesteryear. For a convenient sweat session at a tiny gym, consider a 5-minute walk to the University Club ($5). Swimmers and serious workout fiends should know the drill by now — head to the Yates Y (5-minute drive).

BEYOND HOTELS DOWNTOWN

Yates YMCA
221 Riverside Avenue, Jacksonville, FL 32202
(904) 355-1436 • firstcoastymca.org/yates

CARDIO
TREADMILLS: **Precor**
UPRIGHT BIKE: **Precor • Fan**
RECUMBENT BIKE: **Precor**
ELLIPTICAL: **Precor**
STEPPER: **Precor • Stepmill**
ROWING: **Concept II**

STRENGTH
FREE WEIGHTS: **Yes**
HAMMER: **Yes**
MACHINES: **Cybex • Paramount • BodyMaster**
DUMBBELLS: **5-125 lbs**

SWIM
GRADE: **C+**
SPECS: **4x25yd • Indoor • 85°**
TOYS: **Kick • Pull • Clock**

OTHER
CLASSES: **Yes**
HOURS: M-TH **5:30a-9:30p** • F **5:30a-8p** • SAT **7a-6p** • SUN **12-6p**
COST: **$10 • $25/week**
TV: **Yes**
EXTRAS: **1/6 mile outdoor track • Racquetball • Basketball • Cafe**

About a mile from the Omni Hotel and 1-1/2 miles from the other hotels listed, this 70,000 square foot YMCA has everything athletic travelers desire at a reasonable $10 price. For those setting up camp in Jacksonville for a longer stay, the Y offers a $25 weekly pass as well.

Before entering this worthy facility, runners will notice a 1/6 mile outdoor running loop that partially follows the north bank of the St. John's River. Inside, fitness-minded folk will find the club loaded with a variety of fresh equipment in a bright and friendly atmosphere. The new and finely tuned cardio machines are almost exclusively Precor. We counted 16 ellipticals, 14 treads, 7 recumbents, 4 uprights and 4 steppers. Balancing this tiptop selection is an ample amount of weight equipment, including at least 10 Paramount machines, several pulley systems and plenty of free weights.

Though the lap pool craves some "TLC," it is certainly better than average. Swimmers flutter in 4 lanes divided by floating lines and bottom stripes. At 85 degrees, the water was a little warm, but definitely not too hot to handle. We noticed the cheaper Styrofoam-type pull-buoys, but the kickboards seemed stiff and the pace clock functioned properly.

YMCA at the Bank of America Tower

50 North Laura Street, Jacksonville, FL 32202
(904) 356-9622 • firstcoastymca.org/bankofamerica.htm

This smaller, executive-size club primarily services the 9-5 white-collar crowd employed in the neighboring downtown office buildings. As a result of its target market, this corporate Y closes on weekends. Visitors not belonging to another Y must pay $10/day for access, but it is a reasonable fee for what is given in return.

Although the club is tiny by Y standards, management has squeezed as much equipment as possible into the "L"-shaped facility. To give you a better sense of its size, we counted a total of 18 cardio machines, 18 stack-loaded weight stations, 2 free weight benches and a pulley system. Most of the machines have been on duty for a year or two, but all appear to be operating well.

Swimmers, no way can a pool fit inside this club. Go to Yates.

CARDIO
TREADMILLS: **StairMaster**
UPRIGHT BIKE: **Stratus • Tectrix**
RECUMBENT BIKE: **Stratus**
ELLIPTICAL: **Precor**
STEPPER: **StairMaster**
ROWING: **Concept II**

STRENGTH
FREE WEIGHTS: **Yes**
HAMMER: **Yes**
MACHINES: **Cybex • BodyMaster**
DUMBBELLS: **5-100 lbs**

OTHER
CLASSES: **Yes**
HOURS: M-F **5:30a-8p** • SAT-SUN **Closed**
COST: **$10**
TV: **Yes**

University Athletic Club at Riverplace Towers

1301 Riverplace Boulevard, Jacksonville, FL 32207
(904) 399-3011 • uc-jacksonville.com/athletics

As the off-site option for the South Bank hotels (Hilton, Hampton and Radisson), University Club is a very, very small gym. All on one level, we estimate the floor space to be about the same size as half a tennis court. Luckily, passage to this petite play is peanuts at $5/day.

The amount of equipment is limited, but adequate to get you through a satisfactory workout. Unfortunately, most of the weight machines are air pressurized, no doubt cheaper than the typical

CARDIO

TREADMILLS: **StarTrac**
UPRIGHT BIKE: **StarTrac**
RECUMBENT BIKE: **StarTrac**
ELLIPTICAL: **Precor • StarTrac**
STEPPER: **StairMaster • StarTrac • Tectrix**
OTHER: **Gravitron**

STRENGTH

FREE WEIGHTS: **Yes**
MACHINES: **Keiser Air Press**
DUMBBELLS: **5-50 lbs**

OTHER

CLASSES: **Yes**
HOURS: M-F **6a-8p** • SAT **9a-1p** • SUN **Closed**
COST: **Free Hampton Inn • $5 Others**
TV: **Yes**

stack-loaded series. Free weights and dumbbells are here, thankfully and they compensate for some of the weight machine disappointment.

Showers and toiletries are provided, so you may clean up on-site.

Note: This Club has limited hours on Saturdays and is closed on Sundays.

PONTE VEDRA BEACH

Ponte Vedra Inn & Club

200 Ponte Vedra Boulevard, Ponte Vedra Beach, FL 32082
(904) 285-1111 • pvresorts.com

The Lodge and Club at Ponte Vedra Beach

607 Ponte Vedra Boulevard, Ponte Vedra Beach, FL 32082
(904) 273-9500 • pvresorts.com

Ponte Vedra Inn & Club

CARDIO

TREADMILLS: **10 Cybex**
UPRIGHT BIKE: **2 Cybex**
RECUMBENT BIKE: **3 Cybex**
ELLIPTICAL: **7 Precor**
STEPPER: **3 StairMaster**
ROWING: **2 Concept II**

STRENGTH

FREE WEIGHTS: **Yes**
HAMMER: **Yes**
MACHINES: **22 Cybex**
DUMBBELLS: **3-100 lbs**

SWIM

GRADE: **B+**
SPECS: **4x25yd pre-expansion • Outdoor • 80°**
TOYS: **Kick • Pull**

OTHER

CLASSES: **Yes**
HOURS: M-F **5:30a-9p** • SAT **5:30a-8p** • SUN **7a-8p**
COST: **$15** • POOL **Free**
TV: **Yes**

If you are in the hunt for a luxurious beach and golf destination that offers state-of-the-art workout facilities, look no further than the Inn or Lodge at Ponte Vedra.

These sister properties are located about 20 miles southeast of Jacksonville on the Atlantic Ocean shores. Within 2 miles of one another, each provides unique, first-class accommodations. The larger Inn showcases its 250 units in low-rise Floridian buildings, while the more intimate 66-room Lodge differentiates itself with a Mediterranean flair. Both hotels continually receive stellar reviews and have collected numerous travel industry awards.

Since this is primarily a fitness book, we will stick to the fitness options and let you have fun exploring these resorts' features online. The exercise centers are similar in size and quality, so guests will receive a lot of bang for their $15/day.

The brand-new high-end equipment in the two immaculate facilities will surely satisfy. An added bonus at the Inn's gym is the endless Atlantic Ocean views, giving it a leg up over the Lodge in the atmosphere category. Classes are offered at both, including aerobics and cycling.

Swimmers are not left out of the fitness festivities, as both resorts boast serious lap-swim options at no cost. Swimmers will happily find floating lane lines and bottom stripes along with kickboards and pull-buoys. Again, the Inn "one-ups" the Lodge with its dramatic ocean setting. In addition, a new pool is expected to be completed June 2004 adding 4 more 25-yard lanes. Its setting should be as spectacular as the existing 4 lane, 25-yard lap option.

While we relished the seclusion of the Lodge, we prefer the Inn for its superior fitness center, proximity to the golf courses and spa (Lodge guests must commute there to golf and get massaged) and greater selection of dining options. We only wish the two resorts resisted charging their guests a $15 gym access fee. At least the pools are free.

Note: Because these two stellar facilities sport similar machine counts of top-level brands and worthy swim venues, we are listing the details for the Inn only.

RUNNING ROUTES

DOWNTOWN

St. John's River

For downtowners, the St. John's River area provides a nice out-and-back venue that can add up to over 10 miles. There is also a smaller 2-mile loop that is popular.

Keep in mind that the River divides the North and South Banks, and there are several convenient crossing points. In addition, Friendship Park on the south side is a good landmark. The Yates YMCA also provides running maps of several other routes.

Omni Route

The downtown Omni hotel provides a map, but the general route is: Water Street to the Acosta Bridge, to Mary to San Marcos to Prudential Drive to Main Street Bridge to Jacksonville landing. While it's not too exciting, the views from the bridges should put a smile on your face. If you find the route confusing, ask the front desk for a map — even if you're not staying at the hotel (they won't know, right?)

You can also add the Yates YMCA's 1/6 mile outdoor track to your run for some interval work. It's adjacent to their outdoor parking lot and free to use.

BEYOND JACKSONVILLE

Jacksonville Beach

Jacksonville Beach is flat and provides miles of meditative running. It's about 15 miles east of Downtown — in your backyard if you're staying at the Ponte Vedra Inn or Lodge.

KANSAS CITY, MISSOURI

As Americans, we expect everything NOW. We like quick cars, fast food, short lines and rapid transit. But when it comes to cooking barbecue, natives of this Midwest town will attest that sloow-ww roastin' is the way to go!

With more BBQ restaurants per capita than any other city in the country, K.C. is the capital of all things lip smackin' and chin dribblin'. Like Hoosiers and their basketball rims, finding a Kansas City native without a backyard grill, smoker or pit is a difficult task indeed. Since the first Kansas City BBQ smoke signals went up in 1908, locals have whiled away countless hours basting and marinating, hoping to discover that perfect sauce for fall-off-the-bone meat.

Every October, smokin' hot shots from around the country come here to compete in the American Royal Barbecue Contest. Not just any slab smacker can sign up for the fun, however. Only winners from state qualifiers can participate in the invitational division. And the open event, now limited to 400 teams, commands an ever-increasing waiting list of hopefuls salivating to square off in this moo and oink extravaganza. With beefy prize packages totaling more than $65,000 in BBQ stained cash, earning the coveted Grand Champion title can mean more than prestige. After winning the first contest in 1980, psychiatrist Rich Davis "shrunk" his medical practice to market his champion sauce, KC's Masterpiece — he's doing pretty well.

Leave your hurries and worries behind and savor your time in this easygoin', finger-lickin' city. Sampling the local slow-fired fare proves that patience can be a mouth watering vir-chew!

EXPENSIVE

GOLD: Fairmont at The Plaza

401 Ward Parkway, Kansas City, MO 64112
(816) 756-1500 • fairmont.com/kansascity

CARDIO

TREADMILLS: **3 Precor**
UPRIGHT BIKE: **1 Tectrix • 1 Fan • 1 Spin**
ELLIPTICAL: **2 Precor • 1 Schwinn**
STEPPER: **1 Tectrix • 1 StairMaster - old**

STRENGTH

MACHINES: **1 Multi**
DUMBBELLS: **10-60 lbs**

SWIM

SPECS: **Outdoor • Not lap**

OTHER

HOURS: **24**
COST: **Free**
TV: **Yes**

We really like this hotel. Sitting on a small hill overlooking Brush Creek and nearby Country Club Plaza's upscale shops and restaurants, this Fairmont often hosts professional athletic teams in town for a game. Fairmont's understated luxury and proximity to Kansas City's best shopping, dining and entertainment attractions earn it a tie for the Gold. Even when business Downtown brings us to K.C., we seek a room in the higher rent Country Club Plaza district. All 366 guest quarters are elegantly decorated with contemporary furnishings, pillow top mattresses, marble baths and phenomenal views. High-speed internet access (surcharge) is provided for the business traveler, and 24-hour room service is available for those late night munchies.

Fairmont's in-house gym is not going to wow you, so we could not give it the all-out victory (see Westin). It is rather small and cramped with machines, but several standouts will service a worthwhile cardio or rudimentary strength routine. All treadmills are in great shape, the ellipticals have been recently purchased, and the upright bikes will suffice. Strength enthusiasts must bear the brunt of the center's shortcomings, as no stack-loaded stations or free weights are here. A multi-gym is the primary weight-bearing apparatus, in addition to a decent range of dumbbells. Though the gym is attended only from 6 a.m. to 2:30 p.m., your room key provides access 24 hours a day.

Swimmers and those wanting a more elaborate workout should head to UMKC's Recreation Center — a 3-minute drive or 10-minute jog away (at 1.25 miles, it's a bit far to comfortably walk, especially in the winter). Additionally, swimmers have another option, driving 5-10 minutes to the Tony Aguirre Community Center.

Those wanting a closer weight training option can head to Universal Fitness instead of UMKC (5-minute walk). Bottom line, if you don't mind commuting to the off-site workout venues, stay in this preferred neighborhood. However, if you want a better gym in your hotel and don't care about the surrounding area, book the Westin.

GOLD: Westin Crown Center

1 Pershing Road, Kansas City, MO 64108
(816) 474-4400 • westin.com/kansascity

CARDIO	
TREADMILLS:	**4 LF • 1 Precor • 1 True**
UPRIGHT BIKE:	**1 LF • 4 LF - old**
RECUMBENT BIKE:	**3 Cybex • 3 LF**
ELLIPTICAL:	**2 LF • 1 Precor**
STEPPER:	**3 LF • 2 StairMaster - old**
ROWING:	**1 Concept II**

STRENGTH	
FREE WEIGHTS:	**Yes**
MACHINES:	**17 Nautilus**
DUMBBELLS:	**3-70 lbs**

SWIM	
GRADE:	**B-**
SPECS:	**3x25yd • Outdoor • 82-85°**
TOYS:	**Kick**

OTHER	
HOURS:	M-F **6a-10p** • SAT-SUN **7a-10p**
COST:	**$7** • POOL **Free**
TV:	**Yes**
EXTRAS:	**Tennis**

While Westin, hands down, boasts the best hotel gym in urban Kansas City, the accommodation's "convention-ish" vibe and less exciting location weaken its appeal. Westin is somewhat separated from downtown's business district (1.5 miles north) and Country Club Plaza's unique shopping and entertainment venues (~3 miles south). While this area features pleasant landscapes, grassy knolls and beautiful trees (not in February, of course!), its cookie-cutter mall and two theaters are not big draws for out-of-towners. This Starwood brand behemoth offers 729 contemporary rooms with pleasing Westin comforts, including its trademark Heavenly Beds. Guests can also count on 24-hour room service to cure those late night hunger pains.

Unlike Fairmont's workout room, this facility will wow you. Eleven brand-new Life Fitness cardio pieces complete with 15-inch plasma screens were added to Westin's stock in March 2004, and additional machines are scheduled for replacement by January 2005. Westin's facility was not in dire need of plastic surgery, but we always welcome a makeover! Muscle heads don't despair. It's not all about endurance in this gym. Plenty of free weights line the separate strength room, and close to 20 stack-loaded weight stations operate with ease.

Rounding out the fitness party, Westin's 25-yard lap pool will entertain swimmers' water aspirations. While 3 lanes are marked with bottom stripes, only one floating line divides the surface. Nevertheless, it is the best *hotel* lap pool in K.C.

In short, stay here if fashionable Country Club Plaza's 5-mile distance from downtown's business center is too far away, or if you desire a full-service fitness facility on premise.

Note: Guests are charged an annoying $7/day to use this fitness facility. The pool is free.

MODERATELY EXPENSIVE

GOLD: Residence Inn C.C. Plaza

4601 Broadway Boulevard, Kansas City, MO 64112
(816) 753-0033 • residenceinn.com

Location, location, location! Residence Inn occupies prime real estate within steps of Country Club Plaza's coffee shops, cafes and swank shops. Although staying here puts you 5 miles away from downtown's business district, we believe this area's attractions are worth the trade-off.

This Marriott brand really knows how to shower guests with comps. Free high-speed internet access, gratis hot breakfasts each morning, weekday happy hours serving complimentary cocktails and free parking are examples. Accommodations with kitchenettes and separate living/sleeping areas top off a very convenient stay.

While the workout room is bare-bones with its one multi-gym, step machine and treadmill, Residence is within a 10-minute jog to UMKC's Recreation Center (plan a) and a 3-minute walk to Universal Fitness Club (plan b).

Swimmers can also consider the Tony Aguirre Community Center (plan c — a 5-10 minute drive).

SILVER: Hyatt Regency

2345 McGee Street, Kansas City, MO 64108
(816) 421-1234 • crowncenter.hyatt.com

CARDIO

TREADMILLS: **4 LF**
UPRIGHT BIKE: **2 LF**
RECUMBENT BIKE: **2 LF**
ELLIPTICAL: **3 LF**
STEPPER: **1 StairMaster - old**
ROWING: **Yes**

STRENGTH

MACHINES: **1 Multi**
DUMBBELLS: **5-50 lbs**

SWIM

GRADE: **D**
SPECS: **1x18yd • Outdoor • 82°**

OTHER

HOURS: **5:30a-10p**
COST: **Free**
TV: **Yes**

Hyatt's large convention hotel suffers the same address challenge as the Westin: Most business action is 12 blocks north, and most shopping and entertainment hoopla is 24 blocks south. Nevertheless, Hyatt's 731 guest quarters and its gym will please your senses. And the attached walkway to Crown Center does afford a number of mall shopping and dining options, including Morton's Steakhouse.

A separate elevator bank transports exercisers to Hyatt's gratis fitness center, which is outfitted with a fair number of new machines. Endurance junkies receive the most attention, with an ample assortment of well-maintained cardio stations. However, weight enthusiasts are this gym's second class citizens. No free weights or separate stack-loaded weight stations are supplied, and the multi-gym is hardly "multi-purposeful."

For swimmers, Hyatt's outdoor water square, with no floating lane lines (it does have a bottom stripe), stretches a meager 56 feet

(~18 yards). So, some short distance lapping is possible here, but hard core swimmers will want to take a dip off site.

Those wanting a full-service workout or a real lap venue should head to UMKC (5-10 minute drive). Swimmers should also consider the closer Tony Aguirre Community Center (5-minute drive).

LEAST EXPENSIVE

GOLD: **Homestead Studio Suites** C.C. Plaza

4535 Main Street, Kansas City, MO 64111
(816) 531-2212 • homesteadhotels.com/plz

GOLD: **Holiday Inn** C.C. Plaza

One East 45th Street, Kansas City, MO 64111
(816) 753-7400 • ichotelsgroup.com

These Country Club Plaza neighbors are budget friendly, so don't hold out for lavish accommodations or a sparkling fitness center. Guests can expect tidy rooms and a perfect home base to enjoy this posh Kansas City neighborhood.

Homestead's front desk clerk heads home after midnight, but the complete kitchens and free local calls are available 24 hours. And free passes to Solid Fitness — a small gym only 4 blocks away — are offered to athletic-minded guests as compensation for Homestead's missing on-site workout room. UMKC is also a short drive or jog away.

The larger and slightly nicer Holiday Inn costs a bit more but offers free continental breakfasts each morning. Its on-site sweat option contains 2 treads, 1 recumbent bike, 1 step machine and a multi-gym. However, only the treads are in good condition. Taking your sweat off-site will cost $10 ($7 IHRSA), since Holiday Inn does not offer free passes to Solid Fitness. Similar to Homestead, Holiday Inn is within a 3-minute drive or 10-minute jog to UMKC's Recreation Center.

Swimmers can also drive 5-10 minutes to the Tony Aguirre Community Center for some lap action.

BEYOND HOTELS

University of Missouri/Kansas City (UMKC) Recreation Center

5030 Holmes, Kansas City, MO 64110
(816) 235-1772 • umkc/src.edu

CARDIO

TREADMILLS: **Woodway • Quinton**
UPRIGHT BIKE: **LF**
RECUMBENT BIKE: **LF**
ELLIPTICAL: **Precor**
STEPPER: **Precor • StairMaster**
ROWING: **Yes**

STRENGTH

FREE WEIGHTS: **Yes**
HAMMER: **Yes**
MACHINES: **Medex**
DUMBBELLS: **3-100 lbs**

SWIM

GRADE: **B**
SPECS: **6x25yd • Indoor • 80-84°**
TOYS: **Kick • Pull • Clock**

OTHER

CLASSES: **Yes**
HOURS: **Vary**
COST: **$5**
TV: **No**
EXTRAS: **1/8 mile indoor track • 1/4 mile outdoor track • Basketball**

This university athletic complex houses everything from a 6 lane, 25-yard competition swimming pool to an indoor 1/8 mile track. When the weather cooperates, the 1/4 mile outdoor track next door is a great addition. Like most university guest policies, non-student visitors seeking access to the center are, technically, supposed to show up with an enrolled co-ed as a "sponsor." But the kids here are pretty relaxed; if you hold out your $5 and tell the undergrad at the counter you need a sponsor, he or she will find someone nearby to do the honors. Skeptical of the process, we discussed it with staff on several occasions and were assured that getting inside should not be a problem. If you encounter any resistance, just inform reception that a sponsor was "found" for you on previous occasions.

Finding the complex can be tricky, so we have included directions in place of our usual witty description of the center's innards. Suffice it to say, the place has everything you will need for a complete workout — though we recommend an expansion and makeover for the drab fitness room décor.

Directions: East on Volker Blvd.; south on Oak St.; east on 50th St.; south on Cherry; park in the first lot on the right in the metered spaces. Walk east across the street and north of the outdoor track (track will be on your right); the Recreation Center is adjacent to the track. Proceed up the stairs and down the hallway to your left; the check-in counter will be at the corner on your right. See, it is quite the treasure hunt, but there is gold at the end of this rainbow. Okay, maybe silver!

Solid Fitness

4711 Central, Kansas City, Mo. 64112
(816) 960-1077 • solidpft.com

The key selling point for this petite club is its ideal location in the heart of Country Club Plaza. Judging by the look of its equipment selection (heavy on weights/light on cardio), the club caters to a weightlifting clientele. When we visited, though, steroid-enhanced "meathead" types were nowhere to be found. Club staff and members were particularly friendly and interested in ensuring our satisfaction and wellbeing. At $10/day, admission is reasonable.

Though many of its endurance machines are Solid's own brand, a few familiar Precor and Life Fitness friends are here, too. Strength enthusiasts will be most satisfied with Universal's free weights, plate-loaded machines, stack-loaded stations and dumbbell selection. Spinning classes are offered three times a week and there are other aerobic and yoga programs. Towels, toiletries and headsets are provided — we just wish they had a few more high-end cardio pieces.

CARDIO

TREADMILLS: **Quinton • Universal**
UPRIGHT BIKE: **Universal**
RECUMBENT BIKE: **Universal**
ELLIPTICAL: **Precor**
STEPPER: **LF • Universal**
ROWING: **Concept II**

STRENGTH

FREE WEIGHTS: **Yes**
HAMMER: **Yes**
MACHINES: **Universal • LF • Free Motion**
DUMBBELLS: **3-90 lbs**

OTHER

CLASSES: **Yes**
HOURS: M-TH **6a-10p** • F **6a-8p** • SAT **8a-6p** • SUN **10a-6p**
COST: **Free Homestead • $7 IHRSA • $10 Others**
TV: **Yes**

Tony Aguirre Community Center

2950 W. Pennway, Kansas City, MO 64108
(816) 784-1300 • kcmo.org/parks.nsf/web/centers

We are patting ourselves on the back for finding this little gem of a pool. Although driving is required, the empty parking lot during lap swim hours is a good indicator of how crowded this place gets — not very!

Despite its short 5-10 minute drive from most Kansas City hotels, the head lifeguard informed us that adult lap swimmers are as rare as a Chicago Cubs World Series appearance. For $2, water worshippers will likely secure a personal lane and enjoy full use of the provided kickboards, pull-buoys and Zoomers. Floating lane lines and bottom stripes guide the way through these calm and often uncharted waters.

Remember, this is a community center. Especially during the summer, call to ensure that a gaggle of rambunctious kids is not going to add P- to your -ool.

Note: Towels and locks are not provided, but most swimmers leave their bags on deck, and the facility is closed Sundays.

SWIM

GRADE: **B**
SPECS: **2x25yd • Indoor • 84°**
TOYS: **Kick • Pull • Fins**

OTHER

HOURS: M/W: **12:30p-7p** • T/TH/F/SAT: **12:30p-5:45p** • SUN **Closed**
COST: **$2**

RUNNING ROUTES

Country Club Plaza

Another positive for this neighborhood is the running routes. Eighty-acre Loose Park and its awesome rose garden, located several blocks south of the Plaza, offer runners several 1+ mile loops. Head west of Loose to pick up Ward Parkway, which will introduce you to one of K.C.'s glitziest neighborhoods. The greenway running down its middle goes from 55th to 75th Street and is popular with the local running club. For longer mileage, consider linking the street car trail (SE end of CC Plaza) to the Brush Creek Waterway.

Crown Center

Washington Park is right near the hotels and looping it will accrue a measly mile or so. While Penn Valley Park behind the Liberty Memorial is an attractive green space and home to the City's first dog park ("Bark Park"), striders' best bet is running the 2.5 miles south along Main Street to Country Club Plaza. It's a busy street with a lot of traffic, so be careful going to and fro.

LAS VEGAS, NEVADA

With all of your drinking, gambling, buffet-eating and second-hand smoke inhaling in Vegas, your heart and arteries are gonna be beggin' for a workout to purge those sins! In this land of bigger is better, you are among the largest resorts in the world — and some of the best hotel workout centers in the country. So take advantage of them. Think how much more you will enjoy that filet and Cosmo with a solid conditioning under your belt.

If you subscribe to the philosophy that "what happens in Vegas stays in Vegas," a daily detox will ensure you don't bring any extra pounds home, either. It's Vegas, baby! Work out hard, play hard!

ALL PRICE CATEGORIES

If you are familiar with Vegas, you know that room pricing for casinos located on the "Strip" (Las Vegas Blvd.) can be all over the map. Depending on conventions, special events, season and promotional offers, the most expensive hotel one week can be the cheapest the next. As a result, our price categories are not relevant for this unique city. Leaving the rate research to you, we have instead listed accommodations in order of the appeal and caliber of each on-site workout option.

To further simplify your fitness quest, we have excluded the usual room descriptions. With the exception of the all-suite Venetian, our recommended properties provide very similar quality accommodations. In addition, all hotels maintain comprehensive websites fully describing their rooms and amenities — some with a 360 degree tour. And this is Vegas! How much time are you going to be spending in your room, anyway?

When checking into your hotel, request a coupon book from guest services. Almost every hotel provides these free money savers. While most of it is junk, a few goodies are usually in the mix. In particular, you may find free passes to the hotel's health club. And, since all Strip hotels charge a fairly substantial fee to work out (unless you have already paid for a spa or salon service that same day), this freebie can be valuable. Daily workout tariffs typically fall into the $20–$30 range, with a few locations offering multi-day discounts. For example, Luxor charges its guests $20/day, but the coupon book yielded 2 free passes with no strings attached. Now that's our type of deal!

#1 Mirage Hotel & Casino

3400 Las Vegas Boulevard South, Las Vegas, NV 89109
(702) 791-7111 • mirage.com

CARDIO

TREADMILLS: **8 StarTrac**
UPRIGHT BIKE: **2 Cybex**
RECUMBENT BIKE: **2 Cybex**
ELLIPTICAL: **2 Precor • 1 Cybex • 1 SciFit**
STEPPER: **2 Cybex**

STRENGTH

FREE WEIGHTS: **Yes**
MACHINES: **21 Cybex**
DUMBBELLS: **5-80 lbs**

SWIM

GRADE: **B**
SPECS: **3x25m • Outdoor • 81-85°**

OTHER

HOURS: GYM **6a–7p** • POOL **9a–5p**
COST: **$20**
TV: **Yes**

Thanks to one ornery tiger, Siegfried and Roy are no longer here, but fortunately the fantastic fitness center, spa and pool remain. Distinguished by its erupting volcano, Mirage's location next to Caesar's Palace Shopping Mall and across the street from the Venetian Resort is a perfect center-of-the-strip location.

Mirage's exercise tax is $20/day, a difficult pill to swallow, we know. But go ahead and take the medicine, because this facility will patch you up in no time. Mirage's large, light, beige-toned room contains an abundance of unbelievably new strength apparatus, including 21 Cybex weight stations, a wide assortment of dumbbells, fixed weight barbells and plenty of free weights for bench press and squat exercises. Equally impressive is the number of high quality cardio machines, all equipped with personal plasma televisions and headphones. While most of the endurance units are manufactured by Cybex (including the fabulous Arc Trainer elliptical), Mirage adds variety with its StarTrac treadmills and Precor ellipticals. Spa attendants circulate to meet all your conditioning needs, so don't even think of getting off that treadmill for a towel or water — have it delivered.

Outside, on the far end of the main pool, 3 lanes of 25-meter lap swimming are available. The pool is well marked with bottom stripes and floating lines, so don't fret the "daytime cocktail" crowd infringing upon your underwater meditation. The pool hours vary by season, but we were assured that it is open year round. Bring your watch for any intervals, because any pace clock is a mirage.

If you find yourself in Vegas for an extended period of time, consider venturing across the street to the Venetian for a workout. While its Canyon Ranch facility costs more and you must trek through the Venetian Mall to get there, this fitness heaven is worth the effort.

#2 MGM Grand Hotel & Casino

3799 Las Vegas Boulevard South, Las Vegas, NV 89109
(702) 891-1111 • mgmgrand.com

Beyond its extraordinary workout options, the MGM's indoor live lion and tiger display, array of upscale restaurants and shops and a few chic nightclubs — especially Studio 54, where circus-like dancers perform to thumping bass beats — lure visitors. Located on the southern end of the Strip, MGM's neighboring properties are not as exciting as those of the Mirage. But New York New York, with its accompanying roller coaster, game room and many restaurants, is directly across the street. We know... get to the important stuff.

CARDIO

TREADMILLS: **11 LF**
UPRIGHT BIKE: **5 LF**
RECUMBENT BIKE: **5 LF • 5 Tectrix**
ELLIPTICAL: **2 Precor**
STEPPER: **4 LF • 2 Tectrix**

STRENGTH

FREE WEIGHTS: **Yes**
MACHINES: **14 LF**
DUMBBELLS: **5-50 lbs**

SWIM

GRADE: **B**
SPECS: **3x30m • Outdoor • 80°**

OTHER

HOURS: GYM **6a-6p** • POOL **Vary**
COST: **$25**
TV: **Yes**

MGM's fitness center charges $25/day, but working out between 6 p.m. and 8 p.m. is complimentary. Extended stay guests can purchase a multi-day pass that comps the 5th workout. Such a deal — who comes to Vegas for more than 4 days anyway? As with the other hotels, paying for a spa service includes same day complimentary admission to the fitness center.

MGM's open and airy cream-toned facility offers a plethora of top-of-the-line equipment. Precor ellipticals, 9500 series Life Fitness bikes and barely used stack-loaded weight machines highlight the room. Some treadmills are in fair condition, and the stepper selection is weak. We would prefer to see heavier dumbbells, but this place is excellent nonetheless. The friendly and knowledgeable attendant, ready to assist exercisers with towels, water or changing the music, is an appreciated touch.

The Producer's Pool lures fish-like friends with its fabulous 3 lanes of 30-meter (approx.) swimming. While no stripes are painted on the pool's bottom, the narrow, floating-line divided lanes make straight swimming a breeze. The sidewalls of the pool have one step just beneath the water's surface, so you may have to slightly adjust your flip-turn. Expect this desirable rectangle to be empty, as most non-swimmers and children are drawn to MGM's 4 other recreational pools and lazy river.

MGM and Mirage are the only two Strip hotels with true lap pools, and MGM's runner-up position is due to its smaller gym, higher fee and less desirable location. Nevertheless, book here in confidence, because we are really splitting hairs.

#3 The Venetian

3355 Las Vegas Boulevard South, Las Vegas, NV 89109
(702) 414-1000 • venetian.com

Canyon Ranch at the Venetian

CARDIO

TREADMILLS: **17 StarTrac**
UPRIGHT BIKE: **4 StarTrac**
RECUMBENT BIKE: **4 StarTrac**
ELLIPTICAL: **3 Precor • 2 LF**
STEPPER: **4 LF • 3 StairMaster • 4 Stepmill**
ROWING: **2 Concept II**

STRENGTH

FREE WEIGHTS: **Yes**
MACHINES: **14 LF • 9 Life Circuit**
DUMBBELLS: **5-65 lbs**

SWIM

SPECS: **Outdoor • Not lap**

OTHER

CLASSES: **Yes**
HOURS: **5:30a-10p**
COST: **$30 • $70/3-day**
TV: **Yes**
EXTRAS: **Climbing wall**

Inside this enormous all-suite resort sits the independently operated Canyon Ranch Spa — a 65,000-square-foot wellness facility adorned with the hottest cardio and weight equipment. In 2005, the 4-story facility will double in size, making the largest fitness facility on the Strip even bigger. To be accurate, much of the present square footage is dedicated to the spa and café, but the fitness center space is by no means tight.

Discounted access for Venetian guests to this fitness find would bring athletic-minded happiness. Alas, no such luck. This sweat option does not come cheap at $30/day ($70/3days, $95/5days). Because exercisers are charged equally no matter where they rest their heads, consider a less expensive hotel for your stay and the Venetian for your play.

Reaching the club requires a lengthy hike through the seemingly endless Venetian Mall, so wear your workout shoes and ask for directions. All fitness equipment is located on Canyon Ranch's lower level.

Descending the stairs, you will notice an enormous 40-foot rock climbing wall that shoots up to the ceiling. Beyond this wall, you will discover Canyon's cardio zone, where late edition treads, bikes, ellipticals and steppers (4400PT) await, all with attached personal plasma screens. In yet another huge space, strength training is the focus, with cutting-edge stack-loaded machines, computerized resistance machines and a healthy supply of free weights. For those with group activity in mind, loads of classes are offered, including cycling, yoga and fitness testing.

Swimmers must give their Speedos a break, however. Despite all the space and more on the way, Canyon Ranch has no intention of installing a lap pool of any size — disappointing, since not one of the 4 outdoor Venetian pools is "lap-swimmable."

#4 Mandalay Bay

3950 Las Vegas Boulevard South, Las Vegas, NV 89119
(702) 632-7777 • mandalaybay.com

Located on the far southern end of the Strip and more isolated from the other hotels, Mandalay Bay is the closest accommodation to the airport. Its monorail system eases the distance to the neighboring Luxor and Excalibur. Try flagging a taxi on a busy night, however, and you may be in for a long wait.

Home to a faux beach and real wave pool, Mandalay also boasts a few favorite restaurants, including Aureole — where harnessed wine stewards rappel a 4-story glass tower to retrieve your favorite vintage. Mandalay's sports book is one of the best venues to catch any major sporting event, especially the NCAA Basketball Tournament.

CARDIO

TREADMILLS: **12 LF**
UPRIGHT BIKE: **4 LF**
RECUMBENT BIKE: **4 LF**
ELLIPTICAL: **2 Precor • 1 LF**
STEPPER: **8 LF • 1 Stepmill**

STRENGTH

FREE WEIGHTS: **Yes**
MACHINES: **15 LF**
DUMBBELLS: **5-80 lbs**

SWIM

SPECS: **Outdoor • Not lap (wave)**

OTHER

HOURS: **5a-10p**
COST: **$27**
TV: **Yes**

At $27/day, Mandalay's beach-level fitness center fee is pricey. Mirage and MGM offer superior gyms for a lower rate, and the Venetian affords the Canyon Ranch experience for only $3 more. But Mandalay's facility is no slouch. Its spacious workout area is comfortable and appealing, with floor-to-ceiling windows overlooking an outdoor lagoon. Thanks to its longer operating hours, fitness fiends can rack up late night cardio miles and body pumps on a variety of new and technologically advanced equipment. Our favorites include the Life Fitness 9500 series upright bikes with pedal straps, fixed weight barbells up to 60 pounds, bench press and squat racks and a Life Fitness 9500 series elliptical.

The spa is one of the coolest, featuring indulgent "baths" with fancy ingredients in a very zen environment. Guys, don't get too excited — the baths are for women, and men have separate tubs.

Swimmers, look elsewhere. Unless you want to practice open water swimming in the wave pool, you are out of luck.

#5 Luxor

3900 Las Vegas Boulevard South, Las Vegas, NV 89119
(702) 262-4000 • luxor.com

An actual 30-story glass pyramid, Luxor does not have elevators inside its trademark hotel — it has "inclinators." That's right. These unique people movers transport guests to their quarters sideways at a 39-degree angle! It is worth stopping in just for the ride.

The Luxor's slanted windows and exterior walls remind guests they are bunking in a pyramid, but for those who find the angles unsettling, the hotel's other tower affords 2,000 traditionally square sleeping spots. Luxor's room rates also tend to hold in the moderate price category, making it a comfortable and fitness friendly option.

Its Oasis Spa houses the only 24-hour hotel fitness center on the Strip (it closes only on Tuesdays from 11:30pm–6am). Twenty bucks

CARDIO
TREADMILLS: **10 LF**
UPRIGHT BIKE: **4 LF**
RECUMBENT BIKE: **4 LF**
STEPPER: **3 LF • 3 Tectrix**

STRENGTH
FREE WEIGHTS: **Yes**
MACHINES: **14 Paramount**
DUMBBELLS: **5-60 lbs**

SWIM
SPECS: **Outdoor • Not lap**

OTHER
HOURS: **24**
COST: **$20**
TV: **Yes**

or a free pass from the coupon book will part the pyramid walls to this neatly organized and cozy room. Luxor did not spring for pricey plasma screens, which is fine by us because the dollars clearly went to the plentiful, brand spankin' new equipment. Life Fitness 9500 series treads, uprights, recumbents and steppers adorn the room. The only missing link is ellipticals, but the center's Life Fitness step machines are worthy substitutes. Strength equipment is also in large supply, with new Paramount stack-loaded machines, 25-70 lbs. barbells, a fair assortment of metal dumbbells and plenty of free weights for bench press and squat exercises.

Swimmers are out of luck. Despite having 4 large pools, a lap lane is not in sight — fitting for an Egyptian desert theme.

Note: Luxor is connected via monorail to Mandalay Bay and the Excalibur hotels.

BEYOND HOTELS

24 Hour Fitness

Las Vegas McCarran Airport
5757 Wayne Newton Boulevard, Las Vegas, NV 89119
(702) 261-3971 • 24hourfitness.com

CARDIO
TREADMILLS: **LF**
UPRIGHT BIKE: **LF**
RECUMBENT BIKE: **LF**
ELLIPTICAL: **Precor**
STEPPER: **StairMaster**

STRENGTH
FREE WEIGHTS: **Yes**
HAMMER: **Yes**
MACHINES: **Cybex**
DUMBBELLS: **5-120 lbs**

OTHER
CLASSES: **Yes**
HOURS: M-TH **24** • F **Closes 11p** • SAT-SUN **6a-9p**
COST: **$15 • $10 IHRSA**
TV: **Yes**

You are stuck at the Las Vegas airport because your flight back to Chicago is snow-delayed. Or you are connecting through Vegas and have 2 hours to burn — enough time to get bored but not enough time to hit the Strip for a little action. While the airport hopes you invest in its "one-arm bandits," which legend has it sport the worst odds in town, you have another option. Invest in some sweat equity and guarantee a payout.

It is likely you have not noticed that the same signs guiding travelers through the airport terminals also provide directions to an on-site health club. And we're not talking about a rinky-dink room with a few lead-filled suitcases, either. 24-hour Fitness has assembled a full gym, complete with massage, sauna and steam options (no lap pool). Most members are airport employees, but any paying customer is welcome. The entry fee is $15 but, if your flight is delayed, airlines often provide $5 coupons for immediate use at the club. And you can monitor your flight's status on up-to-the-minute wall displays.

No workout gear? No problem. For an additional $10, the club will sell you a shirt, shorts, socks and a sweat towel to take home. Staff will even let you borrow shoes and a shower towel.

The gym itself has modern versions of all the equipment you expect to see at a burgeoning national franchise, including Life Fitness bikes, Precor ellipticals, Cybex weight machines and plenty of free weights. So forget about eating pretzels in the Red Carpet Club. Spend your extra time here and fill up on the trail mix en route.

RUNNING ROUTES

THE STRIP

Websites

In the City that never sleeps, the early bird not only gets the worm, but the run, too. Taking to the streets while most are heading to bed is a surefire strategy for an unimpeded 6-mile roundtrip Strip run. If you would like some company for your pavement pounding, check out the websites provided below for sponsored group runs:

lvtc.org/training.htm

and

lasvegasrunningteam.com/training.htm

Track Options

There are two track options near the Strip. Located just east of Paradise Road (which is east of the Strip) at Harmon & Swenson, next to the UNLV Baseball Stadium, the Myron Partridge Stadium boasts a state-of-the-art polyurethane surface. There are 9 lanes, each 48 inches wide, gracing this oval, which debuted in 1998.

The Hilton near the convention center has a 1/3 mile paved path that circles the buildings and parking lot.

OUTSIDE THE CITY

Red Rock Canyon Trails

If you have wheels, look to Red Rock Canyon for long, scenic and challenging trails. While this is primarily a hiking/biking venue, many runners seek the area's diversity of trails, beautiful scenery and varied plant and animal life. There are 22 listed routes — check the Visitor Center for a map. Keep in mind that, while some trails are quite easy to navigate, others are extremely challenging. Mind your footing. The park is located about 15 miles west of the Strip and is worth the trip.

LOS ANGELES, CALIFORNIA

L.A. is a funny place, but you gotta love it. Natives drive 3 blocks to get a morning cup of joe and, like Corey Hart's song, people really do wear sunglasses at night. Tupperware parties have matriculated into Botox fetes with hosts clamoring to secure the hottest plastic surgeon's attendance. Pet owners don heels and Armani to exercise their four-legged friends at $100/month "health clubs" and, no matter where you go, everyone could be someone. Only in L.A.!

It's a land of hard bodies and healthy diets — where working out is more than a recreational pursuit; it's a way of life, and often part of the job description. And since Hollywood stars often assume athletic roles on the big and small screens (or credit their fit body to an exercise device via a 20-minute infomercial), we investigated how many Tinseltown thespians have achieved significant athletic feats in real life. Here's who impressed us:

- **Will Ferrell**
  Boston, New York and Stockholm Marathons
- **Alexandra Paul** *(Baywatch)*
  Ironman Hawaii and Boston Marathons
- **David James Elliott** *(JAG)*
  Boston Marathon and 2 x L.A. Marathon
- **Oprah Winfrey**
  Marine Corps Marathon
- **David Duchovny**
  Triathlete
- **Geena Davis**
  U.S. Olympic Team Finalist (archery)
- **Robin Williams**
  Hard core cyclist
- **Queen Latifah**
  State high school basketball champ
- **Matthew Perry**
  Top ranked Canadian Junior Tennis player (#17 in Canada)
- **Lisa Ling**
  Boston Marathon

BEVERLY HILLS/CENTURY CITY

In a place where 2,200 square foot homes average $1.1 million and driving a Ferrari is passé, you would think finding extravagant hotels with phenomenal workout options would be a piece of high-priced, low-carb cake. Surprisingly, it's not. And, because most residents have their own backyard swimming holes, those attempting to track down a 90210 lap pool have a better chance of becoming an American Idol. Swimmers, we've got you covered, but you'd better cozy up to those rental car keys.

EXPENSIVE

GOLD: Hyatt Regency Century Plaza

2025 Avenue of the Stars, Los Angeles, CA 90067
(310) 277-2000 • centuryplaza.hyatt.com

CARDIO

TREADMILLS: **7 Cybex**
UPRIGHT BIKE: **2 Cybex**
RECUMBENT BIKE: **3 Cybex**
ELLIPITCAL: **7 Precor**
STEPPER: **1 Cybex - old**
ROWING: **1 Concept II**

STRENGTH

FREE WEIGHTS: **Yes**
MACHINES: **14 Cybex**
DUMBBELLS: **3-90 lbs**

SWIM

SPECS: **Outdoor • Not lap**

OTHER

CLASSES: **Yes**
HOURS: M-SAT **5a-9p** • SUN **7a-7p**
COST: **$12 Plaza** • **$30 All others**
TV: **Yes**

One mile from Beverly Hills shopping and within walking distance of Westfield's Shoppingtown Mall (Macy's, Bloomingdale's, Houston's & AMC-16 Theater), Century Plaza offers a fantastic respite for business and leisure travelers. While Century City's high-rise, office tower setting is not nearly as pristine as nearby Beverly Hills neighborhoods, you will quickly forget the steel and asphalt once you encounter this hotel's resort-like grounds.

Century Plaza decorates its 7-acre urban getaway with 5 reflecting pools, a host of tropical plants and greenery, quaint outdoor cafés and a 35,000 square foot spa. All 727 rooms have balconies, and those facing west overlook the Plaza's expansive real estate. The guest quarters' décor is equally appealing. Contemporary furnishings, crisp beige and crème tones, pillow top mattresses, down comforters and dual showerhead baths are interior details.

The Plaza also boasts the best hotel gym in L.A. As part of the Mystique Spa, guests can shape up for $12/day. We found the usage fee — on top of the pricey nightly rates — vexing, but the Plaza tempered our annoyance with its fantastic facility. The charming room, with its giraffe-spotted carpeting and airy high ceilings, contains over 35 cardio and strength machines, a bench and squat rack, and a vast array of dumbbells. Except for slightly worn upright bikes and an even older stepper, the endurance machines are impressively new. Building muscle here requires little creativity, with Century's generous supply of stack-loaded stations and free weights — comparable to many full-service health clubs. Finally, lonely travelers in search of workout buddies can take advantage of Plaza's cardio classes.

In Beverly Hills, public lappers are in short supply. If you require a convenient regulation option, consider staying at the Beverly Hilton. Otherwise, plan to drive 2-5 miles for the next closest alternative (24 Hour Fitness-West Hollywood or Santa Monica College).

SILVER: Four Seasons

300 S. Doheny Drive, Los Angeles, CA 90048
(310) 273-2222 • fourseasons.com

CARDIO

TREADMILLS: **5 LF**
UPRIGHT BIKE: **2 Precor**
RECUMBENT BIKE: **1 Precor**
ELLIPTICAL: **5 Precor**
STEPPER: **2 StairMaster**

STRENGTH

FREE WEIGHTS: **Yes~400 lbs.**
MACHINES: **5 Cybex**
DUMBBELLS: **3-60 lbs**

SWIM

GRADE: **D**
SPECS: **3x18yd • Outdoor • 80°**
TOYS: **Kick**

OTHER

HOURS: **5:30a-10p**
COST: **Free**
TV: **Yes**

Often the empress of the hotel pyramid, in posh Beverly Hills Four Seasons battles with other worthy adversaries. Even here, however, Four Seasons stands tall against its competition. Located within a mile of famous Rodeo Drive, this high-end accommodation is convenient to Beverly Hills' businesses and shopping, but far enough away to avoid its traffic.

All 285 modern rooms charm with European décor, French doors that open to spacious balconies, high thread count sheets, premium bedding and spa-like marble baths. Of course, 24-hour in-room dining is available.

The hotel's indoor/outdoor gym is partially enclosed by a tent and canopy and faces the pool deck. One side can be opened to SoCal's sunshine and cool breezes. Only L.A.'s near-perfect year-round weather allows for such a pleasing perk. New cardio and weight machines line the inside of the little "big top," and plenty of free weights are offered as well. While the endurance machine spacing is rather cozy, the stack-loaded weight station and free weight areas are more comfortable. Fitness fans can look forward to Life Fitness' 9500 series, along with StairMaster's 4400PT steppers and approximately 400 pounds of plate weights for bench press and the like.

Four Seasons' 18-yard (53 feet to be exact), 3-lane lapper with bottom stripes will not inspire, but in this diamond-adorned neck of the woods, it is a very convenient option. No floating lines or pace clock are served up in this leisure-focused lap pool. Water lovers seeking a more serious lap swim must drive 2 miles to West Hollywood's 24-Hour Fitness ($15, see our West Hollywood description). Or, if you don't mind a longer commute, drive 15-20 minutes for the best lap venue around, Santa Monica College's tremendous aquatic facility (see Santa Monica).

MODERATELY EXPENSIVE

GOLD: **Park Hyatt** Century City

2151 Avenue of the Stars, Los Angeles, CA 90067
(310) 277-1234 • parklosangeles.hyatt.com

CARDIO

TREADMILLS: **4 LF**
UPRIGHT BIKE: **2 LF**
RECUMBENT BIKE: **3 LF**
ELLIPITCAL: **3 LF**

STRENGTH

MACHINES: **10 LF**
DUMBBELLS: **5-50 lbs**

SWIM

SPECS: **Outdoor • Not lap**

OTHER

HOURS: **5a-11p**
COST: **Free**
TV: **Yes**

While Park Hyatt rarely lands in the moderate price category, its $300-$400+ a night Beverly Hills neighbors make this place seem like a bargain. Typically priced in the $200/night range, Park Hyatt is near the Century Plaza Hotel, the 20th Century Fox movie studio lot and the Westfield shopping mall. Conservative beige tones, attractive furnishings, 300 thread count sheets and marble baths decorate the 367 rooms. Large balconies offer city views and 24-hour in-room dining is handy for nights when you prefer to stay in. When you do venture out, take advantage of Park Hyatt's complimentary car service, which will transport you (7 a.m.-7 p.m.) anywhere within a 1.5 mile radius, including famous Rodeo Drive. (You can also arrange a return.)

Park Hyatt's gym is a good one. On the 2nd floor, the assortment of "just out of the box" machines will start the athletic-minded traveler's day on firm footing. All cardio pieces are Life Fitness' new 95re series, and the stack-loaded weight stations are equally young. Although free weights are absent, a decent range of dumbbells supports a full body strength session.

Swimmers must drive 3 miles to West Hollywood's 24-Hour Fitness or 5 miles to Santa Monica College. Park Hyatt's short (50 feet) outdoor pool is not lap designed — no lane lines or stripes.

SILVER: **Beverly Hilton**

9876 Wilshire Boulevard, Los Angeles, CA 90210
(310) 274-7777 • hilton.com

This famed property is a half-mile from Rodeo Drive's glitter and is home to the Golden Globe Awards. The aging Beverly Hills grand dame received a much needed $60 million facelift during 2004 and '05. Thankfully, Hilton's 579 refurbished guest quarters now display a contemporary style with tropical accents — a welcome change from their former 1980-ish tackiness.

The athletic highlight here continues to be the one true hotel lap pool in all of L.A. While Hilton describes it as "Olympic size," it's well short of 50 meters. However, it is longer than 25 yards (we estimate at approx. 31 yards) and, like the current rooms, the decorating is just fine. Swimmers can count on 4 bottom striped lanes with at least one having floating lines.

The gym is a good option, too, with new Precor cardio equipment intermixed with new Paramount strength machines. The ceilings are low and the separate dumbbell room is a little dark, but the plasma TVs on the wall are a nice touch. Runners should remember that they are in Southern California — so keep in mind your outdoor option: jogging to the nearby Beverly Hills High School 1/4-mile track or through the million-dollar neighborhood of 90210.

CARDIO
TREADMILLS: **3 Precor**
UPRIGHT BIKE: **1 Precor**
RECUMBENT BIKE: **1 Precor**
ELLIPTICAL: **2 Precor**

STRENGTH
MACHINES: **9 Paramount**
DUMBBELLS: **5-70 lbs**

SWIM
GRADE: **B**
SPECS: **4x31yd • Outdoor • 80-83°**

OTHER
HOURS: **6a-11p**
COST: **Free**
TV: **Yes**

LEAST EXPENSIVE

In Beverly Hills? Keep Dreaming!

DOWNTOWN

If business, a convention or sporting event brings you to L.A., Downtown is a practical and convenient home base. While regentrification efforts continue and some progress is evident, Downtown has a long way to go before it will be a sought after leisure destination. If you don't have to be down here, don't — at least, not yet.

MODERATELY EXPENSIVE

GOLD: Wilshire Grand

930 Wilshire Boulevard, Los Angeles, CA 90017
(213) 688-7777 • wilshiregrand.com

Located four long blocks from the Staples Center and L.A. Convention Center (still walkable), Wilshire Grand caters to conventioneers and business travelers. That's not a surprise, since Downtown's tourist attractions are few and far between — are there any?

The Grand extends its hospitality throughout this 896-room, 16-story high-rise. The light and airy guest quarters approach studio apartment size, and some entry level units have two bathrooms. Decorated with contemporary furniture and soft beige tones, the accommodations are

CARDIO
TREADMILLS: **5 Cybex - 2 old**
UPRIGHT BIKE: **2 Precor • 2 LF - old**
ELLIPITCAL: **2 Precor**
STEPPER: **2 LifeStep**

STRENGTH
MACHINES: **9 Maxicam - old**

SWIM
SPECS: **Outdoor • Not lap**

OTHER
HOURS: **24**
COST: **Free**
TV: **Yes**

neither lavish nor overly plush, but you are not paying for such treatment, either.

Guests have two workout options. First, the lobby-level gym is worth a quick hit. Inside this expansive room, which is nowhere near filled with equipment, exercisers will find a mix of old and new machines. Highlights include great condition ellipticals, a couple of appealing bikes and 2 decent treadmills. The Maxicam stack-loaded weight stations may appear worn, but they function well. Second, is the wonderful Gold's Gym ($10) located directly across the street. Both endurance and swim junkies will be smiling there.

SILVER: The Standard Downtown

550 South Flower Street, Los Angeles, CA 90071
(213) 892-8080 • standardhotel.com

CARDIO
TREADMILLS: **2 Precor**
RECUMBENT BIKE: **1 Precor**
ELLIPITCAL: **2 Precor**

STRENGTH
MACHINES: **4 Cybex**
DUMBBELLS: **3-40 lbs**

SW IM
SPECS: **Outdoor • Not lap**

OTHER
HOURS: **24**
COST: **Free**
TV: **Yes**

If you need to be Downtown and are burned out with business-like hotels, let the Standard rescue you. About 6 blocks from Staples Center and the L.A. Convention Center, guests are front and center to downtown businesses and attractions. But, unlike its massive, conservatively decorated neighbors, this young property (2002) brings a West Hollywood vibe into the City and affords an experience in stark contrast to any run-of-the-mill conventioneer lodging. *Modern, minimalist* and *moody* are the adjectives that come to mind when describing this 21st Century creation. All 207 rooms are an experience in gray — light gray walls, darker gray bedding and even darker gray carpet. Surprisingly comfortable platform beds, plastic chairs with cushions, glass enclosed bathrooms and 1970s-style mood lighting create Standard's anything but ordinary accommodation. Think Jetson's redux.

Fortunately for the athletic-minded, Standard extends the fun to its useful, in-house gym. The 3rd floor sweathouse sports all new equipment, but cyclists must recline and serious weight buffs will hanker for more.

However, Standard's fitness facility will certainly suffice for a mild tune-up. Lap swimmers and those craving more should walk 5 minutes to Gold's Gym ($10). While Standard sports a rooftop pool, it is more of an accoutrement to the hip bar scene than anything else.

BRONZE: Westin Bonaventure

404 South Figueroa Street, Los Angeles, CA 90071
(213) 624-1000 • westin.com

The largest downtown hotel property with 1,354 rooms, Westin Bonaventure is almost too big. Connected to the World Trade Center via pedestrian bridge and about a mile from the L.A. Convention Center, it is easy to get lost in its concrete abyss. While you may need signs to locate your room, once inside you'll be glad you came. Count on tastefully outfitted and designed guest quarters with floor-to-ceiling windows, upscale furnishings, wood accents and Westin's trademark Heavenly Beds. Pillow top mattresses, triple sheets and down comforters are pleasing companions — and, if you have a roommate, the generous floor plans are an added bonus.

CARDIO

TREADMILLS: **3 Total - old • LF • Cybex • Trotter**
UPRIGHT BIKE: **1 Tectrix - old**
RECUMBENT BIKE: **1 Tectrix**
ELLIPITCAL: **1 LF**
STEPPER: **1 Tectrix**

STRENGTH

MACHINES: **6 Paramount**

SWIM

SPECS: **Outdoor • Not lap**

OTHER

HOURS: **24**
COST: **Free**
TV: **Yes**
EXTRA: **$10 Pass to YMCA**

Westin's workout facility is an odd duck. On the atrium's 3rd level, the small, glass-enclosed room houses a scattered assortment of old and worn machines. The only breathing option is one Life Fitness elliptical machine — the rest have flatlined. Outside this tiny fishbowl, in the center of the hotel atrium, a so-called "jogging track" (maybe 1/30 mile?) curves around the hotel's concrete support pylons. Six new stack-loaded weight machines are evenly spaced around its perimeter. This unconventional set-up is anything but user friendly. Westin's saving grace is a pedestrian bridge that provides a traffic-free, 3-minute thoroughfare to downtown's YMCA. Ten bucks is the going rate, and we recommend the investment (a lap pool is offered at the Y, too).

LEAST EXPENSIVE

GOLD: Holiday Inn City Center

1020 South Figueroa Street, Los Angeles, CA 90015
(213) 748-1291 • hicitycenter.com

Make sure you book the right Holiday Inn! Downtown has two, and you want the one with "City Center" in its name. Its across-the-street location from Staples Center and the convention center is ideal for those in town for a Lakers game or an expo. No frills and nothing fancy, it's a very good representative for this budget franchise. The common areas and 195 rooms have been renovated over the last several years and are bright and cheerful. While the décor will not garner any L.A. magazine style awards, each large guest unit offers everything you expect to find in a modern hotel with an added touch of flair — rare for a Holiday Inn.

Skip the hotel's 5-piece workout room. The treadmills are old and strength equipment is absent. Instead, take advantage of Holiday's free passes to Gold's Gym, only a 5-minute walk away. Show your room key to the health club's reception desk and prepare for a phenomenal workout experience — lap swim included.

BEYOND HOTELS DOWNTOWN

Gold's Gym

735 South Figueroa Street, Los Angeles, CA 90017
(213) 688-1441 • goldsgym.com

CARDIO

TREADMILLS: **LF**
UPRIGHT BIKE: **LF**
RECUMBENT BIKE: **LF**
ELLIPITCAL: **LF • Precor**
STEPPER: **StairMaster • Stepmill**

STRENGTH

FREE WEIGHTS: **Yes**
HAMMER: **Yes**
MACHINES: **LF • Free Motion • Icarian**
DUMBBELLS: **3-100 lbs**

SWIM

GRADE: **B**
SPECS: **3x25yd • Indoor • 82°**
TOYS: **Kick • Clock**

OTHER

CLASSES: **Yes**
HOURS: M-TH **5a-11p** • F **5a-9p** • SAT-SUN **7a-9p**
COST: **Free Holiday Inn • $10 Other hotels • $20 Others**
TV: **Yes**
EXTRAS: **Boxing ring • Juice bar**

If the "Gold's" name conjures images of intimidating muscle-heads pumping iron in a sweaty, bodybuilding type gym, you have this club pegged all wrong. The newer Gold's facilities are more health club than gym, and this downtown L.A. location fits the new and improved mold. On 7th and Fig Plaza's lower level, Gold's serves up a full plate of modern strength and cardio machines, an ample assortment of classes and a top-notch indoor lap pool. Aesthetically, the full-service center's industrial loft vibe creates a serious environment to work your body and rest your mind.

Although we always prefer to swim outdoors — especially in weather-friendly cities — Gold's indoor lap pool is a sight to be seen. Only in L.A. are we not surprised to see a pool's water glowing from "mood lighting." But it's not all vibe. Floating lines and bottom stripes part the lanes, and a pace clock keeps your time.

Holiday Inn guests receive complimentary access, all other downtown hotel patrons pay $10 and others must part with $20.

Stuart M. Ketchum Downtown YMCA

401 South Hope Street, Los Angeles, CA 90071
(213) 624-2348 • ymcala.org

Recommended primarily for Westin guests whose access to this exceptional and convenient facility runs a very reasonable $10 (all others must pay a steep $25), this Downtown Y boasts an endless quantity of high-grade fitness opportunities.

California sunshine spills into the exercise area via floor-to-ceiling windows and reflects off the brand new cardio machines. Life Fitness' latest and greatest 95ci series treadmills, upright bikes, ellipticals and steppers outnumber other impressive machinery that includes Precor ellipitcals, Cybex Arc Trainers and StairMaster's 4400PT Free Climbers and Stepmills. Plenty of strength apparatus will satisfy any iron pumping desires, and a wide range of classes adds a group option.

Lap swimmers are not left high and dry, as the Y supplies 4 lanes of 25-yard water fun in an appealing pool. Floating lane lines, bottom stripes and backstroke flags will assist with your wet workout, but call ahead if sharing a lane is not your cup of tea — the pool can get crowded.

CARDIO

TREADMILLS: **LF • StarTrac**
UPRIGHT BIKE: **LF**
RECUMBENT BIKE: **LF**
ELLIPITCAL: **LF • Precor • Cybex**
STEPPER: **LF • StairMaster • Stepmill**
ROWING: **Concept II**
OTHER: **Gravitron • Crossrobic**

STRENGTH

FREE WEIGHTS: **Yes**
HAMMER: **Yes**
MACHINES: **LF • Life Circuit**
DUMBBELLS: **3-100 lbs**

SWIM

GRADE: **B-**
SPECS: **4x25yd • Indoor • 82°**
TOYS: **Kick • Pull • Fins • Clock**
MASTERS: **Yes**

OTHER

CLASSES: **Yes**
HOURS: M-TH **5:30a-11p** • F **5:30a-9p** • SAT **8a-6p** • SUN **11a-6p**
COST: **$10 Westin • $25 Others**
TV: **Yes**
EXTRAS: **1/16 mile indoor track • Basketball • Racquetball**

SANTA MONICA

Santa Monica offers balance. Still hip, urban and fun, yet happily removed from Beverly Hills' traffic snarls, Downtown's concrete and Hollywood's hoopla. Its oceanfront shopping and dining attractions, Third Street Promenade and plethora of outdoor amusements make Santa Monica one of our favorite spots in the country.

Consider renting a convertible and heading up the coast to Malibu and Zuma beach, or keep on driving and savor California's coast!

EXPENSIVE

GOLD: **Loews Santa Monica Beach Hotel**
1700 Ocean Avenue, Santa Monica, CA 90401
(310) 458-6700 • loewshotels.com

Set amidst several other hotels, just one alleyway from the Pacific Ocean and Santa Monica's golden beaches, Loews is a fantastic vacation getaway or business home base (1 block from Santa Monica Convention Center). The hotel can get busy, creating potential long waits for taxis and other service requests. However, patient guests will be rewarded by this wonderful 342-room accommodation's upscale beachfront setting, plush rooms and worthy fitness venue.

Many of the guest quarters afford incredible deep blue ocean

CARDIO

TREADMILLS: **7 StarTrac • 5 LF - old**
UPRIGHT BIKE: **2 Precor • 1 LF**
RECUMBENT BIKE: **3 Precor**
ELLIPITCAL: **4 Precor**
STEPPER: **4 LF • 1 Precor**

STRENGTH

FREE WEIGHTS: **Yes**
MACHINES: **9 Cybex**
DUMBBELLS: **5-60 lbs**

SWIM

SPECS: **Outdoor • Not lap**

OTHER

CLASSES: **Yes**
HOURS: M-F **6a-10p** • SAT-SUN **6a-9p**
COST: **Free**
TV: **Yes**

views and all draw California's coastline inside with sand tones, plenty of light and balconies with sliding glass doors. Premium furnishings, including stylish beds with padded headboards and down comforters, contribute to the property's oasis setting.

Exercisers are treated to the best *hotel* gym in Santa Monica and one of the top 3 in L.A. Complimentary to Loews guests, the comfortably large facility is outfitted with the most technologically advanced equipment on the market. Except for a few of the treadmills, the machines are barely worn and ready for action. We always admire a hotel gym that provides free weights to its guests along with a wide variety of stack-loaded machines — kudos to Loews. Classes are also available, including twice weekly spinning. And do not forget, Loews' beachfront location offers some of the best jogging routes in all of L.A.

Although the 63-foot (~21 yards) length of Loews' outdoor pool may tempt lap swimmers, the absence of floating lines and bottom stripes makes straight freestyling difficult. We suggest rewarding yourself with a true lap experience at Santa Monica College's fantastic outdoor pools (5-minute drive).

MODERATELY EXPENSIVE

GOLD: Huntley Santa Monica Beach

1111 Second Street, Santa Monica, CA 90403
(310) 394-5454 • thehuntleyhotel.com

Location, location, location. Two blocks from Santa Monica's popular Third Street Promenade shopping and dining district and 3 blocks from the beach, the best feature of the Huntley is... you guessed it... the location.

This former apartment building is now home to Huntley's 213 rooms and occupies a quiet piece of real estate on a tree-lined residential street. With so much fun just outside the door, guests will likely not spend too much time in their plush rooms. Oh, but the poofy white comforters, plasma televisions, and stylish decor may tempt you. Huntley's common areas are appealing in their own right, but with a bit of dreamy and 70s flair. Take a look at our pics and you'll see what we mean. To top your experience off, Huntley sports a romantic 18th floor rooftop restaurant/lounge that has phenomenal ocean views.

Skip the on-site workout room. Most equipment is old, run down and in need of corrective surgery. Instead, runners should head to the beach, swimmers should drive 10 minutes to Santa Monica College or jog 10 minutes to the YMCA, and those looking for the most convenient huff and puff should walk 5 minutes to Easton Gym. Class dismissed!

LEAST EXPENSIVE

GOLD: Best Western Ocean View Hotel

1447 Ocean Avenue, Santa Monica, CA 90401
(310) 458-4888 • bestwestern.com/oceanviewhotel

Wow! A Best Western with an ocean view and appealing accommodations to match — now that's worth a daytime Emmy! Dollar for dollar, this may be the best place to stay in Santa Monica. Across the street from sandcastles and surfing, a block away from Third Street's liveliness and within a 5-minute walk of Santa Monica Pier's roller coaster and rides, Best Western guests are within arm's length of all the fun.

Only 66 rooms are offered at this, dare we say, "upscale" property, and it fills quickly. Okay, so upscale may be a push, but the guest quarter furnishings are significantly nicer than its typical brand brethren. Light, bright and possessing a modestly modern flair, we were pleasantly surprised by the aesthetics.

With no workout room in-house, your sweat options are identical to the Radisson's: Run along the ocean shore, swim at Santa Monica College (5-10 minute drive) or the YMCA (3-minute drive, 10-minute jog) or strength/cardio train at Easton Gym (5-minute walk).

BEYOND HOTELS SANTA MONICA

Santa Monica College

2225 16th Street, Santa Monica, CA 90405
(310) 458-8700 • swim.santa-monica.org

Fantastic public swimming and running facilities are available to all comers on the campus of this 2-year junior college. Our fish-like friends will flip over the 50-meter pool, which is set up for several hours of long course swimming 5 days a week. At all other times, lappers must "settle" for 15 lanes of 25-yard swimming in this competition-quality venue. Just be sure you don't end up in the mixed-use pool that shares lap space with the kids. The college sports two water boxes, but only one is a pure lapper. Kickboards, pull-buoys and pace clocks are provided in both areas. Your fee will be $5.

SWIM

GRADE: **A**
SPECS: **8x50m • Outdoor • 80°**
TOYS: **Kick • Pull • Clock**
MASTERS: **Yes**

OTHER

HOURS: POOL **Vary, call** • TRACK **See text**
COST: SWIM **$5** • TRACK **Free**
EXTRAS: **1/4 mile outdoor track**

If running on a top grade 1/4-mile track is on your wish list, this 7-lane surface is Santa Monica's finest. Open during daylight hours during the week and 6am-4pm on weekends, this oval plays host to many fleet feet.

Note: During the week, park in metered spaces along 16th Street or Pico Blvd. On weekends, parking in the garage is allowed and free.

Easton Gym

1233 Third Street Promenade, Santa Monica, CA 90401
(310) 395-4441 • eastongym.com

CARDIO

TREADMILLS: **LF**
UPRIGHT BIKE: **LF**
RECUMBENT BIKE: **LF**
ELLIPITCAL: **LF • Precor**
STEPPER: **StairMaster**

STRENGTH

FREE WEIGHTS: **Yes**
HAMMER: **Yes**
MACHINES: **BodyMaster**
DUMBBELLS: **5-100 lbs**

OTHER

CLASSES: **Yes**
HOURS: M-F **6a-12a** • SAT-SUN **7a-10p**
COST: **$15 • $10 IHRSA**
TV: **Yes**

Above the Adidas store on the east side of Santa Monica's Third Street Promenade, Easton maximizes its diminutive floor space by providing an impressive array of new cardio and weight equipment. The fitness area is aesthetically pleasing, with higher than average ceilings and second floor French doors that open to ocean breezes.

Life Fitness is the primary brand of choice, but Precor ellipticals and StairMaster's 4600PT series step machines make an appearance. All machines are new and, with plenty of strength apparatus, muscle pumpers will not suffer any iron deficiency. Yoga, spin and other classes are offered as well. If you belong to an IHRSA club back home, you'll save $5 off the $15 admission fee (www.healthclubs.com). You must bring a photo I.D.

Note: Starbucks is just down the block for a post-workout caffeine jolt.

Santa Monica YMCA

1332 Sixth Street, Santa Monica, CA 90401
(310) 393-2721 • ymcasm.org

Recommended primarily for Radisson and Best Western guests (Loews is equidistant) as a closer lap swim than Santa Monica College, the Y sports an aesthetically pleasing indoor lap pool with high ceilings and good lighting. Six lanes of 25-yard swimming are offered to water lovers, along with a full assortment of toys and extras (e.g., clock and backstroke flags). The College is definitely a preferable swim experience, but those without wheels (15-20 minute walk) or pressed for time will find the Y's pool more convenient.

While the YMCA also supplies a small selection of cardio and strength equipment, the much closer Easton Gym is a better health club bet. But Y swimmers are afforded the necessary land tools for a double-up routine ($15 for all visitors).

Note: Swimmers, you must wear a swim cap in this pool. Bring your own or be faced with a $3 purchase at the Y's front desk.

CARDIO

TREADMILLS: **StarTrac - old**
UPRIGHT BIKE: **LF**
RECUMBENT BIKE: **LF**
ELLIPITCAL: **Precor**
STEPPER: **LF • Precor**

STRENGTH

FREE WEIGHTS: **Yes**
MACHINES: **Cybex • Icarian**
DUMBBELLS: **3-90 lbs**

SWIM

GRADE: **B**
SPECS: **6x25yd • Indoor • 81°**
TOYS: **Kick • Pull • Clock**

OTHER

CLASSES: **Yes**
HOURS: M-F **6a-10p** • SAT-SUN **8a-8p**
COST: **$15**
TV: **No**

WEST HOLLYWOOD

This is the place you read about in *US* and *People* — home to uber-trendy clubs, endless nightlife possibilities and loads of beautiful people. It's also where you're most likely to spot a few stars. Contain your enthusiasm, play it cool, and you will fit right in.

EXPENSIVE

GOLD: Sunset Marquis

1200 North Alta Loma Road, West Hollywood, CA 90069
(310) 657-1333 • sunsetmarquishotel.com

So you wanna be a rock star, huh? How about living like one for a night or two? As one of the most frequented hotels for actors, musicians and reality show personalities (are they actors?), Sunset Marquis is an alluring destination. Located on a relatively quiet residential street off busy Sunset Boulevard, a Marquis stay places you in one of LA's exclusive domains. Trendy restaurants and clubs, Melrose Avenue's shopping and other attractions are within a quick commute. Understated and tattooed, Marquis' clientele are more apt to sport bed heads and grunge than Chanel or Hugo while savoring java poolside.

CARDIO

TREADMILLS: **1 Precor**
RECUMBENT BIKE: **1 Tectrix**
ELLIPITCAL: **1 Precor**

STRENGTH

MACHINES: **1 multi**
DUMBBELLS: **5-50 lbs**

SWIM

SPECS: **Outdoor • Not lap**

OTHER

HOURS: **7a-10p**
COST: **Free**
TV: **Yes**
EXTRAS: **Free pass to Equinox**

Catering to its celebrity base, the Marquis provides high quality accommodations. All 127 guest rooms offer separate sleeping and living areas, high thread count sheets, 24-hour room service, refrigerators and expensive furnishings with a retro flair. Entry level rooms resemble a studio apartment layout; those wanting a larger floor plan can select among a variety of options, including a $1,000/night two bedroom villa.

Unlike its on-site recording studio, Sunset Marquis' in-house gym will not inspire song lyrics. However, true to its top service mentality, Marquis compensates guests for its off key facility with complimentary passes to the wonderfully convenient and cutting-edge Equinox Fitness — a 3-minute walk. Although it has no lap pool, this recently opened, state-of-the-art health club has everything else.

Swimmers should head to 24 Hour Fitness ($15). Gliding downhill to 24 should only take 5 minutes, but double that for your return trek. Consider a stop at 24's neighboring Jamba Juice or Starbucks to propel you back up the hill.

MODERATELY EXPENSIVE

GOLD: The Standard

8300 Sunset Boulevard, West Hollywood, CA 90069
(323) 650-9090 • standardhotel.com

If you're in search of a very "L.A." experience, and Sunset Marquis' rates are budget busting, consider the Standard. On the famous Sunset Strip, this modish accommodation will put you in the middle of everything cool, hip and trendy. It is within a couple blocks of Sunset Marquis, so a Standard stay also affords the same neighborhood perks — albeit a bit noisier than its higher-priced competitor.

The Standard is an exhibit in shades of blue and gray. Walls, carpets, floors, bedding — who knew so many different hues existed. And though we typically associate these colors with rainy days and gloomy moods, Standard pulls off an aesthetically upbeat environment by adding a whimsical mix of minimalist furnishings and playful accents. For example, all 139 rooms pair contemporary platform beds with retro bean bags. The lobby combines sharp-edged furniture with shag carpet, and various lamp styles from the last 3 decades set the mood. Only the orange bathrooms (yes, orange!) interrupt the blue and gray motif.

The workout room is not blue and gray — because there is none. Although staff will likely refer guests to the 3-block-away Crunch Gym, Equinox Fitness (3 blocks in the opposite direction) is a much better alternative. It will cost more ($25 vs. $11), but it will be the best extra 14 bucks you spend in LA.

Swimmers, head to 24 Hour Fitness on Santa Monica Boulevard ($15, 15-minute walk).

GOLD: Chamberlain

1000 Westmount Drive, West Hollywood, CA 90069
(310) 657-7400 • chamberlainwesthollywood.com

CARDIO
TREADMILLS: **2 ST**
RECUMBENT BIKE: **1 ST**
ELLIPITCAL: **1 ST**

STRENGTH
DUMBBELLS: **5-40 lbs**

OTHER
COST: **Free**
TV: **Yes**

On a quiet residential street 2 blocks up the hill from busy Santa Monica Boulevard, Chamberlain presents a fantastic accommodation and a convenient locale. Only 2 blocks from the "expensive" Sunset Marquis, Chamberlain shares the same location benefits as its pricier rival — within walking distance of Sunset Strip restaurants, clubs and attractions.

As a former apartment building, all 111 rooms boast separate sleeping and living areas, microwave ovens, refrigerators and fireplaces.

Exercisers will find a few worthy machines in Chamberlain's small fitness center, but most will want to head straight downhill to 24 Hour Fitness. It's only a 2-minute walk and you can stop at Jamba Juice or Starbucks before trudging back up the hill ($15 for a workout and/or swim).

BEYOND HOTELS WEST HOLLYWOOD

Equinox Fitness West Hollywood

8590 Sunset Boulevard, West Hollywood, CA 90069
(310) 289-1900 • equinoxfitness.com

CARDIO
TREADMILLS: **LF • True**
UPRIGHT BIKE: **LF**
RECUMBENT BIKE: **LF**
ELLIPITCAL: **LF • Precor • Cybex**
STEPPER: **Life Step • Stepmill**
OTHER: **Ergometer**

STRENGTH
FREE WEIGHTS: **Yes**
HAMMER: **Yes**
MACHINES: **LF • Cybex • Icarian**
DUMBBELLS: **3-100 lbs**

OTHER
CLASSES: **Yes**
HOURS: M-TH **5:30a-10:30p** • F **5:30a-9:30p** • SAT **7a-8p** • SUN **8a-7p**
COST: **Free Sunset Marquis • $25 Select hotels only**
TV: **Yes**
EXTRAS: **Cafe**

With staff that look like Leo DiCaprio and Mandy Moore, and members who resemble TV and movie stars (because they really are), this place is a true Hollywood scene. However, the crowd here is friendly, the plasma screens are huge, the environment is contemporary and the equipment is as good as it gets — it's the best club in this area of Tinseltown. Guests of Sunset Marquis enjoy complimentary access, and patrons of a select few other hotels may exercise here for $25 (e.g., Standard).

The club is divided into two stories, with cardio and strength equipment organized on each floor. Both levels are spacious and have plentiful cutting-edge machines, but we were a tad perturbed by the disorganized layout of the stack-loaded weight stations, requiring a trip up/down the staircase to complete our routine — not a big deal for a workout or two, but annoying if this is your home club. We realize this criticism is getting picky, so plan on enjoying a wonderful workout experience.

Swimmers are not treated as well as other sweat addicts. In fact, they are not accommodated here at all. Water-loving ones should head to 24 Hour Fitness for a proper swim.

Note: Bring your own headphones for the televisions.

24 Hour Fitness Sport

8612 Santa Monica Boulevard, West Hollywood, CA 90069
(310) 652-7440 • 24hourfitness.com

CARDIO

TREADMILLS: **LF • StarTrac**
UPRIGHT BIKE: **LF - old**
RECUMBENT BIKE: **LF • StarTrac**
ELLIPITCAL: **LF • Precor**
STEPPER: **StairMaster • Stepmill**
OTHER: **Crossrobic**

STRENGTH

FREE WEIGHTS: **Yes**
HAMMER: **Yes**
MACHINES: **Cybex • BodyMaster**
DUMBBELLS: **5-115 lbs**

SWIM

GRADE: **B**
SPECS: **4x25m • Outdoor • 82°**
TOYS: **Clock**

OTHER

CLASSES: **Yes**
HOURS: M-F **5a-12a** • SAT-SUN **6a-11p**
COST: **$15 • $10 IHRSA**
TV: **Yes**

Far from Equinox's panache, this club's trusty yet unimpressive facility will get you through any sweat routine — including a swim. All guests pay $15/day ($10 IHRSA) to access the mix of older and newer cardio machines, plenty of young weight apparatus and a wide range of classes. Upright cyclists will be disappointed by the older model, brown Life Fitness bikes — the only uprights offered. Everyone else should be satisfied, including swimmers.

An outdoor lapper in the middle of West Hollywood is a rare find. 24 Hour Fitness boasts 4 lanes of 25-meter swimming divided by floating lane lines and bottom stripes. We did not see any toys, but a pace clock was hanging on the wall.

RUNNING ROUTES

Beverly Hills

The best Beverly Hills route is a loop through, and gawk at, the residential setting south of Wilshire Blvd. You can then easily access the Beverly Hills High School's 1/4-mile track (241 Moreno Drive, Beverly Hills, 90212). After your interval work, head back the way you came. If you elect to drive to the track, parking usually is not a problem in this area.

Another Beverly Hills option is running through the neighborhoods north of Santa Monica Boulevard. Just pick your street and plan on viewing mansion after mansion and estate after estate. The farther north of Santa Monica Boulevard you run, the hillier it gets. So have those quads ready for a little work.

Downtown

Downtown LA's running potential is poor, save for a couple miles of paths through nearby Elysian Park. It is the closest green patch to the concrete jungle, but you may have to bank 4 miles or so to get there, and some of the neighborhoods didn't look too great.

Instead, drive the rental and pull over anywhere inside the park. Since Elysian offers little mileage, consider adjacent Dodger Stadium for some add-ons. Better yet, stick to the treadmill.

Santa Monica

Thankfully, Los Angeles does have a running oasis — Santa Monica. It's as easy as making a beeline for the beach. You can pick up the path virtually anywhere. It begins north of Pacific Palisades at Will Rogers State Beach (~4 miles from the Santa Monica Pier) and ends far south, past famed Venice Beach.

Along the route in between, you're likely to see camera crews filming commercials, beach volleyball players, vacationing tourists at the Santa Monica Pier and a variety of characters hanging about the Venice Beach Boardwalk.

The pavement is flat throughout but, if you want to add a real climb or two, consider running up the hills into Pacific Palisades. You will have to run about a quarter-mile up Chautauqua Boulevard, but the neighborhood streets on top are less crowded, and quite nice for house viewing.

If you elect to continue south of Venice, you will encounter alleyways and residential streets, so we recommend turning around.

Santa Monica College

Santa Monica College has a 1/4-mile track open daily. It's a great locale for Fartlek sessions and interval training. Just look for the pool, drive through the parking garage, and it will be right there. You'll have to park on the nearby streets and feed the meters during the week, as the campus garages are permit only. Weekend runners may park in the garages for free.

West Hollywood

Running in West Hollywood? Forget it. If you get up early, you can beat the crowds to Sunset Boulevard's sidewalks and log a few miles. Your best bet is to head toward the nearby residential streets of the Hancock Park neighborhood. Otherwise, get in the car and drive to Lake Hollywood Reservoir, where a 2-3 mile path encircles the fenced-off water.

Griffith Park

You'll find L.A.'s best trail running in 4,000 acre Griffith Park.

Wheels — the kind with an engine — will be required to get there. But plenty of parking is available, as are running routes. Be prepared for hills, however, as this territory is some of LA's steepest.

LOUISVILLE, KENTUCKY

"And they're off!"

These three words launch the Run for the Roses, the most exciting 2 minutes in sports. It's probably the only time during all of Derby week when not one thoroughbred racing fan or Derby party fanatic is sipping the cocktail of choice — the Mint Julep.

As the Kentucky Derby's traditional libation, creating the Mint Julep is an event unto itself. Those elixirs served on the infield of Churchill Downs are a toxic, quick mix of Bourbon, syrup and water but, as julep connoisseurs will inform you, they're not the "official" Kentucky Mint Julep. Concocting the authentic version is considered an art form, not horseplay. The festive brew demands tremendous preparation and precision. Purchasing, washing and tearing mint leaves, boiling water and adding specific sugars, soaking and refrigerating the mint overnight and determining the appropriate brand of Bourbon... This is just a sampling of the elaborate undertaking required to perfect this spring spirit.

Serving a julep appears nearly as complicated as its creation. Snooty-toots profess that full appreciation of this refreshment can only be achieved if proper etiquette is followed: The ice must be crushed, not shaved; the julep must be served in a chilled, sterling silver cup; the cup should be held by the rim so as not to disturb the frosty sides; and, assuming a straw is used, it must be short enough to smell the mint's "bloom" when slurping.

All this work just to have a "special" drink in hand for two minutes? We need a beer!

Traveling athletes visiting downtown Louisville may want to indulge in the Derby delight prior to reviewing the workout options. While "mint" may symbolize hospitality, the odds of finding a hospitable hotel gym in the Derby City are long. Serious exercisers must saddle up and head over to the YMCA, the only race in town. Finally, despite varying quality, all recommended hotels fall in the same price category of "Moderately Expensive."

MODERATELY EXPENSIVE

GOLD: Hyatt Regency

320 West Jefferson, Louisville, KY 40202
(502) 587-3434 • louisville.hyatt.com

CARDIO

TREADMILLS: **2 Cybex**
UPRIGHT BIKE: **2 Cybex**
ELLIPTICAL: **1 True**
STEPPER: **2 Cybex**

STRENGTH

MACHINES: **1 Multi**
DUMBBELLS: **3-50 lbs**

SWIM

SPECS: **Indoor • Not lap**

OTHER

HOURS: **5a-10p**
• Will open after hours
COST: **Free**
TV: **Yes**
EXTRAS: **Tennis**

Connected via walkway to the Kentucky Convention Center in the heart of Louisville, Hyatt is a large, business style accommodation that hosts the best hotel gym in Downtown — which isn't saying much, but good news is on the way.

Hyatt's 392 rooms and corridors received a much needed renovation. Guests are spoiled with Hyatt's Grand Beds (which include a pillow top mattress, down blanket and plenty of pillows), elegant custom designed chairs and lamps, and an ergonomically designed workspace featuring wireless internet service.

Just beyond the lobby, guests will find Hyatt's average, yet functional, workout facility. In an area about the size of a small guest room, Hyatt supplies several good condition cardio machines, a fair assortment of dumbbells, and a useless multi-gym. The endurance equipment appears several years old, but the upright bikes are a highlight (they even have pedal straps). Traveling athletes in need of a quick energy boost will find this gym sufficient. Those wanting a more elaborate conditioning or swim must walk 10 minutes to the YMCA. Water worshipers not adverse to a 10-minute car ride can check out the fantastic Mary Meagher Aquatic Center.

Note: The hotel has an outdoor tennis court on the 4th floor and will have a new fitness experience by late 2006 with brand new Life Fitness equipment. Check athleticmindedtraveler.com for updates.

SILVER: The Brown

335 West Broadway, Louisville, KY 40202
(502) 583-1234 • brownhotel.com

CARDIO

TREADMILLS: **2 Trotter**
RECUMBENT BIKE: **2 Cybex**
STEPPER: **2 Tectrix**

STRENGTH

DUMBBELLS: **5-40 lbs**

OTHER

HOURS: **24**
COST: **Free**
TV: **Yes**

Built in 1923, the historic Brown offers rooms in Louisville's quaint Theater Square — a block-long area with a cobblestone street and a few art attractions and shops. Instead of Hyatt's modern business theme, Brown guests enjoy classic Victorian-style accommodations with antique furnishings and Old World features. The 293 standard rooms are large and fairly attractive, but for a few dollars more guests can upgrade to Brown's enhanced "club-level" rooms, which include amenities such as complimentary continental breakfasts, midday snacks and evening refreshments. The slightly more expensive quarters also afford 250 thread count sheets, down comforters and fresh flowers. Our research reveals a $20-$40/night premium for the upgrade, well worth the extra green.

The workout room breaks this hotel's dominant vintage theme and goes for minimalist — unfortunately, not in a Zen way. Only 6 cardio machines call the tiny room home, and not one is new or in great condition. Upright bikes and ellipticals are noticeably absent and the dumbbell set is an insufficient primary strength conditioner.

Fortunately, the Brown is close to downtown's YMCA — closer than the Hyatt, in fact. So, if Hyatt's exercise room will not satisfy your workout demands and you plan to seek the Y's services, Brown will be a better choice. Staying at the Brown will cut your YMCA commute by half, but neither walk is unbearable (5 minutes from Brown versus 10 minutes from Hyatt).

Swimmers can frolic at the Y or hop in the car to Mary Meagher Aquatic Center (10-minute drive).

BRONZE: **Holiday Inn** Downtown

120 West Broadway, Louisville, KY 40202
(502) 582-2241 • holiday-inn.com

By far the least plush of the three recommended hotels, Holiday Inn makes our cut solely for its proximity to the YMCA. Frankly, we would only stay here if the other two hotels were booked. Holiday's unpleasantly decorated rooms and cavernous common areas are a bit depressing. And those who equate Holiday Inn to a guaranteed bargain should think again. This hotel's nightly rates are within $20-$30/night of the Hyatt's.

The so-called workout room is a glass-enclosed cube adjacent to the indoor pool, containing 6 worn cardio machines begging for an upgrade. Since you are staying here because this hotel is the closest to the Y, you'd better use it — you can see it from the driveway.

BEYOND HOTELS

YMCA Downtown

555 South Second Street, Louisville, KY 40202
(502) 587-6700 • ymcalouisville.org

Evidently, local hotels view their gyms as an afterthought, and it's a shame. Thank goodness for the Louisville Y! Without this full-service fitness option, athletic-minded travelers to the Derby City would be out of luck. A room key and $10 provide access to the facility's 8 floors of fitness fun. The mega-center's two hotspots are its 4th floor wellness center and ground-level lap pool.

YMCA's recently renovated wellness center is bright and cheer-

CARDIO

TREADMILLS: **Cybex • Precor • Trotter**
UPRIGHT BIKE: **Cybex • Fan**
RECUMBENT BIKE: **Cybex • Tectrix**
ELLIPTICAL: **Precor**
STEPPER: **StairMaster**
ROWING: **Concept II**
OTHER: **Crossrobic**

STRENGTH

FREE WEIGHTS: **Yes**
HAMMER: **Yes**
MACHINES: **Cybex • Magnum • Nautilus**
DUMBBELLS: **5-95 lbs**

SWIM

GRADE: **B**
SPECS: **5x25yd • Indoor • 86º**
TOYS: **Kick • Pull**
MASTERS: **Yes**

OTHER

CLASSES: **Yes**
HOURS: M-TH **5a-10p** • F **5a-8p** • SAT **6a-6p** • SUN **9a-6p**
COST: **$10**
TV: **Yes**
EXTRAS: **1/19 mile indoor track • Basketball • Racquetball • Climbing wall**

ful. This expansive room, about the length and width of half a tennis court, is stocked with a ton of new cardio and strength equipment. Twenty-five stack-loaded weight stations, 10 treadmills and 9 ellipticals are a few of the center's highlights.

While the Y's aesthetic appeal diminishes on the other floors, the amount of equipment does not. The 5th, 6th and 7th levels house a 30-foot climbing wall, basketball court, free weight area and indoor track. If you're still not impressed, classes such as yoga, step and spinning (Reebok bikes) are offered in the Y's aerobic studio.

Swimmers can join the fitness party in the 25-yard lap pool. With a 20-foot ceiling and 5 lanes divided by floating lines and bottom stripes, we give it a "B" on our grading scale. If swim intervals are on your agenda, bring your watch, as we did not notice a pace clock. Because a Masters team frequents this pool, we suspect a clock was just not on deck at the time of our visit. Fortunately, kickboards and pull-buoys were in full view.

Mary T. Meagher Aquatic Center

201 Reservoir Avenue, Louisville, KY 40206
(502) 897-9949
lexdolphins.org/directions.pdf (for directions only)

SWIM

GRADE: **A**
SPECS: **11x50m • Indoor • 83º**
TOYS: **Kick • Pull • Clock**
MASTERS: **Yes**

OTHER

HOURS: M-F **5a-9p** • SAT **9a-6p** • SUN **12-6p**
COST: **$4.50**

An easy 10-minute drive from downtown Louisville, lap swimmers should seriously consider this phenomenal Aquatic Center for their water workout. The public facility schedules lap swim hours throughout the day and boasts a 50-meter pool used by a Masters group and several local high school teams.

Housed in a building with a high, warehouse-type roof, swimmers will feel anything but cramped in this liquid heaven. Wide bottom stripes and competition-quality floating lane lines will keep swimmers of all abilities in a straight line. Depending on the hour, the

11-lane behemoth can be divided into 22 lanes of 25-yard/25-meter swimming or kept at long course. Of course, all of the necessities are here, including kickboards, pace clocks, backstroke flags and the like. According to staff, your best chance for an uncrowded dip is between 8 a.m. and 3 p.m. The shower facilities are bare bones — good for a quick chlorine rinse.

The center also houses a small fitness room, but most of the equipment is old and worn. Still, those in desperate need of a daily double workout will find 8 Cybex stack-loaded machines, free weights with an accompanying bench and squat rack, 5-70 pound dumbbells, 3 old Precor treadmills, 2 Concept II rowers, a couple of old step machines and a few fan bikes. Certainly not much to drool over, but something is better than nothing, right? Come here for the pool only.

Directions: Take I-71 North from Downtown to exit #2, which is Zorn Avenue. After exiting, turn right on Zorn and drive for ~ 1 mile — you will drive up a slight hill. At Brownsboro, turn left and immediately pull into the right lane. About 2 blocks from Brownsboro, turn right on Reservoir — this street comes up quickly, so be looking for it. Follow Reservoir for 1/4 to 1/2 mile; the Aquatic Center and its parking lot will be on your left.

Note: As with any public facility, call to verify hours, lap swim schedule, etc.

RUNNING ROUTES

RiverWalk

For a downtown run, the 20+ miles along the RiverWalk multi-use path originating in Waterfront Park is a worthy option. This 50+ acre park is a downtown favorite. Lunch-breaking workers, families and sports enthusiasts seek the ample greenery for fun, rest or a picnic. The park's Ohio River setting affords boating opportunities and other water festivities. Several 1-2 mile courses run through it.

The path follows the Ohio River and can be picked up in a variety of spots — for Hyatt guests, a 5-minute saunter will get you there. Brown guests have a little farther to go, but it is still convenient. Several parks are along the way, and river and skyline views allow for a meditative sweat.

Cherokee Park (Willow Park)

Runners will enjoy the shorter, 2.5-mile paved loop in this hilly retreat. Other trails meander along Beargrass Creek and, with the park's abundance of trees, cool shade is plentiful. Cherokee's 409 acres also sport horse trails, an archery range, 9 holes of golf, ball fields, tennis courts and more.

Needless to say, locals flock here for their recreation fun — and you can, too. Runners will find the park at Willow and Cherokee Parkway, about 5 miles southeast of the Ohio River (downtown part). Holiday Inn guests are closer (~3 miles away).

Note: A popular trail begins behind Hogan's fountain.

Madison

MADISON

As America's Dairyland and the country's largest purveyor of cheese (2.2 billion lbs. in 2002), Wisconsin and its natives have endured derogatory "cheesehead" references and cheesy ridicule since... well, forever. Never one to have a cow over name-calling, former cabinet maker and resident cheesemeister Ralph Bruno created his own specialty cheese topping to rebut these critics.

Before heading to a Milwaukee Brewers baseball game in 1987, this whiz carved a wedge from his mother's sofa cushion, spray-painted it bright yellow, added some holes and wore it as a hat during the game. Fans instantly took to his creative "Cheesehead" couture, transforming this once stinky slur into an icon of Wisconsin pride — and a booming business for the crown's craftsman.

Bruno's Foamation Incorporated has been cutting the cheese ever since for Packer fans, Fortune 500 companies and California movie studios. Foamation has even expanded its product line to include cowboy hats, firefighter helmets and baseball caps.

Although the Cheesehead now comes in a variety of shapes and sizes, Bruno's original is on display at the Wisconsin Historical Museum in the state capital of Madison. When taking your picture along side this memorable headgear, make sure you don't forget to say, "cheeeese!"

31 Locations Reviewed

DOWNTOWN

MODERATELY EXPENSIVE

GOLD: Hilton Madison

9 East Wilson Street, Madison, WI 53703
(608) 255-5100 • hilton.com

CARDIO

TREADMILLS: **1 LF • 1 StarTrac**
RECUMBENT BIKE: **2 LF**
ELLIPTICAL: **1 LF**

STRENGTH

MACHINES: **1 LF Multi**
DUMBBELLS: **5-50 lbs**

SWIM

SPECS: **Indoor • Not lap**

OTHER

HOURS: **5a-11p**
COST: **Free**
TV: **Yes**

This 14-story Hilton, located across the street from Lake Monona and a short walk to State Street and Capitol Square, oozes class with its un-chain-like Old World charm and décor. The elegant lobby beckons travelers with comfy chairs and a cozy fireplace, and all 240 rooms are accented with mahogany and maple wood. Guests can expect weekday newspaper delivery, high-speed internet access (fee), capitol or lake views and 24-hour room service.

Although this Ironman Wisconsin host hotel's fitness facility lacks step machines and upright bikes, it does provide several good quality cardio and weight-lifting options in a bright and cheerful room. The Life Fitness endurance machines are the recent 9500 series, and the multi-gym, though not a strength favorite, is better than most.

Hilton's best workout feature is its proximity to Lake Monona. Open water freestyling during Madison's summers is a swimmer's treat, and the 11+ mile perimeter path is a year-round favorite for joggers. Those looking for a more serious sweat or strength routine can trek 10 minutes to Capital Fitness on Butler Street ($10/day).

To satisfy their water frolicking desires more traditionally, lap swimmers must endure a 10-15 minute drive to either Princeton West or East ($20/day).

LEAST EXPENSIVE

GOLD: Madison Concourse Downtown

1 West Dayton Street, Madison, WI 53703
(608) 257-6000 • concoursehotel.com

In the heart of downtown Madison, the Concourse is within steps of the Capitol, State Street and the University of Wisconsin campus. While the 13-story exterior resembles a college dormitory, the upscale interior will quickly affirm that your co-ed days are long gone. Concourse's 360 rooms are tastefully furnished with basic amenities. For an upgraded stay, consider the hotel's VIP level, where each day guests can enjoy complimentary continental breakfasts, evening cocktails and hors d'oeuvres.

Adjacent to the hotel's indoor non-lap pool is its glass-enclosed exercise room. This "mini-greenhouse" will not satisfy athletic-minded travelers needing a full body conditioning. The few useful cardio machines and decent dumbbell set will service a quick tune-up at best. Instead, purchase a discounted $6 pass to either of the two downtown Capital Fitness Clubs (both within a 5-minute walk), from Concourse's front desk.

Swimmers can either head to Lake Monona for an open water session or to one of the Princeton Clubs for a traditional lap routine (10-15 minute drive to either Princeton East or West, $20).

CARDIO

TREADMILLS: **1 LF • 1 Trotter**
UPRIGHT BIKE: **1 Tectrix**
ELLIPTICAL: **1 LF - old**
STEPPER: **1 Tectrix - old**

STRENGTH

MACHINES: **1 Multi**
DUMBBELLS: **5-50 lbs**

SWIM

SPECS: **Indoor • Not lap**

OTHER

HOURS: **5a-11p**
COST: **Free**
TV: **Yes**
EXTRA: **$6 pass to Capital Fit.**

SILVER: Doubletree Madison

525 West Johnson Street, Madison, WI, 53703
(608) 251-5511 • doubletree.com

As the closest hotel to Madison's eclectic State Street, the Kohl Center and the University of Wisconsin's Southeast Recreation Facility (SERF), this Doubletree sits in a great location.

A $4 million renovation to this previous Howard Johnson has transformed it from a no frills budget accommodation to a comfortable on-the-road retreat. Guests will enjoy Doubletree's trademark "Sweet Dreams" beds with down comforters and 250 thread count sheets, along with stylish furnishings that include ergonomic work spaces. A restaurant is on-site, and Doubletree provides free shuttle service to Monona Terrace and other close venues.

CARDIO

TREADMILLS: **2 LF**
UPRIGHT BIKE: **1 LF**
ELLIPTICAL: **2 LF**
STEPPER: **1 LF**

STRENGTH

MACHINES: **1 Multi**
DUMBBELLS: **Yes**

SWIM

SPECS: **Indoor • Not lap**

OTHER

HOURS: **6a-11p**
COST: **Free**
TV: **Yes**

On site, exercise fiends will find quite a few fabulous machines. Brand new Life Fitness equipment was stocked in Spring 2006. We have quite a few photo images of all the machines, but suffice it to say you should not be disappointed. It's great to see such high quality machinery in a smaller market city. The dumbbells may not be enough for your strength session, however. If not, you will have to look off-site to SERF or the other nearby health clubs.

SERF is the closest option (read our review), but staff is very strict about letting anyone inside for a sweat unless you are a student or faculty member — or show up with someone who is such. We understand from management that any written proof of on-campus business (including department letters, convention brochures, etc.) along with some begging and pleading may help. Working out at UW's excellent facility is worth the effort for both cardio and swim fiends, and the price is a bargain at $5/day. If SERF is not an option, sweat seekers can hoof it to Capital Fitness ($10; no pool), about a mile away.

WESTSIDE

LEAST EXPENSIVE

GOLD: **Radisson West Madison**
517 Grand Canyon Drive, Madison, WI 53719
(608) 833-0100 • radisson.com

GOLD: **Hampton Inn West Towne Mall**
516 Grand Canyon Drive, Madison, WI 53719
(608) 833-3511 • hamptoninn.com

Located across the street from one another in the midst of Madison's West Towne Mall (Starbucks, Barnes & Noble and Olive Garden), Radisson and Hampton are recommended for their proximity to the massive and brand new Princeton Club West. Each accommodation is typical for its brand. Expect clean rooms, courteous service and, at Hampton Inn, a free continental breakfast each morning.

Neither has a workout center worth using or mentioning, so plan to drive 5 minutes to Princeton West's fitness utopia ($20/day) — not cheap but well worth the investment.

EASTSIDE

LEAST EXPENSIVE

GOLD: **Crowne Plaza**
4402 E. Washington Avenue, Madison, WI 53704
(608) 244-4703 • crowneplaza.com

This hotel is a good deal for travelers to Wisconsin's capital who do not mind a more isolated location. It's not as if Crowne is in the middle of rural Wisconsin — exactly. But, except for the phenomenal Princeton Club East across the street (5-minute walk), Madison's eastside "walk to" dining and shopping attractions are less appealing than those found Downtown and in the western section of the City.

The accommodation itself is nice, but nothing special — clean rooms, standard floor plans and average service. We recommend Crowne because guests receive discounted access to the Princeton Club — $5 instead of $20. Now, that's a deal! Purchase your pass from the hotel front desk.

BEYOND HOTELS

Princeton Club West

8080 Watts Road, Madison, WI 53719
(608) 833-2639 • princetonclub.net

Princeton Club East

1726 Eagan Road, Madison, WI 53704
(608) 241-2639 • princetonclub.net

Although Princeton West had yet to open its doors at the time of our visit, we reviewed its plans and checked out the facility's exterior. Additionally, we toured its sister club across town and confirmed with staff that the quality levels of the two clubs are comparable, which is good news!

Both fitness centers strive to provide members with a convenient and first rate exercise experience. Massive in size, each club resembles a strip mall from the outside. With round-the-clock hours for members (see chart for guests), free on-site childcare, loads of classes and multiple sport courts, they've got everything. Some features are even on the rooftop (tennis and soccer).

Inside, sweat fiends can feast on a plethora of state-of the-art cardio machines (e.g., more than 30 treads, 30 ellipticals and 30 steppers at each), a ton of weights (actually, more than 40,000 lbs.) and 6-lane, 25-yard competition-quality pools. They are easily the best indoor workout options in Madison — and possibly the state. We could hardly contain our enthusiasm.

The only Princeton detractor is the steep guest fee and the 10-15 minute drive from Downtown to either club. However, free and ample parking and easy navigation will ease your commute.

According to staff, rush hours are 4:30-8 p.m. While some hotels (e.g., Crowne Plaza) do issue discounted passes, the customary entry cost is $20 with photo ID. Since both clubs offer a similar workout experience with almost identical equipment, we have included one chart only.

CARDIO

TREADMILLS: **Precor • Woodway • Quinton**
UPRIGHT BIKE: **Stratus • Tectrix**
RECUMBENT BIKE: **Stratus • Tectrix • Reebok**
ELLIPTICAL: **Precor • Cybex**
STEPPER: **StairMaster • LF • Stepmill**
ROWING: **Concept II**
OTHER: **NordicTrack • Gravitron**

STRENGTH

FREE WEIGHTS: **Yes**
HAMMER: **Yes**
MACHINES: **Cybex • Free Motion • Nautilus**
DUMBBELLS: **3-140 lbs**

SWIM

GRADE: **B**
SPECS: **6x25yd • Indoor • 84°**
TOYS: **Clock**

OTHER

CLASSES: **Yes**
HOURS: M TH **9a-8p** • F **9a-6p** • SAT **9a-5p** • SUN **12p-5p**
COST: **$5 Crowne (East) • $20 Others**
TV: **Yes**
EXTRAS: **1/10 mile indoor track • Basketball • Racquetball • Tennis**

Capital Fitness Butler Plaza

302 East Washington, Madison, WI 53703
(608) 251-1245 • capitalfitness.net

CARDIO

TREADMILLS: **StarTrac**
UPRIGHT BIKE: **Stratus**
RECUMBENT BIKE: **Stratus**
ELLIPTICAL: **Precor • LF**
STEPPER: **StairMaster • Stepmill**
ROWING: **Concept II**

STRENGTH

FREE WEIGHTS: **Yes**
HAMMER: **Yes**
MACHINES: **Magnum**
DUMBBELLS: **5-100 lbs**

OTHER

CLASSES: **Yes**
HOURS: M-TH **5:30a-11p** • F **5:30a-9p** • SAT-SUN **7a-9p**
COST: **$6 Concourse • $10 Others**
TV: **Yes**

Capital Fitness Butler Plaza and Capital Fitness on the Square, located only 3 blocks from one another, are the only private health clubs in downtown Madison. Unfortunately, neither has a pool, and both are small in size. The Butler Plaza branch is the newer and nicer of the two and is open on weekends. Its drawback is its distance (6 blocks) from the Capitol and Concourse hotel — potentially significant during Wisconsin's frigid winters.

Butler confirms its superiority where it counts — equipment quantity and quality. This younger club offers 17 treads, 18 Precor ellipticals and 7 StairMaster 4600 series steppers. Weather permitting, we strongly recommend the slightly longer walk to Butler Plaza.

Capital Fitness On the Square (WOMEN ONLY)

44 East Mifflin Street, Madison, WI 53704
(608) 256-5656

CARDIO

TREADMILLS: **StarTrac**
UPRIGHT BIKE: **LF**
RECUMBENT BIKE: **LF**
ELLIPTICAL: **Precor**
STEPPER: **StairMaster**
ROWING: **Concept II**

STRENGTH

FREE WEIGHTS: **Yes**
HAMMER: **Yes**
MACHINES: **Magnum**
DUMBBELLS: **5-140 lbs**

OTHER

CLASSES: **Yes**
HOURS: M-TH **5:30a-11p** • F **5:30a-9p** • SAT-SUN **Closed**
COST: **$6 Concourse • $10 Others**
TV: **Yes**

Capital Fitness on the Square is 3 blocks from its sister club, Capital Fitness Butler Plaza. Neither Downtown club has a pool, and both are small in size.

Mifflin Street's lower ceilings and older equipment is mitigated by its closer proximity (3 blocks) to the Capitol and Concourse hotel — potentially significant during Wisconsin's frigid winters.

While Butler has more and better equipment, this older club offers 7 treads, 6 Precor ellipticals and 5 StairMaster 4600 series steppers as well as 7 Life Fitness 9500 series upright bikes, a decent assortment of free weights and effective Magnum stack-loaded weight machines.

It should satisfy, but it's closed on weekends. Overall, we favor Butler Plaza.

SERF - University of Wisconsin SE Recreation Facility

715 West Dayton Street, Madison, WI 53706
Hotline/daily activity schedule (608) 262-4756
Recreational Sports Office (608) 262-8244
http://wiscinfo.doit.wisc.edu/recsports/

SERF is located on the eastern edge of campus near the Kohl Center basketball arena and 3 blocks from the Howard Johnson Hotel. Although you need not be a student or alum to work out here, a strict admission policy requires guests to supply written proof that University business brought them to town. An event/presentation schedule printed on university stationary should do the trick. Once you have cracked the entrance code and paid your $5, an impressive facility, renovated mid-2003, awaits. SERF's exercise equipment is located in 3 separate rooms: cardio, free weights and stack-loaded machines. Each area holds an impressive volume of workout hardware, including 12 mixed brand treadmills, 8 Precor ellipticals, 6 Cybex ArcTrainers, 3 Life Fitness 9500 series upright bikes and 10 Free Motion stack-loaded weight machines.

CARDIO

TREADMILLS: **Mix**
UPRIGHT BIKE: **LF**
RECUMBENT BIKE: **LF**
ELLIPTICAL: **Precor • Cybex**
STEPPER: **StairMaster**
ROWING: **Concept II**

STRENGTH

FREE WEIGHTS: **Yes**
HAMMER: **Yes**
MACHINES: **Cybex • Free Motion**
DUMBBELLS: **3-125 lbs**

SWIM

GRADE: **A**
SPECS: **8x50m • Indoor • 78-80°**
TOYS: **Kick • Pull • Clock**

OTHER

CLASSES: **Yes**
HOURS: **Vary**
COST: **$5 w/Univ affiliation only**
TV: **Yes**
EXTRAS: **1/9 mile indoor track • Basketball • Racquetball**

The 50-meter pool is home to the University's swim team and is Big Ten Conference quality. There is no set schedule for the competition-level water box's set up (long or short course); it just depends on the swim team's practice needs. Regardless of the course distance, this pool receives our top grade. Call ahead to verify lap availability, admission policy and rental lock availability.

Note: Avoid most of the late-sleeping undergrads by working out prior to 10 a.m.

Also: We've heard that SERF is becoming even more stringent with its guest policy, so you may have to beg or come in with a student or faculty member.

RUNNING ROUTES

Downtown

Big cheese runners should stay in the heart of Madison. Its isthmus location affords guests staying in downtown hotels convenient access to miles of lakefront mileage. A Madison favorite is Lake Monona's 11+ mile loop. Lake Wingra, located near the University of Wisconsin and the 1,200+ acre Arboretum, is a worthy runner-up with its 6+ mile course.

West Side

A Westside base camp is more appealing than an Eastside, but neither rivals the premium downtown selection. Radisson and Hampton guests can seek out Elver Park and its paved trails 1.5 miles away. However, if you don't mind the 3 miles of street running it will take to reach Lake Wingra and the Arboretum, go for it. It is worth the trip.

East Side

Eastsiders, you will be cheesed off to learn that a 4-mile pavement pound is your course to Lake Monona. If you anticipate that this long commute will curdle your fun, consult with the hotel front desk for a traffic-free route around the hotel. Better yet, just run at Princeton East!

Memphis

MEMPHIS, TENNESSEE

Guess which "house" is the most visited in the United States. If you thought, "the White House," good job! Now, which house do you think is the runner-up? If you said, "Graceland," you are correct. Elvis' 1957 purchase receives more than 600,000 visitors annually. Dead or alive, the King continues to be Memphis' most popular tourist attraction, but this birthplace of Blues and Rock and Roll offers travelers a whole lot more.

Strolling along famous Beale Street, you will encounter an assortment of music and entertainment options ranging from large-scale nightclubs to hole-in-the-wall bars. Food is a big attraction too, featuring some of the best barbeque in the world! Our favorite is served at Rendezvous (www.hogsfly.com or 888-hogsfly), known for its charcoal-broiled dry ribs and other finger lickin' BBQ dishes. But don't show up hungry on a Sunday or Monday, when the hogs are grounded and the restaurant is closed.

Finally, if you are Downtown during the summer and a baseball fan, taking in a Memphis Redbird game at Autozone Park is a treat. The AAA stadium holds over 20,000 fans, is located within a short walk of most hotels, and is a fascinating experience for the sport's purists.

So slip on those blue suede shoes when it's time to have some Memphis fun and lace up a second pair for your elliptical, stepper, bike or run.

18 Locations Reviewed

EXPENSIVE

GOLD: Madison Hotel

79 Madison Avenue, Memphis, TN 38103
(901) 333-1200 • madisonhotelmemphis.com

CARDIO

TREADMILLS: **2 Precor**
RECUMBENT BIKE: **1 Precor**
ELLIPTICAL: **2 Precor**

STRENGTH

MACHINES: **1 Precor Multi**
DUMBBELLS: **3-50 lbs**

SWIM

SPECS: **Indoor • Not lap**

OTHER

HOURS: **24**
COST: **Free**
TV: **Yes**
EXTRA: **$10 pass to Six50**

In the heart of the business district and only steps from renowned Beale Street, the Madison transformed an early 20th Century bank building into a swank, boutique hotel. Opened in May 2002, the Madison is the most luxurious lodging option in Memphis.

The 110 guest rooms are decorated with chic furniture, expensive bedding and powerful colors. A picture is worth a thousand words, so check out the Madison's website, where you can view photos of the hotel's guest rooms, lobby and fitness center. While you will not see pictures of cereal, muffins or juice, Madison does offer guests a free continental breakfast each morning and high tea service in the afternoons.

The complimentary gym is located in the hotel's basement in what was once the bank vault. Rather than disguising the space, Madison cleverly emphasizes its features with the spindle wheel lock as a centerpiece. The vault's cash has been replaced with 5 expensive Precor cardio machines, all in fantastic condition. Though weights are scarce, the dumbbells and multi-gym suffice for a light muscle pump session.

Those looking for something more significant can walk across the street, pay $10 and exercise at Six50 Health and Fitness. Because Madison's indoor pool is not lap-designed, swimmers must trek a little farther (10 minutes) to the Downtown YMCA's 25-yard lapper. It's nothing fancy, but it will get the job done on the cheap ($8).

SILVER: The Peabody

149 Union Avenue, Memphis, TN 38103
(901) 529-4000 • peabodymemphis.com

It is a choice of old versus new with the Peabody and Madison hotels. Unlike the chic Madison boutique, Peabody dazzles guests with Old World elegance and charm, historic tradition and a greater number of rooms (468). Peabody's location is slightly more convenient to Memphis' attractions, but we are really splitting hairs.

Though we believe Madison's accommodations are a tad above its luxury rival, the major reason Peabody gives up the Gold is its inferior workout options. The ergonomically challenged fitness center has more equipment than Madison's vault, but our comparison takes into account the neighboring Wellworx, which we view as an extension to Madison's workout option. Your right to sweat at Peabody is on the house, while 10 bucks at the Madison grants access to "the vault" and a health club across the street.

Nevertheless, with a host of modern machines and a large assortment of weights, Peabody still offers a better than average hotel workout alternative, justifying our recommendation.

Swimmers, your suggested route remains the same at either hotel, go to the Y.

CARDIO

TREADMILLS: **2 LF**
UPRIGHT BIKE: **1 Cybex • 2 Spin**
RECUMBENT BIKE: **1 Cybex**
ELLIPTICAL: **2 LF**
STEPPER: **3 StairMaster**
ROWING: **2 Concept II**

STRENGTH

FREE WEIGHTS: **Yes**
MACHINES: **12 Cybex**
DUMBBELLS: **3-90 lbs**

SWIM

SPECS: **Indoor • Not lap**

OTHER

HOURS: M-F **5:30a-10p** • SAT-SUN **8a-9p**
COST: **Free**
TV: **Yes**

MODERATELY EXPENSIVE

GOLD: Hampton Inn & Suites Peabody Place

175 Peabody Place, Memphis, TN 38103
(901) 260-4000 • hamptoninn.com

What is this — a Hampton property in the "Moderately Expensive" category?

That's right! This is the nicest Hampton Inn we have seen. While we stop short of using the "L" word (luxury), this franchise comes close with its warm, lodge-like lobby and fireplace, attractive guest quarters and free continental breakfasts. Unfortunately, the exercise room does not contribute to its appeal.

Hampton's 5 Life Fitness cardio machines have seen better days. Lacking any strength equipment, muscle buffs will likewise have to resort to the YMCA. From Hampton Inn, it's a 7-10 minute walk.

SILVER: Holiday Inn Select Downtown

160 Union Avenue, Memphis, TN 38103
(901) 525-5491 • holiday-inn.com

SILVER: Doubletree Hotel

185 Union Avenue, Memphis, TN 38103
(901) 528-1800 • doubletree.com

Because Madison and Peabody are the only downtown hotels that offer useful on-site workout options, the relevant question for those staying elsewhere becomes, "how far is the Downtown YMCA?" From the Holiday Inn Select and Doubletree, the walk is 3-5 minutes.

Both of these hotels previously offered similar lodging experiences until Doubletree poured about $8 million into a complete renovation, giving the hotel a fresh and appealing feel. Guests can count on friendly and helpful staff and central locations at both, but the bright red carpeted rooms with busy bed comforters at Holiday Inn could use a renovation as well. Since neither offers worthwhile exercise machinery onsite, workout plans mandate a trip to the Y.

LEAST EXPENSIVE

GOLD: Best Western Benchmark Hotel

164 Union Avenue, Memphis, TN 38103
(901) 527-4100 • bestwestern.com

Warning! This hotel is for extreme budget seekers only. The property is in need of a major makeover, but if you want a great location at bare bones pricing ($65/night), this is your place.

The guest room doors open into interior hallways, and the interior of your unattractive quarters. Off-white walls and dreary gray carpets provide a stage for the rooms' cheap furniture and homely bedding. If your expectations are low, these rooms will meet them.

A Denny's off the lobby is this hotel's highlight. And forget about a workout room. The YMCA is a 3-minute walk.

BEYOND HOTELS

Wellworx

1 North Maine, Memphis, TN 38103
(901) 526-7966 • wellworxsportingclubs.com

CARDIO

TREADMILLS: **LF**
UPRIGHT BIKE: **LF**
RECUMBENT BIKE: **LF**
ELLIPTICAL: **LF**
STEPPER: **LF**

STRENGTH

FREE WEIGHTS: **Yes**
HAMMER: **Yes**
MACHINES: **LF**
DUMBBELLS: **5-120 lbs**

OTHER

CLASSES: **Yes**
HOURS: M-TH **5:30a-11p** • F **5a-8p** • SAT **7a-8p** • SUN **8a-6p**
COST: **$10 Madison • $20 Others**
TV: **Yes**

A nice supplement to Madison's on-site gym, Madison guests receive discounted entry at $10 (normally $20). This modern club opened in September 2003 and supplies oodles of new machines on two floors of studio space.

Unfortunately, Wellworx decided to stock Life Fitness equipment exclusively. While a high quality manufacturer, we prefer a wider assortment of machines to accommodate exercisers' diverse preferences. That said, come here with high expectations and high energy for a complete workout.

Swimmers, go to the Y, because Wellworx has no pool.

Fogelman Downtown YMCA

245 Madison Avenue, Memphis, TN 38103
(901) 527-9622
ymcamemphis.org/locations/folgelman.html

We always enjoy walking into YMCAs because the staffs are so polite and helpful. Fogelman Y is no exception. Housed in this multi-level building since 1909, the Y underwent a $4.5 million interior overhaul in 1989 and continues to raise money for a desperately needed interior renovation. Like an old and cherished holey t-shirt, this decaying Y provides comfort with its well-tailored selection of high-level machines and nurturing lap pool.

Indicative of the Y's ongoing equipment replacement process, the fitness area mixes old and new. Sixteen Paramount stack-loaded weight machine "newbies" sit beside 15 BodyMaster veterans. Next to 11 older Precor treadmills rest 7 newer Precor ellipticals. Windows throughout the facility afford plenty of sunlight during the day, and a few even overlook the AAA baseball park, so game watching calorie burning is a distinct possibility.

CARDIO

TREADMILLS: **Precor**
UPRIGHT BIKE: **Precor • Tectrix • Fan**
RECUMBENT BIKE: **Stratus • Precor**
ELLIPTICAL: **Precor**
STEPPER: **StairMaster**
ROWING: **Concept II**
OTHER: **Free Runner**

STRENGTH

FREE WEIGHTS: **Yes**
HAMMER: **Yes**
MACHINES: **Paramount**
DUMBBELLS: **3-100 lbs**

SWIM

GRADE: **C**
SPECS: **6x25yd • Indoor • 82°**
TOYS: **Kick • Pull • Clock**
MASTERS: **Yes**

OTHER

CLASSES: **Yes**
HOURS: M-TH **5:30a-10p** • F **5:30a-9p** • SAT **8a-6p** • SUN **12-5p**
COST: **$5-$8**
TV: **Yes**
EXTRAS: **Basketball • Racquetball**

No different from the rest of the building, the pool is worn and needs a fresh coat of paint. But the appearance did not affect our 3500-yard swim session. Floating lane lines, bottom stripes, toys and a pace clock are all here. And the water temperature was fine.

Admission fees will vary depending on the hotel you select. Eight bucks is the norm, but Holiday Inn Select, Radisson and Hampton Inn all receive a $3 discount. Towels are provided and the locker rooms/showers are adequate for a simple clean-up.

RUNNING ROUTES

The Mississippi River

The river is a runner's best bet in this BBQ loving town. The Tom Lee Park has a paved 1-mile shorty and Harbor Town, on the residential side of Mud Island, has a similarly length-challenged path. Our advice? Consult with the hotel front desk.

Overton Park

About 3 miles east of Downtown Memphis is the 90-year-old mature forest of Overton Park. Replete with nature trails, jogging paths and bike routes, this is a popular destination for visitors and locals looking to "recreate." The park is also home to a public golf course, museum and zoo.

MIAMI, FLORIDA

Once Dictator Fidel Castro seized power in 1959, Cubans began fleeing their homeland in record numbers, setting their sights, hopes and dreams on 90-mile-away Florida soil and American freedom. Through hard work and U.S. government sponsorship, many of these refugees made Miami their home, and were instrumental in transforming the City from a sleepy vacation destination to an economically booming cosmopolitan center. "Little Havana" is emblematic of this blossoming and enduring Hispanic culture.

The Cubans' success inspired Colombians, Guatemalans and Nicaraguans, among others, to escape and plant roots in America's "Magic City." Like the Cubans before them, they enriched Miami with their customs, food and language.

One Hispanic pastime has captivated both this city and the rest of Florida — the little-known sport of Jai Alai. Literally a "merry festival," the game was first seen at religious and holiday festivals in the Basque mountains of Spain and France. The Latinos introduced the sport to North America, where the action and legalized wagering attracted a mass following. Florida supports more Jai Alai (*fronton*) arenas than anywhere else in the world, and downtown Miami is the sport's mecca.

Jai Alai is a rugged form of racquetball, where two teams compete by slinging a ball (*pelota*) from a sickle-shaped wicker basket (*cesta*) affixed to players' wrists. Points are scored when one team shoots the ball off the arena's front wall and the other team fails to catch and sling it back before it bounces twice on the floor. Spectators get in on the action by making win, place or show bets on any of the eight players.

With ball speeds reaching 190 mph, professional Jai Alai is dangerous. Four men have been killed and many others severely injured, usually from high-velocity ball strikes to the head. Oddly enough, player's salaries average $40,000 per year, hardly compensating for these risks.

In the 21st Century's "Gateway to South and Central America," Jai Alai is but one adrenaline-rushing pursuit. This city bursts with energy, style and opportunity. Your only holdback will be time and budget. So get going!

SOUTH BEACH

A popular destination for the international jet-set, chic "SoBe" is a fashion and entertainment nucleus where late nights are as common as National Enquirer scandals. Donning your sneakers and cap for a morning jog on the beach is just fine, but don't even think of sporting them out to dinner or a club. In this style capital, such a major fashion faux pas is almost a crime!

EXPENSIVE

GOLD: **Shore Club**

1901 Collins Avenue, Miami Beach, FL 33139
(305) 695-3100 • shoreclub.com

CARDIO

TREADMILLS: **6 LF**
UPRIGHT BIKE: **3 LF**
RECUMBENT BIKE: **3 LF**
ELLIPTICAL: **4 Precor**
STEPPER: **3 StairMaster**

STRENGTH

FREE WEIGHTS: **Yes**
MACHINES: **9 Cybex**
DUMBBELLS: **5-50 lbs**

SWIM

SPECS: **Outdoor • Not lap**

OTHER

HOURS: **24**
COST: **Free**
TV: **Yes**

On the north end of Collins Avenue, this recent addition to the South Beach strip epitomizes Miami's hip style and culture. Visitors flock to Shore Club's over-the-top trendy property for reasons beyond the minimalist art deco rooms and 400 thread count Egyptian linens. Its "in" restaurants, chic bars and swank outdoor pool are prime attractions.

No matter what time of day, this hotel is teeming with the "to be seen" crowd. Professional athletes dine in the extravagant Nobu restaurant, supermodels and wannabes sip martinis at the indoor/outdoor Skybar, Hollywood celebrities get rubbed the right way at Christy Turlington's rooftop Sundari Spa and average Joes like us pull up a seat and take it all in.

Though not great, Shore Club's complimentary exercise facility is about as good as you're going to find in a South Beach hotel. The basement-level club lacks natural light, but the high-end machines will brighten your workout. Plenty of barely-used free weights are supplied, along with a flat bench, an incline bench and barbells. While all of the cardio machines are youthful and in excellent condition, beautiful Miami Beach is your backyard! This is the place to run on the beach, swim in the ocean or even drop to the sand for some pushups.

Shore Club is outfitted with two pools, the main pool and a 20-yard rectangle that could serve as a desperate lap option. There are no lines or lanes, but at least the European guests will not raise their eyebrows when you prance around the deck in your Speedo. Swimmers wanting to get wet in a regulation lap pool should drive to Flamingo Park. By the way, don't forget about the salty open-water alternative known as the Atlantic Ocean.

SILVER: **Delano**

1685 Collins Avenue, Miami Beach, FL 33139
(305) 672-2000 • ianschragerhotels.com

This hyper-chic beachfront hotel offers its very own South Beach experience, one in stark contrast to the Shore Club's omnipresent scene.

Within a block of Lincoln Road boutiques and restaurants, Delano is a bit more centrally located than the Shore Club. Its showcase indoor/outdoor lobby sets the tone for the hotel's fresh air and natural light theme. Ocean breezes whisper through the lobby, gently rustling the white, mosquito-net-like curtains, encouraging you to surrender all worries to the wind — even if only for a night or two. The all-ivory 206 guest rooms perpetuate Delano's halcyon motif. The rooms are truly "heavenly" with their white walls, white floors, white bedding and white furniture. Guest comforts also include 24-hour room service and a 1,500 volume movie library for the in-room VCRs.

CARDIO

TREADMILLS: **5 LF**
UPRIGHT BIKE: **3 LF - old**
RECUMBENT BIKE: **4 LF - old**
ELLIPTICAL: **4 LF**
STEPPER: **6 StairMaster**

STRENGTH

FREE WEIGHTS: **Yes**
HAMMER: **Yes**
MACHINES: **8 LF**
DUMBBELLS: **5-100 lbs**

SWIM

SPECS: **Outdoor • Not lap**

OTHER

CLASSES: **Yes**
HOURS: M-F **6a-12a**
• SAT-SUN **8:30a-9:30p**
COST: **Free Hotel Guests**
• **$25 Others**
TV: **Yes**

Delano's complimentary workout room is the one place where the "pure white" theme is broken. Ironically accented in black, the below-ground fitness center is comprised of two small rooms with low ceilings. Though stocking a great assortment of weight machines, free weights and dumbbells, Delano slips into the #2 slot due to its inferior cardio equipment and cramped atmosphere. Specifically, a mix of old bikes and newer ellipticals run uncomfortably close to one another, forcing exercisers within whiffing distance. Fortunately, this is South Beach, so the prevailing scent is more likely Chanel or Hugo Boss, but you never know. Nevertheless, this gym remains a good workout option and one of the best in the area. For endurance and strength junkies wanting an off-site indoor sweat, Crunch Fitness is your only option.

Swimmers should head to Flamingo Park or the Atlantic Ocean. The former is a 5-minute drive/20-minute walk. The latter is in your backyard.

Note: For complimentary access to Delano's workout center, guests must bring their "privilege card," provided by the front desk at check-in.

BRONZE: **Ritz Carlton** South Beach

One Lincoln Road, Miami Beach, FL 33139
(786) 276-4000 • ritzcarlton.com/resorts/south_beach

At close to $500/night, the Ritz certainly fits the high price category bill. This handsome property opened to the public on New

CARDIO

TREADMILLS: **4 LF**
UPRIGHT BIKE: **2 LF**
RECUMBENT BIKE: **2 LF**
ELLIPTICAL: **4 LF**

STRENGTH

FREE WEIGHTS: **Yes**
MACHINES: **7 LF**
DUMBBELLS: **5-50 lbs**

SWIM

SPECS: **Outdoor • Not lap**

OTHER

HOURS: **6a-11p**
COST: **Free**
TV: **Yes**

Year's Eve 2003 and boasts a prime beachfront location within steps of tony Lincoln Road.

According to the Ritz's website, the 375 guest rooms "are inspired by the staterooms of a luxury liner with dark cherry furniture and nautical blue and gold color schemes." We don't know about the "luxury liner" part, but the rooms are certainly elegant, contemporary and those colors. Do not expect the glitz, glamour and drama of the Shore Club or Delano. This is a Ritz, and it looks like a Ritz.

We love recently opened hotels because new exercise equipment is guaranteed. The Ritz stocks its attractive fitness center with the Life Fitness brand, which is fine by us. Stack-loaded weight machines, a decent assortment of dumbbells and 12 gleaming cardio pieces grace the tasteful room. The hotel's full-service spa is also available for full-price pampering.

At these prices, it's hard to imagine bothering with an off-site option, but Crunch Fitness is a good South Beach sweat/lift prospect. No doubt the Ritz is a wonderful stay and play destination, but the more unique accommodations, lower prices and comparable gyms of the other two hotels in this category will provide a more lasting impression for your SoBe sabbatical.

Swimmers, head to the ocean or Flamingo Park — same travel times as from Delano (5-minute drive or 20-minute walk).

MODERATELY EXPENSIVE

GOLD: National Hotel

1677 Collins Avenue, Miami Beach, FL 33139
(305) 532-2311 • nationalhotel.com

CARDIO

TREADMILLS: **1 StarTrac**
RECUMBENT BIKE: **1 StarTrac**
STEPPER: **1 StarTrac**

STRENGTH

MACHINES: **1 Icarian Pulley**
DUMBBELLS: **5-45 lbs**

SWIM

GRADE: **C-**
SPECS: **0x70yd • Outdoor • 84–86°**

OTHER

HOURS: **6:30a-11p**
COST: **Free**
TV: **Yes**

A beautiful oceanfront hotel, National's unique feature is its 70-yard long outdoor pool (205 feet, to be exact). Although the narrowly-stretched rectangle does not have lane lines or bottom stripes, we easily visualized ourselves accruing yardage in its waters — and, at 140 per lap, they add up fast. Our guess is an early arrival will ensure a clear path. Check out the hotel's website for pictures of this massive pool, as well as the rest of the hotel. This attractive property actually provides another pool for its guests, but the second is your run-of-the-mill leisure version.

The 150 guest rooms are stylish, with modern furnishings in cream and brown tones. Since thread counts usually drop in proportion to room rates, you will have to settle for a good 250-count here rather than Shore Club's amazing 400. DVD and VCR players are provided in all rooms, and room service is at your beck and call 24 hours a day.

Like the sheet thread count, the quality of workout rooms also diminishes once guests start booking hotels for under $200/night (depending on the season). National's version just barely makes the grade, housing 3 average cardio machines, a mediocre weight pulley system and a passable dumbbell set, all in a fairly small room. While runners should head to the beach, swimmers can sample the outdoor pool or drive 5 minutes to Flamingo Park.

Those desiring a more elaborate weight lifting session or a class should walk next door to Delano's gym, where 25 bucks will get you in the door.

LEAST EXPENSIVE

GOLD: **Albion Hotel**

1650 James Avenue, Miami Beach, FL 33139
(305) 913-1000 • rubellhotels.com/albion.html

So you want to do South Beach on a budget, huh? Good luck. Miami Beach, and SoBe in particular, are areas where it really pays to pay up. We toured a number of "low-rent" hotel options and unearthed rooms that were small, dirty, plain and/or uncomfortable. Without slumbering at any of these risky businesses, we are reluctant to recommend any. However, we did bunk at the Albion and found it safe, convenient and tidy. Just make sure your expectations are looowwwerrred.

Two blocks from the beach and 10 paces from trendy Lincoln Road, Albion's location is its best feature. While the lobby and bar are handsomely decorated with marble-like flooring, leather seating and designer architecture, the same attractive style does not carry over to the rooms. The 96 guest quarters are clean and quiet with comfortable beds. The white walls, white bedding and plastic seating attempt funky, minimalist styling but end up looking bare and tacky. Luckily, this is South Beach, so most of your time will be spent at the beach, beside the pool, on the streets, in the restaurants and at the clubs. Who cares what the room looks like while you're sleeping?

Adjacent to the pool deck, the workout room is less appealing than the guest quarters. Three old StarTrac cardio machines sit next to a rickety multi-gym in an area the size of a large walk-in closet. The rectangular pool at 20 yards could provide determined swimmers with a little cardio work but, for a proper swim, we recommend a 5-minute drive/20-minute walk to Flamingo Park. For a real workout, walk 10 minutes to Crunch Fitness — the closest full-service health club (w/o pool). At $21, the fare is not cheap, but we found no less expensive or better alternative.

Albion is the best budget hotel in South Beach. However, "budget" in South Beach is way down the food chain from luxury.

BEYOND HOTELS SOUTH BEACH

Flamingo Park Pool

11th Street at Jefferson Avenue, Miami Beach, FL 33139
(305) 673-7750 • miamibeachparks.com

SWIM

GRADE: **B**
SPECS: **8x25yd • Outdoor • 83°**
TOYS: **Kick • Pull • Clock**

OTHER

HOURS: **Vary**
COST: **$6**
EXTRAS: **1/4 mile outdoor track**

We had an incredibly difficult time finding a regulation lap pool in South Beach. Countless inquisitions of hotel concierges, front desk staff and health club personnel came up empty. A typical exchange went something like this: "Where can we find a lap pool?" "Oh, our hotel has one and so do many of the hotels." "No, I mean a competition lap pool. You know, one with lines that mark lanes for swimmers." "Hmmm, lines? You mean like a drawing or picture on the bottom of the pool?" "Uh, no, we're talking about the kind you see on TV during the Olympics." "Oh, our pool is Olympic size." "Actually, Olympic size is 50 meters, not 15 yards but, that's okay, thanks for your help."

And just as we were abandoning our lap pool quest, a pamphlet on one of those freebie magazine racks caught our eye. We picked up the 20-page booklet titled "Recreation Review" and, voila! Inside was a description of Flamingo Park, a public facility with tennis courts, park grounds, a 400-meter paved track and a 25-yard outdoor lap pool!

The pool is a bit of a hike (approximately 20 minutes) from the hotels on Collins Avenue, so we recommend driving 5 minutes and parking in the large lot adjacent to the complex. The facility is clean, well-maintained and staffed with a lifeguard. We would have no problem accepting this water gem as our home pool. Eight lanes are created with floating lines and bottom stripes. Except for overhead flags, all of the other swim extras are provided, including a pace clock, kickboards and pull-buoys.

Despite the separate children's pool, the lapper can get crowded during peak summer months, so arrive early to increase your chance of a solitary swim. Bring $6, a towel and a lock if you want to stow your stuff.

Crunch Fitness

1259 Washington Avenue, Miami Beach, FL 33139
(305) 674-8222 • crunch.com

CARDIO

TREADMILLS: **LF - old**
UPRIGHT BIKE: **LF**
RECUMBENT BIKE: **LF**
ELLIPTICAL: **LF • Precor**
STEPPER: **StairMaster - old • Stepmill**
ROWING: **Concept II**

STRENGTH

FREE WEIGHTS: **Yes**
HAMMER: **Yes**
MACHINES: **LF • Icarian • Cybex**
DUMBBELLS: **5-110 lbs**

OTHER

CLASSES: **Yes**
HOURS: M-F **6a–12a** • SAT **8a-9p** • SUN **9a-8p**
COST: **$21 • $50/3 days**
TV: **Yes**

A few blocks west of the beach on Washington Street, Crunch is the only "big" gym option for guests of the ocean-front hotels. The $21/day access fee ($50/3 days) hurts because Crunch is not a top-of-the-line facility. However, it does carry an adequate assortment of new Life Fitness and Precor ellipticals (8 and 4 respectively), a fair number of late-model Life Fitness recumbent and upright bikes (9 and 3) and a ton of free weights, Hammer Strength machines and stack-loaded weight stations. It is a small club, and the environment is friendly and gay. Bring your own headphones to listen to the televisions, or leave the earpiece at home and tune into the potentially entertaining Crunch reality show. With the hip and colorful locals populating this club, a little strategic eavesdropping can be quite intriguing.

Note: Bring your own towel.

DOWNTOWN

In contrast to South Beach's jet-set oceanfront scene, Downtown is more typical of a modern U.S. city with its high-rise hotels, skyscraping office towers and miles of concrete. The business district's otherwise bland landscape is broken only by the deep blue waters of Biscayne Bay.

Bayside Marketplace is Downtown's main dining and entertainment venue, offering 16 acres of retail shops, a concert pavilion, food court, outdoor cafés and restaurants. The 6-mile commute from South Beach can be "trafficky," so if you have early morning business here and want to maximize your zzzz's, stay at one of our recommended downtown hotels. Otherwise, SoBe is the place to be.

EXPENSIVE

GOLD: **Four Seasons Miami**

1435 Brickell Avenue, Miami, FL 33131

(305) 358-3535 • fourseasons.com • thesportsclubla.com

Sports Club/LA

CARDIO

TREADMILLS: **Precor**
UPRIGHT BIKE: **LF**
RECUMBENT BIKE: **LF**
ELLIPTICAL: **Precor**
STEPPER: **StairMaster**
ROWING: **Concept II**

STRENGTH

FREE WEIGHTS: **Yes**
HAMMER: **Yes**
MACHINES: **LF • Cybex • Free Motion**
DUMBBELLS: **3-95 lbs**

OTHER

CLASSES: **Yes**
HOURS: M-F **5a–11p** • SAT-SUN **7a-8p**
COST: **Free Four Seasons only**
TV: **Yes**

The Four Seasons' accommodations are at the top of the food pyramid and are difficult to outshine. Although a few of this luxury chain's locations did not make our list for one reason or another, the Miami representative definitely scores.

Occupying floors 20 through 29 of a 70-story skyscraper, Four Seasons' 221 hotel rooms offer magnificent views of Downtown and Biscayne Bay. The living quarters are also easy on the eyes, with tasteful décor and expensive furnishings. Guests are pampered with high thread count sheets, marble baths, 24-hour room service, CD/DVD players and complimentary access to the unbelievable Sports Club/LA (connected via elevator).

This 45,000 square foot workout nirvana opened its doors in late 2003. Fitness fanatics will drool over the scads of cutting-edge machines, weights and over-the-top features. Everything about the club screams 21st Century technology. Daily class schedules are displayed via interactive 50-inch plasma touch screens. Each of the over 70 cardio machines comes equipped with its own satellite-receiving LCD screen. Large windows flood the facility with Florida sunshine. And the shower area resembles a luxurious spa.

If only this top dog had a lap pool! Swimmers will need to drive 20 minutes to Flamingo Park in South Beach.

After experiencing the best health club in all Miami, you will dread returning to your relatively mundane hometown gym. We apologize in advance for putting you through that torture.

SILVER: Mandarin Oriental

500 Brickell Key Drive, Miami, FL 33131
(305)913-8288 • mandarinoriental.com

One of the latest buildings to decorate downtown Miami's skyline, Mandarin opened its doors to discriminating travelers in November 2000. On the shores of Biscayne Bay, this 5-star property is a convenient choice for those with business in the neighboring office towers, but it's a good 20 minute drive (without traffic) from South Beach's fun and flavor. You will not find anything close to SoBe's unique art deco buildings and picturesque beaches in this part of the city. Nevertheless, Mandarin provides a desirable refuge from its adjacent concrete jungle.

CARDIO

TREADMILLS: **4 LF**
UPRIGHT BIKE: **2 LF**
RECUMBENT BIKE: **2 LF**
ELLIPTICAL: **2 LF**
STEPPER: **2 LF**

STRENGTH

MACHINES: **9 LF**
DUMBBELLS: **5-40 lbs**

SWIM

SPECS: **Outdoor • Not lap**

OTHER

CLASSES: **Yes**
HOURS: **24/7**
COST: **Free**
TV: **Yes**

The private grounds are fabulously designed, allowing guests to appreciate and enjoy the Florida sunshine on Mandarin's man-made beach, beautiful sunrises and water views along Biscayne Bay, and poolside lounging around its infinity-edge pool.

Inside, the luxurious and tasteful display continues. All 327 rooms resemble pages from your favorite interior design magazine. Beautifully flowing tones, hardwood floors, sleek furnishings, marble baths with separate tubs and showers, high ceilings and balconies overlooking the Bay make this place special.

Mandarin's fitness center is part of its 15,000 square foot spa. Unfortunately, given the 300+ room accommodation, the gym and amount of equipment inside is somewhat undersized. While the room itself has a spectacular display of water views and a plush atmosphere, many of the machines were occupied during our 5pm tour — and we wouldn't be surprised if there were times when travelers had to work in with others or wait for a particular piece of equipment. The sweat apparatus is top notch, and adds to the allure of the facility. We just wish they had supplied a few more machines, especially ellipticals. Plasma televisions are attached to the machines, but we didn't see whether headphones are provided (so, bring yours just in case). Yoga, Meditation, Pilates and other classes are offered for a fee ($20-25).

Lap swimmers are out of luck in this part of town, but outdoor runners have a great option that we've mapped out for you in our online "Work Out" section.

MODERATELY EXPENSIVE

GOLD: Intercontinental Hotel

100 Chopin Plaza, Miami, FL 33131
(305) 577-1000 • intercontinental.com

CARDIO

TREADMILLS: **6 StarTrac - old**
RECUMBENT BIKE: **2 Tectrix**
ELLIPTICAL: **2 True**
STEPPER: **2 StairMaster • 2 Tectrix**

STRENGTH

FREE WEIGHTS: **Yes**
HAMMER: **Yes**
MACHINES: **17 Cybex**
DUMBBELLS: **5-80 lbs**

SWIM

SPECS: **Outdoor • Not lap**

OTHER

HOURS: **24**
COST: **$10**
TV: **Yes**

The Intercontinental rises 34 stories above Biscayne Bay and is centrally located in downtown Miami near Bayfront Park and the Bayside Marketplace dining and entertainment complex. Room décor is a tad dated with retro 1980s patterns and furnishings, but all 641 rooms offer attractive views.

For $10/day, hotel patrons receive access to Intercontinental's 5th floor fitness center. While the relatively large gym (about the size of a 7-Eleven) contains a significant quantity of equipment, weights and weight machines are favored at the expense of the cardio selection. The wide selection of dumbbells, free weights and new Cybex stack-loaded weight machines is sure to satisfy, but the older treadmills, missing uprights and lesser brand-quality ellipticals leave our metabolisms hungering for more. Miami's outdoors will rescue the runner, with the Bay and Brickell Street providing a convenient substitute for those sub-par treads. Cardio connoisseurs looking for more selection or less impact can walk 7 minutes to the Fitness Company or consider staying at the Doubletree across town.

Unfortunately, swmmers are left out of the fun in downtown Miami. If you can't go cold turkey, South Beach's Flamingo Park is a 20-minute drive.

Doubletree Grand Hotel Biscayne Bay

1717 North Bayshore Drive, Miami, FL 33132
(305) 372-0313 • doubletree.com

An interesting mix of single rooms and rental condo units, this 42-story Doubletree property is just north of the 395 highway and somewhat isolated from downtown's dining and entertainment attractions. Standard guest rooms are offered on floors 4 through 9, while the condos view the City and Biscayne Bay from floors 10 and higher. All are furnished in a contemporary taupe and cream with wood accents.

Doubletree's workout option is a good one. Access is complimentary for those staying in a standard room and $15/day for those residing in a condo. Unofficially, we were told that condo guests frequently cut deals so, if you are not averse to a little haggling, have at it.

Doubletree's gym is smaller than the Intercontinental's, but offers a superior cardio selection of newer bikes, ellipticals and treadmills, with some older machines thrown into the mix. While not as impressive as Intercontinental's plentiful weight collection, Doubletree's selection is no slouch. Nine new Cybex machines, plenty of free weights with barbells and a good-size dumbbell set decorate the room. Packed with equipment, some areas are a bit cozy, but our impression was that the club rarely attracts crowds.

CARDIO

TREADMILLS: **6 Total - • LF • Precor**
UPRIGHT BIKE: **2 LF • 1 Fan**
RECUMBENT BIKE: **1 LF**
ELLIPTICAL: **1 Precor**
STEPPER: **5 StairMaster - old • 1 LF • 1 Stepmill**
OTHER: **2 Gravitron - old**

STRENGTH

FREE WEIGHTS: **Yes**
MACHINES: **9 Cybex**
DUMBBELLS: **5-80 lbs**

SWIM

SPECS: **Outdoor • Not lap**

OTHER

CLASSES: **Yes**
HOURS: M-F **6:45a-10p • SAT 8a-5p • SUN 8a-4p**
COST: **Varies**
TV: **Yes**

Swimmers, your only viable option requires a 20-minute commute to Flamingo Park (see South Beach for details).

LEAST EXPENSIVE

GOLD: **Courtyard by Marriott**

200 SE Second Avenue, Miami, FL 33131
(305) 374-3000 • courtyard.com

Opened in 2003 and within a half-mile of the Bayside Marketplace dining and entertainment complex, Courtyard is a reliable lodging option in downtown's business hub. Guests can expect tastefully garnished rooms and typical Courtyard perks. All units provide complimentary high-speed internet access, views of the City and/or Biscayne Bay and step-out balconies.

Courtyard makes our list despite its meager workout room's few cardio pieces and small dumbbell set because of its proximity to the Fitness Company. This worthwhile facility provides the athletic-minded traveler with a convenient and pocket-book-friendly option. So bring $8 and plan to walk 3 minutes.

Swimmers, you are out of luck, unless you fancy a 20-minute drive to Flamingo Park (see South Beach for details).

BEYOND HOTELS DOWNTOWN

Executive Health Club Fitness Company

Bank of America Tower
100 SE 2nd Street, 19th Floor, Miami, FL 33131
(305) 539-2183

CARDIO

TREADMILLS: **LF - old**
UPRIGHT BIKE: **LF - old**
RECUMBENT BIKE: **LF**
ELLIPTICAL: **LF**
STEPPER: **StairMaster - old**

STRENGTH

FREE WEIGHTS: **Yes**
HAMMER: **Yes - 1**
MACHINES: **15 LF**
DUMBBELLS: **5-90 lbs**

OTHER

CLASSES: **Yes**
HOURS: M-TH **6a-9p** • F **6a-8p** • SAT-SUN **Closed**
COST: **$8**
TV: **Yes**

On the 19th floor of the Bank of America building, the Fitness Company is small on size, large on strength equipment and big on classes. If only they would super size the supply of cardio machines! Closed on weekends, this club caters primarily to the surrounding business crowd but welcomes out-of-towners with open arms and available machines. Your $8 entry fee includes access to the club's classes, including yoga, cycling and Pilates.

With no lap pool in the downtown area, swimmers are compelled to go "on the wagon" for the duration of their Miami stay. If severe chlorine withdrawal overcomes you, your agua fix is a 20-minute drive to Flamingo Park in South Beach.

Note: The Club is considering weekend hours.

RUNNING ROUTES

South Beach

It can't get any easier or better. If you're in South Beach, the no-brainer is the beach. Take to the sand for some cushioning or hit the boardwalk for firmer footing. Either way, think of your out-and-back as another great opportunity to soak up the sun and South Beach atmosphere.

Downtown

For those bunking Downtown, your run is a city street pavement route. Unfortunately, Bay Front Park does not offer anything but scenery. For any decent mileage, your best bet is to find your way to Brickell Street and head south for as long as your heart desires — then turn around. Brickell is a main thoroughfare and sports the Four Seasons Hotel among others, but traffic during non-rush hours tends to be light.

Milwaukee

MILWAUKEE, WISCONSIN

Touring this city will remind you that this is America's beer capital. The Milwaukee Brewers play at Miller Park, Pabst Theater is the local entertainment host, countless taprooms and microbreweries line the streets and intoxicating references to early brewing powerhouses Blatz, Pabst, Miller and Schlitz abound in Milwaukee's historical records. What was it about this small metropolis on the shores of Lake Michigan that fostered such a blue ribbon climate for cooking up brewskis?

While some argue it's the area's superior hops, barley and water, these theories are only drunken lore. Milwaukee's rise to the rim is due in large part to its small town stature. In the early beer trade days, stout production was typically driven by local demand. With its small population, Milwaukee brewers were forced to look beyond their community to sell enough suds to survive. Long before "marketing" and "distribution" became common business buzz words, these savvy barley barons were merchandising and promoting their lager throughout the country.

Over the years, historic events further strengthened these malt-makers as lead beer exporters. After the Chicago Fire decimated local suppliers, Milwaukee stepped in to feed the Windy City's barley sandwich appetite and, during World War II, Miller secured a U.S. Army contract to serve soldiers their cold ones. With the advent of television in the 1950s, Milwaukee's already developed promotion and advertising strategies solidified its market clout and national appeal.

Today, mergers and acquisitions have consolidated the number of draft producers into a few mega-breweries, and Milwaukee's top dogs continue to reign supreme — although St. Louis' Anheuser Busch may argue this point. Visitors to this beer burg can expect a revitalized downtown, entertaining attractions, friendly locals and good exercise options — proving that you can have your beer and brat, and work out, too.

22 Locations Reviewed

MODERATELY EXPENSIVE

GOLD: **Courtyard** Downtown

300 West Michigan Street, Milwaukee, WI 53203
(414) 291-4122 • courtyard.com

Built in 1999, this centrally located Courtyard receives the Gold crown primarily due to its connection to Downtown's best health club, the YMCA. While Courtyard's accommodations will not match the elegance and luxury afforded to Pfister guests, its dramatically superior and convenient workout alternative vaults it to the top. All 169 guest quarters are Courtyard typical — catering to the business traveler with standard floor plans, tidy accommodations and furnishings. We also appreciate the complimentary high-speed internet access provided in all rooms.

Adjacent to the lobby is the hotel's 24-hour workout room, which fit ones will surely skip once they lay eyes on the deficient 4 cardio pieces and one multi-gym. Instead, make a beeline along the indoor passageway to the stellar Y. Bring your hotel key and $5 for a proper and exceptional workout.

Unfortunately for swimmers, this 2-minute commute does not afford a pool. Your water frolicking requires a 10-15 minute walk to Marquette University's Rec Plex ($5 and room key).

SILVER: **Pfister**

424 East Wisconsin Avenue, Milwaukee, WI 53202
(414) 273-8222 • pfister-hotel.com

CARDIO

TREADMILLS: **4 Trotter • 2 Precor**
RECUMBENT BIKE: **3 Precor**
ELLIPTICAL: **2 Precor**
STEPPER: **1 LF**

STRENGTH

MACHINES: **1 Multi**
DUMBBELLS: **5-50 lbs**

SWIM

SPECS: **Indoor • Not lap**

OTHER

HOURS: **5:30a-10p**
COST: **Free**
TV: **Yes**

Pfister is downtown Milwaukee's most upscale accommodation, yet travelers should not expect Four Seasons or Ritz Carlton equivalent luxury — or prices, for that matter. The hotel's 23rd floor bar, ground level restaurant and common areas are impressive, but the 307 guest rooms are only moderately attractive. Heavily decorated in a 19th Century Victorian style, the maroon and dark green guest quarters are adorned with antique furnishings and floral patterns — nice, but not worth any significant pricing premium.

The 23rd floor fitness center's views are exceptional, but the equipment inside is marginal. Though it is the best *hotel* gym in the City, this distinction is easy to achieve. Two good condition Precor ellipticals and 6 decent treadmills are the highlights. With no upright bike, free weights or separate weight stations, this facility will certainly leave guests looking for more. Luckily, a quick jaunt across the street to the Wisconsin Athletic Club resolves the workout quandary ($10). Walking a little farther brings athletes to the Milwaukee YMCA, where $5 will buy you access to a larger and more complete club (plan on 10 minutes by foot).

Swimmers must commute to Marquette University's Rec Plex for the nearest regulation lap pool. Pfister is a good 13 blocks from campus so, if you plan to hoof it, allow 20 minutes. Otherwise, we suggest a $5 fare taxi ride (Pfister has a 24-hour cab stand). Available parking is scarce and Pfister does not provide shuttle service. Marquette's $5 with room key admission won't break the bank but, with round-trip cab fare, your swim will run $15 per dip.

LEAST EXPENSIVE

GOLD: Hampton Inn

176 West Wisconsin Avenue, Milwaukee, WI 53203
(414) 271-4656 • hamptoninn.com

Located directly across the street from the Downtown YMCA, this hotel is a good pick for those in search of a marvelous workout option and sound bargain.

While the least expensive rooms (non-suites) provide bare-bones furnishings and amenities, you can count on clean and comfortable accommodations. And you can savor free breakfast, to boot.

Forget about the paltry 2-treadmill, 2-bike, in-house exercise room. The $5 Y is only 20 paces from Hampton's front door — look both ways before crossing the street!

Note: Swimmers, head to Marquette — 15 minutes on foot and bring your room key ($5).

BEYOND HOTELS

Downtown YMCA

161 W. Wisconsin Avenue
Suite 4000
Milwaukee, WI 53203
(414) 291-9622
http://downtown.ymcamke.org

Of all the health clubs we have visited across the country, this club's staff was the most paranoid about granting a tour, apparently worried that we might "feature" their club in some unsavory publication. We were given the 3rd degree but, after much deliberation, they relented and chaperoned us around. Rest assured, with your picture I.D., hotel room key and $5, your admission to Milwaukee's best facility will be hassle free.

CARDIO

TREADMILLS: **LF • Precor**
UPRIGHT BIKE: **LF**
RECUMBENT BIKE: **LF**
ELLIPTICAL: **Precor • LF**
STEPPER: **LF • StairMaster**
ROWING: **Yes**

STRENGTH

FREE WEIGHTS: **Yes**
HAMMER: **Yes**
MACHINES: **Cybex**
DUMBBELLS: **3-120 lbs**

OTHER

CLASSES: **Yes**
HOURS: M-F **5a-10p** • SAT **6a-10p** • SUN **11a-8p**
COST: **$5 w/room key • $10 Others • $20/week**
TV: **Yes**
EXTRAS: **1/6 mile indoor track • Climbing wall**

With a rock climbing wall, indoor track, classes (extra fee may apply), childcare, massage services and cardio/weight equipment, this Y provides every workout modality imaginable, except a pool. Its 4th floor downtown business building setting is urban and cozy. Athletes will find plenty of new strength and cardio stations lining the fitness deck.

To maximize the available square footage, the Y is forced to organize its industry-leading machines fairly close together, but there is enough room to avoid feeling cramped.

Towels and locker keys are provided, and hair dryers and toiletries are available in the locker room.

Note: The Y's larger size and greater quantity of equipment make it a better choice than the Wisconsin Athletic Club.

Marquette University Rec Plex

915 West Wisconsin (Straz Tower), Milwaukee, WI 53233
(414) 288-7778
gomarquette.edu/recsports/pages/facilities.htm

SWIM

GRADE: **B-**
SPECS: **4x25yd • Indoor • 80-83°**

OTHER

HOURS: **Vary**
COST: **$5 w/room key • No others**

Recommended primarily as a swim option, the Rec Plex houses the only regulation lap pool in downtown Milwaukee. Inside the Straz Tower, a dorm-like building on the campus' eastern edge, the Rec Plex is a 10-15 minute walk from the Courtyard and Howard Johnson hotels. Those staying at the Pfister should take a taxi, especially during winter's chill. Though not exactly convenient, the 25-yard lapper will provide an adequate venue for your swim routine. The lighting could be brighter and toys (kickboards, pull-buoys etc.) are not provided, but the 80-degree water separated by floating lines and bottom stripes is there for the taking.

In addition, the facility offers a fair number of newer cardio and weight machines, free weights and athletic courts for basketball, racquetball and squash. So if you want to pull a back-to-back workout before or after your swim, go for it! They have a little bit of everything. However, the more convenient YMCA and Wisconsin Athletic Club are superior weight and cardio facilities, so we recommend those clubs if getting wet is not in your plan.

Note: Along with your I.D., room key and $5, bring your own towel and lock to this facility. Unfortunately admission is only granted to those staying at downtown hotels.

Wisconsin Athletic Club (WAC)

411 E. Wisconsin Ave. (6th Floor), Milwaukee, WI 53202
(414) 212-2000 • milwaukee.wisconsinathleticclub.com

The WAC offers another full-service health club option (sans pool) in downtown Milwaukee.

Though the Y is larger, less expensive and more elaborate than its cross-town rival, we mention the WAC because it is located across the street from the Pfister hotel. Except during those brutal Milwaukee winter days, Pfister guests will find the extra 5-minute stroll to the Y well worth the trouble.

Inside its small facility, the WAC assembles an ample variety of cardio and strength equipment. All machines are new and most of the fitness industry's leading brands are here.

Classes are offered, including spin and yoga, but swimmers must look elsewhere.

Ten bucks is the going rate for out-of-towners ($20/week).

CARDIO

TREADMILLS: **LF**
UPRIGHT BIKE: **LF**
RECUMBENT BIKE: **LF**
ELLIPTICAL: **Precor**
STEPPER: **StairMaster**
ROWING: **Yes**

STRENGTH

FREE WEIGHTS: **Yes**
HAMMER: **Yes**
MACHINES: **Magnum**
DUMBBELLS: **3-105 lbs**

OTHER

CLASSES: **Yes**
HOURS: M-TH **5a-10p** • F **5a-9p** • SAT-SUN **6:30a-7p**
COST: **$10** • **$20/week**
TV: **Yes**

RUNNING ROUTES

Lake Michigan

Lake Michigan is a runner's best bet in this brew town, and downtown hotels are less than a mile away. So head east and pick a direction (north or south), either way you will be treated to lakefront homes, parks and beaches.

Veteran's Park

Heading north along Lincoln Memorial Drive will quickly bring you to Veteran's Park with its 3-mile loop and 20-station exercise course. This park also connects into the Oak Leaf Trail, a former railroad line converted for bicycle use (also known as the 76 Bike Trail).

Summerfest Island

If you elect a southerly direction, follow Harbor Drive to the Summerfest grounds where you can pick up a paved path out to Summerfest Island.

Milwaukee River

Lastly, you can always look to the trails along the Milwaukee

River for some fun, but the footing is a little trickier. And only in Milwaukee would there be an annual Beer Run. It takes place every June at the Locust Street Festival. The under 2-mile jog includes quarter mile beer stops!

MINNEAPOLIS, MINNESOTA

Too hot or too cold is the common visitor complaint about this extreme climate city. Interestingly, Minneapolis' all-time record high and low temperatures occurred in the same year — 1936 (July 108°F, Jan. -34°F).

Although locals learn to tolerate Minneapolis' muggy summer nights and bitter winter days, first-timers to this city's heart need only pack for 70° no matter what time of year.

Huh?

Downtown guests can find sanctuary in nearly seven miles of indoor skybridges networked throughout Minneapolis' office high-rises, shops, restaurants, apartments and hotels. Weather wimps can conduct their city business without ever breaking a sweat or donning a heavy coat. And acrophobes (those with a fear of heights) can take comfort that their perch above terra firma is usually a mere one story.

But beware! Foot-traffic congestion is a surprising rush hour reality in this above-ground world — especially on those extreme climate days. If the overhead signs fail to point you in the right direction and you find yourself frazzled in the maze, ask for directions. Despite their frequently frigid town, Minnesotans are some of the warmest folk in the country.

EXPENSIVE

GOLD: Grand Hotel Downtown

615 2nd Avenue South, Minneapolis, MN 55402
(612) 288-8888 • grandhotelminneapolis.com
mltac.com (Fitness Center)

CARDIO

TREADMILLS: **Woodway**
UPRIGHT BIKE: **LF • Cybex**
RECUMBENT BIKE: **LF • Cybex**
ELLIPTICAL: **Precor • Cybex**
STEPPER: **Stepmill**
ROWING: **Concept II**

STRENGTH

FREE WEIGHTS: **Yes**
HAMMER: **Yes**
MACHINES: **Cybex • Free Motion • LF**
DUMBBELLS: **3-130 lbs**

SWIM

GRADE: **C**
SPECS: **6x20yd • Indoor • 84°**
TOYS: **Kick • Pull • Clock**

OTHER

CLASSES: **Yes**
HOURS: M-F **5a-10:30p** • SAT **7:30a-6:30p** • SUN **8a-6p**
COST: **Free Grand Guests • $20 IHRSA • No others**
TV: **Yes**
EXTRAS: **1/17 mile indoor track • Racquetball • Indoor driving range**

In the heart of downtown Minneapolis, The Grand affords a lavish accommodation stocked with all the amenities you expect from a luxury hotel — including a stellar fitness center. Inside its 140 rooms, guests are pampered with Egyptian cotton linens, down comforters, marble bathrooms, CD players and 24-hour room service. Conservative beige tones color the walls and complimentary high-speed internet access is provided. Grand even delivers complimentary coffee to those requesting a wake-up call.

Hotel patrons receive free privileges to the 58,000 square-foot facility owned by Lifetime Fitness Corporation. This stately health club maintains an entrance adjacent to and downstairs from the hotel lobby. We were awed by the opulent design. For example, the main fitness floor's cherry wood paneled walls, art deco railings, plasma TVs and 30-foot ceiling reminded us of a private theater rather than a public sweat house. While surroundings are important, good equipment seals the deal — and Lifetime comes through with flying colors. No expense was spared in stocking the gym with top-of-the-line cardio machines, weight stations and free weights. Precor, Cybex, Life Fitness and Free Motion are all here in force. Plenty of classes are offered, and sport courts top off the center's athletic options.

Only serious swimmers will feel slighted. Though the lap pool is ornate, the length comes up short at 20 yards. Great pictures of the 6-lane lapper are shown on Lifetime's website, but you don't see the awkward location of the locker rooms. Patrons must traipse past the pool to reach the changing rooms. With a little more length, this pool would get more praise — but isn't that always the case?

Note: With so many machines in stock, we have listed brands only.

MODERATELY EXPENSIVE

GOLD: Residence Inn Downtown

45 South Eighth Street, Minneapolis, MN 55402
(612) 677-1000 • residenceinn.com

Be sure to book the right Residence Inn. Two of these Marriott-owned hotels call downtown Minneapolis home, and we are NOT recommending the Residence Inn at the Depot. Residence Inn Downtown opens its doors to the core of Minneapolis' financial and shopping hub and is connected via skywalk to American Express and Target corporations.

As is typical with this reliable chain, 124 guest quarters are offered with separate living and sleeping rooms. Fully equipped kitchens give extended stay patrons the ability to store snacks in their refrigerator, heat items in the microwave or prepare meals. Don't worry about breakfast, however. Residence Inn has got you covered with its full, hot, breakfast buffet.

Not surprisingly, this hotel's workout room is threadbare. Your time will be better spent working out at the impressive Downtown YMCA. "Skywalking" will get you there in less than 3 minutes and a pass from the hotel front desk gets you in free.

SILVER: Hyatt Regency

1300 Nicollet Mall, Minneapolis, MN 55403
(612) 370-1234 • minneapolis.hyatt.com

This large Hyatt is located 2 skybridge blocks away from Minneapolis' Convention Center. The 533 rooms underwent a welcome renovation in 2002, with the final product revealing comfortable guest quarters sporting a contemporary flair. This appealing accommodation affords some of the best views of downtown — especially from the higher floors. High-speed internet is available in the rooms and common areas, and the on-site restaurants and bar can be convenient distractions.

Hyatt steers fitness-minded guests to the Regency Athletic Club on its 6th floor. The privately run center is better than most hotel gyms. Before your sweat begins, however, prepare to pay a $10/day ($20/3 days) admission fee at the club's front desk. You are then free to play as much as your heart desires on Regency's fine

Regency Athletic Club

CARDIO

TREADMILLS: **7 Precor**
UPRIGHT BIKE: **3 Precor**
RECUMBENT BIKE: **4 Precor**
ELLIPTICAL: **8 Precor**
STEPPER: **3 StairMaster - old**

STRENGTH

FREE WEIGHTS: **Yes**
MACHINES: **~10 Cybex & Paramount**
DUMBBELLS: **3-85 lbs**

SWIM

SPECS: **Indoor • Not lap**

OTHER

CLASSES: **Yes**
HOURS: M-F **6a-10p** • SAT-SUN **8:30a-6p**
COST: **$10 • $20/3 days**
TV: **Yes**
EXTRAS: **Basketball • Racquetball • Boxing Ring**

cardio and weight equipment. Besides not having a lap pool, the only chink we could find in Hyatt's fitness armor was its collection of old step machines. All other apparatus is new and running great. Classes are offered too, so those looking for a little group therapy will find it here as well.

LEAST EXPENSIVE

GOLD: Radisson Metrodome

615 Washington Avenue SE, Minneapolis, MN 55414
(612) 379-8888 • radisson.com

We are really proud of ourselves for finding this fantastic accommodation located on the University of Minnesota campus. Only a couple miles from downtown Minneapolis' hustle and bustle, the Radisson is convenient for those conducting business in the City's financial and retail center. A complimentary shuttle delivers you Downtown in under 5 minutes.

Modern on the outside but country-style inside, Radisson's 304 guest quarters come at affordable prices.

While you receive no significant freebies or high-end luxury within these hotel walls, you are furnished with complimentary access to the University of Minnesota's state-of-the-art recreation center, located a mere 100 yards behind the hotel. Just pick up a pass from Radisson's front desk and you'll be on your way to fitness bliss.

CARDIO

TREADMILLS: **StarTrac**
UPRIGHT BIKE: **LF**
RECUMBENT BIKE: **LF • StarTrac**
ELLIPTICAL: **Precor • StarTrac**
STEPPER: **StairMaster**
ROWING: **Concept II**

STRENGTH

FREE WEIGHTS: **Yes**
MACHINES: **Cybex • Nautilus**
DUMBBELLS: **1-125 lbs**

SWIM

GRADE: **B+**
SPECS: **6x25yd • Indoor • 82-84°**
TOYS: **Kick • Pull • Clock**
MASTERS: **No - Group Swim**

OTHER

CLASSES: **Yes**
HOURS: M-F **5:30a-9:30p** • SAT **7a-7p** • SUN **8a-7p**
COST: **Free Residence Inn • No others**
TV: **Yes**
EXTRAS: **1/10 mile indoor track • Basketball • Racquetball**

BEYOND HOTELS

YMCA Downtown

30 S. 9th Street
Minneapolis, MN 55402
(612) 371-8765
ymcatwincities.org

Given its location in the midst of downtown's high-rises, we were surprised by the Y's enormous square footage and full menu of athletic options. Guests of the Residence Inn can get to it via skywalk. Just follow the overhead signs and you will never leave your perfect indoor climate.

This modern facility covers every workout option from A to Z and will satisfy any exercise craving. Gently used cardio machines, newer weight equipment and a tremendous lap pool are highlights, while basketball, racquetball and squash courts add a competitive group option. A full slate of classes is also offered, including cardio-kick and spinning.

Our favorite feature of the Downtown Y is its fantastic 25-yard lap pool. Six lanes separated by floating lines and bottom stripes are surrounded by a huge deck and high ceiling. A pace clock will keep your time while freestyling, fluttering with the provided kick-boards or pulling with the furnished pull-buoys.

The pool comes ever so close to receiving our highest grade, but its yard-not-meter measurement system brings it down a notch in our book.

Note: Only Residence Inn patrons receive guest access to the Downtown Y. Swimmers, bring a swim cap just to be safe, because many Ys require one.

University of Minnesota Recreation Center

1906 University Avenue SE, Minneapolis, MN 55455
(612) 626-9222 • recsports.umn.edu

Major universities rarely grant access to their recreation centers without accompaniment by an enrolled student, and UM breaks this rule for Radisson guests only. Patrons of that nearby accommodation receive a pass from Radisson for complimentary admission and full Rec Center privileges.

As one of the nicest university complexes that we have toured, this massive facility provides cutting-edge cardio and weight equipment, modern racquetball/squash courts, a 25-foot rock climbing wall and 2 competition swimming pools — one of which is housed in the several-thousand-seat Natatorium adjacent to the complex.

In case you needed a little more persuasion, the nearby University Fieldhouse sports a 200-meter indoor track — perfect for running intervals, and access is free.

CARDIO

TREADMILLS: **Woodway**
UPRIGHT BIKE: **LF**
RECUMBENT BIKE: **SciFit**
ELLIPTICAL: **Precor**
STEPPER: **StairMaster**
ROWING: **Concept II**

STRENGTH

FREE WEIGHTS: **Yes**
HAMMER: **Yes**
MACHINES: **Cybex • LF**
DUMBBELLS: **5-170 lbs**

SWIM

GRADE: **A**
SPECS: **8x50m • Indoor • 80°**
TOYS: **Kick • Pull • Clock**

OTHER

CLASSES: **Yes**
HOURS: **Vary, check web**
COST: **Free Radisson • No others**
TV: **Yes**
EXTRAS: **200 meter indoor track**
- **Racquetball**
- **Climbing wall**

Note: Check the website or call for pool hours and class schedules.

RUNNING ROUTES

The River

In the Twin Cities there are a number of running venues, all convenient from downtown area hotels. Minneapolis' Mississippi River location means scenic parks and fairly flat miles. Of course, the chain of lakes is equally worthy and offers loop runs of varying lengths. And if you prefer to just clock in miles with an out and back, head to the river and run in either direction. Add some variety by crossing any of the pedestrian friendly bridges.

Loring Park

Just east of the Hyatt (1/4 to one mile from other hotels on the river's east side) and en route to Lake Isles is Loring Park. Loring sports several bike and walking paths that wind around a lake and garden. At 800 acres, the Park is not huge, but mileage can be conveniently added by making your way across the Sculpture Bridge to Kenwood Parkway and Lake of the Isles in the stately Kenwood neighborhood. The lake perimeter loop is approximately 2.8 miles. The lakes all connect, so adding significant mileage is easy.

Boom Island Trail

The Boom Island Trail is convenient to hotels on either side of the River. There is an easy-to-navigate 5 to 7 mile loop. Starting on the west side of the Mississippi, take 4th Avenue to the River Parkway north and cross the river at the Plymouth Ave Bridge. Go south to Boom Island Park and Nicollet Island. Your return bridge is Hennepin Ave. Within the Park, there are a number of trails to explore.

NASHVILLE, TENNESSEE

Arguably the most transformed City in our nation, Nashville has evolved from a 1700s French and Indian trading post to a Civil War battleground to a cotton industry heavyweight to its present designation as the world's Country Western Music Capital. Most influential in this latest makeover has been the creation and fabulous success of The Grand Ole Opry.

Introduced into homes across the country in 1925 as a live music radio broadcast, The Grand Ole Opry soon attracted admirers to its studio. As the audience grew, programmers agreed to allow them inside. An ever-increasing gaggle of fascinated fans continued to mob the production and its performers, even after the program began charging 25 cents a head. This surging popularity forced the studio to find larger broadcast venues until 1974, when the performance finally landed a permanent home in the 4,400-seat Grand Ole Opry House. The longest-running radio program in history, Grand Ole Opry broadcasts can be heard on Clear Channel's radio network, via internet at opry.com and on the Country Music Television channel (CMT).

Pulling away from its industrial roots and refashioning itself as a champion for the creative arts, Music City U.S.A. bursts with business and tourist appeal. Nashville's Second Avenue and Church Street are alive with dance clubs, cultural galleries, entertaining restaurants and live performance stages. Downtown's performing arts centers are consistently packed with visitors and locals. And, in what some consider the true measure of a city's success, Tennessee's capital has imported both NFL (Titans) and NHL (Predators) franchises.

Nashville is a prime example that change is a good thing.

27 Locations Reviewed

EXPENSIVE

GOLD: Renaissance

611 Commerce Street, Nashville, TN 37203
(615) 255-8400 • renaissancehotels.com

CARDIO

TREADMILLS: **5 True**
UPRIGHT BIKE: **1 True**
RECUMBENT BIKE: **1 True**
ELLIPTICAL: **2 True**
STEPPER: **2 StairMaster**

STRENGTH

MACHINES: **3 BodyMaster**
DUMBBELLS: **3-40 lbs**

SWIM

SPECS: **Indoor • Not lap**

OTHER

HOURS: **24**
COST: **Free**
TV: **Yes**

Location and a gym that slightly outshines the also Gold-rated Hermitage are winning attributes for this massive hotel. Attached to the Nashville Convention Center and only blocks away from vibrant Second Avenue, Renaissance has the conventioneer in mind. While we recognize that styling a 673-room hotel with a unique flavor is an arduous task, it would have been nice to find some signs of life in Renaissance's "flat-line" quarters. Drab blues dominate the visual landscape, which sorely needs a "Fab 5" makeover. Thankfully, these chambers are brightened with natural sunshine via large windows. Renaissance's aesthetic challenges were enough to create a toss-up in this price category between it and the Hermitage.

The hotel's second floor, 24-hour workout room is predominantly stocked with the less popular and less expensive True brand aerobic machines. Highlights include very good treadmills, new 4600 series StairMaster steppers and a decent assortment of dumbbells. This equipment will "work out" for non-nitpickers. While the other machines are in fair condition, we are just not crazy about the quality of True's bikes and ellipticals.

Fortunately, a more elaborate gym and swim venue are nearby. Within a 10-minute walk, the Downtown YMCA's fitness equipment will satisfy aforementioned nitpickers. However, swimmers may prefer the 5-minute drive to the Vanderbilt area, where Sportsplex's competition lap pool is slightly better and less crowded than the YMCA's.

Note: With its more appealing rooms and more desirable workout option (M-F), the moderately priced Courtyard is a better weekday alternative.

GOLD: Hermitage

231 Sixth Avenue North, Nashville, TN 37219
(615) 244-3121 • thehermitagehotel.com

Across the street from the State Capitol and a 10-minute walk to Second Avenue's shopping and entertainment venue, the Hermitage is Music Town's most upscale and poshest accommodation. The 2003 guest room renovation means fresh décor, premium bedding and complimentary high-speed internet access. Additionally,

Hermitage differentiates itself with its cooking demonstrations, room-service pet menu and personal shopping services — all for a charge, of course. So why does Hermitage share the first place podium? Despite Renaissance's less attractive accommodation, its in-house gym is a slight cut above Hermitage's — although that's not saying much.

CARDIO
TREADMILLS: **2 LF - old**
ELLIPTICAL: **1 LF - old**
STEPPER: **1 LF**

STRENGTH
MACHINES: **4 LF**
DUMBBELLS: **2.5-55 lbs**

OTHER
HOURS: **24**
COST: **Free**
TV: **Yes**

With all the luxury and fanfare throughout the rest of this hotel, the Hermitage's workout room is disappointing. Rather than spending on individual plasma screens for its 4 cardio machines, an investment into more, and better, equipment (e.g., a bike) would have produced greater returns. All apparatus is in fair condition, and the televisions are a nice addition, but serious athletes will be challenged to complete a full exercise routine.

If you plan a quick sweat or a brief strength session, this gym should get you by. A more elaborate conditioning program will compel you to join Renaissance guests at the Downtown YMCA. The distance to the Y is about the same for both the Hermitage and Renaissance (10-minute walk). Swimmers can lap it up at the Y or drive to Sportsplex's slightly superior pool.

Note: Online photos of Hermitage's exercise room show a recumbent bike, but we did not see one during our tour.

SILVER: Marriott at Vanderbilt University
2555 West End Avenue, Nashville, TN 37203
(615) 321-1300 • marriott.com

Only two miles from the heart of Nashville, the Vanderbilt area hotels present viable lodging alternatives for downtown visitors. Built in 2001, Marriott is the most impressive hotel in this area. Inside its 307 rooms, guests will enjoy pillow top bedding, contemporary furnishings and marble bathroom vanities. The quarters are certainly attractive, and the colorful accents fend off franchise blandness.

CARDIO
TREADMILLS: **2 Precor**
UPRIGHT BIKE: **2 Precor**
RECUMBENT BIKE: **1 Precor**
STEPPER: **1 Precor**

STRENGTH
MACHINES: **1 Multi**

SWIM
SPECS: **Indoor • Not lap**

OTHER
HOURS: **24**
COST: **Free**
TV: **Yes**

The petite workout center filled with new Precor equipment is a solid cardio prospect. However, the absence of dumbbells, free weights and separate weight stations is an iron pumping obstacle. Swimmers and those looking to balance the cardio work with a legitimate strength session should head to Sportsplex (10-minute walk, 2-minute drive).

Note: Don't miss the neighboring Starbucks and P.F. Chang's.

MODERATELY EXPENSIVE

GOLD: **Courtyard Nashville Downtown**

170 Fourth Avenue North, Nashville, TN 37219
(615) 256-0900 • courtyard.com

This hotel represents the best *weekday* lodging and workout combination in Nashville due to its proximity and free access to the Uptown YMCA (closed on weekends). Not endowed with the same glamour or character as its higher priced rivals, Courtyard's heart of downtown location and thrifty rates make it a worthy challenger 5 days a week. Only a 5-minute walk to Second Avenue's dining and entertainment district, guests can conveniently sample Music Town's menu of fun.

The 192 guest quarters are typical for this Marriott-owned chain, with tidy accommodations, standard amenities and free high-speed internet access.

Bypass the in-house gym and its 5 threadbare cardio machines. Instead, stop by the front desk to retrieve your free pass to Uptown YMCA, located across the street on the 30th floor of the Sun Trust Financial Building (lobby elevators go to 29, then take 29th floor elevator to 30). The walk will take you less than a minute, so your allotted workout time can be spent productively inside this desirable YMCA. However, weekend travelers pay attention! The Uptown YMCA closes on Saturdays and Sundays — the reason why Courtyard is the best *weekday* choice. Though not nearly as convenient but still a good deal, guests can use Courtyard's freebie pass at the Downtown Y on weekends.

Since the weekday Uptown Y has no pool, swimmers should drive to Sportsplex (5-10 minutes) or walk to the Downtown Y (10-15 minutes). We suggest driving to the Sportsplex's slightly nicer and likely less crowded lapper.

SILVER: **Loews Vanderbilt**

2100 West End Avenue, Nashville, TN 37203
(615) 320-1700 • loewshotels.com/hotels/nashville

CARDIO

TREADMILLS: **3 LF**
UPRIGHT BIKE: **2 Tectrix**
RECUMBENT BIKE: **1 LF**
ELLIPTICAL: **2 LF**
STEPPER: **1 Tectrix**

STRENGTH

MACHINES: **1 LF Multi**
DUMBBELLS: **5-40 lbs**

OTHER

HOURS: **6a-10p**
- **Will open after hours**

COST: **Free**
TV: **Yes**

We rarely find a Loews hotel with rates appropriate for our "Moderate" category. Across the street from "Harvard of the South," this Nashville representative is a sensible choice for travelers with business on Vanderbilt's campus or downtown Nashville (2 miles away). With room rates plunging as low as $132/night (internet), guests can get some bang out of their bucks thanks to Loews' accommodating quarters and upscale service. Simply decorated in shades of cream and brown, the 354 rooms have a country home feel. We are especially fond of the hotel's 24-hour room service, complimentary bottled water and free shuttle service (5-mile radius).

Sadly, the workout room does not make our list of raves. The Life Fitness treadmills are new, but the other machines are marginal and worn. A quick tune-up is possible, but for a longer or more intense strength, cardio or swim session, drive 5 minutes or take Loews' shuttle to the Sportsplex.

LEAST EXPENSIVE

GOLD: Holiday Inn Express

920 Broadway, Nashville, TN 37203
(615) 244-0150 • hiexpress.com

Precor and Holiday Inn Express? Who knew that these two brands could come together under one roof? As possibly the best Holiday Inn Express gym in the country, this franchise takes the cake for Nashville travelers in search of a good workout option and budget prices.

In addition to free breakfasts and high-speed internet access, guests receive complimentary admission to the hotel's large workout room filled with high-quality cardio gear.

CARDIO
TREADMILLS: **2 Precor**
RECUMBENT BIKE: **1 Precor**
ELLIPTICAL: **4 Precor**

STRENGTH
MACHINES: **1 Precor Multi**
DUMBBELLS: **5-50 lbs**

SWIM
SPECS: **Outdoor • Not lap**

OTHER
HOURS: **24**
COST: **Free**
TV: **Yes**

All of the Precor machines are new, and included in the line up is a Precor multi-gym. Similar to their treads and ellipticals, this weight apparatus is first class and, along with Holiday Inn's dumbbells, serve up a basic strength option. But, if you have read our other hotel reviews, you should know the drill by now. Go to the Downtown YMCA if you want more — more weights, more machines or a swim. From Holiday Inn Express, it will be about a 10-15-minute walk.

SILVER: Hampton Inn at the University

2330 Elliston Place, Nashville, TN 37203
(615) 320-6060 • hamptoninn.com

There are two Hampton Inns in the Vanderbilt area. Book this one to have Sportsplex in your backyard and Vanderbilt University a block away. Expect typical Hampton service and amenities from this reliable and wallet-friendly hotel. Clean rooms, warm service and free continental breakfasts are highlights.

Hampton's workout room is standard fare as well. Diminutive in size, 5 ramshackle cardio pieces hug its walls. So jaunt 2 minutes to Sportsplex.

Note: 53 restaurants are located within a one-mile radius of this hotel, including Fleming's Prime Steakhouse and PF Chang's.

BRONZE: Embassy Suites Vanderbilt

1811 Broadway, Nashville, TN 37203
(615) 320-8899 • embassysuites.com

This atrium hotel is all about the freebies. Free made-to-order breakfasts, free happy hours with cocktails and free passes to the Sportsplex (2 per stay). The all-suite guest accommodations are not too shabby, either!

Even if you would rather skip the 3-5 minute drive to Sportsplex (it's too far to walk), the in-house fitness center will not suffice. While the room is attractive and airy, the equipment is better suited as replacement parts. Head to Sportsplex!

Note: While Embassy also provides guests with a free pass to the closer Baptist Hospital Health Club, we checked it out, and Sportsplex is superior.

BEYOND HOTELS

Downtown YMCA

1000 Church Street, Nashville, TN 37203
(615) 254-0631 • ymcamidtn.org/downtown

CARDIO

TREADMILLS: **True • StairMaster**
UPRIGHT BIKE: **LF • Fan**
RECUMBENT BIKE: **StairMaster**
ELLIPTICAL: **Precor • LF • Cybex • StarTrac**
STEPPER: **StairMaster • Stepmill**
ROWING: **Concept II**

STRENGTH

FREE WEIGHTS: **Yes**
HAMMER: **Yes**
MACHINES: **Nautilus**
DUMBBELLS: **5-100 lbs**

SWIM

GRADE: **B+**
SPECS: **8x25m • Indoor • 82°**
TOYS: **Kick • Pull • Clock**

OTHER

CLASSES: **Yes**
HOURS: M-F **5:15a-9p** • SAT **7a-5p** • SUN **1-5p**
COST: **Free Courtyard • $15 Others**
TV: **Yes**
EXTRAS: **1/18 mile outdoor track • Basketball • Racquetball**

The only disadvantage to this Y is its location. This large, multi-level facility is at least 5 walking minutes away from all of Nashville's lodging options, not just those appearing on our list.

After paying the $15 entry fee, athletes receive access to the entire club and its array of equipment, courts, pool and classes. Most fitness apparatus is on one floor. The cardio machines are new, top-grade and come in a variety of forms. Ellipticals are here in force with 7 Precors, 4 StarTracs, 6 Life Fitness 9500s and 4 Cybex Arc Trainers awaiting your arrival. The collection of weight options is impressive too, especially for a YMCA. Iron-pumpers will find 17 Nautilus Nitro machines, 1 Nautilus pulley system, 5 benches and a few Cybex free weight leg units.

The lap pool should please even hard core swimmers — those persnickety ones who feel that the difference between a 25-yard and a 25-meter pool is material. Okay, we agree, those extra seven feet can add up! Rest assured, all you need to worry about for this swim workout is your Speedo and goggles.

The lanes are separated by floating lines and bottom stripes, and all of the extras are provided, including a pace clock, kickboards and pull-buoys.

Centennial Sportsplex

222 25th Avenue North, Nashville, TN 37203
(615) 862-8480 • centennialsportsplex.com

Most space in this enormous indoor public facility is dedicated to its 2 swimming pools, diving well and ice skating rink (used as a practice facility by the NHL's Nashville Predators). Local high schools and Masters groups train and compete in the main pool. Though 50 meters long, it is typically set up for 22 lanes of 25-yard short course. Some pull-buoys and kickboards are usually on deck, but don't be surprised if you have to do without. Of course, as a competition pool, swimmers can count on staples such as pace clocks.

A practice pool is also onsite, but its 88-degree temperature is warm for any serious swimming.

CARDIO

TREADMILLS: **StairMaster • Quinton - old**
UPRIGHT BIKE: **Stratus**
RECUMBENT BIKE: **Stratus**
STEPPER: **StairMaster**
ROWING: **Concept II**

STRENGTH

FREE WEIGHTS: **Yes**
MACHINES: **BodyMaster**
DUMBBELLS: **2-110 lbs**

SWIM

GRADE: **A**
SPECS: **22x25yd • Indoor • 79°**
TOYS: **Kick • Pull • Clock**
MASTERS: **Yes**

OTHER

CLASSES: **Yes**
HOURS: M-TH **6a-9p** • F **6a-7p** • SAT **8:30-6p** • SUN **Closed**
COST: **$6**
TV: **Yes**
EXTRAS: **Ice Rink**

Receiving less attention, money and space, the fitness areas stock a disorganized collection of old and new equipment. Its 4 StairMaster treads, 4 StairMaster 4600 steppers, 2 Stratus recumbent bikes and 2 Stratus upright bikes are all gently used and should get your heart pumping. The other endurance equipment, however, is old or non-functional. And Sportsplex does not have any ellipticals!

Alongside the cardio equipment, strength buffs will find modern BodyMaster stack-loaded weight stations. Additional strength equipment can be found on the opposite side of the pool deck in a room that recalled our days of lifting in our high school buddy's garage. Be careful not to trip over scattered dumbbells and try to ignore the rust growing on the plate weights. Although they may not look pretty, the good thing about free weights is that they never wear out. Dull your senses and you will be okay. At $6/day, your wallet will be okay, too.

Uptown YMCA

SunTrust Center, 30th Floor
424 Church Street, Nashville, TN 37219
(615) 251-5454 • ymcamidtn.org/uptown

CARDIO

TREADMILLS: **Precor • StarTrac**
UPRIGHT BIKE: **Precor • Fan**
RECUMBENT BIKE: **Precor**
ELLIPTICAL: **Precor • Cybex • StarTrac**
STEPPER: **StairMaster • StarTrac**
ROWING: **Concept II**

STRENGTH

FREE WEIGHTS: **Yes**
MACHINES: **Cybex • Free Motion**
DUMBBELLS: **5-100 lbs**

OTHER

CLASSES: **Yes**
HOURS: M-TH **5:15a-8p** • F **5:15a-7:30p** • SAT-SUN **Closed**
COST: **Free Courtyard • $15 Others**
TV: **Yes**
EXTRAS: **Basketball 1/2 court**

Although named Uptown, this YMCA is also located in the midst of downtown Nashville. Offered and used as a weekday executive fitness center, this 30th floor skyscraping Y is a convenient and worthwhile option for Courtyard guests. Unfortunately, this nifty facility is closed on weekends. But Courtyard guests can use the free pass ($15 for all others) at the Downtown Y when Uptown is closed (10-15 minute walk). Monday through Friday, guests will be pleased with Uptown's splendid offering of cardio/weight machines, free weights and classes. This Y features 11 Cybex weight stations, 7 Precor ellipticals, 5 Precor treads, 3 Precor upright bikes and plenty more.

With no pool, swimmers must look for a dip at the Downtown Y or Sportsplex. You may be able to use your Courtyard freebie at the Downtown YMCA as well even when Uptown is open.

After your workout here, clean up in the Y's locker room. A full assortment of amenities is provided, including hair dryers and Q-tips.

Note: Those not staying at the Courtyard (the only recommended hotel near this Y) will be better served by the larger, full-service Downtown YMCA.

RUNNING ROUTES

Riverfront Park

Within blocks of the downtown hotels is Riverfront Park, where athletes can cross the Shelby Street Pedestrian Bridge to Nashville's east bank. Striders should follow the Davidson Street Connector route (hang a right on So. 2nd to Davidson) to Shelby Bottoms Greenway and Nature Park — just under 4 miles. You will be heading in an easterly direction along the Cumberland River. Once you reach your destination, you will be treated to another 5 miles of paved paths and 4+ miles of trails. You will actually reach Shelby Park first. The Bottoms is behind the park.

NEW ORLEANS, LOUISIANA

Note: Along with the rest of the country and world, we sympathize for everyone who endured the recent tragedies in New Orleans. We hope that our information will encourage travelers to head back to the Big Easy and help revitalize its people and economy.

As of midsummer 2006, other than the Loews and Omni, most hotels are not quite ready for public use, but check athleticmindedtraveler.com for updates.

Everyone knows the "Big Easy" is home to the most popular Mardi Gras celebration in North America. But are you familiar with these tidbits about New Orleans and its traditions?

• The Mardi Gras official colors are purple, green and gold, representing justice, faith and power, respectively.

• Bead throwing caught on in the late 1800s after a krewe member (guy on a float) dressed as Santa Claus tossed trinkets into the crowd. The spectators loved it, and a tradition was born.

• Consuming alcohol while roaming the streets is legal, provided your cocktail is in a "go-cup" — readily available at all liquor establishments.

• Each year, over 500,000 King cakes are gobbled from January 6th until Fat Tuesday. These round, brightly decorated treats are baked with a small plastic baby hidden inside to symbolize the Three Kings' search for newborn Jesus and the circular route they traveled. Receiving the gift-bearing slice is said to bless the eater with good fortune and obligates them to host the next week's King Cake festivities.

• Fifteen percent of this city's people practice the ancient religion of Voodoo. It is not uncommon to see locals with small, herb-filled "gris-gris" pouches attached to their belts to bring good luck or ward off the evil eye. The Christianity-based Voodoo is often wrongly confused with the magical tradition of Hoodoo, which draws upon spells, curses, potions and other forms of witchcraft to influence a particular behavior. Hoodoo uses Voodoo dolls, but Voodoo does not.

Confused? Yeah, we thought so. But at least you won't have to rely on magic to make good workout options appear in this bewitching city — though swimmers may want to think about it.

79 Locations Reviewed

EXPENSIVE

GOLD: **Ritz Carlton New Orleans** (RE-OPENING EARLY 2007)

921 Canal Street, New Orleans, LA 70112
(504) 524-1331 • ritzcarlton.com/hotels/new_orleans

CARDIO

TREADMILLS: **9 Cybex**
UPRIGHT BIKE: **1 Cybex**
RECUMBENT BIKE: **3 Cybex**
ELLIPTICAL: **3 Precor**
STEPPER: **2 StarTrac**

STRENGTH

FREE WEIGHTS: **Yes**
HAMMER: **Yes - 1**
MACHINES: **8 Cybex**
DUMBBELLS: **3-70 lbs**

SWIM

GRADE: **C**
SPECS: **Resistance Pool**
TOYS: **Kick**

OTHER

CLASSES: **Yes**
HOURS: **6a-10p**
COST: **Free Ritz & Maison • $10 Iberville**
TV: **Yes**

Only steps from Bourbon Street, three Ritz-owned hotel properties inhabit the same block-long building on a quiet edge of the French Quarter. While still expensive, the room rates at the Ritz New Orleans fall between the more costly Ritz Maison and cheaper Ritz Iberville Suites.

As expected with this luxury chain, guest rooms are meticulously decorated with the finest comforts, including soundproofed walls, 300 thread count Frette linens, goose down pillows, CD players and high speed internet access (surcharge). Though the décor's accent is upper class, it is the 20,000-square-foot workout space that is uppermost in our minds.

The immaculate fitness center and spa (shared by all 3 Ritz properties) is a complimentary oasis to patrons of the two higher-priced hotels, but requires a $10/day fee for those staying at the less expensive Iberville. Three large rooms divide the exercise space: cardio, resistance pool and weights. Nearest to the reception desk, the bright and expansive cardio area houses modern machines with attached individual plasma television screens. On the far end of the gym, the weight room provides an impressive selection of cutting-edge stack-loaded machines, free weights and dumbbells.

Between the cardio and weight rooms is the facility's most unique feature — a 10-foot-long resistance pool. One of these pricey swim-in-place toys has been #1 on our Christmas list for some time. We're not sure whether Endless Pools manufactured this particular unit, but it works the same — with controllable, jet propelled water resisting forward motion while you swim (think swimming treadmill). The water seemed a tad warm and kickboards are provided to round out this unique immersion. Ritz's upscale day spa also provides a full menu of pampering to reward your exercise diligence.

Sadly, this pool is the best swim option in all of downtown New Orleans (health clubs included). It is hard to believe, but the closest regulation pool requires a 15-minute drive beyond the French Quarter to the Kiefer U.N.O. Lakefront Arena.

SILVER: Ritz Carlton Maison Orleans

(RE-OPENING EARLY 2007)

904 Rue Iberville, New Orleans, LA 70112
(504) 670-2900 • ritzcarlton.com/hotels/maison_orleans

As the priciest of the 3 Ritz neighbors, Maison attempts to legitimize its steep rates by overloading guests with amenities such as 5 complimentary food and beverage services a day, extravagant French furnishings, an expensive art collection and Italian Frette linens.

The 75-room boutique hotel is beautiful and private, but we do not understand why anyone would pay an extra $100/night when the luxurious and less expensive Ritz New Orleans' rooms are literally next door. And, since all 3 Ritz properties share the same great workout and spa facility, traveling athletes can rest easy that they have not forsaken workout quality to save accommodation dollars.

Note: Read Ritz New Orleans for Maison's health club description.

MODERATELY EXPENSIVE

GOLD: Loews New Orleans

300 Poydras Street, New Orleans, LA 70130
(504) 595-3300 • loewshotels.com/hotels/neworleans

This Loews property opened its doors in late 2003. The hotel is centrally located across the street from Harrah's Casino and 3 blocks from the convention center. Although not within the French Quarter, straying a few blocks outside this noisy and hectic district suits us just fine. Bourbon Street and the Quarter are great party places, but terrible sleeping spots. Even one block can mean the difference between a raucous crowd keeping you awake all night and a peaceful night of zzz's.

CARDIO

TREADMILLS: **3 Cybex**
UPRIGHT BIKE: **1 Cybex**
RECUMBENT BIKE: **2 Cybex**
ELLIPTICAL: **2 Cybex**

STRENGTH

MACHINES: **7 Cybex**
DUMBBELLS: **5-50 lbs**

SWIM

SPECS: **Indoor • Not lap**

OTHER

HOURS: **5a-10p**
COST: **Free**
TV: **Yes**

Loews is contemporary, with rooms marked by clean lines in crisp brown and white shades. Don't be surprised if you see Fido or Filbert roaming the halls. Pet-friendly Loews accommodates critters of all shapes and sizes, but they cannot use the fitness center or pool.

You will be in the doghouse if working out escapes your daily routine. So heed our command and hightail it to the hotel's 8th floor fitness center and spa. This expansive and sparkling room, filled with the latest in cardio and weight technology, will have you panting in no time. While free weights are AWOL, Loews' assortment of stack-loaded machines and dumbbells are acceptable substitutes. The large space can accommodate more machines, so perhaps by the time you are reading this page the young Loews will have ordered and received additional equipment. After eyeing the selection, if you find yourself barking for more machines or an obedience... sorry, aerobics class, walk 10 minutes to Elmwood Fitness.

Swimmers, you are out of luck. The only lap pool Downtown is a 20-yard, pathetic water box at the private New Orleans Athletic Club. Not only is the club a pit ("F" on our grading scale), but they have the audacity to charge a ridiculous $20 admission! If dehydration sets in and you have a car, driving 15 minutes to the Kiefer U.N.O. Lakefront Arena ($20 by taxi) is your only other option.

SILVER: Hotel Monaco (AWAITING RE-OPENING NEWS)

333 St. Charles Avenue, New Orleans, LA 70130
(504) 561-0010 • monaco-neworleans.com

CARDIO

TREADMILLS: **2 StarTrac**
UPRIGHT BIKE: **1 StarTrac**
RECUMBENT BIKE: **2 StarTrac**
ELLIPTICAL: **2 StarTrac**

STRENGTH

MACHINES: **4 Paramount**
DUMBBELLS: **5-35 lbs**

OTHER

HOURS: **24**
COST: **Free**
TV: **Yes**

One thing you can look forward to with this hotel brand is fun, fun, fun! New Orleans' version upholds this trademark with peach and yellow rooms, decorative mosquito nets above each bed and leopard-print upholstery.

But the amusement hardly stops there. Complimentary wine and happy hour, free chair massages and an open invite for your pet guarantee a creative and unique stay. Finally, for those lonely travelers looking for a quiet companion, goldfish can be provided.

With high ceilings, yellow walls and loads of space, Monaco's workout facility looks like it once functioned as a fashionably small ballroom. The area is bright and cheerful, but Monaco's small selection of exercise equipment hardly fills it up. However, enough gently-used StarTrac and Paramount machines line the floor to satisfy fitness fans. And those unsatisfied with Monaco's in-house gym can walk 3 minutes to Elmwood Fitness, located around the corner.

Swimmers, you know the drill. If you are desperate and have a car, start driving to Kiefer U.N.O.

BRONZE: Omni Royal Orleans

621 St. Louis Street, New Orleans, LA 70140
(504) 529-5333 • omnihotels.com

This hotel is for those wanting to be front and center of the French Quarter hoopla. Light sleepers are forewarned — you may need earplugs for those nights when Hurricane (the drink, not the storm) influenced revelers and other festive folk flood the streets. This noise potential may lead you toward a listing on the Quarter's fringe.

Formerly the Louisiana state capitol building, the Royal Orleans' stretches over an entire city block. Fifty paces from Bourbon Street, the 346 gold and cream guest rooms come with antique furnishings and free high-speed internet access.

Omni's exercise center is the best you will find in the heart of the Quarter, which is not saying much. Located on the hotel's roof and adjacent to the outdoor pool, the 15x20 hut barely holds the equipment inside. Although the 7 Cybex weight machines are new, the same cannot be said for the cardio apparatus. The treads, bikes and ellipticals all work, but should be replaced with more recent models.

CARDIO
TREADMILLS: **2 Cybex**
UPRIGHT BIKE: **1 Tectrix**
RECUMBENT BIKE: **1 Tectrix**
ELLIPTICAL: **1 Cybex • 1 Precor - old**

STRENGTH
MACHINES: **7 Cybex**
DUMBBELLS: **15-50 lbs**

SWIM
SPECS: **Outdoor • Not lap**

OTHER
HOURS: **24**
COST: **Free**
TV: **Yes**

Swimmers, the outdoor pool is nothing close to a lapper, so your dilemma remains the same — whether to drive or cab to Kiefer U.N.O.

LEAST EXPENSIVE

GOLD: **Iberville Suites** (RE-OPENING EARLY 2007)

910 Iberville Street, New Orleans, LA 70112
(504) 523-2400 • ibervillesuites.com

As our third and least expensive Ritz listing, Iberville may be the best overall hotel choice in New Orleans for the money. On the edge of the French Quarter and in the same building as the Ritz New Orleans and Ritz Maison, Iberville grants guests many of the same comforts as its sister properties, but for prices in the $90-$140/night range as opposed to $199-$300/night. Although not decorated with the same luxurious flair, all accommodations are suites with separate sleeping and living areas, mini-refrigerators, antique furnishings and 24-hour room service. And Iberville treats hotel guests to a complimentary breakfast buffet each morning.

For your workout, Iberville shares the same fitness center and spa with the 2 other Ritz properties. Although guests of the Ritz New Orleans and Ritz Maison get in for free, Iberville travelers are charged $10/day. Since you are saving at least $50-$100/night on your room, this tack-on should not break the budget.

Note: Read our Ritz New Orleans review for a detailed description of the exercise facility.

SILVER: **Drury Inn and Suites**

820 Poydras Street, New Orleans, LA 70112
(504) 529-7800 • druryhotels.com/properties/neworleans.cfm

Located in the central business district and 5 blocks from the

French Quarter, this Drury Inn makes our list for being across the street from Elmwood Fitness, its inexpensive room rates and its load of freebies. It's easier to forgive Drury for its ugly rooms when you consider the free local calls, free high-speed internet access, in-room microwaves and refrigerators, free evening beverages and snacks (M-Th) and free hot breakfast buffets. Belgian waffles, scrambled eggs, sausage and other treats make up Drury's morning feast.

After stuffing yourself, do not bother with Drury's measly in-house workout room. Instead, waddle across the street to the 13th floor of One Shell Center to exercise at Elmwood Fitness for $10.

BEYOND HOTELS

Elmwood Fitness Downtown

(AWAITING RE-OPENING NEWS)

701 Poydras Street, Suite 1300, New Orleans, LA 70139
in One Shell Square
(504) 588-1600 • elmwoodfitness.com

CARDIO

TREADMILLS: **10 StarTrac**
UPRIGHT BIKE: **3 Tectrix**
RECUMBENT BIKE: **3 Technogym - old**
ELLIPTICAL: **8 Precor**
STEPPER: **8 StairMaster - old**
ROWING: **1 Concept II**
OTHER: **Crossrobic • XC Ski**

STRENGTH

FREE WEIGHTS: **Yes**
HAMMER: **Yes**
MACHINES: **16 Icarian**
DUMBBELLS: **5-100 lbs**

OTHER

CLASSES: **Yes**
HOURS: M-F **5:30a-9p** • SAT **8a-4p** • SUN **Closed**
COST: **$10**
TV: **Yes**
EXTRAS: **Racquetball • Smoothie Bar**

Finding Elmwood's 13th-floor fitness center can be tricky, so ask hotel staff or any security personnel you come across for help. Once you have made it to the gym and paid $10, you will be greeted by new strength equipment and semi-new cardio machines strewn across the club's 2 floors.

The gym's upper level is actually a loft-like area suspended above a portion of the main floor. Although Elmwood claims that the club is 16,000 square feet, a good amount is dedicated to 3 racquetball courts. But its wide-open fitness areas, attractive city views and acceptable range of equipment get the workout job done.

You can sneak a peek on their user-friendly website.

With no pool, swimmers can give their Speedos a day off.

Note: Since Elmwood is small, we have included the number of machines in our equipment breakdown.

Kiefer University of New Orleans
Lakefront Arena Aquatic Center

(AWAITING RE-OPENING NEWS)

East Campus of the University of New Orleans
6801 Franklin Avenue, New Orleans, LA 70122
(504) 280-7238 • arena.uno.edu

SWIM

GRADE: **#1 A • #2 B**
SPECS: **#1 8x50m • Indoor • 82°**
#2 6x25yd • Outdoor • 82-86°
TOYS: **Kick • Pull • Clock**

OTHER

HOURS: **Vary - call**
COST: **$3**

Dashing to make our flight out of New Orleans, we missed visiting this pool located 6 miles and a 15-minute drive outside the French Quarter (cab fare $20 — prearrange a ride home). But our solid research on this swim-only option and the aquatic center's website should provide enough information to guide you here with confidence.

Two pools are available at this university facility. As the host of local swim meets and competitions, the deeper indoor 50-meter version is preferable to the outdoor 6-lane, 25-yard alternative. Unfortunately, a bulkhead usually divides the indoor pool into 16 lanes of short course (25-yard) swimming, so you will not gain any length inside.

Kickboards, pull-buoys and pace clocks are available. Three bucks is the going rate and the facility is open year round, 7 days/ week, so give it a go.

Note: Since this pool hosts swim meets and other competitions, call ahead to ensure that lap swimming is available during your desired time. This is especially important, considering the commute.

RUNNING ROUTES

Esplanade Avenue

The Big Easy is also "easy" on the running. Both Esplanade Avenue and St. Charles Avenue boast wide dirt medians for a more cushioned jaunt (always run against trolley traffic!). Runners can pick up Esplanade on the north end of the Quarter and take it west to the 1,500 acre City Park and its 2.5-mile Arboretum Trail.

For those staying at one of the Ritz properties, taking Rampart north about 12 blocks will hook you up with Esplanade.

Audubon Park

Starting at Lee Circle and following St. Charles Avenue's dirt median in a southerly direction to Audubon Park and back provides a very nice 7 miler. This 400-acre park located at St. Charles between Walnut and Calhoun has a 1.8 perimeter loop. In addition, the park has 3 lagoons, gardens, bridle paths, a golf course and a zoo. Watch out for Fido, as Audubon is a popular dog exercise venue.

River Road

Lastly, head to River Road and follow the levee along the mighty Mississippi for as many flat miles as you can take.

NEW YORK, NEW YORK

"Start spreading the news...
I'm leaving today..."

Are you tapping your foot yet? What does New York City mean to you? It must be something, because 40 million people visit the Big Apple each year. For us, those two words, "New... York" elicit a stream of images, impressions and reactions.

New York is where:

- All of our hearts bled on 9/11/01
- Tycoons and socialites have names like "the Donald" and "Paris"
- The ball drops every new year
- "Yogi-isms" have nothing to do with Yoga
- On marathon day, locals actually wear something besides black
- A borough is where you live, not an animal you ride
- Jackie Robinson pioneered, The Babe astonished, Namath predicted and Steinbrenner spends
- The Arts are center stage and "Page Six" tries to upstage, and
- Anything is possible.

But time is money and money is time... which is a good reminder for us to get down to business.

CENTRAL PARK WEST

In a city that never sleeps and daily life is acutely urban, Central Park provides calming balance. Its trails, ponds and rolling hills attract natives and visitors in search of something more natural. Apart from a boating, horseback riding and ice skating oasis, Central Park's miles of tree-lined roads create a runner's sanctuary in the midst of New York's skyscrapers and city grit.

Locals know such paradise does not come cheap. In this metropolis, status rules — and proximity to the Park is another measuring stick. Neighborhoods bordering the City's outdoor playground host the Big Apple's elite, and an address on Central Park West is arguably the crown.

Hotels follow suit in this high stakes game of real estate. So, while staying in this part of town will provide convenient access to the Park's wonderful refuge, you'll end up paying more for the perk.

EXPENSIVE

GOLD: Mandarin Oriental

80 Columbus Circle at 60th Street, New York, NY 10023
(212) 805-8800 • mandarinoriental.com/newyork

CARDIO

TREADMILLS: **5 LF**
UPRIGHT BIKE: **2 LF**
RECUMBENT BIKE: **2 LF**
ELLIPTICAL: **3 LF**
STEPPER: **1 LF**

STRENGTH

MACHINES: **7 LF**
DUMBBELLS: **5-50 lbs**

SWIM

GRADE: **C**
SPECS: **2x25yd • Indoor • 86°**
TOYS: **Kick • Pull**

OTHER

HOURS: M-F **7a-9p**
• SAT-SUN **7a-7p**
COST: **Free**
TV: **Yes**

Opened in late 2003, the Mandarin is an impressive addition to Manhattan's hotel market and skyline. Located at Columbus Circle on the southwest corner of Central Park, Mandarin's 251 guest rooms and suites are the ultimate lap of luxury and sophistication. You know you are in a stylish accommodation when the room inspires home decorating ideas. Keep in mind, because Manhattan real estate is some of the most expensive in the world, even the pricey hotel rooms will be smaller than you are accustomed to. Fortunately, the incredible Park views and abundant natural light expand these quarters.

The 36th floor fitness center is immaculate. As part of a 14,500 square foot spa, the complimentary 6,000 square foot exercise center and lap pool offer high-tech workouts in a true state-of-the-art facility. Delivered in December of 2003, the Life Fitness cardio machines all have plasma LCDs and look great atop the center's Asian bamboo flooring. Although free weights are missing, we think the decent dumbbell set and 7 stack-loaded weight machines will adequately service your major muscle groups.

We are pleased to see a hotel offer a regulation length lap swim option, especially at these prices. Even though the 25-yard water box does not have floating lane lines, the two bottom stripes are sufficient lap-swim markings. At 86°, the water is a little warm, but tolerable for a moderate effort workout.

Finally, it is always refreshing to find a fitness center staff that is helpful, polite, and interested in your workout and well-being. Confucious says, "Staying here will bring a fitness fortune."

SILVER: Trump International Hotel & Towers

One Central Park West, New York, NY 10023
(212) 299-1000 • trumpintl.com

Across the street from Central Park, this hotel is slightly "trumped" by new entrant and neighbor, the Mandarin.

While its competitor edges out Trump on the exercise option, guests can rest easy that all the luxuries of a high-end, pricey, Central Park hotel are here: plush duvets, Frette linens, 24-hour room service (from none other than the famous Jean Georges Restaurant), complimentary internet access and, believe it or not, complimentary fresh flowers delivered daily! In fact, if you would like a truly relaxing dining experience, don the slippers and bathrobe — because, with a little advance notice, an in-room chef will be at your service.

CARDIO

TREADMILLS: **4 Quinton**
UPRIGHT BIKE: **2 Cybex**
RECUMBENT BIKE: **1 Cybex**
ELLIPTICAL: **3 Precor**
STEPPER: **1 StairMaster • 1 Tectrix** - old
ROWING: **1 Concept II**
OTHER: **1 VersaClimber**

STRENGTH

FREE WEIGHTS: **Yes**
MACHINES: **14 Cybex**
DUMBBELLS: **3-80 lbs**

SWIM

GRADE: **C-**
SPECS: **2x18yd • Indoor • 83°**
TOYS: **Kick • Pull • Clock**

OTHER

HOURS: M-F **6:30a-9p** • SAT-SUN **8a-8p**
COST: **Free**
TV: **Yes**

Although all rooms take on a contemporary style with beige tones dominating the walls, floors and bedding, only 38 of the 167 units fall into the lesser price category of "superior/deluxe." The other quarters are 1 and 2 bedroom suites and cost a mint!

Trump's workout facility has slightly more equipment than the Mandarin, but the machines are not as new, the lap pool is shorter (2 bottom stripes, no floating lines) and the lower level venue provides no view. That said, this accommodation remains a solid second-place selection in this high price category.

But before you take out the plastic, be advised that the moderately priced Phillips Club offers a workout option that surpasses both luxury properties.

MODERATELY EXPENSIVE

GOLD: Phillips Club at Lincoln Square

155 West 66th Street, New York, NY 10023
(212) 835-8800 • phillipsclub.com/nyc/split.html

Phillips Club management has informed us that, while hotel rooms are still offered at their property, they will take reservations only 10 days or less in advance of your arrival. If they have a vacancy, you will get a room. It's worth the call, since this stay and play option is one of the best in all of NYC.

At around $300/night during the week, Phillips Club is the best stay and play option, not just in this neighborhood, but in all of Manhattan. The Lincoln Square address affords New York convenience: Subway stop across the street, Balducci's market off the lobby, Lincoln Center around the corner and a host of dining spots within shouting distance. The contemporary, uncluttered guest suites create a Manhattan apartment feel, complete with full kitchens, refrigerators, silverware and microwaves. Don't let the Residence Inn type perks mislead you. Phillips Club's Frette linens, Matelasse coverlets, Herman Miller Aeron chairs and stylish furniture are reminders that this is no cookie-cutter franchise property.

Without a fitness center on-site, Phillips Club went to bat for its athletic-minded guests by arranging guest privileges at the best workout destination in all of Manhattan — Reebok Sports Club/NY. It is less than a 3-minute walk to this country club-like facility, which we understand has a two-year waiting list to join! Phillips guests simply show Reebok reception their room key and picture I.D. and are granted complimentary access to the gym's 140,000 square-feet of workout bliss.

Note: On weekends, Phillips' room rates can jump to the $400/night price range.

SILVER: Le Parker Meridien (LPM)

118 West 57th Street
New York, NY 10019
(212) 245-5000
leparkermeridien.com

With a mix of business and leisure clientele, the LPM's "uptown, not uptight," theme shows throughout. Only blocks south of Central Park and near Times Square, this hotel provides ergonomic rooms at moderate Manhattan prices.

The smallish guest quarters are accented with cherry and cedar woods, Aeron chairs, 32-inch televisions and low-lying platform beds. Think Scandinavian design. Technologically savvy, the hotel offers patrons free high-speed internet access and CD/DVD players in every room. If you love breakfast as much as we do, check out Norma's off the hotel lobby. This all-day ('til 3pm) breakfast spot has been rated by several sources as the best in New York City.

Guests also receive complimentary access to the chic Gravity Health Club on LPM's lower level. A separate bank of elevators transports you to this impressive 15,000 square foot spa and gym. Inside, the floor space is loaded with new equipment of every brand and model. We especially were keen on the 11 Hammer Strength machines and numerous stack-loaded weight stations. Classes are offered here, too, including cycling and aerobics.

Swimmers are provided a pool option on the 42nd PH floor of the hotel. This 40-foot shorty is nothing to get excited about, but can be used in a pinch. Bring your calculator to keep track of the laps. If you want a longer lap pool (not nicer), the West Side YMCA is a 10-minute walk.

CARDIO

TREADMILLS: **12 LF**
UPRIGHT BIKE: **4 LF**
RECUMBENT BIKE: **1 LF**
ELLIPTICAL: **4 LF • 2 Precor • 2 Reebok**
STEPPER: **2 Tectrix**
ROWING: **2 Concept II**
OTHER: **2 Gravitron**

STRENGTH

FREE WEIGHTS: **Yes**
HAMMER: **Yes**
MACHINES: **15 Cybex**
DUMBBELLS: **1-80 lbs**

SWIM

GRADE: **D**
SPECS: **3x13yd • Indoor • 86°**
TOYS: **Kick • Pull • Clock**

OTHER

CLASSES: **Yes**
HOURS: M-F **6a-10:45p** • SAT-SUN **8a-8:45p**
COST: **Free Le Parker • $25 Others**
TV: **Yes**

BRONZE: Sheraton Manhattan & New York Hotels

811 7th Avenue, New York, NY 10019
(212)581-1000 • sheraton.com

It's not often that you'll find two hotels of the same brand located directly across the street from one another, but these two Sheratons are just that — positioned on opposite sides of 7th Avenue in Manhattan. Convenient to Midtown's businesses and Central Park's serenity, these neighboring hotels are centrally located for a home base.

Rooms at both accommodations are essentially designed and decorated the same: conservative color tones and patterns, standard furnishings, and basic floorplans. Guests will appreciate the comfortable Sheraton "Sweet Sleeper" beds, 24-hour room service and high speed internet access (fee).

Each Sheraton has its own gym, but the New York Hotel and Tower version has the better workout option by far. Guests of either property can work out at New York's fitness club for a $10/day fee ($20/stay). On the lower level of the hotel, the privately operated facility re-opened after renovation in March 2006. All cardio and strength equipment has been replaced with new Life Fitness apparatus. Some of the older machines were carried across the street to

Manhattan's relatively puny workout room. Your dollars will be well spent here whether you're looking for high octane pulse beating, group classes (yoga, pilates, kick-boxing) or a muscle pump.

LEAST EXPENSIVE

Westside YMCA

5 West 63rd Street, New York, NY 10023
(212) 875-4206 • ymcanyc.org/westside

Warning! This hotel recommendation is directed only at those athletic-minded travelers who are on a really tight budget, willing to stay in a hotel that may not please the senses, and are okay sharing a bathroom with their fellow hotel guests.

In the lobby of this hotel/health club/youth center, we noticed foreign travelers and college-age kids checking into their rooms, suggesting a hostel type crowd — which makes sense given the price and accommodations. For working out, however, this is a phenomenal deal. Along with your cheap room, you also get free access to the Y's health club and pool located in the same building as the hotel.

BEYOND HOTELS CENTRAL PARK WEST

CARDIO

TREADMILLS: **LF**
UPRIGHT BIKE: **LF**
RECUMBENT BIKE: **LF**
ELLIPTICAL: **LF • Precor**
STEPPER: **StairMaster**
ROWING: **Concept II**
OTHER: **VersaClimber • NordicTrack • Crossrobic • Ergometer**

STRENGTH

FREE WEIGHTS: **Yes**
HAMMER: **Yes**
MACHINES: **Cybex • LF • Nautilus**
DUMBBELLS: **3-110 lbs**

SWIM

GRADE: **B**
SPECS: **4x25yd • Indoor • 81°**
TOYS: **Kick • Pull • Clock**

OTHER

CLASSES: **Yes**
HOURS: M-TH **5a-11p** • F **5a-10p** • SAT-SUN **7a-9p**
COST: **Free Phillips Club only**
TV: **Yes**
EXTRAS: **1/6 mile outdoor track • Basketball • Climbing wall**

Reebok Sports Club/ NY (LA)

160 Columbus Avenue, New York, NY 10023 at 67th Street
(212) 362-6800 • sportclubla.com

Sports Club/LA sets the standard for a truly upscale and premium health club experience. All of their unbelievable facilities are essentially the same: a huge space, tons of equipment, loads of classes, fantastic pools and plush locker rooms. This Reebok-sponsored, Upper West Side location is no different. One of the lap pools even has underwater music piped in to enliven your swim!

We don't know about you, but heading out to exercise for the first time at a club of this caliber gave us that same feeling of anticipation as when we "toe it up" at a race's starting line. Simply put, Reebok Sports Club/NY is the finest fitness facility in Manhattan, which puts it in high demand during workout rush hours. So plan accordingly.

Your Phillips Club room key and a picture I.D. are all you need for complimentary access to this workout paradise. Unfortunately the restrictive guest policy prohibits any other non-members.

Swimmers Note: A swim cap is required for everyone.

Westside YMCA

5 West 63rd Street, New York, NY 10023
(212) 875-4100 • ymcanyc.org/westside

Despite the shabby accommodations, the YMCA's fitness center is a really good option for those in search of total body conditioning. The small wood-paneled workout rooms and early 20th Century photographs showing the center and its original members provide a historic feel. Fortunately, the machines have been replaced since these pictures were taken.

In fact, the equipment here is new — really new. Twenty-four Cybex machines, 15 Life Fitness treads, 12 Concept II rowers and 9 Precor ellipticals are just samples of the high-end apparatus you will find in this unique Y.

And, in case the abundant 21st Century machinery has distracted you from your ancestral surroundings, the lap pool will take you right back in time. The carnival-themed tile decorating the walls is reminiscent of when the club was originally designed. The ceiling is a bit low and the room a little dark, but floating lines and bottom stripes mark the way. Set your expectations low and you should not be disappointed. Surprisingly, the admission fee for those not staying at the Y is a steep $25.

CARDIO

TREADMILLS: **LF**
UPRIGHT BIKE: **LF**
RECUMBENT BIKE: **LF**
ELLIPTICAL: **Precor**
STEPPER: **StairMaster • LF • Tectrix**
ROWING: **Concept II**
OTHER: **Gravitron**

STRENGTH

FREE WEIGHTS: **Yes**
HAMMER: **Yes - 1**
MACHINES: **Cybex • Free Motion**
DUMBBELLS: **1-120 lbs**

SWIM

GRADE: **C-**
SPECS: **4x25yd • Indoor • 80°**
TOYS: **Kick • Pull**
MASTERS: **Yes**

OTHER

CLASSES: **Yes**
HOURS: M-F **6a-11p** • SAT-SUN **8a-8p**
COST: **Free w/YMCA stay • $25 Others**
TV: **Yes**
EXTRAS: **Basketball • Racquetball**

MIDTOWN

In the Big Apple's core, tourist attractions such as Times Square, Rockefeller Center and the Empire State Building share real estate with corporate heavyweights in the world of finance, fashion and technology. State, federal and international government offices such as the United Nations call this area home, too. It's the busiest section in Manhattan, so travelers should be prepared to cover ground on foot, since available taxis are often difficult to find.

EXPENSIVE

GOLD: Grand Hyatt

Park Avenue at Grand Central Station, New York, NY 10017
(212) 883-1234 • grandnewyork.hyatt.com

CARDIO

TREADMILLS: **5 LF**
UPRIGHT BIKE: **2 LF**
RECUMBENT BIKE: **1 LF**
ELLIPTICAL: **3 LF**
STEPPER: **1 StairMaster**

STRENGTH

MACHINES: **8 LF**
DUMBBELLS: **5-40 lbs**

OTHER

HOURS: **5:30a-11p**
COST: **Free**
TV: **Yes**
EXTRAS: **$10 pass to Bally**

Despite a noisy yet convenient location next to Grand Central Station, the Hyatt's soundproof walls ensure that the commotion on the street stays outside. Inside, Grand Hyatt completed a renovation in 2004, and it shows. Tastefully decorated rooms mesh well with the rest of this upscale property. Additional perks include 24-hour room service as well as 3 on-site restaurants.

Grand Hyatt's 35th floor fitness center sounds its horn with a sizable offering of new machines in an attractive space. While sweating through your routine, you can watch 1 or all 7 plasma television screens hanging on the gym's walls. For those in search of a more significant weight workout or swim, Hyatt has arranged a deal with the nearby Bally Fitness at Madison and 43rd ($10 admission). While Grand Central's busses and trains are right next door, your feet are adequate for this less than 3-minute commute.

MODERATELY EXPENSIVE

GOLD: Affinia Dumont

150 E. 34th Street, New York, NY 10016
(212) 481-7600 • affinia.com

This is our favorite hotel in the Midtown area. Affinia's brochure describes itself as "New York's first executive fitness suite hotel." While it may not actually be the first or only, we applaud the concept. In a quieter part of central Manhattan, yet only 3 blocks from the Empire State Building, Affinia has created a fine lodging/workout option for fit travelers.

All 243 guest rooms have kitchens accessorized with microwaves, refrigerators, stoves, toasters and dishware. The style speaks a contemporary language, using earth tones, upholstered headboards, ergonomic desk chairs and custom window shades.

The connected Barking Dog Restaurant with its canine theme is an added convenience for an inexpensive meal.

The health and wellness center is petite but packs a strong

punch. Inside, a fitness concierge eagerly awaits to assist with jogging maps, access to the wellness library, arranging fitness activities, or simply spotting you on the free weights. All of the top-notch machines are just off the delivery truck, and many have plasma screens attached. Although we did not see any step machines, all other equipment modalities are there.

Swimmers must go to the nearest full-service health club to get wet. The Bally Fitness on West 32nd is probably your closest option (5-minute taxi ride), but getting through the door will cost $25.

CARDIO

TREADMILLS: **3 LF**
UPRIGHT BIKE: **1 LF**
RECUMBENT BIKE: **1 LF**
ELLIPTICAL: **3 LF**

STRENGTH

FREE WEIGHTS: **Yes**
MACHINES: **15 LF**
DUMBBELLS: **3-50 lbs**

OTHER

HOURS: M-F **6a-10p** • SAT-SUN **8a-6p** • **Will open after hours**
COST: **Free**
TV: **Yes**

SILVER: Crowne Plaza Times Square

1605 Broadway, New York, NY 10019 Between 48th and 49th
(212) 977-4000 • manhattan.crowneplaza.com

Need to be in the thick of NYC's most frenzied tourist trap, a.k.a. Times Square? Then Crowne Plaza is your best lodging and workout option. Far from a boutique hotel, Crowne's 770 humdrum rooms are basic, with beige-toned walls and light-hardwood furnishings. While the rooms and common areas do not make much of an impression, the exercise facility does. Located on the hotel's 15th floor, the 29,000 square-foot, full-service, private gym is independently operated by New York Sports Club. The up-to-date and cutting-edge equipment will no doubt elevate your heart rate, and the Club's modern design ensures that your workout will not be retro.

Access is complimentary to the marginal 4-lane, 4-foot deep pool. Floating lane lines and bottom stripes help swimmers navigate these calm, chlorinated waters. But if your workout calls for more than 2,000 yards, consider popping a Dramamine to fend off the flip-turn induced dizziness you may suffer in this 17-yard shorty.

Since this is one of the busiest gyms in Manhattan, expect to "work-in" with others. You know the crowd risk is high when the host offers a sweetener to sweat off-peak. If your schedule is flexible, accept the bribe and work out for free. Otherwise, pay $10 to

CARDIO

TREADMILLS: **LF • StarTrac**
UPRIGHT BIKE: **LF • StarTrac**
RECUMBENT BIKE: **LF • StarTrac**
ELLIPTICAL: **LF • Precor**
STEPPER: **StairMaster • Stepmill**
ROWING: **Concept II**

STRENGTH

FREE WEIGHTS: **Yes**
HAMMER: **Yes**
MACHINES: **Cybex • Icarian • Nautilus**
DUMBBELLS: **1-130 lbs**

SWIM

GRADE: **D+**
SPECS: **4x17yd • Indoor • 80-83°**
TOYS: **Kick • Pull • Clock**

OTHER

CLASSES: **Yes**
HOURS: M-F **6a-9:30p** • SAT **8a-8p** • SUN **8a-6p**
COST: **Varies**
TV: **Yes**

join the primetime clique.

To summarize guest pricing options:

FREE 8:30-11 a.m. • 2-4 p.m. • 8:30-9:30 p.m. • Weekends

$10 All other times

If you are a Crowne Priority Club member, you can skip deciphering the pricing grid, because access is always on the house.

BRONZE: Avalon

16 East 32nd Street, New York, NY 10016
(212) 299-7000 • avalonhotelnyc.com

For a hotel experience completely opposite of Crowne Plaza's, a respite at the quaint European-style Avalon may be in order. Within 4 blocks of the Empire State Building and Penn Station, this boutique property offers a convenient location for both business and leisure travelers. Avalon's 100 rooms are very "cozy" (marketing speak for small), but they are attractively appointed with marble bathrooms, Egyptian cotton linens and free high-speed internet access. Speaking of freebies, the hotel offers a gratis continental breakfast each morning and a complimentary pass to Bally Total Fitness, 3 blocks away on 32nd. Without a gym of its own, Avalon demonstrates its business savvy by extending the Bally comp to guests.

LEAST EXPENSIVE

GOLD: Helmsley Middletowne

148 East 48th Street, New York, NY 10017
Between Lexington and 3rd Avenues
(212) 755-3000 • helmsleyhotels.com

On the east side of Midtown Manhattan, this 192-room hotel is short on frills but easy on the pocketbook. Guests can choose from studio, one-bedroom and two-bedroom units, all of which would benefit from Queer Eye Guy makeovers. Those patrons looking to save more cash can store their eats in the convenient mini-refrigerators. The hotel provides a complimentary continental breakfast each morning with bagels, Danish pastries, coffee and orange juice.

No workout room is on-site, but Middletowners receive $10 discounted access to the Vanderbilt YMCA, a 3-block and 5-minute walk from the hotel's doorstep.

SILVER: Hotel Pennsylvania

401 Seventh Avenue at 33rd Street, New York, NY 10001
(212) 736-5000 • hotelpenn.com

At 1,700 rooms, the "Penn" is one of the largest hotels in New York City. Just steps away from the trains at Penn Station, this hotel was built by the Pennsylvania Railroad Company in 1919. Although we are not crazy about its enormous size and bare-bones rooms, we cannot argue with its bottom-dollar prices and next-door location to Bally Total Fitness on 32nd Street. Avoid Penn's barren workout room and dilapidated equipment. Instead, purchase a $12 pass from Penn's front desk and shuffle 15 paces out the front door to Bally.

BEYOND HOTELS MIDTOWN

Bally Total Fitness Biltmore

Bank of America Plaza, 43rd & Madison
335 Madison Avenue, New York, NY
(212) 983-5320 • ballyfitness.com

Like the yellow cabs on the street, Bally clubs are scattered throughout Manhattan. Most are fairly unappealing and not worth the price of admission but, luckily, a few break this mold. This smaller, executive-size club caters primarily to the Midtown business crowd and offers an assortment of high quality machines in an intimate environment. Although the club's walls are painted in Bally's ugly trademark colors of black and red, the cardio and weight areas do not feel as confined as some New York City gyms.

While water in the 2-lane lap pool appeared a little green, we are confident this coloring effect is due to the pool's mint-green painted walls and bottom rather than spoiled agua. The 25-yard option should service most swimmers quite well, but be aware that the pool closes a bit earlier than the rest of the club. Call to verify specific hours.

CARDIO

TREADMILLS: **LF • Precor • StarTrac**
UPRIGHT BIKE: **LF**
RECUMBENT BIKE: **LF**
ELLIPTICAL: **LF • Precor**
STEPPER: **LF • StairMaster**
ROWING: **Concept II**

STRENGTH

FREE WEIGHTS: **Yes**
HAMMER: **Yes**
MACHINES: **LF • Icarian • Magnum**
DUMBBELLS: **2-50 lbs**

SWIM

GRADE: **C**
SPECS: **2x25yd • Indoor • 82°**
TOYS: **Kick • Pull**

OTHER

CLASSES: **Yes**
HOURS: M-F **6a-10p** • SAT-SUN **9a-6p**
COST: **$10 Hyatt • $25 Others**
TV: **Yes**
EXTRAS: **Juice Bar**

At a discounted $10 fee, the 43rd Street locale is a good value for Grand Hyatt guests. The $25/day tariff for all others is excessive for this or any Bally club in Manhattan. But other choices, especially for lap swimmers, are few and far between.

Bally Total Fitness Penta

139 West 32nd Street, New York, NY
(212) 465-1750 • ballyfitness.com

As one of the larger New York City Bally clubs, the 32nd Street location offers a convenient workout option for those out-of-towners staying at the Avalon or Hotel Pennsylvania. The club's appeal is enhanced by the discounted $10 access fee enjoyed by guests of these two properties, particularly since the customary daily rate for others is an exorbitant $25. Nevertheless, keep your expectations in check. All of the latest cardio and weight equipment is stocked

CARDIO

TREADMILLS: **LF • StarTrac**
UPRIGHT BIKE: **LF**
RECUMBENT BIKE: **LF**
ELLIPTICAL: **LF • Precor**
STEPPER: **StarTrac • Stepmill**

STRENGTH

FREE WEIGHTS: **Yes**
HAMMER: **Yes**
MACHINES: **LF • Icarian • Magnum**
DUMBBELLS: **2-85 lbs**

SWIM

GRADE: **C-**
SPECS: **3x25yd • Indoor • 82°**
TOYS: **Kick • Pull**

OTHER

CLASSES: **Yes**
HOURS: M-F **5:30a-10p** • SAT-SUN **9a-6p**
COST: **$10 Avalon & Penn • $25 Others**
TV: **Yes**

inside, but the drab red and black gym has low ceilings and little space between machines. In typical New York fashion, the place can get crowded, so be prepared to "work-in" with others and share lanes while swimming.

The dark and dreary lap pool offers 3 lanes divided by floating lines and bottom stripes, but during rush hours swimmers may be limited to 30 minutes of splash time. We do not know how strictly this time limit is enforced, but your best bet is to avoid the busy times altogether. Call the club to find out the best hours to head over.

Vanderbilt YMCA

224 East 47th Street, New York, NY 10017
(212) 756-9600 • ymcanyc.org/vanderbilt

CARDIO

TREADMILLS: **LF**
UPRIGHT BIKE: **LF**
RECUMBENT BIKE: **LF**
ELLIPTICAL: **LF • Precor**
STEPPER: **StairMaster**
ROWING: **Concept II**
OTHER: **Crossrobic**

STRENGTH

FREE WEIGHTS: **Yes**
MACHINES: **Cybex • Icarian**
DUMBBELLS: **5-110 lbs**

SWIM

GRADE: **C+**
SPECS: **6x25yd • Indoor • 80-83°**
TOYS: **Kick • Pull • Clock**
MASTERS: **Yes**

OTHER

CLASSES: **Yes**
HOURS: M-F **4:30a-12a** • SAT **7a-7p** • SUN **7a-9p**
COST: **$25**
TV: **Yes**
EXTRAS: **1/27 mile indoor track**

After seeing the number of people coming through this fitness center's turnstiles, we thought the Vanderbilt YMCA should be renamed the "Grand Central Station Y." During peak hours (before work, during lunch, immediately after work), cardio machine time limits, "working-in" on weights, and sharing swim lanes are standard practices. During non-rush hours, things calm down a bit, but the term "empty" could never describe this notable facility.

We recommend this Y to those staying at the Helmsley for its close proximity and fantastic equipment. New cardio and weight machines captivate exercisers, while an above-average lap pool entertains swimmers. As long as you are a "people person," you should have a happy workout experience here.

Note: All Manhattan YMCAs were offering a free one-week trial pass online at the time of printing. Check their website for details.

UNION SQUARE/CHELSEA

Though hotels in this predominantly residential zone are few and far between, Union Square and its neighboring Chelsea and East Village neighborhoods are some of our favorite bites of the Big Apple. Hip New Yorkers donning different shades of black (yes, there are varying shades!) flood these sidewalks instead of wide-eyed, picture-taking tourists.

Independent boutiques and street retailers are more prevalent than premium 5th Avenue mega-stores. And 4 days a week, 6 months a year, Union Square itself is transformed into an urban farmers' market, where local sellers offer produce, baked goods, flowers and clothing at bare bones prices. Get there early — because in today's fast-paced, get-it-now culture, veggie eaters reserve their orders in advance, and the good stuff sells out in a New York minute.

What keeps us coming back to this part of New York is the neighborhood's friendly vibe and colorful people.

EXPENSIVE

GOLD: **W Hotel Union Square**
201 Park Avenue South, New York, NY 10003
(212) 253-9119 • starwood.com/whotels

Our only Union Square hotel recommendation, this W combines its trademark stylish flair with a stellar location, offering guests a worthy stay, play and exercise option. Across the street from Union Square's hustle and bustle and within 3 blocks of trendy Chelsea and the East Village, W guests can experience Manhattan — local style.

Though nicely appointed and thoroughly hip, W guest quarters are small, even by New York standards. But this is the Big Apple! How much time are you really going to spend in your room?

CARDIO
TREADMILLS: **3 Cybex**
UPRIGHT BIKE: **1 Cybex**
RECUMBENT BIKE: **2 Cybex**
ELLIPTICAL: **4 Precor**

STRENGTH
DUMBBELLS: **5-50 lbs**

OTHER
HOURS: **24**
COST: **Free**
TV: **Yes**

Do not squander your New York minutes in W's "Sweat" room either, especially given our nearby fitness find. This hotel's basement fitness center does possess a few decent machines and is useful for a jiffy aerobic session, but a 10-minute walk away you'll find the McBurney YMCA — the best Y in Manhattan and one of the nicest in the country. Ten bucks will get you in the door, and we highly recommend the donation. The W concierge may steer you toward the closer New York Health and Racquet Club, but this Y is better and $20/day cheaper.

Note: For unrivaled people watching and a unique atmosphere, sip your evening cocktail at Underbar, W's swank lounge.

BEYOND HOTELS UNION SQUARE/CHELSEA

McBurney YMCA

125 West 14th Street, New York, NY 10011
(212) 741-9210 • ymcanyc.org/mcburney

CARDIO

TREADMILLS: **Precor**
UPRIGHT BIKE: **Precor**
RECUMBENT BIKE: **Precor**
ELLIPTICAL: **Precor**
STEPPER: **StairMaster • Stepmill**
ROWING: **Concept II**
OTHER: **Crossrobic**

STRENGTH

FREE WEIGHTS: **Yes**
MACHINES: **Magnum**
DUMBBELLS: **5-120 lbs**

SWIM

GRADE: **B+**
SPECS: **7x25yd • Indoor • 81-83°**
TOYS: **Kick • Pull • Clock**
MASTERS: **Yes**

OTHER

CLASSES: **Yes**
HOURS: M-F **5:30a-11p** • SAT-SUN **8a-8p**
COST: **$10**
TV: **No**
EXTRAS: **1/10 mile indoor track • Basketball**

By far the nicest YMCA in New York City, McBurney could be one of the best Ys in the country. This Y has been in its home for just over a year, which means new stuff for the traveling athlete. No chipped paint, rusty dumbbells, awkwardly low ceilings or strange musty smells at this state-of-the-art health club. In fact, several of our City-dwelling friends are members and rave about the cutting-edge equipment, bright atmosphere and low-key crowd.

Topping it off, McBurney also houses one of the best lap pools on the Island — which means getting an empty lane is about as likely as finding an available taxi after a Broadway show. Our local amigos advise any weekday after 8 p.m. as your best bet to avoid lane mates.

Admission for $10 is a bargain, considering the prize exercisers receive and the ridiculous rates charged by other New York facilities (e.g., $50/day at Chelsea Piers). However, fitness buffs may be able to sidestep the guest fee altogether by logging on to McBurney's website and printing the complimentary 1-week pass (available at the time of our book's printing). A freebie in New York City? Now that's a deal!

LOWER MANHATTAN

Staying on the south end (lower) of Manhattan Island is best for those who want to be as close as possible to their business in Wall Street's high-rises. Leisure travelers are better off in more tourist-friendly Manhattan neighborhoods. However, a taxi or subway ride will provide easy access to Lower Manhattan's sights, such as the Statue of Liberty and Ground Zero. This is an area of New York where the hip vibe gives way to the business suit. Weekdays bring sidewalks teeming with workers, but on weekends the suits are gone and the scene is rather dull.

EXPENSIVE

GOLD: Embassy Suites

102 North End Avenue, New York, NY 10282
(212) 945-0100 • embassysuites.com
(212) 945-3535 Gym

CARDIO

TREADMILLS: **LF • StarTrac**
UPRIGHT BIKE: **LF**
RECUMBENT BIKE: **LF**
ELLIPTICAL: **LF • Precor**
STEPPER: **StairMaster**
ROWING: **Yes**

STRENGTH

FREE WEIGHTS: **Yes**
HAMMER: **Yes**
MACHINES: **Cybex • Free Motion**
DUMBBELLS: **5-110 lbs**

OTHER

CLASSES: **Yes**
HOURS: M-TH **5:30a-10p** • F **5:30a-9p** • SAT-SUN **8a-6p**
COST: **Free Embassy • $25 Others**
TV: **Yes**

On the banks of the Hudson River and within 2 blocks of Ground Zero, the flagship Embassy presents a fantastically modern 463 suite high-rise hotel. Opened in 2000, this accommodation far exceeds all other Lower Manhattan options for the athletic-minded traveler.

Inside, Embassy's standard two-room suites are appointed with contemporary furnishings, microwaves, refrigerators and large windows that open.

Our favorite Embassy hotel feature is its complimentary cooked-to-order breakfast. After a calorie burn session, fitness addicts can devour waffles, French toast, omelets and breakfast meats without worrying about who is picking up the tab. And if you find it raining on your vacation parade, Embassy's pipeline of indoor pursuits comes to the rescue. Six restaurants, a 16-screen cinema and a top-notch health club are all under its roof.

Of course, from our perspective, the most magnetic attraction is the sparkling New York Sports Club connected via the 5th floor walkway. Hotel patrons receive free access to this grade "A" facility and will eat up the industry-leading equipment. It is a full-size club with too many machines to count, so rest assured that it will fully minister to your workout sermon.

Swimmers, no good lap-pool options exist in this slice of the Big Apple. Plan on cross-training or taking the subway uptown to the McBurney YMCA in Chelsea.

LEAST EXPENSIVE

GOLD: Manhattan Seaport Suites

129 Front Street, New York, NY 10005
(212) 742-0003 • manhattanseaport.citysearch.com

No danger of finding Embassy-like amenities here! But for those trying to do downtown Manhattan on a budget, your ship will come in at Seaport Suites.

One block from Wall Street, this low-priced hotel has only 56 rooms, so fish one out as early as possible. Several floor plans are available, including deluxe rooms with mini-refrigerators, studios with kitchenettes and one-bedrooms with full kitchens. Guest accommodations have cathedral ceilings and marble baths, and patrons are treated to complimentary continental breakfasts.

With no exercise room under its roof, Seaport has intelligently negotiated a discounted $10/day rate at the New York Sports Club on Water Street, a 3-minute walk away.

BEYOND HOTELS LOWER MANHATTAN

New York Sports Club (NYSC)

160 Water Street, New York, NY 10038
(212) 363-4600 • mysportsclubs.com

CARDIO

TREADMILLS: **LF • StarTrac**
UPRIGHT BIKE: **LF • Cycle Plus**
RECUMBENT BIKE: **LF**
ELLIPTICAL: **LF • Precor**
STEPPER: **StairMaster • Stepmill**
ROWING: **Concept II**

STRENGTH

FREE WEIGHTS: **Yes**
HAMMER: **Yes**
MACHINES: **Cybex • Nautilus • Hammer**
DUMBBELLS: **3-120 lbs**

OTHER

CLASSES: **Yes**
HOURS: M-TH **5:30a-10p** • F **5:30a–9p** • SAT **8a-1p** • SUN **Closed**
COST: **$10 Seaport • $25 Others**
TV: **Yes**

Smaller than its sister club in the Embassy Suites, the NYSC Water Street offers the same desirable high-end equipment and bright environment for its exercisers.

Seaport Suites' discounted $10 pass is a reasonable fare for your workout ride, and the 3-minute walk over should not discourage you either. Of all the clubs we viewed in Manhattan, this one appeared the least crowded.

There is no pool inside for swimmers, so we recommend cross training or taking the subway up to the McBurney YMCA.

NOTE: While touring this part of the City, we happened upon a great dining option: Café World (Deli, Sandwiches, Mexican & Tex-Mex, Sushi), 50 Trinity Place, New York, NY 10006, (212) 269-4355.

RUNNING ROUTES

CENTRAL PARK WEST/MIDTOWN

Central Park

Central Park is clearly the "it" place to run and recreate in this hulking city. The outer loop is a friendly 6 miler with some nice inclines. If you fancy less footwork, wind your way inward and create your own loop. Most hotels will have maps handy, but if not, no worry, the park is easy to navigate.

The four main city streets bordering the park are: Central Park West, Central Park South, Fifth Avenue and Cathedral Parkway. The 72nd Street entrance is likely to be your starting point.

Even if the need for exercise escapes your mind, head to Central Park just to see this 843-acre green zone surrounded by New York City's skyscrapers. Consider a horse-drawn carriage as your touring mode. Year round visitors can find willing guides lined up, ready for action on Central Park South (59th Street, between Fifth and Sixth Avenues). While the $55 cost for a park tour (45-50 minutes) may be somewhat steep, you can always give haggling a shot.

Keep in mind that Central Park is a frequent host to movies and TV shows. For some reason, visitors are often keen to find Balto, the sled dog. An animated 1995 movie featured the statue, which is located northwest of the Children's Zoo, where 66th would cross if it went through the park.

Riverside Park

Riverside Park — about a half-mile west of Central Park — is also off 72nd (and goes to 116th). It provides another run venue along the Hudson River, about 4 miles one way. The park stretches from 72nd to 158th streets and is frequented by local dog owners (great dog run), joggers and skateboarders (there is a skate park here, too). History buffs may want to check out Grant's Tomb to finally put to rest the frequently asked question, "Who is buried in Grant's Tomb?"

CHELSEA

In Chelsea, runners trade cool running for an even cooler neighborhood. Luckily, the Y is a very good workout spot. So take to the treadmill or get up at the crack of dawn and take your chances on the streets.

Chelsea Piers

If you're willing to try running on the streets of New York, head east toward Chelsea Piers and run along the Hudson. Several of the Chelsea Piers are now home to wonderfully landscaped parts (e.g., Christoper Street) that will help distract you during a run.

LOWER MANHATTAN

Battery Park

Battery Park is your best bet in Lower Manhattan. Follow it north along the Hudson River. The 21-acre park affords decent views of Lady Liberty and is a popular tourist destination — primarily because of its proximity to the Ellis Island and Statue of Liberty ferry. Continuing our history lesson, the reddish, circular edifice is Castle Clinton, designed in 1807 as a defense fortress. It also served as the New York immigration center before Ellis Island. Today, it operates as a museum.

OAKLAND, CALIFORNIA

While this Cinderella town may dwell in the cultural shadow of its glamorous half-sister San Francisco, Oakland can lay claim to surviving perhaps the most contentious sports owner ever — and it's not Al Davis. As the controversial owner of the NFL's Oakland Raiders, Al Davis has cultivated a tough, shrewd and sometimes ornery reputation for himself and his team — envied by some and criticized by many. Yet the dubious honor of "most contentious" goes to Charlie O. Finley, owner of the Oakland A's from 1960-1981. Described by many as a "cantankerous buffoon," his ideas and behavior ranged from asinine to zany.

One of Finley's favorite stunts was parading his mule "Charlie O" all about town and into reporter-filled press rooms just after feeding time. (You can guess what happened next.) Courting the media, he invented catchy nicknames for his players, and then concocted elaborate faux boyhood stories to explain how they came to be (e.g., Jim "Catfish" Hunter). One year, Finley offered to pay each player a $300 bonus to grow a moustache before the team picture was taken. Since $300 was equal to a week's salary for some, all but one obliged.

An oddball innovator, Finley campaigned for orange baseballs, 3-ball walks, ball girls and mechanical rabbits to transport baseballs to the home plate umpire between innings. Rather entertaining was his 5th inning delivery of home made cookies to the umpires, baked by none other than A's employee Debbie Fields — recognize the name?

Finley's personality also had a vindictive side. He fired his 2nd baseman immediately after a World Series game for making 2 errors. He threatened to send Hall of Famer Reggie Jackson to the minors after a 47 home run season. He publicly berated any player in a slump and was known to keep his best players out of the line-up to "teach them a lesson."

Former player Sal Bando summed it up best when asked if it were difficult to leave the A's and Finley. Bando responded, "Was it hard to leave the Titanic?"

To prevent you from making any Finley-esque workout decisions, we have covered Oakland's fitness bases.

15 Locations Reviewed

EXPENSIVE

GOLD: **Marriott** City Center

1001 Broadway, Oakland, CA 94607
(510) 451-4000 • marriott.com

CARDIO

TREADMILLS: **4 StarTrac**
UPRIGHT BIKE: **1 StarTrac**
RECUMBENT BIKE: **1 StarTrac • 1 LF**
ELLIPTICAL: **1 StarTrac**
STEPPER: **1 Tectrix**

STRENGTH

MACHINES: **1 Hoist Multi**
DUMBBELLS: **3-50 lbs**

SWIM

SPECS: **Outdoor • Not lap**

OTHER

HOURS: **24**
COST: **Free**
TV: **Yes**
EXTRAS: **$10 pass Club One**

Marriott, located in the heart of Downtown and connected to the City's convention center, is Oakland's largest hotel. Since this 21-story property is fairly new, its 484 rooms are modern, clean, and typical of Marriott's conservative décor. In addition, the 12th Street rapid transit station across the street makes commuting to the East Bay or San Francisco cheap and easy.

The 24-hour exercise room is Oakland's best *hotel* gym. While it provides plenty of new workout machines in a hospitable 2nd floor environment, we strongly recommend walking 5 minutes to perhaps the best health club in the Bay Area — Club One. It will cost $10 (with the hotel discount), but what you will receive is well worth the Alexander Hamilton.

Although Marriott insists it has a lap pool, this short, outdoor square without lane lines misses the mark. Swimmers, go to Club One. You will not be disappointed.

MODERATELY EXPENSIVE

GOLD: **Courtyard** Downtown

988 Broadway, Oakland, CA 94607
(510) 625-8282 • courtyard.com

CARDIO

TREADMILLS: **2 StarTrac**
UPRIGHT BIKE: **1 StarTrac**
STEPPER: **2 StarTrac**

OTHER

HOURS: **6a-11p**
• Will open after hours
COST: **Free**
TV: **Yes**
EXTRAS: **$10 pass to Club One**

A less expensive alternative to the Marriott, this 2-year old hotel will likely save you $40/night. Also located in the City's hub, Courtyard is convenient to Downtown's businesses and attractions. Additionally, the nearby 12th Street rapid transit station will transport you anywhere in the East Bay as well as to San Francisco.

Courtyard bills itself as the business travelers' hotel, but nothing special is offered, unless a desk with an ergonomic chair (think Aeron) and 24-hour complimentary coffee in the lobby qualify. Don't get us wrong, the hotel is reliable, and we often accept the franchise's invite. We just do not understand what the "business" hoopla is all about.

Courtyard's fitness room consists of 5 barely-used machines squeezed into a small, ground floor area near the lobby. Fortunately, guests receive discounted access to the spectacular Club One. Venture out of your "Courtyard" — it's worth the $10 and 5-minute walk.

BEYOND HOTELS

Club One City Center

1200 Clay, Oakland, CA 94612
(510) 895-1010 • clubone.com

This 64,000 square foot facility has been rated by local sources as the Bay Area's "Best Health Club." Although not quite reaching the fitness facility summit of San Francisco's Sports Club/LA, we wholeheartedly endorse this club and echo its praise.

Located in the midst of downtown Oakland's city center retail district, the Club's atmosphere is light, bright and playful. Sun shines through large windows as exercisers sweat on phenomenal new machines while surfing channels on the attached individual plasma screens. Basketball players run on an indoor NBA-size court, and muscle buffs pump up on ample cutting-edge weight equipment.

The pool is outside, but swimmers are not left out in the cold. They can "lap it up" in Club One's 25-yard pool. With 3 lanes divided by floating lines and bottom stripes, the swim box is near competition grade. Kickboards and pull-buoys are provided, so no need to bring your own.

In Club One's lobby, the Surf City Café offers healthy lunch fare and smoothies to cure any post-workout munchies.

CARDIO

TREADMILLS: **StarTrac • Quinton**
UPRIGHT BIKE: **StarTrac**
RECUMBENT BIKE: **StarTrac**
ELLIPTICAL: **Precor**
STEPPER: **StairMaster**
ROWING: **Concept II**
OTHER: **NordicTrack**

STRENGTH

FREE WEIGHTS: **Yes**
HAMMER: **Yes**
MACHINES: **LF • Cybex**
DUMBBELLS: **3–120 lbs**

SWIM

GRADE: **B**
SPECS: **3x25yd • Outdoor • 79–82°**
TOYS: **Kick • Pull • Clock**

OTHER

CLASSES: **Yes**
HOURS: M-F **5a-10p** • SAT **7a-6p** • SUN **8a-6p**
COST: **$10 Marriott & Courtyard • $20 Others**
TV: **Yes**
EXTRAS: **1/16 mile indoor track • Basketball • Racquetball • Cafe**

RUNNING ROUTES

Merritt Lake

Located between Broadway and Lakeshore, Merritt Lake is about a 10-minute jog from Downtown. The 155-acre retreat boasts a nice 3-mile paved perimeter loop that introduces striders to its scenic saltwater lake and the Bay's breezes. We recommend this as a daytime route only. After dark, its clientele is a bit "iffy."

Alameda

Only a 5-10 minute highway drive from downtown Oakland, the Bay area's island city of Alameda offers a scenic beach run or paved path jog. Grassy fields, playgrounds and a bird sanctuary provide distractions along the route and the infamous breezes can play havoc with your easy run.

Take the Webster Tube, a tunnel that goes beneath the Oakland Inner Harbor Channel, and follow signs to Alameda Beach. Parking is plentiful near Washington Park. Remember to confirm directions with your hotel's front desk.

Omaha

17 Locations Reviewed

OMAHA, NEBRASKA

With a per capita income almost double the national average, Omaha quietly prospers as a middle-American city where family values run as high as portfolio values. Successful hometown companies like Berkshire Hathaway, ConAgra and Peter Kiewit Sons have spawned a litter of millionaire (and even a few billionaire) residents with money to burn, invest or donate. Most in this understated neck of the woods would rather help than hoard, so hosts of charities, cultural and humanitarian organizations and, of course, the University of Nebraska football program share in this good fortune.

With no professional sports franchise calling Nebraska home, the Cornhusker football team garners a cult-like following that cherishes game day services and professes that their program reigns supreme. Big Red fans proudly eulogize their Huskers' record 38 NCAA consecutive winning seasons, 32 consecutive bowl game appearances and 31 straight seasons with 9 or more victories. Diehards also preach the grandeur of the athletic department's weight room, which is the largest in the country, covering an astonishing 3/4 acre. True to their values, these Midwesterners are proudest that their team has more Academic All-Americans than any other Division I school.

To their credit, Husker hysteria is not a fair-weather fad. On home game days, Memorial Stadium becomes the 3rd largest populated area in the State (behind the cities of Omaha and Lincoln). Additionally, this NFL-quality arena holds the record for the most consecutively sold-out football games — 220 since 1962.

So, if you're trying to score a few extra points with the locals, give up the safety brown-nosing. Instead, strike up a conversation salted with your newly-acquired Husker football knowledge — it might just seal your deal.

MODERATELY EXPENSIVE

GOLD: Courtyard

101 South 10th Street, Omaha, NE 68102
(402) 346-2200 • courtyard.com

Within 2 blocks of the newly constructed Qwest Center concert venue and a short walk from Omaha's Old Market dining and shopping district, Courtyard puts guests in the middle of Downtown's entertainment attractions. Constructed inside a restored historic building, Courtyard's 181 rooms cater to the business traveler by providing complimentary high-speed internet access, an ergonomic office chair and an in-room coffee maker. Free parking is an added perk.

Though the workout room is nothing to write home about, it is the second best *hotel* gym in the area (Harrah's being first). If you are pressed for time and need a "quickie," this scantily clad room will suffice. The upright bike and one of the treadmills (StarTrac) are your best cardio bets, and the multi-gym will shoulder a minimal strength routine. The only other machine is a StarTrac stepper.

Those with more time and more in mind for their workout can take Courtyard's complimentary shuttle to the nearby Pinnacle Club. More than a mile away, it is a little far to walk. Access typically costs $8, but you may be able to get in for free.

Note: Before booking, check out our Harrah's review.

SILVER: Sheraton

1615 Howard Street, Omaha, NE 68102
(402) 342-2222 • sheraton.com

CARDIO

TREADMILLS: **1 True**
UPRIGHT BIKE: **1 LF - old**
STEPPER: **1 Schwinn - old**

STRENGTH

MACHINES: **1 Multi**
DUMBBELLS: **10-50 lbs**

OTHER

HOURS: **24**
COST: **Free**
TV: **Yes**

Not quite in the luxury category, Sheraton comes closer than any other downtown Omaha hotel. Situated about a half mile from the Old Market entertainment and dining district, Sheraton is near Omaha's theater and museums.

The motif appears "stately," with mahogany furnishings and conservative tones throughout the 145 rooms. Normally, we like to refer you to the property's website for a sneak preview of the accommodations, but Sheraton only showcases its premium, 2-story suites — hardly a realistic benchmark for a standard room here.

While we cannot complain about the size of Sheraton's workout room, we can and will grumble that it is mostly empty. The multi-gym and dumbbells will suffice for a lazy man's strength session, but the 3 decrepit cardio machines will only serve a corpse. Exercisers in search of any legitimate fitness equipment or lap pool should walk a half-mile to the Pinnacle Club or get a lift in the hotel's free shuttle.

Note: Read our description of Harrah's before booking here.

BRONZE: Embassy Suites

555 South 10th Street, Omaha, NE 68102
(402)346-9000 • embassysuites.com

As part of Omaha's Old Market shopping, dining and entertainment district, Embassy Suites is an appealing lodging option in a convenient location.

The hotel's 249 guest rooms offer typical Embassy features: separate living and sleeping areas, refrigerators and microwaves. In the lobby, guests can enjoy a java fix at the Starbucks Internet Cafe in addition to complimentary cooked-to-order breakfasts served each morning.

Embassy's workout room is spatially challenged by the 6 machines squeezed inside. The 2 StarTrac treadmills are the center's highlight, with the other equipment in barely working condition — some missing parts (e.g., bike pedal straps). Athletic ones will want to either drive 5 minutes to the privately owned Pinnacle Club or hop on the hotel's free shuttle for round-trip transportation. With limited parking at Pinnacle, the shuttle may be the way to go.

Finally, before booking your reservation here, check out our Harrah's review. Although an extra mile or two of driving is required, Harrah's cheaper room rates, better in-house workout room, fantastic buffet spread and gambling option make it a winner.

LEAST EXPENSIVE

GOLD: Harrah's

One Harrah's Boulevard, Council Bluffs, IA 51501
(712) 329-6000 • www.harrahs.com/our_casinos/cou

Do not let the fact that it's in a different state fool you — Council Bluffs, Iowa is just across the Missouri River from downtown Omaha. Embassy Suites and other Omaha hotels are merely 200 yards away "as the crow flies." We believe Harrah's is the best lodging option in Omaha for several reasons. First, the room rates are below $100/night, making them some of the least expensive in the area. Second, despite their budget price, Harrah's guest quarters are stylishly colored and attractively furnished. Third, the crowd at Harrah's 240-room casino is a bit grayer than your typi-

CARDIO
TREADMILLS: **2 Precor • 1 True**
UPRIGHT BIKE: **1 LF**
RECUMBENT BIKE: **1 LF**
STEPPER: **1 LF • 1 Tectrix - old**

STRENGTH
MACHINES: **1 Hoist Multi**
DUMBBELLS: **5-45 lbs**

OTHER
HOURS: **24**
COST: **Free**
TV: **Yes**

cal Vegas or Atlantic City rowdies, so hallways are usually quiet overnight.

Fourth, the hotel's 24-hour workout room is the best *hotel* gym in the area, boasting cutting-edge treadmills and bikes as well as adequate strength equipment.

Those desiring a more elaborate fitness session can still drive to the Pinnacle Club across the Missouri. Finally, what really elevated our heart rates was the hotel's gambling option and unbelievable "All You Can Eat" buffet.

We admit to being picky at chowtime and the red flag goes straight up when we hear the term "buffet." Harrah's blew us away with healthy offerings from its aptly-named "Fresh Market Square Buffet." In the midst of Omaha Steak country, we plunked freshly-cut turkey breast, lean pork, steamed broccoli and baked potatoes onto our plates, then splurged on Bananas Foster. Brisket, peel-n-eat shrimp, chicken noodle soup and made-to-order pasta are other yummy eats available. Iceberg lettuce was the only food item on the massive buffet that turned up our noses. And we cannot complain about the prices either, ranging from $7.99 to $14.99 – all three meals served.

BEYOND HOTELS

Pinnacle Club

2027 Dodge Street, Omaha, NE 68102
(402) 342-2582

CARDIO

TREADMILLS: **Cybex**
UPRIGHT BIKE: **LF**
RECUMBENT BIKE: **LF**
ELLIPTICAL: **Cybex • Precor**
STEPPER: **StairMaster**

STRENGTH

FREE WEIGHTS: **Yes**
HAMMER: **Yes**
MACHINES: **Cybex**
DUMBBELLS: **3-100 lbs**

SWIM

GRADE: **B**
SPECS: **3x25yd • Indoor • 81°**
TOYS: **Kick • Clock**

OTHER

CLASSES: **Yes**
HOURS: M-TH **6a-10p** • F **6a-9p** • SAT **8a-7p** • SUN **10a-6p**
COST: **$8 • $30/5 days**
TV: **Yes**
EXTRAS: **1/22 mile indoor track**

Pinnacle is the best private health club in downtown Omaha. Unfortunately, no hotel is within convenient walking distance (Sheraton is closest), so car, hotel shuttle or a short jog is your best transportation bet. If you drive, bring along some quarters to feed a street meter, because the parking lot can fill up fast.

Once inside this rather nondescript, yet cheerful, full-service facility, you will find friendly staff eager to improve your workout experience. While the spacing of machines in some areas is a bit cozy, we were pleased with the wide assortment of high-end equipment. New treadmills, bikes, ellipticals and step machines fill the cardio areas. Plenty of free weights, dumbbells and 18 stack-loaded Cybex machines wait for muscle buffs.

Swimmers should get excited by Pinnacle's 25-yard lap pool. The 3 lanes are separated by floating lines and bottom stripes, and its temperature is good. We noticed several kickboards on deck but did not see pull-buoys or fins.

Saturdays from 8 a.m. to noon kids are allowed in for family day, so serious athletes should plan accordingly.

Note: Although the entrance fee is $8, we found a website that offers a printable coupon for a free, two-week trial membership (omahacoupons.com).

RUNNING ROUTES

Elmwood Park

Omaha is working on its trail system, and over the next several years it will sport miles of paved running paths that will conveniently connect in all parts of this city.

As it stands now, while there is a host of trails, not one is especially convenient to Downtown or Council Bluffs (Harrah's). The 12-mile Keystone Trail is the most popular, but the nearest connector is Elmwood Park, 4–5 miles from downtown hotels. Getting to this park, which offers a 2-mile loop run, requires a less-than-scenic pavement pound west on Leavenworth to 60th. The trail begins at Pacific Street and 67th.

Heartland of America Park

Our suggestion for downtowners is to trot over to nearby Heartland of America Park, within 1 mile of all hotels (8th and Douglas). The 15-acre park hooks into the Back-to-the-River Trail, which currently runs south along the Missouri River for approximately 3 miles. Once the expansion project is complete, this trail will afford Huskers and visitors 15 to 20 miles of running distance.

Field Club Trail

Another option off of Leavenworth at 38th is the Field Club Trail, which is a 1.5 mile shorty along an abandoned railroad. At about 1.5 miles from the hotels, the upside is its closer proximity and traffic escape once you arrive.

Western Historic Trails

Looking to burn buffet calories? Harrah's guests' most convenient option is the 5+ mile trail that originates at the Western Historic Trails Center.

This riverfront trail was completed in 2003 and runs right past the Casino. The actual trail center is 3.25 miles from the hotel. Farther away (6 miles) is an access point to the 63-mile limestone Wabash Trace Nature Trail at Lewis Central Middle School (2000 Hwy

275). While only convenient for those willing to drive for their run, this trail cuts a scenic southwesterly path through Iowa's countryside. It's a very well maintained trail and especially popular with mountain bikers.

Orlando

ORLANDO, FLORIDA

So the kids finally talked you into visiting Mickey, Donald, Minnie and Pluto, huh? Well, perk up those mouse ears, because this trip does not have to be all about the rug rats. Choose one of our recommended hotels and guarantee your own "moment" each day before or after the little ones enjoy hundreds of their own.

Accommodations on Walt Disney World Resort's property are likely the most fun — and the most expensive. But we also found appealing alternatives in the Sea World/Convention Center area. And, never forgetting our business traveler, we covered Downtown, too.

Enjoy the sun, have a magical trip and, if you don't bring any kids along, we promise not to tell!

DISNEY WORLD RESORT

Opened in 1971, Walt Disney World Resort has blossomed into 47 square miles of fun and fantasy. The property features four theme parks (Magic Kingdom, Epcot, Disney-MGM Studios and Animal Kingdom), two water parks (Blizzard Beach and Typhoon Lagoon) and 30 resort hotels.

As a site for athletic dreams as well, Disney hosts a marathon in January, a Half-Ironman triathlon in May and spring training baseball in March for the Atlanta Braves.

57 Locations Reviewed

EXPENSIVE

GOLD: Grand Floridian

4401 Grand Floridian Way, Orlando, FL 32830
(407) 824-3000 • disneyworld.com

CARDIO

TREADMILLS: **4 LF - 2 old**
UPRIGHT BIKE: **1 Precor**
RECUMBENT BIKE: **4 Precor**
ELLIPTICAL: **3 Precor**
STEPPER: **4 StairMaster**

STRENGTH

FREE WEIGHTS: **Yes**
MACHINES: **11 Cybex**
DUMBBELLS: **5-50 lbs**

SWIM

SPECS: **Outdoor • Not lap**

OTHER

HOURS: **6a-9p**
COST: **Free**
TV: **Yes**

Closest to the Magic Kingdom, this Disney accommodation is one monorail stop away from Mickey Mouse's home turf. The Grand Floridian takes guests back to the 19th Century, with Victorian-styled rooms, old-fashioned furnishings and staff dressed in knickers and knee-high stockings.

The 867-room property's common areas are Southern plantation in style, and its restaurants follow themes of yesteryear.

Grand Floridian's spa and fitness facility is an exercise wonderland. The full-service center supplies popular cardio machines and a broad selection of strength apparatus in a space about the size of two hotel rooms. Except for a couple of treadmills, all equipment is top drawer, and we especially enjoyed finding 4600 series StairMasters and Precor ellipticals. Strength buffs will have a magical workout as well. Plenty of free weights are on deck for bench pressing, an ample range of dumbbells indulge isolation exercises and a full mix of stack-loaded weight stations will round out your overall muscle conditioning.

Swimmers will not be spellbound by Grand Floridian's pool. Though nearly 50 meters in length, its rubber ducky shape is hardly conducive to straight swimming. Plus, the absence of bottom stripes and lane lines make an already difficult lap swim even more trying. Our suggestion? Drive and park in either the Swan or Dolphin's free lots and walk to their legitimate lapper. (Nobody appeared to be checking IDs or room keys, but you didn't hear that from us.)

Note: Grand may be our #1 hotel in this price category, but we recommend either the Swan or Dolphin as better athletic-minded alternatives overall.

MODERATELY EXPENSIVE

GOLD: Swan and Dolphin Resorts

1500 Epcot Resorts Boulevard, Orlando, Florida 32830
(407) 934-4000 • swandolphin.com/home.html

Located across a small lake from one another, these Starwood mega-hotels (over 750 rooms each) commingle their operations despite different branding (Swan is Westin and Dolphin is Sheraton).

Choose either to enjoy the best workout options Disney offers. You are in Magic Kingdom Land, so expect festive colors and creative designs in whimsical quarters.

CARDIO

TREADMILLS: **4 LF**
UPRIGHT BIKE: **2 LF**
RECUMBENT BIKE: **2 LF**
ELLIPTICAL: **3 LF**
STEPPER: **1 LF**

STRENGTH

FREE WEIGHTS: **Yes**
MACHINES: **11 LF**
DUMBBELLS: **10-85 lbs**

SWIM

GRADE: **B+**
SPECS: **3x33yd • Outdoor • 80°**

OTHER

HOURS: **6a-9p**
COST: **Free**
TV: **Yes**

The only appreciable room difference is Swan's trademark Westin Heavenly Beds. With its 250 thread count sheets, pillow top mattresses and down filled comforters, these adult cradles afford a comfy respite after a full day's mouseketeering. Otherwise, what's good for the mammal is good for the bird — both hotels offer 24-hour room service, complimentary transportation to the parks and a combined total of 17 restaurants and lounges.

The main fitness center and lap pool are on Dolphin's side of the lake — walking over from Swan will take no more than 2-3 minutes. Luckily for fitness fans, management was not goofying around when equipping this complimentary and well-stocked exercise facility. Admission is included in each hotel's $10/day "resort fee." Athletes can look forward to new, 9500 series Life Fitness cardio machines, approximately 400 pounds of free weights for benching and squatting, a good range of dumbbells and recently purchased stack-loaded weight stations. It is not a huge space, but it's organized and comfortable.

Swan's compound houses a tiny workout room but, when lobster is across the lake, why settle for catfish?

When we see a body of water, our first thought is not, "Oh, how beautiful." Rather, we wonder, "Open water swimming?" Unfortunately, no stroking is allowed in the lake separating the two hotels, despite its attractive sand beach and shallow water play area. Fellow agua amigos should not despair — 3 lanes of 33-yard outdoor bliss beckon just beyond the fitness center. Bottom stripes are not marked, but lanes are divided by high-quality floating lines. Bring your own toys to kick or pull and a watch if you plan on doing intervals (no pace clock). With Dolphin's separate kids' pool, your 3,000-yard session should afford a "moment" to yourself.

SILVER: Disney's Wilderness Lodge

901 Timberline Drive, Orlando, FL 32830
(407) 824-3200 • disneyworld.com

Unique and imaginative, the Wilderness Lodge is for those looking to "rough it" Disney style. In its wild frontier, guests camp with Chip n' Dale during the day and then get cozy in their amenity-filled hotel rooms at night. The resort's 728 rooms follow a log cabin motif sporting quilts, wildlife imagery and 19th Century furniture.

CARDIO

TREADMILLS: **3 LF**
UPRIGHT BIKE: **3 LF**
RECUMBENT BIKE: **2 LF**
ELLIPTICAL: **2 LF**
STEPPER: **2 LF • 2 StairMaster**

STRENGTH

FREE WEIGHTS: **Yes**
MACHINES: **14 Cybex**
DUMBBELLS: **3-50 lbs**

SWIM

SPECS: **Outdoor • Not lap**

OTHER

HOURS: **6a-9p**
COST: **Free**
TV: **Yes**

Fortunately for athletic-minded travelers, Davy Crockett left behind a state-of-the-art exercise center in this neck of the woods. Workout hounds will appreciate the Lodge's low mileage cardio machines and marvelous strength apparatus. You will find Life Fitness' 9500 series and StairMaster's 4600 model cardio equipment throughout, as well as plenty of free weights and stack-loaded stations.

Any lap pool sighted in the middle of a forest is a mirage, so don't expect one among this Lodge's trees. Both water options have the kids in mind, with rock formations and a 15-foot water slide. Water-logged friends should drive 5 minutes to Dolphin's lapper — park in their free lot (or the Swan's) and walk to the pool. It's probably not against the rules, since all hotels are on Disney property.

LEAST EXPENSIVE

GOLD: Coronado Springs Resort

1000 West Buena Vista Drive, Orlando, FL 32830
(407) 939-1000 • disneyworld.com

CARDIO

TREADMILLS: **5 LF - 3 old**
RECUMBENT BIKE: **1 LF**
ELLIPTICAL: **1 Precor - old**
STEPPER: **2 StairMaster • 1 LF**

STRENGTH

FREE WEIGHTS: **Yes**
MACHINES: **14 Cybex**
DUMBBELLS: **3-50 lbs**

SWIM

GRADE: **C-**
SPECS: **3x25m • Outdoor • 78-82°**

OTHER

HOURS: **6a-9p**
COST: **Free**
TV: **Yes**

A mile or two from Dolphin and Swan, Coronado Springs is Disney's Spanish, Mexican and American Southwest-themed resort. Be prepared to walk a lot — and we don't mean around the theme parks. This massive accommodation is spread over serious acreage, and ambling from guest quarters to lobby can easily take 5 minutes.

Coronado's 1,921 rooms surround the scenic but un-swimmable Lago Dorado (Lake of Gold). The tidy and colorful accommodations provide a welcome budget balance to Disney's not-so-imaginary steep prices.

Coronado's workout option is notable. Slightly larger than a typical hotel room, this gym stocks an ample supply of high-end strength and cardio equipment. Weights are definitely the highlight, with more than 800 pounds of free plates, a useful dumbbell set and a large assortment of stack-loaded stations. About half of the endurance apparatus are newer machines, including 4400 and

4600 series StairMaster Free Climbers, 2 treadmills and 1 recumbent bike. Cyclists, no upright bikes are on-site, so pedal pushing is a reclined activity only.

Adjacent to the fitness center, Coronado provides a lap pool that may work for many swimmers. We could not get accurate length information from the hotel, but our eagle eyes estimated it at about 25 meters (one wall is angled). Although no floating lines are present, 3 lanes are marked by stripes on the pool's bottom, so lapping is possible. For a more legitimate rectangle, drive 3 minutes to Dolphin.

SEA WORLD/CONVENTION CENTER

After Disney's success, a crop of overflow theme parks emerged in the area bordering its Resort. Sea World and Universal Studios have proven successful, as have other, lesser-known carnival-type attractions. Most hotels in this zone are within 5 miles of Disney property, so they are convenient lodging alternatives for vacationers.

Conventioneers should certainly consider staying in this area, too, if walking distance to the Convention Center is a priority.

EXPENSIVE

GOLD: Ritz Carlton & JW Marriott Grande Lakes

4012 & 4040 Central Florida Parkway, Orlando, FL 32837
(407) 206-1100 • grandelakes.com

Sharing a Greg Norman designed 18-hole golf course, 3 lighted tennis courts, 2 swimming pools and 11 restaurants, these two neighboring Marriott-owned luxury accommodations are the latest arrivals in Orlando's upscale hotel market. Guests staying at either will enjoy lavish quarters, a variety of recreational pursuits and tremendous service at similar nightly rates. Although Ritz's rooms typically run $20/night more than JW's, its higher thread count bedding and smaller size (584 rooms vs. 1,000) are worth the slight premium. Guests at both hotels have complimentary access to the pleasing on-site spa and health club housed in a separate building.

CARDIO

TREADMILLS: **14 StarTrac**
UPRIGHT BIKE: **2 StarTrac**
RECUMBENT BIKE: **2 StarTrac**
ELLIPTICAL: **8 Precor**
STEPPER: **2 StarTrac**

STRENGTH

FREE WEIGHTS: **Yes**
MACHINES: **17 LF**
DUMBBELLS: **3-100 lbs**

SWIM

GRADE: **C**
SPECS: **4x25m • Outdoor • 78-80°**

OTHER

HOURS: **5a-11p**
COST: **Free**
TV: **Yes**
EXTRAS: **Golf • Tennis • Spa**

The large and airy fitness space contains a multitude of cutting-edge sweat equipment. All treadmills have attached plasma screens (headphones provided), and the other cardio units are new, new, new, with Precor ellipitcals offered in force. A combination aerobic and strength routine is no problem here, as a ton of weights in varying forms is supplied.

Lap swimmers should pack their Speedos. Ritz/JW boast two pools, and one is a lapper located adjacent to the spa, between the hotels. Although the 4 lanes are divided by bottom stripes, floating lane lines do not stretch across the pool's 25-meter length. And no toys or pace clock are provided. Still, this aesthetically pleasing outdoor lap pool is a worthy option in Grand Lakes land. Speaking of which, your freestyling should be serene, because the kids will undoubtedly flock to the "fun" pool — also between both hotels.

Note: For a fantastic swim in a more traditional pool, drive 10 minutes to the YMCA Aquatic Center ($10). The Y's cardio and strength equipment is comparable to what you have on-site.

MODERATELY EXPENSIVE

GOLD: The Peabody Orlando

9801 International Drive, Orlando, FL 32819
(407) 352-4000 • peabodyorlando.com

CARDIO

TREADMILLS: **2 Precor**
UPRIGHT BIKE: **2 Precor**
RECUMBENT BIKE: **2 Precor**
ELLIPTICAL: **2 Precor • 1 LF**
STEPPER: **1 StairMaster • 1 LF**

STRENGTH

FREE WEIGHTS: **Yes**
MACHINES: **12 Nautilus**
DUMBBELLS: **5-75 lbs**

SWIM

GRADE: **C+**
SPECS: **2x33yd • Outdoor • 82-85°**

OTHER

HOURS: M-F **6a-9p** • SAT-SUN **7a-8p**
COST: **$9 • $22/week • $13 Others**
TV: **Yes**
EXTRAS: **Tennis**

Located across the street from the Orange County Convention Center, Peabody is an attractive option for both business and leisure travelers. While its quarters are not outfitted with the same extravagant amenities as the Ritz or JW, Peabody's 891 rooms promote relaxation with warm beige tones, down comforters, pillow top mattresses and bathroom televisions.

Peabody's workout facility impresses as well. With barely used Precor equipment and a 4600 series StairMaster, cardio buffs will leave here huffing and puffing — in a good way. Although the 12 Nautilus stack-loaded weight stations are old, we were pleasantly surprised by their ease of use and effectiveness. And the marvelous stock of free weights should fill any strength voids.

Freestylers will appreciate Peabody's lap pool. On one side of the 60-yard behemoth, 2 lanes marked with bottom stripes provide about 33 yards of lap swimming. The shape is difficult to describe--one side of the pool is 60 yards long and the other is 33. Only the shorter side has lane stripes (no floating lines). We did not find any toys or pace clock, so it's BYO for any variety or intervals.

Note: Drive 5 minutes and pay $10 for a more traditional swim at the YMCA Aquatic Center. The Y's cardio and strength equipment is comparable to the on-site option.

LEAST EXPENSIVE

GOLD: Radisson Barcelo

8444 International Drive, Orlando, FL 32819
(407) 345-0505 • radisson-orlando.com

Radisson Barcelo occupies prime real estate on International Drive. The hotel is across the street from many of Orlando's popular restaurants and attractions, 3 miles from Sea World and, most importantly, immediately adjacent to a full-service YMCA. Its 522 rooms are divided between a mid-rise tower and a low-rise lodge. We suggest reserving a tower room — quieter, and doors open to interior corridors. Regardless of which building, all guest quarters offer nothing but the basics — this is a budget-friendly accommodation, after all. But expect clean rooms and a friendly staff. The Starbucks and snack shop off the lobby are convenient for a cup of joe or sweet treat.

Radisson's on-site gym is the YMCA, and access to Radisson's backyard facility is free! Guests simply furnish their IDs and room keys to the hotel front desk in exchange for complimentary passes to YMCA's workout fun.

Note: This hotel has outdoor tennis courts.

BEYOND HOTELS

YMCA Aquatic & Family Center

8422 International Drive, Orlando, FL 32819
(407) 363-1911 • ymcaaquaticcenter.com

We love seeing "Aquatic" in a facility's name because it almost always means a top-notch swim venue. Happily, this theory holds true here. If this Y is good enough for the U.S.A. Junior National Competitions, it should be good enough for you, right? A picture is worth 1,000 words, so check out its website and feast your eyes on the main pool.

Y's field-house type building harbors 3 water boxes: the 50-meter main pool, a 25-yard teaching pool and a large diving well (platforms up to 10 meters in height). Local swim teams practice here year round, but lanes are always made available for adult lap swimmers. Count on all the bells and whistles — kickboards, pull-buoys and a pace clock. This is probably the best Y swimming option in the country so, if you are close, come for a dip (free for Radisson guests and a few other non-recommended hotels, $10 everyone else).

CARDIO

TREADMILLS: **StarTrac**
UPRIGHT BIKE: **StarTrac**
RECUMBENT BIKE: **StarTrac**
ELLIPTICAL: **Precor • StarTrac**
STEPPER: **StairMaster • LifeStep**
ROWING: **Concept II**
OTHER: **XC Ski**

STRENGTH

FREE WEIGHTS: **Yes**
MACHINES: **Cybex • BodyMaster**
DUMBBELLS: **3-100 lbs**

SWIM

GRADE: **A**
SPECS: **8x50m • Indoor • 82°**
TOYS: **Kick • Pull • Clock**
MASTERS: **Yes**

OTHER

CLASSES: **Yes**
HOURS: M-F **6a-9p** • SAT **8a-9p** • SUN **12-4p**
COST: **Free Radisson & select hotels • $10 Others**
TV: **Yes**
EXTRAS: **Racquetball**

The Y's fitness floor is no slouch either, offering a mix of old and new equipment. Exercisers will not search long before finding a well-running machine. Six new StarTrac bikes and 8 Precor ellipticals were recently delivered and sparkle beside other old cardio friends. Pumping iron is no problem, with the Y's generous supply of free weights, dumbbells and stack-loaded machines.

We just wish the ceilings were a little higher.

Note: Bring your own towel.

DOWNTOWN

As Orlando grows, so does its business district. We recommend a stay in this area only if downtown meetings are on your agenda. Otherwise, more desirable hotel options exist elsewhere.

EXPENSIVE

GOLD: **Westin Grand Bohemian**
325 S. Orange Avenue, Orlando, FL 32801
(407) 313-9000 • grandbohemianhotel.com

This upscale Euro-style hotel emphasizes culture and the arts with its stunning architecture, striking art collection and classical and contemporary music offerings. With its creative surroundings and edgy atmosphere, we thought we were back in South Beach. The Grand Bohemian is just that — non-conformist in its style. However, the workout room is also off-beat... way off. All 250 guest rooms are comfortably modern, with red and purple color schemes, velvet drapes and cushions, quilted headboards and Westin's signature Heavenly Beds. Techies must pay a surcharge for high-speed internet access, but it is available in all rooms. Late night munchies will be appeased by this Starwood property's 24-hour in-room dining.

After oohing and ahhing over the common areas and rooms, we anticipated an equally impressive fitness center. While the equipment is new, especially the four 9100 series Life Fitness cardio units, the machines are crammed into a space smaller than a hotel room. A cardio or weight quickie is possible here, but those longing for more should go elsewhere. The Citrus Club, located across the street in the Republic Bank Building's basement, admits Westin patrons for $10/day — and, while it's nothing great, it is certainly better than Westin's in-house gym. However, the Citrus Club is closed on weekends. If you want a guaranteed "A" rated health club, pull out the car keys and drive to the YMCA. The trip will take about 5-10 minutes, and your first visit is free ($12/day thereafter).

CARDIO

TREADMILLS: **2 LF**
UPRIGHT BIKE: **1 LF**
ELLIPTICAL: **1 LF**

STRENGTH

MACHINES: **1 LF Multi**
DUMBBELLS: **5-50 lbs**

SWIM

SPECS: **Outdoor • Not lap**

OTHER

HOURS: **24**
COST: **Free**
TV: **Yes**
EXTRAS: **$10 access Citrus**

Lap swimmers should seek the Y or Lake Highland Prep Academy.

MODERATELY EXPENSIVE

GOLD: Embassy Suites

191 East Pine Street, Orlando, FL 32801
(407) 841-1000 • embassyorlandodowntown.com

Located in the most appealing slice of downtown Orlando, Embassy is 2 blocks from Lake Eola Park and Church Street. Typical Embassy floor plans and amenities are provided in all 167 rooms. Expect plain business décor, separate living and sleeping quarters, microwaves and refrigerators. And, of course, Embassy serves up yummy and free hot breakfast buffets.

CARDIO

TREADMILLS: **2 Precor**
UPRIGHT BIKE: **1 Precor**
ELLIPTICAL: **1 Precor**

SWIM

SPECS: **Outdoor • Not lap**

OTHER

HOURS: **24**
COST: **Free**
TV: **Yes**

Embassy's exercise room supplies a few high-end cardio pieces, and that's it. If you only have 20-30 minutes to sweat on an elliptical, it will do. Otherwise, plan on walking 10 minutes to Metro Muscle ($10/day), running a few times around Lake Eola or driving 5 minutes to the YMCA (first visit is free).

Lap swimmers can go to the Y but, if your priority is the swim, you'll be happier at the outdoor Lake Highland Aquatic Center (smaller crowd and better pool — but closed weekends).

LEAST EXPENSIVE

GOLD: Courtyard by Marriott

730 North Magnolia Avenue, Orlando, FL 32803
(407) 996-1000 • courtyard.com

Although Courtyard is beyond any "walkable" restaurants or entertainment attractions, it's less than 10 minutes on foot to Lake

Highland Prep Academy's fantastic lap pool and running track. In typical Courtyard fashion, guests can count on standard rooms, basic décor, free high-speed internet access and overall reliable service. This particular property is easy on the wallet, with rates often under $100/night.

Courtyard's Gold standing is certainly not due to its on-site fitness option. With 2 shabby treadmills and a ramshackle multi-gym, using the word "fitness" to describe this room is a mistake. Fortunately, your off-site health options are solid and convenient. In addition to Lake Highland, the Downtown Y is less than 1.5 miles away (we recommend driving this busy street), and the Courtyard's surrounding residential neighborhood offers some great urban (i.e., asphalt), yet tree-lined, running routes — nothing too long, but loops are easily created.

BEYOND HOTELS

Citrus Club

255 South Orange Avenue, Orlando, FL 32801
(407) 843-1080 • citrus-club.com

CARDIO

TREADMILLS: **4 StarTrac**
UPRIGHT BIKE: **2 Cybex • 2 Fan**
RECUMBENT BIKE: **3 Cybex**
ELLIPTICAL: **2 Precor**
STEPPER: **5 StairMaster**
ROWING: **1 Concept II**
OTHER: **Crossrobic • NordicTrack • Gravitron**

STRENGTH

FREE WEIGHTS: **Yes ~450lbs**
MACHINES: **13 Cybex**
DUMBBELLS: **3-60 lbs**

OTHER

CLASSES: **Yes**
HOURS: M-F **6a-8p** • SAT-SUN **Closed**
COST: **$10 Westin only**
TV: **Yes**

This aesthetically-challenged health club caters to local office workers and is both light on equipment and short on space. However, Citrus is a clear step up from Westin Grand Bohemian's in-house facility.

To give you a better sense of its size, we have included the number of machines as well as brands in our chart. Westin guests are welcome after paying $10 — just keep your expectations in check.

Note: If you have time and wheels, the Y is a better workout alternative.

YMCA Downtown

433 North Mills Avenue, Orlando, FL 32803
(407) 896-6901 • centralfloridaymca.org

This Y is typically jammed with members during its rush hours (6-8 a.m., 4:30-7:30 p.m.), which is not too surprising because it is a phenomenal, full-service club. Unfortunately, no hotels are within walking distance, so you need wheels to get here.

This modern facility is stocked with the latest and greatest cardio and strength equipment. Endurance junkies can choose from two floors of youthful treadmills (18), ellipticals (16), bikes (10) and StairMaster 4600 series steppers (10). Separate rooms house the Y's unbelievable supply of 38 new Cybex stack-loaded weight stations, free weights and Hammer Strength machines.

Swimmers are afforded a rarity — the choice between an indoor or outdoor lapper. Both water boxes sport 5 lanes of 25-yard swimming complete with floating lines and bottom stripes. All toys are supplied and a Masters group also splashes here. Your first time at this location is on the house, but thereafter the going guest rate is $12/day or $20/week.

CARDIO

TREADMILLS: **StarTrac**
UPRIGHT BIKE: **StarTrac • Fan**
RECUMBENT BIKE: **StarTrac**
ELLIPTICAL: **Precor • StarTrac**
STEPPER: **StairMaster**
ROWING: **Concept II**

STRENGTH

FREE WEIGHTS: **Yes**
HAMMER: **Yes**
MACHINES: **Cybex**
DUMBBELLS: **5-120 lbs**

SWIM

GRADE: #1 **B+** • #2 **B+**
SPECS: #1 **5x25yd • Outdoor • 79°**
#2 **5x25yd • Indoor • 84°**
TOYS: **Kick • Pull • Clock**
MASTERS: **Yes**

OTHER

CLASSES: **Yes**
HOURS: M-F **5a-10p** • SAT **7a-8p** • SUN **12p-6p**
COST: **Free 1st time • $12 Other • $20/week**
TV: **Yes**

Metro Muscle

133 East Robinson Street, Orlando, FL 32801
(407) 481-0507

Within a half mile of Embassy Suites, this one-room club is reminiscent of an old-school sweat shop. The atmosphere has an industrial warehouse vibe with barren walls and tightly packed exercise machines. Split in half by a narrow aisle, the fitness floor provides nearly 20 stack-loaded weight stations, 5 Hammer Strength machines and a ton of free weights on one side, and 8 bikes, 7 ellipticals and 6 treads on the other — all newer 9500 series models. A live DJ spins House music on Mondays and Tuesdays, which can be good or bad. No pool and admission is $10/day.

CARDIO

TREADMILLS: **LF • StarTrac - old**
UPRIGHT BIKE: **LF**
RECUMBENT BIKE: **LF**
ELLIPTICAL: **LF**
STEPPER: **LF • Stepmill • StairMaster - old**

STRENGTH

FREE WEIGHTS: **Yes**
HAMMER: **Yes**
MACHINES: **LF**
DUMBBELLS: **5-145 lbs**

OTHER

CLASSES: **Yes**
HOURS: **24**
COST: **$10**
TV: **Yes**

Lake Highland Prep Academy

901 North Highland Avenue, Orlando, FL 32803
(407) 206-1900 • lhps.org

One of Orlando's esteemed private schools, Lake Highland has excellent athletic facilities. Unfortunately, the aquatics department

SWIM

GRADE: **A**
SPECS: **8x50m • Outdoor • 78-82°**
TOYS: **Kick • Clock**

OTHER

HOURS: M/T/TH/F **5:30-7:30a** • M-F **11a-1p** • M-F **5-6:30p**
EXTRAS: **1/4 mile outdoor track**

is terrible at returning phone calls, so we were unable to confirm the cost to swim. Nevertheless, a fantastic 50-meter pool with floating lines and bottom stripes sits in front of the school's main entrance — you can't miss it.

The 1/4-mile track is a great venue for joggers staying at the Courtyard. Both facilities are less than a half-mile from the hotel.

Note: We recommend verifying hours, etc. before planning a workout.

RUNNING ROUTES

Disney

Those holed up in Mickey's backyard, take to the roads. They meander across miles of land, are mostly flat with moderate traffic.

Sea World/Convention Center

Your best bet is to strategize with the hotel concierge for suggested routes. With the exception of Ritz and JW, which sport a 1.75 mile path, most routes will go through business-heavy areas.

Downtown

Lake Eola Park and its ~1-mile perimeter loop is within a hop, skip and stride from both Embassy and Westin (Downtown). The scenic 20-acre park is popular with locals. Courtyard guests can explore the relatively quiet residential area surrounding their temporary home. Head north for about 2 miles, where you will find the 45-acre Loch Haven Park's lakes, trees and gardens.

West Orange Trail

If you really need a serious run and you have wheels, the wonderful 18+ mile West Orange Trail runs along Lake Apopka through Oakland, Winter Garden and Apopka. But it is a good 10-25 miles from the accommodations we recommend. This venue is especially popular with cyclists.

PHILADELPHIA, PENNSYLVANIA

After receiving the dubious "America's fattest city" distinction in 1999 from Men's Health Magazine, Philadelphia civic leaders launched a battle of the bulge by funding a number of healthy lifestyle and obesity awareness programs. While these politically correct initiatives have reined in Philadelphians' expanding girth to a certain extent (in 2004, Philly dropped to #7), we believe the City of Brotherly Love would greatly benefit from a few additional enactments:

a) Limit cheese-steak and hoagie intake to one weekly serving. While enforcement may be difficult, roadblocks and random blood cholesterol screenings could be conducted by the police.

b) Restrict all smoking activity to the now-vacant site of Veterans Stadium — thus providing a destination for puffers to reminisce about the days of Ron Jaworski and Steve Carlton while intoxicating the canine-size rats with second-hand smoke.

c) Ban all alcohol sales in the week following a Philadelphia Eagles loss — reducing calorie consumption while simultaneously rallying this city's fair-weathered fans behind their team even during a losing season.

A keen reader will notice that our pontificating excluded hotels and health clubs, and that's good news for athletic-minded travelers. Philly's accommodations are ahead of the waistband curve when it comes to providing out-of-town guests with convenient and worthy fitness facilities.

EXPENSIVE

GOLD: Park Hyatt

Broad & Walnut Streets, Philadelphia, PA 19102
(215) 893-1234 • philadelphia.hyatt.com

This upscale, turn-of-the-century style hotel is smack dab in the middle of downtown Philly. The 172 plush guest rooms occupy the top 7 floors of the historic 19-story Bellevue Building, affording views of either the City or the hotel's inner court. Added conveniences are the shops and eateries located in the Bellevue Building's lower floors.

Park Hyatt does not dazzle with modern technology or chic motifs. Instead, we felt like guests to somebody's millionaire grandparents' home, where you can sense the furnishings are expensive, but they are simply not your taste. The richly decorated rooms are elegant and comfortable, just not our cup of tea — which, incidentally, is complimentary at the hotel, along with coffee and evening champagne. Pillow top mattresses, down duvets, deep closets and CD/VCR players remind us how the wealthy must live. And, for those wanting a spritz under the hood, the bidet is a fringe benefit.

With all of this luxury inside the hotel, Park Hyatt outdoes itself by providing complimentary access to the adjoining 93,000-square-foot Sporting Club at Bellevue. The best health club in Philadelphia, it may be better than any gym you've seen in a long time, and only Park Hyatt guests are granted this privilege.

SILVER: Four Seasons

One Logan Square, Philadelphia, PA 19103
(215) 963-1500 • fourseasons.com/philadelphia

CARDIO

TREADMILLS: **3 Precor**
UPRIGHT BIKE: **3 Precor**
ELLIPTICAL: **2 Precor**
STEPPER: **1 Precor**

STRENGTH

MACHINES: **4 Cybex**
DUMBBELLS: **3-50 lbs**

SWIM

GRADE: **D**
SPECS: **3x15yd • Indoor • 84°**
TOYS: **Kick**

OTHER

HOURS: **5:30a-10p**
COST: **Free**
TV: **Yes**

Because Park Hyatt is such a category stand-out and the Loews such an ideal moderately-priced alternative, we debated the need for a runner-up in this "Expensive" category. But everyone prefers options, right? So, in the event the Park and Loews are booked and you have the bullion to bankroll a highbrow experience, Four Seasons fits the bill.

The Philadelphia version of this 5-star chain adheres to the City's colonial past with a Federal-style room décor. In addition to attractive city or courtyard views, the luxury property boasts the customary Four Seasons high thread count sheets, restful mattresses, neutral décor and 24-hour room service.

Unfortunately, the first class accommodations and amenities are not equaled by the workout experience. Housed in a petite and unsightly "L" shaped room, the cardio and weight machines are scattered about. Treadmills are lined up along a narrow, mirrored corridor that will likely deter claustrophobics. Though athletes will find a small number of stack-loaded weight stations and dumbbells, free weights are noticeably missing.

Swimmers fare no better with the spatially-challenged lap pool. At 15 yards, it may suffice for 1,000 yards or so, but a longer workout's flip-turning will induce dizziness.

If you need any additional incentive to stay at Park Hyatt, consider that your room at the Four Seasons will probably run an extra $100/night.

MODERATELY EXPENSIVE

GOLD: **Loews**

1200 Market Street, Philadelphia, PA 19107
(215) 627-1200 • loewshotels.com/hotels/philadelphia
balancespaandfitness.com

This hotel rightfully earns the Gold medal as well as our "cool" award... if we had one. Strikingly modern in a sea of Renaissance-era inspired hotels, this renovated bank building is a National Historic Landmark and home to the luxurious Loews. Guests will relish a full menu of amenities at this centrally located property, 1 block from City Hall and 2 blocks from the convention center. All 583 guest quarters are attractively furnished in a contemporary style, with 10-foot ceilings, upscale baths and purple-toned colors. The least expensive rooms contain a queen-size sofa bed only, so be sure to reserve the exact sleeping arrangement you desire. Loews aims to please the "techie" by providing a few toys in each room — fax machine, printer and T1 line.

CARDIO
TREADMILLS: **6 Cybex**
UPRIGHT BIKE: **2 Cybex • 1 LF**
RECUMBENT BIKE: **2 Cybex**
ELLIPTICAL: **2 Reebok**
STEPPER: **2 Cybex**

STRENGTH
FREE WEIGHTS: **Yes**
MACHINES: **12 Cybex**
DUMBBELLS: **3-80 lbs**

SWIM
GRADE: **B-**
SPECS: **2x20m • Indoor • 80-84°**

OTHER
CLASSES: **Yes**
HOURS: M-SAT **6a-10p** • SUN **7a-7p**
COST: **$10 • $30/week**
TV: **Yes**

The sleek styling extends to the fully-stocked 5th floor Balance Spa and Fitness Center. Cybex manufactured equipment dominates this 15,000 square foot space, so athletes partial to Precor ellipticals or StairMaster climbers may want to consider the Park Hyatt. The equipment is not "brand" new, but the machines' year or two of miles will not hamper any workout. A sufficient supply of free weights and the 12 stack-loaded weight stations are ample for any strength routine.

Swimmers will enjoy the 2-lane, 20-meter lap pool with regulation stripes, a roped lane-line and abundant light from tall windows. After your workout, shower in the full-amenity locker rooms and take advantage of Balance's complete offering of spa and salon services.

The only drawback to this tip-top center is an irritating $10 access fee ($30/week). Fortunately, an above average product is provided in return.

SILVER: Crowne Plaza Center City

1800 Market Street, Philadelphia, PA 19103
(215) 561-7500 • crowneplaza.com

While it's within walking distance of most downtown businesses and attractions, visitors to this mid-grade accommodation trade posh for price. Crowne's 445 rooms convey an appealing business-hotel vibe with a renovation completed in 2005. Fresh white linens and comforters cover the beds and work well with the other tasteful decor.

Crowne's mediocre 8th floor fitness center's couple of cardio machines and dumbbells may satisfy some athletic-minded travelers, but more will consider this hotel for its proximity and reduced admission price to the full-service Philadelphia Sports Club across the street. At the time of our tour, guests of the Crowne could exercise at PSC for $10 ($15 discount). However, we understand a new deal was being finalized that may even provide for complimentary access — call to find out for sure.

Note: Because Crowne negotiates an arrangement with PSC on a year-to-year basis, there could be periods when no discount is available for guests.

LEAST EXPENSIVE

GOLD: Holiday Inn Express Midtown

1305 Walnut Street, Philadelphia, PA 19107
(215) 735-9300 • hiexpress.com

Why this hotel has "Midtown" in its name is a mystery. The Holiday Inn Express is located in the heart of downtown Philly and neighboring hotels also use a "downtown" reference.

Like kids gathering candy after breaking a piñata, staying at a Holiday Inn Express is all about hoarding the freebies. In return for sacrificing premium bedding and upscale furnishings, guests to Express' 160-room property receive free local calls and free continental breakfasts.

Holiday Inn Express does not have a workout room on-site, but atones for its fitness black hole with a much appreciated complimentary pass to Bally Fitness — only 5 minutes away on foot.

BEYOND HOTELS

Sporting Club at Bellevue

220-224 South Broad Street, Philadelphia, PA 19102
(215) 985-9876 • sportingclubbellevue.com

Hotel guests rarely have the opportunity to sample a city's most exclusive health club for free. When we get the chance, we jump all over it. So, too, should Park Hyatt guests, who are granted complimentary access to this adjoining 93,000 square foot awe-inspiring facility. While the enormous size can be intimidating, the club's multi-level atrium floor plan is extremely organized, with an NBA-size basketball court on the lowest level and huge surrounding balconies on the way up (think rectangle with the middle cut out). An indoor track, weight and cardio areas, racquet sport courts and a café/juice bar are on the upper levels.

CARDIO

TREADMILLS: **StarTrac**
UPRIGHT BIKE: **LF**
RECUMBENT BIKE: **LF • Stratus**
ELLIPTICAL: **Precor • Reebok • LF**
STEPPER: **StairMaster • Reebok**
ROWING: **Concept II**
OTHER: **NordicTrack**

STRENGTH

FREE WEIGHTS: **Yes**
HAMMER: **Yes**
MACHINES: **Cybex • Free Motion • Nautilus**
DUMBBELLS: **3-150 lbs**

SWIM

GRADE: **B+**
SPECS: **4x25m • Indoor • 82°**
TOYS: **Kick • Pull • Fins • Clock**
MASTERS: **Yes**

OTHER

CLASSES: **Yes**
HOURS: M-TH **5a-11p** • F **5a-10p** • SAT-SUN **8a-8p**
COST: **Free Park Hyatt • No others**
TV: **Yes**
EXTRAS: **1/12 mile Indoor track • Racquetball • Basketball • Cafe**

Sporting Club's fitness floor is adorned with a ton of the industry's latest technology and exercise favorites. Those wishing to push their anaerobic threshold can choose among more than 20 treadmills, nearly 20 recumbent bikes, around 15 ellipticals, a dozen upright bikes and seven 4400 PT series StairMaster Free Climbers — many of which have individual plasma televisions. The club's weight selection is just as impressive, with close to 50 stack-loaded weight stations, 15 Hammer Strength machines, 8 benches, 2 squat racks and plenty of other equipment. Over 90 group exercise classes are offered, so those looking for strength in numbers will find it here.

Swimmers are included in the fun. Sporting Club's 25-meter competition-level lap pool is easily the best around. Fins, kickboards, pull-buoys and a pace clock sit on deck of this 4-lane beauty containing floating lines and bottom stripes. A Masters program is even available from 6:30 p.m. to 8 p.m. (call to confirm time).

We could easily spend all day here — especially given the fully-stocked, plush locker rooms and spa services. Unfortunately, due to the exclusivity of the club, only Park Hyatt visitors, members and members' guests receive access privileges.

Philadelphia Sports Club (PSC)

1735 Market Street, Philadelphia, PA 19103
(215) 564-5353 • mysportsclub.com

CARDIO

TREADMILLS: **LF • StarTrac**
UPRIGHT BIKE: **LF**
RECUMBENT BIKE: **LF**
ELLIPTICAL: **Precor**
STEPPER: **StairMaster**

STRENGTH

FREE WEIGHTS: **Yes**
HAMMER: **Yes**
MACHINES: **Cybex • Nautilus**
DUMBBELLS: **5-115 lbs**

OTHER

CLASSES: **Yes**
HOURS: M-TH **5a-10p** • F **5:30a-9p** • SAT-SUN **8a-4p**
COST: **$25 • TBD Crowne Guests**
TV: **Yes**

Though the club's name may bring to mind hunting season, leave the shotgun and fluorescent orange vest at home. There are a number of PSC facilities throughout Philly, and this location in the basement of Mellon Bank Centre (corner of 18th and Market and across the street from Crowne Plaza) provides great endurance and strength options.

The facility's bright walls and spacious workout areas compensate for the lack of windows and natural light. While small in terms of overall square footage, its one large room stocks an impressive supply of useful machinery. Fitness fans will have a wide variety of manufacturers competing for their sweat equity, in addition to a large selection of classes.

Those looking to get wet in a chlorinated way must search elsewhere, as this club is "pool-free."

Twenty-five bucks will provide access, unless you are staying at the Crowne Plaza. Guests of this hotel, located across the street, often receive a discount, depending on the current arrangement with PSC.

Bally Total Fitness Drexel Building

1435-1441 Walnut Street, Philadelphia, PA 19102
(215) 564-2121 • ballyfitness.com

While this is a perfectly acceptable club, especially for the Bally brand, we like the equipment selection and atmosphere better at the more aesthetically pleasing and fully stocked Philadelphia Sports Club. In addition, you are likely to encounter a smaller crowd there. However, this club is a great option for Holiday Inn Express guests because:

a. It is free
b. It is free
c. It is free
d. It is only a 5-minute walk
and
e. Plenty of popular cardio and weight machines are offered inside, including Precor ellipticals and Life Fitness bikes.

For those not staying at Holiday Inn Express, this Bally Fitness does not have a set access charge for non-members. However, we confirmed that out-of-towners desiring a sweat can come over for a day or two and work out for free. You will have to fill out some paperwork (they don't check your phone number or email), endure a short tour and dismiss a quick membership pitch, but afterward you're in like Flynn. Just to be certain, though, we would call before heading over to confirm the procedure.

Note: No pool for swimmers, and you should bring your own towel and lock.

CARDIO

TREADMILLS: **LF**
UPRIGHT BIKE: **LF**
RECUMBENT BIKE: **LF**
ELLIPTICAL: **Precor**
STEPPER: **StairMaster**

STRENGTH

FREE WEIGHTS: **Yes**
HAMMER: **Yes**
MACHINES: **LF**
DUMBBELLS: **5-80 lbs**

OTHER

CLASSES: **Yes**
HOURS: M-TH **6a-11p** • F **6a-10p** • SAT **8a-8p** • SUN **8a-7p**
COST: **Free Holiday Inn Express • Others free for a visit or two**
TV: **Yes**

RUNNING ROUTES

Fairmount Park

Runners are in luck. Despite its bustling financial center complete with the usual urban hazards, downtown Philly is ideally situated near the 8,900-acre Fairmount Park on the Schuylkill River, affording runners a scenic 8+ mile loop. From Logan Square, head toward the Art Museum via Benjamin Franklin Parkway. Kelly Drive and West River Drive will be your primary thoroughfares on each side of the River. Falls Bridge is your turnaround, assuming you are up for the full loop. Fairmount Park is home to a zoo, music center, zoological garden, tennis courts and much more.

Franklin Field

For a circular sweat, check out the all weather track at University of Pennsylvania. Home to the historic Penn Relays, Franklin Field's 400-meter surface has witnessed its share of competitive running history — not too surprising, since it has hosted the event for over 100 years!

National Historic Park

Those athletes with a penchant for our nation's history will undoubtedly enjoy a jog through the 45-acre National Historic Park, also known as "the birthplace of our nation." The park is home to the Liberty Bell, Independence Hall and a multitude of other historic buildings. This brief route is located between 5th and 6th streets and Chestnut and Walnut Street.

Note: See the City's Visitor Center map for other run options and more specific information.

Pennypack Park

For those with wheels, a 13-mile side trip to the northeast side of Philly (near the Delaware River) offers loads of outdoor pursuits, including canoeing, biking, fishing and, of course, running. A 9-mile paved trail cuts directly through the park, and there are a number of off road trails for varied terrain. With 1,600 acres to play in, we are confident you will find a path to your liking.

Phoenix

79 Locations Reviewed

PHOENIX, ARIZONA

"Yeah, but it's a dry heat," is the popular platitude outsiders recite when pointing out the positives of desert living. But spend some time here in July, when the average temperature sizzles at 106F, and you may witness some peculiar events and behaviors that will quickly debunk this "dry heat" adage. For example, Phoenicians have been known to don oven mitts to open car doors, mow lawns at 4 a.m., cook TV dinners on car backseats and suffer first degree burns attempting to "barefoot it" across a parking lot — at 11 p.m. These daredevils have endured melting windshield wipers, exploding car batteries and quadruple-digit air-conditioning bills.

Phoenix's urban sprawl and steadfast growth haven't caused a cool draft, either. Quite the opposite. Engineers and climatologists agree that the nation's 6th largest city's clustered home communities with their tile roofs and stucco walls, unshaded streets and miles of asphalt create an enormous "sponge," absorbing daylight's blazing heat and retaining the swelter overnight. In fact, recent studies show that Phoenix posts temperatures 5-10° hotter overnight than many smaller nearby communities.

These desert dwellers fortify for summer much like Minnesotans brace for winter, when avoiding the outdoors is a common theme. Nevertheless, before and after Phoenix's 90 days of searing heat (June through August), this town is an outdoor enthusiast's delight. Miles of paved bike routes, mountain hiking trails, dirt jogging paths and fresh water lakes are accompanied by a myriad of golf courses and spring baseball stadiums. The outdoors becomes center stage and its entertainment is endless.

So, next time you hear the "dry heat" theory, just reply, "So is the heat in your oven!"

SCOTTSDALE

Those of you expecting to find the Phoenician and Biltmore high on our list might be surprised. While these are wonderful resorts (we've enjoyed both), when it comes to hotels with the best fitness and accommodation combos, the following selections outshine.

EXPENSIVE

GOLD: Sanctuary Camelback Mountain

5700 East McDonald Drive, Paradise Valley, AZ 85253
(480) 948-2100 • sanctuaryaz.com

CARDIO

TREADMILLS: **4 Precor • 1 NordicTrack**
UPRIGHT BIKE: **1 Cybex**
RECUMBENT BIKE: **3 Cybex**
ELLIPTICAL: **4 Precor**
STEPPER: **1 StairMaster • 1 Stepmill**

STRENGTH

FREE WEIGHTS: **Yes**
HAMMER: **Yes**
MACHINES: **9 Free Motion**
DUMBBELLS: **3-60 lbs**

SWIM

GRADE: **B**
SPECS: **2x25yd • Outdoor • 82-84º**
TOYS: **Kick • Pull • Clock**

OTHER

CLASSES: **Yes**
HOURS: **5a-11p**
COST: **Free**
TV: **Yes**
EXTRAS: **Tennis**

Seldom does a name so perfectly characterize a resort. Nestled against Camelback Mountain, Sanctuary's 98 suite-and-casita hideaway is wonderfully secluded and offers zen-like tranquility to discriminating guests.

Sanctuary's pampering commences with first-class service and plush accommodations. Fifty-three beautifully landscaped acres set the scene for relaxing by the infinity pool, enjoying a rubdown in the full-service spa or sweating in the desert sun. Sanctuary's guest rooms continue the sense of wellbeing with 300 thread count linens, marble baths, soft desert-toned décor and contemporary furnishings.

While there is much to praise at this boutique resort, nothing elevates our heart rates more than its exceptional fitness facilities and nearby mountain trails. Sanctuary's cozy indoor gym houses a perfect quantity and variety of equipment to satisfy even the most finicky workout junkie. Though the machine numbers are not huge, Sanctuary's intimate size ensures availability. All cardio and strength apparatus are sparkling new and only premium brands are stocked. Plasma televisions are attached to ellipticals and treadmills. A high-quality stereo system pumps in music (headphones are provided as well).

The hotel's infinity pool is beautifully enticing, but it's the 2-lane, 25-yard lap pool that attracts us. Complete with floating lines, a pace clock and toys, Sanctuary's outdoor water box is a true lapper.

For those in search of more adventure, head straight up — Camelback Mountain that is. Attack these trails via bike or foot, bring water and don't forget sunblock. Several paces off Sanctuary's lush grounds will quickly remind you that this is the hot and dry desert. The hotel offers guided hikes and bike rides for a fee, but of course you can strike out on your own for free!

SILVER: Westin Kierland Resort & Spa

6902 East Greenway Parkway, Scottsdale, AZ 85254
(480) 624-1000 • westin.com/kierlandresort

Equivalent in stature to the Sanctuary but vastly different in size and style, the 735-room Westin glimmers. While this top-grade accommodation is elegant throughout, those in search of a serene retreat should stay elsewhere. The luxurious property covers a vast piece of real estate near Scottsdale Airport and Kierland Commons — an upscale shopping center that includes retailers Anthroplogie, French Connection, Tommy Bahama and Z Gallerie as well as eateries PF Chang's and Morton's. Westin's guest quarters speak a sophisticated language. Warm desert shades of cream and brown, premium bedding and linens, leather upholstered furniture and private balconies or patios comfort travelers.

CARDIO
TREADMILLS: **5 Precor**
UPRIGHT BIKE: **2 Precor**
RECUMBENT BIKE: **2 Precor**
ELLIPTICAL: **5 Precor**
STEPPER: **2 Precor**

STRENGTH
MACHINES: **12 LF**
DUMBBELLS: **5-50 lbs**

SWIM
GRADE: **C+**
SPECS: **1x24yd • Outdoor • 79-83°**

OTHER
CLASSES: **Yes**
HOURS: **24**
COST: **Free**
TV: **Yes**
EXTRAS: **Tennis • Golf**

Adjacent to the main outdoor pool, Westin provides athletic-minded travelers with a worthwhile fitness center and spa. Open 24 hours, its workout facility contains a solid number of top-of-the-line Precor cardio machines and Life Fitness weight stations. Although free weights are noticeably absent, an array of dumbbells will round out your muscle work.

The swimmers' lap option along one side of the main pool is appealing. Though stripes are not painted on the bottom, a floating lane line guides you through a 24-yard chlorinated course.

Westin's 27 hole golf course is spectacularly manicured and conveniently located just outside the hotel's front door — too bad running trails do not surround the fairways!

MODERATELY EXPENSIVE

GOLD: Scottsdale Resort & Athletic Club

8235 East Indian Bend Road, Scottsdale, AZ 85250
(480) 344-0600 • scottsdaleresortandathleticclub.com

We pat ourselves on the back for finding this moderately priced gem. Opened in May 2003, the Scottsdale Resort and Athletic Club is a petite 56 all-suite accommodation that rivals many five-star ho-

CARDIO

TREADMILLS: **8 LF**
UPRIGHT BIKE: **2 Cybex**
RECUMBENT BIKE: **4 Cybex**
ELLIPTICAL: **4 Precor • 1 LF**
STEPPER: **2 StairMaster • 1 Stepmill**
OTHER: **1 Ergometer**

STRENGTH

FREE WEIGHTS: **Yes**
HAMMER: **Yes**
MACHINES: **15 Total • LF • Magnum**
DUMBBELLS: **2.5-80 lbs**

SWIM

GRADE: **B**
SPECS: **3x25m • Outdoor • 84º**
TOYS: **Kick**

OTHER

CLASSES: **Yes**
HOURS: M-F **5:30a-10p • SAT 7a-9p • SUN 7a-7p**
COST: **Free**
TV: **Yes**
EXTRAS: **Tennis • Golf**

tels. Although it may not wow you with external beauty or a million-dollar landscape, dollar for dollar it could be the best resort in all of Phoenix.

The building's design requires guests to enter their chambers via motel-like outside doors, but once inside travelers are instantly aware that this is no budget lodging. Full kitchenettes, high quality furnishings, working fireplaces and huge floor plans with separate living and sleeping areas create a home away from home. All bedrooms boast premium mattresses, high thread count sheets and tasteful décor. In addition, most one-bedroom units can be expanded into 2-bedroom suites to accommodate families or larger groups. Despite the resort's timeshare set-up, one-night rentals are available and no sales pitches, thankfully, are given unless requested.

The resort's owner is a talented tennis fanatic, and the meticulously maintained outdoor-lighted hard courts evidence his addiction. This pristine racquet facility is adjacent to a 2-story full-service athletic club that is complimentary to resort guests. Inside the immaculate club, athletic-minded travelers are treated to many of the latest and greatest cardio machines, weight equipment and a full slate of exercise classes, including spin. Life Fitness 95Ti series treadmills, Cybex bikes and 15 stack-loaded weight stations are samples of the club's stellar supply.

Swimmers are included in the fun. The 25-meter outdoor lap pool contains only one floating lane line, but stripes are marked on its bottom to create 3 lanes total.

Complete spa services top off a worthy fitness experience, not to mention the Club's tasty restaurant, which serves Eurasian cuisine well into the night.

Note: Golfers will be happy to learn that discounted greens fees and preferential tee-times are available at the neighboring par 70 Silverado Golf Course.

SILVER: Embassy Suites Scottsdale

4415 E. Paradise Village Pkwy South, Phoenix, AZ 85032
(602) 765-5800 • embassysuitesaz.com

Located a block from Paradise Valley Mall and 6 miles from Kierland Commons, Embassy is a legitimate contender in the battle for your desert travel dollars. While not nearly as luxurious or pampering as the Sanctuary or Westin, guests may rest easier here knowing that half as much cash is set loose each night.

As is customary for this Hilton brand, all 270 suites offer separate living and sleeping areas, refrigerators, microwaves and private balconies. Though you may be tempted to zap a few nibbles, let Embassy cover your breakfast and happy hour feasts with its complimentary chow and beverage offerings. Each morning, guests wake up to Embassy's trademark hot breakfast buffet — made to order omelets, waffles, cereals and juices. In the evenings (5:30-7:30 p.m.), the Manager's reception serves free hors d'oeuvres and drinks.

Workout rooms are rarely Embassy's focus, and this Scottsdale representative is no exception. The miniscule and under-equipped room (3 old cardio machines and 10-45 lbs. dumbbells) does not merit your sweat. Instead, we recommend a 5-minute walk to LA Fitness. This facility, which opened its doors in 2002, stocks the latest in cardio and weight technology — and has a lap pool.

When we first toured this Embassy, guests were granted free access privileges at LA Fitness. However, this "deal" has since fallen through, so exercisers must now pay $20/day or $40/week (IHRSA members $15/day). But even with an Andrew Jackson added to your daily tab, you're still nowhere near luxury resort prices.

Note: Embassy sits on an 18-hole Scottish links-style golf course.

LEAST EXPENSIVE

GOLD: **Fairfield Inn North**

13440 North Scottsdale Road, Scottsdale, AZ 85254
(480) 483-0042 • fairfieldinn.com

So you want to vacation in Scottsdale but do not want to pay Scottsdale resort prices, huh? Don't worry, we have you covered. This Fairfield Inn offers nothing but the basics — clean rooms, good service and standard furnishings. But its wallet-friendly attitude and great location on Scottsdale Road two miles from Kierland Commons (see Westin) are winning attributes.

Fairfield piles on the perks, including free local calls, free continental breakfasts, free parking and, most importantly, free passes to a fantastic 24 Hour Fitness health club — a 5-minute walk away!

Note: Request a 3rd floor room with a door opening into an interior hallway to insulate yourself from noisy Scottsdale Road.

BEYOND HOTELS SCOTTSDALE

LA Fitness Paradise Valley

11630 Tatum Road, Phoenix, AZ 85028
(602) 404-4700 • lafitness.com

Opened in 2002, this LA Fitness sparkles with new equipment

CARDIO
TREADMILLS: **StarTrac**
UPRIGHT BIKE: **LF**
RECUMBENT BIKE: **LF**
ELLIPTICAL: **LF • Precor**
STEPPER: **Cybex**
ROWING: **Concept II**

STRENGTH
FREE WEIGHTS: **Yes**
HAMMER: **Yes**
MACHINES: **Cybex • Nautilus**
DUMBBELLS: **5-150 lbs**

SWIM
GRADE: **B**
SPECS: **3x25m • Indoor • 78-80°**

OTHER
CLASSES: **Yes**
HOURS: M-F **5a-10p** • SAT-SUN **7a-8p**
COST: **$20 • $15 IHRSA**
TV: **Yes**
EXTRAS: **Basketball • Racquetball**

in a great workout environment — some machines even overlook Embassy Suites' golf course. While a $20/day guest fee is rather steep, we can swallow the pricey pill knowing that LA's equipment and facilities are top-notch. Inside, exercisers will happily discover an enormous quantity of new machines (e.g., >20 treadmills), a ton of free weights and a wide assortment of classes.

The lap pool is a winner, too, with 3 lanes of 25-meter swimming separated by floating lines. Bring a wristwatch if you plan on swimming base intervals as no pace clock is on deck.

Note: $40/week pass is also available, and IHRSA members receive a $5 discount off the daily rate (go to IHRSA's website at healthclubs.com).

24 Hour Fitness Sport Scottsdale

13220 N. Scottsdale Rd.
Scottsdale, AZ 85254
(480) 951-8883
24hourfitness.com

CARDIO
TREADMILLS: **LF**
UPRIGHT BIKE: **LF**
RECUMBENT BIKE: **LF**
ELLIPTICAL: **LF • Precor**
STEPPER: **StairMaster**
ROWING: **Concept II**

STRENGTH
FREE WEIGHTS: **Yes**
HAMMER: **Yes**
MACHINES: **Cybex • Free Motion • Nautilus**
DUMBBELLS: **3-120 lbs**

SWIM
GRADE: **B**
SPECS: **4x25m • Indoor • 82°**
TOYS: **Kick • Clock**

OTHER
CLASSES: **Yes**
HOURS: M-F **24** • SAT-SUN **6a-9p**
COST: **Free Fairfld • $15 IHRSA • $20 Others**
TV: **Yes**

As 24 Hour's upscale brand, "Sport" typically means a larger footprint, more classes and a regulation lap pool. During our swim and sweat, we were impressed by 24's equipment set-up, pool and overall facility quality.

The club's 2 stories of fitness bliss will have traveling athletes grinning. Cardio, weights and classrooms are upstairs, with the lap pool on the ground level. Expect ultramodern endurance apparatus, youthful strength stations and plenty of free weights ready to whip you into shape.

Our agua amigos receive a little bonus length in 24 Hour's 25-meter lap pool. Floating lines and bottom stripes mark the territory, so no crooked swimming excuses. Kickboards and a pace clock are provided as well.

Note: Fairfield Inn guests get to enjoy the sweat action for free — all others must pay $20/day.

DOWNTOWN

Here's the scoop on downtown Phoenix: If you don't have to stay there, opt for Scottsdale or Tempe. Why? With only 6 lodging options dotting downtown's map, the hotel selection is weak. Two potential venues (Ramada and Best Western) are in dire need of renovation, and a third (Holiday Inn Express) is outside comfortable walking distance to attractions such as the Civic Plaza and America West Arena. So that leaves 3 candidates in the nation's 6th largest city. Talk about slim pickings!

The Hyatt is the nicest of the three, and usually costs the most. Wyndham often charges as much as Hyatt but offers less in amenities and workout facilities. San Carlos is the least expensive but has no workout option. Guests of all three seeking a more serious fitness fix should plan on a 10-minute walk to the Downtown YMCA ($4 with room key).

MODERATELY EXPENSIVE

GOLD: Hyatt Regency

122 North 2nd Street, Phoenix, AZ 85004
(602) 252-1234 • phoenix.hyatt.com

As the most upscale accommodation in the heart of Phoenix, Hyatt is conveniently located across the street from Phoenix's convention center and 2 blocks from the Arizona Center — Downtown's only shopping mall. America West Arena and Bank One ballpark are a short walk away as well.

Catering primarily to a business and convention set, this high-rise hotel can support large numbers with its 712 rooms. Despite this size, Hyatt deserves credit for offering upscale accommodations decorated with creativity and flair. Stylish armoires, leather upholstered headboards, sofa chairs and ottomans as well as ergonomic office chairs distinguish this hotel.

CARDIO
TREADMILLS: **3 LF**
UPRIGHT BIKE: **2 LF**
RECUMBENT BIKE: **1 LF**
ELLIPTICAL: **3 LF**
STEPPER: **1 LF**

STRENGTH
MACHINES: **4 Paramount**
DUMBBELLS: **5-50 lbs**

SWIM
SPECS: **Outdoor • Not lap**

OTHER
HOURS: **5a-10p**
COST: **Free**
TV: **Yes**
EXTRAS: **$4 YMCA**

Hyatt's fitness center received a much-needed facelift in Spring

2006. New Life Fitness cardio machines adorn the room and all have visual entertainment built in. Dumbbells are also on-site for a limited strength session, but the cardio equipment is certainly the highlight.

Those desiring a lap swim or a more health club-like workout should head to the YMCA (10-minute walk). While the hotel may direct you to the closer Phoenix Suns Health Club, the Y's newer equipment is worth the longer commute — and PSHC has no lapper.

SILVER: **Wyndham**

50 East Adams Street, Phoenix, AZ 85004
(602) 333-0000 • wyndham.com

CARDIO

TREADMILLS: **4 Cybex**
RECUMBENT BIKE: **4 Total - • Cybex • Tectrix**
ELLIPTICAL: **2 Precor**

STRENGTH

MACHINES: **1 Multi**

SWIM

SPECS: **Outdoor • Not lap**

OTHER

HOURS: **6a-10p**
COST: **Free**
TV: **Yes**
EXTRAS: **$4** YMCA

Wyndham is another large business hotel competing for conventioneers and business travelers. Like Hyatt, it is located a short walk from Downtown's shopping, entertainment and dining attractions.

Since its renovation in 2003, Wyndham guests can anticipate premium bedding, Herman Miller desk chairs, charming décor and cozy earth tones in all 532 rooms. Techies will appreciate complimentary high-speed internet access and multi-line phones.

Sadly, Wyndham does not serve up any better fitness offering than Hyatt. In fact, with no useful strength equipment, muscle work is not an option. While the cardio machines are in fair condition, the absence of an upright bike and a step machine are additional flaws. Exercisers' best in-house sweat is on the slightly worn Precor ellipticals. Most guests will welcome the 10-minute jaunt to the Downtown YMCA. Your room key and 4 bucks get you in the door.

LEAST EXPENSIVE

GOLD: **Hotel San Carlos**

202 North Central Avenue, Phoenix, AZ 85004
(602) 253-4121 • hotelsancarlos.com

The San Carlos has been around for awhile (since 1928), and it shows. Despite a $1 million renovation in 2002, the guest rooms' garish bedspreads stand out against bland vanilla walls. Still, you cannot beat the hotel's location if being Downtown is a must, and the nightly tariffs are cheap, cheap, cheap! Free continental breakfasts are offered, scoring another point in the "positives" column.

At bare bones prices, a workout room is a fantasy, so athletic-minded travelers should head to the Downtown YMCA. Again, 10 minutes and 4 bucks (bring your room key and I.D.) is the not-so-secret combination.

BEYOND HOTELS DOWNTOWN

Downtown YMCA

350 North 1st Avenue, Phoenix, AZ 85003
(602) 257-5138 • valleyymca.org

Summer 2004 brings exciting changes to this public facility. Renovations are needed and, thankfully, they're on the way! The gym will remain open during the spruce-up, so try to overlook any design flaws because this Y's inventory of cardio and strength equipment is ample and satisfying — especially for the $4/day bargain admission (with hotel room key; $8/day all others).

Although the ground level cardio room is a bit tight with machines, most apparatus is in good condition and well maintained. Top-of-the-line Life Fitness and Precor brands are represented, in addition to a few StairMaster units. Similar to the cardio space, YMCA's downstairs strength area has its aesthetic moles (e.g., low ceilings and plain colors), but we cannot complain about the equipment supply. Plenty of free weights, stack-loaded stations and plate-loaded machines give the room the personality and character we care about.

The 4 lane, 25-yard lap pool will not captivate you with its charm, but your time will be spent staring at the bottom stripes and lane lines, anyway. A few toys were on deck during our tour, so plan on mixing up that 4,000 yards with a little kick and pull. Bring your watch if intervals are on the training schedule — we did not see a pace clock. Towels and locks are provided, but bring your flip-flops for the showers.

CARDIO

TREADMILLS: **LF**
UPRIGHT BIKE: **LF**
RECUMBENT BIKE: **LF**
ELLIPTICAL: **LF • Precor**
STEPPER: **StairMaster • Stepmill**
ROWING: **Concept II**

STRENGTH

FREE WEIGHTS: **Yes**
HAMMER: **Yes**
MACHINES: **Cybex**
DUMBBELLS: **5-110 lbs**

SWIM

GRADE: **C-**
SPECS: **4x25yd • Indoor • 85°**
TOYS: **Kick • Pull**
MASTERS: **Yes**

OTHER

CLASSES: **Yes**
HOURS: M-F **5:30a-9:45p** • SAT **5:30a-7p** • SUN **11a-5p**
COST: **$4 Hotels • $8 Others**
TV: **Yes**
EXTRAS: **1/19 mile outdoor track • Racquetball**

RUNNING ROUTES

Scottsdale

Best bets will depend upon where you choose to rest your head each night. Given this city's topography, most accommodations will likely be close to a trailhead, park or runner-friendly bike path. In terms of paved paths, the top two are the Grand Canal (200+ mile system running through all Phoenix) and the Indian Bend Multi-Use Path (runs 10+ miles from Shea south to Tempe, paralleling Hayden Road). Consult with your hotel front desk and rest easy. In the Valley of the Sun, running routes are plentiful.

Downtown

The more desirable running venues are elsewhere, but Downtown hotels will provide street routes for you to clock mileage. If you have a car, consider driving to the Phoenix Mountain Preserve or the very popular South Mountain Park (8 miles).

PITTSBURGH, PENNSYLVANIA

While Burger King is "Home of the Whopper," Pittsburgh is where the "Big Mac Attack" began. Losing sales to rival Big Boy, Jim Delligatti, one of McDonalds' earliest owner/operators, was convinced that, to boost revenue, he must broaden his Steel City fast food menus. In 1967, he persuaded the golden arches to let him sell a double patty/triple bun burger that he cleverly coined the "Big Mac." The burger pioneer's business increased 12% and sales in other Mickey D test markets jumped 10%. By 1968, Americans' diets were changed forever.

Ironically, not too many years after Big Mac's debut transformed the fast food industry, Pittsburgh medical professionals conceptualized and created Mr. Yuk stickers. Research had demonstrated that the customary skull and cross-bones image failed to deter children from ingesting household chemicals. In fact, it actually suggested adventure and pirates to its target tots. As a result, the Children's Hospital of Pittsburgh set out to develop and promote a more effective symbol — Mr. Yuk. These no-nonsense, neon-green frowning faces with big tongues sticking out pack a powerful anti-poison message, and have kept children away from all things poisonous.

Today, over 40 million Mr. Yuks are distributed annually throughout the U.S. and Europe. Fortunately, we did not have to order any to describe downtown Pittsburgh's hotel and health club workout options.

MODERATELY EXPENSIVE

GOLD: Renaissance Downtown

107 6th Street, Pittsburgh, PA 15222
(412) 562-1200 • renaissancehotels.com

CARDIO

TREADMILLS: **3 StarTrac**
UPRIGHT BIKE: **1 StarTrac**
RECUMBENT BIKE: **1 StarTrac**
ELLIPTICAL: **2 Sohn**

STRENGTH

MACHINES: **1 Sohn Multi**
DUMBBELLS: **5-50 lbs**

OTHER

HOURS: **24**
COST: **Free**
TV: **Yes**
EXTRAS: **Free Pass to Bally**

As the best place to stay in Pittsburgh, we give Renaissance a hearty pat on the back for creating a 300-room luxurious hotel with a fantastic workout option. In other cities, this Renaissance would likely command an "Expensive" category, but in Pittsburgh its rates are under $200/night. That's fine by us — extravagance at a discount is as rare as a Cleveland Browns Super Bowl appearance (sorry, Drew Carey)! In a renovated 14-story structure originally built in 1906, Renaissance pampers guests with an abundance of 19th Century elegance with 21st Century quality. Twelve foot ceilings, bay windows, premium bedding, CD players and upscale baths create the perfect comfort zone.

Renaissance's lower level fitness center is more than adequate for a quck tune-up. The spacious and attractive room houses an array of good quality endurance and weight equipment. All cardio machines are new and in great condition, but the Sohn ellipticals are not brand favorites. Strength apparatus is even weaker, so those looking for a serious muscle pump should head straight to the hotel's "fitness annex," Bally Total Fitness. Literally 10 paces from Renaissance's front door, complimentary access to this full-service club, which includes an appealing lap pool option, more than compensates for any perceived deficiencies in the Renaissance's on-site room. Just show your hotel room key, sign a waiver and you're in!

SILVER: Hilton

600 Commonwealth Place
Gateway Center
Pittsburgh, PA 15222
(412) 391-4600 • hilton.com

CARDIO

TREADMILLS: **4 LF - 2 old**
UPRIGHT BIKE: **1 LF**
RECUMBENT BIKE: **1 LF**
ELLIPTICAL: **2 LF • 1 Precor**
STEPPER: **2 Tectrix**

STRENGTH

MACHINES: **1 Multi**
DUMBBELLS: **5-40 lbs**

OTHER

HOURS: **24**
COST: **Free**
TV: **Yes**
EXTRAS: **Free Bally Pass**

We recommend the Hilton only if the Renaissance is full or if a significant price advantage exists. Located on the edge of Downtown, Hilton comes up short in every category compared to its cross-town rival. Expect 713 standard rooms with plain colors and patterns, elementary furnishings and basic amenities. A lack of flair and perks is expected and acceptable for budget accommodations, but encountering such conditions here at $180-$200/night is difficult to swallow.

Hilton's saving grace is its above-average workout room. Heavy on cardio and light on weights, Hilton stocks the 4th floor facility with a decent selection of youthful treadmills, bikes and elliptical machines. However, the small assortment of dumbbells and an older multi-gym will limit strength buffs. Fortunately, those looking for a swim or more equipment have an option within a 7-10 minute walk. As it is for Renaissance patrons, access to Bally Fitness is on the house for Hilton guests.

LEAST EXPENSIVE

GOLD: Hampton Inn University Center

3315 Hamlet Street, Pittsburgh, PA 15213
(412) 681-1000 • hamptoninn.com

Located near Carnegie Mellon and the University of Pittsburgh, Hampton is only a 10-minute cab ride from the heart of Downtown, making it a convenient home base for downtown business. In typical Hampton Inn fashion, guests receive reliable rooms and amenities for a reasonable price. Complimentary wireless internet access is offered to all guests, and the Hampton's trademark, free continental breakfast will get your day started right.

Skip the hotel's 3-machine workout room and walk 3 minutes to Three Rivers Fitness, an "everything but a pool" gym. Actually, patrons of this gym also receive access to St. Joseph's pool on the campus of Carlow College, but its hours are limited.

SILVER:

Ramada Plaza Suites

One Bigelow Square
Pittsburgh, PA 15219
(412) 281-5800 • plazasuites.com
Downtown Athletic Club
(412) 560-3488 • dacpittsburgh.com

If only this place were as nice as the pictures! Before arriving, we thought Ramada might be the best place to stay in Pittsburgh, but reality quickly set in during our tour. "Inconsistent" is the description that comes to mind for this 307-room downtown hotel. While the rooms are pleasantly presented with antique furniture, conservative décor, refrigerators and microwaves, some of the common areas are not as cheery. En route to the on-site, independently operated Downtown Athletic Club, the

CARDIO

TREADMILLS: **8 Cybex**
UPRIGHT BIKE: **2 Tectrix**
RECUMBENT BIKE: **5 - LF & others**
ELLIPTICAL: **3 LF • 3 Precor**
STEPPER: **4 StairMaster - 2 old**
ROWING: **2 Concept II**

STRENGTH

FREE WEIGHTS: **Yes**
MACHINES: **Nautilus • LF • Icarian**
DUMBBELLS: **2-100 lbs**

SWIM

SPECS: **Indoor • Not lap**

OTHER

CLASSES: **Yes**
HOURS: M-F **5:30a-9p** • SAT-SUN **8a-9p**
COST: **$5 Ramada • $15 IHRSA • No others**
TV: **Yes**

dark hallways and worn carpeting reminded us of a college dorm. And, although the fitness center's interior is pleasing to the eye, being buzzed in through a locked door and screened by a security camera made us wonder whether the facility is just extra careful or potentially unsafe.

The hodge-podge continues inside the gym, where many of the machines are dated, and bikes are missing pedal straps. Enough diamonds are scattered among the rough to justify inclusion on our list, including good Precor ellipticals, decent StairMaster Free Climbers and newer Life Fitness stack-loaded weight machines.

Lap swimmers will have to look elsewhere, as the Downtown Athletic Club's indoor pool is short and oval in shape. Head to Bally Fitness ($15). In addition, Ramada's website describes the Downtown Athletic Club as "downtown Pittsburgh's largest health club." Au contraire! Bally Fitness is more than twice its size.

Note: Access to the Athletic Club is granted to Ramada guests ($5) and IHRSA club affiliate members ($15, healthclubs.com) only.

BEYOND HOTELS

Bally Total Fitness

119 Sixth Street, Pittsburgh, PA 15222
(412) 391-3300 • ballyfitness.com

CARDIO

TREADMILLS: **LF • StarTrac**
UPRIGHT BIKE: **LF • Cybex**
RECUMBENT BIKE: **LF**
ELLIPTICAL: **Precor • LF**
STEPPER: **StairMaster**
ROWING: **Yes**

STRENGTH

FREE WEIGHTS: **Yes**
HAMMER: **Yes**
MACHINES: **Nautilus • Life Circuit**
DUMBBELLS: **5-110 lbs**

SWIM

GRADE: **B**
SPECS: **3x25yd • Indoor • 81-84°**
TOYS: **Kick • Pull • Clock**

OTHER

CLASSES: **Yes**
HOURS: M-TH **5:30a-10p** • F **5:30a-9p** • SAT **8:30a-5p** • SUN **8:30a-3p**
COST: **Free Renaissance & Hilton • $15 Others**
TV: **Yes**
EXTRAS: **1/18 mile indoor track**

Definitely one of the better Bally clubs we have toured. If you are a Renaissance or Hilton guest, just sign in, show your room key and you are on your way. Others must pay $15/day.

To the right of reception is the club's 3-lane lap pool, divided by bottom stripes and floating lines. Kickboards, pull-buoys and a pace clock are all on deck. Although this aquatic facility is a tad dark, we would have no qualms swimming here for a week, let alone a day.

Just beyond the pool, cardio connoisseurs will appreciate the plentiful supply of the latest in endurance equipment housed in a large, cheerful space. Bally provides a good mix of brands, too. Precor, Life Fitness and StairMaster are well represented. Six televisions provide entertainment in this area, but don't forget your own headphones.

Weights rule the downstairs turf and, like upstairs, a wide variety of equipment is available. While we are not crazy about Bally's stock of 13 older Nautilus stack-loaded weight machines, they get the job done. Most of the other strength equipment is significantly younger.

The showers and locker rooms are convenient for post-workout primping. We were pleasantly surprised by the cleanliness and selection of toiletries (e.g., shampoo, conditioner, hairdryers, mouthwash and gel).

Three Rivers Fitness

3216 5th Avenue, Pittsburgh, PA 15213
(412) 621-8380 • threeriversfitness.com

Located near Carnegie Mellon and the University of Pittsburgh campuses, the first-class Three Rivers Fitness opened in 2003. Although small in size, the club packs a whopping punch of equipment with 2 floors full of state-of-the-art Life Fitness strength and cardio machines. Other than 5 Hammer Strength free weight machines, all apparatus comes only in the Life Fitness flavor. If you need a Precor elliptical or Cybex bike, you're out of luck. But Life Fitness makes a great product, so your disappointment should be short lived.

CARDIO

TREADMILLS: **LF**
UPRIGHT BIKE: **LF**
RECUMBENT BIKE: **LF**
ELLIPTICAL: **LF**
STEPPER: **LF**

STRENGTH

FREE WEIGHTS: **Yes**
HAMMER: **Yes**
MACHINES: **LF**
DUMBBELLS: **5-100 lbs**

OTHER

CLASSES: **Yes**
HOURS: M-TH **5:30a-10p** • F **5:30a-9p** • SAT **8a-6p** • SUN **10a-5p**
COST: **Free Hampton • $10 Others**
TV: **Yes**
EXTRAS: **Access to Carlow College Pool**

Although Three Rivers has no swim option, the club extends privileges to the St. Joseph pool on the Carlow College campus. It's a bit of a hassle, but a nearby alternative nonetheless. First, you must obtain a pool pass from Three Rivers. Then, walk 5 minutes to the pool entrance in St. Joseph Hall. The pool has limited hours and was closed at the time of our visit, so we were unable to view it. However, a virtual tour of the pool is online at ecampustours.com. Just type in Carlow College and look for the St. Joe's pool link. You will see what looks to be a 20-yardish pool divided by 3 lanes without floating lines. It's not a great option, but it will satisfy swimmers in a pinch.

RUNNING ROUTES

Point State Park

Point State Park is downtown runners' best bet. The Park is located where the Allegheny, Monongahela and Ohio Rivers meet at Pittsburgh's Golden Triangle. Unfortunately, the 36-acre park does not sport much mileage, but there is a paved path and the views are tremendous. For an additional 3 to 5 miles, hook into the Eliza Furnace Path (aka Jail Trail), part of Three Rivers Trail. The trailhead is located behind the PNC building at First Ave. and Grant Street, just south of Point State Park along the Monongahela River.

Schenley Park

Those bunking near Carnegie Mellon and the University of Pittsburgh have far superior running options. Within a mile is Schenley Park, a 456-acre expanse that sports a 5-mile course and, for speedsters, a 400-meter oval track. Runners and cyclists gravitate to Schenley Drive, the main thoroughfare that runs through the middle of this hilly and scenic park.

Frick Park

If you continue east from Schenley, you will reach the 480-acre Frick Park, which serves up additional trails through its wooded nature preserve. Schenley Drive will hook into Forbes Avenue, which runs straight into this beautiful and solitary retreat. It is roughly a mile between the two parks.

PORTLAND, OREGON

As the business and tourist hub of the most mispronounced state in the country, Portland, (Or-ih-gun, not Or-ih-gahn) occupies some of the most beautiful territory in the U.S. It is set among towering pine and fir trees, the Willamette and Columbia Rivers, and Mts. Hood, Jefferson and St. Helens. Flying over this city on a sunny day is simply awesome.

Oregonians are a unique breed — strong in their beliefs, confident in their abilities and unabashed in their fun. Beavers and Ducks fight the in-state rivalries, and Portland is the state's largest "dam" and "pond."

Downtown Portland offers visitors an array of attractions, including funky retail boutiques, large department stores, quaint cafés, remarkable restaurants and beautiful scenery. Shoppers appreciate Oregon's lack of sales tax, but travelers fueling the rental car must pay full-service prices. As if caught in a time warp with no self-service option, gas station attendants pump the premium and take your cash (it creates jobs).

Considering our high opinion of the Rose City, and knowing that headquartered athletic giants Nike and Adidas significantly contribute to this community's active lifestyle, we were disappointed by the downtown lodging and workout options. After visiting many antiquated hotel fitness centers, we wondered whether we'd arrived via 21st Century Boeing 737 or the Oregon Trail.

Of course, we unearthed a few worthy options. But, like Oregon politicians, downtown Portland visitors are forced to make tradeoffs. Before booking a hotel, you must decide which is more important: lodging within steps of the best downtown workout option OR having the shopping district just outside your hotel entrance. Read on — you'll see that you cannot have your duck and eat it, too.

Note: All desirable hotel options fall into the Moderate and Least Expensive price categories.

35 Locations Reviewed

MODERATELY EXPENSIVE

GOLD: RiverPlace Hotel

1510 SW Harbor Way, Portland, OR 97201
(503) 228-3233 • riverplacehotel.com

RiverPlace is a charming and elegant accommodation located along the western bank of the Willamette River with its popular Riverwalk running path. A boutique hotel with only 84 guest quarters, RiverPlace imparts a European flavor to colorfully presented rooms, premium bedding and 24-hour room service. Staying here will make you feel like a visitor in a friend's home.

This winning accommodation has no on-site workout option. However, if you reserve your room through the hotel's reservation department, your "package" should include free passes to the RiverPlace Athletic Club — a full-service health center and lap pool 3 minutes walk away. If you book through an online source, you may miss the complimentary workout perk, but RiverPlace will sell you a discount pass for $8 (normally $15).

RiverPlace's tradeoff is its 1-1.5 mile distance to Downtown's shopping and restaurants. But we think the scales tip in this property's favor with its peaceful setting, upscale accommodations and fantastic fitness benefits.

SILVER: 5th Avenue Suites

506 SW Washington, Portland, OR 97204
(503) 222-0001 • 5thavenuesuites.com

CARDIO

TREADMILLS: **2 LF - old**
UPRIGHT BIKE: **1 LF**
RECUMBENT BIKE: **1 LF**
ELLIPTICAL: **1 LF**
STEPPER: **2 Tectrix**
ROWING: **1 Concept II**

STRENGTH

MACHINES: **1 Multi**
DUMBBELLS: **10-40 lbs**

OTHER

HOURS: **24**
COST: **Free**
TV: **Yes**
EXTRAS: **$10 Pass to Bally**

As the most upscale hotel in Portland's vibrant shopping district, 5th Avenue Suites is short on fitness equipment but tall on understated elegance and sophisticated service. The 221 rooms are posh — Portland style. Instead of over-the-top, trendy décor, guests are assuaged by soft yellow and cream tones, premium linens and padded headboards.

Creativity abounds in this Kimpton lodge, and we loved it. Complimentary yoga baskets equipped with a mat, block and strap are available upon request, and guests can tune into free yoga instruction on the TV. Gratis wine tastings are held each evening around the warm glow of the lobby fireplace. Easels, paints and brushes are on hand during this happy hour. Some visitors' creations even decorate the hotel walls.

An Aveda Spa offering skin and body care services is located off the lobby and is a nice touch. But 5th Avenue's creativity plunges dramatically in its mediocre 9th floor fitness center, foiling its contention for Gold. Expect fair condition cardio equipment, an awkward multi-gym and a simple set of dumbbells. Guests trade fitness quality for upscale fun.

5th Avenue acknowledges its sub-par fitness offering and provides guests $10/day passes to Bally Fitness, 5 minutes away on foot. Swimmers must commute a little farther to 24 Hour Fitness (1 mile) or RiverPlace Athletic Club (3/4 mile), as Bally Fitness has no lap pool.

SILVER: Westin Portland

750 Southwest Alder Street, Portland, OR 97205
(503)294-9000 • westin.com

Westin Portland sits in the heart of urban downtown. The upscale accommodation is a wonderful blend of classical character with modern style and is convenient to the city's shopping boutiques and restaurants.

All 205 rooms welcome guests with a comforting vibe. Westin's trademark Heavenly beds are always a welcome sight, with their puffy white comforters and high thread count sheets. Marble baths are also standard here, along with separate showers and tubs. Some rooms have a less desirable "colonial" color palette with blue carpeting, but others are more chic and attractively toned. 24 hour room service, high speed internet access (fee applies) and CD players are additional welcome amenities.

CARDIO
TREADMILLS: **3 LF**
UPRIGHT BIKE: **1 LF**
ELLIPTICAL: **1 LF**
STEPPER: **1 LF**

STRENGTH
DUMBBELLS: **5-50 lbs**

OTHER
HOURS: **24/7**
COST: **Free**
TV: **Yes**

All Westins are transforming their gyms into "Westin Workout Centers Powered by Reebok," and Portland's version has already been completed. That means white walls, a black mat floor, and top-of-the-line Life Fitness cardio equipment. The room has one window for some natural light to peek inside, which is always preferred. But the space is still relatively small and holds only a half dozen cardio machines in total. That could mean having to wait for your favorite piece of equipment. Strength sessions here are limited somewhat by a small selection of weight apparatus. Nevertheless, Westin's hotel gym is still one of the better options in downtown Portland.

Lap swimmers should head to Riverplace and joggers should consider our online custom routes with maps included — see the "work out" tab.

LEAST EXPENSIVE

GOLD: Four Points Downtown

50 SW Morrison, Portland, OR 97204
(503) 221-0711 • fourpoints.com/portlanddowntown

The least expensive hotel choice near Portland's appealing shopping district, Four Points' exterior resembles an upscale motor lodge

— if there is such a thing. The hotel's interior is without the trappings of its more lavish competitors, so expect simple décor, light wood furniture and basic amenities inside all 140 rooms. Freebies include high-speed internet access, bottled water and newspapers — not bad tradeoffs for a room that should run less than $110/night.

Four Points has a small gym on-site, but it does provide one additional comp — free passes to the across-the-street Bally Fitness. This health club will not blow you away, but it will work you out when you're visiting Portland. Swimmers, 24 Hour Fitness and RiverPlace Athletic Center are your only lap options.

SILVER: **Days Inn** City Center

1414 SW Sixth Avenue, Portland, OR, 97201
(503) 221-1611 • daysinn.com

As the least expensive hotel on our list, Days provides affordable accommodations about a mile from Downtown's shopping and entertainment hub. Its best feature, and the primary reason for our recommendation, is its next-door location to an above-par 24 Hour Fitness. Days' 173 guest quarters are motel-esqe in appearance, furnished with the basics — bed, desk and armchair. However, the rooms' doors open into interior corridors, not to the outside. Parking is on-site, and room service is available.

Not only is 24 Hour Fitness next door, but Days' guests receive complimentary access to all its exercise fun. And, since the club has a desirable lap pool, swimmers can dive in.

BEYOND HOTELS

RiverPlace Athletic Club

0150 SW Montgomery, Portland, OR 97201
(503) 221-1212 • therac.com

Complimentary to guests booking directly with the RiverPlace Hotel and $15/day for guests of other downtown hotels (with room key), this full-service health club caters to Portland area families. Despite a somewhat disorganized equipment layout and some general sprucing needs (downstairs weight room and locker rooms), fitness fans will find everything they require for a complete and satisfying workout.

The main cardio area sits behind a concrete wall adjacent to the basketball courts. The aesthetics are not great, but we cannot complain about the equipment. Six good treads, 4 desirable 4400 series StairMaster steppers, and several exceptional Precor ellipticals exemplify the first-class selection. A separate endurance space above the café contains high-quality bikes and a few Keiser pressurized strength machines (not favorites).

Luckily, strength sessions are aided by a large assortment of sound apparatus in the club's basement, including plenty of free weights, a wide range of dumbbells and several brands of effective stack-loaded weight stations. Noticeably absent, however, are any Hammer Strength free weight machines.

Swimmers, break out your Speedos for this impressive 25-yard water box. Floating lines and bottom stripes divide its 5 lanes, and every toy necessary for workout variety is on deck. A Masters group swims here Monday through Thursday (contact club for specific times), so those looking to accrue yardage while meeting a few locals can join in the fun.

CARDIO

TREADMILLS: **Precor**
UPRIGHT BIKE: **Precor**
RECUMBENT BIKE: **Precor**
ELLIPTICAL: **Precor**
STEPPER: **Precor • StairMaster • Stepmill**
ROWING: **Concept II**
OTHER: **NordicTrack**

STRENGTH

FREE WEIGHTS: **Yes**
MACHINES: **Cybex • Paramount • Keiser Pressure**
DUMBBELLS: **3-100 lbs**

SWIM

GRADE: **B**
SPECS: **5x25yd • Indoor • 82°**
TOYS: **Kick • Pull • Fins**
MASTERS: **Yes**

OTHER

CLASSES: **Yes**
HOURS: M-F **4:30a-10p** • SAT **7a-8p** • SUN **8a-8p**
COST: **Free w/RiverPlace direct book • $15 Other hotels & IHRSA • No others**
TV: **Yes**
EXTRAS: **1/16 mile indoor track • Basketball • Cafe**

24 Hour Fitness Sport

1407 SW 4th Avenue, Portland, OR 97201
(503) 224-2233 • 24hourfitness.com

A modern health club with a techno vibe, this 24 Hour Fitness is our favorite gym in the downtown area. Unfortunately, its loca-

CARDIO

TREADMILLS: **Precor • StarTrac**
UPRIGHT BIKE: **LF • Cybex**
RECUMBENT BIKE: **LF • Cybex**
ELLIPTICAL: **LF • Precor**
STEPPER: **Cybex • Reebok • Stepmill**
ROWING: **Concept II**

STRENGTH

FREE WEIGHTS: **Yes**
HAMMER: **Yes**
MACHINES: **Cybex • Paramount • BodyMaster**
DUMBBELLS: **5-120 lbs**

SWIM

GRADE: **B-**
SPECS: **2x25m • Indoor • 79-82°**
TOYS: **Kick • Clock**

OTHER

CLASSES: **Yes**
HOURS: M-F **~ 24** • SAT **6a-9p** • SUN **6a-8p**
COST: **Free-Days Inn • $10 IHRSA • $15 Others**
TV: **Yes**

tion is somewhat inconvenient to every hotel except the Days Inn. But the place is loaded with the latest and greatest exercise equipment, and its lap pool is clean, inviting and seldom crowded.

We give 24 the edge over RiverPlace Athletic Club because it carries a greater quantity of cutting-edge equipment in a more workout-friendly atmosphere. Athletic-minded travelers can anticipate too many aerobic machines to count (e.g., ~ 21 treadmills) and a ton of daily classes to enjoy. We know 15 bucks is a steep price to pay for an hour or two of sweating ($10 IHRSA), but 24's top-dog facility delivers an exceptional fitness experience.

At 25 meters, swimmers get a little extra length over RiverPlace's 25-yard lapper, but the only toys on deck are kickboards. A pace clock is here for interval training as well.

If you are driving, metered parking is available on the roads or in the self-park garage across the street ($1/hr). No car? Consider a cab (it's 1 mile from 5th Ave. Suites and 3/4 mile from Four Points).

Bally Total Fitness Yamhill

110 SW Yamhill Street
Portland, OR 97024
(503) 223-0088 • ballyfitness.com

CARDIO

TREADMILLS: **LF**
UPRIGHT BIKE: **LF**
RECUMBENT BIKE: **LF**
ELLIPTICAL: **LF**
STEPPER: **StairMaster**
ROWING: **Concept II**

STRENGTH

FREE WEIGHTS: **Yes**
HAMMER: **Yes**
MACHINES: **LF • Icarian • Magnum • Hammer**
DUMBBELLS: **3-130 lbs**

OTHER

CLASSES: **Yes**
HOURS: M-TH **5a-10p** • F **5a-9p** • SAT-SUN **7a-7p**
COST: **Free Four Points • $10 Others**
TV: **Yes**

This Bally Fitness is one of only 2 health clubs in the entire country that refused to let us in for a look. We offered to sign their waiver and promised not to bother anyone, but the answer was a resounding no!

Setting aside our egos, we still recommend it because, other than handing over your free pass or cash, you likely will not have any contact with the foolish personnel. And complimentary admission to a conveniently located club is always welcome (e.g., Four Points, $10 all others).

We peeked through the windows, followed up with several investigative calls and determined that this club is like most of its Bally brethren — far from a workout utopia. Older cardio machines (e.g., StairMaster 4000PT) are mixed with new (e.g., Life Fitness 9500 series treads and bikes), and the weight selection is plentiful. No pool is on-site. Based on our research, this is a very average Bally club, so expect mediocre quality.

RUNNING ROUTES

Oregon is green for a reason... it rains an awful lot. The upside is that Portland's frequent drizzly days are rarely too cold for a run. Pack the winter rain gear, and you will be set to stride in the Rose City. On a more positive note, summers here are pleasant and warm, and the rain often subsides for days. With its riverfront paths, parks and hills, no matter your preferred running surface, Portland's got you covered!

Flat

All downtown hotels are conveniently located to flat mileage along the Willamette River. Heading north or south, you can't go wrong. A roughly 3+ mile loop is easily created using the Hawthorne (south) and Steel (north) Bridges as your River crossing points.

On the other side of the river, you will be greeted by the Eastside Esplanade, a 1.5 mile paved path that runs between the two bridges. Need more miles? No problem. For 9+ miles, stay on the Westside and run south to Sellwood Bridge (roughly 3/4 mile south of the 30-acre Willamette Park). Cross over, head north and re-cross at the Steel Bridge. It is not a perfect, traffic-free corridor, but it's easy to navigate, scenic and flat.

Track

A little over a mile southwest of Downtown's shopping hub is Duniway Park and its 9 lane, 400-meter state-of-the-art track. With a surface made largely from recycled rubber (mostly donated by Nike), the mystery of running shoe heaven is solved. If you are completing your riverside circuit, head west and you will find the park at SW 4th and Sheridan (roughly between the Hawthorne and Ross Island Bridges). There is even a large digital clock to time your laps!

Hills

Terwilliger Boulevard's wide bike lane is not only great for testing your hill endurance, it provides a runner-friendly route to the beautiful, 645-acre Tryon Creek Park (6 miles) and Lake Oswego. You can pick up the path in Duniway Park and, along the way, you will be treated to amazing mountain and skyline views... assuming it is not raining.

Trails

A 5-10 minute drive over to trendy NW Portland brings you to 2 heavily forested running trails that are part of Forest Park — over 5,000 wooded acres!

The 11+ mile Leif Erikson Trail (NW Thurman) and the 25+ mile Wildwood Trail (NW 23rd) are Portland distance runners' favorites. The Leif Erikson route is an all-weather, relatively flat road. Both trails have mile markers every quarter-mile. We recommend carrying water.

Sacramento

35 Locations Reviewed

SACRAMENTO, CALIFORNIA

Known as the "River City" for its thousand miles of flowing waterways, Sacramento nearly lost its designation as California's capital soon after it was so named in 1854. Torrential winter rains in the late 1850s caused overflowing rivers to deluge the City, wreaking havoc on its citizens and businesses. Even after the rivers crawled back to their beds, there was no relief. Sacramento became an underwater realm plagued by fatal cholera outbreaks bred by the bacteria-infested standing water.

With the City's survival in question, most Californians agreed that Sacramento was a terrible choice for the state's capital and organized a significant movement to relocate it 90 miles east in the rapidly growing and flood-resistant city of San Francisco. In an effort to hold on to power, Sacramento's leaders proposed erecting 10-foot high brick walls along all streets and raising the City above the flood line, in effect reconstructing the entire City on top of a "basement." Former building front doors would now open into brick walls and prior second floors would become first floors.

When the "taller" city plan was finally completed 13 years later, it left behind an underground world of tunnels and catacombs that harbored Sacramento's sordid side. Chinese opium dens, gambling outlets, prostitution rings and outlaws are all rumored to have flourished in the capital's dark underbelly. Even today some of these passageways remain and are said to be haunted by spirits from the underground.

So, for those of you in search of a running partner during your travels, Sacramento appears to have a limitless number of potential training buddies. We understand that the immortals can be a little cranky in the morning, however, so you might want to bring them a hot cup of joe.

EXPENSIVE

GOLD: Hyatt Regency Downtown

1209 L Street, Sacramento, CA 95814
(916) 443-1234 • sacramento.hyatt.com

CARDIO

TREADMILLS: **2 LF**
UPRIGHT BIKE: **1 LF**
RECUMBENT BIKE: **2 LF**
ELLIPTICAL: **2 LF • 2 Precor • 2 Reebok**
STEPPER: **1 LifeStep**

STRENGTH

MACHINES: **6 Paramount**
DUMBBELLS: **5-50 lbs**

SWIM

SPECS: **Outdoor • Not lap**

OTHER

HOURS: **5a-10p**
COST: **Free**
TV: **Yes**
EXTRAS: **$15 Access Capital Ath. Club**

As the host hotel for NBA teams in town to challenge the Sacramento Kings (Denver Nuggets were checking in during our tour), the Hyatt Regency really is a traveling athlete hotel. Hyatt describes its 500 plus room lodging option as "Mediterranean-styled," but it did not give us that impression. No matter, the rooms and common areas are upscale, with contemporary furnishings, marble floors and checkerboard bed comforters. We are especially fond of the Hyatt's location — across the street from scenic Capitol Park (too small for a run), across from the Capitol building and a 2-minute stroll from the Sacramento Convention Center.

To access Hyatt's recently renovated fitness center, guests must walk outside the hotel and enter through a door on the street using their room key. The equipment inside is the latest and greatest in workout apparatus from Life Fitness. Most machines have personal television screens built in, so you can be distracted during your sweat. Adequate strength options are also on site, but if you desire a true health club experience, consider the 7-minute hike and $15/day investment for the Capital Athletic Club ($10/day if you belong to an IHRSA club at home).

SILVER: Sheraton Grand

1230 J Street
Sacramento, CA 95814
(916) 447-1700
sheraton.com/sacramento

CARDIO

TREADMILLS: **4 StarTrac - old**
UPRIGHT BIKE: **2 StarTrac**
RECUMBENT BIKE: **2 StarTrac**
STEPPER: **2 StarTrac**

STRENGTH

MACHINES: **9 Paramount**
DUMBBELLS: **5-50 lbs**

SWIM

SPECS: **Outdoor • Not lap**

OTHER

HOURS: **24**
COST: **Free**
TV: **Yes**

Within a block of the Hyatt and directly across from the Sacramento Convention Center, Sheraton is a modern luxury high-rise hotel suited to business and leisure travelers. The guest rooms impart a Scandinavian feel, with light-toned wood, gray and cream décor and ergonomic furniture. Pet lovers will appreciate the royal treatment afforded to their four-legged friends. Canine companions are indulged with plush dog sleepers, kibble and water saucers and temporary I.D. tags listing the hotel's "411."

Unfortunately, Sheraton's in-house workout center is also for the dogs. Though we are being a bit facetious, the 4th floor gym is certainly not impressive. Muscle pumpers make out the best, with the facility's 9 new Paramount weight machines and good set of dumbbells. Cardio buffs may want to take to the outdoors, as the StarTrac equipment is adequate for a light sweat session only. Since guests here are not granted access to the Capital Athletic Club (unless your home gym is a member of IHRSA, e.g., 24 Hour Fitness), those intent on a real workout can walk 15 minutes to 24 Hour Fitness. Fifteen bucks will get you in that door.

Swimmers note: The Sheraton does not have a pool. If you belong to an IHRSA club, go to Capital. If not, the next closest option is 24 Hour Fitness, but the pool is only ~20 yards. A third option is driving 10 minutes to the Central Family YMCA for a 6-lane, 25-yard alternative.

MODERATELY EXPENSIVE

GOLD: **Embassy Suites Riverfront**

100 Capitol Mall, Sacramento, CA 95814
(916) 326-5000 • emabassysuites.com

On the banks of the Sacramento River, Embassy provides guests with its typical two-room quarters and free, made-to-order breakfasts. Better suited for the leisure traveler, the hotel's best feature is its proximity to the quaint shops and restaurants on the touristy Old Sacramento Promenade. T-shirt, knickknack and coffee retailers line the wooden sidewalks and brick-inlay streets of this old-west themed district. Although this is a favorable location for Sacramento shoppers, business travelers and those with a penchant for exercise will be better served by the other hotels on our list.

Embassy's in house fitness room stocks older equipment useful only as a last resort. But the hotel's relative isolation may compel guests to use the sub-par facility, since the nearest gym (24 Hour Fitness, $15) is a mile and a 15-minute walk away — depending on your stride.

LEAST EXPENSIVE

GOLD: **Holiday Inn Express Downtown**

728 16th Street, Sacramento, CA 95814
(916) 444-4436 • hiexpress.com

Your lungs and sinuses will thank you for staying at this 100% smoke-free hotel. Located next to the Clarion, Holiday Inn Express sits 4 blocks from the convention center, 5 blocks from the Capitol, and it's a 15-minute walk to 24 Hour Fitness. With marble flooring and upscale wood paneling, the lobby of this Express looks more like a Westin than a budget accommodation. After checking in, relax and let the freebies begin! The hotel showers guests with free parking, free local calls, free daily newspaper and free continental breakfasts.

However, working out in the hotel's gym might give you a free headache. Management crammed four cheap cardio machines into a "Napoleonic" room that faces a charming parking lot. Although 24 Hour Fitness is not exactly close, its relative proximity makes it the best option for athletic guests. Bring $15 and your room key.

Swimmers, read our note in Sheraton's description, as you face the same issues.

SILVER: Clarion Hotel Mansion Inn

700 16th Street, Sacramento, CA 95814
(916) 444-8000 • clarionhotel.com

Several online travel websites attest that Clarion provides guests with a "complimentary pass to a nearby health club." We are not sure where these booking services get their information, but we can tell you for certain that this is not the case. Clarion patrons are advised to take the 15-minute hike to 24 Hour Fitness and pay the $15/day access fee for their sweat.

Clarion is less expensive than the neighboring Holiday Inn Express, but Express' accommodations are nicer, and the freebies make up most of the room rate disparity.

We have not mentioned Clarion's own exercise room because it does not exist. Guests are pointed across the parking lot to Express' mini-gym, and if you've read that hotel's description, you already know how we feel about it, so go to 24 Hour Fitness.

BEYOND HOTELS

The Capital Athletic Club

1515 8th Street, Sacramento, CA 95814
(916) 442-3927 • capitalac.com

The best private health club in Sacramento, Capital maintains its exclusivity by restricting hotel guest access to only those staying at the Hyatt. Patrons of all other hotels must look elsewhere for their workout, unless their home health club belongs to IHRSA. For example, 24 Hour Fitness is a part of this organization, but we suggest you contact your gym directly to confirm its status, or look online at healthclubs.com.

Inside Capital's 52,000 square foot facility, newer cardio and weight equipment is arranged in several areas. Our favorite is the weight space with its arched passageway and vaulted ceiling that reminded us of a chapel. All high-end brands are represented, so expect to find equipment that will tickle your fancy.

Swimmers, Capital is also home to the best lap pool in town. A Masters team works out here daily, and the pool's 4 lanes are marked by floating lines and bottom stripes. Other than the Y, which is 3 to 4 miles from Downtown, no other health club or hotel possesses a 25-yard or longer lapper.

CARDIO

TREADMILLS: **Trackmaster**
UPRIGHT BIKE: **LF • Scifit**
RECUMBENT BIKE: **Reebok • LF - old**
ELLIPTICAL: **Reebok • Precor • LF**
STEPPER: **StairMaster**
ROWING: **Concept II**
OTHER: **Gravitron • XC Ski**

STRENGTH

FREE WEIGHTS: **Yes**
HAMMER: **Yes**
MACHINES: **BodyMaster • Nautilus**
DUMBBELLS: **3-110 lbs**

SWIM

GRADE: **B**
SPECS: **4x25yd • Outdoor • 82°**
TOYS: **Kick • Pull • Fins • Clock**
MASTERS: **Yes**

OTHER

CLASSES: **Yes**
HOURS: M-F **5:30a-10p** • SAT **8a-6p** • SUN **Closed**
COST: **$15 Hyatt • $10 IHRSA**
TV: **Yes**
EXTRAS: **Basketball • Racquetball**

24 Hour Fitness Sport

1020 7th Street, Sacramento, CA 95814
(916) 658-1626 • 24hourfitness.com

A newer site for this rapidly growing chain, the Sacramento version offers 24's standard fare of high-end, wide-ranging equipment that will not disappoint. The downside for this attractive club is its unfriendly location. Sacramento's hotels are clustered in two areas: around the Capitol and near Old Sacramento's Promenade. Unfortunately, 24 Hour sits in between, so hotel-goers are faced with long walks in either direction (1 mile from Embassy, 1/2-mile-ish from the Capitol).

Swimmers, we thought 24's pool would be a good option for you until we paced it off at 20 yards, saw it divided by a rope and found no toys on deck. With the $15 fee and long walk, wet ones deserve better.

CARDIO

TREADMILLS: **LF • StarTrac**
UPRIGHT BIKE: **LF**
RECUMBENT BIKE: **LF**
ELLIPTICAL: **LF • Precor**
STEPPER: **StairMaster • Stepmill**
ROWING: **Yes**

STRENGTH

FREE WEIGHTS: **Yes**
HAMMER: **Yes**
MACHINES: **LF • Cybex • BodyMaster**
DUMBBELLS: **5-150 lbs**

SWIM

GRADE: **C**
SPECS: **2x20yd • Indoor • 83°**

OTHER

CLASSES: **Yes**
HOURS: **24**
COST: **$15**
TV: **Yes**

Central Family YMCA

2021 W Street, Sacramento, CA 95818
(916) 452-9622 • sacymca.org/central_branch.htm

SWIM

GRADE: **C+**
SPECS: **6x25yd • Indoor • 83º**
TOYS: **Kick • Pull • Clock**

OTHER

HOURS: M-TH **5:30a-10p** • F **5:30a-8p** • SAT **8a-6p** • SUN **12-6p**
COST: **$10**

Located about 3 to 4 miles from most hotels, we recommend this mediocre Y for swimmers exclusively. Holding the only 25-yard pool in town besides Capital Athletic Club, Y's slightly above-average swim alternative has a large warehouse feel with its bright white tones and 30-foot ceiling. The 6 lanes are not always set up for lap swimming but, unless you are staying at the Hyatt or come from an IHRSA Club, this is your only regulation length swim option in downtown Sacramento.

RUNNING ROUTES

You can always run the local Downtown streets, but those with wheels should drive 6 miles east to the American River Parkway, home of 31 miles of running bliss. We understand mileage markers and water stops are on the route.

Salt Lake City

SALT LAKE CITY, UTAH

Skiers flock to Salt Lake City seeking its awesome peaks and powder, and many associate Utah's capital with the 2002 Olympic Games. However, less familiar and often misconstrued are the City's unique laws, customs and attributes. To test your knowledge of this friendly mountain town, take our true or false quiz, which will also help set the record straight — on a few issues at least:

1. **True or False:** The term "Mormon"refers to members of The Church of Jesus Christ of Latter Day Saints.
2. **True or False:** Polygamy is accepted by the Mormon religion.
3. **True or False:** Utah has the highest literacy rate and youngest population in the nation.
4. **True or False:** Because drinking alcohol is frowned upon by SLC's large religious population, private clubs were established to sell the hard stuff. Visitors wishing to tip a toddy can do so only at such establishments — and only after purchasing temporary membership.
5. **True or False:** The Great Salt Lake has twice the salt content of an ocean.
6. **True or False:** The Great Salt Lake is a popular fishing spot and underwater habitat for a variety of saltwater creatures.
7. **True or False:** The people of Salt Lake City consume more Jell-O per capita than any other city in the U.S.
8. **True or False:** Salt Lake City provides desirable hotels and health clubs for athletic-minded travelers.

Answers: 1. T; 2. F, polygamy has been denounced by the church's leadership; 3. T; 4. F, though visitors will find hard liquor served only in private clubs, these establishments were formed to get around the state's ban on smoking in public places. Smoking is also only permitted in "private" clubs. 5. T; 6. F, brine shrimp are the only creatures that can survive the Lake's harsh conditions; 7. T; 8. Very true!

28 Locations Reviewed

EXPENSIVE

GOLD: The Grand America Hotel

555 South Main Street, Salt Lake City, UT 84111
(801) 258-6000 • grandamerica.com

CARDIO

TREADMILLS: **8 StarTrac**
UPRIGHT BIKE: **2 StarTrac**
RECUMBENT BIKE: **3 StarTrac**
ELLIPTICAL: **2 Reebok**
STEPPER: **2 Cybex**

STRENGTH

MACHINES: **9 Cybex**
DUMBBELLS: **3-60 lbs**

SWIM

SPECS: **Indoor/Outdoor • Not lap**

OTHER

CLASSES: **Yes**
HOURS: **6a-10p**
COST: **$10**
TV: **Yes**

Those flush with funds and in search of the City's most luxurious hotel need look no further — the Grand is for you. Just a half-mile south of Downtown's hub, you cannot miss this towering European palace stretching across an entire block.

Opened in 2001, this hotel dazzles. Oak paneled hallways, overstuffed furniture, premium bedding, marble bathrooms, balconies and antique-style furnishings outfit all 775 pastel-colored quarters. The Grand showers guests with perks, including an afternoon tea and pastry service, 24 hour in-room dining, free local calls, complimentary high-speed internet access and free airport shuttle service. And, to top it all off, Grand is a complete non-smoking hotel — so puffers must part with their packs.

One perk Grand left off the list is free access to its 3rd floor spa and fitness center. Before touching a treadmill, exercisers must pay the $10/day sweat tax — vexing when room rates are north of $200/night. After lightening your wallet, head downstairs to Grand's fitness room. It's an expansive area where impressive new cardio and strength machines are well organized. Endurance enthusiasts can distract themselves with personal plasma television screens and, although free weights are AWOL, enough stack-loaded weight stations and dumbbells are here for a full body muscle pump.

Swimmers must be content with paddling about, as neither of Grand's pools is lap-style and there's no lapper within easy commuting distance.

MODERATELY EXPENSIVE

GOLD: Marriott City Center

220 South State Street, Salt Lake City, UT 84111
(801) 961-8700 • marriott.com

The Marriott City Center may not be as decadent as Grand America, but it occupies more centrally located real estate, costs less and provides the best hotel workout room in Salt Lake City.

In the heart of Downtown, this Marriott's 359 rooms are modern and equipped with down comforters, pillow top mattresses and complimentary high-speed internet access. Our recent stay was more than comfortable.

Not only does Marriott's exercise option blow away its rivals, but it houses one of the best hotel gyms in the Mountain Time zone. Perched on the 2nd floor overlooking State Street through floor-to-ceiling glass windows, fitness fiends will feast on the ample cardio and strength equipment comfortably distributed across the "L" shaped room. This hotel's owner and the current general manager are both fitness enthusiasts, and it shows in their open all night gym. We especially appreciate the abundance of free weight equipment, which hotels rarely stock. Though it would be nice to see more than one upright bike and step machine, it is easy to let this small deficit slide since all other apparatus is truly state-of-the-art.

CARDIO

TREADMILLS: **4 Precor**
UPRIGHT BIKE: **1 Precor**
RECUMBENT BIKE: **2 Precor**
ELLIPTICAL: **3 Precor**
STEPPER: **1 Precor**

STRENGTH

FREE WEIGHTS: **Yes**
MACHINES: **9 Icarian**
DUMBBELLS: **5-50 lbs**

SWIM

SPECS: **Indoor • Not lap**

OTHER

HOURS: **24**
COST: **Free**
TV: **Yes**

Swimmers, Marriott has no lap pool, and there's no good alternative in the area.

Finally, do not confuse this preferred Marriott with its sister hotel, the Marriott Salt Lake City Downtown. The quality differences are huge despite a similar name and pricing.

SILVER: Hilton City Center

255 South West Temple, Salt Lake City, UT 84101
(801) 328-2000 • hilton.com

Hilton's central downtown location, adjacent to the Salt Palace Convention Center, is also convenient to other Salt Lake City attractions, including Temple Square, the Delta Center and, most importantly, to our off-site workout options! A distant second to the Marriott City Center, Hilton's standard accommodations are forgettable. Expect the basic bed, desk and armoire — comfortable but nothing special.

Though the guest rooms garner no style awards, management deserves kudos for its generous investment in the fitness center. Large windows surround the 2nd story black-floored room located next to Hilton's pool. Thankfully, the glass walls separating the exercise area from the recreational water box keep out chlorinated air and humidity. Sweat-aholics will be pleased to find a decent mix of newer cardio and strength machines. Treadmills, bikes and stack-loaded weight machines are

CARDIO

TREADMILLS: **4 StarTrac**
UPRIGHT BIKE: **2 LF**
RECUMBENT BIKE: **2 StarTrac**
ELLIPTICAL: **1 StarTrac**
STEPPER: **1 Tectrix - old**

STRENGTH

MACHINES: **6 Paramount**
DUMBBELLS: **3-30 lbs**

SWIM

SPECS: **Indoor • Not lap**

OTHER

HOURS: **5a-11p**
COST: **Free**
TV: **Yes**

the best prospects. All apparatus, other than the stepper, are in good condition.

Swimmers have no lapper available in the downtown area.

Athletic-minded travelers might like to sample several of Salt Lake's clubs. Plaza Club and SportsMall/Metro are within a 10-minute stroll.

SILVER: **Hotel Monaco**

15 West 200 South, Salt Lake City, UT 84101
801-595-0000 • Monaco-saltlakecity.com

CARDIO

TREADMILLS: **2 LF**
UPRIGHT BIKE: **2 LF**
RECUMBENT BIKE: **2 LF**
ELLIPTICAL: **2 Precor**
STEPPER: **1 StairMaster**

STRENGTH

DUMBBELLS: **5-40 lbs**

OTHER

HOURS: **24/7**
COST: **Free**
TV: **Yes**
EXTRAS: **$10 to SportsMall**

If you're like us, you are always on the hunt for unique accommodations when away from home. Standard business hotels are functional, but boring. Hotel Monaco Salt Lake City is one of those properties that just makes us smile.

From the street, this 14-story edifice resembles yet another historic, Victorian-esque hotel. Once inside, travelers quickly realize that looks can be deceiving. This is no stodgy, cookie-cutter accommodation. Gone are the traditional style and classic furnishings of so many hotels, replaced by vibrant colors, whimsical décor, and charming splashes of character. Unique hotel services such as complimentary chair massages and glasses of wine during evening social hours, a pet friendly policy welcoming dogs/cats of all sizes (yes, even your Great Dane can check-in), and "goldfish rental" for those traveling without a four-legged friend but desiring a roommate are Monaco trademarks. Practical amenities are on-site as well. We especially appreciate the WiFi internet access throughout the building.

All 225 rooms will keep you entertained with vertically striped wallpaper, trendy brown carpeting with orange stars, and white bedding (Frette linens) accented with red-patterned throws. "Tall rooms" are even available for those athletic-minded travelers exceeding 6 feet. These super-sized quarters were custom designed with 9-foot King beds and heightened showerheads. Add to the mix 24-hour room service and the always available Yoga channel, and you can see that Monaco sits squarely outside the proverbial "box."

In addition to the in-room Yoga channel exercise option, Monaco provides sweat-minded individuals with two other possibilities. There's the on-premise diminutive gym with its busy floor, mirrors, and half dozen cardio machines — sufficient for some, but many may want more (especially AMT-ers desiring muscle pumping). Or there's the $10/day discounted access to SportsMall/Metro — a full-service gym (sans pool) within a 5-minute walk of the hotel (see our review). Don't forget about our outdoor run routes and the nearby 400 meter track.

Swimmers are out of luck. No lap pool is available downtown SLC.

LEAST EXPENSIVE

GOLD: Little America

500 South Main Street, Salt Lake City, UT 84101
(801) 363-6781 • littleamerica.com/slc

CARDIO
TREADMILLS: **4 StarTrac**
RECUMBENT BIKE: **3 StarTrac**
STEPPER: **2 Reebok**

STRENGTH
MACHINES: **6 Cybex**
DUMBBELLS: **5-50 lbs**

SWIM
SPECS: **In/Out • Not lap**

OTHER
HOURS: **5:30a-11p**
COST: **Free**
TV: **Yes**
EXTRAS: **$10 Grand America pass**

Once a 1950s truck stop, the now 850-room hotel offers a variety of sleeping arrangements. Literally in the shadow of the luxurious Grand, Little America offers the same convenient location at thrifty rates. Travelers can select among 3 room options: Courtside, Garden and Tower, with the first 2 falling into our less expensive category. These budget-friendly quarters are housed in separate buildings spread across a square block parking lot, which gives them a motor-lodge vibe.

Courtside rooms open to the outside and offer 1 queen or 2 double beds. Garden units are a little larger and can be reserved with 1 king or 2 queen beds. The unattractive floral-pattern décor in both floor plans is rather dowdy, but the units are tidy and comfortable.

In Little America's upscale Tower, the workout center is surprisingly extensive. The large room houses new cardio and strength equipment and is cheery and attractively decorated. Although upright bikes and ellipticals flew the coop, Little America's remaining endurance machines are forehead sweatin' good. In addition, its 6 stack-loaded stations and ample range dumbbell set make full-body conditioning achievable.

Swimmers, your fun awaits at Metro Sports Club. Allow 5 minutes by taxi and have your room key and $11 ready.

Note: Little America guests may access Grand America's spa and fitness center for $10/day — the same price paid by those staying at the Grand!

BEYOND HOTELS

The Plaza Executive Health Club

40th East Gallivan, Salt Lake City, UT 84111
(801) 961-1300 • plazaexecutiveclub.com

CARDIO

TREADMILLS: **Precor**
UPRIGHT BIKE: **Precor**
RECUMBENT BIKE: **LF**
ELLIPTICAL: **Precor**
STEPPER: **Precor**

STRENGTH

FREE WEIGHTS: **Yes**
MACHINES: **Cybex**
DUMBBELLS: **5-100 lbs**

OTHER

CLASSES: **Yes**
HOURS: M-TH **5:30a-9p** • F **5:30a-8p** • SAT **8a-1p** • SUN **9a-2p**
COST: **$8**
TV: **Yes**

This little-known gem is located behind Marriott City Center on a small "L" shaped avenue off of State Street between South 2nd and 3rd Streets. Eight bucks a day grants entry to Plaza's petite and contemporary two-floor club. Catering to executives working in the surrounding office towers, this sparkling new facility dropped a wad of cash on high-end equipment. The club demonstrates that top-notch Precor is its brand of choice, with 8 ellipticals, 6 treads, 3 uprights and 2 steppers. Strength enthusiasts are not left out. Upstairs is filled with plenty of weight apparatus to make your muscles sore.

No lap pool is on-site, so swimmers can give their Speedos the day off or look to Metro Sports Club for water frolicking. Post-workout primping is an option here with complimentary towels, locks, hair dryers and toiletries. (We give this club a slight nod over Apple Fitness.)

Note: Exercisers should notice Plaza's limited weekend hours and plan accordingly.

SportsMall/Metro

324 South State Street, Salt Lake City, UT 84111
(801) 521-9400

CARDIO

TREADMILLS: **StarTrac**
UPRIGHT BIKE: **LF**
RECUMBENT BIKE: **StarTrac**
ELLIPTICAL: **LF • Precor • Reebok**
STEPPER: **StairMaster**

STRENGTH

FREE WEIGHTS: **Yes**
HAMMER: **Yes**
MACHINES: **Cybex**
DUMBBELLS: **3-100 lbs**

OTHER

CLASSES: **Yes**
HOURS: M-TH **4:30a-11p** • F **4:30a-10p** • SAT **7a-9p** • SUN **8a-6p**
COST: **$10 w/room key** • **$20/day Others** • **$35/week All**
TV: **Yes**

Sportsmall/Metro's vibe is more urban and "techno" than its nearby rivals. Divided into two floors, Metro's street level glass-enclosed "fish bowl" allows passers-by to gawk at the athletic-minded. Despite the audience, we enjoyed Metro's selection of newer machines with the ellipticals and treadmills as our favorites.

In contrast to upstairs, privacy is the rule in the lower level, loft-like room. Its high ceilings and exposed air ducts create a pleasing environment for weight routines. Plenty of benches and squat racks sit beside youthful stack-loaded machines and a large quantity of dumbbells. Classes are also offered downstairs for those in search of a little group therapy.

Bring your hotel room key for $10 discounted access, regular Janes are charged $20/day.

RUNNING ROUTES

For those challenged by our quiz, you can relax. Figuring out where to run in this town is a no-brainer. Several good prospects are convenient to Downtown with a satisfying variety of flat and hilly routes.

Remember, Downtown Salt Lake City sits at 4,000 feet of elevation — just enough altitude to make your aerobic system work harder than at sea level.

There are several good prospects convenient to Downtown.

Memory Grove Park

Located east of the Capitol, Memory Grove Park is roughly 1 mile north of the Grand and Little America hotels and under a half mile from our other listings. Follow State Street to North Temple to Canyon Road to the Park's entrance. The path will run into City Creek Canyon's trail, which serves up ample mileage, good scenery and varied terrain — meaning uphill! You can clock up to 10 miles round-trip.

Liberty Park

Southeast of town (within 1-2 miles of all hotels) striders may prefer Liberty Park's two short, shaded and flat perimeter loops (1.3 and 1.5 miles). Keep an eye out for the 450 birds that call this 110-acre green spot home. If running in circles is your thing, there is also Sugar House Park (another 2 miles southeast) with its 2+ mile loop — it's a local favorite.

Red Butte Garden

Lastly, for those who like to stop and smell the roses, consider heading east toward the University of Utah where, behind campus, you will be treated to 4 miles of scenic trails through Red Butte Garden's 150 lush acres. Approximately 4 miles from Downtown, your mileage will accrue fast, but we think you'll enjoy the Garden's amazing colors and stunning city views.

San Antonio

41 Locations Reviewed

SAN ANTONIO, TEXAS

Downtown San Antonio is a party waiting to happen. Along the meandering River Walk, fiesta opportunities abound. Restaurants, bars, nightclubs and hotels make this area a fantastic destination for both conventioneers and leisure travelers. Attractions vary from the historical (the Alamo) to the whimsical (Fiesta Texas) with a great deal in between.

Prepare to have your healthy diet challenged in this "Tex-Mex" cuisine capital. Southern Texan and Mexican flavors combine to create mouthwatering breakfast, lunch and dinner fare that you can fully indulge in knowing that we have your workout options covered.

The expression "Tex-Mex" surfaced in the early '70s, when cooking aficionados fixated on distinguishing between authentic Mexican food and the "mixed plates" served at so-called Mexican restaurants in the U.S. Mexican culinary fanatics cringed at the thought that they could be labeled as the creators of such "un-Mexican" Texan creations like hard shell tacos, chips and salsa, chile con carne, barbacoa and breakfast burritos. Incidentally, these North-of-the border delights are now enjoyed throughout the world. Just don't expect to find them in Mexico — unless, of course, you are in a tourist zone.

All this food talk has made us hungry — so here are the recommendations.

EXPENSIVE

GOLD: Watermark Hotel & Spa

212 West Crockett, San Antonio, TX 78205
(210) 223-8500 • watermarkhotel.com

CARDIO

TREADMILLS: **5 LF**
UPRIGHT BIKE: **1 LF**
RECUMBENT BIKE: **1 LF**
ELLIPTICAL: **4 LF**
STEPPER: **1 LF**

STRENGTH

FREE WEIGHTS: **Yes ~ 340 lbs**
MACHINES: **8 LF**
DUMBBELLS: **5-50 lbs**

SWIM

SPECS: **Outdoor • Not lap**

OTHER

CLASSES: **Yes**
HOURS: **24**
COST: **Free**
TV: **Yes**

As you step into the lobby of San Antonio's most luxurious hotel, you immediately realize the Watermark is someplace special. Its casual elegance, with a hint of Southwest charm, is only improved upon by Watermark's perfect location in the heart of Downtown and across the street from the renowned River Walk.

Pleasing shades of brown and white give the 99 guest rooms a clean, contemporary feel. Comfortable bedding and high thread count sheets top it all off.

On the 8th floor, Watermark enhances your paradisiacal experience with a marvelous fitness center and spa. Although only Life Fitness cardio and weight machines are supplied (with attached plasma screens), the equipment is as new as a baby's first tooth. Free weights are a hotel workout room rarity, but Watermark has them, complete with bench rack and 340 lbs. of plates.

Additional touches include an impressive aerobics studio offering classes such as yoga and Pilates, and a first-class assortment of massage and salon services.

With no lap pool on-site, we recommend that swimmers drive 5 minutes to the San Antonio Natatorium.

SILVER: La Mansion Del Rio

112 College Street, San Antonio, TX 78205
(210) 518-1000 • lamansion.com

Surrender your worries to the wind at this Spanish colonial River Walk hotel where, at each night's turndown service, a box of mythical worry dolls is left behind. Legend has it each worry doll under your pillow will remove one worry from your mind. More worries, more dolls beneath the pillow. Before a competition, some of us might need two or three pillows, right?

La Mansion is the across-the-river sister property to the Watermark. Though it does not provide the same luxurious accommodations, visitors will enjoy attractive old Spanish style rooms for about half the cost. Each room is uniquely decorated, and all have beamed ceilings, custom cotton bedding and double French doors that open to an outdoor balcony.

From our perspective, La Mansion's best perk is the complimentary access to Watermark's top-notch fitness center and spa. that alternative across the river, no need to trouble with La sion's feeble in-house exercise room, where 2 Life Fitness treadn 2 Life Fitness recumbent bikes and a small set of 5-40 pound du bells are crowded into a room slightly larger than a closet.

Swimmers should drive to the Natatorium, because La Ma sion's advertised outdoor "lap pool" is a short rectangle withou lines or stripes.

MODERATELY EXPENSIVE

GOLD: **Residence Inn** San Antonio Alamo Plaza

425 Bonham Street, San Antonio, TX 78205
(210) 212-5555 • residenceinn.com

CARDIO

TREADMILLS: **2 LF - old**
UPRIGHT BIKE: **1 LF**
RECUMBENT BIKE: **1 LF**
ELLIPTICAL: **1 Precor - old**
STEPPER: **1 LF**

STRENGTH

MACHINES: **1 Multi**
DUMBBELLS: **5-50 lbs**

SWIM

SPECS: **Outdoor • Not lap**

OTHER

HOURS: **24**
COST: **Free**
TV: **Yes**

Be sure to book the right downtown San Antonio Residence Inn. You want the location named above, not the downtown Market Square Inn, which is located at least a mile from the famed River Walk.

Once hotel shoppers drop out of the "Expensive" category, in-house exercise room quality deteriorates dramatically all over town. This Residence Inn is no exception. Indeed, being number one without a good quality on-site workout option highlights the extent of this deficit.

Residence Inn does not afford a unique stay or that San Antonio flavor, but its reasonable location (3 blocks from Alamo & River Walk), complete in-room kitchenettes and free, hot, full breakfasts justify its category leader spot. If these benefits still leave you wanting for a little more pizzazz, check out the Emily Morgan Hotel.

The on-site gym's few moderately-used cardio pieces and small set of dumbbells may be adequate for a quick tune-up. But if you crave an all-encompassing workout or a more pleasing exercise environment, set out for the Downtown YMCA. Walking will take approximately 10 minutes, driving less than 5 (6/10 mile). Swimmers can head to the Y as well, but we think you will be happier driving 10 minutes to the San Antonio Natatorium.

SILVER: **Emily Morgan Hotel**

705 East Houston, San Antonio, TX 78205
(210) 225-5100 • emilymorganhotel.com

Across the street from the Alamo and a couple blocks from the River Walk, Emily treats guests to a unique hotel experience. The modern guest rooms are outfitted with 250 thread count sheets, Aveda bath products, a CD player and a 27-inch television. In a ho-

...ool, the minimal lighting creates a chic night- ... picture is worth a thousand words, so check out ...nd detailed website, where you will also find guar- ... room rates.

...the category nod to franchise Residence Inn primarily ...er on-site workout option and free hot meals. But we actu- ...r Emily's swank and tony accommodations, and especially ...nend this hotel if you are planning to sweat off-site. Then, ...esidence's in-house gym edge becomes a non-factor.

...o not bother with Emily's barren fitness room, stocked with ...ired Tectrix upright bike, 1 average step machine, 2 sub-par re- ...umbent bikes and 2 treadmills. Five bucks and a 10-minute walk to the Downtown YMCA offer so much more.

LEAST EXPENSIVE

GOLD: Hawthorn Suites

830 North St. Mary's Street, San Antonio, TX 78205
(210) 527-1900 • hawthorn.com

Attention! Do not let this hotel's confusing promotional language fool you. Yes, it is located on the River Walk. But it is 7 to 8 blocks away from the "real" River Walk, which means the main attractions stop more than a mile short of this hotel. Tricky, huh?

Hawthorn is isolated on the outskirts of Downtown, but its across-the-street proximity to the Downtown YMCA makes it a fine location for the traveling athlete on a budget. Two or three other hotels also call this area home, so you will not be too lonesome.

At these rates, do not expect anything close to a worthy in-hotel workout option. Hawthorn holds true to form with 2 junky treads and 2 Diamondback bikes crammed into an 8x10 closet of a room. Go to the Y, it is right across the street!

SILVER: Crowne Plaza River Walk

111 Pecan Street East, San Antonio, TX 78205
(210) 354-2800 • crowneplaza.com

CARDIO
TREADMILLS: **5 LF**
RECUMBENT BIKE: **5 LF**
ELLIPTICAL: **2 LF**
STEPPER: **2 LF**

STRENGTH
MACHINES: **1 Multi**

SWIM
SPECS: **Outdoor • Not lap**

OTHER
HOURS: **6:30a-12a**
COST: **Free**
TV: **Yes**

On the southern edge of the River Walk and Downtown, this 21-story hotel is a refuge for those on a budget. The room rate savings compensate for the 7-block distance to the Alamo and the 4 blocks to River Walk's heart of commotion. Just don't forget to pack the walking shoes.

Completing a $6.5MM renovation has provided this hotel with a much needed facelift. The on-site gym serves up a surprisingly impressive number of cardio machines, creating a usable exercise option for fitness fans. All equipment is manufactured by Life Fitness, and only 3 of the treadmills are older models. Without any upright bikes in the room, cyclists will have to go recumbent for their pedal pushing. Those not satisfied by Crowne Plaza's selection can drive 5 minutes to the Downtown YMCA (too far to walk).

Lap swimmers should also entertain driving to the Natatorium.

BEYOND HOTELS

San Antonio Natatorium

1430 West Durango Boulevard, San Antonio, TX 78207
(210) 226-8541 • sanantonio.gov/sapar/swimming.asp

SWIM

GRADE: **B+**
SPECS: **8x25yd • Indoor • 82°**
TOYS: **Kick • Pull • Clock**

OTHER

HOURS: **Vary** • SUN **Closed**
COST: **$1.50**

Ahhh, words like Natatorium and Aquatic Center are music to our ears whenever we are in search of lap swimming options. It sounds even better when we discover that the prospect is publicly funded.

Approximately 2 miles south of the Alamo, this public facility hosts USA junior swim meets and other water competitions. Although swimmers will have to settle for 25-yard short course, the $1.50 entry fee is a bargain, given the pool's star quality and ample supply of swimming toys. Sunday lapping is not available, and lap swim hours vary throughout the week, so we suggest calling to confirm times. After your swim, modest showers are suitable only for a quick chlorine rinse.

Although the Natatorium is only 2 miles from Downtown's hub, we recommend driving. It has a large parking lot and, because of the precarious surrounding neighborhood, jogging to and fro may not be the best choice.

Downtown YMCA

903 North St. Mary's Street, San Antonio, TX 78215
(210) 246-9600 • ymcasatx.org/downtown

Traveling athletes, rein in your expectation. Calorie burners, be prepared to sweat on older equipment. Although the bright and clean cardio area is filled with popular brands such as Precor, Cybex and Life Fitness, most machines are older models without the bells and whistles of their younger siblings. Age aside, all of the equipment works well and is properly cared for, alleviating our main concerns.

Weight lifters are treated better, with late model apparatus including free weights, dumbbells and 19 Cybex machines that still smell new.

Swimmers inherit an average-size pool with an average atmosphere. Floating lane lines and bottom stripes mark the course,

CARDIO

TREADMILLS: **StarTrac - old**
UPRIGHT BIKE: **LF**
RECUMBENT BIKE: **LF - old**
ELLIPTICAL: **Cybex • Precor - old**
STEPPER: **StairMaster**
ROWING: **Concept II**
OTHER: **NordicTrack**

STRENGTH

FREE WEIGHTS: **Yes**
HAMMER: **Yes**
MACHINES: **Cybex**
DUMBBELLS: **5-75 lbs**

SWIM

GRADE: **C+**
SPECS: **4x25yd • Indoor • 82°**
TOYS: **Kick • Clock**
MASTERS: **Yes**

OTHER

CLASSES: **Yes**
HOURS: M-F **5:30a-9p** • SAT **9a-6p** • SUN **Closed**
COST: **$5**
TV: **Yes**
EXTRAS: **Racquetball**

while a pace clock will keep your time. Kickboards are available to break up the monotony of long distance sessions.

For a better liquid experience, visit the San Antonio Natatorium.

If you drive to the YMCA and cannot find a metered parking space on the street, parking in the lot costs $1. Admission to the club is $5.

Note: This Y is closed Sundays.

RUNNING ROUTES

Seek out potential routes from your hotel front desk. The River Walk may be a good early morning bet but, as the sun rises, the multitudes will clog your path. If you do have a car, we understand that the 900-acre McAllister Park, just north of San Antonio International Airport, has more than 3 miles of pathways.

DINING

Cool place for a drink or dinner – Hotel Valencia's "Citrus" restaurant and bar.

SAN DIEGO, CALIFORNIA

San Di·e·go (san′ dē ā′gō), *n.*, the 7th largest city in the U.S., located 15 miles north of Mexico and, according to residents, a world away from LA. Noted for its temperate year-round climate. Pristine beaches line its coast, rolling waves pound its sand and scores of surfers — including lunching office workers — decorate its waters. Natives are friendly, laid back and content. Most share a common story of seeking a better life and lifestyle, adopting "America's Finest City" by design rather than compelled by job or circumstance. A breeding ground for technological innovation, medical discovery and music creativity — and where a flowered Hawaiian shirt is the common business attire. Also a home to many professional athletes who fight battles for fun, and military heroes who fight battles for real. A high cost of living is the primary detractor, but locals insist it keeps the population in check. Warning: Be careful when you visit — you may want to move.

U·to·pi·a (yoo tō′pē′ə), *n.*, see San Diego, above.

DOWNTOWN/CORONADO

Not so long ago, downtown San Diego's streets were populated by a scant number of office towers, few hotels and a handful of run-of-the-mill shops and restaurants. Today, Downtown and its Gaslamp Quarter boast a multitude of dining and entertainment attractions. This area bustles morning, noon and night. The 2004 premier of Petco Park and the advent of multiple condominium high-rises confirm that San Diego's urban heart is not revitalizing — it is revitalized.

In contrast, Coronado's serene beach setting is another highly sought-after San Diego tourist destination. Yet its short, 2.5-mile bridge-assisted distance from Downtown makes it a legitimate option for business travelers, too.

EXPENSIVE

GOLD: Manchester Grand Hyatt

One Market Place, San Diego, CA 92101
(619) 232-1234 • hyatt.com

CARDIO

TREADMILLS: **6 StarTrac**
UPRIGHT BIKE: **2 LF**
RECUMBENT BIKE: **2 LF**
ELLIPTICAL: **3 LF • 2 Precor**
STEPPER: **Stepmill**

STRENGTH

FREE WEIGHTS: **Yes**
MACHINES: **9 LF • 1 Free Motion**
DUMBBELLS: **5-80 lbs**

SWIM

SPECS: **Outdoor • Not lap**

OTHER

HOURS: **5:30a-10p**
COST: **$5**
TV: **Yes**
EXTRAS: **Tennis**

Overlooking breathtaking San Diego Bay and its resident cruise liners and Navy aircraft carriers, the twin tower Grand Hyatt is a San Diego skyline landmark. In addition to its appealing waterfront location, the hotel is convenient for conventioneers (one block from the convention center), shoppers, club-hoppers (2 blocks to the lively Gaslamp Quarter) and baseball fans (3 blocks from Padres' Petco Park). This massive 40-story hotel's 1,625 rooms are rather disappointing when compared to its opulent common areas, incredible views and first-class restaurants and lounges (don't miss the rooftop bar). The antique furnishings, plain ambiance and standard amenities are overly modest. Despite Hyatt's excellent in-house gym, the lagging guest quarters preclude a stand-alone Gold — Omni quite deservedly shares the podium.

Hyatt's fitness center is one of the best in all of San Diego — not just Downtown. For $5, guests can sample the wares — and there are many. All machines are new, new, new, and most cardio apparatus have plasma screens attached for individual viewing. A full set of free weights is always a welcome sight, and Hyatt delivers.

The only missing feature is a lap pool — despite Hyatt's website's claim to the contrary. The outdoor square (well short of 25 yards) has no floating lines or bottom stripes. Lap swimmers can hoof it 10 minutes to Pure Fitness or drive 10-15 minutes to Coronado's Community Pool. Both are good options.

GOLD: Omni Hotel

675 L Street, San Diego, CA 92101
(619) 231-6664 • omnihotels.com

Opened in April 2004, Omni's skybridge connection to Padres' Petco Park creates a convenient accommodation for visiting major league baseball teams and their fans. Situated on the Gaslamp Quarter's fringe and across the street from the convention center, the Omni also serves as a wonderful home base for Joe and Jane business/leisure travelers. Omni's 511 rooms are magic, cleverly drawing in the outdoors with a contemporary, zen-like style. Floor-to-ceiling windows offer marvelous city and bay views, and carpeting that mimics the ocean's grooved sand bottom indulges fancy footing. Open and airy baths hint of South Beach with an Art Deco flair. Tropical plants add a welcome dash of green, and zzz's come easy on Omni's premium pillow top bedding with 320 thread count Egyptian cotton sheets. So, why an "extra inning" tie for the Gold? Despite its far superior accommodations, Omni only hits a double with its gym, while Grand Hyatt smacks a home run.

CARDIO
TREADMILLS: **5 Precor**
RECUMBENT BIKE: **2 Precor**
ELLIPTICAL: **4 Precor**
STRENGTH
MACHINES: **5 Cybex**
DUMBBELLS: **5-50 lbs**
SWIM
SPECS: **Outdoor • Not lap**
OTHER
HOURS: **24**
COST: **Free**
TV: **Yes**

Omni's 6th floor fitness facility may, however, satisfy most athletic-minded travelers with its decent assortment of 2004 machines. The 24-hour modern sweat room's gray floors and plain walls are drab. Ejected from Omni's exercise game are upright bikes and step machines, though plenty of other endurance alternatives are in the dugout. Most iron-pumpers should get by on the combination of dumbbells and stack-loaded machines, but dedicated lifters will be better served by Grand Hyatt's free weight selection and wider range of dumbbells. Omni's outdoor pool is pure leisure, so our aquatic friends and others yearning for another gym should taxi ($5) to Pure Fitness. Lappers should also consider driving to Coronado's Community Center for a fabulous swim option.

Play ball!

SILVER: Hotel Del Coronado

1500 Orange Avenue, Coronado, CA 92118
(619) 435-6611 • hoteldel.com

Note: The Del's gym is currently under renovation and will re-open at the end of 2006. A temporary gym under a large tent on the pool deck is currently offered with the below-listed equipment.

Across the Bay is quaint and beautiful Coronado Island — technically a peninsula. The 2.5-mile landmark Coronado Bridge connects this laid back beach town with the urban and lively heart of San Diego. A favorite vacation destination, Coronado's proximity to Downtown makes it a potential option for business travelers, too. Legendary and historic, the Hotel Del Coronado is the best place to stay on the island. Located on the main drag of Orange Avenue and boasting 31 acres of beautiful sand beach in its backyard, the "Del" delights with Old World charm, modern conveniences and a multitude of

CARDIO
TREADMILLS: **4 Matrix**
UPRIGHT BIKE: **3 Matrix**
RECUMBENT BIKE: **2 Matrix**
ELLIPTICAL: **3 Matrix**
STEPPER: **1 StarTrac**
STRENGTH
MACHINES: **6 Cybex**
DUMBBELLS: **3-50 lbs**
SWIM
SPECS: **Outdoor • Not lap**
OTHER
HOURS: **6a-8p**
COST: **$10 • $12/room**
TV: **Yes**
EXTRAS: **Tennis**

active pursuits. Its 688 rooms vary in size and décor depending on whether you stay in the original Victorian main building, the Towers or the Cabana building. We recommend avoiding the entry level "Victorian" rooms, which are small and without a view.

The resort affords numerous athletic opportunities: running on the beach or along Coronado's Silver Strand (9-mile running/bike path), tennis, cycling, boating and, of course, sweating and lifting. The Del's newly renovated and re-stocked fitness center (March 2004) sports expensive machines in a bright environment with awesome ocean views. While we were not familiar with Del's cardio brand of choice, Matrix, we tested several of the machines, liked how they performed and appreciated the attached plasma screens. Del's Cybex stack-loaded weight stations are familiar friends, and its dumbbell selection will help round out a strength routine.

Lap swimmers can brave the Pacific's crisp temperatures or lap it up in the new Coronado Community Center pool (5-minute walk). Its former 50-meter outdoor box was pretty darn good — and the new 52-meter beauty, along with a separate 25-yard warm-up pool, is stellar. Also, a 3 lane, 25-yard lap pool can be found at the Marriott on the other side of downtown Coronado (pool is just right of Marriott's front driveway); it is free and easy to get into. But that pool is for Marriott guests only — wink, wink.

MODERATELY EXPENSIVE

GOLD: **Wyndham at Emerald Plaza**

400 West Broadway, San Diego, CA 92101
(619) 239-4500 • wyndham.com

CARDIO

TREADMILLS: **2 True**
UPRIGHT BIKE: **3 Sohn**
ELLIPTICAL: **2 Sohn**
STEPPER: **2 StairMaster - old**

STRENGTH

FREE WEIGHTS: **Yes**
MACHINES: **12 Polaris - old**
DUMBBELLS: **3-90 lbs**

SWIM

GRADE: **B-**
SPECS: **2x22.5yd • Outdoor • 82°**

OTHER

CLASSES: **Yes**
HOURS: **6a-9p**
COST: **$10 • $21 3/day**
TV: **Yes**

In the midst of downtown San Diego's office towers and within a 10-minute walk of the convention center, this 26-story high-rise hotel is a great choice for athletic-minded business travelers. Wyndham's 436-room accommodation offers various floor plans and views, pillow top mattresses, comfortable sheets, oversized desks, Herman Miller office chairs and contemporary, earth-toned décor.

A functional in-house gym and lap pool are offered on the hotel's 3rd floor. Before paying the $10/day fee ($21/3-day), scope out the mix of older and newer machines and free-weight assortment. If you need more, head over to Pure Fitness (less than a 3-minute walk) for a greater selection of high end endurance machines and newer stack-loaded weight stations

— admission is about the same. Swimmers receive free access to Wyndham's two-lane, 22.5-yard lap pool with floating lane lines. If that extra 2.5 yards makes a difference to you, seek Pure Fitness for its 25-yard lapper.

SILVER: Westgate Hotel

1055 Second Avenue, San Diego, CA 92101
(619) 238-1818 • westgatehotel.com

Across the street from Horton Plaza Mall (Nordstrom and Macy's) in the heart of Downtown, Westgate offers a classic European lodging experience in a modern 19-story high-rise. The hotel's afternoon tea service is popular with the downtown crowd.

All 223 rooms are oversized and elegantly adorned with French and English furnishings, Italian marble baths and draped floor-to-ceiling windows. We also appreciate Westgate's non-smoking policy throughout the hotel... not to mention California's non-smoking policy for all restaurants and bars!

Skip the hotel's lower level in-house fitness room, unless you are very pressed for time. The 5 StarTrac cardio pieces and scant strength apparatus are squeezed inside a small room. Instead, head across the street to 24 Hour Fitness for a real sweat. Westgate's fitness room attendant may have a coupon for free admission, so it is worth the trip downstairs to check. Otherwise, plan on paying $20 for your 24 Hour workout, or $15 if you belong to an IHRSA club back home (www.healthclubs.com).

Swimmers must trek a little farther (still under 10 minutes in the San Diego sunshine) to Pure Fitness, where you will find a 25-yard lapper ($12).

LEAST EXPENSIVE

GOLD: Best Western Bayside Inn

555 West Ash Street, San Diego, CA 92101
(619) 233-7500 • baysideinn.com

Three blocks from San Diego Bay on the north side of Downtown, this 12-story Best Western is a great option for athletic-minded business travelers on a budget. Walking to the convention center is a 10-minute jaunt, and a safe stroll into the Gaslamp's heart can be clocked under 15.

Best Western's 122 rooms are devoid of any real style, but the picturesque views through floor-to-ceiling windows and the attached balconies help beautify unattractive quarters. Microwaves and refrigerators are provided in all units, and a complimentary continental breakfast is served each morning.

With no in-house workout facility, Best Western treats exercising guests to free access at Pure Fitness — located 4 blocks from the front door. Also, don't forget about the fantastic jogging route along the sidewalks bordering the Bay.

BEYOND HOTELS DOWNTOWN/CORONADO

Pure Fitness

501 West Broadway, San Diego, CA 92101
(619) 231-8991 • purefitness.cc

CARDIO

TREADMILLS: **LF • StarTrac • Precor**
UPRIGHT BIKE: **LF - old**
RECUMBENT BIKE: **StarTrac**
ELLIPTICAL: **LF • Precor • Cybex**
STEPPER: **LifeStep • StairMaster - old • Stepmill**
OTHER: **Gravitron**

STRENGTH

FREE WEIGHTS: **Yes**
HAMMER: **Yes**
MACHINES: **Icarian**
DUMBBELLS: **10-95 lbs**

SWIM

GRADE: **B**
SPECS: **3x25yd • Outdoor • 80°**
TOYS: **Kick • Pull • Fins**

OTHER

CLASSES: **Yes**
HOURS: M-TH **5a-9:30p** • F **5a-8:30p** • SAT **8a-5p** • SUN **9a-3p**
COST: **Free Best Western • $12 Hotels • $20 Others**
TV: **Yes**
EXTRAS: **Basketball**

If you walk to Pure Fitness, enter the Koll Building and proceed through the lobby to the garage parking elevators. Press the "AC" button to bring you up to the health club's rooftop location.

This small executive health club caters to downtown office workers and presents a convenient sweat and swim venue. San Diego's year-round favorable weather permits an indoor/outdoor equipment arrangement. Sun worshipers can sweat under blue skies, but SPF 30 disciples need not worry, as most newer equipment remains inside, including 12 stack-loaded weight stations, 11 ellipticals (7 Precor), 8 treadmills, 4 bikes and plenty of free weights.

Pure's 25-yard outdoor lap pool is impressive, with 3 lanes separated by floating lines and bottom stripes. Water toys are provided, but bring a watch if intervals are in your plan — a pace clock is not on deck.

Note: If you're looking for a pick-up game, consider coming over for some hoops. Pure's outdoor basketball court is terrific.

Coronado Community Center

1845 Strand Way, Coronado, CA 92118
619)522-2464 • coronado.ca.us

The city of Coronado filled its old 50-meter pool and leveled the building in preparation for a new, state-of-the-art community center which opened in the Summer of 2005. Down the street from Hotel Del Coronado, the new facility consists of a 52-meter lap pool with a movable bulkhead, a separate warm up and water polo pool with 25-yard lap swimming, a fitness center with first class cardio and strength equipment, a climbing wall, basketball court and locker/shower facilities. Whew! This could be the best lap pool facility in the U.S. We enjoy swimming here because it runs long course lap swimming on M,W,F and Sundays. Times vary throughout the year. We have always urged swimmer friends staying Downtown to drive across the Bridge to this true Olympic-size pool. And if you are staying at the Hotel Del, it's a no-brainer.

24 Hour Fitness Sport

1 Horton Plaza, San Diego, CA 92101
(619) 232-4024 • 24hourfitness.com

On the ground level of Horton Plaza Mall's west side (near the Westin), this 24 Hour Fitness opened in 2003. "Sport" in the burgeoning franchise's name usually means a larger, nicer and pool-equipped facility. Unfortunately, this 24 breaks convention and sports no water option. It does, however, provide a vast array of cutting-edge machines inside a roomy, two-story space. All the top dogs from the fitness world are here, including Life Fitness 9500 series bikes, StairMaster 4600PT steppers, Precor ellipticals and Hammer Strength free weight plate-loaded stations.

CARDIO

TREADMILLS: **LF**
UPRIGHT BIKE: **LF**
RECUMBENT BIKE: **LF**
ELLIPTICAL: **LF • Precor**
STEPPER: **StairMaster • Stepmill**
ROWING: **Concept II**

STRENGTH

FREE WEIGHTS: **Yes**
HAMMER: **Yes**
MACHINES: **LF • Nautilus**
DUMBBELLS: **3-125 lbs**

OTHER

CLASSES: **Yes**
HOURS: **24**
COST: **$15 IHRSA • $20 Others**
TV: **Yes**

The going fare for out-of-towners is 20 bucks but, if you come from an IHRSA club (www.healthclubs.com), you will save $5. Although Westgate guests may get lucky with a fitness freebie from the hotel fitness center attendant, no hotels have standing discounts or free pass policies, not even the neighboring Westin — which we did not recommend due to superior and similarly priced alternatives.

MISSION BAY/HOTEL CIRCLE

Staying in Mission Bay will keep you close to Sea World and put some of San Diego's best running, cycling and rollerblading routes outside your door. However, everything else requires a drive — restaurants, nightlife, business offices, etc.

Hotel Circle is convenient for travelers with meetings in corporate-heavy Mission Valley and economical for those on a tight expense account. Leisure travelers trying to save some dough may may want to choose Hotel Circle if staying near Sea World and Mission Bay is a priority. There are two major shopping centers in the area, with multiplex theaters and plenty of dining options. Downtown is 3 miles away.

EXPENSIVE

GOLD: Paradise Point

1404 West Vacation Road, San Diego, CA 92109
(858) 274-4630 • paradisepoint.com

CARDIO

TREADMILLS: **3 Cybex**
RECUMBENT BIKE: **2 Cybex - old**
ELLIPTICAL: **2 Precor**
STEPPER: **2 StairMaster - old**

STRENGTH

MACHINES: **7 Cybex**
DUMBBELLS: **3-60 lbs**

SWIM

SPECS: **Outdoor • Not lap**

OTHER

HOURS: **6a-9p**
COST: **$10**
TV: **Yes**
EXTRAS: **Tennis**

Green grass, full flower beds and lush tropical plants wind alongside the entry route that brings guests to this secluded resort. It is one of the most beautiful hotel introductions in all San Diego. On the shores of Mission Bay and down the road from Sea World, Paradise Point is a wonderful destination for vacation travelers.

Guest quarters are housed in 3-4 unit bungalows scattered throughout the 44-acre property. The 462 rooms are refreshingly colorful and country-home in style.

The workout facility is good, but not great. A mix of old and new machines is offered in an aesthetically pleasing room. Cyclists must ride recumbent and strength enthusiasts must settle for dumbbells and stack-loaded weight stations. Free weights are missing in action — likely with the uprights! However, the ellipticals are in great condition, and so are the Cybex weight machines. For runners, San Diego's best jogging paths around Mission Bay and Pacific Beach are at your doorstep.

Swimmers face a challenge. Despite Paradise Point's 5 pools, not one is "lappable," and locals typically avoid swimming in Mission Bay. While the water quality is fine for some beach play and water sports, most serious swimmers question the wisdom of lengthy immersion. So, what to do? Live dangerously — or, better yet, drive 10 minutes to Clairemont Community Pool ($5). For an even nicer facility, drive 20 minutes to the La Jolla High School pool ($5). If you elect the latter, you have the added benefit of shopping along La Jolla's famed Prospect Avenue before or after you get wet.

MODERATELY EXPENSIVE

GOLD: Hilton San Diego Resort

1775 East Mission Bay Drive, San Diego, CA 92109
(619) 276-4010 • sandiegoresort.hilton.com

"Resort" may not accurately describe this large hotel complex, whose best feature is its Mission Bay location. If you want great exercise options at your fingertips and are not in search of luxury, stay here. But keep in mind that top dining, shopping and entertainment attractions will require a commute. While not nearly as lush and secluded as Paradise Point, Hilton's 18 acres present a charming escape from the run-of-the-mill hotel property. Festively decorated with bright colors, all 357 guest quarters are equipped with refrigerators and walk-out balconies. To avoid potential noise, we suggest requesting a room away from the highway.

CARDIO

TREADMILLS: **4 StarTrac**
UPRIGHT BIKE: **1 StarTrac**
RECUMBENT BIKE: **3 StarTrac**
ELLIPTICAL: **3 Precor**
STEPPER: **1 StarTrac • 1 Stepmill**
OTHER: **Gravitron**

STRENGTH

FREE WEIGHTS: **Yes**
HAMMER: **1 Leg**
MACHINES: **6 Hoist • 4 Cybex**
DUMBBELLS: **5-70 lbs**

SWIM

GRADE: **B-**
SPECS: **2x23yd • Outdoor • 79-82°**

OTHER

HOURS: M-SAT **6a-9p** • SUN **6a-8p**
COST: **$12 • $25 3/day**
TV: **Yes**
EXTRAS: **Tennis**

Mission Bay is a favorite training and racing site for many San Diego locals, and the Hilton is front and center. Joggers, cyclists and rollerbladers zip along the area's roads and sidewalks. Water sport enthusiasts (kite surfers, jet skiers and sailors) flock to the shallow Bay. Because the water quality can be questionable, we do not recommend extended swimming sessions (e.g., open water freestyle for an hour). Hilton rents all the toys except running shoes, so plan to sample the Bay's goodies.

On-site, Hilton sports one of the best hotel gyms in San Diego. New cardio machines and youthful weight stations sparkle in this cozy "L"-shaped room. We also appreciated the ample set of free weights for bench press, squat exercises and leg press work. The sweat tariff is an annoying $12/day, but swallow the pesky pill because this Hilton prescribes an excellent remedy.

Swimmers can "lap it up" in Hilton's main pool. On one side, 2 lanes are divided from the rest of the pool by floating lines. Stripes are not marked on the bottom and one wall is angled, so the length comes up short of 25 yards — our guess is 23 in one lane and 24 in the other. Nevertheless, it's a functional option for hotel swimmers.

SILVER: Residence Inn

1865 Hotel Circle South, San Diego, CA 92108
(619) 582-7500 • residenceinn.com

One of the most recent additions to San Diego's Hotel Circle Drive, Residence Inn opened its doors in spring 2003. Since this part of town does not lend itself to "out the door" exploring, we recommend this property primarily for business travelers. However, its full kitchens, separate living areas and free breakfasts make it a worthy competitor for all travelers on a budget. In addition, it is convenient to both Sea World and Downtown.

The Inn is set back halfway up a hill, isolating it from Interstate 8's traffic noise. Bright, colorful and cheery are dominant themes throughout the property's common areas and 192 rooms. All guests will appreciate the wall hanging plasma screen in the dining area and the free high-speed internet access.

With a "born on" date of 2003, you know how old — or, in this case, how young — the fitness equipment is. Residence stocks a few good quality machines in its small workout room, including 2 Life Fitness 8500 series bikes and an 8500 series elliptical. The Life Fitness multi-gym will get you by in a pinch but don't bother with the treadmills. They are new, too, but this is San Diego! Head outdoors for a run into neighboring Mission Hills, a beautiful residential area (run west along Hotel Circle Drive, and take the first road on your left — adjacent to the softball fields).

Lap swimmers and those yearning for a health club experience can walk 5 minutes to Frog's Club One ($10) — we know, it's a funny name, but a good gym nonetheless.

LEAST EXPENSIVE

GOLD: Holiday Inn Select

595 Hotel Circle South, San Diego, CA 92108
(619) 291-5720 • holidayinnselectsd.com

GOLD: Mission Valley Resort

875 Hotel Circle South, San Diego, CA 92108
(619) 298-8282 • missionvalleyresort.com

These two business traveler-oriented hotels are recommended for their cheap rates and proximity to Frog's Club One, a full-service health club with lap pool. Do not expect too much in the way of amenities or freebies from these frugal finds.

Completing a 2003 renovation, the Holiday Inn provides 318 rooms in a high-rise building. All guest quarters open to interior corridors and offer standard floor plans and features. A walk to Frog's will take less than 5 minutes and admission costs $10/day.

If you don't mind motel-like accommodations and room doors that open to the outside, consider Mission Valley Resort for its next door proximity to Frog's and free workout pass. We favor the slightly more upscale Holiday Inn Select, but both are reliable athletic-minded options.

Note: See our Residence Inn description for a suggested running route.

BEYOND HOTELS MISSION BAY/HOTEL CIRCLE

Clairemont Community Pool

3600 Clairemont Drive, San Diego, CA 92117
(858) 581-9923

San Diego manages a vast number of community pools year round, and Clairemont is one of them. We swim here occasionally and enjoy its empty lanes and easy access. For $5, water loggers will get 3 to 5 lanes of 25-yard lap swimming with each lane separated by floating lines and bottom stripes. A pace clock is on the wall, and toys are provided — kickboards and pull-buoys.

SWIM

GRADE: **B**
SPECS: **5x25yd • Outdoor • 82°**
TOYS: **Kick • Pull • Clock**

OTHER

HOURS: **Vary**
COST: **$5**

Directions: I-5 North to Balboa; exit east (away from ocean); up the hill and turn south (right) on Clairemont; drive about a mile, and the pool is on your left. Only the building is visible, not the pool. Park in adjacent lot.

Frog's Club One

901 Hotel Circle South, San Diego, CA 92108
(619) 291-3500 • clubone.com

This notable club is tricky to find. You will see it after driving or walking to the back of Mission Valley Resort's parking lot. It sports one of the area's few regulation size lap pools, and its cardio and strength inventory makes it a solid option for land athletes, too.

There are no floating lines in the 2 lane, 25-yard liquid lapper; however, stripes are painted on the pool's bottom. Bring a watch if base intervals are in your plan, as the clock is tough to read through goggles.

All fitness machinery is located on the club's second floor. The environment is dull and industrial, but the quality of equipment is first rate. Expect to be worked by Life Fitness 9500 series bikes and ellipticals, StairMaster 4600PT model Free Climbers and a slew of useful strength apparatus. The treadmills are relatively old and worn, but who travels to San Diego to run indoors on a treadmill? Runners, get outside!

Admission for all hotel guests is $10, except for patrons of the Mission Valley Resort — these lucky ducks get into Frog's for free.

CARDIO

TREADMILLS: **StarTrac - old**
UPRIGHT BIKE: **LF**
RECUMBENT BIKE: **LF**
ELLIPTICAL: **LF • Precor**
STEPPER: **StairMaster • Stepmill**

STRENGTH

FREE WEIGHTS: **Yes**
HAMMER: **Yes**
MACHINES: **Hoist**
DUMBBELLS: **5-120 lbs**

SWIM

GRADE: **C+**
SPECS: **2x25yd • Outdoor • 79-82°**
TOYS: **Kick**

OTHER

CLASSES: **Yes**
HOURS: M-TH **5a-10:30p** • F **5a-9p** • SAT-SUN **7a-8p**
COST: **Free MV Resort • $10 Hotels • $15 Others**
TV: **Yes**
EXTRAS: **Tennis**

LA JOLLA/TORREY PINES

Here's the rub on lovely La Jolla. It boasts fantastic upscale shopping, incredible art galleries, wonderful dining and entertaining nightlife. However... this lap of luxury is not a typical Southern California beach town.

The nearby coves and rocky ocean inlets are breathtaking, but if you want sand outside your door, both Coronado and Del Mar are better beach venues. Staying outside of downtown La Jolla may be prudent — close enough to enjoy the attractions, but far enough to avoid the traffic and crowd.

EXPENSIVE

GOLD: Estancia La Jolla Hotel and Spa

9700 North Torrey Pines Road, La Jolla, CA 92037
(858) 550-1000 • estancialajolla.com

CARDIO

TREADMILLS: **3 LF**
UPRIGHT BIKE: **1 LF**
RECUMBENT BIKE: **1 LF**
ELLIPTICAL: **2 LF**

STRENGTH

MACHINES: **4 LF**
DUMBBELLS: **5-50 lbs**

SWIM

GRADE: **C**
SPECS: **3x20yd • Outdoor • 79-82°**
TOYS: **Kick • Pull**

OTHER

HOURS: **TBD**
COST: **Free**
TV: **Yes**

We toured this luxury property a month before its June 28th, 2004 grand opening. And, while the hotel was still in the final stages of construction, we saw enough to go out on a very short limb and award Estancia Gold. The accommodations, location and nearby fitness options are tremendous.

The former family equestrian ranch preserves its heritage with rustic accents, barn-themed doors (upscale California horse ranch, not red farm barns) and exposed wooden beams. The original stable's white bricks were used to construct the main building's edifice. Several restaurants and state-of-the-art conference facilities make Estancia's lush 9.5 acres a natural destination for both the business and leisure traveler.

Guests of all 210 rooms will appreciate California country home décor, 300 thread count bedding, lavish furnishings and 24-hour room service. Though strategic landscaping with dense plant life and trees insulate the hotel from busy Torrey Pines Road, we suggest a room away from the traffic.

An Estancia stay affords athletic-minded travelers a diverse menu of workout opportunities. The complimentary on-site fitness center will stock an impressive array of cutting-edge equipment. Although step machines and free weights are not in the plans, the University of California-San Diego's (UCSD) Recreation Center ($10) is right across the street! Runners will enjoy UCSD's competition quality 1/4 mile track — frequented by many professional endurance athletes. Swimmers can perform flip turns in Estancia's 20-yard rectangle, which we were assured will sport floating lane lines for several hours each day. Other water options include UCSD's outdoor 50-meter pool, home to many local triathletes and a Masters swim program, and La Jolla Cove (open water swimming from the beach to the pier — not walkable).

Finally, La Jolla is loaded with unique outdoor pursuits, including sea kayaking, motorized gliding, Torrey Pines golfing, hiking and cycling. Estancia plans to organize "Extreme Packages," or you can venture out on your own with ease.

SILVER: Grande Colonial

910 Prospect Street, La Jolla, CA 92037
(858) 454-2181 • thegrandecolonial.com

On Prospect Avenue in the heart of La Jolla's shopping and dining district, this boutique hotel is perfectly situated for a weekend getaway. La Jolla's hub is hardly urban, but it is in high demand. Unfortunately, traffic jams, crowded sidewalks and nightlife noise are common detractors for this wealthy town, especially on weekends. However, in addition to placing you within an easy walk to fancy clothing, art and furniture galleries and tremendous restaurants, a Prospect Street home base provides incredible views of the Pacific Ocean, rocky shores and seal-filled coves.

Colonial's 75 quaint guest units are Victorian in style, with pale yellow tones, large windows and country home furnishings. Goose down comforters and premium bedding create a cozy respite.

Since no workout room is offered on-site, guests looking for an indoor sweat can walk 3-5 minutes to Frog's Club One. Lacking a pool, it's an otherwise full-service gym with modern equipment.

Runners are encouraged to head outside and hit La Jolla's residential streets and hills, big hills — or La Jolla High School's 1/4-mile track.

Swimmers with a wetsuit or thick skin can take to the Cove, where open water freestylers share space with the wildlife (5-minute walk). Swimming to the pier is a local favorite route, but have someone pick you up on the other side.

For a measurable swim session, head to La Jolla High School's new 50-meter lap pool. It's normally set up for short course, and adult lap swim hours are available throughout the day — it's about a mile and a half south on Fay street ($5).

MODERATELY EXPENSIVE

GOLD: Hyatt Regency La Jolla at Aventine

3777 La Jolla Village Drive, La Jolla, CA 92122
(858) 552-1234 • hyatt.com

This hotel, though catering to the business set, offers one of the best and most convenient stay and play (workout wise) options in the San Diego area. Just east of Interstate 5, Hyatt is under 3 miles from downtown La Jolla, within 2 miles of the UTC shopping mall (Macy's, Nordstrom, Crate & Barrel) and close to many corporate offices. An adjacent complex houses four popular high-end restaurants serving a variety of cuisines — Asian fusion, steak, Italian and Californian.

Often booked by NFL teams in town to play the Chargers (the Raiders stayed here during the 2003 Superbowl), Hyatt's 419 rooms are upscale. Décor is modern and zen-like, with floor-to-ceiling windows, wispy see-through drapes and sharp furnishings in crisp brown and cream tones.

But Hyatt's real treat is its affiliation with the attached Sporting Club at Aventine. As one of San Diego's most exclusive health clubs, the Sporting Club boasts the most elaborate and aesthetically pleasing fitness complex around ($12).

SILVER: **Empress Hotel**

7766 Fay Avenue, La Jolla, CA 92037
(858) 454-3001 • empress-hotel.com

If you want to be within walking distance of downtown La Jolla's upscale shopping and dining, but need to adhere to a conservative budget, Empress is a great, moderately-priced alternative to the more expensive Colonial. (See "Colonial" for more La Jolla town description.) Empress' 73 rooms are tidy and contemporary in design, but they are not 5 star accommodations by any means — you are not paying for such luxury, either. All guest units stock refrigerators, hair dryers, coffee makers and Starbucks brand coffee. Bring your cup of homemade joe down to the outdoor sun deck each morning, where complimentary continental breakfast is served.

Across the street, fitness-minded travelers can work out at La Jolla Sports Club, with its decent assortment of cardio machines, strength equipment and classes — a necessary alternative to Empress' dysfunctional in-house exercise room. Ten bucks gets you in LJSC's door. Runners, skip the treadmills. Instead, explore the surrounding neighborhoods for beautiful residential scenery and hill work. La Jolla High School's 1/4-mile track is another possibility.

Swimmers with a wetsuit or a penchant for cold water (avg. 68° in summer) can open water freestyle at La Jolla Cove — a popular local swim spot. Or, for a more comfortable water experience, head to La Jolla High School's fantastic outdoor lap pool open 7 days a week (south ~1mile; $5).

LEAST EXPENSIVE

GOLD: **Best Western Inn by the Sea**

7830 Fay Avenue, La Jolla, CA 92037
(858) 459-4461 • bestwestern.com/innbythesea

Less than a block away from the Empress Hotel and similarly located off La Jolla's main shopping and entertainment drag of Prospect Avenue, the Inn By the Sea is a good representative for this wallet-friendly franchise. The hotel exterior resembles a residential apartment mid-rise.

Interior corridors, walk-out balconies and standard guest room floor plans are features of this 5-story, 132-unit property. Free continental breakfast is served each morning. During summer weekends, this place can get expensive, so compare its rates to the Empress and do not hesitate to elect Empress as your hotel queen.

With no exercise room on-site, Best Western directs guests across the street to La Jolla Sports Club. Ten bucks provides access to this pleasing gym with the latest fitness equipment. Runners should simply head to the hilly La Jolla community or La Jolla High School's 1/4-mile track. Swimmers can go to La Jolla High School's lap pool (~1 mile away from the hotel; $5) or take a chilly dip in the salty bay waters of La Jolla Cove — swimming to the pier is a popular open-water route for locals.

BEYOND HOTELS LA JOLLA/TORREY PINES

University of California San Diego (UCSD)

RIMAC Arena Fitness Center
(858) 534-3570
Outdoor 1/4-mile track **(just NE of Visitor Information Center)**
Canyonview Aquatics & Activities Ctr
(858) 534-6034
rec.ucsd.edu

An educational breeding ground for tomorrow's scientists and engineers, UCSD is also an athletic playground for local residents and out-of-town visitors. Professional triathletes and Olympic track and fielders train on the quarter-mile oval. Elite swimmers work out in the 50-meter outdoor pool and take advantage of the 3 daily Masters swims. Students and adult members get fit at RIMAC Arena — the campus' health and wellness center.

These state-of-the-art facilities are supported by private and state funding and are available to the traveling public. Circular running is free, and admission to RIMAC and the pools is $10/day. Parking on campus can be a challenge, but temporary permits can be purchased at the Visitor Informa-

CARDIO

TREADMILLS: **LF**
UPRIGHT BIKE: **LF**
RECUMBENT BIKE: **LF**
ELLIPTICAL: **LF**
STEPPER: **StairMaster**
ROWING: **Concept II**
OTHER: **Ergometer**

STRENGTH

FREE WEIGHTS: **Yes**
HAMMER: **Yes**
MACHINES: **LF • Cybex • Icarian**
DUMBBELLS: **5-120 lbs**

SWIM

GRADE: **A**
SPECS: **8x50m • Outdoor • 79°**
TOYS: **Kick • Pull • Clock**
MASTERS: **Yes**

OTHER

CLASSES: **Yes**
HOURS: **Vary**
COST: **$10 • $35/month**
TV: **Yes**
EXTRAS: **1/4 mile outdoor track • Basketball • Racquetball**

tion Center on the campus' NW side (some meter spots are located near each of the athletic venues).

Running on the meandering roads and tree-lined trails (east of Hopkins Drive) is a hilly treat. Maps are available at the Visitor Information Center. Estancia guests are closest to all the fun, although anyone in the San Diego area can enjoy the facilities — we do all the time.

La Jolla Sports Club

7825 Fay Avenue, La Jolla, CA 92037
(858) 456-2595

CARDIO

TREADMILLS: **StarTrac - old**
UPRIGHT BIKE: **LF**
RECUMBENT BIKE: **LF**
ELLIPTICAL: **LF • Precor • StarTrac**
STEPPER: **StairMaster**
ROWING: **Concept II**
OTHER: **VersaClimber**

STRENGTH

FREE WEIGHTS: **Yes**
HAMMER: **Yes**
MACHINES: **Cybex • Hoist • Free Motion • Icarian**
DUMBBELLS: **5-140 lbs**

OTHER

CLASSES: **Yes**
HOURS: M-F **5:30a-9p** • SAT **6:30a-6p** • SUN **7a-6p**
COST: **$10 All hotels • $15 Others**
TV: **Yes**

This diminutive facility may be short on space, but it stocks a powerful punch of new cardio machines and strength equipment. Most endurance apparatus is offered on the smaller, ground floor including Life Fitness 9500 series bikes and ellipticals, new Precor EFX ellipticals and StairMaster 4600PT model steppers. A few more cardio pieces are stocked in the large below-ground room, but it is primarily a strength venue. We stopped counting stack-loaded weight stations after 20 and noticed a ton of free weights as well. Swimmers, this club is water-phobic, i.e., no pool on-site.

All area hotel guests get in for $10 ($15 if you're not in a hotel). Be prepared to show your room key. Overall, LJSC is a convenient health club option for those staying in downtown La Jolla.

La Jolla High School
Coggan Family Aquatic Center & Track

800 Nautilus Street, La Jolla, CA 92037
(858) 456-0945 • cfaquatics.org

SWIM

GRADE: **A**
SPECS: **8x50m • Outdoor • 79°**
TOYS: **Kick • Pull • Fins • Clock**
MASTERS: **Yes**

OTHER

HOURS: **Vary**
EXTRAS: **1/4 mile outdoor track**

On the corner of Fay and Nautilus Streets, this public pool (completed late 2002) is a fantastic outdoor swimming facility. As the site of national water polo tournaments, regional swim meets and professional endurance athletes' training sessions, expect competition quality.

During the school year, the 50-meter pool is typically set up with 16 lanes of 25-yard short course but, in the summer, a long course pattern is more standard. Hours vary, especially with scheduled competitions, so call before heading over. Five bucks is all you need for this stellar and convenient pool. Plenty of parking is available.

A quarter-mile, foam-surfaced track was also recently completed. Adjacent to the pool, you will find that the fencing surrounding the track is typically unlocked along the southeast side. The available hours seem sporadic, especially during the school year, so we cannot guarantee access.

If you run to the track and can't get in, take it in stride and modify your workout into a hill repeat — run to Nautilus Street and turn left (east). You will find a MONSTER of a climb! Be careful on the way down.

The Sporting Club at Aventine

8930 University Center Lane, San Diego, CA 92122
(858) 552-8000 • thesportingclub.com

A workout at this prime facility is a real treat. Adjacent to the Hyatt Regency at Aventine, it has an atrium-like floor plan. The second story forms a wide, circular balcony around the main level, creating an expansive workout space with high ceilings and contemporary décor.

The Sporting Club stocks nothing but the latest in cutting-edge equipment, including brand-new StarTrac treads, Life Fitness 9500 series bikes and ellipticals, StairMaster 4400 model steppers and recently purchased Technogym stack-loaded weight stations. Tons of plate weights and dumbbells are on-site, along with a snack/juice bar and group exercise studios.

The going rate for Hyatt guests is 12 bucks, and it's well worth the green. Hyatt reward members receive a slight discount.

CARDIO

TREADMILLS: **StarTrac • NordicTrack**
UPRIGHT BIKE: **LF • StarTrac • Spin**
RECUMBENT BIKE: **LF • Reebok**
ELLIPTICAL: **LF • Precor**
STEPPER: **StairMaster • Stepmill**
ROWING: **Concept II**

STRENGTH

FREE WEIGHTS: **Yes**
HAMMER: **Yes**
MACHINES: **Cybex • Free Motion • Technogym**
DUMBBELLS: **3-150 lbs**

SWIM

GRADE: **B+**
SPECS: **4x25m • Outdoor • 80°**
TOYS: **Clock**
MASTERS: **Yes, $5**

OTHER

CLASSES: **Yes**
HOURS: M-F **5a-10p** • SAT **6a-8p** • SUN **7a-8p**
COST: **$12 Hyatt • $24/3-day Hyatt • $25 Others** • POOL **Free**
TV: **Yes**

The Club and Hyatt share a pool, which means hotel guests receive complimentary access to the 25-meter lapper. Four lanes are divided with floating lines and bottom stripes. And the rectangle is wide enough for kids and families without churning lappers' water. We noticed no kickboards or pull-buoys, but a Masters group works out here twice a week, so toys are likely close. You can join in the Masters fun for $5.

Runners should jog west across I-5 and make your way to UCSD campus where trails and a competition quarter-mile track await (1 mile to campus).

RUNNING ROUTES

DOWNTOWN

We've included running routes in the hotel descriptions for the Coronado, Mission Bay, Sea World, Hotel Circle and La Jolla areas.

Balboa Park

Those staying Downtown have two running options: First, seek Sixth Avenue and head north until you begin a gradual ascent (about a mile from most hotels) to where tree-lined Balboa Park begins. Turn right (east) at Laurel Drive, which places you on the Park's main drag. After passing two fountains, a pedestrian bridge will take you over Park Blvd. After crossing, head north (museum and zoo will be on your left) as far as the grass will take you, then drop down into some hilly trails on the right (east).

Continuing east from here will provide additional miles through the park — trails are all over, so keep your eyes peeled.

Embarcadero/Harbor Drive

The Embarcadero paved path runs along San Diego Bay. Head west from your hotel to the water, then jog north past the cruise liners and pirate ships. As you approach the airport, the sidewalk curves west; you can follow it for miles.

San Francisco

SAN FRANCISCO, CALIFORNIA

Ahh, San Francisco. In the words of Elizabeth Barrett Browning, "How do I love thee? Let me count the ways." The West Coast's urban playground, this City by the Bay captivates with its cosmopolitan lifestyle, cultural opportunities and quirky attractions. Although the City is renowned for its liberal politics, breathtaking scenery and romantic allure, San Francisco's Golden Gate Bridge is often the first image that comes to mind. However, while this architectural masterpiece and modern Wonder of the World is an engineering beauty, it is only one of this city's treasures.

There's Alcatraz Island, where residents were once granted million-dollar views from cozy quarters they could not leave — now a swim start for racing triathletes who prove that they could have escaped. There's Chinatown, the largest Chinese community outside of the mainland, where shoulder-to-shoulder crowds flood a 24-block maze and fortune cookies are sold hot off the press (Golden Gate Cookie Factory in Ross Alley). In colorful Haight Ashbury, the free-loving, hippie vibe beats loudly in a place where tie-dye is worn by more than a few grizzly old Ruperts. And San Francisco's long arms of acceptance embrace gay and lesbian activists who thrive well outside the walk-in closet. There are the trolley cars, the "crookedest" street, the touristy Wharf and Ghirardelli's chocolate. And those hills, oh those mini-mountain hills, which are good for two things: views at the top and glute-building on the way up.

Like New York, this city is so deep in character and spirit, you just have to visit. And we have to stop — writing, that is.

UNION SQUARE

This is where the action lies. If you want to stay in the middle of it all — upscale shopping, fancy dining, cultural attractions and China Town, Union Square is your destination. Rooms are small, hotel rates expensive and streets crowded, but the exercise options are high quality and convenient. Bring your workout gear and your wallet — you'll need both.

114 Locations Reviewed

EXPENSIVE

GOLD: Four Seasons

757 Market Street, San Francisco, CA 94103
(415) 633-3000 • fourseasons.com/sanfrancisco

Do we really need to expound on the delights of this epic hotel brand? We envy those with the means, because a Four Seasons experience is icing on any cake. While some properties outshine others, San Francisco's version glitters.

This lavish urban retreat occupies floors 5 through 17 of a 42-story skyscraper. Above are private residences, below is the dazzling Sports Club/LA. Four Seasons delicately adorns its 277 guest quarters with contemporary furnishings and ultra premium bedding in light and airy tones. Self-billed as the "largest rooms in the city," they are certainly spacious. Marble baths with deep soaking tubs and separate glass-enclosed showers will energize you for a night out — in a location where everything is outside your door.

Luxury accommodations are not enough to satiate well-heeled athletic-minded travelers, and Four Seasons' unparalleled hospitality ensures your fitness craving is caviar fed. Sports Club/LA, San Francisco's most elaborate and exclusive health club, grants Four Seasons patrons complimentary access to its unbelievable wealth of fitness opportunities. And it's right downstairs!

SILVER: Palace Hotel

2 New Montgomery Street, San Francisco, CA 94105
(415) 512-1111 • sfpalace.com

CARDIO

TREADMILLS: **1 LF • 2 StarTrac**
UPRIGHT BIKE: **1 LF**
RECUMBENT BIKE: **1 LF • 1 StarTrac - old**
ELLIPTICAL: **1 LF • 1 Precor - old**
STEPPER: **1 LF**

STRENGTH

MACHINES: **4 LF**
DUMBBELLS: **5-50 lbs**

SWIM

GRADE: **D**
SPECS: **3x20yd • Indoor • 81°**

OTHER

HOURS: M-F **5a-10p** • SAT-SUN **6a-10p**
COST: **Free**
TV: **Yes**
EXTRAS: **$10 Access to Crunch**

In contrast to Four Seasons' 21st Century luxury, Palace's restored 1875 grand dame offers an Old World setting. This regal hotel is 3 blocks from Union Square and within a mile of Downtown's financial district. Nearly covering a city block, its immensity is astounding — both inside and out. The hallways are wide enough to drive a Mini-Cooper through and the doorways are tall enough to grant NBA players entry without their customary hunching. Three restaurants are included in this massive building as well. All 552 guest quarters impress with 14-foot ceilings, Egyptian cotton sheets and comfortable down bedding. Palace's conservatively plain décor and antique furnishings lack pizzazz but fall in line with the accommodation's historic theme.

The hotel's largesse extends to sweat purveyors. Exercising guests will be pleased to find a satisfactory equipment mix in the 4th floor fitness center. Although we expected more machines and a larger space, we compliment the Palace for affording guests a basic cardio and strength routine. Life Fitness' 9500 series is emphasized in the endurance zone, and good condition dumbbells and stack-loaded weight stations are ready for muscle pumpers. However, serious power lifters and cardio connoisseurs preferring a wider brand selection can cross New Montgomery Street and workout at Crunch Fitness for $10 (closed Sundays).

Online pool photos heightened our expectations for the Palace's lap option. Alas, after viewing it in person, our hopes for a proper swim were dashed. This water box is 5 yards short of regulation length, and floating lines are not installed. Therefore, our fish-like friends must frolic in a 20-yard venue with 3 black stripes painted on the bottom — not ideal, but certainly not hopeless. Hard core swimmers should journey uphill 10-15 minutes on foot to the legitimate lapper at Club One on Mason Street ($15).

MODERATELY EXPENSIVE

GOLD: **Argent**

50 Third Street, San Francisco, CA 94103
(415) 974-6400 • argenthotel.com

CARDIO

TREADMILLS: **2 Precor**
UPRIGHT BIKE: **2 LF - old**
RECUMBENT BIKE: **3 - mix**
ELLIPTICAL: **2 Precor**
STEPPER: **2 StairMaster - old**

STRENGTH

MACHINES: **8 Paramount**
DUMBBELLS: **5-20 lbs**

OTHER

HOURS: **24**
COST: **Free**
TV: **Yes**
EXTRAS: **$25 Access to Sports Club/LA • Organized runs M-F 6:30a**

Looking for a truly fitness oriented hotel, but don't want to pay Four Seasons prices? We have found it for you. Argent's one-block proximity to the convention center makes it a popular choice for conventioneers, but athletic-minded travelers may also flock here after discovering its exercise treasures.

By no means a boutique accommodation, Argent's 36-stories house 667 rooms, one restaurant and a lounge. Modern and convenient describe this bustling property. Guests can expect larger than average San Francisco-sized units (350 square feet), elegant décor and premium bedding, which will soothe those sore muscles after you go crazy with the fitness options.

On-site, exercisers are given free reign over Argent's diminutive yet useful 4th floor workout room. New ellipticals, treadmills and stack-loaded weight stations share space with an older mix of bikes and steppers, all of which present a viable cardio or strength quick hit. For those seeking more (and there will be many), a stay here includes a standing invitation to the best health club in the entire Bay Area — Sports Club/LA. Argent guests are among a privileged few who, along with Four Seasons patrons, receive access to this exclusive club, located one block away. Your aerobic fun will not come cheap ($25), so consider booking a "stay in shape" package which eases the sticker shock by 5-10 bucks/night — more if you have a companion.

Runners also receive a rare perk from the conditioning-conscious Argent — organized morning runs. Monday through Friday at 6:30 a.m. a knowledgeable guide whisks runners away on an awakening stride — that was 6:30 a.m.!

Swimmers should head straight to Sports Club/LA's highly rated 25-yard lapper; you will not be disappointed.

SILVER: Clift Hotel

495 Geary Street, San Francisco, CA 94102
(415) 775-4700 • clifthotel.com

CARDIO

TREADMILLS: **4 Cybex**
RECUMBENT BIKE: **2 Cybex**
STEPPER: **2 Cybex**

STRENGTH

MACHINES: **1 Cybex multi**
DUMBBELLS: **2-90 lbs**

OTHER

HOURS: **24**
COST: **Free**
TV: **Yes**

Looking back and forth from Clift's street address written on our note pads and the buildings within view, we were perplexed. Where was the hotel?

Frustrated, we finally sought assistance from a nice-looking gentleman standing outside one of San Francisco's many architecturally rich and historic high-rises. "Hey bud, know where the Clift is?" we inquired.

With a grin on his face, he simply said, "Why, yes. I'm the doorman, and I'm standing in front of the entrance."

Without a blatant sign or crude canopy announcing its presence, Clift's façade blends in a little too well.

A completely unique hotel experience, this Ian Schrager property (LA's Mondrian and South Beach's Shore Club) in the heart of Union Square's hustle and bustle will transform even serious fuddy-duddys into chic and cool players. A younger and less "business-y" crowd fills these rooms during the day and the hotel's swank Redwood Room bar at night. We recommend sipping a cocktail at this tony watering-hole, if only to check out the digital wall portraits, whose expressions actually change.

One of the glowing green, red or orange elevators transports you to Clift's 363 guest quarters. While the rooms are small, especially the entry-level "standards" at 250 square feet (consider paying more for an extra 65 square feet), we were happy to find as much attention and detail dedicated to the accommodations as to the lobby, restaurant and bar. Cool and crisp tones color the walls, sleigh beds with light hardwood frames and high thread count Egyptian cotton sheets create a comfy on-the-road respite. The in-room DVD/CD players offer additional distraction, and Clift's video library serves up an entertaining selection.

Sweat fiends will discover a mediocre exercise option on the hotel's 2nd floor. Although the machines inside are in good condition, upright bikes, elliptical trainers and separate stack-loaded weight machines are noticeably absent. The plasma TV-attached cardio pieces might satisfy a mini-workout, but most (including lap swimmers) will want to walk 5 minutes to Union Square's Club One, where 15 bucks will get you in.

BRONZE: Hotel Monaco

501 Geary Street, San Francisco, CA 94102
monaco-sf.com • (415) 292-0100

This whimsical property within 2 blocks of Union Square is all about fun, fun, fun. Where Argent is contemporary and elegant, and Clift hip and trendy, Monaco is a circus.

Seeking a quiet companion? Pet gold fish are available. Weighing a big decision? Tarot card readings are held in the fireplace lounge. Traveling with Fido this time? Reserve the "Bone-A-Petit" package for you and your four-legged friend.

CARDIO

TREADMILLS: **2 StarTrac • 2 LF - old**
UPRIGHT BIKE: **1 LF**
RECUMBENT BIKE: **2 StarTrac**
ELLIPTICAL: **2 LF • 1 StarTrac**
STEPPER: **3 Tectrix - old**

STRENGTH

MACHINES: **5 LF**
DUMBBELLS: **2-50 lbs**

OTHER

HOURS: **6a-10p**
COST: **Free**
TV: **Yes**

Although the entry level accommodations are the smallest in this category at 200 square feet, the bold patterns and loud pigments decorating the 200 guest quarters divert your attention away from any spatial challenges. Basic furnishings? No way. Instead, guests are treated to an eclectic mix of canopy beds, bamboo desks, pillow top mattresses and Chinese armoires.

Monaco recently ordered new equipment for its attended lower level workout center and spa. Delivery is expected prior to publication, so the accompanying chart details the anticipated inventory. At present, the center is not a total slouch and provides a decent sweat prospect with a number of treadmills, a couple of recumbents and one elliptical.

While the new machinery will enhance the room's appeal, and most cardio apparatus will have personal plasma viewing screens, strength enthusiasts (now and in the future), will want to look elsewhere.

Lap swimmers and guests who desire a more serious body sculpt can walk 5 minutes to the Club One in Union Square — $15 is the tariff.

LEAST EXPENSIVE

GOLD: Hotel Rex

562 Sutter Street, San Francisco, CA 94102
(415) 433-4434 • thehotelrex.com

One of our favorite properties, Hotel Rex is the best dollar for dollar "stay n' play" deal in all of San Francisco. Only 2 blocks from Union Square's luxury shopping attractions and within a 5-minute walk of Chinatown, Rex's location is wonderfully convenient for leisure travelers. Complimentary Towncar service, available weekday mornings (M-F 7:30-8:30 a.m.), makes it a practical base for business travelers as well.

Rex's boutique accommodation houses 94 rooms on 7 floors. The single elevator works overtime transporting patrons up and down, but an adjacent staircase reliably serves less patient folk. The staff's friendly approach and the hotel's cozy, living-room-like aura greet weary travelers. Complimentary evening wine receptions, packages that include parking discounts and the artsy café create a vibe that is more home than hotel.

Creativity is evident throughout all guest quarters. While entry level rooms are small (225 square feet) and come with queen-size beds only, the king bed "deluxes" are larger. Request a high floor for the preferred rooms (room numbers 13 or 14 if possible) — they will not guarantee it, but will try their best. Additionally, we've had luck asking Rex to match online travel service rates which often price rooms $20-$30/night less — don't be bashful.

Once you settle on your sleeping arrangement, you can expect warm and deep tones complemented by pillow top mattresses and high thread count sheets. High-speed internet access and CD players with one or two music selections are nice touches.

Without a fitness room on-site, Rex takes care of athletic-minded guests with discounted access to the full-service Club One — it's less than a 2-minute walk. Pay for a pass at the hotel front desk ($10) and head on over. The club's 25-yard lap pool makes it a great option for swimmers, too.

SILVER: Handlery Union Square Hotel

351 Geary Street, San Francisco, CA 94102
(415) 781-7800 • handlery.com

A distant second to Rex's dominant showing, but a respectable and thrifty accommodation, Handlery offers similar location benefits — a couple blocks from Union Square, a few more to Chinatown and a few more to the financial district.

Rooms are located in two connected buildings — the Historic Tower and Club Tower. We recommend paying a slight premium ($20-$30) for the larger, more comfortable and quieter (if on the pool side) Club quarters. At 400-450 square feet, these relative behemoths outsize the Historic Tower's little guys by nearly 150 square feet. Handlery does not dazzle with flair nor spoil with amenities, but its reliable quality, solid service and attention to detail are valued attributes, especially in this price category.

Handlery has no workout room on-site so, like many other hotel guests in this neck of the San Francisco woods, heading a few blocks to Club One is your best option (purchase a $10 pass from the front desk — $5 discount).

BEYOND HOTELS UNION SQUARE

Sports Club/LA

747 Market Street, San Francisco, CA 94103
(415) 633-3900 • thesportsclubla.com

Four Seasons (free) and Argent ($25) guests will be spoiled by the prodigious Sports Club/LA, which is hands down the best and most extensive health club in the Bay Area. Other visitors are not allowed unless accompanied by a member.

The club boasts over 100,000 square feet of health conscious opportunities in a museum-like environment. Workout addicts will never want to leave. Despite the rich décor and trappings, members are here to sweat. Hundreds of the latest cardio machines, many with attached plasma screens, sparkle like new. Any strength routine is possible in the 10,000 square foot weight training gym — the size of some entire health clubs.

Whatever your passion, you'll find it here, including Life Fitness 9700 series treads and 9500 series computerized bikes, StairMaster 4600PT model steppers, fixed weight barbells and Lemond spinning bikes. Group therapy makes a strong showing, too, with endless class options displayed on wall-hanging 42-inch interactive plasma screens.

With all the space, there had better be a true lapper, right? The Sports Club comes through with an 8 lane, 25-yard water box marked with floating lines and bottom stripes. Narrow lanes preclude sharing, but they are wide enough for one hard-core swimmer. Check out the website for a good visual.

CARDIO

TREADMILLS: **Precor**
UPRIGHT BIKE: **LF**
RECUMBENT BIKE: **LF**
ELLIPTICAL: **Precor**
STEPPER: **StairMaster • Stepmill**
ROWING: **Concept II**
OTHER: **Gravitron**

STRENGTH

FREE WEIGHTS: **Yes**
HAMMER: **Yes**
MACHINES: **LF • Cybex • Free Motion • Icarian**
DUMBBELLS: **3-110 lbs**

SWIM

GRADE: **B+**
SPECS: **8x25yd • Indoor • 81°**
TOYS: **Kick • Pull • Fins • Clock**

OTHER

CLASSES: **Yes**
HOURS: M-F **5a-11p** • SAT-SUN **7a-8p**
COST: **Free Four Seasons • $25 Argent • No others**
TV: **Yes**
EXTRAS: **Basketball • Cafe**

Crunch Fitness Sharon

61 New Montgomery Street, San Francisco, CA 94105
(415) 543-1110 • crunch.com

CARDIO
TREADMILLS: **LF**
UPRIGHT BIKE: **LF**
RECUMBENT BIKE: **LF**
ELLIPTICAL: **LF • Precor**
STEPPER: **StairMaster - old • Stepmill**

STRENGTH
FREE WEIGHTS: **Yes**
HAMMER: **Yes**
MACHINES: **LF • Magnum • Icarian**
DUMBBELLS: **5-100 lbs**

OTHER
CLASSES: **Yes**
HOURS: M-F **5:30a-9:30p** • SAT **7a-6p** • SUN **Closed**
COST: **$10 Palace • $16 IHRSA • $24 Others**
TV: **Yes**

Recommended primarily as an off-site fitness alternative for Palace Hotel guests, this Bally's owned club resembles a tiny old theater. The main fitness floor is bordered by two overhead balconies, while the middle is left open to 30-foot ceilings. The black walls create a nightclub-ish vibe, but Crunch's decent assortment of modern workout gear enlivens the room. The endurance and strength industries' most popular brands are well represented, including Precor, Life Fitness and StairMaster.

This Crunch is too small for a pool, so lap swimmers must look elsewhere for a dip; consider Club One.

Palace guests get in for $10, members of a home IHRSA club are charged $16 (healthclubs.com) and everyone else must sacrifice $24 for this mediocre workout venue.

Note: This club is closed on Sundays.

Club One Union Square

535 Mason Street
San Francisco, CA 94102
(415) 337-1010
clubone.com

CARDIO
TREADMILLS: **8 StarTrac**
UPRIGHT BIKE: **4 LF**
RECUMBENT BIKE: **3 LF**
ELLIPTICAL: **4 LF • 4 Precor**
STEPPER: **5 StairMaster**
ROWING: **1 Concept II**

STRENGTH
FREE WEIGHTS: **Yes**
MACHINES: **13 LF • 1 Free Motion**
DUMBBELLS: **5-100 lbs**

SWIM
GRADE: **B-**
SPECS: **3x25yd • Indoor • 80°**
TOYS: **Kick • Pull • Clock**

OTHER
CLASSES: **Yes**
HOURS: M-F **5:30a-10p** • SAT-SUN **7a-7p**
COST: **$10 Select hotels • $15 Other hotels & IHRSA • $20 Others**
TV: **Yes**

This amazingly convenient gym opens its doors to both members and guests and obliges athletic-minded travelers with a worthy swim and/or sweat venue. The small facility packs a strong punch of cardio and strength equipment in a pleasing, contemporary environment. Concerned about crowd potential, we asked several staff members about waiting for machines, rush hours, etc. Their puzzled look and verbal denials assured us that this club does not "pack 'em in." Our chart includes the exact machine count at the time of our most recent visit. All apparatus are new models such as Life Fitness' 9500 series and StairMaster's 4400PT, and many sport mini-screens for visual programming.

A regulation lap pool in this dense section of San Francisco is a rare find, and Club One has it. Three lanes are divided by floating lines and bottom stripes across its 25-yard chlorinated course. We understand that swimmers may reserve lanes up to one day in advance, so if you are really organized, dial the 7 "D's" to ensure yourself a slot. However, in our 3 visits to this club, we saw only one swimmer, so supply and demand appears to work in your favor.

Note: Towels are provided and the locker rooms are first class .

EMBARCADERO/FINANCIAL DIST.

This is where stocks are traded and business is done. Local financial whizzes living in the Pacific Time Zone punch in at 4 a.m. And you thought you woke up early! Stay here to be in the midst of the working crowd and the Embarcadero's piers, and not far from Union Square's daytime shopping and nighttime entertainment.

MODERATELY EXPENSIVE

GOLD: **Hotel Griffon**

155 Steuart Street, San Francisco, CA 94105
(415) 495-2100 • hotelgriffon.com

Most convenient to the financial district's office high-rises and Embarcadero's piers, this European-style boutique accommodation suits up nicely for the business traveler. While somewhat distant to Union Square shopping or theater district entertainment, nearby trolley lines and a BART station (subway) offer traffic-free transportation throughout the City.

With soaring real estate prices, space is a premium in San Francisco, so expect guest quarters to be small — very small. Griffon's 62 rooms, outfitted with mahogany desks and colorful bedding, are no exception. The upside is that this is no cookie-cutter accommodation. Many rooms sport unique whitewashed 1906 brick walls and fabulous views of the bridge — Oakland's Bay, that is. Other Griffon spoils include free continental breakfasts 7 days a week, morning weekday newspapers and weekday Towncar service within a half-mile of the hotel (7:30-9 a.m. only).

With the first-rate Embarcadero YMCA next door, business savvy Griffon does not try to compete by offering an on-site facility. Instead, its guests can walk 10 paces out the front door and pay $15 for a full-service workout (some frequent-stay guests can get in free with an ongoing corporate account). Frankly, this hotel is interchangeable with Harbor Court for the top slot — both deserve the Gold. Book either with confidence and keep in mind the Y's $15 fee in your calculations. If you reserve directly with Harbor Court, your Y access is free.

GOLD: Harbor Court

165 Steuart Street, San Francisco, CA 94105
(415) 882-1300 • harborcourthotel.com

If Griffon's 10-step commute to the Y is still too far, consider Harbor Court's 5 paces. Offering the same location positives and negatives as its financial district neighbor — in the midst of Downtown's corporate hustle and bustle, but farther from Union Square and other popular San Francisco neighborhoods — this friendly and quaint accommodation is twice the size of nearby Griffon, but it successfully preserves a boutique character.

Harbor mixes contemporary furnishings with Old World charm in its 131 rooms by providing canopied beds, modern desks and soothing Bay views (most rooms). Close to the trolleys and BART, Harbor also offers weekday morning Towncar service (7-9 a.m.); however, breakfast eaters are left in a lurch without a free morning bite.

Like Griffon, Harbor Court passes on an in-house fitness option and directs exercising guests to the Embarcadero YMCA. Unlike Griffon, if you book directly with Harbor Court, complimentary access will be granted to this Y — a considerable perk if you will be purposefully sweating for a few days.

CARDIO

TREADMILLS: **Precor**
UPRIGHT BIKE: **LF**
RECUMBENT BIKE: **LF**
ELLIPTICAL: **Precor • Cybex • Reebok**
STEPPER: **StairMaster - new & old**
ROWING: **Concept II**

STRENGTH

FREE WEIGHTS: **Yes**
HAMMER: **Yes - Leg only**
MACHINES: **Cybex • Life Circuit**
DUMBBELLS: **3-100 lbs**

SWIM

GRADE: **B**
SPECS: **5x25m • Indoor • 84º**
TOYS: **Kick • Pull • Clock**
MASTERS: **Yes**

OTHER

CLASSES: **Yes**
HOURS: M-F **5:30a-10p** • SAT **8a-8p** • SUN **9a-6p**
COST: **Free Harbor • $15 Others**
TV: **No**

BEYOND HOTELS

EMBARCADERO/ FINANCIAL DISTRICT

Embarcadero YMCA

169 Steuart Street
San Francisco, CA 94105
(415) 957-9622
ymcasf.org/embarcadero

Amazingly convenient for guests of the Griffon and Harbor Court, the Embarcadero Y passes our athletic "white glove" test. Although the full-service health club is often brimming with locals during rush hours (before 9 a.m. and after 4 p.m.), avoiding these times is simple when you are staying next door. In addition to the Y's vast array of high-end cardio machines and modern strength apparatus, which we applaud, we especially appreciated the 4-foot hinged windows that overlook the Bay. On beautiful San Francisco days, the windows swing open to whisk in a bay breeze on the heels of harbor sounds... okay, back to business.

The Y's endurance machines are all newer models. Life Fitness 9500 series bikes, StairMaster 4600PT model steppers and the latest Precor treadmills are primed for action. Weight buffs will not be disappointed, with plenty of free weights, a plethora of stack-loaded stations and a large range of dumbbells all rallying to your cause.

Judging from the number of swimmers sharing lanes, lappers may endure the largest crowd. If possible, be strategic with your timing. Nevertheless, this water rectangle is functional and appealing with its 5 lanes stretching over 25 meters. Floating lines and bottom stripes get you from end to end, and an assortment of toys and a pace clock are available as well (see website for a good visual).

The going rate for a day pass is 15 bucks, but guests of Harbor Court and certain guests of Hotel Griffon can get in for free — check with each.

PACIFIC HEIGHTS/PRESIDIO

Compared to Union Square and Embarcadero, Pacific Heights is more residential, more subdued and more local in its vibe. This neighborhood boasts fantastic shops and eateries along Union and Fillmore Streets and is the most sought-after real estate in the City. Despite a 2-3 mile distance to Union Square and Downtown's corporate action, it is a hilly commute. While we have you covered for whatever your fitness fetish, your other obvious option is simply to walk the hills.

EXPENSIVE

BRONZE: **Hotel Drisco**

2901 Pacific Avenue, San Francisco, CA 94115
(415) 346-2880 • hoteldrisco.com

No, your eyes are not deceiving you. We award Drisco Bronze, despite the fact that there are no Gold or Silver listings in this high-price category. Along with Drisco's many positives, too many detractions hinder a higher ranking. At one of the highest points in ritzy Pacific Heights, the petite, 43-room Drisco occupies a corner of the Bay area's most expensive and coveted real estate. Surrounded by luxury homes in a quiet neighborhood, it is more of an early 20th Century mansion than 21st Century hotel. Creaking floors and handcrafted detail create a cozy and homey ambiance. The common areas may bespeak its 100+ year age, but the quarters have been renovated to uphold modern standards.

Keep in mind that, in urban San Francisco, rooms are small. And, while good things often come in small packages, you may disagree if you are greeted unexpectedly with twin bed sleeping arrangements. Because Drisco's accommodations vary, we strongly urge guests to reserve directly with the hotel. If you need further motivation, consider that the six 2-bedroom suites are sometimes rented as separate 1-bedroom units — leaving one party without a commode. Don't worry, it's just outside the hallway door.

For those who cherish an intimate and regal rest and do not mind the hilltop locale (which puts guests a steep mile away from any diversion), Drisco offers impeccable service and a number of goodies, including complimentary gourmet breakfast buffets, morning Towncar service to Union Square and/or the financial district (M-F, 7:30-9 a.m.), afternoon tea and pastries and free access to the Presidio YMCA.

Athletes will want to take advantage of this last comp, because Drisco's basement "exercise" room is circa 1903. Plan for a 5-minute drive or taxi (plenty of parking spaces are available at the Y), or a 10-minute HILLY run.

LEAST EXPENSIVE

GOLD: **Laurel Inn**

444 Presidio Avenue, San Francisco, CA 94115
(415) 567-8467 • thelaurelinn.com

A bargain accommodation in one of this city's less urban areas, the Laurel is happily removed from commercial Union Square and Downtown's hustle and bustle. Although this part of Pacific Heights is certainly not isolated, you will find less traffic and fewer tourists. Laurel does not suffer from the same hill climbing challenge as Hotel Drisco, and a number of coffee houses, boutiques and restaurants are nearby. Still, top shopping and dining spots are beyond comfortable walking distance. If you are driving, this is your place. Laurel's free parking perk is a hot commodity in a city where hotel parking charges often run up to $40/night.

This 49-room charmer has generously-sized guest quarters with creative décor, though not quite as crisp and colorful as Laurel's website portrays. We suggest requesting a room on the backside of the hotel to avoid potential overnight noise from the bordering streets, especially Presidio Boulevard. Or ask for one of the 18 rooms with a kitchenette. Complimentary muffins, coffee and juices are convenient for a quick bite as you head out the door.

Laurel's workout option is a good one. With nothing on-site, exercising patrons receive discounted admission to the phenomenal Jewish Community Center across the street. Opened in 2004, this JCC is a state-of-the-art fitness facility and a whole lot more.

BEYOND HOTELS PACIFIC HEIGHTS/PRESIDIO

Presidio Community YMCA

Fitness Center
Lincoln & Funston Sts., Bldg. 63, San Francisco, CA 94129
(415) 447-9622
Pool
Bldg. 1151, Gorgas Street, San Francisco, CA 94129
(415) 447-9680
ymcasf.org/presidio

This YMCA is located inside the Presidio, once a sprawling military base and now a national park. The Y covers two separate buildings approximately a half-mile from one another: building #63 (main gym) and building #1151 (pool). Feeling energetic? Put on the running shoes and jog here from Hotel Drisco or the Laurel Inn, but be mindful of your descent en route, because it is all uphill for the return trip.

Inside the white-painted fitness center with its 30-foot ceilings, exercising recruits will salute a fine troop of new cardio machines, free weights and stack-loaded weight stations. We called to attention more than 25 Cybex and Free Motion machines, 14 Life Fitness 9500 series bikes, 10 treadmills, 10 ellipticals and six 4600 model StairMaster steppers. Only one flat and one incline bench are in the Y's arsenal, but plenty of dumbbells save the day.

Commendations are given to the separately housed pool with its 6 lanes of 25-yard navigable waters. Floating lines and bottom stripes map your route, and scores of toys are on deck for your pleasure. At ease, soldier!

CARDIO

TREADMILLS: **Precor**
UPRIGHT BIKE: **LF**
RECUMBENT BIKE: **LF**
ELLIPTICAL: **Precor • LF**
STEPPER: **StairMaster**
OTHER: **NordicTrack**

STRENGTH

FREE WEIGHTS: **Yes**
MACHINES: **Cybex • Free Motion**
DUMBBELLS: **3-100 lbs**

SWIM

GRADE: **C+**
SPECS: **6x25yd • Indoor • 79-82°**
TOYS: **Kick • Pull • Clock**
MASTERS: **Yes**

OTHER

CLASSES: **Yes**
HOURS: M-F **5:45a-9:30p** • SAT **7a-7p** • SUN **8:30a-7p** **Pool closes 30 minutes earlier**
COST: **Free Drisco • $12 Others**
TV: **Yes**
EXTRAS: **Basketball • Tennis**

Directions: *FITNESS CENTER - Follow Presidio Blvd. down a long and winding hill (the road becomes Lincoln Blvd.). Turn left on Funston; you will see a parking lot and a "Post Gymnasium" building on the left before making your turn. POOL - On Lincoln, after passing the Gym and Funston make a soft right (unnamed road); right on Gorgas before underpass; right on Halleck St. Follow Halleck to just before the end. Pool building is on the left (parking near the pool is limited).*

Jewish Community Center JCC

3200 California Street, San Francisco, CA 94118
(415) 292-1234 • jccsf.org

CARDIO

TREADMILLS: **StarTrac**
UPRIGHT BIKE: **StarTrac**
RECUMBENT BIKE: **StarTrac**
ELLIPTICAL: **Precor**
STEPPER: **StairMaster • Stepmill**
ROWING: **Concept II**

STRENGTH

FREE WEIGHTS: **Yes**
HAMMER: **Yes**
MACHINES: **LF • Hoist • Icarian**
DUMBBELLS: **3-100 lbs**

SWIM

GRADE: **B+**
SPECS: **5x25yd • Indoor • 80°**
TOYS: **Kick • Pull • Paddle**
MASTERS: **Yes**

OTHER

CLASSES: **Yes, call ahead**
HOURS: M-F **5:30a-10p**
• SAT-SUN **7a-7p**
COST: **$10 Laurel • $15 Others**
TV: **Yes**
EXTRAS: **Basketball**

This place is pretty darn spectacular and recommended over the Y. Reopened in January 2004, the new and improved JCC attracts a diverse crowd to its immaculate and hospitable facility. While lectures, community events and classes are hosted year round, our interests relate solely to the fitness center and lap pool.

All your favorite cardio machines are here, and most of these late 2003 and early 2004 models have entertainment attached (e.g., individual plasma screens). Strength enthusiasts do not get short changed, either. Au contraire, the JCC boasts plenty of free weights, 25-115 lbs barbells, 3 Hammer Strength machines and a litany of stack-loaded weight stations.

Swimmers are treated just as well. Five 25-yard lanes are separated by floating lines and bottom stripes. Paddles, kickboards and pull-buoys are on the menu. Bring a watch if intervals are your main course, because our tour revealed no pace clock.

The going guest rate is 15 bucks. Laurel Inn patrons receive a $5 discount. Shalom.

RUNNING ROUTES

The most convenient run is along the waterfront, accessible from all neighborhoods. Those staying in Union Square and Downtown will want to begin at the Embarcadero and run northwest past Fisherman's Wharf, Fort Mason, through Crissy Field and across the Golden Gate Bridge's pedestrian lane (~6-7 miles total, one way). Those staying in Pacific Heights/Presidio can jog through hilly Presidio Park and pick up the route in either direction at Crissy Field.

Golden Gate Park

If you have a car, you'll find the City's best running trails here. As the largest man-made park in the world, it has no shortage of paved, grass and dirt running routes. Park anywhere, get out and explore!

San Jose

SAN JOSE, CALIFORNIA

While the high tech and internet bubble may have burst a few years ago, the heart of Silicon Valley still beats loudly as America's business capital (sorry, New York). Downtown continues to attract a growing number of business and convention travelers with powerful companies like Ebay, Cisco, Sun and Adobe dotting (or, should we say, "dot.com-ing") the San Jose landscape. As new companies sprout into big plants, thanks to an infusion of venture seed money, San Jose's future looks as bright as a plugged-in LCD.

Those traveling to San Jose should not expect the glitz, glamour and nightlife of big sister San Francisco. Cultural attractions, shopping boutiques and the urban vibe have not yet arrived. However, natives insist that these big city staples are on the way. For the time being, Downtown continues to sleep after midnight, when restaurants close and streets go silent. Our late night travels in the City certainly confirm the zzzz's.

14 Locations Reviewed

EXPENSIVE

GOLD: Fairmont

170 South Market Street, San Jose, CA 95113
(408) 998-1900 • fairmont.com/sanjose

CARDIO
TREADMILLS: **6 Precor**
UPRIGHT BIKE: **2 Cybex**
RECUMBENT BIKE: **2 Cybex**
ELLIPTICAL: **4 Precor • 1 LF - old**
STEPPER: **3 Cybex**

STRENGTH
MACHINES: **6 Cybex**
DUMBBELLS: **5-50 lbs**

SWIM
SPECS: **Outdoor • Not lap**

OTHER
HOURS: **5:30a-9p**
COST: **Free**
TV: **Yes**

Across the street from San Jose's retail and dining options at the Pavilion and a block from the convention center, the Fairmont is San Jose's most luxurious hotel.

While its 808 guest quarters are plain vanilla in color, Fairmont is Neapolitan with its furnishing flavors. The attractive rooms feature premium bedding with high thread count sheets, free bottled water, 24-hour room service, large bathrooms with separate shower and tub, free local calls and refrigerators.

The 3rd floor exercise center is a double-scoop of fitness fun. Although free weights are noticeably absent, Fairmont stocks a wide assortment of modern weight and cardio machines for a full body conditioning. Only the Life Fitness elliptical gets an "old" tag in our book; the other cardio units run efficiently in a room full of good humor.

Swimmers and those looking for a free weight workout must look off-site to complete their sweat sessions. Water seekers should walk 10 minutes to San Jose State's Aquatic Center. Weight buffs, head for Pinnacle Fitness (3-minute walk).

MODERATELY EXPENSIVE

GOLD: Marriott

301 South Market Street
San Jose, CA 95113
(408) 280-1300 • marriott.com

CARDIO
TREADMILLS: **4 Body Guard**
UPRIGHT BIKE: **2 Body Guard**
RECUMBENT BIKE: **2 Body Guard**
ELLIPTICAL: **2 SciFit**
STEPPER: **2 Body Guard**

STRENGTH
MACHINES: **7 Paramount**
DUMBBELLS: **Uni**

SWIM
SPECS: **Outdoor • Not lap**

OTHER
HOURS: **24**
COST: **Free**
TV: **Yes**

This 26-story modern hotel opened its doors in spring 2003 and still looks and smells new. Connected to the convention center and a short walk from Downtown's small retail district, this high-rise Marriott is an attractive lodging option for business and leisure travelers.

Marriott's 506 colorful rooms speak a fresh and stylish language. Red desk chairs, blue lounges and honeycomb yellow down comforters cheerfully decorate the interior. We give management credit for stepping outside the convention hotel box.

The in-house fitness center will satisfy most guests. While Marriott provides a wide assortment of cardio modalities in a large and welcoming room, it skimped on brands. Body Guard is the manufacturer of choice and the equipment is simply not as good as Precor, Life Fitness or StarTrac. Nevertheless, all of the machines are as young as the hotel, so give them a whirl. Those with a strength session in mind have nothing to worry about — Marriott spent a good chunk of cash on high quality Paramount stations.

Swimmers and exercisers turning their noses up at the Body Guard brand should walk to San Jose State's Aquatic Center and Pinnacle Fitness, respectively (5 minutes and 10 minutes).

LEAST EXPENSIVE

GOLD: The Sainte Claire

302 South Market Street, San Jose, CA 95113
(408) 298-1234 • thesainteclaire.com

An historic landmark within a short walk of Downtown's convention center and Pavilion retail shops, the Sainte Claire is a good bet for those with a penchant for a touch of yesteryear.

Since the Sainte Claire was built in 1926, expect rooms smaller than those in newer accommodations. While not tiny, we definitely noticed the spatial challenges in the bathrooms — especially counter space. All 171 units are clean and attractively decorated, but they are not nearly as sunny and cheery as the online pictures represent.

Sainte Claire recently purchased a few new machines, and we award management kudos for doing so. However, the basement level work out room may not please all athletic-minded travelers. The machines inside are good quality, but there is no upright bike, and you are likely to find that someone has already laid claim to the one elliptical. In that case, your best bet will be to head to Pinnacle Fitness — an upscale club less than 5-minutes' walk away that has everything but a pool.

If it's water that you desire, you will not find a better swim option than San Jose State's Olympic-size lapper. This, too, is within walking distance of the hotel, but it will take around 10 minutes rather than 5 to get there.

Note: Il Fornaio restaurant is located inside the hotel.

BEYOND HOTELS

San Jose State Aquatic Center

Sports Club at the Event Center
One Washington Square, San Jose, CA 95192
(408) 924-6368 – Sports Club
(408) 924-6341 – Aquatic Center
sjsu.edu (follow quick link to event center)

CARDIO

TREADMILLS: **StairMaster**
UPRIGHT BIKE: **Cybex • Schwinn**
RECUMBENT BIKE: **Cybex • Schwinn**
ELLIPTICAL: **Precor**
STEPPER: **StairMaster**
ROWING: **Concept II**

STRENGTH

FREE WEIGHTS: **Yes**
MACHINES: **Cybex**
DUMBBELLS: **3-110 lbs**

SWIM

GRADE: **B+**
SPECS: **8-20x25 yards • Outdoor • 80°**
TOYS: **Kick • Pull • Clock**

OTHER

CLASSES: **Yes (Extra $)**
HOURS: **Vary - call**
COST: POOL **$3** • GYM **$8**
TV: **No**

Within 100 yards of one another, both the Aquatic Center and Sports Club are within a 10-minute walk of the listed hotels. Walking to either workout option is a must, as available parking is in extremely short supply. Even the surrounding residential streets are permit-only during the day. If you insist on driving, seek out the 7th Street parking garage.

The Aquatic Center's 50-meter pool is a reasonably cheap swim option at $3/day. Short course is always the pattern here, so swimmers will stroke along the 25-yard width of the pool. Depending on lessons and swim team practices, the Center will have 8 to 20 lanes available for lap swim. Make sure to call ahead for the current schedule.

The Sports Club is a small, 5,000-square-foot gym used primarily by students. But guests are allowed to enjoy the modern weight and cardio machines after paying an $8 entrance fee. The usual suspects of the exercise equipment world are here, including Precor ellipticals and Cybex stack-loaded weight machines.

Walking to both of these locations from our listed hotels is a simple jaunt down San Carlos Street. The Aquatic Center is at 8th and San Salvador and the Sports Club entrance is on the street level at 7th and San Carlos.

Note: Both SJSU facilities have varying hours, especially on weekends. Call before you set out.

Pinnacle Fitness Pavilion

150 South First Street, San Jose, CA 95113
(408) 924-0500 • ballyfitness.com

As Bally's upscale brand, Pinnacle Fitness Clubs are typically much more hospitable workout environments than the traditional gyms carrying the Bally name. This Pinnacle is no exception. Located in the middle of the Pavilion retail mall (Starbucks is there), this 2-floor gym is a welcoming, bright and clean exercise venue with one-year-old equipment. The admission fee is a little steep at $15/day but, without any nearby competition, Pinnacle can dictate the market. Plan on getting a lot of exercise luxury for your money — cutting-edge cardio machines and exceptional weight apparatus are on hand. And the large quantity of equipment eliminates waiting.

Pinnacle has no pool, but swimmers have a nearby venue at San Jose State's Aquatic Center or the San Jose Athletic Club.

CARDIO

TREADMILLS: **StarTrac**
UPRIGHT BIKE: **LF**
RECUMBENT BIKE: **LF**
ELLIPTICAL: **LF • Precor**
STEPPER: **StairMaster**
ROWING: **Concept II**

STRENGTH

FREE WEIGHTS: **Yes**
HAMMER: **Yes**
MACHINES: **TechnoGym**
DUMBBELLS: **5-100 lbs**

OTHER

CLASSES: **Yes**
HOURS: M-TH **5a-10p** • F **5a-9p** • SAT-SUN **7a-7p**
COST: **$10 Bally member** • **$15 Other**
TV: **Yes**

San Jose Athletic Club

196 North Third Street, San Jose, CA 95112
(408) 292-1281

Inside an older building, this private club allows out-of-towners to use its facility for $20/day along with members of IHRSA ($15, check with your home club). While SJAC is a good fitness experience, those staying at any of our recommended hotels may find that there are more convenient exercise options.

New management has improved the club's stuffy image and updated some of the equipment. The strength selection does not disappoint, offering a wide variety of Cybex stack-loaded machines, plenty of free weights and a large range of dumbbells. Classes are also offered, so those fed up with "alone time" can join in the group fun.

Swimmers should appreciate the club's 25-yard outdoor lap offering. Floating lines and stripes mark the course, while a full set of toys is available to provide variety. Though staff tries to keep the water temperature at 80 degrees, we were told the liquid can get a little chilly at times — down to 76-ish. Although San Jose State does own a more appealing pool, swim-

CARDIO

TREADMILLS: **StarTrac**
UPRIGHT BIKE: **Tectrix**
RECUMBENT BIKE: **StarTrac**
ELLIPTICAL: **StarTrac • Reebok**
STEPPER: **StairMaster**
ROWING: **Yes**

STRENGTH

FREE WEIGHTS: **Yes**
HAMMER: **Yes**
MACHINES: **Cybex**
DUMBBELLS: **5-130 lbs**

SWIM

GRADE: **B-**
SPECS: **5x25yd • Outdoor • 78°**
TOYS: **Kick • Pull • Clock**
MASTERS: **Yes**

OTHER

CLASSES: **Yes**
HOURS: M-F **5a-10p** • SAT-SUN **8a-6p**
COST: **$20/day, $15/day IRHSA**
TV: **Yes**

mers may find that the lap swim hours here are more convenient than those at San Jose State's Aquatic Center.

RUNNING ROUTES

Los Gatos Creek Trail

Downtown San Jose is a thriving business destination, but this city's recreational activities are works in progress, especially for runners! The 9-mile Los Gatos Creek Trail is the best nearby jogging route, with water and bathrooms along the path. Unfortunately, a quick car ride is in order to access the trailhead — unless you are marathon training and don't mind the 3-4 miles (one way) you will have to cover from the downtown hotels. Park near the trailhead beside Leigh Street at Willow — look for Blackford Elementary School.

San Jose State University

For those wanting to hit the pavement straight away, we suggest running the 1.5-mile perimeter of San Jose State University. It is a very obvious rectangle, so at least you can zone out.

SJSU's Track

If a track workout sounds appealing, SJSU's outdoor oval (10th Street) is an alluring destination, and it should be open during most daytime hours.

Santa Fe

SANTA FE, NEW MEXICO

Are you like us? Two plus years in the same abode and still no dining room chandelier or wall hangings...

In this adobe-style town, the decorating challenged will be inspired. Santa Fe's Plaza is unparalleled in its artsy offerings. Countless galleries, shops and restaurants line the capital city's center. Canyon Road, less than a mile from the Plaza, is considered Santa Fe's true cultural focus. And, at 7,000 feet elevation, the thin air may finally loosen your purse strings.

Not surprisingly, this city's preferred hotels congregate near the Plaza as well but, unless you are bunking at La Posada, be ready to commute for a full-service workout. Downtown Santa Fe is long on Southwestern charm but short on fitness options. Many accommodations, including the most expensive, have nothing on-site. Those few that advertise this perk fail to fully satisfy athletic-minded travelers. But, before you leave the gym shoes at home, consider this: A 10-15 minute drive south of the Plaza is the best community center workout facility in the country!

Fit ones can have it all here — a unique accommodation, a nearby top-notch workout alternative and the prospect of finally adorning those walls!

38 Locations Reviewed

EXPENSIVE

GOLD: Inn of the Anasazi

113 Washington Avenue, Santa Fe, NM 87501
(505) 988-3030 • innoftheanasazi.com

While this small luxury hotel had no gym at the time of publishing, we understand from management that plans are in the works to transform a guest suite into a small fitness center. It is unlikely that this new offering will awe athletic-minded travelers, but it will add a convenient on-site option. So check on the progress, and keep in mind that, whether or not Anasazi has an exercise room, its fantastic on-the-Plaza locale and premier accommodations make it a lock for a luxurious stay. Just be prepared to spend a wad of dough.

Its 59 guest units reflect the Native American and Southwest style of this region. Hand-crafted furnishings, four-poster beds, gas fireplaces and hand-woven rugs create a warm, homey and comfortable environment. The attention to detail and overall room design are impressive. The Inn also boasts the only 4-star, 4-diamond restaurant in New Mexico. Simply named "Anasazi," the upscale eatery serves Southwest style breakfast, lunch and dinner emphasizing fresh fruits, vegetables and organic meats and poultry.

Without a current on-site workout option, Anasazi visitors must drive 10-15 minutes to the Chavez Community Center for a full-service fitness fix.

While there are closer options (Fort Marcy's pool and the Santa Fe Spa), these also require a short drive. And, once you are behind the steering wheel, there's no sense in settling for a mediocre venue when an extra 5-10 minutes will zip you to the top of the health club food chain.

MODERATELY EXPENSIVE

GOLD: La Posada de Santa Fe

330 East Palace Avenue
Santa Fe, NM 87501
(505) 986-0000
laposada.rockresorts.com

CARDIO

TREADMILLS: **2 Trotter**
RECUMBENT BIKE: **1 Tectrix - old**
ELLIPTICAL: **2 Precor**
STEPPER: **1 Tectrix - old**

STRENGTH

MACHINES: **6 Cybex**
DUMBBELLS: **2-50 lbs**

SWIM

SPECS: **Outdoor • Not lap**

OTHER

HOURS: **6:30a-8p**
COST: **Free**
TV: **Yes**

Two blocks from the Plaza, La Posada is an intimate hotel spread across 6 acres of landscaped grounds. Each room has unique design touches that reflect an authentic Southwestern adobe style. However, "unique" and "authentic" can, unfortunately, also mean noisy, potentially small and inconsistent. We recommend requesting a room away from Paseo de Peralta (busy street) and on the top floor. The hand-crafted, beamed ceilings are appealing to the eyes but fail to insulate the ears. We also suggest spending a little extra time with reservations to ensure your desired room type. Complimentary shuttles, wine tasting and margarita-making instruction are unique guest perks.

Both the fitness center and spa are located in the same attractive building. La Posada's gym is currently the best hotel offering in Santa Fe, which is disheartening because upright bikes, free weights and newer steppers are missing. Fitness fans will find 6 sturdy Cybex stack-loaded weight machines, an adequate dumbbell set, 2 ellipticals with attached TV screens and 2 treadmills in fair condition.

After a sweat, guests can reward themselves with a gourmet rub down. The spa offers a wide selection of massages and body treatments to pamper both body and soul. Swimmers and those looking for a more elaborate workout should drive 10-15 minutes to Chavez Community Center.

Note: With nightly rates close to the "Expensive" category, we struggled with La Posada's appropriate classification. Often rooms here are available at $60-$70/night under Anasazi, placing it in the "Moderately Expensive" category.

LEAST EXPENSIVE

GOLD: Any hotel near the Plaza

Except for the two hotels listed above, the remaining are indistinguishable from one another and have poor or no workout facilities. So pick a hotel near the Plaza that satisfies your budget needs and plan on driving to the Chavez Community Center (10-15 minute drive from the Plaza) to satisfy your exercise cravings.

BEYOND HOTELS

Genoveva Chavez Community Center

3221 Rodeo Road, Santa Fe, NM 87505
(505) 955-4000 • chavezcenter.com

Driving 10-15 minutes for a workout is frustrating, and we strive to avoid this necessity. But you must see this place to believe it! Pulling into the ample and free parking lot, this athletic center could easily be mistaken for an NBA arena. Our first thought was, "Why is this place so enormous?"

Once inside, we were blown away by 4 acres of recreation space that include an ice skating rink, gymnasium and pool — all in an architecturally stunning space. Natural light spills in via plentiful skylights and windows, art hangs from the 57-foot ceiling and Santa Fe's beautiful landscape is visible throughout. Like most community centers, Chavez was designed as a venue for people to gather. With its more than 350,000 visitors each year, it is a roaring success.

CARDIO

TREADMILLS: **StairMaster • Matrix**
UPRIGHT BIKE: **Stratus**
RECUMBENT BIKE: **Stratus**
ELLIPTICAL: **LF • Matrix**
STEPPER: **StairMaster**
OTHER: **Gravitron**

STRENGTH

FREE WEIGHTS: **Yes**
MACHINES: **LF**
DUMBBELLS: **5-90 lbs**

SWIM

GRADE: **A**
SPECS: **8x50m • Indoor • 82º**
TOYS: **Kick • Pull • Clock**
MASTERS: **No • 6a Group swim**

OTHER

CLASSES: **Yes**
HOURS: M-F **6a-10p** • SAT **8a-8p** • SUN **10a-6p**
COST: **$4**
TV: **No**
EXTRAS: **1/10 mile indoor track • Racquetball • Basketball • Ice Skating**

In the Center's core, between the ice rink and lap pool, exercisers sweat using a moderate supply of satisfying cardio and strength machines. Five StairMaster Stratus uprights, 5 StairMaster 4400PT series steppers and 4 Life Fitness 9500 series ellipticals highlight the endurance options. Those looking to get strong can choose from an even better variety of equipment, including 10 Life Fitness stack-loaded weight stations, plenty of free weights and a wide assortment of dumbbells.

The indoor, 8 lane, 50-meter competition-quality lap pool with its 50-foot high ceiling (separate kids' pool with water slide) is fantastic. Even better, most of the time this fabulous lapper is configured for long course swimming — a rare treat for water worshippers. We do not use the term "competition-quality" lightly, so expect the best of everything.

A welcome respite from hot August days, the NHL-size skating arena, complete with stadium seating and skate rentals, is open year round. Chavez's endless facility also contains 3 basketball courts, a 1/10 mile indoor jogging track, 2 glass-enclosed racquetball courts and an aerobics/spinning studio.

Community center? Where are we, Beverly Hills? At $4, this bargain admission makes it quite clear we are nowhere near 90210.

Note: Keep in mind that at 7,000 ft elevation, Santa Fe's thin air will make a moderate workout difficult.

Fort Marcy Recreation Complex

490 Washington Avenue, Santa Fe, NM 87501
(505) 955-2500

SWIM

GRADE: **C+**
SPECS: **6x25yd • Indoor • 83º**
TOYS: **Kick • Pull • Clock**

OTHER

HOURS: M-F **6a-8:30p** • SAT **8a-6:30p** • SUN **12-5:30p**
COST: POOL **$2 • $4 w/Fitness Center**

We recommend the Fort Marcy swim option as a distant runner-up to Chavez's Olympic-size stunner. Marcy's 25-yard lapper is nothing special, but it is within one mile of the Plaza. Its regulation length and 6 lanes marked by floating lines and bottom stripes present a worthy get-wet alternative. Aesthetically, this water rectangle does not impress, but it does not depress either. Bottom line, it's a functional choice for lap swimmers looking for a convenient workout.

Note: There is also a small fitness space with exercise equipment, but its anemic supply won't satisfy most. Expect to find only a couple of decent ellipticals and steppers.

Santa Fe Spa

786 North Saint Francis Drive, Santa Fe, NM 87501
(505) 984-8727

Although this small club has no pool, it is the closest health club to the Plaza (5-minute drive). We strongly recommend Chavez for any workout, but if you are pressed for time and need a quick health club hit, Santa Fe Spa will substitute nicely. Sweat fiends will find 5 new Life Fitness 9100 series treads, good quality Precor ellipticals, fantastic Hammer Strength stack-loaded isolation weight machines and a ton of free weights. Disappointing is the club's offering of 3 older upright bikes and several 4000PT series steppers. Your $10/day access fee includes all classes, including spin.

CARDIO

TREADMILLS: **LF**
UPRIGHT BIKE: **LF • Universal**
RECUMBENT BIKE: **LF • StarTrac**
ELLIPTICAL: **Precor**
STEPPER: **StairMaster** - old
ROWING: **Yes**

STRENGTH

FREE WEIGHTS: **Yes**
MACHINES: **BodyMaster • Hammer • Keiser Pressurized**
DUMBBELLS: **3-120 lbs**

OTHER

CLASSES: **Yes**
HOURS: M-F **5:30a-9p** • SAT **8a-8p** • SUN **9a-5p**
COST: **$10**
TV: **Yes**

RUNNING ROUTES

Santa Fe Striders

Not much rainfall, 7,000 feet elevation and amazing trails and scenery create a serious running town. The Santa Fe Striders host group runs throughout the week. Wednesdays these fit folk gather at 6 p.m. at the Plaza (across from the clock) for varying distance circuits.

Santa Fe River Path

Other prospects include the Santa Fe River Path, which runners can hook into a few blocks from the Plaza. Three paved miles follow along Downtown, and additional mileage can be added along the River. Also convenient to the Plaza is the Old Santa Fe Trail which has paved and dirt sections.

La Tierra Foothills Trail

For those looking for altitude and/or off-road surfaces, check out La Tierra Foothills Trail, which can be accessed behind the Santa Fe Spa, just north of the Plaza (~1.5 miles). The single-track and fire road course is approximately 11 miles long — expect a lot of hills.

Seattle

48 Locations Reviewed

SEATTLE, WASHINGTON

In Southern California, weather wimps deem a little mist to be legitimate cause to cancel plans and remain indoors. Seattleites cannot afford such luxury. Located on the Puget Sound, bordered by two lakes (Washington and Union) and frequently rained upon from above, Emerald City residents have no choice but to embrace water — and do they ever! Seattle boasts more pleasure boat owners per capita than any other city in the country. Runners enthusiastically squish through city streets each November during Seattle's popular Marathon — scheduled smack dab in the middle of the rainy season. Weekenders seek adventure and challenge on Mt. RAINier's terRAIN — note the first and last four letters. Professional athletes' uniforms sport emblems of Mariners, Seahawks and the Storm (WNBA). And Seattle is home of the only rained-out NBA basketball game — in 1986, due to a leaky roof.

Surprisingly, Seattle is not a rainy town by volume (it receives significantly less than New York City or Atlanta). Month-long drizzles and mere 69 days of sunshine earn the Microsoft and coffee capital of the world its dreary reputation. Natives, with their Pillsbury Doughboy "tans," brag they can identify the arrival of summer by the warmer rain. Yet, if you find yourself in the Emerald City on a sunny day, it is one of the most beautiful places in the world.

EXPENSIVE

GOLD: **Grand Hyatt**

721 Pine Street, Seattle, WA 98101
(206) 774-1234 • grandseattle.hyatt.com

CARDIO

TREADMILLS: **3 Precor**
UPRIGHT BIKE: **1 Precor**
RECUMBENT BIKE: **2 Precor**
ELLIPTICAL: **2 Precor**
STEPPER: **2 Precor**

STRENGTH

MACHINES: **5 Technogym**
DUMBBELLS: **5-25 lbs**

OTHER

HOURS: **24**
COST: **Free**
TV: **Yes**

Adjacent to the Washington Convention Center in the heart of Downtown, Grand Hyatt is the epitome of 21st Century high-tech luxury. All 425 tan and black toned guest quarters are minimalist in style and come furnished with generous bathrooms (separate showers and baths), refrigerators and floor-to-ceiling windows that frame beautiful mountain views (higher floors). Tech savvy Seattle is addicted to gadgetry, and Grand Hyatt showcases switch-operated blackout blinds, complimentary in-room high-speed internet access and wireless internet capabilities that operate through the TV (fee).

Grand Hyatt's 4th floor fitness center gets kudos for its high-end equipment and creative décor. The room's seductive mood lighting is unique and will not keep exercisers from reading. Newly purchased Precor machines, each with attached plasma television screens, decorate the immaculate Koa wood floor. However, its 5 stack-loaded weight stations, small dumbbell set and absent free weights make the moderately priced Inn at Harbor Steps an overall better athletic-minded option. Hyatt guests looking for a more elaborate sweat session or swim are advised to walk a half-mile to the full-service 24 Hour Fitness Club ($15).

Note: A Gold's gym is closer, but the superior 24 is worth the extra few minutes walk. Swimmers — no pool at Gold's.

SILVER: **Westin**

1900 Fifth Avenue, Seattle, WA 98101
(206) 728-1000 • westin.com

CARDIO

TREADMILLS: **5 LF**
UPRIGHT BIKE: **2 LF**
RECUMBENT BIKE: **3 LF**
ELLIPTICAL: **3 LF**
STEPPER: **2 LF**

STRENGTH

MACHINES: **5 LF**
DUMBBELLS: **5-50 lbs**

SWIM

SPECS: **Indoor • Not lap**

OTHER

HOURS: **24**
COST: **Free**
TV: **Yes**

As the Seattle Marathon's host hotel, this Westin is definitely in sync with the athletic crowd. Its 40-story twin towers, located within 6 blocks of Pike Place Market and the convention center, are a convenient home base. The 891 rooms are modern and contemporary, with earth-tone colors, trademark premium Heavenly Beds and Baths and 24-hour room service. The hotel's cylindrical shape graces all guest units with fabulous mountain views.

The North Tower's 5th floor exercise center reaffirms that Westin prioritizes fitness. The separate cardio and weight rooms are decked out with black rubber floors and snow-white walls. A renovation and equipment purchase was completed in 2003, so every cardio and strength apparatus is new, new, new. Individual plasma screens are attached to each treadmill and recumbent bike, and headphones are supplied.

Westin's runner-up tag in this category is largely because Grand Hyatt stocks the premium Precor brand in a more appealing workout environment. Regardless, book here with confidence.

Those desiring a more elaborate health club or regulation lap swim should walk 10-15 minutes to 24 Hour Fitness Sport ($15).

MODERATELY EXPENSIVE

GOLD: Inn at Harbor Steps

1221 First Avenue, Seattle, WA 98101
(206) 748-0973 • foursisters.com

Northeast Tower (Pool is SE)

CARDIO

TREADMILLS: **2 LF**
UPRIGHT BIKE: **1 LF**
RECUMBENT BIKE: **1 LF**
ELLIPTICAL: **2 Precor**
STEPPER: **1 StairMaster**

STRENGTH

FREE WEIGHTS: **Yes**
MACHINES: **6 LF**
DUMBBELLS: **5-75 lbs**

SWIM

SPECS: **Resistance Pool**

OTHER

HOURS: **6a-11p**
• Will open after hours
COST: **Free**
TV: **Yes**

Don't let the "Inn" reference, or the fact that you may not recognize the name, deter you from Seattle's best athletic-minded traveler accommodation. The 28-room Inn (not a B&B) is situated on the 1st and 2nd floors of a 4-tower residential high-rise complex in the heart of Seattle's chic arts and business district. Though the Inn's ground-level courtyard views are mediocre, you cannot beat this location — steps from Pike Place Market, Seattle's Art Museum and the waterfront.

We liked Harbor's pampering. In place of typical hotel amenities (marble baths, spa services, etc.), the Inn showers guests with what counts — true home comforts. Huge country-influenced suites with kitchenettes; mini-fridges stocked with complimentary water and soft-drinks; in-room gas fireplaces; free hot breakfasts; complimentary happy hours with wine and hors d'oeuvres; room service from the neighboring Wolfgang Puck restaurant; and 24-hour on-site workout access are this hotel's travel perks!

Three of the complex's towers house workout centers, and Inn guests have privileges at all of them. The northeast tower's gym outshines the other two. Its expansive, window-less room is somewhat dim, but the exposed ceiling ducts and open space create a pleasing loft vibe. While most cardio machines are recent purchases, the Life Fitness 9100 series bikes and StairMaster 4200PT free climbers outshine the older Life Fitness treadmills — consider an outdoor jog. The Inn's stack-loaded weight stations do impress, and approximately 225 pounds of free weights are available for bench and squat routines. Take the northeast elevators to level "A" (down), and follow the signs.

In the southeast tower, swimmers will have fun not flip-turning in the adjustable current pool. We are unsure whether this stationary swim is an Endless Pool, but we cranked up the jets and it appeared to function well.

Those seeking a private health club experience or a regulation lap pool should taxi to Allstar Fitness or 24 Hour Fitness — both are about 5-10 minutes ride away and offer commendable facilities, though we slightly favor the more exclusive Allstar.

Note: With only 28 rooms, this place fills up fast during the summer! Plan ahead and book early. You won't regret it.

SILVER: Renaissance

515 Madison Street, Seattle, WA 98104
(206) 583-0300 • marriott.com

CARDIO

TREADMILLS: **4 Precor**
RECUMBENT BIKE: **2 Precor**
ELLIPTICAL: **1 Precor**
STEPPER: **2 Precor**

STRENGTH

MACHINES: **1 Multi**

SWIM

SPECS: **Indoor • Not lap**

OTHER

HOURS: **5a-11p**
COST: **Free**
TV: **Yes**

Renaissance guests are near one of the best private health clubs in Seattle (Allstar Fitness), as well as within a half-mile of Downtown's major business and tourist attractions.

The 28-story modern high-rise's 553 rooms are contemporary and elegant, decorated in conservative brown tones. We loved the fact that the windows opened for a breath of fresh Seattle air. Premium bedding tops off the peaceful surroundings.

Renaissance does a fair job assembling a small number of expensive cardio machines in a cherry wood-floored workout room. The center's 28th floor ambiance is wonderful and its views fantastic, but fitness essentials such as upright bikes, free weights and dumbbells are missing. Nevertheless, the cardio machines that are here should satisfy a worthwhile endurance session.

Serious weight buffs and lap swimmers should walk 5 minutes to Allstar Fitness ($10). Renaissance's mini 10-yard (approx.) pool is not a lap option.

LEAST EXPENSIVE

GOLD: Springhill Suites by Marriott Downtown

1800 Yale Avenue, Seattle, WA 98101
(206) 254-0500 • springhillsuites.com

This clean, relatively new hotel's only disadvantage is its location. Just west of I-5, Springhill is about a half-mile outside of Downtown's shopping and business districts and a mile from Pike Place

Market. However, while beyond easy walking range of Seattle's top attractions, the hotel is nicely situated across the street from a full-service health club.

Springhill's guest suites with separate living and sleeping areas, microwaves, mini-refrigerators, free high-speed internet access and complimentary downtown shuttle service are great features for families or larger groups. To avoid potential overnight noise from the neighboring highway, request a room on the "quieter" side of the hotel. Otherwise, you might be a little cranky during your free continental breakfast.

CARDIO

TREADMILLS: **2 Precor**
RECUMBENT BIKE: **1 Precor**
STEPPER: **1 Precor**

STRENGTH

DUMBBELLS: **5-25 lbs**

SWIM

SPECS: **Indoor • Not lap**

OTHER

HOURS: **5:30a-11p**
COST: **Free**
TV: **Yes**
EXTRAS: **$10 Pass to 24 Hour**

The in-house exercise room presents several good Precor cardio prospects, but those looking for a more serious sweat routine, lap swim or strength equipment can pay $10 at the fantastic 24 Hour Fitness across the street ($5 discount).

SILVER: Executive Pacific Plaza

400 Spring Street, Seattle, WA 98104
(206) 623-3900 • pacificplazahotel.com

This centrally located, inexpensive hotel has no on-site exercise option, but its convenient proximity to Allstar Fitness makes it a notable athletic-minded budget option. With Executive as a home base, guests can easily walk to all of downtown Seattle's attractions (e.g., Pike Place is 5 blocks).

After a renovation in early 2001, all of Executive's rooms are clean and smoke-free — gotta love that! Typically under a "C" note/night, you are not going to be pampered, but the hotel's 160 Northwest-flavor green and brown rooms are nice enough.

While hotel staff may refer those desiring a workout to the non-recommended Pure Fitness on 2nd and Columbia, you will be happier at Allstar at 5th and Columbia — a more complete club ($10). In addition, Allstar is a closer and less hilly pedestrian commute.

Swimmers should head Allstar's way, too, since neither Executive nor Pure Fitness has a pool. Allow 10 minutes to walk there.

BEYOND HOTELS

Allstar Fitness Key Tower

700 5th Avenue, 14th Floor, Seattle, WA 98104
(206) 343-4692 • allstarfitness.com

Located on a high-rise office building's 14th floor, this executive-style club supplies the latest in cardio and weight equipment, a fantastic lap pool, an extensive selection of classes and an upscale locker/shower facility.

Due to the club's smaller size, the equipment spacing is tight-

CARDIO

TREADMILLS: **LF**
UPRIGHT BIKE: **LF**
RECUMBENT BIKE: **LF**
ELLIPTICAL: **LF • Precor**
STEPPER: **StairMaster • Stepmill**

STRENGTH

FREE WEIGHTS: **Yes**
HAMMER: **Yes**
MACHINES: **Nautilus**
DUMBBELLS: **3-125 lbs**

SWIM

GRADE: **B+**
SPECS: **5x25yd • Indoor • 81°**
TOYS: **Kick • Pull**

OTHER

CLASSES: **Yes**
HOURS: M-F **5a-10p** • SAT-SUN **8a-8p**
COST: **$10**
TV: **Yes**

er than we prefer, but walls of large windows expand the rooms. We have no complaints about the unbelievable quality of Allstar's fitness technology. Highlights include state-of-the-art Nautilus Nitro stack-loaded weight machines, StairMaster 4600PT series steppers and Life Fitness' latest aero-shaped upright bikes. Website photos provide a useful peek.

Allstar's competition-quality lap pool's floating lines and bottom stripes divide 5 lanes over 25 yards. Floor-to-ceiling windows with spectacular views running along deck are an added aesthetic bonus — too bad you can't enjoy the view face down.

The club is walking distance from several hotels listed here. Free parking is available on weekends (and some weekday hours) — check its website. Because the club caters to a business crowd, the place is typically empty on weekends and weekdays after 7 p.m.

24 Hour Fitness Sport Downtown

1827 Yale Avenue, Seattle, WA 98101
(206) 624-0651 • 24hourfitness.com

CARDIO

TREADMILLS: **LF • StarTrac**
UPRIGHT BIKE: **LF**
RECUMBENT BIKE: **LF**
ELLIPTICAL: **LF • Precor**
STEPPER: **StairMaster • Stepmill**
ROWING: **Yes**

STRENGTH

FREE WEIGHTS: **Yes**
HAMMER: **Yes**
MACHINES: **Cybex • Paramount • BodyMaster**
DUMBBELLS: **3-125 lbs**

SWIM

GRADE: **B+**
SPECS: **4x25m • Indoor • 81°**
TOYS: **Kick • Pull**

OTHER

CLASSES: **Yes**
HOURS: **24**
COST: **$10 Springhill • $7.50 IHRSA • $15 Others**
TV: **Yes**

This club opened in 2002 and is one of the larger 24s we have toured. For this burgeoning fitness franchise, "Sport" in a facility's name usually implies a larger and more upscale site. Visitors to downtown Seattle's version can expect nicer locker rooms, a good lap pool and typical 24 Hour techno-industrial décor. Fifteen bucks gets you in the door ($7.50 with proof of IHRSA).

When it comes to equipment, 24 does not hold back on the supply. Top-of-the-line everything decorates the floor, including the latest in Life Fitness bikes, Precor ellipticals, StairMaster steppers, Hammer Strength free weight stations and a ton of free weights.

Swimmers, bring the Speedo. Any workout is possible in this 25-

meter water gem. Floating lines and bottom stripes guide the way, and kickboards and pull-buoys provide variety.

Parking in the neighboring garage is free with club validation from 5-9 a.m. and 5-10 p.m. At all other times, you must pay. Though the center is open 24 hours, the garage closes at 10 p.m. Limited parking is available on the street.

RUNNING ROUTES

Unless you are coming to town during the summer months, don't forget to pack the slicker and water-resistant cap. We don't know about you, but we always view running in a light rain as a welcome adventure, and Seattle's just the place for it. Heavy downpours that soak the socks are another story, but chances are you will not confront a deluge during your run. Do bring a couple extra pair of running socks — you will want to wear a pair that is clean and dry to start.

With an average annual temperature of 53 degrees, at least Jack Frost will not nibble at your nose, even though the City practically kisses the Canadian border.

Alaskan Way

From your hotel door, the most convenient route parallels Alaskan Way, with Elliot Bay to the west. It's about a 3 mile stretch total from the Pioneer Square District (~ Pier 48) through the 5-acre Myrtle Edwards Park to the north. Fairly flat and mostly urban except for the 1.25 miles through the park.

Burke-Gilman/Sammamish River Trail

Those looking for more mileage must first endure a short drive (~ 10-15 minutes). The Burke-Gilman/Sammamish River Trail is a 27-mile paved path that follows an old railroad right of way around Lake Washington. Closest access and parking to Downtown is Gasworks Park on the north shore of Lake Union (2101 N. Northlake Way - not to be confused with Northlake Place). Heading north from there will keep you running 'til the path ends in Redmond — about 25 miles later!

Discovery Park

Seattle's largest park is an urban retreat for runners, hikers and mountain bikes. With over 500 acres, it has an extensive trail system, including a 2.8-mile loop from the Visitor's Center and a 6-mile loop. The park boasts Puget Sound views and access to secluded beaches. The heavily wooded area is also home to a variety of wildlife.

Distance runners can easily clock the 5+ miles to reach the park, located at the western tip of the chichi Magnolia neighborhood. Simply head north along Elliott to Dravus and follow the signs. Others may want to drive.

ST. LOUIS, MISSOURI

As the 1904 host city for the 3rd Olympiad, St. Louis didn't exactly attract a diverse field. Of the 689 amateur athletes who competed (681 men and 8 women), 525 were Americans. It was not until years later that the Games evolved into a serious country versus country competition.

Despite the geographically biased representation, St. Louis' Games marked a few firsts: These were the first Olympics held in North America and the first time that Gold, Silver and Bronze medals were awarded. Boxing, freestyle wrestling and decathlon debuted and, by sending two hopefuls to compete in what was then deemed the premier event, Africa made its inaugural marathon appearance — a race shrouded in controversy.

As the first competitor to cross the finish line (in just over 3 hours), New Yorker Fred Lorz received a standing ovation from the crowd, posed for pictures with celebrities and accepted a laurel wreath from President Theodore Roosevelt's daughter. Just before awarding Lorz a Gold medal, however, officials discovered that 11 of his 26.2 miles were covered by car. Only after the vehicle overheated and broke down at mile 22 did he resume running. Caught red-handed, Lorz admitted the deceit and was promptly issued a lifetime ban from competition. (He won the following year's Boston Marathon after the ban was lifted.)

The already tarnished event suffered another blow when the second man to cross the finish line also had some... shall we say... help. At mile 16, Thomas Hicks was literally given a second wind when friends along the course loaded him with a dose of strychnine, a central nervous system stimulant. They also provided several glasses of cognac as a chaser, then dragged Hicks across the finish line.

The Africans finished 9th and 12th, after the faster of the two was chased a mile off course by a wild dog.

While the Arch may signify that this city is the "Gateway to the West," it is certainly not a preview of the West Coast's workout mentality. After a marathon search and a rather meager list of entrants, we managed to identify only a few strong finishers.

EXPENSIVE

GOLD: **Westin** Downtown

811 Spruce Street, St. Louis, MO 63102
(314) 621-2000 • westin.com/stlouis

CARDIO

TREADMILLS: **5 Precor**
UPRIGHT BIKE: **2 Cybex**
RECUMBENT BIKE: **2 Cybex**
ELLIPTICAL: **2 Precor**
STEPPER: **2 Precor**

STRENGTH

FREE WEIGHTS: **Yes**
MACHINES: **13 Cybex**
DUMBBELLS: **5-50 lbs**

OTHER

CLASSES: **Yes**
HOURS: M-F **5a-11p** • SAT-SUN **6a-8p**
COST: **Free**
TV: **Yes**

Opened in 2001, the Westin's beautifully modern hotel is located within several blocks of Downtown's businesses, government offices and tourist attractions. Its 256 magnificently designed guest quarters offer contemporary furnishings in soothing shades of taupe and brown. Since the hotel is relatively new, the carpets, bedding and bathrooms are spotless.

Westin provides fitness-minded guests with complimentary access to the connected Solera Health Club and Spa. This independently-run facility is a wonderful workout venue with bright, pastel-colored walls that separate the cardio and strength areas.

Though the club is rather petite, there is a third area devoted to yoga, Pilates and aerobic classes. Just prior to opening its doors for business in 2002, Solera procured a wide array of new, high-quality cardio and weight machines and free weights. If you have money to burn and time to spare, a relaxing massage is a great reward after a strong workout, and Solera's full service affords pampering for the weary traveler.

Despite not having a pool, the Westin, without question, has the best hotel workout facility in downtown St. Louis. Swimmers must look to the YMCA for a fix — we recommend driving or hailing a cab (5 minutes).

SILVER: **Hyatt Regency** Union Station

One St. Louis Union Station
St. Louis, MO 63103
(314) 231-1234
stlouis.hyatt.cm

CARDIO

TREADMILLS: **4 LF**
UPRIGHT BIKE: **2 LF**
RECUMBENT BIKE: **2 LF**
ELLIPTICAL: **2 LF**
STEPPER: **2 LF**

STRENGTH

DUMBBELLS: **5-50 lbs**

SWIM

SPECS: **Outdoor • Not lap**

OTHER

HOURS: **6a-10p**
COST: **Free**
TV: **Yes**

Incessant shoppers will delight in Hyatt's proximity to the connected Union Station retail and entertainment complex. But we believe the guest room doors are a little too close to this 11-acre zoo, where noise is prevalent and hallway wanderers frequent. While Hyatt claims that their 539 units are "soundproofed," it is hard to imagine that the clamor can be fully blocked out — especially on busy weekends. Nevertheless, the Victorian-style rooms are attractive, tidy and well-proportioned.

Hyatt's workout room adds to this destination's appeal. Cardio fiends especially will be satisfied by the hotel's top-of-the-line Life Fitness 9500 series treads, bikes, ellipticals and steppers. Without much space left in the small room for weights, Hyatt squeezes in an adequate dumbbell set for some added muscle burn. Of course, we prefer to see a few stack-loaded weight machines and/or free weights but, despite these shortcomings, the on-site gym is a reliable and functional option in downtown St. Louis.

Swimmers, plan to walk 10 minutes to downtown's YMCA.

MODERATELY EXPENSIVE

GOLD: Sheraton City Center

400 South 14th Street, St. Louis, MO 63103
(314) 231-5007 • sheraton.com

The only weakness of this Gold medal winner is its off-the-beaten-path location. Downtown's popular destinations are not far, but they are not very close, either, at a half-mile away. However, Sheraton does deliver with its attractive accommodations and even more attractive pricing. Because Renaissance Grand runs such a close second, if you notice a significant price discrepancy, feel comfortable selecting the cheaper option.

CARDIO

TREADMILLS: **4 StarTrac**
UPRIGHT BIKE: **1 StarTrac**
RECUMBENT BIKE: **1 StarTrac**
ELLIPTICAL: **2 StarTrac**

STRENGTH

MACHINES: **10 StairMaster**
DUMBBELLS: **5-50 lbs**

SWIM

GRADE: **D**
SPECS: **0x25 yd • Indoor • 80-82°**

OTHER

HOURS: **5a-10:30p**
COST: **Free**
TV: **Yes**

Sheraton's 288 guest rooms are more appealing than the Grand's, with deep tones of amber and maroon, dark wood furnishings and ample space. Refrigerators are also convenient for that milk and O.J. stash.

When it comes time to sweat, Sheraton's large and bright 13th floor workout center will put a smile on your face. Plentiful windows invite daytime sunshine and afford a city-lights view after sunset. All of the machines, especially the rarely seen StairMaster brand stack-loaded weight stations, are youthful and in excellent condition. Happily, plenty of space remains for athletes to stretch, hold yoga poses or crunch abs.

Although not technically a lap pool, Sheraton's indoor long and narrow rectangle could suffice for desperate swimmers in a pinch. We estimate the length at 20 yards, but the absence of lane lines and bottom stripes may test your straight swimming skills.

For a regulation lapper, drive or taxi 5 minutes to the Downtown YMCA.

SILVER: Renaissance Grand

800 Washington Avenue, St. Louis, MO, 63101
(314) 621-9600 • renaissancehotels.com

CARDIO
TREADMILLS: **4 LF**
UPRIGHT BIKE: **2 LF**
RECUMBENT BIKE: **2 LF**
STEPPER: **1 LF**

STRENGTH
MACHINES: **5 LF**
DUMBBELLS: **5-45 lbs**

SWIM
SPECS: **Indoor • Not lap**

OTHER
HOURS: **24**
COST: **Free**
TV: **Yes**

Two downtown hotels carry the Renaissance name. Avoid confusion and notice that we recommend Renaissance Grand, not Renaissance Suites. While the Suites are a far cry from a Motel 6, the Grand's accommodations and fitness center are a cut above its sister property.

We value the Grand's central location (adjacent to America's Convention Center) and the marble-filled common areas (Starbucks inside), but the 875 guest rooms' décor is disappointing. Drab blue and rust tones combined with vintage furnishings inspire visions of the days before electricity... these rooms look better in the dark.

Luckily, the hotel's exercise option inspires visions of a different kind. This room is "grand" indeed, with Life Fitness' cutting-edge 9500 series of cardio machines alongside new stack-loaded weight stations. Dumbbells round out a strength session. Noticeably absent was any brand of elliptical machine — which is surprising, since Life Fitness offers a worthy model. Those looking for a swim or more elaborate workout should head to the Downtown YMCA. It's only about a half-mile away, and walking should take less than 10 minutes.

LEAST EXPENSIVE

GOLD: The Roberts Mayfair

A Wyndham Historic Hotel

806 Saint Charles Street, St Louis, MO 63101
(314) 421-2500 • wyndham.com

CARDIO
TREADMILLS: **2 LF**
RECUMBENT BIKE: **1 LF**
ELLIPTICAL: **1 LF**

STRENGTH
MACHINES: **1 LF Multi**
DUMBBELLS: **5-50 lbs**

SWIM
SPECS: **Outdoor • Not lap**

OTHER
HOURS: **24**
COST: **Free**
TV: **Yes**

A block from America's Convention Center and within Downtown's heart, the Mayfair is conveniently located and presents an affordable option, with rooms priced under $100/night. While this budget accommodation does not offer many fancies or frills, the 182 guest quarters are clean and conservatively furnished. Guests should note that Mayfair's standard rooms come with queen-size beds only, so book accordingly.

After a ride on the painfully slow elevators, visitors eventually arrive at the 18th floor fitness center. Inside this 24-

hour facility, a few newer Life Fitness cardio machines await your arrival, along with an average multi-gym and good size dumbbell set.

Serious exercisers will not be impressed — and, while hotel guests receive a $5 discount to Gold's gym, this weight-intensive club is several blocks farther than the YMCA's superior workout facility. So plan to walk 10 minutes to the Y, with $10 and a picture I.D. in tow.

BEYOND HOTELS

YMCA Downtown (NOT Marquette)

1528 Locust, St. Louis, MO 63103
(314) 436-4100 • ymcastlouis.org

Because this facility is approximately a half-mile from all hotels, exercisers intending to visit the Y should consider whether to walk or ride. Our recommendation depends upon the time of day you will be heading over. On a block that appears nearly abandoned, driving or cabbing after dusk is the safe choice in our minds. But we certainly have no qualms walking while the sun is up.

Regardless, do not be scared away from this oldie but goodie workout option.

Although the club's interior could use some refreshing, the warm and friendly staff needs no makeover. Inside the Y's cardio room, newer machines are surrounded by dark wood-paneled walls, imparting a "Clue Game" library feel. It is not a large room, so expect to see less than a half dozen of each machine type. The same cannot be said for the weight room, where you will find ample free weights, a wide assortment of dumbbells and newer Cybex stack-loaded machines.

The Y's weakest link is its lap pool but, because this is the only regulation water box in town, swimmers have no choice but to tolerate the low ceilings and paint-chipped walls. Its 3 lanes separated by floating lines and bottom stripes can get crowded during rush hour. Staff advised us to avoid lapping between 4:30 p.m. and 7 p.m. if possible.

Note: Find another workout alternative on Sundays. This Y is closed.

CARDIO

TREADMILLS: **Cybex**
UPRIGHT BIKE: **Cybex**
RECUMBENT BIKE: **Cybex**
ELLIPTICAL: **Cybex • Precor**
STEPPER: **Cybex**

STRENGTH

FREE WEIGHTS: **Yes**
MACHINES: **Cybex • Universal**
DUMBBELLS: **3-100 lbs**

SWIM

GRADE: **C-**
SPECS: **3x25yd • Indoor • 84°**
TOYS: **Kick • Pull • Clock**
MASTERS: **Yes**

OTHER

CLASSES: **Yes**
HOURS: M-F **5:30a-9p** • SAT **9a-6p** • SUN **Closed**
COST: **$10**
TV: **Yes**

RUNNING ROUTES

Jefferson Expansion Park

Unfortunately, runners best bet is a pavement pound in this Gateway City. However, within a mile or so of most hotels is the 91-acre Jefferson Expansion Park and Arch. Market Street east to Memorial Drive will get you there. The Park serves up a short 2+ mile stride. Additional miles will be on city streets.

Forest Park

The far better venue is the 1,300-acre Forest Park (at Forest Park Ave. and Kingshighway Blvd.) located approximately 4 to 5 miles west of downtown hotels. Running bliss awaits in this wooded and lake filled green space that is the 7th largest in the country. The 7.5-mile perimeter loop will introduce you to the Park's other attractions including, an art museum, zoo, golf course and outdoor theater.

TAMPA, FLORIDA

This city loves pirates. Since 1904, Tampa has revered Jose Gaspar, "the last buccaneer." And every February, more than 400,000 people are drawn to this city and its waterways to partake in Gasparilla Pirate Fest. The festival has grown into a three-month-long celebration, making the pirate a permanent part of Tampa's culture and identity. Year-round swashbuckling events include the Gasparilla Distance Classic (5K to marathon), a children's parade, a night light festival, an art show and, of course, a 16-week cheer-fest for the NFL's Tampa Bay Buccaneers.

Legend has it that Gaspar, a former Spanish naval officer turned pirate, looted merchant ships while patrolling Florida's western shore during the late 18th and early 19th Centuries. This heartless tyrant is said to have captured over 400 vessels, killing the crew and most of the passengers while saving the "booty" for himself — both money and female. Gaspar flourished as a pirate until misidentifying the armed *U.S.S. Enterprise* as an unarmed merchant ship, losing his first, last and only battle. Rather than surrender, he tied himself to his boat's anchor and jumped overboard, vowing to die on his own terms. His treasures are said to be buried in the Tampa area but have never been recovered.

DOWNTOWN

There is not a whole lot to downtown Tampa other than a convention center, a few office highrises and some expansive hotel room views. However, our glass is always half full, and this scarcity of diversion bodes well for workout time. Never mind Gaspar's buried loot, your treasures will be found at the Marriott or Wyndham and inside the awesome Harbour Club.

33 Locations Reviewed

EXPENSIVE

GOLD: **Marriott Waterside Hotel & Marina**

700 South Florida Avenue, Tampa, FL 33602
(813) 221-4900 • marriott.com

CARDIO

TREADMILLS: **5 StarTrac**
UPRIGHT BIKE: **2 StarTrac**
RECUMBENT BIKE: **2 StarTrac**
STEPPER: **1 StarTrac • 2 LF**

STRENGTH

MACHINES: **7 Hoist**
DUMBBELLS: **3-50 lbs**

SWIM

POOL: **Outdoor • Not lap**

OTHER

HOURS: **24**
COST: **Free**
TV: **Yes**

Marriott Waterside's location on the Garrison Channel, just across the bridge from Harbour Island, provides a beautiful setting to the massive 717-room property. Despite its size, Marriott disguises its convention hotel outer shell with inner boutique-style accommodations.

The 24-hour 3rd floor fitness center and spa is an open and airy destination for guests desiring a mildly challenging workout. All of the equipment is relatively new and in good condition. However, other than 2 Life Fitness Cross Trainers (not ellipticals), the cardio machines are exclusively StarTrac. Precor and Life Fitness addicts should make the sunny 7-minute walk to the Harbour Island Athletic Club for their fix (cost $15 + tax). Those interested in free weights, classes and/or a lap pool should journey across the Harbour Island Bridge, too.

If you elect to remain in-house, refresh and rejuvenate post workout by choosing from an assortment of massage and salon services in the same 3rd floor center.

MODERATE & LEAST EXPENSIVE

GOLD: **Wyndham Harbour Island**

725 South Harbour Island Boulevard, Tampa, FL 33602
(813) 229-5000 • wyndham.com

The Wyndham is the only other downtown hotel that offers a worthwhile exercise option, thanks to its close proximity to Harbour Island Athletic Club.

The 299 attractive guestrooms contain Herman Miller Aeron office chairs, large windows and Golden Door Spa toiletries. But, with room rates as volatile as an internet stock, it was a challenge to fit this hotel into a price category. Our online search yielded rates ranging from $85-$170/night, depending upon the date.

Skip the in-house fitness room with its 2 old treadmills, 2 sub-par step machines and limited set of dumbbells. Heck, the Wyndham's offering makes some home gyms look like a 24 Hour Fitness. Besides, the "A" rated Harbour Island Athletic Club is only a 2-minute walk away. With all the money saved staying at the Wyndham, the $15 entry fee is a bargain.

BEYOND HOTELS DOWNTOWN

Harbour Island Athletic Club

900 South Harbour Island Boulevard, Tampa, FL 33602
(813) 202-1950 • harbourislandac.com

Fifteen bucks plus tax gains you access to the best health club in Tampa. This top-of-the food-chain facility is upscale without being snooty. While this is urban Tampa, it is still the South, so expect laid-back staffers and fellow exercisers. The Club's full service includes an outdoor café that offers yummy meals and a "kid zone" which provides babysitting for $5/hour.

With indoor and outdoor athletic space of 150,000 square feet, traveling athletes will feel like kids in an ice cream shop with so many workout flavors to choose from. There are 15 clay tennis courts, a full basketball court, racquetball and squash courts, a cardio and weight area and a lap pool. The workout equipment and sporting courts are in great shape, like most of those who use it. Despite all this well-deserved praise, one item on our wish list would be more brand variety within each equipment type. For example, Harbour stocks a more-than-sufficient 21 treadmills, but all are the StarTrac brand — a good manufacturer, but not preferred by everyone.

Harbour's 25-yard, outdoor lap pool is a superb swimming venue with floating lane lines and bottom stripes. See a photo online.

CARDIO

TREADMILLS: **StarTrac**
UPRIGHT BIKE: **LF**
RECUMBENT BIKE: **LF**
ELLIPTICAL: **LF • Cybex**
STEPPER: **StairMaster**
ROWING: **Concept II**

STRENGTH

FREE WEIGHTS: **Yes**
HAMMER: **Yes**
MACHINES: **Cybex • Nautilus**
DUMBBELLS: **10-100 lbs**

SWIM

GRADE: **B+**
SPECS: **4x25yd • Outdoor • 82°**
TOYS: **Kick • Pull • Clock**

OTHER

CLASSES: **Yes**
HOURS: M-F **5:45a-10p** • SAT **7:45a-8p** • SUN **7:45a-7p**
COST: **$15 + tax**
TV: **Yes**
EXTRAS: **Basketball • Racquetball • Tennis • Cafe**

WESTSHORE

Don't be duped by this fancy "Westshore" label. A more accurate description is "Tampa Airport." Within a few miles of the flying zone, hotels in this area are surrounded by concrete buildings and paved roads, not palm trees and sandy beaches. However, the Buccaneers' home and Yankees' spring ball stadium are not far.

Westshore is devoid of a single hotel with a solid in-house workout room or conveniently located off-site option, but we did find a decent Bally Total Fitness reasonably nearby. We suggest selecting the hotel closest to Bally that meets your needs.

BEYOND HOTELS WESTSHORE

Bally Total Fitness

14350 North Dale Mabry, Tampa, FL 33618
(813) 908-8307 • ballyfitness.com

CARDIO

TREADMILLS: **LF**
UPRIGHT BIKE: **LF**
RECUMBENT BIKE: **LF**
ELLIPTICAL: **Precor • LF**
STEPPER: **StarTrac**
OTHER: **Gravitron**

STRENGTH

FREE WEIGHTS: **Yes**
HAMMER: **Yes**
MACHINES: **LF • Icarian**
DUMBBELLS: **5-85 lbs**

SWIM

GRADE: **B**
SPECS: **5x25yd • Indoor • 82°**

OTHER

CLASSES: **Yes**
HOURS: M-F **5a-10p** • SAT-SUN **8a-7p**
COST: **Free w/local hotel stay & ID**
TV: **Yes**
EXTRAS: **1/15 mile indoor track**

While Bally does maintain free admission deals with a few hotels/motels (Chase Suites, Days Inn, Suburban Lodge and Homestead Suites), staff told us they will give anyone coming to this location one complimentary day pass. Talk to a manager when you arrive.

The club itself is a good representative of this hit-or-miss franchise. It stocks a huge amount of equipment in a two-story space and maintains an indoor 25-yard lap pool as well. Forty weight machines, 21 treadmills, 12 Hammer Strength machines and 10 Precor ellipticals are just a sampling of the voluminous equipment inside the wide-open space. Most equipment is new or slightly used, and everything appeared to be in good condition.

The lap pool is an appealing swim spot, with floating lane lines and bottom stripes. Adjacent to the main weight/cardio area, it receives plenty of light and ample maintenance. Unfortunately, kickboards and buoys are not provided, and we did not see a pace clock, so bring your wristwatch. Do yourself a favor and avoid the locker rooms and shower facilities. Towels and locks are not provided.

RUNNING ROUTES

Bayshore Boulevard

The best running in downtown Tampa borders the Bay. Follow Bayshore Boulevard for nearly 7 miles of undisturbed strides while you take in the city landscape. This flat promenade is popular with walkers, cyclists and inline skaters. Runners can pick up the path in a variety of spots, including behind the convention center.

Al Lopez Park

Another favorite is the 1.8 mile loop through Al Lopez Park, located next to the football Stadium (Himes Ave.). The park often hosts 5K races and other sporting events.

TUCSON, ARIZONA

Quick, close your eyes and picture in your mind a cactus.

Brief pause.

Okay, do you have it? We bet most of you visualized a tall, green, prickly version with a few "J" shaped appendages "arming" out from both sides — right? As the most recognizable cactus in the world, it is interesting that the Saguaro is actually one of this species' rarer breeds. And, as North America's hottest desert, Tucson's Sonoran is the only locale in the world where the giant Saguaro naturally grows.

Reaching heights exceeding 50 feet and weights of 10 tons, the Saguaro's life expectancy is 200 years. While its wildly branching arms are its most familiar feature, the first of these appendages does not typically debut until age 65. A true late bloomer, this massive cactus takes an average of 5 years to grow its first 5 inches.

Survival in the desert is all about water storage. The Saguaro's complex network of roots branches out more than 50 feet wide of its base, never dipping more than 3 feet beneath the surface. This shallow but sprawling system lets the king of the cactus world soak up water from even the briefest rains, storing up to 200 gallons at a time.

Come to think of it, the Saguaro's life cycle is very similar to a marathon experience. You start off slowly and progressively become faster; you drink and store plenty of water throughout the race; and, toward the finish, your arms flail with reckless abandon.

Of course, modern day Tucson has a lot more to offer visitors than desert and cacti. The outskirts are home to several of the world's most luxurious resorts and spas. And why not? With over 300 days of sunshine each year, adventuresome desert topography and stunning sunsets, Tucson certainly is an alluring destination.

Note: During peak season (February through April), many of the resorts will have similar room rates, so our price points may not be as helpful. However, for the other 9 months of the year, the hotels tend to fall into the cost categories listed below.

Tucson

21 Locations Reviewed

EXPENSIVE

GOLD: Miraval Life in Balance Resort & Spa

5000 East Via Estancia Miraval, Catalina, AZ 85739
(520) 825-4000 • miravalresort.com

CARDIO

TREADMILLS: **4 LF**
UPRIGHT BIKE: **2 LF**
RECUMBENT BIKE: **2 LF**
ELLIPTICAL: **3 LF**
STEPPER: **2 LF**
OTHER: **Ergometer**

STRENGTH

FREE WEIGHTS: **Yes**
MACHINES: **16 Nautilus**
DUMBBELLS: **5-50 lbs**

SWIM

GRADE: **B**
SPECS: **6x25yd • Outdoor • 84°**
TOYS: **Kick • Pull • Clock**

OTHER

CLASSES: **Yes**
HOURS: **5a-10p**
COST: **Free**
TV: **No**
EXTRAS: **Tennis • Outdoor climbing wall**

Add another item to the wish list. Together with the Range Rover, the $10,000 Pinarello bicycle and the closet full of Dolce & Gabbana clothing, etch Miraval Spa into your slate of extravagant desires. This all-inclusive resort is not at all haughty, it is just really expensive. Your pampering will run around $1,000/night per couple, but these prices afford everything under the Tucson sun. Top-of-the-food-chain delights include spacious, Southwestern style accommodations, 3 gourmet and healthy "all you can eat" meals a day, hundreds of interesting activities and classes (from rock climbing to sex therapy), round-trip airport transportation, unlimited access to the resort's fitness facilities and one of the following for each hedonistic night: spa service, private wellness consultation or golf round on a Tom Weiskopf designed course. That's a lot!

Miraval's exercise center will not blow you away, but its sufficient supply of new cardio and weight equipment in a light and airy space will get athletes through any workout. Life Fitness cardio machines are the brand of choice, so those hoping for other top manufacturers will have to broaden their horizons. TV multitaskers must settle for the view or a good book, because at Miraval it's all about being mindful of your body and television is deemed an undesirable distraction. Yoga is a major attraction here, with a large, separate studio.

Swimmers will find the 6-lane, 25-yard pool adequate but must rely on bottom stripes to keep straight, as floating lines are absent. A pace clock, kickboards and pull-buoys are available.

MODERATELY EXPENSIVE

GOLD: Loews Ventana Canyon Resort

7000 North Resort Drive, Tucson, AZ 85750
(520) 299-2020 • loewshotels.com/hotels/tucson

Set in the foothills of the Catalina Mountains, this newly renovated 395-room resort is a wonderful retreat for athletes and nonathletes alike. The 93-acre property is breathtaking and the workout options are endless. The mauve and sage guest rooms are tastefully decorated and loaded with every convenience. You will enjoy 24 hour room service, high thread count sheets and private balconies. But don't get too comfortable inside. What awaits beyond your door will make fitness fanatics even happier.

CARDIO

TREADMILLS: **4 StarTrac**
UPRIGHT BIKE: **2 StarTrac**
RECUMBENT BIKE: **2 Precor**
ELLIPTICAL: **3 Precor**
STEPPER: **3 StarTrac**

STRENGTH

FREE WEIGHTS: **Yes**
MACHINES: **11 Cybex**
DUMBBELLS: **5-100 lbs**

SWIM

GRADE: **C-**
SPECS: **3x18yd • Outdoor • 77-82°**
TOYS: **Kick • Pull**

OTHER

CLASSES: **Yes**
HOURS: **6a-8p**
COST: **$12** • POOL **Free**
TV: **Yes**
EXTRAS: **Tennis • Golf**

A short stroll from the hotel lobby brings you to the Loews Spa reception desk and the starting point for all things aerobic. Although Loews commits a pet peeve by charging guests $12/day for use of the fitness center, we can swallow the tack-on a little easier knowing the gym is top-of-the-line. Inside the facility, athletes will be delighted by an impressive number of modern cardio machines, useful weight stations and plenty of free weights. The equipment is dispersed in an ergonomic fashion throughout the pleasantly designed room. Classes are offered as well, so those wanting a little group therapy can join in the fun.

Just outside the fitness center is the resort's 18-yard, 3-lane lap pool. Kickboards and pull-buoys are provided and, unlike the fitness center, freestyling is free. While only one lane is separated with a floating line, the other 2 are adequately marked with regulation stripes on the pool's bottom. Unfortunately, the length is a little short, but here is a tip: The neighboring Wyndham Lodge at Ventana Canyon sports a fantastic 8 lane, 25-yard competition pool. Loews guests can access this pool by contacting Wyndham's guest services department, or just show up in your Speedo and tell the attendant you were informed you could come for a dip.

Runners will be amazed by the beautiful desert country, and are treated to a short, on-property trail. The meandering path is a little curvy for our taste, so we recommend heading down Loews' driveway and logging any major miles along Kolb Street. A good mix of hills will heat up your desert jaunt.

SILVER: Westin La Paloma

3800 East Sunrise Drive, Tucson, AZ 85718
(520) 742-6000 • westinlapalomaresort.com

As a distant runner-up to Loews, this contemporary and pleasing 487-room Westin lacks the panache of its desert rival. The rooms and common areas are classy but look and feel similar to other Westin hotels. The grounds are well kept but not stunning. Fortu-

CARDIO

TREADMILLS: **4 total - StarTrac & LF**
UPRIGHT BIKE: **2 Tectrix**
RECUMBENT BIKE: **2 Tectrix**
ELLIPTICAL: **3 Precor**
STEPPER: **2 Tectrix - old**

STRENGTH

FREE WEIGHTS: **Yes**
MACHINES: **10 total –**
• Cybex • Paramount
DUMBBELLS: **3-65 lbs**

SWIM

GRADE: **B**
SPECS: **6x25yd • Outdoor • 83°**
TOYS: **Clock**

OTHER

CLASSES: **Yes**
HOURS: **6a-8p**
COST: **Free**
TV: **Yes**
EXTRAS: **Racquetball • Tennis • Golf**

nately, the staff is typically Westin — warm and friendly.

The hotel's fitness center is housed in a private country club located on the back side of Westin's grounds. The complimentary workout facility is worthy of an athlete's time but, like many country clubs, the golf courses and tennis courts are the meat on its bones. Weight machines, cardio equipment and free weights are organized into 3 separate rooms. All areas are petite, but the gear is well spaced to avoid discomfort. The cardio machines are a mix of steppers in poor condition, bikes in fair condition and treads and ellipticals in good condition. The stack-loaded weight machines and free weights are the gym's highlight.

The best feature at this Westin is the club's outdoor lap pool, located adjacent to the fitness center. In the 83 degree year-round temperature, swimmers will enjoy 6 lanes of 25-yard lapping, complete with floating lane lines and bottom stripes.

A jogging route that starts at the hotel drive and runs through a residential area provides a welcome outdoor aerobic pursuit. While not as scenic as the Loews' Kolb Street course, it is enjoyable nonetheless.

LEAST EXPENSIVE

GOLD: Omni Tucson National Golf Resort & Spa

2727 West Club Drive, Tucson, AZ 85742
(520) 297-2271 • tucsonnational.com

Golf is clearly the focus (27 PGA Tour level holes) of this Spanish hacienda-style resort, so we were pleasantly surprised by the additional recreational opportunities available to guests. On the grounds beyond the tastefully decorated, but rather plain accommodations, Omni provides lighted tennis, basketball and volleyball courts, 2 outdoor heated pools and a full-service spa and fitness center.

The exercise facility is much smaller than those listed above, but Omni capitalizes on the available space with its recently purchased cardio and weight equipment. In an area the size of a standard hotel room, Omni supplies workout hounds with 10 stack-loaded weight machines, good condition Precor ellipticals and Cybex recumbent bikes. Unfortunately, cycling nuts are forced to recline, but those intent on a traditional ride can hit the nearby roads and trails (more pavement than dirt) on a rental mountain bike.

Swimmers will be content, not thrilled, with the lap swim area — an undivided portion of the main pool. To keep you going straight, the lap swimming section is marked by two 25-yard bottom stripes without floating lines. Logging your 3,000 yards in the morning before the kids arrive is your best bet for solitary strokes.

Runners can obtain a jogging map from the concierge or head out on your own to discover the desert's delights.

Note: Depending on the days you travel, you can book the Omni at budget pricing. However, if the cost here is anywhere near the Loews or Westin (it often is) choose one of those two in an elevated heartbeat.

CARDIO

TREADMILLS: **4 Cybex**
RECUMBENT BIKE: **3 Cybex**
ELLIPTICAL: **3 Precor**

STRENGTH

FREE WEIGHTS: **Yes**
MACHINES: **10 total - • Cybex • Eagle**
DUMBBELLS: **5-65 lbs**

SWIM

GRADE: **C**
SPECS: **2x25yd • Outdoor • 80-84°**
TOYS: **Clock**

OTHER

CLASSES: **Yes**
HOURS: **6a-8p**
COST: **Free**
TV: **Yes**
EXTRAS: **Tennis • Golf**

SILVER: Westward Look Resort & Spa

245 East Ina Road, Tucson, AZ 85704
(520) 297-1151 • westwardlook.com

Similar to the Omni, Westward's room rates vary significantly by season. During the "high" months of February and March, prices can exceed $200/night. Come June, the cost consistently idles under a "C-Note." We like the Westward, but not enough to recommend it at $150-$200/night. So keep this in mind when looking and booking.

Of all the places we visited in Tucson, Westward reminded us the most of an Old World Southwest ranch. The owners have embraced the property's historic heritage by maintaining the 1912 homesite. In fact, the original living room is still located off the hotel's lobby, and much of the retreat's adobe style is inspired by the native homestead. The suite-size guestrooms clustered throughout the 80-acre grounds offer se-

CARDIO

TREADMILLS: **1 Precor • 1 StarTrac**
UPRIGHT BIKE: **1 Tectrix**
ELLIPTICAL: **1 Precor**
STEPPER: **1 Precor**

STRENGTH

MACHINES: **1 Vectra Multi**
DUMBBELLS: **3-35 lbs**

SWIM

GRADE: **C**
SPECS: **5x20yd • Outdoor • 81-85°**
TOYS: **Kick**

OTHER

CLASSES: **Yes**
HOURS: **6a-10p • Will open after hours**
COST: **Free**
TV: **Yes**

clusion in a natural habitat. All have a private balcony or patio and some an outdoor hot tub. Contributing to the resort's ranch character are its on-site stables, offering guests the option of exploring the countryside on horseback. Of course, the dirt trails also make for a nice hike (too curvy and not long enough for most joggers).

Away from the main pool and on the far end of the property, a fitness center and lap pool await exercisers. Privacy and seclusion are this area's most appealing features, and a decent workout is possible, too. The 5-lane, 20-yard lapper, complete with floating and bottom lines, is the more desirable fitness option — we just wish it were 5-yards longer.

Inside the tiny exercise area, athletes can sweat using the small number of mixed-quality cardio machines. The atmosphere and quantity of machines are passable. The treadmills, steppers and ellipticals will raise the metabolism, but those looking to pump iron are left out in the desert heat with Westward's weak dumbbell selection and tired multi-gym.

Runners must get a little creative. The on-property trails are short and twisty and the nearby road (Ina St.) can get busy with traffic. Those accruing more mileage will find themselves running past the urban congestion and into the desert calm. Ask hotel staff for suggested routes.

Note: Spa services are offered at this property's wellness center, as well as a few aerobic and yoga classes.

RUNNING ROUTES

Tucson is all about your resort destination. No matter where you land, your running route is out the front door. Consult the concierge for mileage and paths.

WASHINGTON, D.C.

After clicking the TV remote to CSPAN recently, we noticed that many D.C. politicians would benefit from our constructive travel suggestions. Though Democrats and Republicans are working hard to tighten the nation's financial belt, they certainly are not doing the same with the belts around their waists. Maybe that's best — the longer it takes our delegates to move from one floor to the next, the fewer problems they can create.

A laggard pace is not confined to the halls of Congress; it is standard for what visitors can expect in this logistics and commuting nightmare. Multitudes of one-way streets change direction throughout the day, European-style roundabout intersections congest like feline hairballs, confusing taxi fares vary according to geographical zones and hawk-like parking enforcers swoop in with tickets the second a meter ticks "empty." So forego the car keys and this headache. Embrace the convenient and user-friendly metro train system which transports riders to virtually every D.C. sightseeing and business destination.

Our recommended hotels are close to two of the City's most desirable neighborhoods, Dupont Circle and Georgetown. Trendy Dupont is centrally located to many businesses and a ton of chic dining and entertainment venues. It is also within walking distance of edgy Adams Morgan and blends into what is called "Downtown." Less urban but with its own panache, historic Georgetown showcases pristine neighborhoods, upscale shops and the University. Although hosting no metro stop, a quick taxi or bus ride provides a smooth commute from Georgetown to the city center. Downtown covers a large area and will include any "monumental" exploration. The White House, the Mall and Capitol Hill are all easily accessible.

In a town filled with heated debates, wheeling-'n-dealing and strong opinions, we don't care whether you side with the donkeys or the elephants — as long as you work out like a horse. Here are some great places to do it.

EXPENSIVE

GOLD: Ritz Carlton

1150 22nd Street NW, Washington, D.C. 20037
(202) 835-0500 • ritzcarlton.com/hotels/washington_dc

Opened in 2000, this 300-room contemporary masterpiece is a paragon of luxury that receives our enthusiastic vote as the athletic-minded traveler's best D.C. hotel.

Centrally located near Dupont Circle, the Ritz dazzles guests with lavish interiors, cozy bedding and impeccable service. An added touch is the freshly baked brownie or pastry visitors receive with evening turndown service. Of course, all this comfort does not come cheap. In fact, it wouldn't hurt to have a budget as large as the U.S. military's.

The real treat for travelers with an urge to sweat is Ritz's discounted access ($10/day) to the attached 100,000 square foot Sports Club/LA — D.C.'s best health club and one of the top workout centers in the country. It has everything fitness fanatics want and need.

SILVER: Four Seasons Georgetown

2800 Pennsylvania Avenue NW, Washington, D.C. 20007
(202) 342-0444 • fourseasons.com/washington

CARDIO
TREADMILLS: **3 Precor**
UPRIGHT BIKE: **2 LF**
RECUMBENT BIKE: **4 LF**
ELLIPTICAL: **3 Precor**
STEPPER: **2 StairMaster • 1 LF**
ROWING: **Concept II**
OTHER: **NordicTrack**

STRENGTH
FREE WEIGHTS: **Yes**
MACHINES: **16 Cybex**
DUMBBELLS: **5-65 lbs**

SWIM
GRADE: **C-**
SPECS: **2x20yd • Indoor • 82°**
TOYS: **Kick**

OTHER
CLASSES: **Yes**
HOURS: **5:30a-10p**
COST: **Free**
TV: **Yes**

If you want less hustle and bustle, we recommend staying in historic Georgetown with its architectural character, endless dining options and eclectic shops. Venturing a few blocks from the cosmopolitan main drag introduces you to pristine row houses, mansions and a revered university campus.

This lap of luxury made our list for a reason beyond the elegance, classic décor and tip-top service we love (and expect) at the Four Seasons – its health club! The hotel hits the workout bullseye by providing guests complimentary access to its 12,500 square foot fitness center and spa.

This urban retreat will please all exercise enthusiasts, including swimmers. As one of a select few D.C. hotels that maintains any form of lap pool, Four Seasons gets extra points for its 20-yard, 2-lane option, complete with floating lane lines and bottom stripes. The 2-story "L" shaped fitness studio offers a generous selection of cardio equipment (some with attached televisions) and weights, as well as a spinning/aerobics studio. Due to the "L" configuration, some machines are positioned directly against the wall, but this undesirable location is the exception rather than the rule.

The Four Seasons spa offers an extensive menu of pampering services for those with a weighty wallet.

BRONZE: Madison Hotel

15th & M Streets NW, Washington, D.C. 20005
(202) 862-1600 • themadisondc.com

In 2003, the Madison underwent an extensive $40 million renovation that reestablished this classic hotel as a Washington, D.C. favorite. Only blocks from the White House, it has played host to every President since 1963. Non-VIPs can indulge in refined pampering with 300 thread count linens and Frette duvets. We especially enjoy entertaining such pleasures for $100-$200/night less than the Ritz or Four Seasons.

CARDIO
TREADMILLS: **3 True**
UPRIGHT BIKE: **1 True**
RECUMBENT BIKE: **1 True**
ELLIPTICAL: **2 True**

STRENGTH
MACHINES: **3 Nautilus • 1 Multi**
DUMBBELLS: **5-50 lbs**

OTHER
HOURS: **24**
COST: **Free**
TV: **Yes**
EXTRAS: **$15 pass to Univ. Club**

The 2nd floor fitness center's atmosphere, with bright walls supporting top-of-the-line plasma television screens, is fantastic. Unfortunately, Madison seems to have over-spent on the visual entertainment at the expense of the exercise equipment. Though a good number of cardio and weight machines are present, Madison skimped by selecting the True brand — a mid-tier line of machines inferior to Precor or Life Fitness. Fortunately, for guests preferring to skip the True experience, Madison staff will arrange $15 access to the private University Club's 3rd floor fitness center and lap pool. It's less than a 5-minute walk.

MODERATELY EXPENSIVE

GOLD: Melrose Hotel

2430 Pennsylvania Avenue NW, Washington, D.C. 20037
(202) 955-6400 • melrosehotel.com

Located one block away from the Foggy Bottom Metro Station (great perk – see intro) and near Dupont Circle, Melrose receives our Gold primarily for its relationship with the nearby Sports Club/LA.

A former apartment building, Melrose's 240 rooms are oversized and pleasantly outfitted. Guests enjoy pillow top mattresses, marble baths and 19th Century style furnishings. The on-site restaurant and bar provide welcome distractions after a day of lobbying. And 24-hour room service will satisfy those late night munchies.

Melrose offers a small exercise room in-house, but our advice is to skip it. The best health club in D.C. is only a 5-minute walk from the hotel's front door — Sports Club/LA. Melrose patrons may purchase a workout pass from the hotel front desk for $10/day. It's a small price to pay for the wealth of fitness pleasures offered down the road.

SILVER: Doubletree Washington

1515 Rhode Island Avenue NW, Washington, D.C. 20005
(202) 232-7000 • doubletreewashington.com

CARDIO

TREADMILLS: **2 LF**
UPRIGHT BIKE: **1 LF**
RECUMBENT BIKE: **1 LF**
ELLIPTICAL: **2 LF**

STRENGTH

MACHINES: **1 Multi**

OTHER

HOURS: **24**
COST: **Free**
TV: **Yes**
EXTRAS: **Free pass to YMCA**

We applaud hotels stepping outside the proverbial box with their design and décor. Doubletree does just that with its colorful 220-room Rhode Island Avenue accommodation. Happily missing are plain vanilla walls and stain-obscuring brown carpet. Instead, guests are treated to unique tones and patterns that flow together.

While the stylish theme carries over to the small lower level exercise room, the limited selection of equipment diminishes its appeal. The Life Fitness machines are in tolerable condition, but the absence of dumbbells and free weights makes us extremely grateful forDoubletree's free passes to the National Capital YMCA at 17th and Rhode Island. This Y is less than a 5-minute walk and offers everything you will need — including a great lap pool.

BRONZE: Marriott

Georgetown University Conference Center
3800 Reservoir Road NW, Washington, D.C. 20057
(202) 687-3200 • marriott.com

CARDIO

UPRIGHT BIKE: **2 StarTrac**
RECUMBENT BIKE: **1 StarTrac**
ELLIPTICAL: **1 Precor**
STEPPER: **1 StarTrac**

OTHER

HOURS: **24**
COST: **Free**
TV: **Yes**
OTHER: **$10 pass to Yates**

Smack dab in Hoya land and tucked behind the Georgetown Medical Center, this Marriott is connected to the University's Leavey Conference Center. The hotel is designed for the business traveler and those University parents tracking how their big tuition bucks are spent. The guest rooms take on a country flavor with down-home bedding and oak furnishings.

You cannot get any closer to Georgetown's campus — you're ON it. And a 15-20 minute walk will take you to Georgetown's entertainment, shopping and dining. While a peaceful D.C. accommodation and a wonderful Georgetown home base, this Marriott is less convenient for those touring the monuments or visiting the White House. For that, you will need to hop in the car, grab a taxi or catch the bus.

The on-site exercise room lends itself to a quick cardio session, but nothing more. Instead, we recommend taking advantage of the

Georgetown University Yates Field House, a hop, skip, and $10 fee away. So you make the call — sweat with the young ones or breathe hard solo (Go, Hoyas!).

Note: For an authentic Hoya dining experience (i.e., beer and burger joint), check out The Tombs, a block from campus. If you would like to go more upscale, 1789 is upstairs.

LEAST EXPENSIVE

GOLD: Hotel Helix

1430 Rhode Island Avenue NW, Washington, D.C. 20006
(202) 462-9001 • hotelhelix.com

Located a block from Washington Terrace on the eastern edge of the Dupont Circle neighborhood, this Kimpton boutique property is all about fun. Because internet sleuthing returned rates in the $120/night range slightly more often than the $180/night level, we placed Helix in the "Least Expensive" category. Everything about the Helix makes you feel like a kid, especially if you "bunk" in one of the specialty rooms that has — you guessed it — bunk beds. But don't worry, side-by-side sleeping is smiled upon in most of Helix's 178 rooms. Bright oranges, cheerful reds and goofy purples work surprisingly well together. Additional perks include free continental breakfasts, evening bubbly hours, free high-speed internet access and in-room cordless speakerphones.

The hotel's small exercise room is not much fun with its 3 Precor cardio units (treadmill, upright bike and elliptical). But a free pass to the YMCA on 17th will turn your workout frown upside down! Give yourself 7 minutes to get there on foot.

SILVER: Beacon Hotel

1615 Rhode Island Avenue NW, Washington, D.C. 20036
(202) 296-2100 • capitalhotelswde.com

The recent name change and renovation of this hotel (formerly Governor's House) is a welcome improvement. The rooms are stylish, functional, and apartment-like in size — some with separate living quarters.

The exercise room is not very useful, offering 2 old treads and an antique bike. Fortunately, guests are provided free access to the 17th and Rhode Island Y—a very convenient 2-minute walk.

BRONZE: Lincoln Suites

1823 L Street NW, Washington, D.C. 20036
(202) 223-4320 • lincolnhotels.com

We debated about including this hotel. Other than its central downtown/Dupont Circle location and the free guest passes to Bally Fitness, no other feature justifies the rates that are often charged. However, Lincoln's rates are volatile, and the fare can be as low as $120/night. The rooms are basic, service mediocre and amenities standard. But in a place like Washington, where political events and conventions often boost rates all over town, Lincoln may end up being your best budget option.

With no on-site workout room, exercisers must look to Bally Fitness for any athletic fix. At less than a 5-minute walk, it is convenient.

Swimmers, Bally has no pool, so take your dip at the National Capital YMCA ($15).

BRONZE: Best Western New Hampshire Suites

1121 New Hampshire Avenue NW, Washington, D.C. 20037
(202) 457-0565 • bestwestern.com

Despite rates that seem overpriced, this property's all-suite accommodations, kitchenettes and boutique 76-room size are qualities we value. The least expensive queen suites sleep 4 (bed & sofa) and provide a practical family option. But before you get too excited, Mom and Dad, your privacy is hardly guaranteed by the room-separating entertainment shelving unit. Darn! At least feeding the rug rats each morning is guaranteed. Best Western provides free continental breakfasts with oatmeal, cereals, fruit, juices and bagels.

With no in-house gym, fitness fans enjoy an adequate off-site option. Guests can work out for free at the nearby Bally's Total Fitness. Just swing by the front desk and pick up your admission pass. The walk over should not take more than 5 minutes.

CARDIO

TREADMILLS: **LF**
UPRIGHT BIKE: **LF**
RECUMBENT BIKE: **LF**
ELLIPTICAL: **Precor**
STEPPER: **StairMaster • Stepmill**
ROWING: **Yes**
OTHER: **XC Ski**

STRENGTH

FREE WEIGHTS: **Yes**
HAMMER: **Yes**
MACHINES: **LF • Cybex • Free Motion • Icarian**
DUMBBELLS: **3-110 lbs**

SWIM

GRADE: **B-**
SPECS: **6x20yd • Indoor • 82°**
TOYS: **Kick • Pull • Clock**

OTHER

CLASSES: **Yes**
HOURS: M-TH **5:30a-10p • F 5:30a-9:30p • SAT-SUN 8a-8p**
COST: **$10 Ritz & Melrose • Up to $25 Select Hotels • No others**
TV: **Yes**
EXTRAS: **Basketball**

BEYOND HOTELS

Sports Club/LA

1170 22nd at "M" Street, NW
Washington, D.C. 20037
(202) 974-6600
thesportsclubla.com

We could go on and on about these amazing clubs, but you must see one for yourself. Because only a handful exist across the country, if you find yourself near one and guest access is permitted, we strongly recommend a field trip.

D.C.'s version tops out at 100,000 square feet. How big is that? Consider that the average U.S. hospital is 75,000 square feet — so it's big! In addition to its impressive size, the number and assortment of equipment and classes are mind-blowing. More than 35 stack-loaded machines, close to 10 Hammer Strength stations and a ton of free weights populate the 10,000 square foot strength area — the size of some entire clubs. In the 4,000 square foot cardio zone, the latest and greatest endurance machines are provided, including Life Fitness 9700 and 9500 series equipment. Every exercise class you have ever heard of convenes under this roof, and we understand the club restricts membership to avoid excessive waiting and overcrowding.

We have only one criticism: With so much space, why did the club design its pool 5 yards short of regulation length? This lowers our rating to a "B-." However, the rest of the lapper is fantastic — aesthetically pleasing, toys supplied, floating lines and stripes. A little more length and we'd be happy campers — but isn't that always the case?

Note: Ritz and Melrose guests pay $10/day for this luxury. A select few other hotel guests pay up to $25. Unfortunately, all others must look elsewhere.

University Club

1135 16th Street NW, Washington, D.C. 20036
(202) 862-8800 • universityclubdc.com

In stark contrast to the massive Sports Club/LA, the diminutive, members-only University Club opens its doors to guests of a select few surrounding hotels. Patrons of the Madison can work out here for $15, but make sure the hotel calls and registers you in advance.

On its 3rd floor, the large, streamlined fitness room is fashionably decorated with contemporary carpeting and olive-toned walls. Due to the club's exclusivity, the new cardio and weight equipment sits largely unused, especially during the day. Endurance junkies will be delighted by 6 bikes, 4 treadmills, 4 ellipticals and 3 step machines. And strength buffs are treated equally well with 13 stack-loaded weight stations, a useful dumbbell set and plenty of free weights.

Here we find another 20-yard pool, but its 4 lanes separated by floating lines and stripes are still a favorable fix. A pace clock is on deck as well as kickboards, but no pull-buoys or fins.

CARDIO

TREADMILLS: **StarTrac**
UPRIGHT BIKE: **StarTrac**
RECUMBENT BIKE: **StarTrac**
ELLIPTICAL: **Precor**
STEPPER: **StairMaster • StarTrac**
ROWING: **Concept II**

STRENGTH

FREE WEIGHTS: **Yes**
MACHINES: **BodyMaster**
DUMBBELLS: **5-85 lbs**

SWIM

GRADE: **C-**
SPECS: **4x20yd • Indoor • 81-84°**
TOYS: **Kick • Clock**

OTHER

CLASSES: **Yes**
HOURS: M-F **6a-10p** • SAT-SUN **9a-7p**
COST: **$15 Madison • No others**
TV: **Yes**
EXTRAS: **Squash**

YMCA National Capitol

1711 Rhode Island Avenue NW, Washington, D.C. 20036
(202) 862-9622 • nationalcapitalymca.org

CARDIO

TREADMILLS: **LF**
UPRIGHT BIKE: **LF**
RECUMBENT BIKE: **LF**
ELLIPTICAL: **LF • Precor - old**
STEPPER: **LF**

STRENGTH

FREE WEIGHTS: **Yes**
HAMMER: **Yes**
MACHINES: **Cybex • Icarian**
DUMBBELLS: **5-120 lbs**

SWIM

GRADE: **B+**
SPECS: **6x25m • Indoor • 81-83°**
TOYS: **Kick • Pull**
MASTERS: **Yes**

OTHER

CLASSES: **Yes**
HOURS: M-F **5:30a-10:30p** • SAT **8a-6p** • SUN **9a-5p**
COST: **Free Some Hotels • $15 Others**
TV: **Yes**
EXTRAS: **1/18 mile indoor track**

The second best health club in town (after Sports Club/LA), this Y deserves kudos for stocking new equipment, maintaining a fantastic lap pool and arranging deals with neighboring hotels.

The Y's 20,000 square foot gym is not undersized by any means, but some space could be used more effectively. For example, a new coat of paint and removing a wall would greatly enhance the small, currently boxed off, free weight room. Although the space is aesthetically challenged, we cannot criticize the Y's equipment supply. Youthful treadmills, bikes and ellipticals reside at this address along with ample weight stations and free weights. Although not huge in quantity (e.g., 6 Life Fitness and 5 Precor ellipticals), the Y's offerings satisfy.

The club highlight is its 25-meter lap pool. Swimmers should consider staying nearby for this treat alone (Washington Terrace, Helix and Governor's House). It is competition grade, so expect the works — floating lines and stripes, a high ceiling and plenty of toys. Bottom line, a great facility when access is on the house.

Georgetown University Yates Field House

37th & O Streets NW, Washington, D.C. 20057
(202) 687-2400 or 2412 • yates.georgetown.edu

Given the posh neighborhood, the Georgetown name and the massive facility size, we expected a high-end health club. Instead, our overall impression was more one of fatigue than fit.

The weight equipment sits on what used to be a basketball court, separated from other areas by a matted curtain. Most free weights and weight stations are at least 10 to 15 years old; those lifting dumbbells had better watch out for rust. The fitness picture brightens for cardio exercisers. About a dozen newer Precor and Life Fitness ellipticals steal the show, and several of the 16 treadmills are recent additions.

By far, Yates' best feature is its 25-yard lap pool. Exceeding our expectations, this top-notch aquatic facility offers 8 lanes of competition-quality swimming and a separate diving well. Unlike the ever-changing direction of D.C.'s traffic lanes, swimmers here can rely on floating lines and bottom stripes to clearly guide their way. Kickboards and pull-buoys are provided for extra swim fun. Lappers will love this pool.

Marriott guests receive access to Yates Field House for a reasonable $10. The facility is located 100 yards southwest of the hotel, just over a large hill on the right.

CARDIO

TREADMILLS: **Precor • Trotter • LifeStep**
UPRIGHT BIKE: **LF**
RECUMBENT BIKE: **LF**
ELLIPTICAL: **Precor • LF**
STEPPER: **StairMaster • Stepmill**
ROWING: **Yes**

STRENGTH

FREE WEIGHTS: **Yes**
HAMMER: **Yes**
MACHINES: **Nautilus • Cybex • BodyMaster**
DUMBBELLS: **5-105 lbs**

SWIM

GRADE: **B+**
SPECS: **8x25yd • Indoor • 81°**
TOYS: **Kick • Pull • Clock**
MASTERS: **Yes, during academic year**

OTHER

CLASSES: **Yes**
HOURS: **Vary**
COST: **$10 Marriott • No others**
TV: **Yes**
EXTRAS: **1/7 mile indoor track • Basketball**

Fairmont

The Fitness Center

2401 M Street, Washington, D.C. 20037
(202) 429-2400 • fairmont.com/washington

Your eyes are not deceiving you. The Fairmont hotel does not appear on our list, but its fitness center does. Due to its expensive room rates and the markedly superior accommodations listed above, the hotel did not make the cut. However, because Best Western guests can purchase a $5 pass at their front desk to access Fairmont's on-site fitness offering (5-minute walk), we have included specs for this gym.

This humdrum club previously functioned as a racquetball center with over a half-dozen courts. Although a few courts remain open to play, others have been converted to fitness rooms. Thirteen Life Fitness stack-loaded weight stations sit in one former court and moderately worn cardio machines (some with televisions) are in another. New

CARDIO

TREADMILLS: **LF**
UPRIGHT BIKE: **LF**
RECUMBENT BIKE: **LF**
ELLIPTICAL: **Precor**
STEPPER: **StairMaster • Stepmill**
ROWING: **Yes**

STRENGTH

FREE WEIGHTS: **Yes**
MACHINES: **LF**
DUMBBELLS: **5-100 lbs**

SWIM

SPECS: **Indoor • Not lap**

OTHER

CLASSES: **Yes**
HOURS: M-F **5:30a-9:45p** • SAT-SUN **7a-7p**
COST: **$5 Best Western • $10 Others**
TV: **Yes**
EXTRAS: **Racquetball**

equipment is the exception, not the rule. Most of the apparatus dates back at least 5 years.

A pool is also inside, but it is short and the water is cloudy.

Bally Total Fitness L Street

2000 L Street NW #1B, Washington, D.C. 20036
(202) 331-7788 • ballyfitness.com

CARDIO

TREADMILLS: **LF**
UPRIGHT BIKE: **LF**
RECUMBENT BIKE: **LF**
ELLIPTICAL: **LF • Precor**
STEPPER: **StairMaster**
ROWING: **Yes**

STRENGTH

FREE WEIGHTS: **Yes**
HAMMER: **Yes**
MACHINES: **LF • Magnum • Icarian**
DUMBBELLS: **3-100 lbs**

OTHER

CLASSES: **Yes**
HOURS: M-F **5a-11p** • SAT **8a-8p** • SUN **8a-6p**
COST: **Free Lincoln Suites • Small retail purchase Others**
TV: **Yes**

This Bally Fitness is a pleasant representative of a franchise that can be, shall we say, unpredictable. Despite its lackluster black and red interior color scheme, the club's bountiful supply of high-end equipment more than compensates for the dreary surroundings. Exercisers have the luxury of choosing among more than 50 stack-loaded weight stations, 15 Precor ellipticals, 10 Hammer Strength pieces and a host of other impressive equipment.

Swimmers have no representation at this pool-free facility. Head to the YMCA.

Those coming to Bally from Lincoln Suites can sweat for free. All others may enter after making a small retail purchase from the counter (e.g., energy bar).

RUNNING ROUTES

The Mall

The roughly 3-mile "Mall," the long, grassy, corridor that houses the capital's monuments, is a favorite local loop. With the Washington Monument on one end and the Capitol on the other, runners can take in the landmarks in between. Swing around the Tidal Basin and the Jefferson Memorial to rack up 2 more miles and head back west to the Lincoln Memorial for more historic fun.

The Towpath

For those staying in Georgetown or on the western fringe of Downtown/Dupont Circle, we suggest the Towpath along the C&O Canal. Runners can pick up this hard-packed dirt trail behind the Four Seasons or under Key Bridge. At nearly 185 miles, distance trainers will be in heaven with the beautiful scenery and convenient mile markers — for the first 20, that is.

Appendix: Ironman

Ironman North America Cities

So you've decided to take the Ironman triathlon plunge, huh? Good for you! Ironman North America is expanding its race schedule each year to accommodate the growing number of athletes taking on this epic challenge. In fact, Tempe, Arizona was recently selected as an upcoming site.

Many races are held in small towns (easier for course layout) that are unfamiliar to most travelers. Spending a week in a new city before the biggest physical challenge of your life can add unwanted anxiety. Will the hotel be okay? Where should I eat? Where should I swim, bike and run, before the race? Which bike shop should I go to? These are common traveling triathlete questions.

While staying at the event's host hotel is typically a safe bet, we have a few other, less obvious recommendations to help you focus on what matters — the race!

Keep in mind: No training you do in the final week prior to an Ironman will positively impact your fitness. In fact, it might be detrimental. Therefore, "when in doubt, leave it out."

Good luck, be smart and have fun!

Note: Although we have listed local bike shops, the good folks at Inside Out Sports will have a cutting-edge shop set up at all event expos to supply every potential product and service you need.

COEUR D'ALENE, IDAHO (CDA)

Thirty minutes east of Spokane, Washington, if you are expecting average June temperatures (78F-high), let the 2003 Ironman event be a lesson. The temperature boiled over at 100°F, turning the course into a scorching desert. Locals confirm that snow on the Fourth of July is not out of the question, so plan for everything!

SWIM

Buoys are put in early during race week to mark the course and distances. Gatorade usually sets up a tent and bag check mid-week and gives out daily freebies.

If you want a measured swim, 24-Hour Fitness is the closest lap option (see below).

BIKE

For a flat saddle session, ride east on Sherman to East CDA Lake Drive, then south to Higgin's Point.

For more ups and downs, go west on Hwy. 95 (careful crossing the bridge), then turn right on Riverview Drive (look for the Upriver sign). If you follow the Ironman course, you'll end up riding a 42-mile loop.

To get a feel for the steepest HILL on the course, drive on I-90 out to Post Falls and exit at Spokane Street. Proceed south, turn right (west) just after crossing the Spokane River on West Parkway Drive and park. Saddle up and ride south on Spokane Street and within a mile you'll be on the course at West Riverview Drive, which bends west up the climb. Continue on the course to Poleline and Spokane Street, where you will turn right (south), and head back to the car for a total of about 21 miles.

RUN

From town, you can run a paved loop west along West Lakeshore Dr. and return on River through the Northern Idaho College campus.

For an off road option, Tubbs Hill is just southeast of the CDA Resort. The perimeter trail is only 2-3 miles, but criss-crossing the forested peninsula will add some hills and a couple more miles.

A longer option? Run east on Mullan to East CDA Lake Drive, turning south on the Centennial Trail that parallels the road and lake and head toward Higgin's Point (~7 miles from town).

BIKE SHOP

Vertical Earth

206 North 3rd Street • (208) 667-5503

Located in the heart of Downtown, these folks understand bikes. Don't let the shop's mountain bike vibe fool you — the staff is well versed on the intricacies of road and tri-bikes. For a reasonable fee, you can ship your bike to Vertical and have it humming for your arrival. They will also re-pack and send your bike home.

EATS

Market Café

1401 North 4th Street • (208) 665-1682

Great for lunch and dinner.

Coeur D'Alene Brewing Company

209 Lakeside Avenue • (208)664-BREW

Good food, great beer and centrally located in Downtown. You're gonna need a brewski after the race, we promise.

GYMS

24 Hour Fitness Sport

208 East Coeur D'Alene Avenue • (208) 667-5010

For a few intervals in a legitimate lap pool, this club is nearby. The 5 lane, 25-yard water box will do, but we always prefer swimming in the lake — might as well get used to it. Your family and friends can enjoy this full-service facility for $15/day.

LODGING

La Quinta Inn and Suites

(208) 667-6777 • lq.com

There are two La Quinta hotels in CDA. Since the Sherman Avenue property is 200 meters from the run course and a mile from the transition area, we give it the nod.

Best Western CDA Inn

(208) 765-3200 • bestwestern.com

Although it's 3 miles from Downtown, this Best Western is appealing and has many conveniences (e.g., high-speed internet access, a restaurant) for a hassle free stay.

Sleep Inn Post Falls, ID

(208) 777-9394 • sleepinn.com

The accommodations within the City's limits often sell out, and the Sleep Inn is a good alternative. While this hotel is 12 miles west of Downtown along I-90, the owner will provide extra rags to wipe down your bike, set out fruit and muffins each morning and even offer access to a storage facility for your bike case. Now that's service!

The Sleep Inn is on the Ironman bike course (~43 & 99 mile marks), about 5 miles from the Liberty Lake Athletic Club, one of the few decent gyms and 25-yard pools in the area, just across the border in Washington (libertylakeathleticclub.com, $10).

LAKE PLACID, NEW YORK

A 2-hour drive north of Albany and 6 from New York City, Lake Placid's northern location and 1,800 feet of elevation create unpredictable weather conditions and a challenging course. The quaint town's accommodations fill quickly, so book your room as soon as you mark this race on your calendar... seriously, we mean it!

SWIM

Mirror Lake is the best swim course on the Ironman circuit. The water is as clear as day, and the U.S. Olympic Kayak team trains here with a marked course above *and* below the water's surface. If you can't swim straight by following the taught underwater lines, you probably swim crooked in a lap pool, too.

North Country Community College Pool

23 Santanoni Avenue, Saranac Lake, NY • (518) 891-2915

A short 10-15 minute drive from town, this facility houses an appealing 6 lane, 25-yard lapper for those wanting a measured race-week swim.

BIKE

If you are not arriving more than 6 days before the race to ride one full loop of this demanding course (56 miles), consider having someone drop you off in Wilmington. From there, ride the rolling out-and-back section on Haselton Rd. followed by the final 11-mile climb back to town for a total of 25 miles.

RUN

Once around Mirror Lake is just under 3 miles and a good route to avoid hills — perfect for an easy 25-30 minute flat jog.

If you like the way dirt feels in between your teeth, turn away from Mirror Lake on Mt. Whitney Drive. This dusty road will take you away from town for as many miles as you like. Turn around when you're ready, or when you need a toothbrush.

Those desiring some single track and uneven surfaces should head to the Jackrabbit Trail, accessed from HoJo's parking lot's northwest side — an escape route that winds away from town.

BIKE SHOP

High Peaks Cyclery

(518) 523-3764 • highpeakscyclery.com

Owner Brian Delaney has been in business for 22 years. In addition to providing great sales and service to the local community, High Peaks hosts weekly mini-triathlons and road/mountain bike rides. High Peaks is also the starting point of the 8 a.m. "Underpants Run" on the Friday before the race? Now you know.

EATS

Nicola's Over Main

90 Main Street • (518) 523-4430

Centrally located Downtown, Nicola's is one of our favorite dinner spots. It features yummy Italian and Greek fare.

Black Bear Restaurant

157 Main Street • (518) 523-9886

Downtown, breakfast at the Black Bear can't be topped.

GYM

Lake Placid Health and Fitness

199 Saranac Avenue • (518) 523-4127 • placidhealth.com

With a 4 lane, 25-yard lap pool, LP Health and Fitness is not the only place to work out in town, but it is definitely at the head of the class.

LODGING

Mirror Lake Inn

(518) 523-2544 • mirrorlakeinn.com

Although it's 1+ miles from the race venue, this great hotel offers rooms on the shores of Mirror Lake — a beautiful scene to come home to each day. The Inn usually sells out close to a year before the race.

Best Western Golden Arrow

(518) 523-3353 • bestwestern.com

Within 200 meters of Lake Placid High School (transition area and finish line), this Best Western is a favorite. The hotel's backyard is Mirror Lake Beach, less than a half-mile from the swim start. Rooms are non-smoking and the adjoining restaurant, Goldberry's, is as good as any for breakfast, lunch and dinner.

PENTICTON, BRITISH COLUMBIA

Penticton has been hosting Ironman races since 1983, making it the third oldest ultra-triathlon race, behind Kona and New Zealand. The town's history and commitment are apparent the moment you arrive. It just might be the most anticipated day of the year for this city of 30,000 friendly Canadians.

SWIM

Lake Okanagan is omnipresent, and that's where you swim —in clean, Canadian water straight out of the Rockies. If it's windy and rough, head 3 miles south to Skaha Lake for a calmer splash.

Community Centre Swimming Pool

325 Power Street • (250) 490-2434 • penticton.ca

Although they spell center "centre" in these parts — this is the best pool in the area. We especially enjoy the rope swing in the deep end! At $3.10 (Canadian dollars, eh?) you can't beat the price — unless perfect weather permits a swim in the free Lake O.

BIKE

While most triathletes are wary of Richter Pass (40-mile mark near Osoyoos), we believe the race really heats up in Keremeos (around mile 80), where the climb to Yellow Lake begins. Get your race map out, drive into Similkameen (say that 5 times fast) Valley and out to Keremeos. Park in town and ride to Yellow Lake (~8miles of climbing), then turn around.

Or have someone drop you off in Keremeos, then pedal back to Penticton (~30 miles total) on the course, riding the descent toward Hwy. 97. The 180° turns can be cornered without brakes with some practice. Keep your intensity down and save it for race day.

RUN

The run course is relatively flat, non-descript asphalt — and so are most of your pre-race jogging route options. One exception is the Okanagan River Channel (west side of town) that connects Lake O with Skaha Lake. This 4-mile dirt trail and parallel paved path are a nice respite from town streets.

BIKE SHOP

Bike Barn

300 Westminster Avenue • (250) 492-4140

The Bike Barn has participated in every Ironman Canada since its inception. Whether you need parts, service or some local advice, these guys and gals will take good care of you.

EATS

Hog's Breath Café

202 Main Street • (250) 493-7800

This central meeting point offers strong coffee, yummy breakfasts and tasty lunches. If you don't make it for anything else, be there at 8 a.m. on Friday for the infamous "Underpants Run."

Earl's

101-1848 Main Street • (250) 493-7455 • earls.ca

For lunch or dinner, the food, service and atmosphere of this Canadian original are tough to beat. Pasta, steak, a good salad — you name it. Even the pints of beer are good.

GYM

City Centre Fitness

301-399 Main Street • (250) 487-1481

One of the most popular fitness centers for locals, City Centre stocks an ample supply of exercise equipment.

LODGING

Slumber Lodge Inns and Motels

(250) 492-4008 • slumberlodge.penticton.com

If you are unable to book a room at the host Penticton Lakeside Resort & Casino, Slumber Lodge is your next best lodging bet. Directly across from the swim start, your location is just as good as the Resort's — minus amenities that you probably will not miss.

Best Western Inn at Penticton

(250) 493-0311 • bestwestern.com

Located about 2 miles from the race venue, a third of BW's rooms have kitchenettes and all offer mini-refrigerators. Its proximity to Skaha Lake on the south side of town makes this property a solid choice. It's still close to the race site, but far enough away to enjoy some peace and quiet — and a less-crowded open-water swim.

MADISON, WISCONSIN

In da land of beer, brats, dairy and cheese, Ironman Wisconsin is quickly becoming a triathlete favorite. Locals gear up for the event with backyard BBQs and town festivals. In particular, cyclists will feel like Tour De France competitors as they race through the streets of Verona, where loads of fans cheer and inspire. We have a feeling that, if you compete in this race once, you'll want to come back again.

SWIM

Other than the obvious — swimming in fresh water Lake Monona — a few measurable lap options exist around town. See our "Madison" chapter for exact locations. Keep in mind that Lake Monona's water pushes the wetsuit temperature threshhold, so a non-wetsuit swim here is more likely than anywhere else on the mainland.

BIKE

Drive to Verona's Fireman's Park to ride the meat of this course — a 40-mile loop where the most significant climbs and descents are found. Only ride the entire loop if you're at least 5 days out from the start. Otherwise, the descent on Garfoot Rd. is worth seeing before race day, as is the climb on Old Sauk Rd. Remember, you'll be going up and down a ton on this course, so riding one gear smaller than you can push will save your legs for the run.

RUN

The best options for running are both out-and-backs along Madison's two beautiful lakes, Monona and Mendota. The Howard Temin bike/pedestrian path meanders beside Lake Mendota for approximately 3 miles. About half the distance is trail, the other half is paved. Finding the path is easy. Just take Park Street north until it ends, then veer left.

Across town, a paved jogging route runs along the shores of Lake Monona (swim start). Pick it up at any point along John Nolen Drive. After a couple of miles, you'll find yourself jogging through Olin Park. Here, a network of trails will add some terrain variety.

BIKE SHOP

Cronometro

1402 Williamson Street • (608) 243-7760

When you think of knowledge and credibility in cycling, this shop comes to mind. Whether it's their bio-dynamic fitting, in-house invented products or patient and detailed service, it's worth the extra mile or two to check 'em out.

GYM

See the Madison chapter in the book's main body.

EATS

Great Dane Pub and Brewing Company

123 East Doty Street • (608) 284-0000

Great for lunch, dinner and, of course, beer. Yes, it's typical brew-pub fare, but good dinner items also make an appearance, including pasta.

Olive Garden

(608) 829-1158 – Mineral Point Road (West Towne Mall)
(608) 249-0340 – East Towne Blvd.

On our last trip to Madison, we noticed two of these safe bets for a pre-race meal. Pastas, vegetable dishes and pork entrees are all pretty good. The free wine sampling can give low-tolerance triathletes a quick buzz.

LODGING

See detailed city and hotel descriptions in the book's main text.

KONA, HAWAII

Revered as a mystical place where Hawaiian gods reign supreme over wind, heat and competition, Kona presents a true test of physical endurance and mental strength. Marked by miles upon miles of volcanic rock, the length along the Queen K and Natural Energy Lab can feel like being atop a fiery charcoal grill — you can actually see the heat rising from the pavement. Luckily, Alii Drive (Kailua-Kona's main drag) and the higher elevation towns offer lush, tree-lined roads, bougainvillea-filled yards and beautiful views of the Pacific. Plan on heat (85-90°F), humidity (80-90%) and wind (20-30mph) for race day. If you have air conditioning in your hotel room, don't use it (at least during the day). You're here a week early to acclimate, remember?

SWIM

Kailua Bay — enough said. Later in the week, the Pier becomes the place to see and be seen — Kona's equivalent of LA's Sky Bar. Hard bodies, free goods (think swim caps and energy bars) and envious bystanders line the wall. This is your 15 minutes!

Kona Community Aquatic Center

75-5530 Kuakini Highway, Kailua-Kona • (808) 327-3500

If it rains heavily in Kailua-Kona, the run-off goes straight into Kailua Bay — not a great place to swim the following morning when you have the biggest race of your life on the near horizon. Instead, consider swimming in the best lap pool on the island. It's only a mile from the pier and admission is free!

BIKE

Though riding from your hotel down the Queen K is convenient, plan on putting your bike in the car and driving to Kawaihae. Park across from the convenience store. Once there, saddle up for the journey to Hawi. This ride is a mere 36 miles but, depending on the wind, could ride like 50. Experiencing this section of the course is vital to a good race. You are likely to encounter similar cross winds and heat conditions. It's also a good idea to ride about the same time you expect to pedal through on race day.

RUN

Running along Alii is a safe bet, but logging some miles in the Natural Energy Lab is more important. Consider driving out and running into, and back out of, this desolate stretch of the run course. Sometimes fear of the known is better than fear of the unknown. If you can persuade a volunteer to provide you with water after each mile, all the better.

BIKE SHOPS

Any of these three shops will do a good job for you. Also, consider shipping to, and sending from, these locations.

B&L Bike and Sport

75-5699 Kopiko Street • (808) 329-3309

Powered by Inside Out Sports, they have 2 locations.

HP Bikeworks

74-5599 Luhia Street • (808) 326-2453

Hawaiian Pedals

75-5744 Alii Drive • (808) 329-2294

EATS

The Aloha Theater & Aloha Angel Café

79-7384 Mamalahoa Highway, Kainaliu • (808) 322-3383

Hands down, this is the best dining option around. It requires a 15-minute drive up the Queen K into the town of Kainaliu, but the views and the food are well worth the trip. Breakfast, lunch and dinner are all served with a smile and health conscious menus. Bring a jacket or sweater (especially at night), just in case. The weather here can be quite a bit cooler than in town.

Sibu Café

75-5695 Alii Drive • (808) 329-1112

Don't let the Indonesian food designation scare you away. Located down the arcade from Big Island Jewelers and across from the swim start, Sibu serves fresh plates according to your tastes. Chicken and beef satay and the Gado Gado salad are a couple of 8-time Ironman Champion Paula Newby-Fraser's favorites. Bring cash — plastic is not accepted.

Kona Inn Restaurant

75-5744 Alii Drive • (808) 329-4455

For a more upscale affair — at least as upscale as it gets in Kailua — enjoy a meal at Kona Inn. Steaks and seafood are served to diners enjoying the phenomenal coastline views. Great burgers are cooked up for lunch in the outdoor dining area.

Lava Java

75-5799 Alii Drive • (808) 327-2161

A favorite hangout and meeting point for triathletes and locals alike, you'll find great coffee, breakfast and lunch options inside. Chances are Jürgen Zack will be sipping a joe right beside you as he holds his "office hours" on the front patio.

LODGING

Kona Alii Condominiums

(800) 800-6202 • Knutson & Assoc., property managers

Location, location, location. Three-quarters of a mile from the Kailua Pier swim start, this condo complex is as close to the main drag as you can get without being on it. Everything is within walking distance, which becomes important later in the week as traffic snarls become more frequent. Some of the lower units are susceptible to street noise, but the ocean helps to drown it out.

Outrigger Royal Sea Cliff

(808) 329-8021

A long time triathlete favorite primarily due to its location just 2 miles from Kailua Pier at the 2-mile mark on Alii Drive, the Royal Sea Cliff is far enough away from the Ironman "village" to afford some peace and quiet but close enough for a quick commute to town, expo and transition area.

Kona Seaside Hotel

(808) 329-2455 • sand-deaside.com/kona_hotels.htm

For a less expensive option, but one that puts you as close as possible to the swim start, transition area and town, Kona Seaside will satisfy. Some rooms have a kitchenette option — a nice perk. Expect basic floor plans and amenities otherwise. Having your own private bathroom to run to on race morning is always another big plus.

PANAMA CITY BEACH, FL

Lovingly referred to as "lower Alabama," Panama City Beach is arguably the most popular Ironman destination in North America. The beautiful sugar sand beaches, the beginner-friendly, flat bike and run course, and the abundance of Waffle Houses lure triathletes. But, with Spring Break well over and the summer crowds long gone, racers and their families can enjoy a small piece of the Panhandle all to themselves in November.

SWIM

If red flags are blowing in the wind, lifeguards will forbid Gulf swimming. If this occurs on your swim day, consider Gulf Coast's lapper — it is open to triathletes the week prior to Ironman daily at 10-11 a.m. and 1-2 p.m. Figure on a worthwhile 15-minute drive.

Gulf Coast Community College Natatorium

5230 West Highway 98 • (850) 872-3832
wellness.gulfcoast.edu/aquatics.htm

BIKE

Riding on Front Beach Road or Thomas Drive at off-peak traffic hours is manageable but still not the safest route. Therefore, we suggest driving out to the town of Ebro (really an intersection). Park here and pedal east on Hwy 20. An out-and-back on this road is the safest riding on the course.

RUN

Drive out to St. Andrews State Park. It will cost ~$5 to enter — $1 if you park outside and jog in. This park is part of the run course — you will see it twice on race day — and the slight grade can be a surprise for those not experiencing it beforehand.

BIKE SHOP

Steve's Bike Shop

1923 West 23rd Street • (850) 769-6808

A shop that understands triathletes, Steve's is on the Panama City side of the causeway (not the Beach side). It's worth the drive if Inside Out Sports does not have what you need under the tent.

GYM

World Gym

8340 Front Beach Road • (850) 249-6753

You are in Panama City Beach to race, not go to a gym. However, your friends and family might like the option. We haven't worked out here, so we cannot testify to its merit.

EATS

Olive Garden

2397 SR 77 • (850) 769-4002

Probably the best food in this healthy cuisine challenged city. It's a good 10-15 minute drive, near the airport, and worth the trip.

Captain Anderson's Restaurant

5551 North Lagoon Drive • (850) 234-2225

Good steak, seafood and pasta, but count on a little more salt and oils than you prefer. Ask for everything plain, and add toppings yourself. Also a bit overpriced.

Waffle House

222 all over the place Drive

You can joke all you want about Waffle House and how there is one on every corner. But we are willing to bet that you eat at one before the weekend is over — and you'll like it!

LODGING

With high-rise condominiums lining miles of the Gulf's shores, a weekly rental in one of these buildings is the smart choice — especially since the hotels are nothing to be impressed by.

Sunbird Condominiums

(888) 782-9722 • sunbird.panamacitybeachreservations.com

A 5-minute walk to the race site, kitchenettes and gorgeous balcony views will be enjoyed by all. Waffle House and Walmart are also within a 10-15 minute walk or short drive.

Regency Towers

(850) 234-3533 • regencytowers.net

Located on the run course 2.5 miles east of the transition area, some athletes may welcome the distance from race central. Having a bad race? Just duck into your room — yeah right!